THE

CRIMINAL JUSTICE

See inside for an illustration of

SYSTEM

Essentials of
CRIMINAL
JUSTICE

tenth edition

LARRY J. SIEGEL
University of Massachusetts, Lowell

JOHN L. WORRALL
University of Texas at Dallas

CENGAGE
Learning®

Australia • Brazil • Mexico • Singapore • United Kingdom • United States

CENGAGE Learning®

Essentials of Criminal Justice, **Tenth Edition**
Larry J. Siegel and John L. Worrall

Product Director: Marta Lee-Perriard

Senior Product Manager:
Carolyn Henderson Meier

Senior Content Developer: Shelley Murphy

Product Assistant: Valerie Kraus

Senior Marketing Manager: Kara Kindstrom

Senior Content Project Manager: Christy Frame

Managing Art Director: Andrei Pasternak

Senior Manufacturing Planner: Judy Inouye

Production and Composition: Jill Traut,
MPS Limited

Photo Development: Kim Adams Fox

Photo Researcher: Pandisathya Paul,
Lumina Datamatics

Text Researcher: Manjula Subramanian,
Lumina Datamatics

Copy Editor: Julie McNamee

Text and Cover Designer: Jennifer Wahi

Cover Images: American flag: milanadzic/Getty
Images; hands: H. Armstrong Roberts/Classic-
Stock/Getty Images

For product information and technology assistance, contact us at
Cengage Learning Customer & Sales Support, 1-800-354-9706

For permission to use material from this text or product,
submit all requests online at **www.cengage.com/permissions**
Further permissions questions can be e-mailed to
permissionrequest@cengage.com

Library of Congress Control Number: 2015944016

Student Edition:
ISBN: 978-1-305-63376-6

Cengage Learning
20 Channel Center Street
Boston, MA 02210
USA

Cengage Learning is a leading provider of customized learning solutions with employees residing in nearly 40 different countries and sales in more than 125 countries around the world. Find your local representative at **www.cengage.com**

Cengage Learning products are represented in Canada by Nelson Education, Ltd.

To learn more about Cengage Learning Solutions, visit **www.cengage.com**

Purchase any of our products at your local college store or at our preferred online store **www.cengagebrain.com**

Unless otherwise noted, all content is © 2017 Cengage Learning

Printed in the United States of America
Print Number: 01   Print Year: 2015

DEDICATION

This book is dedicated to my kids, Eric, Andrew, Julie, and Rachel and her husband Mace; my grandkids, Jack, Kayla, and Brooke Macy; and to my wife, Therese J. Libby.

L. J. S.

This book is dedicated to my wife, Sabrina. Thank you for your continued love and support.

J. L. W.

ABOUT THE AUTHORS

LARRY J. SIEGEL was born in the Bronx. While living on Jerome Avenue and attending City College of New York in the 1960s, he was swept up in the social and political currents of the time. He became intrigued with the influence contemporary culture had on individual behavior: Did people shape society, or did society shape people? He applied his interest in social forces and human behavior to the study of crime and justice. Graduating from college in 1968, he was accepted into the first class of the newly opened program in criminal justice at the State University of New York at Albany, where he earned both his MA and PhD degrees. Dr. Siegel began his teaching career at Northeastern University, where he was a faculty member for nine years. He also held teaching positions at the University of Nebraska–Omaha and Saint Anselm College in New Hampshire before being appointed a full professor in the School of Criminology and Justice Studies at the University of Massachusetts–Lowell. Dr. Siegel retired from full-time classroom teaching in 2015 and now teaches exclusively online. He has written extensively in the area of crime and justice, including books on juvenile law, delinquency, criminology, criminal justice, corrections, and criminal procedure. He is a court-certified expert on police conduct and has testified in numerous legal cases. The father of four and grandfather of three, Larry Siegel and his wife, Terry, now reside in Naples, Florida, with their two dogs, Watson and Cody.

JOHN L. WORRALL is Professor of Criminology at the University of Texas at Dallas. A Seattle native, he received a BA, double majoring in psychology and law and justice, from Central Washington University in 1994. Both his MA (criminal justice) and PhD (political science) were received from Washington State University, where he graduated in 1999. From 1999 to 2006, he was a member of the criminal justice faculty at California State University, San Bernardino. He joined UTD in Fall 2006. Dr. Worrall has published articles and book chapters on topics ranging from legal issues in policing to crime measurement. He is the author of *Crime Control in America: What Works?* (3rd ed., Pearson) and *Criminal Procedure: From First Contact to Appeal* (5th ed., Pearson); coauthor of several texts, including most recently, with Jennifer L. Moore, *Criminal Law and Procedure* (Pearson, 2014); and editor of the journal *Police Quarterly*.

BRIEF CONTENTS

CONTENTS

9 PUNISHMENT AND SENTENCING 208

PART 4 CORRECTIONS AND ALTERNATIVE SANCTIONS 235

10 COMMUNITY SENTENCES: PROBATION, INTERMEDIATE SANCTIONS, AND RESTORATIVE JUSTICE 236

14 CRIME AND JUSTICE IN THE NEW MILLENNIUM 344

PREFACE

I n 2015, nine senior officials of FIFA (the Fédération Internationale de Football Association), the organization responsible for the regulation and promotion of soccer worldwide, were indicted on racketeering, wire fraud, money laundering, and other charges. They were accused of involvement in a decades-long scheme to corrupt the sport through bribes, kickbacks, and other criminal activity whose aim was controlling lucrative marketing rights to international tournaments such as the World Cup. In all, more than $150 million in bribes and kickbacks were paid or agreed to be paid to obtain media and marketing rights to international soccer tournaments.

How did the conspiracy unfold? A key way FIFA makes money is by selling media and marketing rights associated with flagship tournaments such as the World Cup. Rights are typically sold through multiyear contracts. Sports marketing companies, in turn, sell the rights to TV and radio broadcast networks, major corporate sponsors, and other sublicensees who want to broadcast the matches or promote their brands. According to federal prosecutors, between 1991 and 2015, the defendants and their co-conspirators abused their positions of trust for personal gain, frequently through alliances with sports marketing executives who shut out competitors and kept highly lucrative contracts for themselves through the systematic payment of bribes and kickbacks.

Empowered by case law and legislation, the criminal justice system routinely processes millions of cases involving fraud, theft, violence, drug trafficking, and other crimes. Some are the products of vast conspiracies, as the FIFA case illustrates. Others are one-time offenses by first-time offenders. The vast majority fall somewhere between each of these extremes. How does the criminal justice system, which costs billions of dollars and involves millions of people, operate? What are its most recent trends and policies? How effective are its efforts to control crime? What efforts are being made to improve its efficiency? We have written the tenth edition of *Essentials of Criminal Justice* in an attempt to help answer these questions in a concise, forthright, and objective manner.

Goals and Objectives

Because the study of criminal justice is a dynamic, ever-changing field of scientific inquiry, and because the concepts and processes of justice are constantly evolving, we have updated *Essentials of Criminal Justice* to reflect the most critical legal cases, research studies, and policy initiatives that have taken place during the past few years. *Essentials of Criminal Justice* lays a foundation for the study of criminal justice by analyzing and describing the agencies of justice and the procedures they use to identify and treat criminal offenders. It covers what most experts believe are the crucial issues in criminal justice and analyzes their impact on the justice system. This edition focuses on critical policy issues in the criminal justice system, including efforts to control and contain terrorism.

The primary goals and objectives of the tenth edition remain the same as they have been for the previous nine:

1. Provide students with a thorough knowledge of the criminal justice system.

2. Be as readable and interesting as possible.

3. Be objective and unbiased.
4. Describe current methods of social control and analyze their strengths and weaknesses.

Every attempt has been made to make the presentation of material interesting, balanced, and objective. No single political or theoretical position dominates the text; we try to be as objective as possible. Accordingly, we have included the many diverse views that are represented within criminal justice and that characterize its interdisciplinary nature.

Focus on Ethics

A key goal of this new edition is to give students an unparalleled opportunity to grapple with some of the ethical issues that agents of the criminal justice system must face every day in their professional lives. The study of ethics is concerned with questions of right and wrong and how we ought to live and behave. In *Essentials of Criminal Justice,* students will be challenged to think about ethical decisions and then be presented with an opportunity to apply their own sense of ethics to everyday decision making in criminal justice. Whether they involve a prosecutor deciding whether to charge a well-known personality or treat the case informally, or a police officer stopping and searching a citizen merely because of his or her race or ethnicity, we believe that understanding ethical issues and being able to think ethically is a key element of the study of criminal justice. To meet this goal, each chapter begins with a vignette that reflects an ethical challenge in criminal justice. In Chapter 3, for example, we begin with the Aaron Hernandez case, the New England Patriot tight end who was convicted of murder. The case and the issues it represents are further referred to in Ethical Reflection boxes that appear throughout the chapter. We address such ethical questions as whether it is fair to equally punish all people involved in a criminal conspiracy even though only one engaged in violence. In other words, should the triggerman be punished more severely than the other conspirators?

Finally, an Ethical Challenge feature also presents students with a controversial topic in criminal justice and asks them to address the ethics of the issue in an essay. Taken together, these elements of the text afford students a much-needed opportunity to think about and practice their own ethical decision-making skills—skills we believe are the cornerstone of an optimally functioning justice system.

Organization of the Text

Essentials of Criminal Justice is a brief introduction to criminal justice. Despite its clear, concise nature, we have made every effort to ensure that the book is informative, complete, interesting, well organized, and impartial as well as stimulating and thought-provoking.

Part One gives the student a basic introduction to crime, law, and justice. The first chapter covers the agencies of justice, outlines the formal justice process, and introduces the concept of the informal justice system, which involves discretion, deal making, and plea bargains. Chapter 1 also examines the major perspectives on justice and shows how they shape justice policy. Chapter 2 discusses the nature and extent of crime and victimization: How is crime measured? Where and when does it occur? Who commits crime? Who are its victims? What social factors influence the crime rate? Chapter 3 provides a discussion of criminal law and its relationship to criminal justice. It covers the legal definition of crime, the types of defenses available to those charged with having committed a crime, as well as issues in constitutional procedural law.

Part Two offers an overview of law enforcement. Three chapters cover the history and development of police departments, the functions of police in modern society, issues in policing, and the police and the rule of law. Special emphasis is placed on community policing and crime prevention, technology and policing, and changes in police procedures.

Part Three is devoted to the court process, from pretrial indictment to the sentencing of criminal offenders. In this section, individual chapters focus on the organization of the court system and the roles of its major participants (judge, prosecutor, and defense attorney), pretrial procedures, the criminal trial, and sentencing. The topics explored include bail, court reorganization, sentencing, and capital punishment.

Part Four focuses on the correctional system, including probation and the intermediate sanctions of house arrest, intensive supervision, and electronic monitoring. Although the traditional correctional system of jails, prisons, community-based corrections, and parole is discussed at length, there is also a focus on restorative justice programs. Such issues as the crisis of overcrowding in prisons and jails, house arrest, correctional workers, super-maximum-security prisons, and parole effectiveness are discussed.

Part Five explores current issues in justice. One chapter deals with the problem of juveniles who break the law by considering what should be done with them, and how they should be treated. Information is also provided on the development of juvenile justice, on waiving youth to the adult court, and on the death penalty for children. Chapter 14 focuses on some of the critical issues currently facing the justice system: terrorism, corporate crime, environmental crime and cyber crime. It illustrates the dynamic nature of the justice process and the fact that the problems it faces are constantly evolving.

Key Changes in the Tenth Edition

In addition to thoroughly updating and revising each chapter, we have included coverage of the hottest topics in criminal justice today, including, but not limited to the following:

- High-profile police shootings
- Lone wolf terrorists
- Recent gun control developments
- Latest on marijuana legalization
- Police technology, including body cameras and drones

- End to prison expansion
- Wrongful convictions
- Youth gangs

Discussions are more concise—leaner than ever before. And the book contains many new graphs, figures, charts, and tables that make the presentation easier to understand. Finally, we have made the following key changes to the text:

Chapter 1, Crime and Criminal Justice, now begins with the shooting of Michael Brown in Ferguson, Missouri, and the resulting backlash against what is perceived as police racial bias. The chapter has also been thoroughly revised and updated with new data on criminal justice expenditures and the numbers of people in the correctional system. The sections on ethics have been revamped and extended.

Chapter 2, The Nature of Crime and Victimization, first covers the terrible case involving the abduction and murder of University of Virginia student Hanna Graham. Data on child abuse and hate crimes have been updated and expanded. New material is provided on recent trends in Uniform Crime Reports (UCR), self-report, and victimization data. For example, the latest national self-report data from the Monitoring the Future program finds that teen alcohol and cigarette use are at their lowest points since the study began 40 years ago. We review crime reporting and find that victims fail to report if they do not trust the police; cities in which people believe the police can help them are more likely to report crime.

Chapter 3, Criminal Law: Substance and Procedure, now begins with the Hernandez case and goes into the legal requirements required for a murder conviction. It also has a boxed feature on gun control and looks at the legal issues that shape this important topic, including the 2015 referendum that asked Colorado voters to repeal gun control laws passed in the wake of the Aurora movie theater shooting. Gun advocates believe that if citizens are armed, they could stop mass shootings. A new Current Issues in Criminal Justice, "Born and Alive," looks at the legal status of a fetus and whether it is considered murder if an unborn child is killed during a criminal act. Criminal defenses have been revised and updated, and we review some of the most important criminal procedure decisions of the past few years.

Chapter 4, Police in Society: History and Organization, includes a new chapter opener that features the tragic 2014 shooting of two New York City police officers, Wenjian Liu and Rafael Ramos. A Criminal Justice and Technology box features the advent of police body cameras, which have become popular in the wake of recent high-profile police shootings.

Chapter 5, The Police: Role and Function, has a new opening vignette about the New York City Police Department work "slowdown," which resulted from a rift between the police union and the city's mayor. Members felt the mayor did not show enough support for the police when riots broke out after officer Daniel Pantaleo was not indicted in the controversial killing of Eric Garner in 2014. Drone use is also covered in this chapter. Drones are ubiquitous these days. How much should police departments rely on them?

Chapter 6, Issues in Policing: Professional, Social, and Legal, features the Eric Garner choking death in the new chapter opener. The incident prompted a backlash and later rioting when the officer who took Garner to the ground was not indicted. Even the shootings of NYPD officers Wenjian Liu and Rafael Ramos was partly attributed to the Garner incident. The latest Supreme Court cases with relevance to law enforcement are included and discussed in this chapter. A new Contemporary Issues in Criminal Justice box focuses on the effectiveness of Tasers.

Chapter 7, Courts, Prosecution, and the Defense, has a new opening vignette that highlights the defense lawyer team in the Dzhokhar Tsarnaev's trial. Tsarnaev was the man charged and ultimately convicted in the Boston marathon bombing in 2013. What kind of person does it take to defend someone involved in such a serious crime? The chapter also includes a feature on specialized courts for drug crimes, domestic violence, and other complex problems.

Chapter 8, Pretrial and Trial Procedures, has a revised opening vignette that considers the latest developments with respect to marijuana legalization. The chapter was updated with the latest developments and court decisions pertaining to trial and pretrial procedures.

Chapter 9, Punishment and Sentencing, includes a new opening vignette that examines the tragic loud music shooting in Florida, a case in which an armed man ended up killing the passenger in an SUV because the car stereo was playing too loudly. A new box features the problem of wrongful convictions—and methods for remedying them. The latest punishment and sentencing data are also included.

Chapter 10, Community Sentences: Probation, Intermediate Sanctions, and Restorative Justice, includes a new chapter opening vignette covering the case of "Real Housewives of New Jersey" stars Teresa and Joe Giudice who pleaded guilty for conspiring to commit wife fraud and failing to file income tax returns. Should nondangerous offenders such as the Giudice's be put in prison, or would they be better served with a community sentence? The Contemporary Issues in Criminal Justice feature, Treating Probationers with Cognitive Behavioral Therapy, has been updated with new data. There is new research on probation styles as well as the number of people on probation and probation effectiveness. New sections cover innovative probation monitoring programs, such as "drive-by" units in which probation officers use a portable device that can be handheld or used in a vehicle with a roof-mounted antenna.

Chapter 11, Corrections: History, Institutions, and Populations, begins with a vignette on the brutal beating of a prison inmate, George Williams, which resulted in the criminal conviction of three correctional officers. The segment on supermax prisons has been expanded, as has the material on private prisons. Statistics on jail and prison populations have been revised and updated. The chapter also reviews the recent stabilization in the prison population after so many years of growth. Although the prison inmate population increases have now begun to slow, there are still far too many people in prison, so we cover legal scholar Michael Tonry's 10-point plan to reduce the prison population over the next five years.

Chapter 12, Prison Life: Living in and Leaving Prison, now begins with the story of Tommy Silverstein, considered one of the most dangerous inmates in the United States, who has been held in solitary confinement for the past 27 years. The section on faith-based treatment has been overhauled, and there is discussion of Corrections Corporation of America's (CCA) intention to employ chaplains and program facilitators, who offer inmate residents a variety of worship services, faith-based counseling, and religious resources to address practical and spiritual needs.

Chapter 13, Juvenile Justice in the Twenty First Century, includes a new chapter opener that features the killing of Elizabeth Thomas by Steven Miles, her boyfriend, who tried to emulate the lead character in the Showtime series, *Dexter.* The latest juvenile delinquency data have been included, as have recent Supreme Court cases relevant to juvenile justice. A new career feature discusses the position of social worker. A new Contemporary Issues box features the state of the youth gang problem.

Chapter 14, Criminal Justice in the New Millennium, addresses such topics as the definitions of terrorism and cyber crime. The opening vignette focuses on a 2015 cyber crime that involved a multimillion-dollar Ponzi scheme. New information is provided on the various forms of cyber crime (including cyber terrorism) and on what law enforcement agencies are doing to thwart cyber criminals. The chapter has a substantial new section on terrorism that covers such issues as the nature and categories of terror groups, efforts to control terror, and terror and the justice system. There is also new material on lone-wolf terrorism, and the section on large-scale corporate crime has been expanded, as has the section on transnational crime.

Boxed Features

Contemporary Issues in Criminal Justice boxed features, highlighting evidence-based criminal justice policies and practices, help students to think critically about current justice issues. For example, a Contemporary Issues box in Chapter 3 reviews the issues surrounding gun control and the Constitution, another in Chapter 11 looks at the problems faced by elderly inmates, and, in Chapter 12, another Contemporary Issues box looks at criminal records and reentry success.

Criminal Justice and Technology boxes review some of the more recent scientific advances that can aid the justice system. In Chapter 12, for example, a feature titled "**Monitoring Parolees with GPS**" looks at how technology now enables correctional administrators to keep track of parolees using GPS technology.

The very popular **Careers in Criminal Justice** boxes have been updated with information on the latest career paths in criminal justice. These boxes contain detailed information on salaries, educational requirements, and future prospects, and we have added to each of these boxes a new "Reality Check" section that discusses the potential pitfalls of that career area,

as well as what might disqualify a person from the career or job highlighted. Careers in Criminal Justice boxes that are new to this edition include loss prevention specialist (Chapter 4), crime analyst (Chapter 5), paralegal (Chapter 7), and social worker (Chapter 13).

Other Important Chapter Features

Every chapter of *Essentials of Criminal Justice* also contains learning tools to enhance student mastery of the material.

- **Learning Objectives.** Each chapter begins with a list of key learning objectives. These objectives are then revisited in the **Summary,** where they are directly tied to the material covered in the text. The learning objectives are also integrated throughout in the text margins, signaling where the learning objective is addressed within the chapter.

- **RealityCheck.** One of the goals of this book is to expose some of the myths that persist about crime, criminals, and the criminal justice system. Given the popularity of television series such as *CSI* and *Law and Order,* which purport to strip away the veneer of the justice system and expose the truth, it has become essential to help students separate rhetoric from reality in the criminal justice system: Is the crime rate really out of control? Are unemployed people more likely than others to commit crime? Do detectives solve the most serious crimes? Does incarceration really work? Does the death penalty deter people from committing murder? Making it clear what is true and what is merely legend is one of the greatest challenges for instructors teaching the first course in criminal justice. The **RealityCheck** feature in *Essentials of Criminal Justice* meets that challenge head on. Its purpose is to separate myth from reality and thereby inform students of the incorrect notions, perceptions, and biases they bring to class as a result of what they see on television or read in fiction and on the Internet.

- **WebApps. New to this edition,** throughout the book are a variety of Web links that help students do further research and reading on the Internet. Some of these are links to websites containing information that can enrich the textual material.

- **Ethical Reflections.** This feature refers back to the ethical issues raised in the opening vignette and links it to the material found within the chapter.

- **Ethical Challenges.** Each chapter presents a writing assignment that challenges students to solve an ethical dilemma they may someday confront while working within the justice system. For example, the ethical challenge posed in Chapter 5 concerns how to deal with two police officers who may have been overzealous in using force on the job.

- **Review Questions**
- **Running Marginal Glossary of Key Terms**

Ancillaries

For the Instructor

MINDTAP FOR CRIMINAL JUSTICE MindTap Criminal Justice from Cengage Learning represents a new approach to a highly personalized, online learning platform. A fully online learning solution, MindTap combines all of a student's learning tools—readings, multimedia, activities, and assessments—in to a singular Learning Path that guides the student through the curriculum. Instructors may personalize the experience by customizing the presentation of these learning tools for their students. MindTap allows seamless introduction of the instructor's own content into the Learning Path via "apps" that integrate into the MindTap platform. Additionally, MindTap provides interoperability with major Learning Management Systems (LMS) via support for industry standards and fosters partnerships with third-party educational application providers to create a highly collaborative, engaging, and personalized learning experience.

INSTRUCTOR'S RESOURCE MANUAL WITH LESSON PLANS AND TEST BANK This manual includes learning objectives, key terms, a detailed chapter outline, a chapter summary, lesson plans, discussion topics, student activities, "What If" scenarios, media tools, a sample syllabus, and an expanded test bank with 30 percent more questions than the prior edition. The learning objectives are correlated with the discussion topics, student activities, and media tools.

Each chapter of the test bank contains questions in multiple-choice, true/false, completion, essay, and new critical thinking formats, with a full answer key. The test bank is coded to the learning objectives that appear in the main text and includes the section in the main text where the answers can be found. Finally, each question in the test bank has been carefully reviewed by experienced criminal justice instructors for quality, accuracy, and content coverage so instructors can be sure they are working with an assessment and grading resource of the highest caliber.

CENGAGE LEARNING TESTING POWERED BY COGNERO This assessment software is a flexible, online system that allows instructors to import, edit, and manipulate test bank content from the *Essentials of Criminal Justice* test bank or elsewhere, including their own favorite test questions, create multiple test versions in an instant, and deliver tests from their LMS, classroom, or wherever they want.

ONLINE POWERPOINT® LECTURES Helping make lectures more engaging while effectively reaching visually oriented students, these handy Microsoft PowerPoint slides outline the chapters of the main text in a classroom-ready presentation. The PowerPoint slides are updated to reflect the content and organization of the new edition of the text, are tagged by chapter learning objective, and feature some additional examples and real-world cases for application and discussion.

For the Student

MINDTAP FOR CRIMINAL JUSTICE MindTap Criminal Justice from Cengage Learning represents a new approach to a highly personalized, online learning platform. A fully online learning solution, MindTap combines all of your learning tools—readings, multimedia, activities, and assessments—in a singular Learning Path that guides you through the course.

Acknowledgments

Thanks to our terrific product manager, Carolyn Henderson Meier, who does it all for us all the time. (She is our unnamed co-author). Plenty of credit for getting this book out must also go to the marvelous Shelley Murphy, content developer extraordinaire, to whom we can never give enough praise no matter how hard we try. Special thanks to our outstanding content project manager, Christy Frame; and to the ever-creative photo researcher, Kim Adams Fox, who brought the book to life with colorful imagery. And, of course, we are totally in debt to our incredible marketing manager, the astonishing Kara Kindstrom. This skilled team's efforts have resulted in an exceptional new edition.

Larry Siegel
Naples, Florida

John Worrall
Dallas, Texas

Essentials of
CRIMINAL
JUSTICE

2

THE NATURE OF CRIME, LAW, AND CRIMINAL JUSTICE

In January of 2015, a controversy developed across the University of Virginia (UVA) campus that had repercussions around the nation. In a letter to 16 UVA sorority chapters, national leaders encouraged members not to participate in activities related to "men's bid night" and instead plan alternative "sisterhood events." The letter was prompted by a recent spate of sexual assaults associated with frat houses and the death of UVA student Hannah Graham. Instead of gaining immediate acceptance, the letter prompted angry responses from students who felt the request treated them as untrustworthy and undermined efforts to reduce the threat of sexual violence.

The UVA incident comes at a time when sexual assaults on campuses have become an issue of growing national concern. All too many high-profile incidents have rocked the nation's campuses, many involving star athletes, as well as frat brothers. Students, such as those shown here at Dickinson College, have organized protests against sexual assault on campus, demanding reforms and calling for the expulsion of perpetrators. Sexual assault on campus and elsewhere is a major concern of those involved in the criminal justice process. Knowing the legal definition of crimes such as sexual assault, when and where crimes like these take place, and how to prevent such criminal activity are significant goals of those who work within the criminal justice system.

To help address these issues, Part 1 of this text covers the basic issues and concepts of crime, law, and justice. Chapter 1 covers the justice process and the organizations that are entrusted with conducting its operations: the police, courts, and corrections. It provides an overview of the justice system and sets out its most important agencies, processes, and concepts. Chapter 2 looks at the nature and extent of crime, and attempts to determine why people commit crimes such as sexual assault. Chapter 3 covers the criminal law, analyzing both its substantive and procedural components, including the legal definition of a crime.

Chapter 1   **Crime and Criminal Justice**

Chapter 2   **The Nature of Crime and Victimization**

Chapter 3   **Criminal Law: Substance and Procedure**

1 Crime and Criminal Justice

REALITY**CHECK**

MYTH OR REALITY?

- Police departments are an American creation, the first having been formed in New York City after the Civil War.

- At its core, the justice system is designed to protect the public from people who cannot abide by or obey the law.

- According to the statute of limitations concept, if a murder isn't solved in 10 years, the killer can no longer be brought to justice.

- There is equal justice under the law, and everyone can expect to get his or her day in court.

- Justice tends to be objective rather than subjective; agents of the justice system put their personal feelings aside in the course of their duties.

- Seeking justice is often confounded by ethical dilemmas that may be difficult to resolve.

- Defense attorneys do not represent clients they know to be guilty.

On August 9, 2014, in Ferguson, Missouri, a suburb of St. Louis, 18-year-old Michael Brown, an unarmed African American, was fatally shot by Darren Wilson, a white police officer. According to most accounts, shortly before the shooting, Michael and a friend Dorian Johnson had stolen some cigars from a local convenience store. Officer Wilson, who at the time was not aware of the theft, encountered the two young men as they were walking down the middle of the street. Wilson ordered them to move to the sidewalk. When the two refused to obey the order, a scuffle broke out during which Michael Brown punched Officer Wilson through the window of the police car. The fight went on until Wilson's gun was fired, and Brown and Johnson fled down the street. Wilson pursued Brown down the street, eventually firing a total of 12 rounds at him from a distance ranging from 30 feet to less than 10 feet. In all, Michael Brown was hit eight times, the last shot causing his death. A grand jury called to review the evidence in the case failed to find sufficient cause to indict Officer Wilson for the death of Michael Brown, a decision that prompted nationwide protests condemning racial bias in the justice system.

The shooting of Michael Brown reminded people of the central role that crime, law, and justice play in their daily lives and how a random encounter can escalate into the death of a young man. Many pertinent issues were raised by the death of Michael Brown. The prosecution employed a grand jury to investigate the case. Required by the Fifth Amendment of the U.S. Constitution in Federal cases, about half the states also make use of a grand jury indictment for prosecution in felony cases. In Missouri, grand juries are used in some but not all cases. When used, the grand jury consists of 12 citizens, of which 9 must vote in favor of an indictment before a case can be brought to trial. Those who considered the shooting of Michael Brown a criminal matter were outraged by the refusal to indict Officer Wilson. Many could not understand how the shooting of an unarmed suspect was not a crime. Legally, the grand jury's decision rested on what happened during the pursuit of Michael Brown: Did he, as some witnesses asserted, have his hands raised in surrender as he moved toward

© Robert Cohen/Corbis, (inset photo) AP Images/Uncredited

LEARNING OBJECTIVES

LO1 Discuss the formation of the criminal justice system in America

LO2 Define the concept of a criminal justice system

LO3 Identify the basic component agencies of the criminal justice system

LO4 Comprehend the size and scope of the contemporary justice system

LO5 Trace the formal criminal justice process

LO6 Articulate what is meant by the term criminal justice assembly line

LO7 Characterize the informal criminal justice system

LO8 Describe the "wedding cake" model of justice

LO9 Discuss the various perspectives on justice

LO10 Discuss the ethical issues that arise in criminal justice

Officer Wilson, or was Michael Brown madly charging at the officer in an attempt to attack him further, as Wilson claimed? If the latter is true, then the officer's behavior may be excused because he acted in self-defense, and the failure to indict was justified. If the former, Wilson's actions amounted to felony murder, and an indictment should have been issued. Members of the jury obviously believed Wilson's story when they failed to indict. Because a grand jury meets behind closed doors, how their decision was made and what evidence they considered remains unknown to all but those directly involved.

The death of Michael Brown also raised issues about the role race plays in the construction and creation of crime and criminality. Would Michael Brown have been stopped by a police officer if he was a white college-aged man? Or a middle-aged white woman who decided to walk down the middle of the street? Protestors claimed that the shooting of Michael Brown was just one of numerous incidents of police harassment and brutality directed at young men of color. The law should and must be colorblind and gender neutral. Did this incident occur because of discrimination and racial profiling? And if so, what can be done to make police officers more sensitive to issues of race and improve police relations with the minority community?

According to the FBI, around 500 incidents of justifiable fatal police shootings occur each year; this number has increased about 10 percent in the past five years.[1] They, along with millions of other cases, fall within the scope of the criminal justice system. Defined as the system of law enforcement, adjudication, and correction that is directly involved in the apprehension, prosecution, and control of those charged with criminal offenses, this loosely organized collection of agencies is responsible for, among other matters, protecting the public, maintaining order, enforcing the law, identifying transgressors, bringing the guilty to justice, and treating criminal behavior. The public depends on this vast system not only to protect them from evildoers and to bring justice to their lives but also to maintain order and protect the fabric of society.

This textbook serves as an introduction to the study of criminal justice. This area of research and scholarship includes describing, analyzing, and explaining the behavior of those agencies authorized by law and statute to dispense justice—police departments, courts, and correctional agencies—and helping these institutions identify effective and efficient methods of crime control.

Myth vs. Reality

As we engage in this study of crime and justice, a unifying theme is exposing, analyzing, and setting straight some of the myths and legends that have grown up about the justice system. Many people form opinions about criminal justice from the media, which often leads to false impressions and unrealized expectations. In the movies and on TV, it takes police about an hour to catch even the most wily criminal. Shootouts and car chases are routine, and every criminal defendant receives a lengthy trial in front of an attentive jury. Journalists and the media as a whole help perpetuate these myths by routinely featuring stories exposing brutal cops and violent prisons. How true are these images of justice? How can we separate myth from reality? Throughout this textbook, we will confront such myths and legends in an attempt to sort the facts from the fiction.

This chapter introduces some basic issues, beginning with a discussion of the history of crime in America and the development of criminal justice. The major organizations and criminal justice processes of the criminal justice system are then introduced as an overview of how the system functions. Because there is no single view of the underlying goals that help shape criminal justice, the varying perspectives on what criminal justice really is, or should be, are set out in some detail.

Developing the Criminal Justice System

During the nineteenth century, America experienced a surge in violent behavior. You have all seen movie westerns featuring bad men such as Jesse James, Billy the Kid, and Butch Cassidy and the Sundance Kid. These outlaws were not merely media legends;

criminal justice system The law enforcement, court, and correctional agencies that work together to effect the apprehension, prosecution, and control of criminal offenders. They are charged with maintaining order, enforcing the law, identifying transgressors, bringing the guilty to justice, and treating criminal behavior.

criminal justice process The decision-making points, from the initial investigation or arrest by police to the eventual release of the offender and his or her reentry into society; the various sequential criminal justice stages through which the offender passes.

they actually robbed trains, rustled cattle, and engaged in western land wars. Bringing them to justice were such legendary lawmen as Wyatt Earp (famed for his part in the "Gunfight at the OK Corral"), Bat Masterson, and Pat Garrett (who shot and killed Billy the Kid).

On the East Coast, large and deadly urban gangs such as the North End Gang, Dead Rabbits, Plug Uglies, and Hudson Dusters set up operations in cities such as New York and Boston. Responding to a public outcry over rising crime rates in the United States and abroad, the first criminal justice agencies began to appear. The emergence of criminal gangs and groups in the nineteenth century and a general sense of lawlessness spurred development of formal agencies of criminal justice. In 1829, the first police agency, the London Metropolitan Police, was developed to keep the peace and identify criminal suspects. In the United States, the first police agencies were created in Boston (1838), New York (1844), and Philadelphia (1854). The penitentiary, or prison, was created to provide nonphysical correctional treatment for convicted offenders; these were considered "liberal" innovations that replaced corporal or capital punishment.

During the first century of their existence, these fledgling agencies of justice rarely worked together in a systematic fashion. Not until 1919, with the creation of the Chicago Crime Commission (a professional association funded by private contributions) did the work of the criminal justice system began to be recognized.[2] This organization acted as a citizens' advocate group and kept track of the activities of local justice agencies. The commission still carries out its work today.

In 1931, President Herbert Hoover appointed the National Commission on Law Observance and Enforcement, which is commonly known today as the Wickersham Commission. This national study group made a detailed analysis of the US justice system and helped usher in the era of treatment and rehabilitation. The final report found that thousands of rules and regulations governed the system and made it difficult for justice personnel to keep track of the system's legal and administrative complexity.[3]

The Modern Era of Justice

The modern era of criminal justice can be traced to a series of research projects begun in the 1950s under the sponsorship of the American Bar Foundation (ABF).[4] Originally designed to provide in-depth analysis of the organization, administration, and operation of criminal justice agencies, the ABF project discovered that the justice system contained many procedures that had been hidden from the public view. The research focus then shifted to an examination of these previously obscure processes and their interrelationship—investigation, arrest, prosecution, and plea negotiations. It became apparent that justice professionals used a great deal of personal choice in decision making, and showing how this discretion was used became a prime focus of the research effort. For the first time, the term *criminal justice system* began to be used, reflecting a view that justice agencies could be connected in an intricate yet often unobserved network of decision-making processes.

Federal Involvement in Criminal Justice

In 1967, the President's Commission on Law Enforcement and Administration of Justice (the Crime Commission), which had been appointed by President Lyndon Johnson, published its final report entitled, *The Challenge of Crime in a Free Society.*[5] This group of practitioners, educators, and attorneys was given the responsibility of creating a comprehensive view of the criminal justice

WEB APP 1.1 Wyatt Earp was one of the most colorful characters in the old West. Read about him at **http://www. wyattearp.net**. To learn more about Wyatt, read this article by his friend and fellow lawman Bat Masterson at **http://www.legendsofamerica.com /we-earpbymasterson.html**. Do you find it amazing that only 150 years ago the West was wild, and gunfights took place on city streets?

REALITY CHECK

MYTH OR REALITY?

Police departments are an American creation, the first having been formed in New York City after the Civil War.

MYTH. The first formal police department was created in London in 1829, headquartered in Scotland Yard.

Police agencies in the United States developed in the latter half of the nineteenth century. What social conditions present at that time encouraged the creation of formal police agencies?

ETHICAL REFLECTION

Police Shootings

When a terrible tragedy such as the shooting death of Michael Brown occurs, people want answers. What can be done to prevent such crimes from occurring? Should all police officers undergo rigorous psychological testing before being sworn in, and should those with identifiable problems be prohibited from joining the force? If so, is it fair and ethical to exclude people from an occupation before they commit a crime, or is that a violation of civil liberties?

REALITYCHECK

MYTH OR REALITY?

At its core, the justice system is designed to protect the public from people who cannot abide by or obey the law.

REALITY. The justice system dispenses formal social control, and is made up of a group of government agencies empowered to control and punish people who violate the criminal law.

What behaviors that are currently illegal would you decriminalize and make legal? Conversely, what behaviors that are now legal do you believe should be criminalized?

process and recommending reforms. In 1968, Congress passed the Safe Streets and Crime Control Act, providing for the expenditure of federal funds for state and local crime control efforts and launching a massive campaign to restructure the justice system.[6] It funded the National Institute of Law Enforcement and Criminal Justice (NILECJ), which encouraged research and development in criminal justice. Renamed the National Institute of Justice (NIJ) in 1979, the Institute has continued its mission as a major source of funding for the implementation and evaluation of innovative experimental and demonstration projects in the criminal justice system.[7]

The Safe Streets Act provided funding for the Law Enforcement Assistance Administration (LEAA), which granted hundreds of millions of dollars in aid to local and state justice agencies. Throughout its 14-year history, the LEAA provided the majority of federal funds to states for criminal justice activities. On April 15, 1982, the program came to an end when Congress terminated its funding. However, the federal government continues to fund innovation in the criminal justice system through the National Institute of Justice (NIJ) and the Bureau of Justice Assistance (BJA).

The Contemporary Criminal Justice System

The criminal justice system is society's instrument of social control. Some behaviors are considered so dangerous that they must either be strictly controlled or prohibited outright, and some people are so destructive that they must be monitored or even confined. The agencies of justice are tasked with preventing or deterring outlawed behavior by apprehending, adjudicating, and sanctioning lawbreakers. Society maintains other forms of informal social control, such as parental and school discipline, but these are designed to deal with moral, not legal, misbehavior. Only the criminal justice system maintains the power to control crime and punish those who violate the law.

Contemporary criminal justice agencies are political entities whose structure and function are lodged within the legislative, judicial, and executive branches of the government. They typically can be divided into three main components (Figure 1.1): law enforcement agencies, which investigate crimes and apprehend suspects; court agencies, in which charges are brought, indictments submitted, trials conducted, and sentences formulated; and correctional agencies, which are charged with monitoring, treating, and rehabilitating convicted offenders.

Because of its varied and complex mission, the contemporary criminal justice system in the United States is monumental in size. At last count, local governments funded half (or $132 billion) of all direct justice system—police protection, all judicial and legal services, and corrections—expenses in the United States. State government spending accounted for 31 percent (or $81 billion), and federal funding accounted for 19 percent (or $50 billion).[8]

These expenses are high because they there are now almost 18,000 local, state, and county law enforcement agencies employing more than 1.1 million people. Of these, almost 800,000 are full-time sworn law enforcement officers, and the remainder are part-time officers and civilian employees. The federal government employs an additional 120,000 sworn law enforcement personnel. The criminal justice system consists of nearly 17,000 courts, more than 8,000 prosecutorial agencies, about 6,000 correctional institutions, and more than 3,500 probation and parole departments.

The system is massive because it must process, treat, and care for millions of people. Although the crime rate has declined substantially, more than 11 million people are still being arrested each year or about 3,700 per 100,000 people. While there has also been a recent decline in the number of cases brought to state courts, about 96 million cases are now being heard each year, including about 20 million that involve criminal matters and 2 million juvenile offenders.[9]

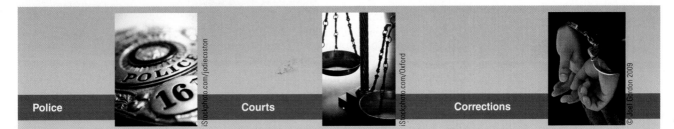

Police

Police departments are those public agencies created to maintain order, enforce the criminal law, provide emergency services, keep traffic on streets and highways moving freely, and develop a sense of community safety. Police officers work actively with the community to prevent criminal behavior; they help divert members of special needs populations, such as juveniles, alcoholics, and drug addicts, from the criminal justice system; they participate in specialized units such as a drug prevention task force or antirape unit; they cooperate with public prosecutors to initiate investigations into organized crime and drug trafficking; they resolve neighborhood and family conflicts; and they provide emergency services, such as preserving civil order during strikes and political demonstrations.

Courts

The criminal courthouse is the scene of the trial process. Here the criminal responsibility of defendants accused of violating the law is determined. Ideally, the court is expected to convict and sentence those found guilty of crimes, while ensuring that the innocent are freed without any consequence or burden. The court system is formally required to seek the truth, to obtain justice for the individual brought before its tribunals, and to maintain the integrity of the government's rule of law. The main actors in the court process are the judge, whose responsibilities include overseeing the legality of the trial process, and the prosecutor and the defense attorney, who are the opponents in what is known as the adversary system. These two parties oppose each other in a hotly disputed contest —the criminal trial—in accordance with rules of law and procedure.

Corrections

In the broadest sense, correctional agencies include community supervision or probation, various types of incarceration (including jails, houses of correction, and state prisons), and parole programs for both juvenile and adult offenders. These programs range from the lowest security, such as probation in the community with minimum supervision, to the highest security, such as 24-hour lockdown in an ultra-maximum security prison. Corrections ordinarily represent the postadjudicatory care given to offenders when a sentence is imposed by the court and the offender is placed in the hands of the correctional agency.

FIGURE 1.1 **Components of the Criminal Justice System**

Considering the massive proportions of this system, it is not surprising that almost 7 million people are under some form of correctional supervision, including more than 2 million men and women in the nation's jails and prisons and an additional 4.75 million adult men and women being supervised in the community while on probation or parole.[10] The size of this massive correctional system is reflected in its cost. States now spend about $50 billion per year on corrections. The mean state corrections expenditure per inmate is now more than $28,000 per year; one-quarter of states spend $40,000 or more.[11]

L04 Comprehend the size and scope of the contemporary justice system

The Formal Criminal Justice Process

Another way of understanding criminal justice is to view it as a process that takes an offender through a series of decision points beginning with arrest and concluding with reentry into society. During this process, key decision makers resolve whether to maintain the offender in the system or discharge the suspect without further action. This decision making is often a matter of individual discretion based on a variety of factors and perceptions. Legal factors, including the seriousness of the charges, available evidence, and the suspect's prior record, are usually considered legitimate influences on decision making. The fact that such extralegal factors as the suspect's race, gender, class, and age may also influence decision outcomes is troubling. Some critics believe that a suspect's race, class, and gender largely determine the direction a case will take, whereas supporters argue that the system is relatively fair and unbiased.[12]

In reality, few cases actually are processed through the entire formal justice system. Most are handled informally and with dispatch. The system of justice has been roundly criticized for its "backroom deals" and bargain justice. Although informality and deal making are in fact the rule, the concept of the formal justice process is important because it implies that every criminal defendant charged with a serious crime is entitled to a full range of constitutional rights under law.

A comprehensive view of the formal criminal process normally includes the following:

1. *Initial contact.* In most instances, an offender's initial contact with the criminal justice system takes place as a result of a police action:

   - Patrol officers observe a person acting suspiciously, conclude the suspect is under the influence of drugs, and take her into custody.
   - Police officers are contacted by a victim who reports a robbery; they respond by going to the scene of the crime and apprehending a suspect.
   - An informer tells police about some ongoing criminal activity in order to receive favorable treatment.
   - Responding to a request by the mayor or other political figure, the local department may initiate an investigation into an ongoing criminal enterprise such as gambling, prostitution, or drug trafficking.
   - A person walks into the police station and confesses to committing a crime—for example, killing his wife after an altercation.

2. *Investigation.* The purpose of the criminal investigation is to gather sufficient evidence to identify a suspect and support a legal arrest. An investigation can take only a few minutes, as in the case where a police officer sees a crime in progress and can apprehend the suspect quickly. Or it can take many years and involve hundreds of law enforcement agents. Dennis Rader, the notorious BTK ("Bind, Torture, Kill") serial killer, began his murderous streak in 1974 and was finally apprehended in 2005 after an investigation that lasted more than 30 years.[13]

3. *Arrest.* An arrest is considered legal when all of the following conditions exist: (1) the police officer believes there is sufficient evidence, referred to as *probable cause,* that a crime is being or has been committed, and the suspect is the person who committed it; (2) the officer deprives the individual of freedom; and (3) the suspect believes that he is now in the custody of the police and has lost his liberty. The police officer is not required to use the word "arrest" or any similar term to initiate an arrest, nor does the officer have to bring the suspect to the police station. To make an arrest in a misdemeanor, the officer must have witnessed the crime personally, a provision known as the **in-presence requirement**. Some jurisdictions have passed laws allowing misdemeanor arrests based on victim complaints in cases involving child abuse or domestic abuse. Arrests can also be made when a magistrate, presented with sufficient evidence by police and prosecutors, issues a warrant authorizing the arrest of the suspect.

4. *Custody.* After an arrest and while the suspect is being detained, the police may want to search for evidence, conduct an interrogation, or even encourage a confession. Witnesses may be brought to view the suspect in a lineup or in a one-on-one confrontation. Because these procedures are so crucial and can have a great impact at trial, the US Supreme Court has granted suspects in police custody protection from the unconstitutional abuse of police power, such as illegal searches and intimidating interrogations.

5. *Charging.* If the arresting officers or their superiors believe that sufficient evidence exists to charge a person with a crime, the case will be turned over to the prosecutor's office. The prosecutor's decision to charge the suspect with a specific criminal act involves many factors, including evidence sufficiency, crime seriousness, case pressure, and political issues, as well as personal factors such as a prosecutor's own specific interests and biases. After conducting a preliminary investigation of its legal

---

in-presence requirement With a few exceptions, in order to make an arrest in a misdemeanor, a police officer must have witnessed the crime personally.

WEB APP 1.2 To read the full story of Dennis Rader and his capture, go to the following websites: **http://murderpedia.org/male.R/r/rader-dennis.htm** **http://www.crimeandinvestigation.co.uk/crime-files/dennis-rader-the-btk-killer** While serial killers such as Rader capture the public's attention, most murders are committed by people who know each other.

REALITYCHECK

MYTH OR REALITY?

According to the statute of limitations concept, if a murder isn't solved in 10 years, the killer can no longer be brought to justice.

MYTH. A statute of limitations is designed to restrict the maximum time after an event that legal proceedings may be initiated; after the period of time is exhausted, legal proceedings can no longer be brought. However, in the United States, there is no statute of limitations for first-degree murder.

Should the statute of limitations be waived for other crimes such as child sexual abuse? This issue will be addressed in Chapter 3.

merits, prosecutors may decide to take no further action in a case; this is referred to as a *nolle prosequi*.

6. *Preliminary hearing/grand jury.* The US Constitution mandates that before a trial can take place, the government must first prove probable cause that the accused committed the crime for which he is being charged. In about half the states and in the federal system, this determination is made by a **grand jury** in a closed hearing. If the prosecution presents sufficient evidence, the grand jury will issue a **true bill of indictment**, which specifies the exact charges on which the accused must stand trial. In the remaining states, the prosecution will file a charging document (usually called an **information**) before a lower trial court, which then conducts an open hearing on the merits of the case. During this procedure, sometimes referred to as a **probable cause hearing**, the defendant and the defendant's attorney may appear and dispute the prosecutor's charges. The suspect will be called to stand trial if the presiding magistrate or judge accepts the prosecutor's evidence as factual and sufficient.

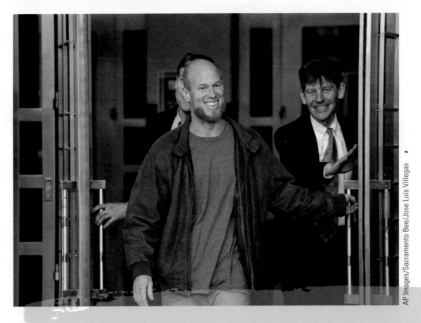

Inmates are released from prison for a number of different reasons: they are granted early release or parole; they have served the maximum sentence; they receive amnesty or a pardon; or they win an appeal. On January 8, 2015, Eric McDavid, 37, was able to walk out of the Federal Courthouse in Sacramento, California, with his attorneys Ben Rosenfeld and Mark R. Vermeulen (right) after being released from prison. McDavid served nine years in federal custody for his involvement in an eco-terrorist plot in the name of the Earth Liberation Front. McDavid was ordered to be released when an appeals judge ruled that at his trial the government had never turned over to his defense attorney documents they were entitled to review.

7. *Arraignment.* Before the trial begins, the defendant will be arraigned, or brought before the court that will hear the case. At this time, formal charges are read, the defendant is informed of his constitutional rights (e.g., the right to be represented by legal counsel), an initial plea (not guilty or guilty) is entered, a trial date set, and bail issues are considered.

8. *Bail/detention.* Bail is a money bond levied to ensure the return of a criminal defendant for trial, allowing the defendant to remain in the community prior to trial. Defendants who do not show up for trial forfeit their bail. Those people who cannot afford to put up bail or who cannot borrow sufficient funds for it will remain in state custody prior to trial. In most instances, this means an extended stay in a county jail or house of correction. If they are stable members of the community and have committed nonviolent crimes, defendants may be released on their own recognizance (promise to the court), without bail.

9. *Plea bargaining.* After an arraignment, or even before, the defense and prosecution will discuss a possible guilty plea in exchange for the prosecution reducing or dropping some of the charges or agreeing to a request for a more lenient sentence. Almost 90 percent of all cases end in a plea bargain, rather than a criminal trial.

10. *Trial/adjudication.* If an agreement cannot be reached or if the prosecution does not want to arrange a negotiated settlement of the case, a criminal trial will be held before a judge (bench trial) or jury, who will decide whether the prosecution's evidence against the defendant is sufficient beyond a reasonable doubt to prove guilt. If a jury cannot reach a decision—that is, if it is deadlocked—the case is left unresolved, leaving the prosecution to decide whether it should be retried at a later date.

11. *Sentencing/disposition.* After a criminal trial, if the accused has been found guilty as charged, he will be returned to court for sentencing. Possible sentencing dispositions include a fine, probation, some form of community-based corrections, a period of incarceration in a penal institution, or, in rare instances, the death penalty.

nolle prosequi The term used when a prosecutor decides to drop a case after a complaint has been formally made. Reasons for a *nolle prosequi* include evidence insufficiency, reluctance of witnesses to testify, police error, and office policy.

grand jury A type of jury responsible for investigating alleged crimes, examining evidence, and issuing indictments.

true bill of indictment A written statement charging a defendant with the commission of a crime, drawn up by a prosecuting attorney and considered by a grand jury. If the grand jury finds sufficient evidence to support the indictment, it will issue a true bill of indictment.

information Charging document filed by the prosecution that forms the basis of the preliminary hearing.

probable cause hearing Term used in some jurisdictions for a preliminary hearing to show cause to bring a case to trial.

12. *Appeal/postconviction remedies.* After conviction, the defense can ask the trial judge to set aside the jury's verdict because the jury has made a mistake of law—for example, by misinterpreting the judge's instructions or convicting on a charge that was not supported by the evidence. Failing that, an appeal may be filed if, after conviction, the defendant believes that his constitutional rights were violated by errors in the trial process. Appellate courts review such issues as whether evidence was used properly, the judge conducted the trial in an approved fashion, jury selection was properly done, and the attorneys in the case acted appropriately. If the court rules that the appeal has merit, it can hold that the defendant be given a new trial or, in some instances, order his or her outright release.

13. *Correctional treatment.* After sentencing, the offender is placed within the jurisdiction of state or federal correctional authorities. The offender may serve a probationary term, be placed in a community correctional facility, serve a term in a county jail, or be housed in a prison. During this stage of the criminal justice process, the offender may be asked to participate in rehabilitation programs designed to help him make a successful readjustment to society.

14. *Release.* Upon completion of the sentence and period of correction, the offender will be free to return to society. Most inmates do not serve the full term of their sentence but are freed through an early-release mechanism, such as parole or pardon or by earning time off for good behavior. Offenders sentenced to community supervision simply finish their term and resume their lives in the community.

15. *Postrelease.* After termination of their correctional treatment, offenders may be asked to spend some time in a community correctional center, which acts as a bridge between a secure treatment facility and absolute freedom. Offenders may find that their conviction has cost them some personal privileges, such as the right to hold certain kinds of employment. These privileges may be restored by court order after the offenders prove their trustworthiness and willingness to adjust to society's rules.

LO5 Trace the formal criminal justice process

The Criminal Justice Assembly Line

To justice expert Herbert Packer, the image that this process evokes is an assembly line conveyor belt down which moves an endless stream of cases, never stopping.[14] According to this view, each of the 15 stages is actually a *decision point* through which cases flow. At the investigatory stage, police must decide whether to pursue the case or terminate involvement because there is insufficient evidence to identify a suspect, the case is considered trivial, the victim decides not to press charges, and so on. At the bail stage, a decision must be made whether to set bail so high that the defendant remains in custody, to set a reasonable bail, or to release the defendant on his or her own recognizance without requiring any bail at all. Each of these decisions can have a critical effect on the defendant, the justice system, and society. If an error is made, an innocent person may suffer or a dangerous individual may be released to continue to prey upon society.

Figure 1.2 illustrates the approximate number of felony offenders removed from the criminal justice system at each stage of the process. As the figure shows, most people who commit crime escape detection, and of those who do not, relatively few are bound over for trial, convicted, and eventually sentenced to prison. About 30 percent of people arrested on felony charges are eventually convicted in criminal court; however, nearly a third of those convicted on felony charges are sentenced to probation and released back into the community without doing time in prison.[15] For every 1,000 crimes, about 20 people are sent to prison.

In actual practice, many suspects are released before trial because of a procedural error, evidence problems, or other reasons that result in a case dismissal by the prosecutor, or *nolle prosequi.* Although most cases that go to trial end in a conviction, others

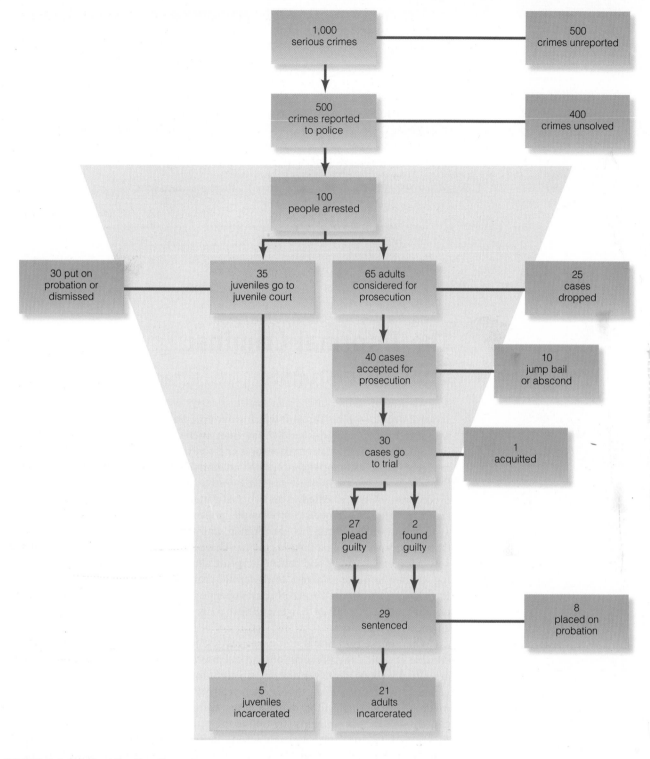

FIGURE 1.2 Criminal Justice Funnel

Sources: Brian Reaves, *Felony Defendants in Large Urban Counties, 2009, Statistical Tables* (Washington, DC: Bureau of Justice Statistics, 2013) http://www.bjs.gov/content/pub/pdf/fdluc09.pdf; Matthew R. Durose, Donald J. Farole, Jr., Sean P. Rosenmerkel, *Felony Sentences in State Courts, 2006 - Statistical Tables* (Washington, DC: Bureau of Justice Statistics, 2009) http://www.bjs.gov/content/pub/pdf/fssc06st.pdf.

are dismissed by the presiding judge because of a witness or a complainant's failure to appear or procedural irregularities. Thus the justice process can be viewed as a funnel that holds many cases at its mouth and relatively few at its end. Concept Summary 1.1 shows the interrelationship of the component agencies of the criminal justice system and the criminal justice process.

L06 Articulate what is meant by the term *criminal justice assembly line*

CONCEPT SUMMARY 1.1 The Interrelationship

The System: Agencies of Crime Control	The Process
1. Police	1. Contact 2. Investigation 3. Arrest 4. Custody
2. Prosecution and defense	5. Complaint/charging 6. Grand jury/preliminary hearing 7. Arraignment 8. Bail/detention 9. Plea negotiations
3. Court	10. Adjudication 11. Disposition 12. Appeal/postconviction remedies
4. Corrections	13. Correction 14. Release 15. Postrelease

The Informal Criminal Justice Process

The traditional model of the criminal justice system depicts the legal process as a series of decision points through which cases flow. Each stage of the system, beginning with investigation and arrest and ending after a sentence has been served, is defined by time-honored administrative procedures and controlled by the rule of law. This "ideal" model of justice still merits concern and attention, but assuming that the system works this way for every case is overly simplistic. Although a few cases exhibit the full array of procedures, many are settled in an informal pattern of cooperation between the major actors in the justice process. For example, police may be willing to make a deal with a suspect in order to gain his cooperation, and the prosecutor may bargain with the defense attorney to gain a plea of guilty as charged in return for a promise of leniency. Law enforcement agents and court officers are allowed tremendous discretion in deciding whether to make an arrest, bring formal charges, handle a case informally, substitute charges, and so on. Crowded courts operate in a spirit of getting the matter settled quickly and cleanly, rather than engaging in long, drawn-out criminal proceedings with an uncertain outcome.

Whereas the traditional model regards the justice process as an adversarial proceeding in which the prosecution and defense are combatants, most criminal cases are actually cooperative ventures in which both the prosecution and defense get together to work out a deal; this is often referred to as the courtroom work group.[16] Made up of the prosecutor, defense attorney, judge, and other court personnel, the courtroom work group helps streamline the process of justice through the extensive use of deal making and plea negotiation. Rather than looking to provide a spirited defense or prosecution, cooperation rather than conflict between prosecutor and defense attorney appears to be the norm. The adversarial process is only called into play in a few widely publicized criminal cases involving rape or murder. Consequently, upward of 80 percent of all felony cases and over 90 percent of misdemeanors are settled without trial.

The "Wedding Cake" Model of Justice

Samuel Walker, a justice historian and scholar, has come up with a rather unique way of describing this informal justice process: he compares it to a four-layer wedding cake, as depicted in Figure 1.3.[17]

courtroom work group The phrase used to indicate that all parties in the adversary process work together cooperatively to settle cases with the least amount of effort and conflict.

LO7 Characterize the informal criminal justice system

LEVEL I The first layer of Walker's model is made up of celebrated cases involving the wealthy and famous, such as O. J. Simpson, or the not-so-powerful who victimize a famous person—such as Jared Lee Loughner, who shot Congresswoman Gabrielle Giffords. Other cases fall into the first layer because they are widely reported in the media and become the subject of widespread media interest. For example, there was an avalanche of media interest in the kidnapping of Elizabeth Smart from her Salt Lake City home on June 5, 2002, and her rescue nine months later. Media attention rebounded in 2010 when her abductors, Brian David Mitchell and Wanda Barzee, were tried and convicted of the crime.[18] Some cases fall into the first level because they involve a large number of victims, such as when James Holmes killed 12 people at a Century movie theater in Aurora, Colorado, on July 20, 2012. Other cases fall into the first tier because they involve the theft of a great deal of money—such as the multi-billion-dollar Ponzi scheme perpetrated by Bernard Madoff who on March 12, 2009, was sentenced to 150 years in prison for his crimes.

FIGURE 1.3 The Criminal Justice "Wedding Cake"

Source: Based on Samuel Walker, *Sense and Nonsense About Crime, Drugs, and Communities* (Belmont, CA: Cengage, 2010).

Cases in the first layer of the criminal justice wedding cake usually receive the full array of criminal justice procedures, including competent defense attorneys, expert witnesses, jury trials, and elaborate appeals. Because of the media focus on Level I cases and the Hollywood treatment they receive, the public is given the impression that most criminals are sober, intelligent people who receive the full range of procedural rights afforded by the justice system and that most victims are members of the upper classes, a patently false impression.

LEVEL II The second layer contains serious felonies—rapes, robberies, and burglaries. Police, prosecutors, and judges all agree that these cases are worthy of the full attention of the justice system. The factors placing them in the Level II category include the following:

- They are committed by experienced, repeat offenders.
- The amount of money stolen in a burglary or larceny is significant.
- Violent acts are committed by a stranger who uses a weapon.
- Robberies involve large amounts of money taken by a weapon-wielding criminal.

Offenders in Level II cases quite often receive a full jury trial and, if convicted, can look forward to a prison sentence.

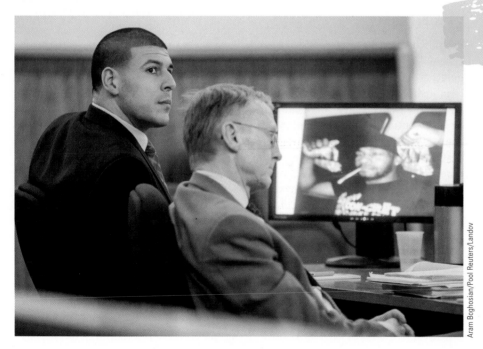

The first layer of the wedding cake involves famous people or those who engage in notorious crime that grab media attention. These defendants receive the most comprehensive criminal defenses and prosecutorial attention. Here former New England Patriots tight end Aaron Hernandez listens next to his attorney Charles Rankin as a photo of witness Darryl Hodge, close friend of Odin Lloyd, is displayed during his murder trial at Bristol County Superior Court in Fall River, Massachusetts, March 31, 2015. Despite his defense attorney's efforts Hernandez was found guilty and received a life sentence.

LO8 Describe the "wedding cake" model of justice

crime control perspective A model of criminal justice that emphasizes the control of dangerous offenders and the protection of society. Its advocates call for harsh punishments as a deterrent to crime and support availability of the death penalty.

LEVEL III Although they can also be felonies, crimes that fall in the third layer of the wedding cake either are less serious offenses, committed by young or first-time offenders, or involve people who knew each other or were otherwise related, such as a domestic abuse case or a drunken brawl involving people in a "love triangle." Level III crimes may be dealt with by an outright dismissal, a plea bargain, a reduction in charges, or, most commonly, a probationary sentence.

LEVEL IV The fourth layer of the cake is made up of the millions of misdemeanors—disorderly conduct, shoplifting, public drunkenness, and minor assault—that are handled by the lower criminal courts in assembly-line fashion. Few defendants insist on exercising their constitutional rights because the delay would cost them valuable time and money, and punishment is typically a fine or probation.[19]

The wedding cake model of informal justice is an intriguing alternative to the traditional criminal justice flowchart. Criminal justice officials handle individual cases quite differently, yet particular types or classes of cases are handled with a high degree of consistency in every legal jurisdiction. For example, police and prosecutors in Los Angeles and Boston will handle the murder of a prominent citizen in a similar fashion. They will also deal with the death of an unemployed street person killed in a brawl in a similar manner. The wedding cake model is useful because it illustrates that public opinion about criminal justice is often formed on the basis of what happened in an atypical case.

Perspectives on Justice

Even though it has been almost 50 years since the field of criminal justice began to be the subject of serious academic study, significant debate continues over the actual meaning of *criminal justice* and how the problem of crime control should be approached. After decades of effort in research and policy analysis, it is clear that criminal justice is far from a unified field. Practitioners, academics, and commentators alike have expressed irreconcilable differences concerning its goals, purpose, and direction. Considering the complexity of criminal justice, it is not surprising that no single perspective or philosophy dominates the field. What are the dominant views of the criminal justice system today? What is the role of the justice system, and how should it approach its tasks? The different perspectives on criminal justice are discussed next.

Crime Control Perspective

People who hold the **crime control perspective** believe that the proper role of the justice system is to prevent crime through the judicious use of criminal sanctions. Because the public is outraged by violent crimes such as the Ferguson shooting, it demands an efficient justice system that hands out tough sanctions to those who choose to violate the law.[20] If the justice system were allowed to operate in an effective manner, unhampered by legal controls, potential criminals would be deterred from violating the law. Those who did commit a crime would be apprehended, tried, and punished so that they would never dare commit a crime again. Crime rates trend upward, the argument goes, when criminals do not sufficiently fear apprehension and punishment. If the efficiency of the system could be increased, and the criminal law could be toughened, crime rates would eventually decline. Effective law enforcement, strict mandatory punishment, incarceration of dangerous criminals, and the judicious use of capital punishment are the keys to reducing crime rates. Crime control may be expensive, but reducing the pain inflicted by criminal activity is well worth the price: if punishments were swift, certain, and severe, few would be tempted to break the law.

Crime control advocates do not want legal technicalities to help the guilty go free and tie the hands of justice. They lobby for the abolition of legal restrictions on a police officer's ability to search for evidence and interrogate suspects. They want law enforcement officers to be able to profile people at an airport in order to identify terrorists, even if it means singling out individuals because of their gender, race, or ethnic origin. They are angry at judges who let obviously guilty people go free because a law enforcement officer made an unintentional procedural error.

Following are the key positions of the crime control perspective:

- The purpose of the justice system is to deter crime through the application of punishment.
- The more efficient the system, the greater its effectiveness.
- The justice system is not equipped to treat people but rather to investigate crimes, apprehend suspects, and punish the guilty.

Rehabilitation Perspective

Advocates of the **rehabilitation perspective** view crime as an expression of frustration and anger created by social inequality. They see the justice system as a means of caring for and treating people who have been the victims of this inequity. According to this view, crime can be controlled by giving people the means to improve their lifestyle and helping them overcome any personal and or psychological problems caused by their life circumstances.

The rehabilitation concept assumes that people are at the mercy of social, economic, and interpersonal conditions and interactions. Criminals themselves are the victims of racism, poverty, strain, blocked opportunities, alienation, family disruption, and other social problems. Violent killers such as James Holmes seem mentally and emotionally unstable. Others live in socially disorganized neighborhoods that are incapable of providing proper education, health care, or civil services. Society must help them in order to compensate for their social problems; proper treatment may prevent their crimes.

Rehabilitation advocates scoff at the notion that crime can be deterred by the threat of punishment alone. Research shows that experienced criminals perceive less risk and more reward from crime, and they are therefore unaffected by the threat of punishments.[21] Even some novice criminals are not easily deterred: they are not well informed about the actual risks of sanctions and believe that crime may actually pay.[22]

Instead of punishment and deterrence, rehabilitation advocates believe that government treatment-oriented programs can help reduce crime on both a societal (macro) and individual (micro) level. On the macro or societal level, rehabilitation efforts are aimed at preventing crimes before they occur. If legitimate opportunities are provided by job training, family counseling, educational services, and crisis intervention, crime rates decline. On a micro or individual level, rehabilitation efforts are aimed at known offenders who have already violated the law. The best way to reduce crime and recidivism (repeat offending) rates is to help offenders adopt prosocial changes in attitudes and improve cognitive thinking patterns through intensive one-on-one counseling.[23] Although the public may want to "get tough" on crime, many are willing to make exceptions, for example, by advocating leniency for younger offenders.[24]

Following are the key provisions of the rehabilitation model:

- In the long run, it is better to treat than to punish.
- Criminals are society's victims.
- Helping others is part of the American culture.
- Convicted criminals can be successfully treated within the confines of the justice system.

Due Process Perspective

According to the **due process perspective**, the justice system should be dedicated to providing fair and equitable treatment to those accused of crime.[25] This means providing impartial hearings, competent legal counsel, evenhanded treatment, and reasonable

ETHICAL REFLECTION

Racial Profiling

Would it be ethical to allow police to stop, search, and interrogate members of racial and ethnic groups who they believe are more likely to be involved in crime? Or does this create a "self-fulfilling prophecy": people in a particular group are arrested more often simply because they are targeted by police. Is racial profiling inherently wrong, or does it have a purpose? Can the death of Michael Brown be linked directly to his being profiled by Officer Darren Wilson?

WEB APP 1.3 Racial profiling is a very troubling issue. To read more about it, go to the ACLU website at **http://www.aclu.org/racial-justice/racial-profiling**. Do you believe it's ever ethical or acceptable for law enforcement officers to be suspicious of someone because of their ethnic or racial profile?

rehabilitation perspective The view that the primary purpose of criminal justice is helping to care for people who cannot manage themselves. Crime is an expression of frustration and anger created by social inequality and can be controlled by giving people the means to improve their lifestyle through conventional endeavors.

due process perspective Due process provides the basic rights of a defendant in criminal proceedings and the requirements for a fair trial.

AP Images/John Minchillo

The due process clause guarantees fairness for all those who come before the law. Sometimes determining what is fair and just can be challenging. Here, Benjamin Carr, stepfather of Eric Garner, leaves the district attorney's office after a grand jury's decision not to indict the officer accused of putting the unarmed Garner in a fatal chokehold after he was arrested for selling cigarettes. The chokehold was applied despite Garner crying out "I can't breathe". Supporters of Garner's family and others have questioned whether due process—both for the family and the officers—is possible in a case that's sparked nationwide protests on excessive force and accusations by NYPD officers and union officials that the officers involved were being railroaded.

sanctions to ensure that no one suffers from racial, religious, or ethnic discrimination and that their basic constitutional rights are respected.

Those who advocate the due process orientation are quick to point out that the justice system remains an adversarial process that pits the forces of an all-powerful state against those of a solitary individual accused of a crime. If concern for justice and fairness did not exist, the defendant who lacked resources could easily be overwhelmed; miscarriages of justice are all too common. Numerous criminal convictions have been overturned because newly developed DNA evidence later showed that the accused could not have committed the crimes; many of the falsely convicted spend years in prison before their release.[26] Evidence also shows that many innocent people have been executed for crimes they did not commit.[27] Because such mistakes can happen, even the most apparently guilty offender deserves all the protection the justice system can offer.

The key positions advocated by due process supporters include the following:

- Every person deserves her or his full array of constitutional rights and privileges.
- Preserving the democratic ideals of American society takes precedence over the need to punish the guilty.
- Because of potential errors, decisions made within the justice system must be carefully scrutinized.
- Steps must be taken to treat all defendants fairly regardless of their sex, socioeconomic status, race, religion, or ethnicity.

Nonintervention Perspective

nonintervention perspective
A view of criminal justice that emphasizes the least intrusive treatment possible. Among its central policies are decarceration, diversion, and decriminalization. In other words, less is better.

Supporters of the **nonintervention perspective** believe that justice agencies should limit their involvement with criminal defendants. They believe that regardless of whether intervention is designed to punish people or to treat them, the ultimate effect of any involvement is harmful and will have long-term negative consequences. Once involved with the justice system, criminal defendants develop a permanent record that follows them for the rest of their lives. They may be watched and kept under surveillance. Bearing an official label disrupts their personal and family life and harms their own self-image; they may view themselves as bad, evil, outcasts, troublemakers, or crazy. Official labels then may promote rather than reduce the continuity in antisocial activities.[28] When people are given less stigmatized forms of punishment, such as probation, they are less likely to become repeat offenders.[29]

Noninterventionists worry that contemporary technology will reduce the privacy of American citizens, especially those convicted of crime who now have a permanent and public record. Take for instance the effort to monitor former sex offenders by requiring them to be placed on Web-based sex offender registration lists. Sex offender registration laws are now used in all 50 states. They appeal to politicians who may be swayed by media crusades against child molesters and appease the public's desire to "do something" about child predators. However, research shows that sex offender registration does not reduce the number of rearrests for sex offenses, nor does it have any demonstrable effect on the time between when sex offenders were released from prison and the time they were rearrested for any new offense, such as a drug offense, theft, or another sex offense.[30]

Fearing the harmful effects of stigma and labels, noninterventionists have tried to place limitations on the government's ability to control people's lives. They have called for the decriminalization (reduction of penalties) and legalization (lawful and noncriminal) of nonserious victimless crimes, such as the possession of small amounts of marijuana. Noninterventionists have sponsored the removal of nonviolent offenders from the nation's correctional system, a policy referred to as deinstitutionalization. They support the placement of first offenders who commit minor crimes in informal, community-based treatment programs, a process referred to as pretrial diversion.

Noninterventionists fear that efforts to help or treat offenders may actually stigmatize them beyond the scope of their actual offense; this is referred to as widening the net of justice. Their efforts have resulted in rulings stating that these laws can be damaging to the reputation and the future of offenders who have not been given an opportunity to defend themselves from the charge that they are chronic criminal sex offenders.[31] As a group, noninterventionist initiatives have been implemented to help people avoid the stigma associated with contact with the criminal justice system.

The key elements of the nonintervention perspective include the following:

- The justice process stigmatizes offenders.
- Stigma locks people into a criminal way of life.
- Less is better. Decriminalize, divert, and deinstitutionalize whenever possible.

decriminalization Reducing the penalty for a criminal act but not actually legalizing it.

legalization The removal of all criminal penalties from a previously outlawed act.

deinstitutionalization The policy of removing as many offenders as possible from secure confinement and treating them in the community.

pretrial diversion A program that provides nonpunitive, community-based alternatives to more intrusive forms of punishment such as jail or prison.

widening the net of justice The view that programs designed to divert offenders from the justice system actually enmesh them further in the process by substituting more intrusive treatment programs for less intrusive punishment-oriented outcomes.

Equal Justice Perspective

According to those who take the equal justice perspective, the greatest challenge facing the American criminal justice system is its capability to dispense fair and equal justice to those who come before the law. It is unfair for police to issue a summons to one person for a traffic violation while letting a second offender off with a warning, or to have two people commit the same crime but receive different sentences or punishments. Unequal and inconsistent treatment produces disrespect for the system, suspiciousness, and frustration; it also increases the likelihood of recidivism. Therefore, law violators should be evaluated on the basis of their current behavior, not on what they have done in the past (they have already paid for that behavior) or on what they may do in the future (because future behavior cannot be accurately predicted). The treatment of criminal offenders must be based solely on their present behavior: punishment must be equitably administered and based on "just deserts."

The equal justice perspective has had considerable influence in molding the nation's sentencing policy. There has been an ongoing effort to reduce discretion and to guarantee that every offender convicted of a particular crime receives equal punishment. A number of initiatives have been designed to achieve this result, including mandatory sentences requiring that all people convicted of a crime receive the same prison sentence.

Following are the key elements of the equal justice perspective:

- People should receive equal treatment for equal crimes.
- Decision making in the justice system must be standardized and structured by rules and regulations.
- Whenever possible, individual discretion must be reduced and controlled.
- Inconsistent treatment produces disrespect for the system.

equal justice perspective The view that all people should be treated equally before the law. Equality may best be achieved through individual discretion in the justice process.

Restorative Justice Perspective

restorative justice perspective
A view of criminal justice that advocates peaceful solutions and mediation rather than coercive punishments.

According to the concept of restorative justice, the criminal justice system should promote a peaceful and just society; the justice system should aim for peacemaking, not punishment.[32] Advocates of the restorative justice perspective view the efforts of the state to punish and control as encouraging crime rather than discouraging it. The violent, punishing acts of the state are not dissimilar to the violent acts of individuals.[33] Therefore, mutual aid rather than coercive punishment is the key to a harmonious society. Without the capacity to restore damaged social relations, society's response to crime has been almost exclusively punitive.

According to restorative justice, resolution of the conflict between criminal and victim should take place in the community in which it originated, not in some far-off prison. Under these conditions, the victim has a chance to tell his story, and the offender can directly communicate his need for social reintegration and treatment. The goal is to enable the offender to appreciate the damage he has caused, to make amends, and to be reintegrated into society.

Restorative justice programs are now being devised to reflect these principles. Police officers, as elements of community policing programs, are beginning to use mediation techniques to settle disputes, rather than resorting to formal arrest.[34] Mediation and conflict-resolution programs are common features in many communities and are being used in efforts to resolve harmful human interactions ranging from domestic violence to hate crimes.[35] Financial and community service restitution programs have been in operation for more than two decades as an alternative to imprisonment.

The most important elements of the restorative justice model are the following:

- Offenders should be reintegrated into society.
- Coercive punishments are self-defeating.
- The justice system must become more humane.

Perspectives in Perspective

Advocates of each view have attempted to promote their vision of what justice is all about and how it should be enforced. During the past decade, the crime control and equal justice models have dominated. Laws have been toughened and the rights of the accused curtailed, the prison population has grown, and the death penalty has been employed against convicted murderers. Because the crime rate has been dropping, these policies seem to be effective; they may be questioned if crime rates once again begin to rise. At the same time, efforts to rehabilitate offenders, to provide them with elements of due process, and to give them the least intrusive treatment have not been abandoned. Police, courts, and correctional agencies supply a wide range of treatment and rehabilitation programs to offenders in all stages of the criminal justice system. Whenever possible, those accused of crime are treated informally in nonrestrictive, community-based programs, and the effects of stigma are guarded against. Although the legal rights of offenders are being closely scrutinized by the courts, the basic constitutional rights of the accused remain inviolate. Guardians of the process have made sure that defendants are allowed the maximum protection possible under the law. For example, criminal defendants have been awarded the right to competent legal counsel at trial; merely having a lawyer to defend them is not considered sufficient legal protection.

In sum, understanding the justice system today requires analyzing a variety of occupational roles, institutional processes, legal rules, and administrative doctrines. Each predominant view of criminal justice provides a vantage point for understanding and interpreting these rather complex issues. No single view is *the* right or correct one. Each individual must choose the perspective that best fits his or her own ideas and judgment—or propose a different view that combines elements of all the perspectives or expresses the individual's own view in a new and unique way.

REALITY**CHECK**

MYTH OR REALITY?

Justice tends to be objective rather than subjective; agents of the justice system put their personal feelings aside in the course of their duties.

MYTH. Agents of the justice system have varied and differing perspectives on what justice is all about and how they should approach their role and duties.

Some police officers, court officers, and correctional personnel practice a "law and order" orientation, whereas others are more interested in helping and treating offenders. What other professions maintain competing values and viewpoints?

LO9 Discuss the various perspectives on justice

Noah Berger/Reuters/Landov

On December 10, 2014, a plain clothes California Highway Patrol detective, who had been marching with anti-police demonstrators, aimed his gun at protesters after some in the crowd identified him and his partner during an arrest in Oakland, California. Chief Avery Browne, commander of the California Highway Patrol's Golden Gate Division, said two plainclothes CHP detectives were surrounded by up to 50 demonstrators who ignored orders to back off, despite one of the officers first taking out his baton and identifying himself as police. Is it ethical for police officers to go undercover in such a volatile situation or does that compromise the political process and the public right to demonstrate against government practices they find objectionable?

Ethics in Criminal Justice

The general public and criminal justice professionals are also concerned with the application of ethics in the criminal justice system.[36] Both would like every police officer on the street, every district attorney in court, and every correctional administrator in prison to be able to discern what is right, proper, and moral; to be committed to ethical standards; and to apply equal and fair justice. These demands are difficult because justice system personnel are often forced to work in an environment where moral ambiguity is the norm. Should a police officer be forced to arrest, a prosecutor charge, and a correctional official punish a woman who for many years was the victim of domestic abuse and who in desperation retaliated against her abusive spouse? Who is the victim here, and who is the aggressor? What about the parent who attacks the man who has sexually abused her young child? Should she be prosecuted as a felon? But what happens if the parent mistakenly attacks and injures the wrong person? Can a clear line be drawn between righteous retribution and vigilante justice? As students of justice, we are concerned with identifying the behavioral standards that should govern each of the elements of justice. If these can be identified, is it possible to find ways to apply these standards to police, court, and correctional agencies around the nation?

Ethics in criminal justice is an especially important topic today because of the power granted to those who control the justice system. We rely on the justice system to exert power over people's lives and to be society's instrument of social control, so we grant the system and its agents the authority to deny people their personal liberty on a routine basis. A police officer's ability to arrest and use force, a judge's power to sentence, and a correctional administrator's ability to punish an inmate give them considerable personal power that must be governed by ethical considerations. Without ethical decision making, individual civil rights may suffer and personal liberties guaranteed by the US Constitution may be trampled upon. The need for an ethical criminal justice system is further enhanced by cyber-age advances in record keeping and data recording. Agents of the criminal justice system now have immediate access to our most personal information, ranging from arrest records to medical history. Issues of privacy and confidentiality, which can have enormous economic, social, and political consequences, are now more critical than ever.

Ethical issues transcend all elements of the justice system. Yet each branch has specific issues that shape its ethical standards, as we will see in the following sections.

Ethics and Law Enforcement

Ethical behavior is particularly important in law enforcement because, quite simply, police officers have the authority to deprive people of their liberty. And, in carrying out their daily activities, they also have the right to use physical and even deadly force.

Depriving people of liberty and using force are not the only police behaviors that require ethical consideration. Police officers exercise considerable discretion when they choose whom to investigate, how far the investigation should go, and how much effort they should spend on a case. They also sometimes are asked to walk a fine line between legal and illegal behavior when they are searching for evidence or interrogating a suspect; for example, claiming a hidden item was actually in "plain view" or that a suspect's confession was freely given when in reality the officer used threats and coercion. In carrying out their duties, police officers must be responsive to the public's demand for protection, while at the same time remaining sensitive to the rights and liberties of those they must deter and/or control. In this capacity, they serve as the interface between the power of the state and the citizens it governs. This duality creates many ethical dilemmas. Consider the following:

- Should law enforcement agents target groups whom they suspect are heavily involved in crime and violence, or does this lead to racial/ethnic profiling? Is it unethical for a security agent to pay closer attention to a young Arab male getting on an airline flight than she pays to a well-groomed American soldier from upstate New York? After all, there have been no terrorist activities among army personnel, and the 9/11 terrorists were of Arab descent. But don't forget that clean-cut Tim McVeigh, who grew up in rural Pendleton, New York, and spent more than three years in the army, went on to become the Oklahoma City bomber. How can police officers balance their need to protect public security with the ethical requirement that they safeguard citizens' legal rights?

- What limits should be placed on the use of technology? Should law enforcement agencies be allowed to use tracking devices to monitor movements, take facial scans, listen in on cell phones, or hack into computers in order to keep watch on potential criminals and terrorists? Does the end justify the means? The accompanying Criminal Justice and Technology feature addresses this issue.

- Should police officers tell the truth even if it means that a guilty person goes free? For example, a police officer stops a car for a traffic violation and searches it illegally. He finds a weapon used in a particularly heinous shooting in which three children were killed. Would it be ethical for the officer to lie on the witness stand and say the gun was resting on the car seat in plain sight (thereby rendering its seizure legal and proper)? Or should he tell the truth and risk having the charges dismissed, leaving the offender free to kill again?

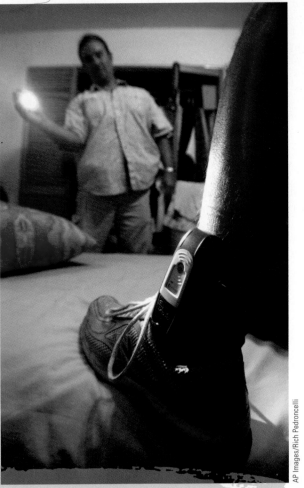

AP Images/Rich Pedroncelli

Parole Agent Steve Nakamura uses a flashlight to inspect a GPS locater worn on the ankle of a sex-offender parolee in Rio Linda, California. As well as wearing GPS locators, paroled California sex offenders are required to periodically take lie-detector tests as part of a stepped-up effort to prevent new sex crimes following several high-profile cases involving parolees who raped and killed. Is it ethical to single out sex offenders for such treatment? Does the severity of their crimes warrant greater scrutiny than that given to other convicted criminals such as robbers, burglars and drug dealers? Do sex offenders deserve a lesser right to privacy than these other criminals?

Ethics and the Courts

Ethical concerns do not stop with an arrest. As an officer of the court and the "people's attorney," the prosecutor must seek justice for all parties in a criminal matter and should not merely be targeting a conviction. To be fair, prosecutors must share evidence with the defense, must not use scare tactics or intimidation, and must represent the public interest. It is inexcusable and illegal for prosecutors to

Monitoring Sex Offenders with GPS technology: Liberty vs. Security

As technology improves, agencies of the criminal justice system must wrestle with the conflict between ensuring the privacy and liberty of even those convicted of criminal offenses with the need for maintaining security and protecting the public.

Take for instance using a Global Positioning System (GPS) to monitor convicted offenders released to the community. This satellite-based navigation system allows receivers to obtain exact location and time information anywhere on Earth where there is an unobstructed line of sight to four or more GPS satellites. The GPS is maintained by the US government and is free to anyone with a GPS receiver.

GPS technology is now being used to monitor offenders in the community. How effective are such efforts, and are they worthwhile? A study of California high-risk sex offenders on parole found that those placed on GPS monitoring had significantly lower recidivism rates than those who received traditional supervision.

Researchers examined the effectiveness of using GPS to monitor 516 high-risk sex offenders who had been released on parole between January 2006 and March 2009. Half of the parolees wore GPS monitoring devices in addition to receiving traditional parole supervision, which involves regular contact by parole agents and weekly sex-offender treatment classes (the "GPS group"); the other half received only traditional parole supervision (the "traditional group"). Researchers tracked each parolee for one year following his initial parole date.

The study assessed both the cost of the GPS program and its effectiveness in reducing the criminal behavior of high-risk sex offender parolees. The researchers collected information from the state's data management system and examined official arrest records, parole supervision records, GPS monitoring data, and state cost information. In addition, they conducted a survey of roughly 1,000 California Department of Corrections and Rehabilitation (CDCR) parole officers. The survey included questions about the GPS monitoring system, caseloads, program staffing, and screening of high-risk sex-offender parolees.

The researchers found that parolees in the traditional group—those not placed on GPS monitoring—committed new crimes and had their parole revoked more often than did parolees in the GPS group. In addition, the traditional group returned to custody at a rate 38 percent higher than the GPS group.

The cost analysis showed that, in California, monitoring parolees using GPS cost approximately $35.96 a day per person, while the cost of traditional supervision is about $27.45 a day. The GPS program is more expensive but more effective. Although the GPS program costs $8.51 more per day than traditional supervision, the GPS approach produced a decrease of 12 percentage points in arrests for any offense (from approximately 26 percent to 14 percent). In addition, offenders who were monitored using GPS complied with the terms of their parole at higher rates than did offenders on traditional parole.

The cost of California's GPS monitoring is lower than the cost of moving parolees to "indefinite civil commitment," that is, sending sex offenders whose prison sentences are over—but who are believed to be too dangerous to release into the community—directly from confinement in prison to confinement in dedicated institutions. Such civil confinement programs can cost an average of more than $100,000 a year per person because of the programming that must be provided.

CRITICAL THINKING

1. Do you think the use of futuristic security methods such as monitoring people's movements will lead to the loss of personal privacy and the erosion of civil liberties?

2. Why should a person's behavior and activities be monitored after they have served their time and left prison? Does the need for security outweigh the right of personal liberty?

3. Should police officers be loyal to their peers even when they know a colleague has violated the law? For example, a new officer soon becomes aware that his partner is taking gratuities from local gangsters in return for looking the other way and allowing their prostitution and bookmaking operations to flourish. Should the rookie file a complaint and turn in his partner? Will he be labeled a "rat" and lose the respect of his fellow officers? After all, gambling and prostitution are not violent crimes and don't really hurt anyone. Or do they?

Source: <u>Philip Bulman</u>, "Sex Offenders Monitored by GPS Found to Commit Fewer Crimes," *NIJ Journal*, No. 271, February 2013, http://www.nij.gov/journals/271/pages/gps-monitoring.aspx.

---

suppress critical evidence, a practice that might mean the guilty walked free and the innocent were convicted.

Prosecutorial ethics are tested when the dual role of prosecutors cause them to experience role conflict. On the one hand, a prosecutor represents the people and has an obligation to present evidence, uphold the law, and obtain convictions as vigorously as possible. In the adversary system, it is the prosecutor who takes the side of victims and on whom the victims rely for justice. Because of overcrowded court dockets and limited resources, prosecutors more often than not seek plea deals, granting more lenient sentences in exchange for an admission of guilt. This can create an ethical dilemma: Is justice being served when a guilty party is allowed to escape the full extent of the law in order to maintain efficiency in the justice process?

But as a fair and impartial officer of the court, the prosecutor must oversee the investigation of crime and make sure that all aspects of the investigation meet constitutional standards. If, during the investigation, it appears that the police have violated the constitutional rights of suspects—for example, by extracting an illegal confession or conducting an illegal search—then the prosecutor has an ethical obligation to take whatever action is necessary and appropriate to remedy legal or technical errors, even if it means rejecting a case in which the defendant's rights have been violated. Moreover, the canon

WEB APP 1.4 What help is available to law enforcement officers in making ethical decisions? Various national organizations have produced model codes of conduct that can serve as behavioral guides. One well-known document created by the International Association of Chiefs of Police (IACP) says, in part, "As a law enforcement officer, my fundamental duty is to serve mankind; to safeguard lives and property; to protect the innocent against deception, the weak against oppression or intimidation, and the peaceful against violence or disorder; and to respect the constitutional rights of all men to liberty, equality, and justice." To learn more, visit their website at **http://www.theiacp.org**.

of legal ethics in most states forbids the prosecutor from pursuing charges when there is no probable cause and mandates that all evidence that might mitigate guilt or reduce the punishment be turned over to the defense.

DEFENSE ATTORNEY As an officer of the court, along with the judge, prosecutors, and other trial participants, the defense attorney seeks to uncover the basic facts and elements of the criminal act. In this dual capacity of being both a defensive advocate and an officer of the court, the attorney is often confronted with conflicting obligations to his client and profession. Suppose a client confides that she is planning to commit a crime. What are the defense attorney's ethical responsibilities in this case? Obviously, the attorney would have to counsel the client to obey the law; if the attorney assisted the client in engaging in illegal behavior, the attorney would be subject to charges of unprofessional conduct and even criminal liability.

What about the situation where an attorney knows that his or her client is guilty because the client admitted as much during pretrial conferences? Should the defense lawyer still try for an acquittal? What is said privately before trial, even at a plea discussion, is never admissible during trial. An attorney would be accused of incompetence if she or he did not try to raise reasonable doubt in every case. The attorney's job is not to decide whether the client committed the offense but to provide a vigorous defense and ensure that the client is not convicted unless the prosecution can prove its case beyond a reasonable doubt. And it is impossible to make the prosecution meet its burden without aggressively challenging the evidence, even if the defender believes the client committed the crime. However, if a client attempted to take the stand and lie about his involvement in the crime, then the attorney would be required to tell the judge.[37]

Ethics and Corrections

Ethical issues do not disappear after a defendant has been convicted. The ethical issues in punishment are too vast to discuss here, but they include the following:

- Is it fair and ethical to execute a criminal? Can capital punishment ever be considered a moral choice? While lethal injections are supposed to be pain free, recent botched executions show that there is no such thing as a painless death. No matter how it is implemented, does the death penalty violate the Constitution's ban on cruel and unusual punishment?
- Should people be given different punishments for the same criminal law violation? Is it fair and just when some convicted murderers and rapists receive probation for their crimes while others are sentenced to prison for the same offense?
- Is it fair to grant leniency to criminals who agree to testify against their coconspirator and therefore allow them to benefit from their perfidy, while others, who are not given the opportunity to "squeal," are forced to bear the full brunt of the law?
- Should some criminal inmates be granted early release because they can persuade the parole board that they have been rehabilitated, while others, who are not as glib, convincing, or well spoken, are forced to serve their entire sentence behind bars?
- Should technology be used to monitor offenders in the community? Would it be ethical to track a probationer's movements with a GPS unit attached to an ankle bracelet she is required to wear at all times? Should her Internet use and computer downloads be monitored?

Ethics are also challenged by the discretion afforded to correctional workers and administrators. Discretion is involved when a correctional officer decides whether to report an inmate for disorderly conduct, which might jeopardize his or her parole. And although the Supreme Court has issued many rulings related to prisoners' rights, no justices are at the scene of the prison to make sure that their mandates are carried out reliably and consistently.

Correctional officers have significant coercive power over offenders. They are under a legal and professional obligation not to use unnecessary force or take

LO10 Discuss the ethical issues that arise in criminal justice

REALITYCHECK

MYTH OR REALITY?

Defense attorneys do not represent clients they know to be guilty.

MYTH. Defense attorneys must provide their clients with a rigorous defense even if they know their client did the act in question.

It is possible that a client is not guilty legally even if they actually did the act for which they are charged, for example, if they acted in self-defense or were legally insane. Therefore, even someone who admits committing a crime requires a rigorous defense.

advantage of inmate powerlessness. Examples of abuse include an officer who beats an inmate or a staff member who coerces sex from an inmate. The possibility that these abuses of power will be perpetrated exists because of the powerlessness of the offender relative to the correctional professional. A recent national survey uncovered evidence that this breach of ethics is significant: An estimated 8,210 allegations of sexual violence were reported by correctional inmates. About 42 percent of the reported allegations of sexual violence involved staff-on-inmate sexual misconduct, and 11 percent involved staff sexual harassment of inmates. In other words, staff members were involved in more cases of sexual violence and harassment in correctional facilities than were inmates![38]

Ethical considerations transcend all elements of the justice system. Making ethical decisions is an increasingly important task in a society that is becoming more diverse, pluralistic, and complex every day.

ETHICAL Challenge

Merchants in Midcity have been complaining to the mayor's office about aggressive and disrespectful youth who are congregating in the downtown retail areas. The merchants believe that the large number of teens hanging out in the area are responsible for scaring away middle-class shoppers and producing a downturn in business. Some owners are even threatening to relocate to a suburban mall unless "something can be done." To counter this threat to the economy, the police chief wants a free hand to clear the streets and make them safe for shoppers. She wants to institute an aggressive policy of stopping and questioning kids she considers troublemakers, especially young black and Hispanic males who have been the main target of merchant complaints. She wants patrol officers to order them off the street because they are "disturbing the peace" and to arrest any person who does not immediately comply with the order to disperse.

Ethical Challenge: Write a memo to the chief listing the ethical pros and cons of allowing patrol officers to use aggressive tactics with youth who have broken no law nor committed any crime. Make sure to address the potential negative side effects of such a police action, even if the street appears safe and business picks up.

You might want to visit these sites before you begin:

http://www.popcenter.org/responses/police_crackdowns/

http://www.children.gov.on.ca/htdocs/English/topics/youthandthelaw/roots/volume5/preventing02_policy_strategiesi.aspx

http://www.academia.edu/6053371/The_Effects_of_Aggressive_Policing_of_Disorder_on_Serious_Crime

http://www.indiana.edu/~atlantic/wp-content/uploads/2011/11/Stoudt-Fine-Fox-Growing-Up-Policed.pdf

SUMMARY

LO1 *Discuss the formation of the criminal justice system in America* There was little in the way of a formal criminal justice system until the nineteenth century when the first police agencies were created. The term *criminal justice system* became prominent around 1967, when the President's Commission on Law Enforcement and the Administration of Justice began a nationwide study of the nation's crime problem.

LO2 *Define the concept of a criminal justice system* The term *criminal justice* refers to both the agencies that dispense justice and the process in which justice is carried out. It is assumed that these agencies work in concert to protect society and dispense fair and equal justice.

LO3 *Identify the basic component agencies of the criminal justice system* On an ideal level, the criminal justice system functions as a cooperative effort among the primary agencies—police, courts, and corrections. All too often, however, these agencies act independently from one another.

LO4 *Comprehend the size and scope of the contemporary justice system* The contemporary criminal justice system in the United States is monumental in size. It now costs federal, state, and local governments more

than $200 billion per year for civil and criminal justice. The system is massive because it must process, treat, and care for millions of people. As a result, the system now employs more than 2 million people.

LO5 *Trace the formal criminal justice process* The criminal justice process consists of the actual steps the offender takes from the initial investigation through trial, sentencing, and appeal. The justice process contains 15 stages, each of which is a decision point through which cases flow. Each of these decisions can have a critical effect on the defendant, the justice system, and society.

LO6 *Articulate what is meant by the term* **criminal justice assembly line** Some experts believe that the justice system processes cases in a routine, ritualized manner resembling an assembly line. Because justice is often dispensed in a hasty fashion, an innocent person may suffer a false accusation while a dangerous individual may be released to continue to prey upon society. The system acts as a "funnel": most people who commit crime escape detection, and of those who do not, relatively few are bound over for trial, convicted, and eventually sentenced to prison.

LO7 *Characterize the informal criminal justice system* A great deal of the criminal justice process is informal, involving deal making and plea bargaining. Rather than engage in the adversarial process, prosecution and defense work together to settle cases efficiently. Bargains and informal negotiations are more common than formal trials.

L08 Describe the "wedding cake" model of justice

There are significant differences in the way each case is treated. Criminal acts that are very serious or notorious may receive the full complement of criminal justice processes, from arrest to trial. However, less serious cases are often settled when a bargain is reached between the prosecution and the defense.

L09 Discuss the various perspectives on justice

The role of the criminal justice system can be interpreted in many ways. People who study the field or work in its agencies bring their own ideas and feelings to bear when they try to decide on the right course of action to take or recommend. Thus, a number of different perspectives on criminal justice exist today, ranging from the most conservative (crime control) to the most liberal (restorative justice).

L010 Discuss the ethical issues that arise in criminal justice

Determining what is fair and just and balancing it with the need to protect the public can be difficult. The police, courts system, and correctional agencies face ethical issues ranging from ethnic and racial profiling to the use of the death penalty.

KEY TERMS

criminal justice system, p. 6

criminal justice process, p. 6

Law Enforcement Assistance Administration (LEAA), p. 8

social control, p. 8

in-presence requirement, p. 10

nolle prosequi, p. 11

grand jury, p. 11

true bill of indictment, p. 11

information, p. 11

probably cause hearing, p. 11

courtroom work group, p. 14

crime control perspective, p. 16

rehabilitation perspective, p. 17

due process perspective, p. 17

nonintervention perspective, p. 18

decriminalization, p. 19

legalization, p. 19

deinstitutionalization, p. 19

pretrial diversion, p. 19

widening the net of justice, p. 19

equal justice perspective, p. 19

restorative justice perspective, p. 20

REVIEW QUESTIONS

1. Can a single standard of ethics be applied to all criminal justice agencies? Or is the world too complex to legislate morality and ethics?

2. Describe the differences between the formal and informal justice systems. Is it fair to treat some offenders informally?

3. What are the layers of the criminal justice "wedding cake?" Give an example of a crime for each layer.

4. What are the basic elements of each model or perspective on justice? Which best represents your own point of view?

5. How would each perspective on criminal justice consider the use of the death penalty as a punishment for first-degree murder?

6. What amendments to the Constitution are most important for the administration of justice?

2 The Nature of Crime and Victimization

REALITY**CHECK**

MYTH OR REALITY?

- Most people report their criminal victimizations to police.
- Crime and violence rates are out of control and getting worse every day.
- The police assign more patrol cars to areas where minority populations are increasing, and white residents have become fearful.
- High unemployment causes crime rates to increase.
- Crime victims are generally people who are in the wrong place at the wrong time.
- The elderly are the age group most vulnerable to predatory criminals.
- Most crimes are committed by strangers.
- Children exposed to lead in their environment will be prone to antisocial behavior as they mature.
- Kids who watch a lot of violence on TV are more likely to eventually get involved in violent behavior themselves.

On September 13, 2014, 18-year-old University of Virginia student Hannah Graham went missing. The night before, Graham had met friends at a restaurant for dinner before stopping by two off-campus parties. She left the second party alone and eventually texted a friend saying she was lost. After a search involving thousands of volunteers, Graham's remains were found on October 18, 2014, near Charlottesville, Virginia, in a spot roughly six miles from where the body of another murder victim, 20-year-old Virginia Tech student, Morgan Harrington, was found after she vanished in 2009.

A lead in the case developed when police examined surveillance videos taken the night Hannah disappeared. In the video, she seems disoriented and can be seen walking unsteadily past a bar and a service station and then onto a seven-block strip of bars, restaurants, and shops. Also caught on the tape was 32-year-old Jesse Leroy Matthew, Jr., who had a long history of violent behavior with women. Matthew became a prime suspect in the case and was eventually arrested in Galveston, Texas, as he planned to leave the country. He was charged with abduction with intent to defile Graham. Forensic evidence linked Matthews to the murder of Graham and Harrington as well as other sexual assaults.[1]

When splashed across the media and rehashed on nightly talk shows, cases such as the murders of Hannah Graham and Morgan Harrington, coupled with incidents of mass killings such as the Boston Marathon bombing, give the public the impression that crime and violence are out of control. How accurate is this vision? Is the crime rate truly skyrocketing, or has intense media coverage given the public a false impression about crime in America? When people read headlines about a violent crime spree, they begin to fear crime and take steps to protect themselves, perhaps avoiding public places and staying at home in the evening.[2] When asked, about two-thirds of Americans believe that crime is increasing despite the fact that we have been in the midst of a two-decade-long crime drop.[3] It is not surprising, then, that more than 40 percent of Americans report having a gun at home or somewhere else on their property.[4]

AP Images/Ryan M. Kelly

LEARNING OBJECTIVES

L01 Discuss how crime is defined

L02 Explain the methods used to measure crime

L03 Discuss the strengths and weaknesses of crime measures

L04 Recognize the trends in the crime rate

L05 Summarize the factors that influence crime rates

L06 Know the various crime patterns

L07 Discuss the concept of the criminal career

L08 Describe the characteristics of crime victims

L09 Discuss the association between crime and mental illness

L010 Distinguish among the various views of crime causation

The public's impression about violent crime may also help shape criminal justice policy. Responding to public fear, lobbying groups are now demanding that state legislators pass legislation not only making it more difficult to buy firearms but also imposing mandatory prison terms on anyone caught with an illegally obtained handgun.

Where do most crimes occur, and what are the patterns and trends in the crime rate? To answer these and similar questions, elaborate methods of crime data collection have been devised. These sources of crime data are essential to get an accurate reading on the nature and extent of crime as well as the nature of crime trends and patterns. Without this data, it is impossible to create crime-control policies and assess their effectiveness.

This chapter reviews some basic questions about crime addressed by criminal justice professionals: How is crime defined? How is crime measured? How much crime is there, and what are its trends and patterns? Why do people commit crime? How many people become victims of crime, and under what circumstances does victimization take place?

How Is Crime Defined?

The justice system revolves around crime and the control of crime. Although for most of us the concept of "crime" seems rather simple—a violation of criminal law—the question remains: Why are some acts considered a violation of the law, while others, seemingly more serious, are considered legal and noncriminal? There are three views of how and why some behaviors become illegal and are considered crimes whereas others remain noncriminal.

Consensus View

consensus view of crime The majority of citizens in a society share common ideals and work toward a common good. Crimes are acts that are outlawed because they conflict with the rules of the majority and are harmful to society.

According to what is known as the **consensus view of crime**, crimes are behaviors that are essentially harmful to a majority of citizens living in society and therefore have been controlled or prohibited by the existing criminal law. Using this definition, criminal law is a set of rules, codified by state authorities, that express the norms, goals, and values of the *vast majority of society*. The definition implies that criminal law and the behaviors it defines as crimes represent the *consensus* of public opinion and that there is general agreement about which behaviors society needs to control and which should be beyond state regulation.

The consensus view rests on the assumption that criminal law has a social control function—restraining those who might otherwise engage in antisocial behavior. Criminal law works to control behaviors that are inherently destructive and dangerous in order to maintain the existing social fabric and ensure the peaceful functioning of society.

Conflict View

conflict view of crime The law is controlled by the rich and powerful who shape its content to ensure their continued economic domination of society. The criminal justice system is an instrument of social and economic repression.

According to the **conflict view of crime**, the content of criminal law, and consequently the definition of crime, are shaped and controlled by the ongoing class struggle between the rich and poor, the haves and have-nots. According to this view, criminal law is created and enforced by the ruling class as a mechanism for controlling dissatisfied, have-not members of society. The law is the instrument that enables the wealthy to maintain their position of power and control the behavior of those who oppose their ideas and values or who might rebel against the unequal distribution of wealth.[5]

Interactionist View

interactionist view of crime Criminal law reflects the values of people who use their social and political power to shape the legal system.

moral entrepreneurs People who wage moral crusades to control criminal law so that it reflects their own personal values.

According to the **interactionist view of crime**, the criminal law is structured to reflect the preferences and opinions of people who hold social power and use their influence to shape the legal process.[6] These so-called **moral entrepreneurs** wage campaigns (moral crusades) to control behaviors they view as immoral and wrong (such as abortion) or, conversely, to legalize behaviors they consider harmless social eccentricities (such as smoking marijuana). In essence, they dedicate themselves to molding the law to reflect their own worldviews. According to the interactionist view, then, many crimes are not

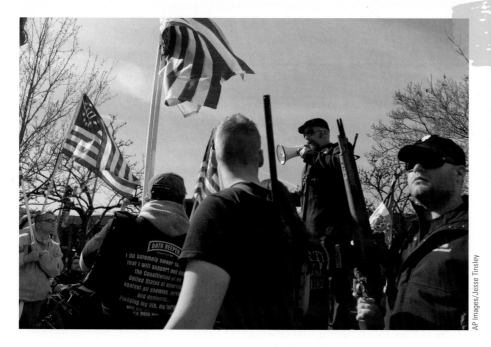

Anthony Bosworth (center with bullhorn) speaks in the plaza of the Spokane Federal Courthouse with other gun protesters during a March 6, 2015, protest of the ban on guns in the plaza, in Spokane, Washington. Bosworth was arrested for openly carrying firearms in the plaza. Why is carrying a gun a crime since the Second Amendment of the U.S. Constitution grants citizens the right to bear arms? How then can an act such as carrying an unlicensed weapon be defined as a crime?

AP Images/Jesse Tinsley

inherently evil or immoral acts but are illegal because they are in conflict with social norms. So, for example, it is perfectly legal to purchase liquor, even though 18 million Americans have alcohol problems and more people die from the effects of alcoholism every year than any other cause.[7]

DEFINING CRIME Although these views of crime differ, they generally agree on four points: (1) criminal law defines crime; (2) the definition of crime is constantly changing and evolving; (3) social forces mold the definition of crimes; and (4) criminal law has a social control function. Therefore, as used here, crime is defined as follows:

> Crime is a violation of social rules of conduct, interpreted and expressed by a written criminal code, created by people holding social and political power. Its content may be influenced by prevailing public sentiments, historically developed moral beliefs, and the need to protect public safety. Individuals who violate these rules may be subject to sanctions administered by state authority, which include social stigma and loss of status, freedom, and, on occasion, their lives.

crime A violation of societal rules of behavior as interpreted and expressed by a criminal legal code created by people holding social and political power. Individuals who violate these rules are subject to sanctions by state authority, social stigma, and loss of status.

LO1 Discuss how crime is defined

How Is Crime Measured?

In addition to understanding how an act becomes a crime, it is important for criminal justice scholars to measure the nature, extent, and trends in the crime rate. They use a variety of techniques to study crime and its consequences. Three principal types of crime data have been developed—official data, victim data, and self-report data—each having particular strengths and weaknesses. The following sections review these methods in some detail and what they tell us about the crime problem in the United States and abroad.

Official Crime Data: The Uniform Crime Reports (UCR)

The FBI's Uniform Crime Reports (UCR) is the best-known and most widely cited source of criminal records. The UCR includes crimes reported to local law enforcement departments and the number of arrests made by police agencies.[8] Data from the UCR are published in an annual volume called *Crime in the United States* and serves as the nation's official crime statistics. The FBI receives and compiles records from more than 17,000 police departments serving a majority of the US population.

Uniform Crime Reports (UCR) The FBI's yearly publication of where, when, and how much serious crime occurred in the prior year.

official crime statistics Compiled by the FBI in its Uniform Crime Reports, these are a tally of serious crimes reported to police agencies each year.

Part I crimes The eight crimes for which, because of their seriousness and frequency, the FBI reports their incidence in its annual Uniform Crime Reports. The Part I crimes are murder, rape, assault, robbery, burglary, arson, larceny, and motor vehicle theft.

murder and nonnegligent manslaughter The willful (nonnegligent) killing of one human being by another.

forcible rape Under common law, the carnal knowledge of a female forcibly and against her will. Many states have made rape a gender-neutral crime. The FBI has created a new definition of rape for its UCR program: "The penetration, no matter how slight, of the vagina or anus with any body part or object, or oral penetration by a sex organ of another person, without the consent of the victim."

robbery The taking or attempting to take anything of value from the care, custody, or control of a person or persons by force or threat of force or violence and/or by putting the victim in fear.

aggravated assault An unlawful attack by one person upon another, accompanied by the use of a weapon, for the purpose of inflicting severe or aggravated bodily injury.

burglary The unlawful entry of a structure to commit a felony or a theft.

larceny The unlawful taking, carrying, leading, or riding away of property from the possession or constructive possession of another.

motor vehicle theft The theft of a motor vehicle.

arson Any willful or malicious burning or attempting to burn, with or without intent to defraud, a dwelling house, public building, motor vehicle or aircraft, or personal property of another.

Part II crimes All other crimes except the eight Part I crimes. The FBI records all arrests made for Part II crimes, including race, gender, and age information.

The FBI tallies and annually publishes the number of reported offenses by city, county, standard metropolitan statistical area, and geographical division of the United States for the most serious crimes. These Part I crimes are murder and nonnegligent manslaughter, forcible rape, robbery, aggravated assault, burglary, larceny, motor vehicle theft, and arson.

In addition to Part I crimes, the UCR also collects data on the number and characteristics (age, race, and gender) of individuals who have been arrested for committing a crime. Included in the arrest data are both people who have committed Part I crimes and people who have been arrested for all other crimes, known collectively as Part II crimes. This latter group includes such criminal acts as sex crimes, drug trafficking, and vandalism.

COMPILING THE UNIFORM CRIME REPORT The methods used to compile the UCR are quite complex. Each month, law enforcement agencies report the number of Part I crimes reported by victims, by officers who discovered the infractions, or by other sources. Whenever criminal complaints are found through investigation to be unfounded or false, they are eliminated from the actual count. However, the number of actual offenses known is reported to the FBI whether or not anyone is arrested for the crime, the stolen property is recovered, or prosecution ensues.

In addition, each month, law enforcement agencies also report how many crimes were cleared. Crimes are cleared in two ways: (1) when at least one person is arrested, charged, and turned over to the court for prosecution; or (2) by exceptional means, when some element beyond police control precludes the physical arrest of an offender (e.g., the offender leaves the country). Data on the number of clearances involving the arrest of only juvenile offenders, data on the value of property stolen and recovered in connection with Part I offenses, and detailed information pertaining to criminal homicide are also reported. Nationwide, slightly less than 50 percent of violent crimes and 20 percent of property crimes are cleared.

Violent crimes are more likely to be solved than property crimes because police devote more resources to these more serious acts, witnesses (including the victim) are frequently available to identify offenders, and, in many instances, the victim and offender were previously acquainted.

The UCR uses three methods to express crime data: (1) the number of crimes reported to the police and arrests made are expressed as raw figures; (2) year over year percentage changes in the number of crimes are computed; and (3) the crime rate per 100,000 people is calculated. The following equation is used:

$$\frac{\text{Number of Repeated Crimes}}{\text{Total US Population}} \times 100{,}000 = \text{Rate per } 100{,}000$$

So, in 2013, there were 14,196 murders, a 4.4 percent decrease from 2012, and a 7.8 percent decrease from 2009. The murder rate was 4.5 per 100,000 people.

HOW ACCURATE IS THE UCR? The UCR's accuracy has long been suspect. Many serious crimes are not reported to police and therefore are not counted by the UCR. The reasons for not reporting vary:

- Victims consider the crime trivial or unimportant and choose not to call the police.
- Some victims fail to report because they do not trust the police or have little confidence in their ability to solve crime. Cities in which people believe the police can help them are more likely to report crime.[9]
- People without property insurance believe it is useless to report theft.
- Victims fear reprisals from an offender's friends or family.
- Victims have "dirty hands" and are involved in illegal activities themselves, so they do not want to get involved with the police.

Because of these and other factors, less than half of all criminal incidents are reported to the police.

The way a police department records and reports criminal activity also affects the validity of UCR statistics. Some departments may define crimes loosely—reporting a trespass as a burglary or an assault on a woman as an attempted rape—whereas others pay strict attention to FBI guidelines. Some make systematic errors in UCR reporting, for example, counting an arrest only after a formal booking procedure, even though the UCR requires arrests to be counted when the suspect is released without a formal charge. These reporting practices may help explain interjurisdictional differences in crime. There may also be differences between the way states define a crime and the definition used in the UCR program. Because many jurisdictions have broadened their classification of rape to include all forms of sexual assault, the FBI has followed suit, changing in 2012 the definition used in the UCR to, "The penetration, no matter how slight, of the vagina or anus with any body part or object, or oral penetration by a sex organ of another person, without the consent of the victim."

Some critics take issue with the way the FBI records data and counts crimes. According to the "Hierarchy Rule," in a multiple-offense incident, only the most serious crime is counted. So if an armed bank robber commits a robbery, assaults a patron as he flees, steals a car to get away, and damages property during a police chase, only the robbery is reported because it is the most serious offense.

Although these issues are troubling, the UCR continues to be one of the most widely used sources of criminal statistics. Because the UCR is collected in a careful and systematic way, it is considered a highly reliable indicator of crime patterns and trends. That is, even if reporting problems compromise computing the exact number of crimes committed in a single year, measurement of year-to-year change should be accurate because measurement problems are stable over time. In other words, half of all burglaries will be reported both in 2014 and 2015, making an accurate count impossible. However, if the number of burglaries increases between the two years, we can conclude that more burglaries were committed in 2014 than in 2015 because half of all the crimes *were reported in both years.*

NIBRS: THE FUTURE OF THE UNIFORM CRIME REPORT Clearly there must be a more reliable source for crime statistics than the UCR as it stands today. Beginning in 1982, a five-year redesign effort was undertaken to provide more comprehensive and detailed crime statistics. The effort resulted in the National Incident-Based Reporting System (NIBRS), a program that collects data on each reported crime incident. Instead of submitting statements of the kinds of crime that individual citizens report to the police and summary statements of resulting arrests, NIBRS requires local police agencies to provide at least a brief account of each incident and arrest, including the incident, victim, and offender information.

In addition to common law crimes such as rape and murder, NIBRS reporting provides information on most of the criminal justice issues facing law enforcement today—terrorism, white collar crime, assaults on law enforcement officers, offenses in which weapons were involved, drug/narcotic offenses, hate crimes, domestic and familial abuse (including elder abuse), juvenile crime, gang-related crime, parental abduction, organized crime, and pornography, as well as arrest data related to driving under the influence. In addition, NIBRS reporting captures whether the offender was suspected of using drugs/narcotics or alcohol during or shortly before the incident and whether the offender used computer equipment to perpetrate the crime; this makes it possible to develop a national database on the nature of crime, victims, and criminals.

To date, the FBI has certified 33 state programs for NIBRS participation that together hold about one-third of the population (about 93 million people). Other state programs are in various stages of testing NIBRS.[10]

National Crime Victimization Survey (NCVS)

Because many victims do not report their experiences to the police, the UCR cannot measure all the annual criminal activity. To address the nonreporting issue, the federal government sponsors the National Crime Victimization Survey (NCVS), a comprehensive, nationwide survey of victimization conducted annually by the US Census Bureau for the Bureau of Justice Statistics (BJS).

National Incident-Based Reporting System (NIBRS) Program that requires local police agencies to provide a brief account of each incident and arrest within 22 crime patterns, including incident, victim, and offender information.

National Crime Victimization Survey (NCVS) A national survey of approximately 90,000 households, used to estimate the frequency of crime victimization, as well as characteristics of victims.

In the most recent survey, 90,630 households and 160,040 persons age 12 or older were interviewed for the NCVS.[11] People are surveyed twice a year, so each interview covers a six-month period, households stay in the sample for three years, and new households are rotated into the sample on an ongoing basis. The NCVS collects information on crimes suffered by individuals and households, whether or not those crimes were reported to law enforcement. It estimates the proportion of each crime type reported to law enforcement and summarizes the reasons that victims give for reporting or not reporting.

There have been numerous methodological changes to the survey over the past decades, including a new sampling method, a change in the method of handling first-time interviews with households, and a change in the method of interviewing: computer-assisted personal interviewing (CAPI) replaced paper and pencil interviewing (PAPI).

Through this massive and complex survey, the NCVS provides information about victims (age, sex, race, ethnicity, marital status, income, and educational level), offenders (sex, race, approximate age, and victim–offender relationship), and crimes (time and place of occurrence, use of weapons, nature of injury, and economic consequences). Questions also cover the experiences of victims with the criminal justice system, self-protective measures used by victims, and possible substance abuse by offenders.

The greatest advantage of the NCVS over official data sources such as the UCR is that it can estimate the total amount of annual crimes, not just those that are reported to police. As a result, the NCVS provides a more nearly complete picture of the nation's crime problem.

Because of the care with which the samples are drawn and the high completion rate, NCVS data is considered a relatively unbiased, valid estimate of all victimizations for the target crimes included in the survey. Yet, like the UCR, the NCVS may suffer from methodological problems. As a result, its findings must be interpreted with caution. Some of the potential problems include the following:

- Victims may overreport as a consequence of their misinterpretation of events; for example, a lost wallet may be reported as stolen, or an open door may be viewed as a burglary attempt.
- Victims may underreport because they are embarrassed about reporting crime to interviewers, fear getting in trouble, or simply forget an incident.
- There may be an inability to record the personal criminal activity of those interviewed, such as drug use or gambling; murder is not included for obvious reasons.
- Sampling errors may produce a group of respondents that does not represent the nation as a whole.
- A faulty question format may invalidate responses; some groups, such as adolescents, may be particularly susceptible to error due to question format.
- For some crimes, such as rape, the number of people reporting victimization is quite small so that even a slight year-to-year change can produce significant results. For example, between 2008 and 2009, the number of rapes declined 39 percent. Although this decline is remarkable, it was based on a drop of 20 cases (from 56 in 2008 to 36 in 2009).

Self-Report Surveys

self-report survey A research approach that requires subjects to reveal their own participation in delinquent or criminal acts.

Self-report surveys, the third source of crime data, ask subjects to describe their past and current criminal activities, including whether they have ever been involved in substance abuse, theft, and/or violence; how often they engage in these activities; what specific kinds of drugs they took; and whether they acted alone or in groups. It is assumed that respondents will be willing to describe their illegal activities accurately because self-report surveys are typically administered in groups, anonymously and unsigned. The idea is to measure crimes that would neither be reported to the police nor show up in victim surveys, such as using cocaine. The capability of self-reports to get at these "dark figures of crime" makes it possible to track the incidence of criminal acts that are not reflected in official statistics.

Most self-report studies are administered among middle school and high school youth. Because school attendance is universal in the United States, a school-based self-report survey represents a cross section of the community. However, self-reports are not restricted to youth crime. They are also used to examine the offense histories of prison inmates, drug users, and other segments of the population.

Although they are widely used, how valid are self-reports? Is it reasonable to expect people to candidly admit illegal acts? They have nothing to gain, and the ones who would be taking the greatest risk are the ones with official records, who may be engaging in the most criminality. Some people may exaggerate their criminal acts, forget some of them, or be confused about what is being asked. Response rate is also critical. Even if 90 percent of a school population voluntarily participates in a self-report survey, researchers can never be sure whether the few who refuse to participate or are absent that day account for a significant portion of the school's population of persistent, high-rate offenders. It is also unlikely that the most serious chronic offenders in the teenage population are the most willing to cooperate with university-based criminologists administering self-report tests.[12] Although these drawbacks are troubling, crime experts have used a variety of techniques to verify the accuracy of self-report data.[13] Although questions remain, as with the UCR, the errors in self-report data remain consistent over time so that self-report surveys that are conducted on a routine basis over a period of years are quite capable of showing trends and patterns in crime and substance abuse over time. Critics may question their validity, but self-reports are reliable and consistent.

LO2 Explain the methods used to measure crime

The Pros and Cons of the Crime Data Sources

Are the various sources of crime data compatible? Each has strengths and weaknesses. The FBI survey is carefully tallied and contains data on the number of murders and people arrested—information that the other data sources lack. However, this survey omits the many crimes that victims choose not to report to police, and it is subject to the reporting caprices of individual police departments.

The NCVS contains unreported crime and important information on the personal characteristics of victims, but the data consist of estimates made from relatively limited samples of the total US population, so that even narrow fluctuations in the rates of some crimes can have a major impact on findings. It also relies on personal recollections that may be inaccurate. Furthermore, the NCVS does not include data on important crime patterns, including murder and drug abuse.

Self-report surveys can provide information on the personal characteristics of offenders that is not available from any other source, such as their attitudes, values, beliefs, and psychological profiles. Yet, at their core, self-reports rely on the honesty of criminal offenders and drug abusers, a population not generally known for accuracy and integrity.

Despite these differences, the data sources seem more compatible than first believed. Although their tallies of crimes are certainly not in sync, the crime patterns and trends they record are often similar.[14] All three sources generally agree about the personal characteristics of serious criminals (such as age and gender) and about where and when crime occurs (such as urban areas, nighttime, and summer months).

LO3 Discuss the strengths and weaknesses of crime measures

Crime Trends

Crime is not new to this century.[15] Studies have indicated that a gradual increase in the crime rate, especially in violent crime, occurred from 1830 to 1860. Following the Civil War, this rate increased significantly for about 15 years. Then, from 1880 up to the time of the World War I, with the possible exception of the years immediately preceding and following the war, the number of reported crimes decreased. After a period of readjustment, the crime rate steadily declined until the Depression (about 1930), when another crime wave was recorded.

Trends in the Uniform Crime Report

As measured by the UCR, crime rates increased gradually following the 1930s until the 1960s, when the growth rate became much greater. The homicide rate, which had actually declined from the 1930s to the 1960s, also began a sharp increase that continued through the 1980s. Crime rates peaked in 1991, when the UCR recorded almost 15 million crimes in a single year. Since then, the number of crimes has been in decline; about 9.8 million crimes were reported in 2013, a drop of more than 5 million reported crimes since the 1991 peak, and this decline occurred despite a boost of more than 50 million people in the general population.

Especially welcome has been a significant drop in UCR violent crimes—murder, rape, robbery, and assault. About 1.16 million violent crimes are now being reported to the police each year, a rate of 368 per 100,000 Americans; there are 800,000 fewer violent crimes being reported today than in 1991, when almost 2 million incidents occurred, and the violence rate was 758 per 100,000.

Not only has violent crime declined, so too have theft offenses. The property crimes reported in the UCR include larceny, motor vehicle theft, and arson. Currently, about 8.6 million property crimes are reported annually to police, a rate of about 2,730 per 100,000 population. Property crimes remain a serious national problem, and losses totaling an estimated $17 billion now result from property crimes each year.

Trends in the Victimization Data

According to the latest NCVS survey, US residents aged 12 or older experienced about 23 million violent and property victimizations.[16] Like the UCR data, NCVS data show that criminal victimizations have declined significantly during the past 30 years (Figure 2.1). In 1973, an estimated 44 million victimizations were recorded, far higher than today; since 1993, the rate of violent victimization has declined about 80 percent. Especially striking has been the decline in the rate of serious violent crime against youth ages 12 to 17, which has declined more than 70 percent since 1994, falling from 62 victimizations per 1,000 youth to around 14 victimizations per 1,000. During this period,

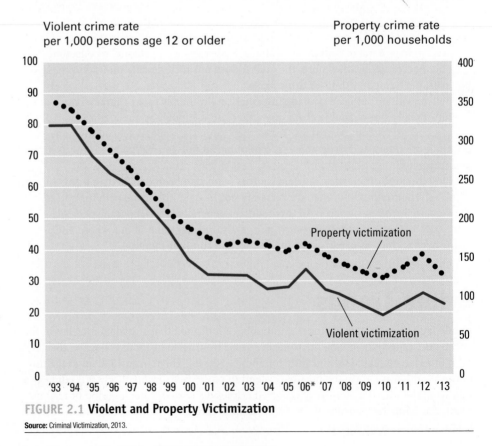

FIGURE 2.1 **Violent and Property Victimization**

Source: Criminal Victimization, 2013.

among serious violent crimes against youth, the rate of rape and sexual assault declined 68 percent, robbery declined 77 percent, and aggravated assault declined 80 percent.[17]

While there have been year to year fluctuations, there is little question that the NCVS data supports the findings of the UCR: the United States has experienced a significant crime drop for more than two decades.

Self-Report Trends

One important source of longitudinal self-report data is the Monitoring the Future (MTF) study that researchers at the University of Michigan Institute for Social Research (ISR) have been conducting annually since 1978. This national survey, which typically involves between 40,000 and 50,000 high school students, is one of the most important sources of trends in self-report data.[18]

The MTF survey shows that a surprising number of teenagers report involvement in serious criminal behavior. About 15 percent reported hurting someone badly enough that the victim needed medical care (7 percent said they did it more than once). About 27 percent reported stealing something worth less than $50, and another 11 percent stole something worth more than $50; 27 percent reported shoplifting one or more times; and 10 percent damaged school property, half more than once.

If the MTF data are accurate, the crime problem is much greater than official statistics lead us to believe. There are approximately 40 million youths between the ages of 10 and 18 in the United States. Extrapolating from the MTF findings, this group accounts for more than 100 percent of all the theft offenses reported in the UCR. About 4 percent of high school students said they had used force to steal (which is the legal definition of a robbery). Half the high school students who reported forcing someone to hand over cash said they committed this crime more than once in a year. At this rate, high school students alone commit more than 1.6 million robberies per year. In comparison, the UCR now tallies about 360,000 robberies for all age groups yearly. While official data show that the overall crime rate is in decline, the MTF surveys indicate that, with a few exceptions, self-reported participation in theft, violence, and damage-related crimes seems to be more stable than the trends reported in the UCR arrest data.

On a more positive note, the most recent MTF study (2014) found that teen alcohol use and cigarette use are at their lowest points since the study began in 1975. Binge drinking (having five or more drinks in a row) fell to about 12 percent of all students from 22 percent a decade earlier. In addition, use of a number of illicit drugs was also in decline, including marijuana use, which had been climbing since 2009. Despite this encouraging news, more than 40 percent of school-age children consumed alcohol in the past year, and 24 percent used marijuana.

The factors that help explain the upward and downward movement in crime rates, as we have experienced for the past two decades, are discussed in Exhibit 2.1.

REALITY**CHECK**

MYTH OR REALITY?

Crime and violence rates are out of control and getting worse every day.

MYTH. Crime rates have been declining recently. Despite what the media tells us, crime rates have been down for almost 20 years.

Do you think this trend will continue? What might cause crime rates to trend upwards?

LO4 Recognize the trends in the crime rate

EXHIBIT 2.1

Factors That Influence Crime Trends

Crime experts have identified a variety of social, economic, personal, and demographic factors that influence crime rate trends. Although crime experts are still uncertain about how these factors impact the trends, directional change seems to be associated with changes in crime rates.

Age Structure

As a general rule, the crime rate follows the proportion of teens in the population: more kids, more crime! Crime rates skyrocketed in the 1960s when the baby boomers became teens and the 13- to 19-year-old population grew rapidly. Crime rate drops since 1993 can be explained in part by an aging society: the elderly commit relatively few crimes.

Immigration

Immigration has a suppressor effect on crime. Research shows that immigrants are less crime prone than the general population, so that as the number of immigrants increases, per capita crime rates decline. During the past two decades, cities with the largest increases in immigration have experienced the largest decreases in crime rates, especially homicides and robberies.

Unemployment

The general public believes that crime rates increase as the economy turns down and unemployment rises. However, there is little correlation between these indicators of economic prosperity and crime rates.

(Continued)

EXHIBIT 2.1 *Continued*

Unemployed people do not suddenly join gangs or commit armed robberies. Criminals are usually unemployed or underemployed and therefore not affected by short-term economic conditions.

Abortion

Evidence exists that the recent drop in the crime rate is linked to the availability of legalized abortion. In 1973, *Roe v. Wade* legalized abortion nationwide, and the drop in crime rate began approximately 18 years later, in 1991. Crime rates began to decline when the first groups of potential offenders affected by the abortion decision began reaching the peak age of criminal activity. It is possible that the link between crime rates and abortion is the result of two mechanisms: (1) selective abortion on the part of women most at risk to have children who would engage in criminal activity, and (2) improved child-rearing or environmental circumstances caused by better maternal, familial, or fetal care because women are having fewer children.

Gun Availability

As recent events show, the association between guns and crime is quite controversial. Those who advocate for the right to own guns claim that the recent spate of mass shootings have occurred at a time when gun control laws have restricted purchases, a fact which proves that criminals will obtain guns while honest citizens are restricted from carrying weapons for self-protection. Gun control advocates claim that the availability of firearms may influence the crime rate: as the number of guns in the population increases, so do violent crime rates. Handguns are especially dangerous if they fall into the hands of teens. Surveys of high school students indicate that between 6 and 10 percent carry guns at least some of the time. Guns also cause escalation in the seriousness of crime. As the number of gun-toting students increases, so does the seriousness of violent crime as a schoolyard fight turns into murder.

Mental Health Treatment Availability

The recent spate of mass killings highlights the fact that the availability of mental health treatment may be linked to violent crime rates. Take for example mass shootings such as the Newtown massacre in 2012 in which the perpetrator, Adam Lanza, is believed to have suffered from mental illness. Adam Lankford studied mass shootings and found that in the 1980s, there were 18; in the 1990s, there were 54; and in the 2000s, there were 87. Counting only such crimes in which 5 or more victims were killed, there were 6 in the 1980s and 19 in the 2000s. At the same time, the availability of mental health treatment has been reduced by budget cuts, and, as a result, the number of state hospital beds in America per capita has dropped to levels that were common in 1850, or 14 beds per 100,000 people. If more treatment becomes available for people like Lanza, incidents of mass shootings may be prevented.

Gangs

Another factor that affects crime rates is the explosive growth in teenage gangs. Surveys indicate that about 800,000 gang members reside in the United States. Data collected by the National Youth Gang Center show that gang members are responsible for a large proportion of all violent offenses committed during the adolescent years. Boys who are members of gangs are far more likely to possess guns than nongang members; criminal activity increases when kids join gangs. Gangs involved in the urban drug trade recruit juveniles because they work cheaply, are exempt from heavy criminal penalties, and are daring and willing to take risks.

Arming themselves for protection, these drug-dealing children present a menace to their community, which persuades adolescents who are not gang affiliated to arm themselves for protection. The result is an arms race that produces an increasing spiral of violence. As gangs become more organized, so too does their level of violence and drug dealing. Without gang influence, the crime rate might be much lower.

Drug Use

Some experts tie increases in the violent crime rate between 1985 and 1993 to the crack epidemic, which swept the nation's largest cities, and to drug-trafficking gangs that fought over drug turf. These well-armed gangs did not hesitate to use violence to control territory, intimidate rivals, and increase market share. As the crack epidemic subsided, so too did the violence rates in New York City and other metropolitan areas where crack use was rampant. A sudden increase in drug use, on the other hand, may be a harbinger of future increases in the crime rate, especially if guns are easily obtained and fall into the hands of gang members.

Media

Some experts argue that violent media can influence the direction of crime rates. As the availability of media with a violent theme skyrocketed with the introduction of home video players, DVDs, cable TV, computer and video games, and so on, so too did teen violence rates. Efforts to curb violence on TV may help account for a declining crime rate.

Medical Technology

Some crime experts believe that the presence and quality of health care can have a significant impact on murder rates. Murder rates might be up to five times higher than they are today without medical breakthroughs in treating victims of violence developed over the past 40 years. The big breakthrough occurred in the 1970s when technology that had been developed to treat injured soldiers in Vietnam was applied to trauma care in the nation's hospitals. Since then, fluctuations in the murder rate can be linked to the level and availability of emergency medical services.

Justice Policy

Some law enforcement experts have suggested that a reduction in crime rates may be attributed to adding large numbers of police officers and using them in aggressive police practices that target "quality of life" crimes such as panhandling, graffiti, petty drug dealing, and loitering. By showing that even the smallest infractions will be dealt with seriously, aggressive police departments may be able to discourage potential criminals from committing more serious crimes. Cities employing aggressive, focused police work may be able to lower homicide rates in the area.

It is also possible that tough laws imposing lengthy prison terms on drug dealers and repeat offenders can affect crime rates. The fear of punishment may inhibit some would-be criminals and place a significant number of potentially high-rate offenders behind bars, lowering crime rates. As the nation's prison population has expanded, the crime rate has fallen.

However, justice policy can sometimes backfire and actually lift crime rates. Take, for instance, the long-term effect of incarceration. The imprisonment boom has resulted in more than two million people behind bars. While this policy may take some dangerous offenders off the street, eventually most get out. About 600,000 inmates are now being released each year, and many return to their communities without marketable skills or resources. Even though the prison population has finally begun to decline, the number of releases will rise for the foreseeable future as more and more sentences bestowed during the high crime rate of the

(Continued)

EXHIBIT 2.1 *Continued*

1990s are completed. The recidivism rate of paroled inmates is quite high, averaging about 40 percent for those released from federal penitentiaries and 67 percent for those released from state custody. Inmates reentering society may have a significant effect on local crime rates.

Sources: Bianca Bersani, "A Game of Catch-Up? The Offending Experience of Second-Generation Immigrants," *Crime & Delinquency*, February 60 (2014): 60–84; David Weisburd, Cody Telep, Brian Lawton, "Could Innovations in Policing Have Contributed to the New York City Crime Drop Even in a Period of Declining Police Strength?: The Case of Stop, Question and Frisk as a Hot Spots Policing Strategy,"

Justice Quarterly 31(2014): 129–153; Richard Rosenfeld and Robert Fornango, "The Impact of Police Stops on Precinct Robbery and Burglary Rates in New York City, 2003–2010," *Justice Quarterly* 31 (2014): 96–122; Patricia L. McCall, Kenneth Land, Cindy Brooks Dollar, and Karen F. Parker, "The Age Structure-Crime Rate Relationship: Solving a Long-Standing Puzzle," *Journal of Quantitative Criminology* 29 (2013): 167–190; Tim Wadsworth, "Is Immigration Responsible for the Crime Drop? An Assessment of the Influence of Immigration on Changes in Violent Crime Between 1990 and 2000," *Social Science Quarterly* 91 (2010): 531–553; David Kopel, "Guns, Mental Illness and Newtown," *Wall Street Journal*, December 17, 2012, http://online.wsj.com/article/SB10001424127887323723104578185271857424036.html.

What the Future Holds

Speculating about the future of crime trends is risky because current conditions can change rapidly. Crime rates may rise in the future if the teenage unemployment rate remains high for a prolonged period of time and the current generation of teens loses hope of ever gaining legitimate employment. Without the hope or possibility of a legitimate job, gang membership may increase, and those involved in gangs may remain active for a longer period time. However, even if teens commit more crime in the future, their contribution may be offset by the aging of the population and the burgeoning number of immigrants, two population groups with relatively low crime rates.[19] The immigrant population is also increasing, which is another factor that may reduce crime rates.

Such prognostications are reassuring, but, of course, no one can predict the changes in store that may influence crime rates. Technological developments such as e-commerce

WEB APP 2.1 To read Donohue and Levitt's famous study of abortion and crime, go to **http://pricetheory.uchicago.edu/levitt/Papers/DonohueLevitt TheImpactOfLegalized2001.pdf.** Do you agree with their findings? Is there a problem with their reasoning? How about this: crime rates for all people of all ages have declined, not just those for people who became teens 18 years after *Roe v. Wade*.

LO5 Summarize the factors that influence crime rates

Some acts previously considered criminal are now legal while others have been criminalized. Rebecca Caine, 24, became the Internet stalking victim of her ex-boyfriend Peter Atkinson, 21. Caine was bombarded with hundreds of texts and calls a day by Atkinson who also posted nude pictures of her online. Atkinson was jailed for 10 months. As people use the Internet to commit crimes, laws must be continually created to remove threats to public safety and individual rights. Some states are starting to criminalize revenge porn such as posting nude photos of ex-girlfriends (or boyfriends) on line or are using existing laws to prosecute people who commit revenge porn. New Jersey's invasion of privacy law, prohibits selling, providing, publishing, distributing, or otherwise disseminating nude or sexual photos of another person without that person's permission. In California it is a crime to photograph or otherwise take private, nude photos of another person and distribute the photos in a way that is intended to and does cause emotional distress. Another new law also makes it a crime to distribute selfies as well as photos taken by someone else.

HotSpot/Landov

on the Internet have created new classes of crime that are not recorded by any of the traditional methods of crime measurement. It's possible that some crimes, such as online fraud, cyber prostitution, website vandalism, Internet stalking, e-tailing fraud, have increased during the past decade but remain undetected because Internet crimes fall under the radar of official crime data. For example, the number of people arrested for prostitution has declined significantly during the past decade. It's possible that (1) there are simply fewer prostitutes, (2) police are less likely to arrest prostitutes than they were a decade ago, or (3) prostitution is booming, but because it's being conducted via the Internet, prostitutes are more likely to avoid detection now.

Crime Patterns

By studying crime data, experts can determine whether stable patterns appear in the crime rate, which may help us to better understand where crime occurs, who commits crime, and why they violate the law. What are these enduring and stable patterns?

Ecological Patterns

Distinct ecological patterns appear in the crime rate:

- Rural and suburban areas have much lower crime rates than large metropolitan centers, suggesting that urban problems—overcrowding, poverty, social inequality, narcotics use, and racial conflict—are related to crime rates.
- Crime rates are highest in the summer months, probably because people spend so much time outdoors and are less likely to secure their homes, and because schools are closed, which provides young people with greater opportunity for criminal activity.
- Crime rates are also related to the region of the country. The West and South usually have significantly higher rates than the Midwest and New England regions.

Gender Patterns

Male crime rates are much higher than those of females. The most recent UCR arrest statistics indicate that males account for about 80 percent of all arrests for serious violent crimes and more than 60 percent of the arrests for serious property crimes. Murder arrests are eight males to one female.

Even though gender differences in the crime rate have persisted over time, there seems little question that females are now involved in serious criminal activities and that there are more similarities than differences between male and female offenders.[20] UCR arrest data show that over the past decade, while male arrest rates have declined by 18 percent, female arrest rates have been more stable, declining by 5 percent. Female arrest rates have actually increased for the crimes of robbery, burglary, and larceny, while at the same time, male rates for these crimes have undergone decline. If these trends continue, gender convergence in crime rates may be a possibility.

A number of views have been put forward to explain the gender differences in crime rates:

- Males are stronger and better able to commit violent crime.
- Hormonal differences make males more aggressive.
- Females are socialized to be less aggressive than males and consequently develop moral values that strongly discourage antisocial behavior.[21]
- Females have better verbal skills and use them to diffuse conflict.
- Males are granted greater personal freedom and therefore have more opportunities to commit crime. Females are subject to greater parental control.

WEB APP 2.2 Read about gender differences at **http://www.education.com/topic/gender-differences/**.
Also, read about the factors related to female crime and delinquency at **http://www.ojjdp.gov/pubs/238276.pdf**.
What biological and social differences help explain differences in crime?

Racial Patterns

Official crime data indicate that members of minority groups are involved in a disproportionate share of criminal activity. African Americans make up about 13 percent of the general population, yet they account for about 39 percent of arrests for Part I violent crime and for 29 percent of property crime arrests. They also are responsible for a disproportionate number of Part II arrests (except for alcohol-related arrests, which involve primarily white offenders).

Self-report studies using large samples also show that about 30 percent of black males have experienced at least one arrest by age 18 (vs. about 22 percent for white males), and, by age 23, almost half of all black males have been arrested (vs. about 38 percent for white males).[22]

Racial profiling creates a cycle of hostility: Young black men see their experience with police as unfair or degrading, so they approach future encounters with preexisting hostility. Police take this as a sign that young black men pose a special danger, so they respond with harsh treatment, and a never-ending cycle of mutual mistrust is created.[23]

Race-based differences are not confined to the arrest process. A significant body of research shows that bias can be found across the entire justice process.[24] Black and Latino adults are less likely than white adults to receive bail in cases of violent crime.[25] African Americans, especially those who are indigent or unemployed, receive longer prison sentences than whites with the same employment status. Recent research conducted in New York City found that when compared to whites, black and Latino defendants were more likely than white defendants to be detained and incarcerated and, if they were sent to prison, to receive especially punitive outcomes, especially if they were convicted of violent crimes. In contrast, Asians received the most lenient treatment in the justice system.[26] There are a number of competing views on this issue, as described next.

INSTITUTIONAL RACISM Racial differences in the crime rate may be a function of racism practiced in the criminal justice system by police, court, and correctional institutions. According to this view, police are more likely to arrest racial minorities because of discriminatory arrest and search practices.[27] Institutional bias creates a vicious cycle: because they are targeted more frequently, young black men are more likely to possess a criminal record, and having a criminal record is associated with repeat stops and searches.[28] This view is so prevalent, that the term **racial profiling** has been used to describe the practice of stopping and searching African Americans without probable cause or reasonable suspicion. Numerous studies find that minority citizens are more likely to be stopped and searched than a member of the white majority, especially if they seem "out of place," that is, driving in a white neighborhood.[29]

According to what is known as the **racial threat hypothesis**, as the percentage of minorities in the population increases, so too does the amount of social control that police direct at minority group members.[30] Police are more likely to aggressively patrol minority neighborhoods; suspect, search, and arrest minority group members; and make arrests for minor infractions, helping to raise the minority crime rate.[31] The result is a stepped-up effort to control and punish minority citizens, which segregates minorities from the economic mainstream and reinforces their physical and social isolation.[32]

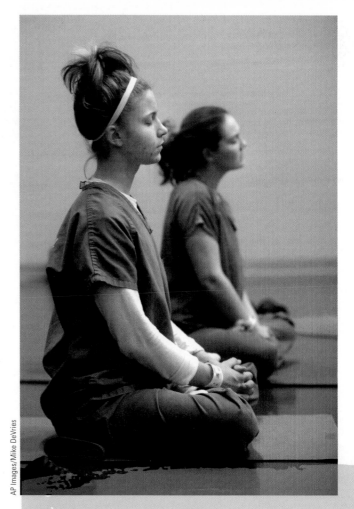

AP Images/Mike DeVries

Because women are committing a significant share of crime, corrections departments are developing programs designed to help female offenders behind bars. Here Wensdae Rauls (left) of Milwaukee, and Linda Miles of Reedsburg, participate in a meditation class held in the gym at the Dane County Jail in Madison, Wisconsin. The stress management and relaxation class that incorporates basic yoga poses is offered to female inmates at the jail.

racial profiling The practice of police targeting minority groups because of a belief that they are more likely to be engaged in criminal activity.

racial threat hypothesis The view that the percentage of minorities in the population shapes the level of police activity.

The treatment of African Americans by police has become a significant national concern. Some high profile cases involving the police shooting of unarmed black men have left the relationship between police and the African American community in tatters. Can anything be done to repair the damage? Here a police officer questions three African Americans stopped on suspicion in Santa Ana, California. Is it possible that the African American crime rate is more a function of police profiling than actual participation in crime? What are your thoughts on this controversial issue?

Marmaduke St. John/Alamy

relative deprivation The view that extreme social and economic differences among people living in the same community exacerbate criminal activity.

broken windows hypothesis The view that deteriorated communities serve as a magnet for criminals and attract criminal activity.

STRUCTURAL RACISM African American families are forced to live in some of the nation's poorest communities that cannot provide economic opportunities. The resulting lack of opportunity creates a sense of hopelessness that serves as an incentive to commit crime. *Racism* infects educational, government, and corporate institutions, creating differential opportunity and powerlessness in the minority community. The high rate of crime committed by African Americans is an expression of their anger and frustration at an unfair social order.[33]

According to most experts, if and when interracial economic, social, and educational differences converge, so too will crime rates.

Social Class Patterns

Although short-term economic trends do not seem to influence crime rates, the official data clearly indicate that crime rates are highest in deprived, inner-city areas. As the level of poverty and social disorganization in an area increases, neighborhood crime rates increase as well. Why are lower-class neighborhoods more likely than affluent communities to be afflicted by crime?

- Communities that lack economic and social opportunities also produce high levels of stress and strain, and residents may then turn to criminal behavior to relieve their frustration.[34]
- Family life is disrupted, and law-violating youth groups and gangs thrive in a climate where adult supervision has been undermined.[35]
- Socially disorganized neighborhoods lack the ability to exert social control over their residents. Lack of informal social control significantly increases the likelihood that residents will engage in criminality.
- Crime rates are high in deteriorated areas where the disadvantaged and the affluent live in close proximity. In these neighborhoods, social differences are magnified, and less affluent residents experience a feeling of relative deprivation that results in a higher crime rate.[36]
- People living in lower-class neighborhoods experience poverty, dilapidated housing, poor schools, broken families, drugs, and street gangs. Deteriorating neighborhoods attract law violators (this is known as the broken windows hypothesis).

An alternative explanation for these findings is that the relationship between official crime and social class is a function of law enforcement practices, not actual criminal behavior patterns. Police may devote more resources to poor areas, and consequently apprehension rates may be higher there. Similarly, police may be more likely to formally arrest and prosecute citizens of lower socioeconomic class than those in the middle and upper classes, which may account for the lower class's overrepresentation in official statistics and the prison population.[37] Self-report data do show that kids in all levels of society and in all social classes commit crime.[38] Therefore, it is possible that the association between class and crime is a function of enforcement practices rather than actual behavior patterns. However, whatever the reason, the crime data tell us that rates of violent and property crime are higher in impoverished areas.

Age Patterns

Official statistics tell us that young people are arrested at a rate disproportionate to their numbers in the population; victim surveys generate similar findings for crimes in which assailant age can be determined. As a general rule, the peak age for property crime is believed to be 16 and for violence 18. In contrast, the elderly are particularly resistant to the temptations of crime; elderly males age 65 and over are arrested predominantly for alcohol-related matters (public drunkenness and drunk driving), and elderly females are arrested mostly for larceny (shoplifting). The elderly crime rate has remained stable for the past 20 years.

When violence rates surged in the 1980s, the increase was due almost entirely to young people; the adult violence rate remained stable. How can the age–crime relationship be explained?

- Young people are part of a youth culture that favors risk taking, short-run hedonism, and other behaviors that may involve them in law violation. The high-risk lifestyle of most youths ends as they mature and become involved in forming a family and a career.[39]
- Adolescents are psychologically immature and are therefore unlikely to appreciate the wrongfulness or destructive consequences of their antisocial acts.
- Youths have limited financial resources and may resort to theft and drug dealing for income.
- Young people have the energy, strength, and physical skill needed to commit crime, and all of these erode with age.[40]
- Adolescents are aware that the juvenile justice system is not as punitive as the adult court system and are therefore more likely to risk committing criminal acts.

Recently, the arrest rate for young people has plummeted. Arrests for those 18 and under is declining at a much faster pace than the decline experienced by those over 18. If this trend continues, the age–crime association will have to someday be reevaluated.

Career Patterns: The Chronic Offender

Chronic offenders commit crime at a very early age, maintain a high rate of criminal violations throughout their lifetime, and are immune to both the ravages of age and the punishments of the justice system. They are responsible for a significant portion of all serious criminal behavior. The chronic offender is one who has serious and persistent brushes with the law, who is building a career in crime, and whose behavior may be excessively violent and destructive.

The concept of the chronic offender is most closely associated with the research efforts of Marvin Wolfgang and his associates at the University of Pennsylvania. In 1972, Wolfgang, Robert Figlio, and Thorsten Sellin published a landmark study entitled *Delinquency in a Birth Cohort*.[41] The researchers used official records to follow the criminal careers of a cohort of 9,945 boys born in Philadelphia in 1945 until they reached age 18 in 1963. Here is what they found:

- About two-thirds of the cohort (6,470) never had contact with police authorities.
- About one-third (3,475) had at least one contact with the police during their adolescence.

MYTH OR REALITY?

High unemployment causes crime rates to increase.

MYTH. Crime rates may actually decline during an economic downturn.

Does it seem possible that one of your relatives or family members would suddenly become a criminal or rob a bank just because they got laid off from their job during a recession?

LO6 Know the various crime patterns

chronic offender A delinquent offender who is arrested five or more times before he or she is 18 and who stands a good chance of becoming an adult criminal; these offenders are responsible for more than half of all serious crimes.

- Of the repeat offenders, a relatively small subgroup (627 boys) was arrested five times or more. These were the chronic offenders, who made up 6 percent of the total (600 out of 10,000).
- The chronic offenders were responsible for 5,305 arrests, or 51.9 percent of the total arrests. They committed 71 percent of the homicides, 73 percent of the rapes, 82 percent of the robberies, and 69 percent of the aggravated assaults.
- Arrest and punishment did little to deter chronic offenders. In fact, punishment was inversely related to chronicity—the stricter the sanctions they received, the more likely they were to engage in repeated criminal behavior.

Since the Philadelphia survey was carried out, a number of other independent studies, including one of a larger Philadelphia cohort of children born in 1958, have confirmed the existence of a repeat offender.[42] Here are some of the key findings about chronic offenders:

- Chronic offender research indicates that young persistent offenders grow up to become adult repeat offenders. This phenomenon is referred to as persistence or continuity of crime.
- Chronic delinquents who commit the most serious violent acts as youngsters have the greatest chance of later becoming adult offenders.[43]
- Youthful offenders who persist are more likely to abuse alcohol, to get into trouble while in military service, to become economically dependent, to have lower aspirations, to get divorced or separated, and to have a weak employment record.

The chronic offender concept has had a great impact on the criminal justice system. If a small group of offenders commits almost all of the serious crime, then it stands to reason that their incarceration might have an appreciable influence on the crime rate. This thought pattern has been responsible for the "get-tough" laws designed to put habitual offenders behind bars for long periods of time. As a consequence of these get-tough sentences, the prison population has trended upward even as crime rates have fallen.

LO7 Discuss the concept of the criminal career

Victim Patterns

In addition to information on the nature and extent of crime, the various sources of crime data, especially the NCVS, can also tell us something about crime victims. How many crime victims are there in the United States, and what are the trends and patterns in victimization? The NCVS data provide a snapshot of the social and demographic characteristics of crime victims.

GENDER Gender affects one's risk of victimization. Men are much more likely than women to be victims of robbery and aggravated assault; they are also more likely to experience theft, but the differences are less pronounced. Although women are far more likely to be victims of sexual assault, thousands of men are sexually assaulted each year.

When men are the victims of violent crime, the perpetrator is usually described as a stranger. Women are much more likely to be attacked by a relative than men are; about two-thirds of all attacks against women are committed by a husband or boyfriend, family member, or acquaintance. In two-thirds of sexual assaults as well, the victim knows the attacker.

AGE Young people face a much greater victimization risk than older persons do. Victim risk diminishes rapidly after age 25. The elderly, who are thought of as being the helpless targets of predatory criminals, are actually much safer than their grandchildren. People over age 65, who make up 14 percent of the population, account for 1 percent of violent victimizations; teens aged 12 to 19, who also make up 14 percent of the population, typically account for more than 30 percent of crime victims.

What factors explain the age–victimization association?

- Adolescents often stay out late at night, go to public places, and hang out in places where crime is most likely to occur.
- Teens spend a great deal of time in the presence of their adolescent peers, the group most likely to commit crime.

INCOME The poorest Americans might be expected to be the most likely victims of crime because they live in inner-city, urban neighborhood areas that are crime prone. The least affluent are by far the most likely to be victims of violent crimes, and this association occurs across all gender, racial, and age groups.

MARITAL STATUS Unmarried or never married people are victimized more often than married people or widows and widowers. These relationships are probably influenced by age, gender, and lifestyle:

- Unmarried people tend to be younger, and young people have the highest victim risk.
- Widows, who are more likely to be older women, suffer much lower victimization rates because they interact with older people, are more likely to stay home at night, and avoid public places.

RACE African Americans are victimized at a higher rate than other racial groups. While interracial theft victimization rates are more similar, blacks are still more likely to suffer violent victimizations than whites. While African Americans make up about 13 percent of the population, they are the victims of more than half of all murders; black males, who are about 6 percent of the population, account for 47 percent of homicide victims.[44]

Crimes committed against blacks tend to be more serious than those committed against whites. About half of all nonfatal violence against blacks can be characterized as a serious violent crime, which includes rape or sexual assault, robbery, and aggravated assault. Robbery accounted for about 15 percent of violent crimes against blacks, a higher percentage than for whites (9 percent). Aggravated assault made up more than a quarter of violence against black victims, compared to 18 percent of violence against white victims.[45]

Why do these discrepancies exist? One clear reason is that young black males tend to live in the largest US cities, in areas beset by alcohol and drug abuse, poverty, racial discrimination, and violence. Because they are forced to live in the most dangerous areas, their lifestyle places them in the highest at-risk population group.

ECOLOGICAL FACTORS The victim rate shows distinct ecological patterns as well:

- Most victimizations occur in large urban areas; rural and suburban victim rates are far lower.
- Most incidents occur during the evening hours (6:00 P.M. to 6:00 A.M.). More serious crimes take place after 6:00 P.M.; less serious crimes before 6:00 P.M.
- The most likely site for a victimization—especially a violent crime such as rape, robbery, or aggravated assault—is an open, public area such as a street, park, or field.
- One of the most dangerous public places is a public school building. Each year about 10 percent of all US youths aged 12 to 19 (approximately 2 million) are crime victims while on school grounds.
- An overwhelming number of criminal incidents involve a solo victim.
- Most victims report that their assailant was not armed (except for the crime of robbery, where about half the offenders carry weapons). The use of guns and the use of knives are about equal, and there does not seem to be a pattern of a particular weapon being used for a particular crime.

REALITY CHECK

MYTH OR REALITY?

Crime victims are generally people who are in the wrong place at the wrong time.

MYTH. Victimization is not random. People who live risky lives—drinking, partying, hanging out with a bad crowd—are most likely to become crime victims.

Comment on how a risky lifestyle influences the chances of becoming a victim. How can a college student avoid victimization risks?

REALITY CHECK

MYTH OR REALITY?

The elderly are the age group most vulnerable to predatory criminals.

MYTH. Young people are much more likely to become victims than the elderly, who, although physically vulnerable, tend to live a low-risk lifestyle.

What can people do to avoid becoming crime victims? How can kids learn from their grandparents to avoid crime?

Former Baltimore Ravens running back Ray Rice (right) walks with his wife Janay Palmer (left) as they arrive for an arbitration hearing with NFL Commissioner Roger Goodell and a judge who heard Rice's arguments that he should not be indefinitely suspended by the league for domestic violence. Rice was caught on an Atlantic City, New Jersey, hotel elevator security video striking and knocking out Palmer, who was his fiancé at the time. Rice was initially given a two game suspension. Additional video released later prompted the league to issue the indefinite suspension and for the Ravens to fire Rice. Later the indefinite suspension was overturned and Rice is currently a free agent. Despite the fact that Rice and Palmer were later married, on March 27, 2014, a grand jury indicted Rice on third-degree aggravated assault with a possible jail sentence of three to five years and a fine of up to $15,000. The case remains unsettled.

Andrew Gombert/Epa/Landov

VICTIM–OFFENDER RELATIONSHIPS The NCVS can tell us something about the characteristics of people who commit crime. This information is available only on criminals who actually came in contact with the victim through such crimes as rape, assault, or robbery.

- About 50 percent of all violent crimes are committed by strangers. The other half of violent crimes are committed by people who were known to the victim, including family members, spouses, parents, children, and siblings.
- Women seem much more likely than men to be victimized by acquaintances; a majority of female assault victims know their assailants.
- A majority of victims report that the crime was committed by a single offender over the age of 20.
- About 25 percent of victims indicate that their assailant was a young person 12 to 20 years of age. This may reflect the criminal activities of youth gangs and groups in the United States.
- While whites are the offenders in a majority of single-offender rapes and assaults, there is no racial pattern in single-offender robberies. However, multiple-offender robberies are more likely to be committed by African Americans.

REPEAT VICTIMIZATION Research shows that individuals who have had prior victimization experiences have a significantly higher chance of repeat victimization than people who have not been victims.[46] Households that have experienced victimization are the ones most likely to experience it again.[47] Some combination of personal and social factors may possibly encourage victimization risk. Repeat victimizations are most likely to occur in areas with high crime rates.[48]

Most revictimizations happen soon after a previous crime, suggesting that repeat victims share some personal characteristics that make them a magnet for predators.[49] Not fighting back, not reporting crime to police, and repurchasing stolen goods may encourage repeat victimization.

LO8 Describe the characteristics of crime victims

Causes of Crime and Victimization

Although the various sources of crime statistics can tell us about the nature of crime patterns and trends, knowing why an individual commits crime in the first place is also important. Such knowledge is critical if programs are to be devised to deter or prevent crime. If, for example, people commit crime because they are poor and desperate, the key to crime prevention might be a job program and government economic aid. If, however, the root cause of crime is a poor family life marked by conflict and abuse, then providing jobs will not help lower the crime rate; family counseling and parenting skills courses are likely to be more effective.

Some criminologists view crime as a social phenomenon and study the social and economic factors that influence human behavior. Others view crime as an individual-level phenomenon and attempt to identify the cognitive and psychological processes that result in antisocial behavior. Regardless of their point of view, criminologists study crime data to identify the factors and motivations that predict crime and to assess the most effective responses to crime by various methods of law enforcement. Because a great deal of uncertainty remains about the "real" cause of crime and the most effective methods of crime prevention, some of the more popular explanations are discussed in the following sections.

Rational Choice Theory

According to rational choice theory, crime is a matter of logical decision making and personal choice. Crime is attractive because it holds the promise of great rewards without corresponding effort. It's a lot easier to steal a car than to earn the money for its purchase. The gains from robbing a bank take a lot less effort than earning the sum through a minimum-wage job.

According to this view, motivated people, after thoughtful consideration, will commit crime if they believe that it will provide immediate benefits without the threat of long-term risks.[50] Take drug dealing for instance. Drug users turn to crime to support their lifestyle when entry into the legitimate job market closes; how else can a heroin user earn enough to support his or her habit?[51] Dealers also display rational thought. Before concluding a drug sale, experienced traffickers will mentally balance the chances of making a large profit against the consequences of being apprehended and punished for drug dealing. They know that most drug deals are not detected and that the potential for enormous, untaxed profits is great. They evaluate their lifestyle and determine how much cash they need to maintain their standard of living, which is usually extravagant. They may have borrowed to finance the drug deal, and their creditors are not usually reasonable if loans cannot be repaid promptly. They also realize that they could be the target of a "sting" operation by undercover agents and, if caught, would get a long mandatory sentence in a forbidding federal penitentiary. They may be aware that law enforcement agents are now using sophisticated technology such as hidden cameras and facial recognition technology to monitor their whereabouts and spy on their drug deals.[52]

If they conclude that the potential for profits is great enough, their need for cash urgent, and the chances of apprehension minimal, they will carry out the deal. If, however, they believe that the transaction will bring them only a small profit and a large risk of apprehension and punishment, they may forgo the deal as too risky. The more often they are arrested, the less likely they are to engage in a risky deal.[53] The decision to commit a crime is similar to a business decision made after weighing potential gains and losses. Criminal groups and gangs may eventually be run like a business enterprise rather than an opportunistic group engaging in random and unplanned crimes.[54]

When deciding to commit crime, potential offenders balance their perceptions of getting caught and punished against the perceived benefits of crime. Benefits include not

rational choice theory People will engage in delinquent and criminal behavior after weighing the consequences and benefits of their actions. Delinquent behavior is a rational choice made by a motivated offender who perceives the chances of gain as outweighing any perceived punishment or loss.

only monetary gains but also psychological rewards such as excitement and increased social status among their peers.[55] Experience may play a hand in the decision-making process. Veteran criminals may not fear some future punishment because they know first-hand that apprehension risk is actually quite low.[56] Some may be deterred in the short run but soon return to their criminal ways.[57] People who are convinced that the pains of punishment outweigh the benefits of crime may become more wary and willing to desist from a criminal career.[58] A central theme of rational choice theory is that people who believe or imagine that they will be punished for crimes in the present will avoid doing those crimes in the future; this is referred to as general deterrence.[59] Even the most committed offenders (e.g., gang members) will forgo criminal activities if they fear legal punishments.[60]

Evidence shows that crime rates fall when police make an effort to concentrate their forces on "hot spots" of crime, convincing would-be criminals that these areas are now unsafe and off limits to criminal activity.[61] Improving police response time, thereby getting to crime scenes quickly, and also increasing the number of patrol cars that respond per crime, may be one way of increasing police efficiency and deterring people from committing crime.[62] Towns and cities have experienced lower crime rates when they increase the visibility of the police force, hire more officers, and use patrol officers in ways that increase the perceived risk of apprehension.[63]

Conversely, if criminals believe that they have only a small chance of suffering apprehension and punishment in the future, they are more likely to engage in crime in the present.[64] It stands to reason that if criminals feared the most severe punishment—the death penalty—they would be reluctant to commit murder. Even if the death penalty could achieve that result, is it an ethical application of punishment?

Biosocial Theory

If criminals choose crime, why do they do so? After all, millions of people live in poverty, yet most choose to live law-abiding, conventional lives. So what causes a relatively few people to select a criminal way of life? According to biosocial theory, elements of the environment (e.g., family life, community factors) interact with biological factors (e.g., diet, neurological makeup) to control and influence behavior.[65] People choose crime because of a preexisting physical condition, present at birth or soon after, that makes them predisposed to being crime prone.

Biosocial theories can be divided into three broad areas of focus: biochemical factors, neurological problems, and genetic abnormalities.

BIOCHEMICAL FACTORS Some criminologists believe that biochemical abnormality may lead to antisocial behaviors. Such biochemical factors as vitamin and mineral deficiencies, hormone imbalance, and environmental contaminants (such as the presence of lead and other metals) have been linked to antisocial behavior.[66] The influence of damaging chemical and biological contaminants may begin before birth: maternal alcohol abuse and/or smoking during gestation have long been linked to prenatal damage and subsequent antisocial behavior in adolescence.[67] Adolescents exposed to harmful chemicals and poor diet may be prone to antisocial behavior choices.[68] Take, for instance, exposure to lead that has been linked to emotional and behavioral disorders and antisocial behaviors.[69] This association is especially important because according to the Center for Disease Control, even low levels of lead has been shown to affect IQ, ability to pay attention, and academic achievement, which are all factors associated with delinquent activity. This is a critical problem because about 2 million kids aged 18 and under have been exposed to dangerously high lead levels according to CDC standards.[70]

NEUROLOGICAL FACTORS Evidence now suggests that decision making may in fact be regulated and controlled by the brain.[71] Some people may engage in antisocial behaviors because some neurological impairment reduces impulse control and self-control, which then leads people to make damaging behavioral choices. For example, there appears to be a link between brain dysfunction and conduct disorder (CD), which is considered a precursor of long-term chronic offending. Children with CD lie, steal, bully other children, get into fights frequently, and break schools' and parents' rules; many are callous and

general deterrence The theory that crime rates are influenced and controlled by the threat of criminal punishment. If people fear being apprehended and punished, they will not risk breaking the law.

biosocial theory Human behavior is a function of the interaction of biochemical, neurological, and genetic factors with environmental stimuli.

conduct disorder (CD) A pattern of repetitive behavior in which the rights of others or social norms are violated.

REALITY CHECK

MYTH OR REALITY?

Children exposed to lead in their environment will be prone to antisocial behavior as they mature.

REALITY. Exposure to lead can cause long-term damage.

Should companies that pollute the environment with lead be held criminally negligent for their actions?

lack empathy and/or guilt.[72] Adolescent boys with antisocial substance disorder (ASD) repeatedly engage in risky antisocial and drug-using behaviors. Research has linked this behavior with misfiring in particular areas of the brain and suppressed neural activity.[73]

Brain dysfunction is sometimes manifested as attention deficit hyperactivity disorder (ADHD), which has been linked to antisocial behavior. About 3 percent of all US children, primarily boys, are believed to suffer from this disorder. Some psychologists believe that the syndrome is essentially a chemical problem, specifically an impairment in the chemical system that supports rapid and efficient communication in the brain's management system.[74] The condition may result in poor school performance, bullying, stubbornness, and a lack of response to discipline.[75]

GENETIC FACTORS Violent behavior is possibly inherited and a function of a person's genetic makeup. The genes–crime association may be either direct or indirect. According to the direct view, (1) antisocial behavior is inherited, (2) the genetic makeup of parents is passed on to children, and (3) genetic abnormality is directly linked to a variety of antisocial behaviors.[76] Although it is possible that genetic makeup is directly linked to aggression, the association may also be indirect: genes are related to some personality or physical trait linked to antisocial behavior.[77] Genetic makeup may shape friendship patterns and orient people toward deviant peer associations, which cause them to become crime prone.[78] Also, adolescent attachment to parents may be controlled by their genetic makeup; attachment that is weak and attenuated has been linked to criminality.[79]

The association between crime and genes is by no means certain, and serious debate continues regarding the influence of genetic heritability on human behaviors such as crime. Some critics argue that the social environment plays a more critical role than genetic makeup in shaping behavior, especially during the critical periods of childhood and adolescence.[80] However, others believe that the evidence is solid and that a great deal of human behavior is shaped by inherited rather than learned traits.[81]

Psychological Theory

Considering incidents such as the Newtown and Aurora massacres, it comes as no surprise that some experts believe criminality is caused by psychological factors. There are actually a number of views on the psychological basis of crime.

PSYCHODYNAMIC THEORY According to the psychodynamic view, some people encounter problems during their early development that cause an imbalance in their personality. The most deeply disturbed are referred to as psychotics, who cannot restrain their impulsive behavior. One type of psychosis is schizophrenia, a condition marked by incoherent thought processes, a lack of insight, and hallucinations. Schizophrenics may suffer delusions and feel persecuted, worthless, and alienated.[82] Other offenders may suffer from a wide variety of mood and behavior disorders that render them histrionic, depressed, antisocial, or narcissistic.[83] They may suffer from conduct disorders, which include long histories of antisocial behavior, or mood disorders characterized by disturbance in expressed emotions. Among the latter is bipolar disorder, in which moods alternate between periods of wild elation and deep depression.[84] Some offenders are driven by an unconscious desire to be punished for prior sins, either real or imaginary. As a result, they may violate the law or even harm their parents to gain attention.

According to this view, crime is a manifestation of feelings of oppression and of the individual's inability to develop the proper psychological defenses and rationales to keep these feelings under control. Criminality may allow these troubled people to survive by producing positive psychic results; that is, it helps them to feel free and independent, and confers an opportunity for excitement and the chance to use their skills and imagination. Criminality also provides them with the promise of positive gain, as well as allowing them to blame others (such as the police) for their predicament. Finally, it gives them a chance to rationalize their sense of failure ("If I hadn't gotten into trouble, I could have been a success").[85] The association between mental illness and crime is discussed further in the following Contemporary Issues in Criminal Justice feature.

WEB APP 2.3 The Minnesota Twin Family Study is fascinating. To read more about it, go to their website at **https://mctfr.psych.umn.edu/**. Do you know any twins, or are you one yourself? If so, do you think twin behavior is a matter of genetics or upbringing?

psychodynamic view Criminals are driven by unconscious thought patterns, developed in early childhood, that control behaviors over the life course.

bipolar disorder A psychological condition marked by mood swings between periods of wild elation and deep depression.

LO9 Discuss the association between crime and mental illness

Mental Illness and Criminal Behavior

You may remember, T.J. Lane, a boy who pled guilty to killing three students in Chardon High School, just east of Cleveland, Ohio, in 2012. Lane made headlines when he showed up in court in 2013 for his sentencing wearing a T-shirt with "killer" scrawled across the front, then cursed the victim's families and gestured obscenely as he was given three life sentences.

Before his trial, Lane had undergone a psychiatric evaluation conducted by Dr. Phillip Resnick, who testified that Lane suffered from mental illness, but his psychosis did not interfere with Lane's ability to understand the charges. Resnick told the court that Lane's symptoms included withdrawal, auditory hallucinations, and involuntary fantasies. Prosecutors asked Resnick if the teen was ever treated for a mental illness prior to this evaluation, and Resnick answered "(Lane) was never treated because he was never diagnosed."

Lane was defiant during the sentencing, smiling and smirking throughout. At one point, he swiveled around in his chair toward the gallery where his own family members and those of the slain teenagers were sitting and spoke suddenly, surprising even his lawyer. "The hand that pulled the trigger that killed your sons now masturbates to the memory," he said, then cursed at and raised his middle finger toward the victims' relatives. Lane was briefly in the news in 2014 when he and two other inmates escaped from prison and remained at large for a day before being recaptured.

Lane's case is certainly not unique. Growing evidence shows that a significant number of law violators, especially those involved in violent crime, suffer from a disproportionate amount of severe mental health problems. Recently, Richard Dorn and his associates, using a longitudinal sample of about 35,000 subjects, examined the association between mental disorder and violence and found that when compared to the mentally sound, people suffering mental illness were significantly more likely to engage in violent episodes, especially if they abused drugs and alcohol. The diagnosed mentally ill also appear in arrest and court statistics at a rate disproportionate to their presence in the population and, if sentenced to prison, are more likely to recidivate upon release.

Although these findings are persuasive, the association between crime and mental illness must be interpreted with some caution. It is possible that the link between crime and mental illness is spurious, and that, in fact, both mental illness and criminal behavior are caused by some other, independent factor:

- People who suffer from prior social problems (e.g., child abuse) may be more likely to commit criminal acts, use drugs and alcohol to cope, and also suffer mental illness; child abuse may be the cause of criminality and mental illness.

- Mentally ill people may also be more likely than the mentally sound to lack financial resources. They are thus forced to reside in deteriorated, high-crime neighborhoods, a social factor that may increase criminal behavior. Living in a stress-filled urban environment may produce symptoms of both mental illness and crime.

- The police may be more likely to arrest the mentally ill, which fosters the impression that they are crime prone.

- Due to their lifestyle, people with severe mental illness are more at risk to victimization than the mentally healthy; victimization has been linked to increased crime rates.

- Those suffering mental illness may self-medicate by using illegal substances, a practice linked to criminal behavior.

Regardless of the association, whether direct or indirect, the weight of the evidence shows a link between mental illness and crime. Whether people like T.J. Lane are better served by prison or residence in a mental health facility is an important issue facing the justice system.

CRITICAL THINKING

Should killers like T.J. Lane or Jared Lee Loughner who are suffering from a mental defect be treated rather than punished and then released back into society after mental health personnel are convinced they no longer pose a threat? Can we ever really be sure when someone is truly rehabilitated?

Source: Michael Ostermann and Jason Matejkowski, "Estimating the Impact of Mental Illness on Costs of Crimes," *Criminal Justice & and Behavior* 41 (2014): 20–40. CBCnews, "Ohio School Shooter Wears 'Killer' T-Shirt to Court," March 19, 2013, http://www.cbc.ca/news/world/story/2013/03/19/us-ohio-school-shooting-sentencing.html (accessed February 2015); Thomas O'Hare, Ce Shen, and Margaret Sherrer, "High-Risk Behaviors and Drinking-to-Cope as Mediators of Lifetime Abuse and PTSD Symptoms in Clients with Severe Mental Illness," *Journal of Traumatic Stress* 23 (2010): 255–263; Tamsin B. R. Short, Stuart Thomas, Stefan Luebbers, Paul Mullen, and James Ogloff, "A Case-Linkage Study of Crime Victimisation in Schizophrenia-Spectrum Disorders over a Period of Deinstitutionalization," *BMC Psychiatry* 13 (2013): 1–9; Tamar Mendelson, Alezandria Turner, and Darius Tandon, "Violence Exposure and Depressive Symptoms Among Adolescents and Young Adults Disconnected from School and Work," *Journal of Community Psychology* 38 (2010): 607–621.

---

social learning theory Behavior patterns are modeled and learned in interactions with others.

BEHAVIORAL/SOCIAL LEARNING THEORY Another psychological view, known as **social learning theory**, is that criminal behavior is learned through interactions with others. One assumption is that people act aggressively because as children they experienced violence firsthand, either observing it at home or being a target of violent parents. Children model their behavior after the violent acts of adults. Observed and experienced violence may have an interactive effect: kids who live in high-crime neighborhoods and witness violence in the community and at home, who are the direct victims of domestic and community-based violence, are the ones most likely to commit crime.[86]

ETHICAL REFLECTION

Punishing the Mentally Ill

In November 2012, Jared Lee Loughner, a diagnosed schizophrenic, was sentenced to life in prison without parole for a shooting spree that severely wounded Congresswoman Gabrielle Giffords and resulted in the death of six others. Would strict punishments deter people such as Loughner from committing horrendous crimes? Or are such criminals immune to the threat of punishment because they suffer from some biological or psychological abnormality? Is it ethical to punish such people, or would we be better off treating them for their psychological problems?

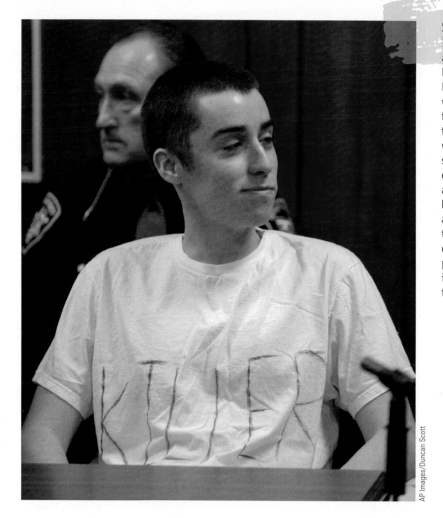

Some crimes appear to be motivated by mental illness. Here T.J. Lane smirks as he listens to the judge during a sentencing hearing on March 19, 2013, in Chardon, Ohio. Lane was given three lifetime prison sentences without the possibility of parole for opening fire in a high school cafeteria in a rampage that left three students dead and three others wounded. Lane, 18, had pleaded guilty to shooting at students at Chardon High School, east of Cleveland. Investigators have said he admitted to the shooting but said he didn't know why he did it. Before the case went to adult court last year, a juvenile court judge ruled that Lane was mentally competent to stand trial despite evidence he suffers from hallucinations, psychosis, and fantasies. Despite his mental issues, Lane was found guilty as charged, rather than incompetent or insane.

AP Images/Duncan Scott

One area of particular interest to social learning theorists is whether the media can influence violence. Some laboratory studies that expose youths to aggressive, antisocial media find that they act more aggressively soon after and act out what they watched on the screen.[87] Nonetheless, millions of kids do not commit violent crimes despite the fact that they routinely watch violent movies and TV shows and play violent video games. There is little evidence that areas which experience the highest levels of violent TV viewing also have rates of violent crime that are above the norm. Nor can the link between media violence and violent behavior explain recent crime trends. Despite a rampant increase in violent TV shows, films, and video games, the violence rate among teens has been in significant decline. The most careful studies looking for a link between violent media and violent behavior have failed to find a significant correlation.[88]

COGNITIVE THEORY Law violators may lack the ability to perform cognitive functions in a normal and orderly fashion.[89] Because they have inadequate cognitive processing, criminals perceive the world as stacked against them; they believe they have little control over the negative events in their life.[90] Some may be sensation seekers who are constantly looking for novel experiences, whereas others lack deliberation and rarely think through problems. Some may give up easily, whereas others act without thinking when they get upset.[91]

This distorted view of the world shapes their thinking and colors their judgments. Crime is viewed as an appropriate means to satisfy their immediate personal needs, which take precedence over more distant social needs and such abstract moral concepts as "obey the law" and "respect the rights of others."[92]

PERSONALITY THEORY It is also possible that people who possess a disturbed personality structure are prone to criminal behavior. For example, people who possess an

REALITY CHECK

MYTH OR REALITY?

Kids who watch a lot of violence on TV are more likely to get involved in violent behavior themselves.

MYTH. Millions of kids watch violent TV shows and remain nonviolent.

The link between violent media and violent behavior is still being debated. In the meantime, should young children be prevented from watching media violence?

antisocial (sociopathic, psychopathic) personality Individuals who are always in trouble and do not learn from either experience or punishment. They are loners who engage in frequent callous and hedonistic behaviors, are emotionally immature, and lack responsibility, judgment, and empathy.

antisocial personality (formerly referred to as sociopathic or psychopathic personality) are believed to be dangerous, aggressive individuals who act in a callous manner. They neither learn from their mistakes nor are deterred by punishment.[93] From an early age, they have had home lives filled with frustration, bitterness, and quarreling.[94] They exhibit low levels of guilt and anxiety, and they persistently violate the rights of others. Although they may exhibit charm and be highly intelligent, these qualities mask a disturbed personality that makes them incapable of forming enduring relationships.[95]

The concept of the antisocial personality is important for understanding the cause of crime because it has been estimated that somewhere between 10 and 30 percent of all prison inmates can be classified as psychopaths, sociopaths, or as having similar character disorders.[96]

Social Structure Theory

social structure theory A person's position in the social structure controls his or her behavior. Those in the lowest socioeconomic tier are more likely to succumb to crime-promoting elements in their environment, whereas those in the highest tier enjoy social and economic advantages that insulate them from crime-producing forces.

Another view is that the basis of crime can be found in the relationship a person has to social structures and institutions. According to social structure theory, the United States is a stratified society, where there are a few thousand "super rich" making more than $5 million per year, and 46 million Americans live beneath the poverty line, which is calculated at about $22,000 per year for a family of four.[97]

Those living in poverty face dead-end jobs, unemployment, and social failure. Because of their meager economic resources, lower-class citizens are often forced to live in poor areas marked by substandard housing, inadequate health care, renters rather than homeowners, poor educational opportunities, underemployment, and despair. Noting the universal association among poverty, neighborhood conditions, and criminal behavior, social structure theorists suggest that antisocial behavior is a direct result of destructive social forces on human behavior.[98]

The problems of lower-class culture are particularly acute for racial and ethnic minorities, who have an income level significantly below that of whites and an unemployment rate almost twice as high. In the inner cities, more than half of all black males do not finish high school. In addition, they face the burden of racism and racial stereotyping. Research shows that whites are averse to living in or visiting black neighborhoods because they consider them crime-ridden, even if these neighborhoods actually have relatively low crime rates.[99]

culture of poverty The crushing lifestyle of slum areas produces a culture of poverty, passed from one generation to the next, marked by apathy, cynicism, feelings of helplessness, and mistrust of social institutions, such as schools, government agencies, and the police.

The crushing burden of urban poverty results in the development of a culture of poverty marked by apathy, cynicism, helplessness, and distrust.[100] The culture is passed from one generation to another such that its members become part of a permanent underclass, "the truly disadvantaged."[101] In these areas, people live in constant fear and suffer social and physical incivilities—rowdy youths, trash and litter, graffiti, abandoned storefronts, burned-out buildings, littered lots, strangers, drunks, vagabonds, loiterers, prostitutes, noise, congestion, angry words, dirt, and stench.[102] Forced to endure substandard housing and schools in deteriorated inner-city, socially disorganized neighborhoods, and cut off from conventional society, the urban poor face a constant assault on their self-image and sense of worth And when they do seek help for their problems, they find that the social support they need to live a conventional life is absent or lacking.[103] The social problems found in lower-class areas have been described as an "epidemic" that spreads through a community, destroying the inner workings that enable neighborhoods to survive; they become "hollowed out."[104] As neighborhood quality decreases, the probability that residents will develop problems sharply increases. Because they lack ties to the mainstream culture, some lower-class people are driven to desperate measures, such as crime and substance abuse, to cope with their economic plight.[105] Crime and violence may also take the form of a "slow epidemic," with a course consisting of stages: onset, peak, and decline. Violence and crime have been found to spread and then contract in a pattern similar to a contagious disease.[106]

Criminal acts and drug dealing provide a means of survival in an otherwise bleak existence. Those living in impoverished neighborhoods are continuously exposed to the opportunity to buy drugs and engage in antisocial acts.[107] It comes as no surprise that gangs develop in poor, deteriorated urban neighborhoods and that gang-related

Les Stone/Do1Thing.org/Redux

homicides are highest in these crowded, inner-city communities.[108] Many kids in these areas grow up hopeless and alienated, believing that they have little chance of being part of the American Dream.[109] Consequently, they become embedded in the gang culture and find it difficult to attain a more conventional life style. The lack of economic opportunity makes the gang world an attractive choice for economic and social success.[110]

A socially disorganized area is one in which institutions of social control, such as the family, commercial establishments, and schools, have broken down and can no longer carry out their expected or stated functions.[111] Living in deteriorated, crime-ridden neighborhoods exerts a powerful influence that is often strong enough to neutralize any positive effects of a supportive family and close social ties.[112]

STRAIN THEORY Social and economic goals are common to people in all economic strata, but the ability to obtain these goals is class dependent. Most people in the United States desire wealth, material possessions, power, prestige, and other comforts.[113] Members of the lower class are unable to achieve these symbols of success through conventional means. Consequently, they feel anger, frustration, and resentment. Lower-class citizens either can accept their condition and live out their days as socially responsible, if unrewarded, citizens, or they can choose an alternative means of achieving success, such as theft, violence, or drug trafficking. Although there are other sources of strain, such as negative life experiences or losing a loved one, the strain imposed by limited opportunities may help explain why lower-class areas have such high crime rates.[114]

CULTURAL DEVIANCE THEORY Combining elements of both strain and social disorganization, cultural deviance theory holds that because of strain and social isolation, a unique lower-class culture has developed in disorganized, poverty-ridden neighborhoods. The independent subcultures maintain a unique set of values and beliefs that are in conflict with conventional social norms. Criminal behavior is an expression of conformity to lower-class subcultural values, which stress toughness, independence, and standing up to authority. These subcultural values are handed down from one generation to the next in a process called cultural transmission. Neighborhood youths who hold these values and incorporate them into their own personal code of behavior are much more likely to join gangs and violate the law than those who reject the deviant subculture.

subculture A substratum of society that maintains a unique set of values and beliefs.

cultural transmission The passing of cultural values from one generation to the next.

Social Process Theory

social process theory An individual's behavior is shaped by interactions with key social institutions—family, school, peer group, and the like.

Still another view, social process theory, holds that people commit crime as a result of the experiences they have while they are being socialized by the various organizations, institutions, and processes of society. People are most strongly impelled toward criminal behavior by poor family relationships, destructive peer-group relations, educational failure, and labeling by agents of the justice system. Although lower-class citizens bear the added burdens of poverty and strain, middle-class or upper-class citizens may turn to crime if their socialization is poor or destructive.

The social process approach has several independent branches. The first branch, social learning theory, as discussed earlier, suggests that people learn the techniques and attitudes of crime from close and intimate relationships with criminal peers; that is, crime is a learned behavior. Kids who have delinquent friends learn both the criminal techniques and antisocial attitudes that help lock them into a delinquent way of life; therefore, the more antisocial the peer group, the more likely its members will engage in delinquency.[115]

The second branch, social control theory, maintains that everyone has the potential to become a criminal, but most people are controlled by their bond to society. Crime occurs when the forces that bind people to society are weakened or broken. The most important version of social control theory was articulated by Travis Hirschi in his influential 1969 book, *Causes of Delinquency.*[116] Hirschi links the onset of criminality to weakening of the ties that bind people to society. He assumes that all individuals are potential law violators, but most are kept under control because they fear that illegal behavior will damage their relationships with friends, family, neighbors, teachers, and employers. Without these social bonds, or ties, a person is free to commit criminal acts. Across all ethnic, religious, racial, and social groups, people who have a weak bond to society may fall prey to criminogenic behavior patterns. People who care little for others are the ones most likely to prey upon them; the lack of social control allows people to engage in antisocial activities without shame or remorse.

social bonds The ties people have to family, peers, social institutions, and significant others.

The third branch, social reaction (labeling) theory, suggests that both crimes and criminals are subjective concepts. The difference between a forcible rape and a consensual sexual encounter often rests on what members of a jury believe and how they interpret the events that took place. The difference between an excusable act and a criminal one is a matter of interpretation. Not only are criminal acts a matter of subjective interpretation, so too are criminal identities. People who run afoul of the law are given negative labels that stigmatize them and reduce their self-image. People labeled "criminals" are assumed to be dangerous, dishonest, unstable, violent, strange, and otherwise unsound. Such labels can have long-term consequences. In a famous statement, Howard Becker sums up the importance of the audience's reaction:

stigmatize To characterize or brand someone as disgraceful in order to make them feel shameful and ruin their reputation.

> Social groups create deviance by making rules whose infractions constitute deviance, and by applying those rules to particular people and labeling them as outsiders. From this point of view, deviance is not a quality of the act a person commits, but rather a consequence of the application by others of rules and sanctions to an "offender." The deviant is one to whom the label has successfully been applied; deviant behavior is behavior that people so label.[117]

Once labeled deviant or criminal, a person becomes locked into a criminal way of life. It's not the quality of the act or the person that counts, but how they are labeled and treated by the rest of society.

Put another way, social learning theory assumes people are born good and learn to be bad; social control theory assumes people are born bad and must be controlled in order to be good; and social reaction theory assumes that whether good or bad, people are controlled by the reactions of others.

Social Conflict Theory

social conflict theory Human behavior is shaped by interpersonal conflict, and those who maintain social power use it to further their own interests.

Social conflict theory views the economic and political forces operating in society as the fundamental causes of criminality. The criminal law and criminal justice systems are viewed as vehicles for controlling the poor members of society. The criminal justice system is believed to help the powerful and rich impose their particular morality and standards of good behavior on the entire society, while it protects their property and physical safety from the have-nots, even though the cost may be the legal rights of the lower class. Those in power control the content and direction of the law and legal system.

Crimes are defined in a way that meets the needs of the ruling classes. Because those in power shape the content of the law, it comes as no surprise that their behavior is often exempt from legal sanctions. Those who deserve the most severe sanctions (wealthy white-collar criminals whose crimes cost society millions of dollars) usually receive lenient punishments, whereas those whose relatively minor crimes are committed out of economic necessity (petty thieves and drug dealers) receive stricter penalties, especially if they are minority group members who lack social and economic power.[118] And after they have done their time, they face a bleak future in a jobless economy in which the poor, minority group members, and those with a criminal record face high levels of unemployment.[119]

While mainstream criminologists focus on the crimes of the poor and powerless, conflict criminologists focus their attention on the law violations of the powerful. One area of concern is referred to as state (organized) crime—acts defined by law as criminal and committed by state officials, both elected or appointed, in pursuit of their jobs as government representatives. Their actions, or in some cases failure to act, amount to a violation of the criminal law they are bound by oath or duty to uphold.[120]

state (organized) crime Criminal acts committed by state officials within the context of their jobs as government representatives.

Developmental Theory

According to developmental theory, even as toddlers, people begin relationships and behaviors that will determine their entire life course. As children, they must learn to conform to social rules and function effectively in society. Later they are expected to begin thinking about careers, complete their schooling, leave their parents' home, enter the workforce, find permanent relationships, and eventually marry and begin their own families.[121] These transitions are expected to take place in an orderly fashion. Disruptions in life's major transitions can be destructive and ultimately promote criminality. Those who are already at risk because of socioeconomic problems or family dysfunction are the most susceptible during these awkward transitions. The cumulative impact of these disruptions sustains criminality from childhood into adulthood.

developmental theory Social interactions that are developed over the life course shape behavior. Some interactions, such as involvement with deviant peers, encourage law violations whereas others, such as marriage and military service, may help people desist from crime.

In some cases, transitions can occur too early—for example, when adolescents engage in precocious sex. In other cases, transitions may occur too late, as when a student fails to graduate on time because of bad grades or too many incompletes. Sometimes disruption of one trajectory can harm another; for example, having a baby while still a teenager is likely to disrupt educational and career development. These negative life experiences can become cumulative: as kids acquire more personal deficits, the chances of acquiring additional ones increase.[122]

Persons who experience significant amounts of anger in early adolescence are more likely to become involved in antisocial behavior as teens and to mature into depressed adults who abuse alcohol.[123] While most adolescents age out of crime and become responsible adults, those growing up in a criminogenic environment and engaging in antisocial behavior as adolescents are the ones who are most likely to engage in antisocial behavior as adults.[124]

Developmental theories also recognize that as people mature, the factors that influence their behavior change.[125] As people make important life transitions—from child to adolescent, from adolescent to adult, from unwed to married—the nature of social interactions also changes.[126] At first, family relations may be most influential; it comes as no shock to life course theorists when research shows that criminality runs in families and that having criminal relatives is a significant predictor of future misbehaviors.[127] In later adolescence, school and peer relations predominate; in adulthood, vocational achievement and marital relations may be the most critical influences. Some antisocial children who are in trouble throughout their adolescence manage to find stable work and maintain intact marriages as adults. These life events help them desist from crime. In contrast, less fortunate adolescents who develop arrest records and get involved with the wrong crowd may find themselves limited to menial jobs and at risk for criminal careers.

One important developmental concept is that the seeds of a criminal career are planted early in life (preschool); early onset of deviance strongly predicts more frequent,

life course theory Theory that focuses on changes in criminality over the life course brought about by shifts in experience and life events.

cumulative disadvantage The tendency of prior social problems to produce future ones that accumulate and undermine success.

propensity theory The view that a stable unchanging feature, characteristic, property, or condition, such as defective intelligence or impulsive personality, makes some people crime prone.

latent trait A hidden trait that guides human behavior.

trajectory theory The view that there are multiple independent paths to a criminal career and different types and classes of offenders.

LO10 Distinguish among the various views of crime causation

varied, and sustained criminality later in life.[128] What causes some kids to begin offending at an early age? Among the suspected root causes are inadequate emotional support, distant peer relationships, and psychological issues and problems.[129] Poor parental discipline and monitoring seem to be a key to the early onset of criminality, and these influences may follow kids into their adulthood.[130] The psychic scars of childhood are hard to erase.

LIFE COURSE, PROPENSITY, AND TRAJECTORY There are actually three independent yet interrelated developmental views. The first, referred to as life course theory, suggests that criminal behavior is a dynamic process, influenced by individual characteristics as well as social experiences, and that the factors that cause antisocial behaviors change dramatically over a person's life span. Kids who get in trouble early, especially those who are arrested early and often, may find it difficult to shake the criminal way of life as they mature.[131] While most kids age out of crime, the ability to change wilts with age as people become embedded in a criminal lifestyle. What may help a person resist a life of crime while they are still in their teens, for example, school achievement and positive family relations, may have little impact after they reach their twenties.[132] As people build up more and more social problems, they often cluster together and create a cumulative disadvantage that makes it more and more difficult to "go straight."[133]

The second view, propensity theory, suggests that human development is controlled by a "master" latent trait, such as impulsivity, intelligence level, or self-control, which remains stable and unchanging throughout a person's lifetime. As people travel through their life course, this propensity is always there, directing their behavior. Because this hidden trait is enduring, the ebb and flow of criminal behavior is shaped less by personal change and more by the impact of external forces such as opportunity. Criminality may increase upon joining a gang, a status which provides more opportunities to steal, take drugs, and attack others. In other words, the propensity to commit criminal acts is constant, but the opportunity to commit them is constantly fluctuating.

A third view, trajectory theory, suggests that subgroups within a population follow distinctively different developmental paths toward and away from a criminal career. Some people may begin early in antisocial activities and demonstrate a propensity for crime, while others begin later and are influenced by life circumstances. Unlike the latent trait and life course views, trajectory theory suggests that there are different types and classes of offenders.[134]

Because a transition from one stage of life to another can be a bumpy ride, the propensity to commit crimes is neither stable nor constant; it is a developmental process. A positive life experience may help some criminals desist from crime for a while, whereas a negative one may cause them to resume their activities. Criminal careers are said to be developmental because people are influenced by the behavior of those around them and in turn influence others' behavior. A youth's antisocial behavior may turn his more conventional friends against him; their rejection solidifies and escalates his antisocial behavior.

ETHICAL Challenge

In a thought-provoking article, Bradley Wilson sets out an argument against the death penalty using an ethical perspective. While the terrible murder of a young woman such as Hannah Graham can anger people enough to demand the killer be executed, the question remains whether capital punishment can be morally justified—that is, the question is whether or not capital punishment is ever permissible. His argument contains five statements:

1. Capital punishment is not morally required in any case, no matter how serious the crime.

2. Mercy is a morally valuable trait; all things being equal, actions that demonstrate mercy have more moral worth than those that do not. Thus, a moral viewpoint that incorporates mercy is preferable to one that does not.

3. Not executing those who have committed capital crimes demonstrates mercy.

4. Just punishment of capital crimes is compatible with showing mercy.

5. Thus, not executing those who have committed capital crimes is morally preferable to executing them.

While this argument is persuasive, Nobel Prize–winning economist Gary Becker disagrees. He says that while opponents of capital punishment frequently proclaim that the state has no moral right to take anyone's life, including that of the most reprehensible murderer, they are absolutely wrong if executions could save the life of only a single person. Even if only one life were saved per execution, the trade-off might still be desirable if the life saved is much better than the life taken, which would usually be the case. Consider a career criminal who robs and kills a victim who led a decent life and left several children and a spouse behind. Suppose it would be possible to save the life of an innocent victim by executing such a criminal. It is obvious, Becker argues, that saving such a victim's life must count for more than taking the criminal's life. Obviously, not all cases are so unambiguous, but a comparison of the qualities of individual lives must be part of any reasonable social policy.

Ethical Challenge: Which argument reflects your own moral values? If we knew for a fact that executing people is an effective crime control policy, would you favor its application? Might there be hidden costs that undermine its effectiveness?

Source: Bradley Wilson, "Justice with Mercy: An Argument Against Capital Punishment," *International Journal of Applied Philosophy* 26 (2012): 119–135; Gary Becker, "The Morality of Capital Punishment," Project Syndicate, 2006, http://www.project-syndicate.org/commentary/the-morality-of-capital-punishment (accessed February 2015).

SUMMARY

LO1 *Discuss how crime is defined* There are three independent views on how behaviors become crimes. The consensus view holds that criminal behavior is defined by laws that reflect the values and morals of a majority of citizens. The conflict view states that criminal behavior is defined in such a way that economically powerful groups can retain their control over society. The interactionist view portrays criminal behavior as a relativistic, constantly changing concept that reflects society's current moral values.

LO2 *Explain the methods used to measure crime* We get our information on crime from a number of sources, including surveys, records, interviews, and observations. One of the most important of these sources is the Uniform Crime Reports (UCR) compiled by the FBI. This national survey compiles criminal acts reported to local police. The acts are called Part I crimes (murder, rape, burglary, robbery, assault, larceny/theft, arson, and motor vehicle theft). All other crimes are referred to as Part II crimes; the FBI reports arrests for Part II crimes. The National Crime Victimization Survey (NCVS) asks people about their experiences with crime. A third form of information is self-report surveys, which ask offenders themselves to tell about their criminal behaviors.

LO3 *Discuss the strengths and weaknesses of crime measures* The validity of the UCR has been suspect because many people fail to report crime to police due to fear, apathy, or lack of respect for law enforcement. Many crime victims also do not report criminal incidents to the police because they believe that nothing can be done or that they should not get involved. Self-reports depend on the accuracy of respondents, many of whom are drug users. While imperfect, the crime patterns found in all three data sources may be more similar than some critics believe.

LO4 *Recognize the trends in the crime rate* Crime peaked in the 1930s and declined afterward. In the 1960s, crime rates began a rapid increase for almost 30 years. Crime rates have been in a downward trend the past two decades. Even violent crimes have dropped significantly.

LO5 *Summarize the factors that influence crime rates* Changes in the crime rate have been attributed to social factors, including the age structure of society. Crime rate increases have been tied to substance abuse levels. While unemployment does not influence crime rates in the short term, long periods of economic decline may promote crime. Crime trends have been linked to abortion: crime began to decline 18 years after abortions became legal. Criminal justice policy may also have an influence on crime rates.

LO6 *Know the various crime patterns* Crime occurs more often in large cities during the summer and at night. Some geographic areas (the South and West) have higher crime rates than others (the Midwest and New England). Arrest data indicate that males, minorities, the poor, and the young have relatively high arrest rates. Victims of crime also tend to be poor, young, male, and members of minority groups.

LO7 *Discuss the concept of the criminal career* One of the most important findings in the crime statistics is the existence of the chronic offender. The data show that repeat, career criminals are responsible for a significant amount of all law violations. Cohort data find that career criminals begin offending early in life and, instead of aging out of crime, continue to commit crimes in adulthood.

LO8 *Discuss the characteristics of crime victims* About 20 million US citizens are victims of crime each year. Data show that, as with crime, victimization has stable patterns and trends. Violent crime victims tend to be young, poor, single males living in large cities. Females are more likely than males to be victimized by someone they know. Adolescents maintain a high risk of being physically and sexually victimized.

LO9 *Describe the association between crime and mental illness* The most recent research suggests that the mentally ill are more crime prone than the mentally sound. Nonetheless, there is no certainty that the relationship is actually causal. It's possible that the mentally ill suffer from other social problems such as drug abuse, poverty, and unemployment that may be the true cause of their antisocial behavior.

LO10 *Distinguish among the various views of crime causation* Diverse schools of criminological theory approach the understanding of the cause of crime and its consequences. Some theories focus on the individual, whereas others view social factors as the most important element in producing crime. Developmental theories integrate variables at the social, individual, and societal levels.

KEY TERMS

REVIEW QUESTIONS

1. Why are crime rates higher in the summer than during other seasons?

2. What factors account for crime rate trends?

3. What factors that are present in poverty-stricken urban areas produce high crime rates?

4. It seems logical that biological and psychological factors might explain why some people commit crime. But if crime is based on individual traits, how would we explain the fact that crime rates are higher in the West and South than the Midwest and East?

5. Considering the patterns that victimization takes, what steps should you take to avoid becoming a crime victim?

3 Criminal Law: SUBSTANCE AND PROCEDURE

On June 18, 2013, Aaron Hernandez, the star New England Patriot tight end, was charged with the murder of his companion Odin Lloyd.[1] Hours after the arrest, the Patriots—a team that had just given him a $40 million contract—dropped him from its roster. Hernandez was accused of shooting his former friend because Lloyd had witnessed Hernandez's involvement in a 2012 drive-by shooting in which two men, Daniel Jorge Correia de Abreu and Safiro Teixeira Furtado, were killed. Odin was then murdered by Hernandez to keep him quiet. The prosecution claimed that Hernandez drove the victim to a remote spot near his home, executed him, took steps to conceal and destroy the evidence, and tried to hush witnesses.[2]

On May 15, 2014, Hernandez was also indicted on murder charges for the killings of Abreu and Furtado. If this was not bad enough for Hernandez, on February 27, 2014, he was sued for $6 million by the victims' family members who claimed that Hernandez "recklessly" and "maliciously" shot a firearm from his vehicle into a vehicle that carried Abreu and Furtado, resulting in their deaths.

Hernandez was tried and convicted of first-degree murder in April of 2015, and he was sentenced to life in prison without the possibility of parole.

According to criminal law, for the jury to convict Hernandez, they had to first determine (1) that he actually committed the crime and then that (2) he intended to kill at the time the murder took place. For him to be found guilty of first-degree murder, the prosecution had to prove that he *maliciously* intended to kill Lloyd and that he had "Express or actual malice" to do so: a state of mind assumed to exist when someone kills another person in the absence of any apparent provocation. Despite the defense efforts, Hernandez was convicted of first-degree murder because the prosecution was able to convince the jury that he had both "premeditation and deliberation." Premeditation means that the killing was considered even briefly beforehand and was not a spontaneous act; deliberation means the killing was planned after careful thought rather than carried out on impulse: To constitute a deliberate and premeditated killing, the offender has the time to weigh and consider using deadly force and, after giving it thought,

Boston Globe/Getty Images

LEARNING OBJECTIVES

LO1 List the similarities and differences between criminal law and civil law

LO2 Discuss the concept of substantive criminal law and its history

LO3 Discuss the sources of criminal law

LO4 Identify the elements of a crime

LO5 Define the term strict liability

LO6 Explain excuses and justification defenses for crime

LO7 Discuss the most recent developments in criminal law reform

LO8 Describe the role of the Bill of Rights in shaping criminal procedure

LO9 List the elements of due process of law

LO10 Explain the role the Supreme Court plays in interpreting the Constitution and shaping procedural law

first-degree murder Killing a person after premeditation and deliberation.

premeditation Considering the criminal act beforehand, which suggests that it was motivated by more than a simple desire to engage in an act of violence.

deliberation Planning a criminal act after careful thought, rather than carrying it out on impulse.

second-degree murder A person's wanton disregard for the victim's life and his or her desire to inflict serious bodily harm on the victim, which results in the victim's death.

substantive criminal law A body of specific rules that declare what conduct is criminal and that prescribe the punishment to be imposed for such conduct.

criminal procedure The rules and laws that define the operation of criminal proceedings. Procedural law describes the methods that must be followed in obtaining warrants, investigating offenses, effecting lawful arrests, conducting trials, introducing evidence, sentencing convicted offenders, and reviewing cases by appellate courts.

civil law All law that is not criminal, including the law of torts (personal wrongs) and contract, property, maritime, and commercial law.

tort A personal injury or wrong for which an action for damages may be brought.

public law The branch of law that deals with the state or government and its relationships with individuals or other governments.

L01 List the similarities and differences between criminal law and civil law

decides to kill. Driving Lloyd to a secluded area, bringing along a gun, destroying evidence, and influencing witnesses are all acts that were both malicious and premeditated and helped convince the jury to find Hernandez guilty of murder in the first.

Now if the jury believed that Hernandez was somehow provoked or goaded by Odin Lloyd and that the killing was a spontaneous act, then they could have found him guilty of **second-degree murder**, a crime that requires the killer to have malice aforethought but not premeditation or deliberation. A second-degree murder occurs when a person's wanton disregard for the victim's life and his or her desire to inflict serious bodily harm on the victim result in the victim's death. Second-degree murder also occurs when the criminal did not intend to kill the victim but exhibited *deliberate indifference* to the danger her or his actions might cause. The deliberate indifference standard is met when a person knows of, and yet disregards or ignores, an excessive risk to another's health or safety.

The Hernandez case shows that subtle differences in the way a person acted or thought before they committed a crime can make a huge difference under law even though the outcome is the same. The punishment for first-degree murder in Massachusetts is life in prison, whereas those convicted of second-degree murder are eligible for early release on parole after 15 years. Hernandez is 25 years old and if he had been convicted of second-degree murder, he would have been out by age 40.

The Hernandez case illustrates how the rule of law governs almost all phases of human enterprise, including crimes, family life, property transfer, and the regulation of interpersonal conflict. It can generally be divided into four broad categories:

- *Substantive criminal law.* The branch of the law that defines crimes and their punishment. It involves such issues as the mental and physical elements of crime, crime categories, and criminal defenses. Exhibit 3.1 sets out the main goals of **substantive criminal law.**
- *Procedural law.* Those laws that set out the basic rules of practice in the government, including the criminal justice system. Some elements of the law of **criminal procedure** are the rules of evidence, the law of arrest, the law of search and seizure, questions of appeal, jury selection, and the right to counsel.
- *Civil law.* The set of rules governing relations between private parties, including both individuals and organizations (such as business enterprises and/or corporations). **Civil law** is used to resolve, control, and shape such personal interactions as contracts, wills and trusts, property ownership, and commerce. The element of civil law most relevant to criminal justice is **torts,** or the law of personal injuries.
- *Public or administrative law.* The branch of law that deals with the government and its relationships with individuals or other governments is known as **public law.** It governs the administration and regulation of city, county, state, and federal government agencies.

Of course, these branches of the law often overlap. In some instances, a person who has been the victim of a criminal act may also sue the perpetrator for damages in a civil tort; some crime victims may forgo criminal action and choose to file a tort claim alone. It is also possible to seek civil damages from a perpetrator even if he or she is found not guilty of the crime because the evidentiary standard in a tort action (by a preponderance of the evidence) is less than is needed for a criminal conviction (beyond a reasonable doubt). Aaron Hernandez is not the only example of a criminal defendant being sued by the victim's family: the families of Nicole Brown and Ron Goldman successfully sued O. J. Simpson for damages, even though he was found not guilty of murder.

People having conflicts with the government may find redress through the administrative law. The government has the option to pursue a legal matter through the criminal process, file a tort action, or both. White-collar crimes, including mail, wire, tax-related, or computer fraud and money-laundering violations, often involve both criminal and civil penalties, giving the government the choice of pursuing one type of action or both.

EXHIBIT 3.1

The Goals of Substantive Criminal Law

Enforce Social Control Substantive criminal law is the main instrument of control at the disposal of an existing government. Those who hold political power use substantive criminal law to eliminate behaviors they believe pose a threat to society or challenge the government's authority.

Distribute Retribution By punishing people who infringe on the rights, property, and freedom of others, the law shifts the burden of revenge from the individual to the state. Although the thought of state-sponsored retribution may be offensive to some, it is greatly preferable to a system in which injured parties or their friends and relatives would seek to redress their injuries through personal vengeance or revenge.

Express Public Opinion and Morality Criminal law reflects public opinions and moral values. It reflects both traditional and contemporary moral values, and it may undergo change according to existing social conditions and attitudes. Criminal law is used to codify changing social values and to educate the public about what is expected of them.

Deter Criminal Behavior Criminal law is designed, through its application of punishment, to control, restrain, and deter illegal acts before they actually occur. During the Middle Ages, public executions drove this point home; today, long prison sentences and an occasional execution are designed to achieve the same result.

Punish Wrongdoing If the deterrent power of criminal law fails to prevent crime, the law gives the state the right to sanction or punish offenders. Those who violate criminal law are subject to physical coercion and punishment.

Maintain Social Order All legal systems are designed to support and maintain the boundaries of the social system they serve. The free-enterprise system is supported and sustained by criminal laws that protect property transfer and control market operations.

Restoration Victims deserve restitution or compensation for their pain and loss. Criminal law can be used to restore to victims what they have lost. Because we believe in equity and justice, it is only fair that the guilty help repair the harm they have caused others by their crimes. Punishments such as fines, forfeiture, and restitution are connected to this legal goal.

Historical Development of the Criminal Law

The roots of contemporary criminal codes can be traced to such early legal charters as the Babylonian Code of Hammurabi (2000 BCE), which rested on the concept of proportionality, *lex talionis* ("an eye for an eye"), that is still the basis of law today. Some of its provisions include the following:

- If a man puts out the eye of an equal, his eye shall be put out.
- If anyone brings an accusation of any crime before the elders and does not prove what he has charged, he shall, if it be a capital offense charged, be put to death.
- If a man knocks the teeth out of another man, his own teeth will be knocked out.
- If the slave of a freed man strikes the body of a freed man, his ear shall be cut off.[3]

The Mosaic Code of the Israelites (1200 BCE), better known today as the Ten Commandments, contains prohibitions against theft, violence, and perjury that still hold sway in the modern criminal law.

The early formal legal codes were lost during the Dark Ages (500–1000 CE). In their place, a legal system featuring monetary compensation, called *wergild* (*wer* means "worth" and refers to what the person, and therefore the crime, was worth), was developed for criminal violations. Guilt was determined by two methods: "compurgation," which involved having the accused person swear an oath of innocence while being backed up by a group of 12 to 25 oath-helpers who would attest to his or her character and claims of innocence, and "ordeal," which was based on the principle that divine forces would not allow an innocent person to be harmed.

Determining guilt by ordeal involved such measures as having the accused place his or her hand in boiling water or hold a hot iron. If the wound healed, the person was found innocent; if the wound did not heal, the accused was deemed guilty. Another ordeal, trial by combat, allowed the accused to challenge his accuser to a duel, with the outcome determining the legitimacy of the accusation.

lex talionis Latin for "law as retaliation." From Hammurabi's ancient legal code, the belief that the purpose of the law is to provide retaliation for an offended party and that the punishment should fit the crime.

 WEB APP 3.1 To read Hammurabi's Code in its entirety, go to **http://eawc.evansville.edu/anthology/hammurabi.htm** Do any of these rules seem similar to what is on the books today? Are there any you might like to adopt?

In ancient legal codes, the standard of "an eye for an eye" was taken literally.

REALITY. In ancient Babylon (modern Iraq), the Code of Hammurabi instructed the removal of an eye for someone who put out the eye of another.

While we don't take out teeth or cut off ears today, can you identify where the contemporary criminal law calls for proportionality in punishment?

stare decisis Latin for "to stand by decided cases." The legal principle by which the decision or holding in an earlier case becomes the standard by which subsequent similar cases are judged.

common law Early English law, developed by judges, that incorporated Anglo-Saxon tribal custom, feudal rules and practices, and the everyday rules of behavior of local villages. Common law became the standardized law of the land in England and eventually formed the basis of criminal law in the United States.

mala in se Refers to acts that society considers inherently evil, such as murder and rape, and that violate the basic principles of Judeo–Christian morality.

mala prohibitum Crimes created by legislative bodies that reflect prevailing moral beliefs and practices.

LO2 Discuss the concept of substantive criminal law and its history

Common Law and the Principle of *Stare Decisis*

Soon after William, Duke of Normandy, conquered England in 1066—a feat that transformed him into William the Conqueror—he sent his royal administrators to travel throughout the land, holding court in each county of his new domain. When court was in session, the royal administrator, or judge, summoned a number of citizens who would, on their oath, tell of the crimes and serious breaches of the peace that had occurred since the judge's last visit. The royal judge then decided what to do in each case, using local custom and rules of conduct as his guide in a system known as *stare decisis* (Latin for "to stand by decided cases").

The present English system of law came into existence during the reign of Henry II (1154–1189), when royal judges began to publish their decisions in local cases. This allowed judicial precedents to be established and a national law to accumulate. Other judges began to use these written decisions as a basis for their decision making, and eventually a fixed body of legal rules and principles emerged. If the new rules were successfully applied in a number of different cases, they would become precedents, which would then be commonly applied in all similar cases. This unified system evolved into a *common law* of the country that incorporated local custom and practice into a national code. Crimes that were *mala in se*, inherently evil and depraved (such as murder, burglary, and arson), and were the cornerstone of the common law, were joined by new *mala prohibitum* crimes such as embezzlement, which reflected existing social and economic conditions.

Before the American Revolution, the colonies, then under British rule, were subject to the common law. After the colonies acquired their independence, state legislatures standardized common-law crimes such as murder, burglary, arson, and rape by codifying them (putting them into statutory form in criminal codes). As in England, whenever common law proved inadequate to deal with changing social and moral issues, the states and Congress supplemented it with legislative statutes, creating new elements in the various state and federal legal codes. Similarly, statutes prohibiting such offenses as identity theft and the pirating of videotapes have recently been passed to control human behavior unknown at the time the common law was formulated.

Sources of Criminal Law

The contemporary American legal system is codified by state and federal legislatures. Each jurisdiction precisely defines crime in its legal code and sets out the appropriate punishments. However, like its English common-law roots, American criminal law is not static and is constantly evolving. A state statute based on common law may define first-degree murder as the "unlawful killing, with malice and premeditation, of one human being by another." Over time, state court decisions might help explain the meaning of the term "malice" or clarify whether "human being" refers only to someone "born and alive" or whether it can also refer to an unborn fetus (this issue is discussed below in the Current Issues in Criminal Justice feature).

CONTEMPORARY ISSUES IN CRIMINAL JUSTICE

"Born and Alive"

After her conviction for manslaughter in 2012, Jennifer Jorgensen, of Miller Place, New York, faced up to 15 years behind bars for a car crash that happened in 2008 when she was eight months pregnant. Jorgenson was driving without a seat belt when she smashed head-on into a car driven by 74-year-old Robert Kelley; both Kelley and his wife Mary died from their injuries. Jorgensen

was originally accused of drunken driving, but at her trial, she claimed that the crash was a result of blacking out from pregnancy complications. She was acquitted of DWI and of charges related to the Kelleys' deaths but was convicted of manslaughter in the death of her unborn child, which is legally permissible in New York; Jorgenson received a three- to nine-year prison sentence.

(Contin

This case is not unique. Under traditional law, a person could not be charged with murder if the victim was not "born and alive." Changing social views in the United States has eroded that restriction. Today, more than two-thirds of the states have expanded their legal codes to include feticide law, which makes the killing of an unborn fetus murder.

At the federal level, the Unborn Victims of Violence Act of 2004 makes it a separate crime to harm a fetus during an assault on the mother. If the attack causes death or bodily injury to a child who is in utero at the time the conduct takes place, the penalty is the same as that for conduct had the injury or death occurred to the unborn child's mother.

State laws vary widely. A Tennessee law considers "a human embryo or fetus at any stage of gestation in utero" as a victim of such offenses as murder, voluntary manslaughter, vehicular homicide, and reckless homicide; prior to 2011, Tennessee law recognized an unborn child as a crime victim only after "viability." In a number of states, recent legislation has created a separate class of crime that increases criminal penalties when a person causes injury to a woman they know is pregnant when the injury results in miscarriage or stillbirth.

These legal changes have sparked heated debates. Those supporting penalizing the death of an unborn fetus claim that both the lives of the pregnant woman and her unborn should be explicitly protected. They assert that fetal homicide laws justly criminalize these cases and provide an opportunity to protect unborn children and their mothers. Those opposed believe that creating laws to protect a fetus could jeopardize a woman's right to choose an abortion and might create an adversarial relationship between a woman and her baby. For example, could a woman be charged with a crime for behavior during her pregnancy that might harm her unborn child, such as smoking, drinking, or using drugs? Some states have taken a middle ground. Texas law extends the protections of the entire criminal code to "an unborn child at every stage of gestation from fertilization until birth." The law does not apply to "conduct committed by the mother of the unborn child" or to "a lawful medical procedure performed by a physician or other licensed health care provider with the requisite consent."

CRITICAL THINKING

How do you stand on this issue? Should a person who causes the death of an unborn fetus be punished the same as someone who kills a 10-year-old child?

Source: News 12 Long Island, "Sentencing Rescheduled for Woman Convicted of Killing Unborn Baby," May 12, 2012, http://longisland.news12.com/news/sentencing-rescheduled-for-woman-convicted-of-killing-unborn-baby-1.3980900 (accessed February 2015); The National Conference of State Legislatures, Fetal Homicide Laws, http://www.ncsl.org/research/health/fetal-homicide-state-laws.aspx (accessed February 2015).

The content of the law may also be influenced by judicial decision making. A criminal offense is no longer enforceable when an appellate judge rules that the statute is vague, deals with an act no longer of interest to the public, or is an unfair exercise of state control over an individual. Conversely, a judicial ruling may expand the scope of an existing criminal law, thereby allowing control over behaviors heretofore beyond its reach.

Michael Democker/The Times-Picayune/Landov

Detectives walk Emilio Calderon into the Jefferson Parish Sheriff's Office Investigations Bureau after being arrested for the murders of Katherine Martinez and her unborn child. Calderon strangled and stabbed his pregnant girlfriend in a rage after learning he was not the unborn baby's father. He was booked on charges of second-degree murder and first-degree feticide. A number of states have passed legislation now making it a crime to kill an unborn child though the common law only considered it murder if the victim was "born and alive".

ex post facto laws Acts that retroactively change the legal status of actions that were committed before the enactment of a law and/or change the consequences after it was enacted.

felony A more serious offense that carries a penalty of incarceration in a state prison, usually for one year or more. Persons convicted of felony offenses lose certain rights, such as the right to vote, to hold elective office, or to maintain certain licenses.

misdemeanor A minor crime usually punished by less than one year's imprisonment in a local institution, such as a county jail.

Constitutional Limits

Regardless of its source, all criminal law in the United States must conform to the rules and dictates of the Constitution.[4] Any criminal law that conflicts with the various provisions and articles of the Constitution will eventually be challenged in the appellate courts and stricken from the legal code by judicial order (or modified to adhere to constitutional principles). The Constitution has been interpreted to forbid any criminal law that violates a person's right to be treated fairly and equally; this principle is referred to as substantive due process. This means that before a new law can be created, the state must show a compelling need to protect public safety or morals.[5]

Criminal laws have been interpreted as violating constitutional principles if they are too vague or broad for their intent to be clear. A law forbidding adults to engage in "immoral behavior" could not be enforced because it does not use clear and precise language or give adequate notice as to which conduct is forbidden.[6] The Constitution also prohibits laws that make a person's status a crime. Being a heroin addict is not a crime, although laws can forbid the sale, possession, and manufacture of heroin. Finally, the Constitution limits laws that are overly cruel and/or capricious.[7]

The Constitution also forbids bills of attainder, which are legislative acts that inflict punishment without a judicial trial. This device, used by the English kings to punish rebels and seize their property, was particularly troublesome to American colonials when it was used to seize the property of people considered disloyal to the crown; hence, attainder is forbidden in the Constitution. Nor does the Constitution permit the government to pass *ex post facto laws*, which are defined as follows:

- A law that makes an action that was done before the passing of the law, and that was innocent when done, criminal and punishes such action.
- A law that makes a crime more serious after the fact than it was when first committed.
- A law that inflicts a greater punishment than was available when the crime was committed.
- A law that makes it easier to convict the offender than it was at the time the crime was committed.[8]

Crimes and Classifications

All states and the federal government have developed their own body of criminal law that defines and grades offenses, sets levels of punishment, and classifies crimes into categories. Crimes are generally grouped into three categories:

- Felonies, the most serious crimes punishable by imprisonment, such as criminal homicide, robbery, and rape, as well as crimes against property, such as burglary and larceny.
- Misdemeanors, less serious crimes punishable by a jail term, including petit (or petty) larceny, assault and battery, and the unlawful possession of marijuana.
- Violations (also called infractions), which are violations of city or town ordinances, such as traffic violations or public intoxication, punishable by a fine. Some states consider violations civil matters, whereas others classify them as crimes.

Distinguishing between a **felony** and a **misdemeanor** is sometimes difficult. Simply put, a felony is a serious offense, and a misdemeanor is a less serious one.

The felony/misdemeanor classification has a direct effect on the way an offender is treated within the justice system. Police may arrest a felon if there is an arrest warrant issued by a court and/or probable cause that he or she committed a crime. In contrast, misdemeanants may be taken into custody only with an arrest warrant or if the police officer observed the infraction personally; this is known as the in-presence requirement. In some instances, however, police can make a misdemeanor arrest without observing its occurrence. For example, a number of jurisdictions have passed domestic violence prevention acts, which allow arrests based merely on the accusation of the injured party. These laws have been created in an effort to protect the target of the abuse from further attacks.[9]

If convicted, a person charged with a felony may be barred from certain fields of employment or some professions, such as law and medicine. A felony offender's status as an alien in the United States might also be affected, or the offender might be denied the right to hold public office, vote, or serve on a jury.[10] These and other civil liabilities exist only when a person is convicted of a felony offense, not of a misdemeanor.

LO3 Discuss the sources of criminal law

The Legal Definition of a Crime

Almost all common-law crime contains both mental and physical elements. For example, to commit the crime of armed burglary, offenders must do the following things:

- Willfully enter a dwelling
- Be armed or arm themselves after entering the house, or commit an actual assault on a person who is lawfully in the house
- Knowingly and intentionally commit the crime

For the prosecutor to prove a crime occurred and that the defendant committed it, the prosecutor must show (1) that the accused engaged in the guilty act (*actus reus*, or guilty act) and (2) that the act was intentional and purposeful (*mens rea*, or guilty mind). Under common law, both the *actus reus* and the *mens rea* must be present for the act to be considered a crime. Thoughts of committing an act do not alone constitute a crime; to be considered a crime, an illegal act must occur. Let us now look more closely at these issues.

actus reus An illegal act. The *actus reus* can be an affirmative act, such as taking money or shooting someone, or a failure to act, such as failing to take proper precautions while driving a car.

mens rea Guilty mind. The mental element of a crime or the intent to commit a criminal act.

Actus Reus

The *actus reus* is a *voluntary and deliberate* illegal act, such as taking someone's money, burning a building, or shooting someone; an accident or involuntary act would not be considered criminal. However, even an unintentional act can be considered a crime if it is the result of negligence and/or disregard for the rights of others. A person cannot be held criminally liable for assault if while walking down the street he has a seizure and as a result his arm strikes another person in the face; his act was not voluntary and therefore not criminal. However, if this same person knew beforehand that he might have a seizure and unreasonably put himself in a position where he was likely to harm others—for instance, by driving a car—he could be criminally liable for his behavior because his actions were negligent and disregarded the rights of others.

In addition, there are occasions when the failure or omission to act can be considered a crime:

- *Failure to perform a legally required duty that is based on relationship or status.* These relationships include parent and child and husband and wife. If a husband finds his wife unconscious because she took an overdose of sleeping pills, he is obligated to save her life by seeking medical aid. If he fails to do so and she dies, he can be held responsible for her death. Parents are required to look after the welfare of their children; failure to provide adequate care can be a criminal offense.
- *Imposition by statute.* Some states have passed laws that require a person who observes an automobile accident to stop and help the other parties involved.
- *Contractual relationship.* These relationships include lifeguard and swimmer, doctor and patient, and babysitter or au pair and child. Because lifeguards have been hired to ensure the safety of swimmers, they have a legal duty to come to the aid of drowning persons. If a lifeguard knows a swimmer is in danger and does nothing about it, and the swimmer drowns, the lifeguard can be held legally responsible for the swimmer's death.

In these cases, the duty to act is a legal and not a moral duty. The obligation arises from the relationship between the parties or from explicit legal requirements. In contrast, a private citizen who sees a person drowning is under no legal obligation to save that person. Although we may find it morally reprehensible, the private citizen could walk away and let the swimmer drown without facing legal sanctions.

Mens Rea

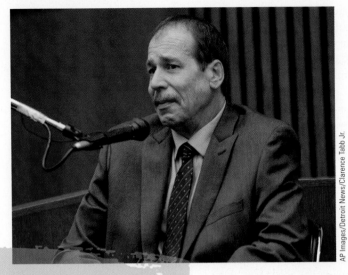

For an act to constitute a crime, it must be done with deliberate purpose or criminal intent. A person who enters a store with a gun with the intention of stealing money indicates by his actions the intent to commit a robbery. Criminal intent is implied if the results of a person's action, though originally unintended, are certain to occur. When Mohammed Atta and his terrorist band crashed an aircraft into the World Trade Center on September 11, 2001, they did not intend to kill any particular person in the building. Yet the law would hold that Atta, and any others conspiring with him, would be substantially certain that people in the building would be killed in the blast and that they therefore had the criminal intent to commit the crime of murder.

On Aug. 4, 2014, Theodore Wafer, of Dearborn Heights, Michigan, testifies in his own defense during his trial for the November 2, 2013, killing of Renisha McBride in Detroit. Wafer claimed he shot the young woman, who was seeking assistance after an auto accident, by accident because he was fearful that his house was being broken into. The jury did not believe his claims and sentenced him to 17 years in prison.

The Relationship between *Mens Rea* and *Actus Reus*

For an act to constitute a crime, the law requires a connection be made between the *mens rea* and the *actus reus,* thereby showing that the offender's conduct was the proximate cause of the criminal act. If a man chases a woman into the street intending to assault her, and the victim is struck by a car and killed, the accused cannot claim at trial that the death was an accident caused by the inopportune passing of the motor vehicle. The law holds that the victim would never have run into the street had she not been pursued by the defendant, and that, therefore, (1) the defendant's reckless disregard for the victim's safety makes him responsible for her death, and (2) his action was the proximate cause of her death.

CRIMINAL HARM Thought alone is not a crime. For a person to be considered to have committed a crime, some act is required to prove the actor's willingness to cause harm. The nature of the harm ultimately determines what crime the person committed. If someone trips another with the intent of making the person fall down and be embarrassed in public, he has committed the crime of battery. If by some chance the victim dies from the fall, the harm caused elevates the crime to manslaughter, even if that was not the intended result.

In the crime of robbery, the *actus reus* is taking the property from the person or presence of another. To satisfy the harm requirement, the robber must acquire the victim's possessions, referred to as "asportation." The legal definition of robbery is satisfied when, even for a brief moment, possession of the property is transferred to the robber. If a robber removes a victim's wallet from his pocket and immediately tosses it over a fence when he spies a police officer approaching, the robbery is complete because even the slightest change in possession of the property is sufficient to cause harm. Nor is the value of the property a consideration; actual value is unimportant as long as the property had some value to the victim.

ETHICAL REFLECTION

The Hernandez Case

The law recognizes that all people involved in a conspiracy to commit a murder are equally guilty even if only one pulled a trigger, and the others merely helped plan the crime and were present during the killing. Knowing about the crime is not enough; the prosecutor must prove that the defendant actually joined in the conspiracy knowing of the unlawful plan *and* intended to take part in it and help carry it out. Is it fair and ethical to punish all conspirators in the same manner even though only one engaged in violence? In other words, should the triggerman be punished more severely than the other conspirators?

Strict Liability

strict liability crime Illegal act whose elements do not contain the need for intent, or *mens rea*; usually, an act that endangers the public welfare, such as illegal dumping of toxic wastes.

In certain statutory offenses, known as public safety or **strict liability crimes**, *mens rea* is not essential. A person can be held responsible for such a violation independent of the existence of intent to commit the offense. Strict liability criminal statutes generally include narcotics control laws, traffic laws, health and safety regulations, sanitation laws, and other regulatory statutes. A motorist could not defend herself against a speeding ticket by claiming that she was unaware of how fast she was going and did not intend to speed, nor could a bartender claim that a juvenile to whom he sold liquor looked quite a bit older. No state of mind is generally required where a strict liability statute is violated.[11]

Criminal Defenses

LO4 Identify the elements of a crime

In 1884, two British sailors, desperate after being shipwrecked for days, made the decision to kill and eat a suffering cabin boy who was on their lifeboat. Four days later, they were rescued by a passing ship and returned to England. English authorities, wanting to end the practice of shipwreck cannibalism, tried the two men and convicted them of murder. Clemency was considered, and a reluctant Queen Victoria commuted the death sentences to six months.[12] Were the seamen justified in killing a shipmate to save their lives? If they had not done so, it is likely they all would have died. Did they act out of necessity or malice? Can there ever be a good reason to take a life? Can we ever justify killing another? Before you answer, remember that we can kill in self-defense, to prevent lethal crimes, or in times of war (more on necessity defenses later).

When people defend themselves against criminal charges, they must refute one or more of the elements of the crime of which they have been accused. Defendants may deny the *actus reus* by arguing that they were falsely accused, and the real culprit has yet to be identified, or that the act was an accident and occurred through no fault of their own. Defendants may also claim that although they did engage in the criminal act they are accused of, they lacked the *mens rea,* or mental intent, needed to be found guilty of the crime. If a person whose mental state is impaired commits a criminal act, it is possible for the person to excuse his criminal actions by claiming he lacked the capacity to form sufficient intent to be held criminally responsible. Insanity, intoxication, and ignorance are also among the types of excuse defenses.[13]

Another type of defense is justification. Here, the individual admits committing the criminal act but maintains that the act was justified and, given the circumstances, anyone would have acted in a similar manner; because her act was justified, she should not be held criminally liable. Among the justification defenses are necessity, duress, self-defense, and entrapment. We will now examine some of these defenses and justifications in greater detail.

Excuse Defenses

Excuses refer to situations in which the criminal defendants admit to performing the physical act of the crime but claim they are not responsible for it because they lacked free will. It is not their fault, they claim, because they had no control over their actions; therefore, they should be "excused" from criminal responsibility.

IGNORANCE OR MISTAKE People sometimes defend themselves by claiming either that their actions were a mistake or that they were unaware (ignorant) of the fact that their behavior was a crime. For example, they did not realize they had stepped onto private property and were guilty of trespassing.

As a general rule, ignorance of the law is no excuse. According to the great legal scholar William Blackstone, "Ignorance of the law, which everyone is bound to know, excuses no man."[14] Consequently, a defendant cannot present a legitimate defense by saying he was unaware of a criminal law, had misinterpreted the law, or believed the law to be unconstitutional.

In some instances, mistake of fact, such as taking someone else's coat that is similar to your own, may be a valid defense; an honest mistake may remove the defendant's criminal responsibility. Mistake can also be used as a defense when the government failed to make enactment of a new law public or when the offender relies on an official statement of the law that is later deemed incorrect.

insanity A legal defense that maintains a defendant was incapable of forming criminal intent because he or she suffers from a defect of reason or mental illness.

self-defense A legal defense in which defendants claim that their behavior was legally justified by the necessity to protect their own life and property, or that of another victim, from potential harm.

entrapment A criminal defense that maintains the police originated the criminal idea or initiated the criminal action.

REALITYCHECK

MYTH OR REALITY?

To commit crime, not only must a person engage in a harmful act, he or she must do so intentionally; unintentional acts don't count.

MYTH. Although most common-law crimes require intent, strict liability crimes do not have a mental requirement. Telling a police officer you did not intend to be speeding when you are stopped on the highway does not help you avoid a ticket.

Should a person on his way to a hospital emergency room be exempt from a speeding ticket? After all, he is endangering other motorists, regardless of his reason for speeding. Is there such a thing as an excuse when you violate traffic laws?

LO5 Define the term *strict liability*

MYTH OR REALITY?

People who are mentally ill cannot be found guilty of a crime.

MYTH. Mentally ill people can be convicted of a crime unless they are legally insane. You can suffer from a mental illness, such as depression or borderline personality disorder, but still be aware of your behavior and be in control of your actions; therefore, you would be legally responsible for your acts.

Do you agree? Or should mental illness excuse guilt? Is it possible to be suffering from severe mental illness yet have the intent to commit crime? Can we really say someone like Jeffrey Dahmer, the cannibal who raped, killed, and ate 17 men and boys, was not insane? Yet, he was found guilty of his crimes and given 15 life sentences; he was later killed in prison.

INSANITY Insanity is a defense to criminal prosecution in which the defendant's state of mind negates his or her criminal responsibility. A successful insanity defense results in a verdict of "not guilty by reason of insanity."[15]

Insanity is a legal category. As used in US courts, it does not necessarily mean that everyone who suffers from a form of mental illness can be excused from legal responsibility. Many people who are depressed, suffer mood disorders, or have a psychopathic personality can be found legally sane. Instead, insanity means that the defendant's state of mind at the time the crime was committed made it impossible for that person to have the necessary *mens rea* to satisfy the legal definition of a crime. A person can be undergoing treatment for a psychological disorder but still be judged legally sane if it can be proved that at the time he committed the crime, he had the capacity to understand the wrongfulness of his actions.

If a defendant uses the insanity plea, it is usually left to psychiatric testimony to prove that the person understood the wrongfulness of her actions and was therefore legally sane or, conversely, was mentally incapable of forming intent. The jury then must weigh the evidence in light of the test for sanity currently used in the jurisdiction. Such tests vary throughout the United States; the commonly used tests are listed in Exhibit 3.2.

INTOXICATION As a general rule, intoxication, which may include drunkenness or being under the influence of drugs, is not considered a defense. However, a defendant who becomes involuntarily intoxicated under duress or by mistake may be excused for crimes committed. Involuntary intoxication may also reduce the degree of the crime; a judgment may be decreased from first- to second-degree murder because the defendant uses intoxication to prove the lack of the critical element of *mens rea*.

AGE The law holds that a child is not criminally responsible for actions committed at an age that precludes full realization of the gravity of certain types of behavior. Under common law, there is generally a conclusive presumption of incapacity for a child under age 7, a reliable presumption for a child between the ages of 7 and 14, and no presumption for a child over the age of 14. This generally means that a child under age 7 who commits a crime will not be held criminally responsible for these actions and that a child between ages 7 and 14 may be held responsible. These common-law rules have been changed by statute in most jurisdictions. Today, the maximum age of criminal responsibility for children ranges from age 14 to 17 or 18, and the minimum age may be set by statute at age 7 or under age 14.[16]

James Holmes and his defense attorney Daniel King (right) sit in court for an advisement hearing at the Arapahoe County Justice Center in Centennial, Colorado June 4, 2013. Holmes, facing execution if convicted of killing 12 moviegoers last summer, entered a plea of not guilty by reason of insanity.

Andy Cross/Pool/Reuters/Landov

Various Insanity Defense Standards

The M'Naghten Rule The M'Naghten rule, first formulated in England in 1843, defines a person as insane if at the time she committed the act she stands accused of, she was laboring under such a defect of reason, arising from a disease of the mind, that she could not tell or know the nature and quality of the act or, if she did know it, that she did not know what she was doing was wrong. In other words, she could not "tell right from wrong." The M'Naghten rule is used in the majority of the states.

The Irresistible Impulse The irresistible impulse test was formulated in Ohio in 1834. It is used quite often in conjunction with M'Naghten and defines a person as insane if he should or did know that his actions were illegal but, because of a mental impairment, could not control his behavior. His act was a result of an uncontrollable or irresistible impulse. A person who commits a crime during a "fit of passion" would be considered insane under this test. One of the most famous cases making use of this defense occurred in 1994, when Lorena Bobbitt successfully defended herself against charges that she cut off the penis of her husband, John, after suffering abuse at his hands.

The Durham Rule The Durham rule, or "product test," was set forth by the US Court of Appeals for the District of Columbia Circuit in 1954 and states that "an accused is not criminally responsible if her unlawful act was the product of mental disease or defect." It was used for some time in the state of New Hampshire.

The Insanity Defense Reform Act The Insanity Defense Reform Act, Title 18, US Code, Section 17, was enacted by Congress in 1984 and states that a person accused of a crime can be judged not guilty by reason of insanity if "the defendant, as a result of a severe mental disease or defect, was unable to appreciate the nature and quality or the wrongfulness of his acts."

The Substantial Capacity Test The substantial capacity test was defined by the American Law Institute in its Model Penal Code. This argues that insanity should be defined as a lack of substantial capacity to control one's behavior. Substantial capacity is defined as "the mental capacity needed to understand the wrongfulness of [an] act, or to conform … behavior to the … law." This rule combines elements of the M'Naghten rule with the concept of irresistible impulse.

Justification Defenses

Justifications arise in situations in which the defendants don't deny they committed a crime but claim that anyone in their situation would have acted in a similar fashion. Justification defenses deny *mens rea*: "I did a bad act, but I did it for all the right reasons."

CONSENT A person may not be convicted of a crime if the victim consented to the act in question. In other words, a rape does not occur if the victim consents to sexual relations; a larceny cannot occur if the owner voluntarily consents to the taking of property. Consent is an essential element of these crimes, and it is a valid defense where it can be proved or shown that consent existed at the time the act was committed. In some crimes, such as statutory rape, however, consent is not an element of the crime and is considered irrelevant because the state presumes that young people are not capable of providing consent.

SELF-DEFENSE Defendants may justify their actions by saying they acted in self-defense. To establish the necessary elements to constitute self-defense, the defendant must have acted under a reasonable belief that he was in danger of death or great harm and had no means of escape from the assailant.

As a general legal rule, a person defending himself may use only such force as is reasonably necessary to prevent personal harm. A person who is assaulted by another with no weapon is ordinarily not justified in hitting the assailant with a baseball bat; a person verbally threatened is not justified in striking the other party. Persons can be found guilty of murder in the first degree if, after being attacked during a brawl, they shot and killed an unarmed person in self-defense. Despite the fact that it was the victim who initiated the fray and pummeled his opponent first, the imbalance in weaponry (gun versus fist) would mitigate a finding of self-defense.[17]

To exercise the self-defense privilege, the danger to the defendant must be immediate; it is not justifiable to kill someone who threatened you with death a year ago. In addition, most jurisdictions require that the defendants prove that they sought alternative means of avoiding the danger, such as escape, retreat, or assistance from others, before they defended themselves with force.

In some instances, women (or men) may kill their mates after years of abuse; this is known as battered-wife syndrome (or, in cases involving child abuse, battered-child syndrome). Although a history of battering can be used to mitigate the seriousness of the crime, a finding of not guilty most often requires the presence of imminent danger and the inability of the accused to escape from the assailant.

STAND YOUR GROUND Most self-defense statutes require a duty to retreat before reacting to a threat with physical violence. An exception is one's own home. According to the "castle exception" ("every man's home is his castle"), a person is not obligated to retreat within his or her residence before fighting back. Some states, most notably Florida, now have "stand your ground" laws, which allow people to use force in a wide variety of circumstances and eliminate or curtail the need to retreat, even if they are not in their own home but in a public place.

Florida's law, enacted on October 1, 2005, allows the use of deadly force when a person reasonably believes it necessary to prevent the commission of a "forcible felony," including carjacking, robbery, and assault.[18] The law allows average citizens to use deadly force when they reasonably believe that their homes or vehicles have been illegally invaded. The Florida law authorizes the use of defensive force by anyone "who is not engaged in an unlawful activity and who is attacked in any other place where he or she has a right to be." Furthermore, under the law, such a person has no duty to retreat and can stand his or her ground and meet force with force. The statute also grants civil and criminal immunity to anyone found to have had such a reasonable belief.[19] The stand your ground law gained national prominence when George Zimmerman shot and killed Trayvon Martin and claimed he was in fear of his life. Zimmerman was found not guilty at trial when the jury supported his self-defense claims.

ENTRAPMENT Defendants can claim their criminal activity was justified because law enforcement agents used traps, decoys, and deception to induce criminal action; this is referred to as entrapment. It is generally legitimate for law enforcement officers to set traps for criminals by getting information about crimes from informers, undercover agents, and codefendants. Police officers are allowed to use ordinary opportunities for defendants to commit crime and to create these opportunities that involve a defendant in a crime. For example, they can pose as prostitutes or drug dealers, hang out in an area known for drug dealing and prostitution, and make an arrest if they are solicited for crime. However, entrapment occurs when the police instigate the crime, implant criminal ideas, and coerce individuals into bringing about crime. In *Sherman v. United States,* the Supreme Court found that the function of law enforcement is to prevent crime and apprehend criminals, not to implant a criminal design originating with officials of the government in the mind of an innocent person.[20]

DURESS To prove duress, defendants must show they have been forced into committing a crime in order to prevent death or serious harm to self or others. For example, a bank employee might be excused from taking bank funds if she can prove

George Zimmerman Legal Defense Fund/Sanford Police Department/Handout/Reuters/Landov

George Zimmerman is shown here with a bloody, swollen nose. This photo was taken on the night he shot and killed unarmed black teenager Trayvon Martin. Zimmerman was found not guilty when a jury believed he acted in self-defense because he thought his life was in danger. What are your thoughts on this case? Was Zimmerman justified in using deadly force, or did he kill in a rage and therefore should have been found guilty of murder?

that her family was being threatened and that consequently she was acting under duress. However, there is widespread general agreement that duress is no defense for an intentional killing.

NECESSITY Sometimes criminal defendants, like the two sailors who killed and ate the cabin boy, argue that they acted out of "necessity." To be successful, a defense of necessity must show that considering the circumstances and conditions at the time the crime occurred, the defendant (or any reasonable person) could not have behaved in any other way. For example, a husband steals a car to take his pregnant wife to the hospital for an emergency delivery, or a hunter shoots an animal of an endangered species that was about to attack his child. The defense has been found inapplicable in cases where defendants sought to shut down nuclear power plants or abortion clinics or to destroy missile components under the belief that the action was necessary to save lives or prevent a nuclear war.

The Evolution of Criminal Law

One day you receive a text message or an automated phone call on your cell phone saying there's a problem with your bank account or your ATM number. The message gives you a phone number to call or a website to log into, and you are then directed to identify yourself so that your account can be "fixed." You might be asked to provide personal identification information—such as a bank account number, ATM PIN number, Social Security number, or credit card number—to fix the problem. The website looks really legitimate and contains a logo that looks exactly like Bank of America, TD Bank, or any other large national bank. Sounds good, but you have just become the victim of a crime called "smishing" or "vishing," and the person monitoring the website is not a bank employee but a criminal intent on collecting your personal information to help themselves to your money via your cell phone. Armed with your personal information, vishers can steal from your bank accounts, charge purchases on your charge cards, create a phony ATM card to drain your account, and so on. If you happened to log on to the phony website with a smartphone rather than your laptop, vishers can begin downloading malicious software that gives them access to anything and anyone in your phone's contact list. With the growth of mobile banking and the ability to conduct financial transactions online, smishing and vishing attacks may become even more attractive and lucrative for cyber criminals.

Vishing and smishing are considered violations of Chapter 63 of the federal criminal code that controls mail fraud.[21] In other instances, new laws must be devised specifically to control criminal innovations. For example, when millions of people were besieged by spam messages, some attempting to get them to give out personal information, Congress passed the CAN-SPAM Act of 2003 (full name, Controlling the Assault of Non-Solicited Pornography and Marketing Act of 2003) to reduce and regulate the use of Internet spam.[22]

Creating new laws to control cyberspace is just one element of the changes that are going on in contemporary criminal law. In recent years, many states and the federal government have been examining their substantive criminal law. In some instances, what was formerly legal is now a crime, and, in other instances, what was previously considered illegal has been legalized or decriminalized (in other words, the penalties have been reduced). An example of the former can be found in changes to the law of rape. In seven states, including California, it is now considered rape when the following sequence of events occurs: (1) the woman consents to sex, (2) the sex act begins, (3) she changes her mind during the act and tells her partner to stop, and (4) he refuses and continues. Before the legal change, such a circumstance was not considered rape.[23]

There are also many instances in which the law has been changed so that what was considered illegal is now legal and noncriminal. Until recently, sexual relations between consenting same-sex adults was punished as a serious felony under sodomy statutes.

LO6 Explain excuses and justification defenses for crime

In an important 2003 case, *Lawrence v. Texas,* the Supreme Court declared that laws banning sodomy are unconstitutional if they restrict adults' private sexual behavior and impose on their personal dignity. As a result of this decision, laws banning same-sex relations between consenting adults in the United States are now unconstitutional and therefore not enforceable.[24]

Creating New Crimes

In some instances, new laws have been created to conform to emerging social issues and to deal with threats to people and the environment. Some of the new crimes and legal categories created in this era of law reform are discussed next.

PHYSICIAN-ASSISTED SUICIDE Doctors helping people to end their lives became the subject of a national debate when Dr. Jack Kevorkian began practicing what he called **obitiatry**, helping people take their lives.[25] In an attempt to stop Kevorkian, Michigan passed a statutory ban on assisted suicide, reflecting what lawmakers believed to be prevailing public opinion; Kevorkian was convicted and imprisoned.[26] He was released on June 1, 2007, on parole due to good behavior and died on June 3, 2011; 44 states now disallow assisted suicide either by statute or common law, including Michigan.[27]

obitiatry Helping people take their own lives.

STALKING More than 25 states have enacted **stalking** statutes that prohibit and punish acts described typically as "the willful, malicious, and repeated following and harassing of another person."[28] Stalking laws were originally formulated to protect women terrorized by former husbands and boyfriends, although celebrities often are plagued by stalkers as well. In celebrity cases, these laws often apply to stalkers who are strangers or casual acquaintances of their victims.

stalking The willful, malicious, and repeated following and harassing of another person.

COMMUNITY NOTIFICATION LAWS These laws require the registration of people convicted of sex-related crimes; they were enacted in response to concern about sexual predators moving into neighborhoods. One of the best-known statutes of this kind, New Jersey's "Megan's Law," was named after 7-year-old Megan Kanka of Hamilton Township, New Jersey, who was killed in 1994. Charged with the crime was a convicted sex offender who (unknown to the Kankas) lived across the street. On May 17, 1996, President Clinton signed Megan's Law, which contained two components:

- *Sex offender registration.* Requires the states to register individuals convicted of sex crimes against children.
- *Community notification.* Compels the states to make private and personal information on registered sex offenders available to the public.

CONTROLLING TECHNOLOGY The new laws created to control such exotic cyber crimes as vishing and smishing are not unique. Such technologies as ATMs and cell phones have already spawned a new generation of criminal acts involving theft of access numbers and software piracy. Identity theft has become a national problem, and, as a result, there has been an ongoing effort by state legislatures to change their criminal codes to penalize sending out bulk e-mail messages designed to trick consumers into revealing bank account passwords, Social Security numbers, and other personal information, as a felony offense.[29]

PROTECTING THE ENVIRONMENT In response to the concerns of environmentalists, the federal government has passed numerous acts designed to protect the nation's well-being. The Environmental Protection Agency has successfully prosecuted significant violations of these and other new laws, including data fraud cases (e.g., private laboratories submitting false environmental data to state and federal environmental agencies); indiscriminate hazardous waste dumping that resulted in serious injuries and death; industry-wide ocean dumping by cruise ships; oil spills that caused significant damage to waterways, wetlands, and beaches; and illegal handling of hazardous substances such as pesticides and asbestos that exposed children, the poor, and other especially vulnerable groups to potentially serious illness.[30]

WEB APP 3.2 To read all about new environmental laws, go to **http://www.epa.gov /lawsregs/laws/** Should people who violate these laws face a prison sentence, or should such cases be handled civilly, with a fine and other penalties?

There are new laws designed to protect the environment. Here fireboat response crews spray water on the burning BP Deepwater Horizon offshore oil rig. An April 20, 2010, explosion at the platform killed 11 men, and the subsequent leak released an estimated 172 million gallons of petroleum into the gulf. BP was forced to pay billions in damages.

LEGALIZING MARIJUANA In 2012, the states of Washington and Colorado voted to legalize marijuana use, and marijuana has been legalized for medical purposes in 18 states; some, including California, allow dispensaries to fill prescriptions.[31] For example, New Jersey Senate Bill 119, signed into law on January 18, 2010, protects "patients who use marijuana to alleviate suffering from debilitating medical conditions, as well as their physicians, primary caregivers, and those who are authorized to produce marijuana for medical purposes" from "arrest, prosecution, property forfeiture, and criminal and other penalties."[32]

While providing medical marijuana has strong public support, the federal government still criminalizes any use of marijuana, and federal agents can arrest users even if they have prescriptions from doctors in states where medical marijuana is legal (though federal guidelines "suggest" to local prosecutors that they concentrate their efforts on abusers and not patients in need). In *Gonzales v. Raich,* the Supreme Court ruled that the federal government can prosecute medical marijuana patients, even in states with compassionate-use laws.[33]

LO7 Discuss the most recent developments in criminal law reform

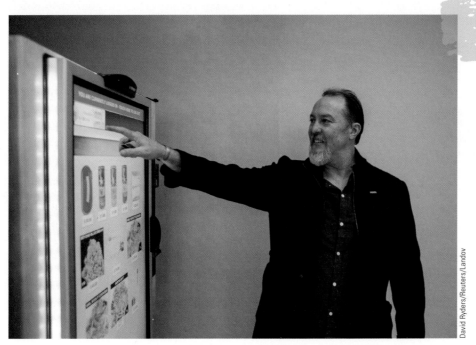

Some states, including Washington and Colorado, have legalized marijuana, prompting new methods of distribution. Stephen Shearin demonstrates the use of a ZaZZZ vending machine that contains cannabis flower, hemp-oil energy drinks, and other merchandise at Seattle Caregivers, a medical marijuana dispensary, in Seattle, Washington on February 3, 2015. Vending machines selling medical marijuana opened for business in Seattle in what the company providing them billed as a first-in-the-state innovation that it expects to expand to other cities and states where pot is legal as medicine. Shearin is the president of technology company American Green Inc., which provides the machines.

Constitutional Criminal Procedure

Whereas substantive criminal law primarily defines crimes, the law of criminal procedure consists of the rules and procedures that govern the pretrial processing of criminal suspects and the conduct of criminal trials. The main source of the procedural law is the body of the Constitution and the first 10 amendments, added to the Constitution on December 15, 1791, which are collectively known as the **Bill of Rights**. The purpose of these amendments is to prevent the government from usurping the personal freedoms of citizens. The most controversial of these rights is the Second Amendment, which deals with gun ownership, a topic discussed further in the Contemporary Issues in Criminal Justice feature.

The US Supreme Court's interpretation of these amendments has served as the basis for the creation of legal rights of the accused. Of primary concern are the Fourth, Fifth, Sixth, and Eighth Amendments, which limit and control the manner in which the federal government operates the justice system. In addition, the due process clause of the Fourteenth Amendment has been interpreted to apply these limits on governmental action to the state and local levels:

- The Fourth Amendment bars illegal "searches and seizures," a right especially important for the criminal justice system because it means that police officers cannot indiscriminately use their authority to investigate a possible crime or arrest a suspect. Stopping, questioning, or searching an individual without legal justification represents a serious violation of the Fourth Amendment right to personal privacy. Under the **exclusionary rule**, evidence seized in violation of the Fourth Amendment cannot be used in a court of law; it is as though it never existed.

- The Fifth Amendment limits the admissibility of confessions that have been obtained unfairly. In the 1966 landmark case *Miranda v. Arizona*, the Supreme Court held that a person accused of a crime has the right to refuse to answer questions when placed in police custody.[34] The Fifth Amendment also guarantees defendants the right to a grand jury hearing and to protection from being tried twice for the same

CONTEMPORARY ISSUES IN CRIMINAL JUSTICE

Gun Control and the Constitution

You may remember the 2014 incident when a Veronica Rutledge, of Blackfoot, Idaho, had gone shopping to Walmart in Coeur d'Alene, Idaho, with her four children. Veronica's 2-year-old son, who was sitting in the shopping cart, reached into her purse, causing the small-caliber handgun to discharge, accidentally killing 29-year-old Veronica. Incidents such as these convince gun control advocates that guns should be banned and that they cause way more harm than good. In contrast, in 2015, Colorado voters were asked to repeal gun control laws passed in the wake of the Aurora movie theater shooting in which James Holmes killed 12 people and wounded 70 others. Colorado has passed measures limiting the size of ammunition magazines and expanding background-check requirements. Gun advocates argue that if citizens were armed they could have stopped someone like Holmes before he had killed so many. Where do the courts stand on this issue?

The Second Amendment states that "a well-regulated Militia, being necessary to the security of a Free State, the right of the people to keep and bear Arms, shall not be infringed." What exactly does this mean? Seventy-five years ago, in *United States v. Miller* (307 US 174 [1939]), the Supreme Court ruled that the Second Amendment must be interpreted as intending to guarantee the states' rights to maintain and train a militia, and not a personal right to bear arms. Miller had wanted to avoid registering a "sawed-off shotgun," which he possessed for personal use. The Court ruled, "In the absence of any evidence tending to show that possession or use of a shotgun having a barrel

of less than 18 inches in length at this time has some reasonable relationship to the preservation or efficiency of a well-regulated militia, we cannot say that the Second Amendment guarantees the right to keep and bear such an instrument." The Court's decision also mentioned that weapons appropriate for the militia at the time were in "common use" and that a sawed-off shotgun was not a weapon that was commonly used or widely possessed.

Because the *Miller* case applied only to sawed-off shotguns, it left the gun possession issue unsettled for seven decades. Then, in the landmark 2008 case *District of Columbia v. Heller,* the Supreme Court put this issue to rest when it held that the Second Amendment protects an individual's right to possess a firearm for private use. Its decision ruled that Washington, DC's Firearms Control Regulations Act of 1975, which banned handgun possession, was unconstitutional and determined that handguns are "arms" that may not be banned by a local jurisdiction. It also struck down the portion of the law that required that all firearms, including rifles and shotguns, be kept "unloaded and disassembled or bound by a trigger lock." The decision clearly declares the Second Amendment protection of "an individual right to possess a firearm unconnected with service in a militia, and to use that arm for traditionally lawful purposes, such as self-defense within the home." It goes on to clarify specific limitations on those Second Amendment protections, and it concludes with a characterization of the District's "total ban on handgun possession in the home (as) amount(ing) to a prohibition on an entire class

(Continued)

of 'arms' that Americans overwhelmingly choose for the lawful purpose of self-defense." Because handguns are commonly used, the *Heller* decision does not conflict with the *Miller* decision's ban on sawed-off shotguns.

In another critical case, *McDonald v. Chicago,* residents of Chicago challenged a local law whose provisions included the following:

- A ban on the registration of handguns
- A requirement that guns be registered prior to purchase
- A requirement to reregister guns yearly
- A law prohibiting any gun from being reregistered if its original registration lapses

The Supreme Court ruled that the right of an individual to "keep and bear arms" was protected by the Second Amendment, incorporated by the due process clause of the Fourteenth Amendment, and therefore applies to the states as well as the federal government. The Court stated that the Second Amendment protects the right to keep and bear arms for the purpose of self-defense, that "individual self-defense is 'the *central component*' of the Second Amendment right," and that self-defense is a basic right, recognized by many legal systems from ancient times to the present day.

Although the *Heller* and *McDonald* decisions prohibit governmental jurisdictions from banning guns outright, the rulings do not prohibit the state and federal governments from regulating gun use and possession. The *Heller* decision stated:

… nothing in our opinion should be taken to cast doubt on longstanding prohibitions on the possession of firearms by felons and the mentally ill, or laws forbidding the carrying of firearms in sensitive places such as schools and government buildings, or laws imposing conditions on the commercial sale of arms.

So while these rulings answer the question of whether gun ownership is a constitutional right (it is), it does not shut the door on governmental regulation and control of that right.

Gun Control Laws

A number of legal attempts have been made to control and regulate gun ownership. The Federal Assault Weapons Ban, enacted in 1994, prohibited the possession and manufacturing of semiautomatic assault weapons that were capable of holding more than 10 rounds of ammunition; it did not restrict semiautomatic assault weapons that had been legally obtained before the ban went into effect. The law had a 10-year sunset clause so it expired in 2004, once again allowing the possession of automatic weapons.

After the expiration of the assault rifle ban, the major federal statutes that regulate the sale and possession of guns were the 1934 National Firearms Act and the Gun Control Act of 1968. The National Firearms Act taxes the manufacturing and sale of guns, and it requires that gun distributors register all guns with the attorney general. The Gun Control Act of 1968 added the requirement that gunmakers and sellers be federally licensed; it prohibits the interstate sale of guns. It also prohibits the direct mail order of firearms (except antique firearms) by consumers and mandates that anyone who wants to buy a gun from a source other than a private individual must do so through a federally licensed firearms dealer. It requires that all dealers be licensed, fill out forms detailing each trade, and avoid selling to people prohibited from owning guns, such as minors, ex-felons, and drug users. Dealers must record the source and properties of all guns they sell and carefully account for their purchase. Gun buyers must provide identification and sign waivers attesting to their ability to possess guns. The act also bans unlicensed individuals from acquiring handguns outside their state of residence, although long guns, such as rifles and shotguns, may be acquired from federally licensed firearms dealers located in other states, provided this is allowed by both the state of purchase and the state of residence.

The Brady Handgun Violence Prevention Act of 1993, amending the Gun Control Act of 1968, imposed a waiting period of five days before a licensed importer, manufacturer, or dealer may sell, deliver, or transfer a handgun to an unlicensed individual. On November 30, 1998, the Brady Law changed, substituting an instant check based on the FBI's National Instant Criminal Background Check System (NICS) on whether a prospective buyer is prohibited from purchasing a weapon. Gun purchases by people convicted of or under indictment for felony charges, fugitives, the mentally ill, those with dishonorable military discharges, those who have renounced US citizenship, undocumented aliens, and illegal drug users, as well as those who have been convicted of domestic violence misdemeanors or are under domestic violence restraining orders are prohibited.

In addition to the federal controls, a number of states have instituted laws restricting access to firearms by individuals who are subject to a restraining order or have been convicted of a domestic violence misdemeanor, or allowing law enforcement officers to confiscate firearms at a domestic violence scene.

States also vary in their control of concealed handguns. All 50 states make some provision for legal concealed carry via a permit or license. Most states have "shall-issue" statutes, which allow people to carry guns if they can meet requirements to obtain a permit; some states, including California, New Jersey, New York, and Massachusetts, have "may-issue" statutes, which typically will issue permits if the applicant provides a documented need for a concealed weapon, such as working in the security industry.

In the wake of the recent spate of mass shootings, gun control and/or restriction has become a hot topic. Those who seek control call for a ban on assault weapons, tightening of background checks, and so on. They note that gun control is an extremely difficult enterprise. Take, for instance, the 2,500 gun shows in which private sellers are able to buy and sell firearms for their personal collections or as a hobby. During many of these shows, sellers are not required to have a federal firearms license, and private sellers are under no legal obligation to ask purchasers whether they are eligible to buy guns or to verify purchasers' legal status through background checks. Guns are part of American life: there are already an estimated 300 million guns in America, and more than 50 million households contain guns. So despite the fact that two-thirds of all murders involve firearms and half by handguns, this problem will not be easily solved.

CRITICAL THINKING

Despite the *Heller* ruling, do you believe that the sale and possession of handguns should be banned outright? Remember, drugs are illegal and yet are commonly possessed. Would a ban on guns take them out of the hands of citizens and place them in the hands of criminals?

Source: *USA Today,* "Toddler Reaches into Purse and Gun Goes Off Killing Mom," http://www.usatoday.com/story/news/nation/2014/12/30/woman-shot-with-own-gun/21062089/ (accessed April 2015); *District of Columbia v. Heller,* 554 US 570 (2008); *McDonald v. Chicago,* 561 US 742 (2010); US Concealed Carry Association, https://www.usconcealedcarry.com/travel/ (accessed February 2015); Bryan Ciyou, "Gun Laws by State 2015," http://www.gunlawsbystate.com/#!/home/terms-of-access-and-use/ (accessed April 2015).

Jeff King (left) of Centralia, Washington, points a rifle towards the state capitol as gun rights advocates rally against Initiative 594, which requires background checks for all gun purchases in Washington state. Despite such efforts, the initiative was voted into law, making the state the first in the country to close the so-called gun-show loophole through popular vote.

Jason redmond/Reuters/Landov

REALITYCHECK

MYTH OR REALITY?

Under the Fourth Amendment, to search a person, the police must first obtain a warrant from a sitting judge.

MYTH. Police can search without a warrant in emergency circumstances or if the courts have granted them permission to do so. This loophole has spurred many legal cases defining when and where police can conduct warrantless searches.

Should a guilty person be allowed to go free simply because police officers made a mistake when they conducted a search? For example, if they opened the trunk of a car and found a dead body in the vehicle, should the driver go free if the search was later ruled illegal? Is there some other possible remedy?

crime (double jeopardy). Its due process clause guarantees defendants the right to fundamental fairness and the expectation of fair trials, fair hearings, and similar procedural safeguards.

- The Sixth Amendment guarantees the defendant the right to a speedy and public trial by an impartial jury, the right to be informed of the nature of the charges, and the right to confront any prosecution witnesses. It also contains the right of a defendant to be represented by an attorney—a privilege that has been extended to numerous stages of the criminal justice process, including pretrial custody, identification and lineup procedures, preliminary hearing, submission of a guilty plea, trial, sentencing, and postconviction appeal.

- According to the Eighth Amendment, "Excessive bail shall not be required, nor excessive fines imposed, nor cruel and unusual punishments inflicted." Bail is a money bond put up by the accused to attain freedom between arrest and trial. Bail is meant to ensure a trial appearance because the bail money is forfeited if the defendant misses the trial date. The Eighth Amendment does not guarantee a constitutional right to bail but, rather, prohibits the use of excessive bail, which is

CAREERS IN CRIMINAL JUSTICE ATTORNEY

Duties and Characteristics of the Job

- Attorneys use their experience and extensive knowledge of the law and the legal system to defend the rights of their clients and protect their best interests either in a legal setting, during a trial, or by settling their grievances in or out of court.

- They also act as legal advisors and engage in such activities as drawing up and/or interpreting a legal document or contract, and they advise clients of changes in existing laws.

- Attorneys will often choose a field of specialization such as tax law or intellectual property and typically work in firms or start their own practice.

- Some work for the federal, state, or local government; others take advantage of increasing opportunities for employment within businesses.

- Attorneys work long hours; especially if a case goes to trial; a workweek of more than 60 hours is not uncommon.

Job Outlook

- Job opportunities are expected to grow at an average rate for the next several years.

- A good academic record from a prestigious law school, as well as work experience, mobility, and additional education in a specialty field, are especially helpful.

(Continued)

- Jobs will be most plentiful in urban areas, where more law firms, big businesses, and government offices are typically located.

Salary

- Attorneys have a median annual salary of about $113,000 per year or about $55 per hour.

- Some partners in the largest national firms in Chicago or New York may have an annual salary in the millions.

- An attorney's salary will depend on type of employer, experience, region, and type of law being practiced. Extremely successful sole practitioners can win millions in tort actions.

Qualifications

- A bachelor's degree in a program that develops strong analytical and writing skills is recommended for preparation for law school.

- Graduating from an accredited law school and passing the bar are required.

Education and Training

- Lawyers must go to an accredited law school and pass the bar.

- Making the law review, publishing law review articles while in school, and obtaining prestigious internships can be helpful in securing coveted jobs.

- Many lawyers use their education and experience as a means of launching careers in business, politics, government, or academia.

Reality Check

- Attorneys must stay informed of the latest developments in law and often attend conferences; many states have continuing legal education (CLE) requirements that must be met.

- For certain positions, such as law school professor and positions focusing on a specialty such as patent law, further experience and education are required.

- Gaining entrance to a law school takes not only hard work and discipline but also good grades and a desirable score on the Law School Admissions Test (LSAT). Start preparing now.

- Be prepared for some long hours at work.

- Be realistic about pay. Not all lawyers start at $160,000 per year, but those hired by top metropolitan firms can expect substantial starting salaries.

- Top grads at top schools get top jobs; the bottom half of the class in the bottom-ranked schools will struggle.

Source: Bureau of Labor Statistics, *Occupational Outlook Handbook, 2014,* http://www.bls.gov/ooh/legal/lawyers.htm (accessed February 2015).

typically defined as an amount far greater than that imposed on similar defendants who are accused of committing similar crimes. The Eighth Amendment also forbids the use of cruel and unusual punishment. This prohibition protects both the accused and convicted offenders from actions regarded as unacceptable by a civilized society, including corporal punishment and torture. Capital punishment, however, is legal unless it is employed in a random, haphazard fashion or if especially cruel means of execution are used.[35] One method used to avoid "cruelty" is lethal injection. In the 2008 case *Baze and Bowling v. Rees,* the Court upheld the use of this method unless there is a "substantial risk of serious harm" that the drugs will not work effectively.[36]

- The Fourteenth Amendment is the vehicle used by the courts to apply the protection of the Bill of Rights to the states. It affirms that no state shall "deprive any person of life, liberty, or property, without due process of law." In essence, the same general constitutional restrictions applicable to the federal government can be imposed on the states.

REALITY CHECK

MYTH OR REALITY?

All US citizens accused of a crime have the right to be released on bail before trial.

MYTH. The Eighth Amendment does not guarantee the right to bail. However, if a person is granted bail, it cannot be excessive.

Due Process of Law

The concept of due process, found in both the Fifth and Fourteenth Amendments, has been used to evaluate the constitutionality of legal statutes and to set standards and guidelines for fair procedures in the criminal justice system. As you may recall from Chapter 1, some criminal justice experts believe that the concept of due process is the lens through which the criminal justice system must be examined. Without the application of due process, civil rights and constitutional protections are meaningless. In seeking to define the term, most legal experts believe that it refers to the essential elements of

LO8 Describe the role of the Bill of Rights in shaping criminal procedure

ETHICAL REFLECTION

The Hernandez Case

Can someone like Aaron Hernandez, whose case has been splashed across the media for over a year, ever hope to get a fair trial? Is it at all logical to suggest that a celebrity and unknown will be treated the same? What would be the most ethical solution: Move the case to a faraway state not filled with Patriot fans such as Washington or Colorado?

fairness under law.[37] This definition basically refers to the legal system's need for rules and regulations that protect individual rights.

Due process can actually be divided into two distinct categories, substantive and procedural. Substantive due process refers to the citizen's right to be protected from criminal laws that may be biased, discriminatory, and otherwise unfair. These laws may be vague or may apply unfairly to one group and not others. The doctrine of substantive due process holds that citizens maintain particular rights, such as freedom of speech and religion, that cannot be controlled or impeded by the government. So we as citizens have the right to criticize government policy without fear of legal retribution. In some instances, the Courts have protected rights, such as the right to marital privacy, that are not mentioned in the Constitution per se, but are considered an essential and undisputed element of American life. Based on this thinking, people have the right to buy and use contraceptives to prevent unwanted pregnancies, something that was not considered by the founding fathers![38]

LO9 List the elements of due process of law

Procedural due process seeks to ensure that no person will be deprived of life, liberty, or property without proper and legal criminal process. Basically, procedural due process is intended to guarantee that fundamental fairness exists in each individual case. Specific due process procedures include the following:

- Freedom from illegal searches and interrogations
- Prompt notice of charges and a formal hearing
- The right to counsel or some other representation
- The opportunity to respond to charges
- The opportunity to confront and cross-examine witnesses and accusers
- The privilege to be free from self-incrimination
- The opportunity to present one's own witnesses
- A decision made on the basis of substantial evidence and facts produced at the hearing
- A written statement of the reasons for the decision
- An appellate review procedure

Interpreting the Constitution

Within the context of due process, how the Supreme Court decides a specific case depends on the facts of the case, the federal and state constitutional and statutory provisions, previous court decisions, and judicial philosophy.[39] The judicial interpretation of the Constitution is not fixed but reflects what society deems fair and just at a particular time and place. The degree of loss suffered by the individual (victim or offender), balanced against the state's interests, also determines how many constitutional requirements are ordinarily applied. When the Supreme Court justices are conservative, they are less likely to create new rights and privileges and more likely to restrict civil liberties. Take the 2009 case of *Herring v. US*, which involved interpretation of the exclusionary rule.[40] Bennie Dean Herring had been searched after the police were informed that there was an outstanding warrant against him on a felony charge. The search turned up methamphetamine and a pistol. Soon after, it was discovered that the warrant had actually been withdrawn five months earlier and had been left in the computer system by mistake. Should the evidence be discarded because the police made an error? Or should it be allowed because they acted in good faith based on existing evidence that later proved inaccurate? The majority decision ruled that "When police mistakes leading to an unlawful search are the result of isolated negligence attenuated from the search, rather than systemic error or reckless disregard of

Pictured here are Oscar Pistorius and Reeva Steenkamp during happier times. South African Olympic athlete Pistorius was found guilty after he fired four shots at Steenkamp through a bathroom door in his Pretoria home. Pistorius claimed he had mistaken her for an intruder but the judge hearing the case found him guilty. He received a five-year prison sentence for culpable homicide and a concurrent three-year suspended prison sentence for a separate reckless endangerment conviction.

Barcroft Media/Landov

constitutional requirements, the exclusionary rule does not apply." The Court ruled that the errors in the *Herring* case did not amount to deliberate police misconduct that should trigger the exclusionary rule.

LO10 Explain the role the Supreme Court plays in interpreting the Constitution and shaping procedural law

ETHICAL Challenge

Prosecuting Celebrities

When the Hernandez case began, one juror had to be dismissed because it turned out he was a greater Patriot fan than he let on. Does sympathy for athletes and other celebrities present an ethical challenge for the justice system?

One prime example of the ethical tangle that occurs when celebrities are on trial can be seen in the 2014 trial of South African athlete Oscar Pistorius, which made headlines around the world. Pistorius, a double-amputee known as the "Blade Runner," was a Paralympics champion who became the first amputee to participate in international competitions, including the Olympics. This world-famous athlete was charged with the murder of his model girlfriend, Reeva Steenkamp, who was killed in the bathroom of his Pretoria home when Pistorius fired shots through the closed door. He claimed to have been awakened by a noise, heard the bathroom window open, believed an intruder had broken into the house and shot to defend himself; he claimed that Reeva's death was a terrible mistake. His story was disputed by prosecutors who argued that Pistorius fought with Steenkamp for some unknown reasons and then shot her in anger when she took refuge in the bathroom. In 2014, Pistorius was found guilty of culpable homicide and sentenced to five years in prison; prosecutors appealed the sentence, which seemed shockingly light considering the crime. Did Pistorius get what he deserved, or did he benefit from being the nation's most famous athlete? Is it ethical to consider a person's accomplishments when deciding on their punishment?

SUMMARY

LO1 *List the similarities and differences between criminal law and civil law* The law today can generally be divided into four broad categories. Substantive criminal law defines crimes and their punishment. Procedural criminal law sets out the basic rules of practice in the criminal justice system. Civil law governs relations between private parties, including both individuals and organizations (such as business enterprises and corporations). Administrative or public law controls the behavior of government agencies.

LO2 *Discuss the concept of substantive criminal law and its history* The roots of the criminal codes used in the United States can be traced to such early legal charters as the Babylonian Code of Hammurabi (2000 BCE) and the Mosaic Code of the Israelites (1200 BCE). In the Middle Ages, societies developed legal systems featuring monetary compensation, called *wergild*. After the Norman Conquest, royal judges would decide what to do in each case, using local custom and rules of conduct as a guide in a system known as *stare decisis* (Latin for "to stand by decided cases"). Eventually, this system evolved into a common law of the country that incorporated local custom and practice into a national code.

LO3 *Discuss the sources of criminal law* The contemporary American legal system was codified by state and federal legislatures. The content of the law may also be influenced by judicial decision making. Regardless of its source, all criminal law in the United States must conform to the rules and dictates of the Constitution.

LO4 *Identify the elements of a crime* Almost all common-law crime contains both mental and physical elements. The *actus reus* is a voluntary and deliberate illegal act, such as taking someone's money, burning a building, or shooting someone. For an act to constitute a crime, it must be done with deliberate purpose or criminal intent, that is, *mens rea.*

LO5 *Define the term* **strict liability** Thought alone is not a crime. For a person to be considered to have committed a crime, some act is required to prove her or his willingness to cause harm. Certain statutory offenses exist in which *mens rea* is not essential. These offenses fall in a category known as public safety or strict liability crimes.

LO6 *Explain excuses and justification defenses for crime* When people defend themselves against criminal charges, they must refute one or more of the elements of the crime of which they have been accused. Defendants may deny the *actus reus* by arguing that they were falsely accused, and the real culprit has yet to be identified. Defendants may also claim that even though they did engage in the criminal act they are accused of, they should be excused because they lacked *mens rea.*

LO7 *Discuss the most recent developments in criminal law reform* Criminal law is constantly changing and being updated. New crimes have been created to control stalking, environmental damage, and cyber crime. Others have been decriminalized or legalized, such as sodomy. In some cases, such as distributing medical marijuana, states may legalize acts that are still banned by federal law.

L08 ***Describe the role of the Bill of Rights in shaping criminal procedure*** The main source of the procedural law is the body of the Constitution and the first 10 amendments—the Bill of Rights—added to the Constitution on December 15, 1791. Of primary concern are the Fourth, Fifth, Sixth, and Eighth Amendments, which limit and control the manner in which the federal government operates the justice system.

L09 ***List the elements of due process of law*** The concept of due process is found in both the Fifth and Fourteenth Amendments. Due process has been used to evaluate the constitutionality of legal statutes and to set standards and guidelines for fair procedures in the criminal justice system.

L010 ***Explain the role the Supreme Court plays in interpreting the Constitution and shaping procedural law*** The law of criminal procedure consists of the rules and procedures that govern the pretrial processing of criminal suspects and the conduct of criminal trials. The Supreme Court is tasked with interpreting the Constitution and setting limits on governmental behavior—for example, limiting the ability of the police in their searching, questioning, and punishing of those suspected of crime.

KEY TERMS

first-degree murder, p. 62

premeditation, p. 62

deliberation, p. 62

second-degree murder, p. 62

substantive criminal law, p. 62

criminal procedure, p. 62

civil law, p. 62

tort, p. 62

public law, p. 62

lex talionis, p. 63

stare decisis, p. 64

common law, p. 64

mala in se, p. 64

mala prohibitum, p. 64

ex post facto laws, p. 66

felony, p. 66

misdemeanor, p. 66

actus reus, p. 67

mens rea, p. 67

strict liability crime, p. 68

insanity, p. 69

self-defense, p. 69

entrapment, p. 69

obitiatry, p. 74

stalking, p. 74

Bill of Rights, p. 76

exclusionary rule, p. 76

REVIEW QUESTIONS

1. What are the specific aims and purposes of criminal law? To what extent does criminal law control behavior?

2. What kinds of activities should be labeled criminal in contemporary society? Why?

3. What is a criminal act? What is a criminal state of mind? When are individuals liable for their actions?

4. Discuss the various kinds of crime classifications. To what extent or degree are they distinguishable?

5. Numerous states are revising their penal codes. Which major categories of substantive crimes do you think should be revised?

6. Entrapment is a defense used when the defendant claims he was entrapped into committing the crime. To what extent should law enforcement personnel induce the commission of an offense?

7. What legal principles can be used to justify self-defense? Given that the law seeks to prevent crime—not promote it—are such principles sound?

8. What are the minimum standards of criminal procedure required in the criminal justice system?

AP Images/Albuquerque Police Department

THE POLICE AND LAW ENFORCEMENT

Every year, approximately 400 people are justifiably killed by police officers. In a country of about 300 million people, that number seems exceptionally low. But police critics think it is too high. Any time a person is fatally shot by the police, whether justified or otherwise, the event is closely scrutinized. The agency for which the officer works typically performs an in-depth investigation. The local prosecutor's office usually investigates to rule out the possibility of criminal behavior. Sometimes federal agencies launch their own probes, as has recently occurred in Albuquerque, New Mexico.

On March 16, 2014, James Boyd, a homeless man who was camping in the Sandia Foothills outside of Albuquerque, was shot following a lengthy and tense standoff with police. Boyd, armed with two small knives, initially threatened to kill police and did not back down when he was ordered to discard his weapon. In their efforts to subdue Boyd, officers fired stun guns, beanbags, and ultimately six live rounds. Boyd was killed. Real-time helmet cam footage was made available by the Albuquerque Police Department and, as of this writing, is available on YouTube (see https://www.youtube.com /watch?v=uAPb04HGwYA). Was the shooting justifiable? Two of the officers were charged with murder, so it is difficult to answer with a yes. Nevertheless, you can watch the video and decide for yourself.

So controversial was the shooting that the Federal Bureau of Investigation launched a criminal probe promptly afterward (and the city eventually entered into an agreement with the US Justice Department to reform its use of force policies). The agency was concerned not just with what happened in the Boyd case, but also with what it felt was an unusually high rate of police shootings in Albuquerque. At the time the probe was launched, 37 people had been shot by Albuquerque police since 2010. In 23 of the shootings, the suspect was killed, giving Albuquerque the dubious distinction of having one of the highest rates of police shootings in the country.[1] But in a city of roughly 550,000 people, some would say 23 deaths are not many. Which perspective is correct? Unfortunately, there are no easy answers.

Part 2 of this text covers policing. Chapter 4 looks at the history and organization of law enforcement organizations at all levels of government. Chapter 5 discusses the role and function of policing, including patrol, investigations, and community policing. Chapter 6 tackles a number of contemporary issues in policing, among them police culture, discretion, stress fatigue, and use of force. Chapter 6 also provides an introduction to the legal environment within which the police must operate.

4 Police in Society:
HISTORY AND ORGANIZATION

On December 20, 2014, two uniformed New York City police officers, Wenjian Liu and Rafael Ramos, were shot dead as they sat in their marked patrol car on a Brooklyn street corner. "No warning, no provocation—they were quite simply assassinated, targeted for their uniform," Commissioner William Bratton told the press.[2] The shooter, Ismaaiyl Brinsley, 28, apparently targeted the officers in retaliation for the deaths of two unarmed black men at the hands of police—Eric Garner on July 17, 2014, in New York City, and Michael Brown in Ferguson, Missouri, on August 9, 2014. Brinsley posted an ominous message on his Instagram page prior to the shooting: "They Take 1 of Ours....Let's Take 2 of Theirs." He also posted pictures of the silver Taurus semiautomatic pistol he used and even posted another message in the moments leading up to the shooting, saying "Watch what I'm going to do." After he shot the officers, Brinsley fled toward the subway, but on seeing that its doors were closed and officers were closing in, he fatally shot himself. Officer Liu left behind his wife of two months, and Officer Ramos left behind a wife and two sons.

Despite terrible events like this, fewer officers are being killed in the line of duty than ever before—about 40 each year. The number rose dramatically in 2001 because 23 officers were killed in the September 11 terrorist attacks, along with 343 firefighters. Before the 2001 spike, the number of officers slain in the line of duty had been trending downward for the previous decade. In 2013, the last year for which data were available as of this writing, 27 law enforcement officers were feloniously killed.[3] Many more officers, though, are assaulted each year (some 50,000 each year), and policing remains a high-risk profession.

The police are the gatekeepers of the criminal justice process. They initiate contact with violators of the law and decide whether to arrest them formally and start their journey through the criminal justice system, to settle the issue in an informal way (such as by issuing a warning), or to take no action at all. The strategic position of law enforcement officers, their visibility and contact with the public, and their use of weapons and arrest power kept them in the forefront of public thought for most of the twentieth century.

REALITY CHECK

MYTH OR REALITY?

- The first modern police force was established in London.
- During the nineteenth century, the police were regarded as competent and professional.
- Federal law enforcement agencies are housed solely within cabinet-level departments (such as the State Department).
- The core mission of the FBI is to enforce the criminal laws of the United States.
- Most metropolitan law enforcement agencies employ fewer than 50 officers.
- There are more private police than public police.

AP Images/John Minchillo

LEARNING OBJECTIVES

L01 *Summarize characteristics of the first law enforcement agencies*

L02 *Discuss the development of law enforcement in the United States*

L03 *Analyze the problems of early police agencies*

L04 *Discuss how reformers attempted to create professional police agencies*

L05 *Describe the major changes in law enforcement between 1970 and today*

L06 *Identify the major federal law enforcement agencies*

L07 *Summarize the differences among state, county, and local law enforcement*

L08 *Explain the role of technology in police work*

This and the following two chapters evaluate the history, role, organizational issues, and procedures of police agents and agencies and discuss the legal rules that control police behavior.

The History of Police

The origin of US police agencies, like the origins of criminal law, can be traced to early English society.[4] Before the Norman Conquest in 1066 BCE, no regular English police force existed. Every person living in the villages scattered throughout the countryside was responsible for aiding neighbors and protecting the settlement from thieves and marauders. This was known as the "pledge system." People were grouped in collectives of 10 families, called **tithings**, and were entrusted with policing their own minor problems. When trouble occurred, the citizen was expected to make a **hue and cry**. Ten tithings were grouped into what was called a **hundred**, whose affairs were supervised by a **constable** appointed by the local nobleman. The constable, who might be considered the first real police officer, dealt with more serious breaches of the law.[5]

Shires, which resembled the counties of today, were controlled by the **shire reeve**, who was appointed by the Crown or by a local landowner to supervise the territory and ensure that order was kept. The shire reeve, a forerunner of today's **sheriff**, soon began to pursue and apprehend law violators as part of his duties.

In the thirteenth century, the **watch system** was created to help protect property in England's larger cities and towns. Watchmen patrolled at night and helped protect the community against robberies, fires, and disturbances. They reported to the area constable, who became the primary metropolitan law enforcement agent. In larger cities, such as London, the watchmen were organized within church parishes and were usually members of the parish they protected.

In 1326, the office of **justice of the peace** was created to assist the shire reeve in controlling the county. Eventually, these justices took on judicial functions in addition to their primary role as peacekeepers. The local constable became the operational assistant to the justice of the peace, supervising the night watchmen, investigating offenses, serving summonses, executing warrants, and securing prisoners. This system helped establish the relationship between police and the judiciary, which has continued for more than 670 years.

Private Police and Thief Takers

As the eighteenth century began, rising crime rates encouraged a new form of private, monied police, who profited both legally and criminally from the lack of formal police departments. These private police agents, referred to as "thief takers," were universally corrupt, taking profits not only from catching and informing on criminals but also from receiving stolen property, theft, intimidation, perjury, and blackmail. They often relieved their prisoners of money and stolen goods and made even more income by accepting hush money, giving perjured evidence, swearing false oaths, and operating extortion rackets. Petty debtors were especially easy targets for those who combined thief taking with the keeping of alehouses and taverns. While prisoners were incarcerated, their health and safety were entirely at the whim of the thief takers, who were free to charge virtually whatever they wanted for board and other necessities. Court bailiffs who also acted as thief takers were the most passionately detested legal profiteers. They seized debtors and held them in small lockups, where they forced their victims to pay exorbitant prices for food and lodging.

The thief takers' use of violence was notorious. They went armed and were prepared to maim or kill to gain their objectives. Before he was hanged in 1725, Jack Wild, the most notorious thief taker, "had two fractures in his skull and his bald head was covered with silver plates. He had seventeen wounds in various parts of his body from swords, daggers, and gunshots, [and] ... his throat had been cut in the course of his duties."[6]

tithing In medieval England, a group of 10 families who collectively dealt with minor disturbances and breaches of the peace.

hue and cry In medieval England, a call for assistance. The policy of self-help that prevailed in villages demanded that everyone respond if a citizen raised a hue and cry to get their aid.

hundred In medieval England, a group of 100 families responsible for maintaining order and trying minor offenses.

constable In medieval England, an appointed official who administered and supervised the legal affairs of a small community.

shire reeve In medieval England, the senior law enforcement figure in a county; the forerunner of today's sheriff.

sheriff The chief law enforcement officer in a county.

watch system During the Middle Ages in England, men were organized in church parishes to guard at night against disturbances and breaches of the peace under the direction of the local constable.

justice of the peace Established in 1326 England, the office was created to help the shire reeve in controlling the county; it later took on judicial functions.

Henry Fielding (famed author of *Tom Jones*), along with Saunders Welch and his brother John Fielding, sought to clean up the thief-taking system. Appointed a city magistrate in 1748, Henry Fielding operated his own group of monied police out of Bow Street in London, directing and deploying them throughout the city and its environs, deciding which cases to investigate and what streets to protect. His agents were carefully instructed on their legitimate powers and duties. Fielding's Bow Street Runners were a marked improvement over the earlier monied police because they actually had an administrative structure that improved record keeping and investigative procedures.

Creating Public Police

In 1829, Sir Robert Peel, England's home secretary, guided through Parliament an "Act for Improving the Police in and near the Metropolis." The Metropolitan Police Act established the first organized police force in London. Composed of more than 1,000 men, the London police force was structured along military lines; its members were known from then on as "bobbies," after its creator. They wore a distinctive uniform and were led by two magistrates, who were later given the title of commissioner. However, the ultimate responsibility for the police fell to the home secretary and consequently to the Parliament.

The early bobbies suffered from many of the same ills as their forebears. Many were corrupt, they were unsuccessful at stopping crime, and they were influenced by the wealthy. Owners of houses of ill repute, who in the past had guaranteed their undisturbed operations by bribing watchmen, now turned their attention to the bobbies. Metropolitan police administrators fought constantly to terminate cowardly, corrupt, and alcoholic officers, dismissing in the beginning about one-third of the bobbies each year.

Law Enforcement in Colonial America

Law enforcement in colonial America paralleled the British model. In the colonies, the county sheriff became the most important law enforcement agent. In addition to keeping the peace and fighting crime, sheriffs collected taxes, supervised elections, and handled a great deal of other legal business.

The colonial sheriff did not patrol or seek out crime. Instead, he reacted to citizens' complaints and investigated crimes that had occurred. His salary, related to his effectiveness, was paid on a fee system. Sheriffs received a fixed amount for every arrest made. Unfortunately, their tax-collecting chores were more lucrative than fighting crime, so law enforcement was not one of their primary concerns. In the cities, law enforcement was the province of the town marshal, who was aided, often unwillingly, by a variety of constables, night watchmen, police justices, and city council members. However, local governments had little power of administration, and enforcement of the criminal law was largely an individual or community responsibility. In rural areas in the South, slave patrols charged with recapturing escaped slaves were an early—if loathsome—form of law enforcement.[7] When these patrols apprehended runaway slaves, they administered "justice" on the spot, often with violence. In the western territories, individual initiative was encouraged by the practice of offering rewards for the capture of felons. If trouble arose, the town vigilance committee might form a posse to chase offenders. These vigilantes were called on to eradicate such social problems as theft of livestock through force or intimidation; the San Francisco Vigilance Committee actively pursued criminals in the mid-nineteenth century.

Early Police Agencies

The modern police department was born out of urban mob violence that wracked the nation's cities in the nineteenth century. Boston created the first formal US police department in 1838. New York formed its police department in 1844, and Philadelphia followed in 1854. The new police departments replaced the night-watch system and relegated constables and sheriffs to serving court orders and running jails.

LO1 Summarize characteristics of the first law enforcement agencies

REALITY CHECK

MYTH OR REALITY?

The first modern police force was established in London.

REALITY. Although there were some signs of organized policing as early as the 1600s, the London Metropolitan Police, formed in 1829, is widely regarded as the first modern organized police force.

What were some of the other early modernized police forces besides the Metropolitan Police?

LO2 Discuss the development of law enforcement in the United States

vigilantes Groups of citizens who tracked down wanted criminals in the Old West.

At first, the urban police departments inherited the functions of the institutions they replaced. For example, Boston police were charged with maintaining public health until 1853, and, in New York, the police were responsible for street sweeping until 1881. Politics dominated the departments and determined the recruitment of new officers and the promotion of supervisors. An individual with the right connections could be hired despite a lack of qualifications. Early police agencies were corrupt, brutal, and inefficient.[8] At first, police were expected to live in the area they patrolled, but as the nineteenth century drew to a close, officers left the most dangerous areas and commuted to work, thereby separating themselves from the people they were being asked to supervise and control.[9]

In the late nineteenth century, police work was highly desirable because it paid more than most other blue-collar jobs. By 1880, the average factory worker earned $450 a year, whereas a metropolitan police officer made $900 annually. For immigrant groups, having enough political clout to be appointed to the police department was an important step up the social ladder.[10] However, job security was uncertain because it depended on the local political machine staying in power.

Police work itself was primitive. There were few of even the simplest technological innovations common today, such as centralized record keeping. Most officers patrolled on foot, without backup or the ability to call for help. Officers were commonly taunted by local toughs and responded with force and brutality. The long-standing conflict between police and the public was born in the

John X. Beidler, pictured here, was leader of the Montana Vigilantes, a secretive band formed to fight crime in Montana in the 1860s. He later became a stagecoach guard and a deputy U.S. marshal. Vigilante groups like Beidler's were precursors to organized police forces in colonial America.

Print Collector/HIP/The Image Works

REALITY**CHECK**

MYTH OR REALITY?

During the nineteenth century, the police were regarded as competent and professional.

MYTH. Policing in the 1800s was anything but professional. Competence often was lacking as well. It would not be until the 1900s that police departments began making major strides toward professionalism.

Is policing a profession today? What are the hallmarks of a profession?

LO3 Analyze the problems of early police agencies

difficulty that untrained, unprofessional officers had in patrolling the streets of nineteenth-century US cities and in breaking up and controlling labor disputes. Police were not crime fighters as we know them today. Their main role was maintaining order, and their power was almost unchecked. The average officer had little training, no education in the law, and a minimum of supervision, yet the police became virtual judges of law and fact with the ability to exercise unlimited discretion.[11]

Police during the nineteenth century were regarded as incompetent and corrupt and were disliked by the people they served. The police role was only minimally directed at law enforcement. Its primary function was serving as the enforcement arm of the reigning political power, protecting private property, and keeping control of the ever-rising numbers of foreign immigrants.

Police agencies evolved slowly through the second half of the nineteenth century. Uniforms were introduced in 1853 in New York. The first technological breakthroughs in police operations came in the area of communications. The linking of precincts to central headquarters by telegraph began in the 1850s. In 1867, the first telegraph police boxes were installed; an officer could turn a key in a box, and his location and number would automatically register at headquarters. Additional technological advances were made in transportation. The Detroit Police Department outfitted some of its patrol officers with bicycles in 1897. By 1913, the motorcycle was being used by departments in the eastern part of the nation. The first police car was used in Akron, Ohio, in 1910, and the police wagon became popular in Cincinnati in 1912.[12] Nonpolice functions, such as care of the streets, had begun to be abandoned by police departments after the Civil War.

The control of police departments by local politicians impeded effective law enforcement and fostered an atmosphere of graft and corruption. In the nineteenth century, big-city police were still not respected by the public, were largely unsuccessful in their role as crime stoppers, and were involved in no progressive activities.

Policing in the Twentieth Century

The modern era of policing can be traced from the turn of the nineteenth century to the present. What are the major events that occurred during this period?

The Emergence of Professionalism

In an effort to reduce police corruption, civic leaders in a number of jurisdictions created police administrative boards to reduce local officials' control over the police. These tribunals were responsible for appointing police administrators and controlling police affairs. In many instances, these measures failed because the private citizens appointed to the review boards lacked expertise in the intricacies of police work. Another reform movement was the takeover of some metropolitan police agencies by state legislators. Although police budgets were financed through local taxes, rural politicians in the state capitals usurped control of the police. New York City temporarily lost authority over its police force in 1857. It was not until the first decades of the twentieth century that cities regained control of their police forces.

The Boston police strike of 1919 heightened interest in police reform. The strike came about basically because police officers were dissatisfied with their status in society. Other professions were unionizing and increasing their standard of living, but police salaries lagged behind. The Boston police officers' organization, the Boston Social Club, voted to become a union affiliated with the American Federation of Labor. The officers went out on strike on September 9, 1919. Rioting and looting broke out, resulting in Governor Calvin Coolidge's mobilization of the state militia to take over the city. Public support turned against the police, and the strike was broken. Eventually, all the striking officers were fired and replaced by new recruits. The Boston police strike ended police unionism for decades and solidified power in the hands of reactionary, autocratic police administrators. In the aftermath of the strike, various local, state, and federal crime commissions began to investigate the extent of crime and the ability of the justice system to deal with it effectively; they then made recommendations to improve police effectiveness.[13] With the onset of the Depression, however, justice reform became a less important issue than economic revival, and little changed in the nature of policing for many years.

At about the same time, a number of nationally recognized leaders called for measures to help improve and professionalize the police. In 1893, the International Association of Chiefs of Police (IACP), a professional society, was formed. The IACP called for creating a civil service police force and for removing political influence and control. The most famous police reformer of the time was August Vollmer. While serving as police chief of Berkeley, California, Vollmer instituted university training for young officers and helped develop the School of Criminology at the University of California at Berkeley. Vollmer's disciples included O. W. Wilson, who pioneered the use of advanced training for officers and was instrumental in applying modern management and administrative techniques to policing. During this period, police professionalism was equated with an incorruptible, tough, highly trained, rule-oriented department organized along militaristic lines. The most respected department was that of Los Angeles, which emphasized the police as incorruptible crime fighters who would not question the authority of the central command.

LO4 Discuss how reformers attempted to create professional police agencies

The 1960s and Beyond

Turmoil and crisis were the hallmarks of policing during the 1960s. Throughout this decade, the Supreme Court handed down a number of decisions designed to control police operations and procedures. Police officers were now required to follow strict legal guidelines when questioning suspects, conducting searches, and wiretapping, among other duties. As the civil rights of suspects were significantly expanded, police complained that they were being "handcuffed by the courts."

Also during this time, civil unrest produced a growing tension between police and the public. African Americans, who were battling for recognition and enforcement of

Police Shootings

Prior to the shooting of officers Liu and Ramos featured in this chapter's opening story, the media extensively reported on the deaths of two unarmed black men at the hands of police officers, one in Missouri and another in New York City. Did the media's coverage of these incidents encourage Brinsley's actions? If so, how? If not, why?

their rights and freedoms in the civil rights movement, found themselves confronting police lines. When riots broke out in New York, Detroit, Los Angeles, and other cities between 1964 and 1968, the spark that ignited conflict often involved the police. When students across the nation began marching in anti-Vietnam War demonstrations, local police departments were called on to keep order. Police forces were ill equipped and poorly trained to deal with these social problems; it is not surprising that the 1960s were marked by a number of bloody confrontations between the police and the public.

Compounding these problems was a rapidly growing crime rate. The number of violent and property crimes increased dramatically. Drug addiction and abuse grew to be national concerns, common among all social classes. Urban police departments could not control the crime rate, and police officers resented the demands placed on them by dissatisfied citizens.

The 1970s witnessed many structural changes in police agencies themselves. The end of the Vietnam War significantly reduced tensions between students and police. The relationship between police and minorities was still rocky, however. Local fears and distrust, combined with conservative federal policies, encouraged police departments to control what was perceived as an emerging minority group "threat."[14]

Increased federal government support for criminal justice greatly influenced police operations. During the decade, the Law Enforcement Assistance Administration (LEAA) devoted a significant portion of its funds to police agencies. Although a number of police departments used this money to purchase little-used hardware, such as antiriot gear, most of it went to supporting innovative research on police work and advanced training of police officers. Perhaps most significant, the LEAA's Law Enforcement Education Program helped thousands of officers further their college education. Hundreds of criminal justice programs were developed on college campuses around the country, providing a pool of highly educated police recruits. LEAA funds were also used to transfer technology originally developed in other fields into law enforcement. Technological innovations involving computers transformed the way police kept records, investigated crimes, and communicated with one another. State training academies improved the way police learned to deal with such issues as job stress, community conflict, and interpersonal relations. More women and minorities were recruited into police work as well. Affirmative action programs helped to slowly alter the ethnic, racial, and gender composition of US policing.

As the 1980s began, the police role seemed to be changing significantly. A number of experts acknowledged that the police were not simply crime fighters and called for police to develop a greater awareness of community issues, which resulted in the emergence of the community policing concept.[15]

Police unions, which began to grow again in the late 1960s, continued to have a great impact on departmental administration in the 1980s. Unions fought for and won increased salaries and benefits for their members. In many instances, union efforts eroded the power of the police chief to make unquestioned policy and personnel decisions. During the decade, chiefs of police commonly consulted with union leaders before making significant decisions about departmental operations.

Although police operations improved markedly during this time, police departments were also beset by problems that impeded their effectiveness. State and local budgets were cut back during the Reagan

Stapleton Historical Collection/Heritage Image Partnership Ltd/Alamy

Great precaution is taken to guard police headquarters in Pemberton Square during the Boston police strike of 1919. Here a cavalryman of the state guard rides a horse previously used by the mounted policemen who went on strike. The Boston police strike ended police unionism for decades and solidified power in the hands of reactionary, autocratic police administrators. In the aftermath of the strike, various local, state, and federal crime commissions began to investigate the extent of crime and the ability of the justice system to deal with it and made recommendations to improve police effectiveness.

administration, and federal support for innovative police programs was severely curtailed with the demise of the LEAA.

Police–community relations continued to be a major problem. Riots and incidents of urban conflict occurred in some of the nation's largest cities.[16] They triggered persistent concern about what the police role should be, especially in inner-city neighborhoods.

The 1990s began on a sour note and ended with an air of optimism. The incident that helped change the face of American policing occurred on March 3, 1991, when Rodney King and his friend Bryant Allen were driving in Los Angeles, California. They refused to stop when signaled by a police car behind them but instead increased their speed; King, the driver, was apparently drunk or on drugs. When police finally stopped the car, they delivered 56 baton blows and 6 kicks to King in a period of two minutes, producing 11 skull fractures, brain damage, and kidney damage. They did not realize that their actions were being videotaped by an observer, who later gave the tape to the media. The officers involved were eventually tried and acquitted in a suburban court by an all-white jury, a decision that set off six days of rioting.[17]

The King case prompted an era of reform. Several police experts decreed that the nation's police forces should be evaluated not on their crime-fighting ability but on their courteousness, deportment, and helpfulness. Interest was renewed in reviving an earlier style of police work featuring foot patrols and increased citizen contact. Police departments began to embrace new forms of policing that stressed cooperation with the community and problem solving. The following are some of the most notable achievements of police departments in the 1990s:

- The intellectual caliber of the police rose dramatically.
- Police began to use advanced management techniques and applied empirical data to their decision making.
- Standards of police conduct climbed. Despite well-publicized incidents of brutality, police tended to treat the public more fairly, more equitably, and more civilly than they did in the 1960s.
- Police became more diverse in race and gender.
- The work of the police became intellectually more demanding, requiring an array of new specialized knowledge about technology, forensic analysis, and crime.
- Police gradually accepted civilian review of police discipline.[18]

LO5 Describe the major changes in law enforcement between 1970 and today

Policing and Law Enforcement Today

Contemporary law enforcement agencies are still undergoing transformation. An effort has been ongoing to make police "user friendly" by decentralizing police departments and making them responsive to community needs. Police and law enforcement agencies are also adapting to the changing nature of crime: they must be prepared to handle terrorism, Internet fraud schemes, and identity theft, as well as rape, robbery, and burglary.[19]

Law enforcement duties are distributed across local, county, state, and federal jurisdictions. Approximately 765,000 sworn law enforcement officers are employed in the United States in almost 20,000 different agencies.[20] Police and law enforcement agencies can be found in a variety of levels of government. No real hierarchy is in place, and each branch has its own sphere of operations, although overlap may occur.

Federal Law Enforcement Agencies

The federal government has a number of law enforcement agencies designed to protect the rights and privileges of US citizens; no single agency has unlimited jurisdiction, and each has been created to enforce specific laws and cope with particular situations. Federal agencies have no particular rank order or hierarchy of command or responsibility; each reports to a specific department or bureau.

Dozens of federal law enforcement agencies exist both inside and outside the cabinet-level departments. Here we focus on law enforcement agencies in two cabinet-level departments: the US Justice Department and the Department of Homeland Security.

REALITYCHECK

MYTH OR REALITY?

Federal law enforcement agencies are housed solely within cabinet-level departments (such as the State Department).

MYTH. Law enforcement agencies exist throughout the federal government.

Many federal law enforcement agencies are not associated with a particular cabinet-level department (an example is the Postal Inspection Service). Try to identify some of the lesser-known federal law enforcement agencies.

FBI Special Agent Eric Perry displays a thumb drive with cell phone records during Aaron Hernandez's murder trial in Fall River, Massachusetts, March 26, 2015. Hernandez was charged with killing semiprofessional football player Odin Lloyd.

Federal Bureau of Investigation (FBI) The arm of the US Justice Department that investigates violations of federal law, seeks to protect America from terrorist attacks, gathers crime statistics, runs a comprehensive crime laboratory, and helps train local law enforcement officers.

Drug Enforcement Administration (DEA) The federal agency that enforces federal drug control laws.

Bureau of Alcohol, Tobacco, Firearms, and Explosives (ATF) Federal agency with jurisdiction over the illegal sale, importation, and criminal misuse of firearms and explosives and the distribution of untaxed liquor and cigarettes.

US Marshals Service Federal agency whose jurisdiction includes protecting federal officials, transporting criminal defendants, and tracking down fugitives.

Department of Homeland Security (DHS) Federal agency responsible for preventing terrorist attacks within the United States, reducing America's vulnerability to terrorism, and minimizing the damage and assisting in recovery from attacks that do occur.

Customs and Border Protection (CBP) Federal agency responsible for the control and protection of America's borders and ports of entry. Its first priority is keeping terrorists and their weapons out of the United States.

US JUSTICE DEPARTMENT AGENCIES The US Justice Department houses four of the better-known federal law enforcement agencies.

- **Federal Bureau of Investigation (FBI)** The FBI is an investigative agency with jurisdiction over all matters in which the United States is or may be an interested party. Its jurisdiction is limited, however, to federal laws, including all federal statutes not specifically assigned to other agencies. The FBI has approximately 33,000 employees, including almost 13,000 special agents and 20,000 support personnel who perform professional, administrative, technical, clerical, craft, trade, or maintenance operations. Since 9/11, the FBI has announced a reformulation of its priorities, making protecting the United States from terrorist attack its number one commitment. It is now charged with coordinating intelligence collection with the Border Patrol, the Secret Service, and the CIA. Among the agency's other activities are gathering crime statistics, running a comprehensive crime laboratory, and training local law enforcement officers.

- **Drug Enforcement Administration (DEA)** DEA agents assist local and state authorities in investigating illegal drug use and carrying out independent surveillance and enforcement activities to control the importation of narcotics. For example, DEA agents work with foreign governments in cooperative efforts aimed at destroying opium and marijuana crops at their source—hard-to-find fields tucked away in the interiors of Latin America, Asia, Europe, and Africa. Undercover DEA agents infiltrate drug rings and simulate buying narcotics to arrest drug dealers.

- **Bureau of Alcohol, Tobacco, Firearms, and Explosives (ATF)** The ATF helps control sales of untaxed liquor and cigarettes and, through the Gun Control Act of 1968 and the Organized Crime Control Act of 1970, has jurisdiction over the illegal sale, importation, and criminal misuse of firearms and explosives.

- **US Marshals Service** The US Marshals Service is America's oldest federal law enforcement agency and one of the most versatile. Its almost 40,000 deputy marshals and criminal investigators perform a number of functions, including judicial security, fugitive investigations, witness protection, prisoner transportation, prisoner services (the agency houses nearly 60,000 federal detainees each day), and administration of the US Justice Department's Asset Forfeiture Program.

HOMELAND SECURITY AGENCIES Soon after the 9/11 attacks on the Pentagon and the World Trade Center towers in New York City, President Bush proposed the creation of a new cabinet-level agency called the **Department of Homeland Security (DHS)**. On November 19, 2002, Congress passed legislation authorizing the creation of the DHS and assigned it the mission of providing intelligence analysis and infrastructure protection, strengthening the borders, improving the use of science and technology to counter weapons of mass destruction, and creating a comprehensive response and recovery division. Rather than working from the ground up, the DHS combined a number of existing agencies into a superagency that carries out a variety of missions from border security to infrastructure protection. Two of the main law enforcement agencies housed within DHS are described in some detail next.

- **Customs and Border Protection (CBP)** After 9/11, the US Border Patrol, portions of the US Customs Service, the Immigration and Naturalization Service, and the Animal and Plant Health Inspection Service were combined into one office of Customs and Border Protection. The agency employs almost 60,000 personnel and is primarily responsible for protection of America's borders and ports of entry. The largest and most visible element of CBP is the Border Patrol. Its approximately 22,000 agents combine to form one of the largest uniformed law enforcement agencies in the United States.

- **Secret Service** The US Secret Service performs two main functions. The more visible of these is protection of national leaders, notably the president but also the vice president, the president-elect, the vice president–elect, the immediate families of these individuals, former presidents and their families, visiting heads of state, and other officials. The Secret Service was first established as a law enforcement entity in 1865 and was tasked with investigating the counterfeiting of US currency. It continues this investigative function today. Since 1984, Secret Service investigative activities have been expanded to include the investigation of financial institution fraud, computer and telecommunications fraud, false identification documents, and other criminal activities.

State Law Enforcement Agencies

Unlike municipal police departments, state police were legislatively created to deal with the growing incidence of crime in nonurban areas, a consequence of the increase in population mobility and the advent of personalized mass transportation in the form of the automobile. County sheriffs—elected officials with occasionally corrupt or questionable motives—had proved ineffective in dealing with the wide-ranging criminal activities that developed during the latter half of the nineteenth century. In addition, most local police agencies were unable to protect effectively against highly mobile lawbreakers who randomly struck at cities and towns throughout a state. In response to citizens' demands for effective and efficient law enforcement, state governors began to develop plans for police agencies that would be responsible to the state, instead of being tied to local politics and possible corruption.

The Texas Rangers, created in 1835, was one of the first state police agencies formed. Essentially a military outfit that patrolled the Mexican border, it was followed by the Massachusetts State Constables in 1865 and the Arizona Rangers in 1901. The states of Connecticut (1903) and Pennsylvania (1905) formed the first truly modern state police agencies.[21]

Today, about 23 state police agencies have the same general police powers as municipal police and are territorially limited in their exercise of law enforcement regulations only by the state's boundaries. They provide investigative services to smaller communities when the need arises. The remaining state police agencies are primarily responsible for highway patrol and traffic law enforcement.

Some state police direct most of their attention to the enforcement of traffic laws. Others are restricted by legislation from becoming involved in the enforcement of certain areas of the law. For example, in some jurisdictions, state police are prohibited from becoming involved in strikes or other labor disputes, unless violence erupts.

The nation's 93,000 state police employees (about 61,000 officers and 32,000 civilians) carry out a variety of functions besides law enforcement and highway safety, including maintaining a training academy and providing emergency medical services.[22] State police crime laboratories aid local departments in investigating crime scenes and analyzing evidence. State police also provide special services and technical expertise in such areas as bomb-site analysis and homicide investigation. Some state police departments, such as California's, are involved in highly sophisticated traffic and highway safety programs, including the use of helicopters for patrol and rescue, the testing of safety devices for cars, and the conducting of postmortem examinations to determine the causes of fatal accidents.

STATE LAW ENFORCEMENT AND THE WAR ON TERROR In the wake of the 9/11 attacks, a number of states have beefed up their intelligence-gathering capabilities and aimed them directly at homeland security. For example, the Texas Homeland Security office coordinates the resources and responses needed to prevent terrorist

Secret Service Federal agency responsible for executive protection and for investigation of counterfeiting and various forms of financial fraud.

WEB APP 4.1 Visit the Department of Homeland Security's website and examine its organizational chart at **http://www.dhs.gov/organizational-chart.** What other law enforcement agencies are part of DHS? Compare and contrast their duties with those of Customs and Border Protection and the Secret Service.

LO6 Identify the major federal law enforcement agencies

LO7 Summarize the differences among state, county, and local law enforcement attacks in the Lone Star state. The state's strategic plan for homeland security prioritizes the following:

1. *Prevent.* Prevent terrorist attacks in Texas, and prevent criminal enterprises from operating successfully in Texas.
2. *Protect.* Reduce vulnerability to natural disasters, criminal and terrorist attacks, and catastrophic events.
3. *Prepare to respond and recover.* Prepare to minimize damage through rapid, decisive response, and quickly recover from terrorist attacks and other disasters.[23]

County Law Enforcement Agencies

The county sheriff's role has evolved from that of the early English shire reeve, whose primary duty was to assist the royal judges in trying prisoners and enforcing sentences. From the time of the westward expansion in the United States until municipal departments were developed, the sheriff was often the sole legal authority over vast territories.

Today, sheriffs' offices contain about 350,000 full-time employees, including about 183,000 sworn personnel. Employment has risen an average of about 4 percent per year since 1990.[24] The duties of a sheriff's department vary according to the size and degree of development of the county. In some jurisdictions, sheriffs' offices provide basic law enforcement services such as performing routine patrols, responding to citizen calls for service, and investigating crimes.

Other standard tasks of a typical sheriff's department are serving civil process (summons and court orders), providing court security, and operating the county jail. Less commonly, sheriffs' departments may serve as coroners, tax collectors, overseers of highways and bridges, custodians of the county treasury, and providers of fire, animal control, and emergency medical services. In years past, sheriffs' offices also conducted executions. Typically, the law enforcement functions of a sheriff's department are restricted to unincorporated areas of a county, unless a city or town police department requests its help.

Some sheriffs' departments are exclusively law enforcement oriented; some carry out court-related duties only; and some are involved solely in correctional and judicial matters and not in law enforcement. However, a majority are full-service programs that carry out judicial, correctional, and law enforcement activities. As a rule, agencies serving heavily populated areas (over 1 million) are devoted to maintaining county correctional facilities, whereas those in smaller population areas are focused on law enforcement.

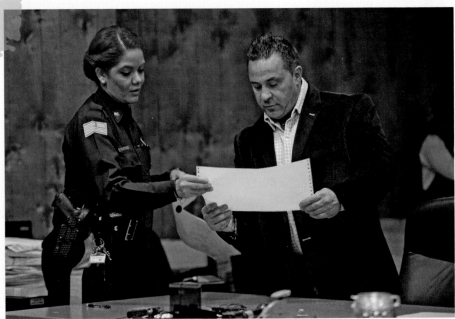

Giuseppe "Joe" Giudice receives information regarding his sentencing from a Passaic County Sheriff Officer in the courtroom of Judge Adam Jacobs in Passaic County (New Jersey) Superior Court. Giudice, of reality television fame (*The Real Housewives of New Jersey*), along with this wife, Teresa, were sentenced to prison for wire and bankruptcy fraud.

Amy Newman/North Jersey/Landov

COUNTY LAW ENFORCEMENT AND THE WAR ON TERROR A number of counties are now engaging in antiterror and homeland security activities. For example, the Harris County, Texas, Office of Homeland Security and Emergency Management (OHSEM) is responsible for an emergency management plan that prepares for public recovery in the event of natural or manmade disasters, catastrophes, or attacks. It works in conjunction with the state, federal, and local authorities, including the city of Houston and other municipalities in the surrounding Harris County area, when required. If needed, OHSEM activates an Emergency Operations Center to allow coordination of all support agencies to provide continuity of services to the public. OHSEM is responsible for advisement, notification, and assembly of services that are in the best interest of the citizens of Harris County. They prepare and distribute information and procedures governing the same.[25]

Similarly, in Montgomery County, Maryland, the Homeland Security Department plans, prevents, prepares, and protects against major threats that may harm, disrupt, or destroy the community, its commerce, and institutions. Its mission is to effectively manage and coordinate the county's unified response, mitigation, and recovery from the consequences of such disasters or events should they occur. It also serves to educate the public on emergency preparedness for all hazards and conducts outreach to diverse and special populations to protect, secure, and sustain critical infrastructures to ensure the continuity of essential services.[26]

WEB APP 4.2 Go to the website for the US Justice Department's Bureau of Justice Statistics at **http://bjs.ojp.usdoj.gov/**. Follow the "Law Enforcement" link, and determine how many law enforcement agencies exist in the United States. Is the number accurate? Why or why not?

Metropolitan Law Enforcement Agencies

Local police form the majority of the nation's authorized law enforcement personnel. Metropolitan police departments range in size from the New York City Police Department, with almost 40,000 full-time officers and 10,000 civilian employees, to rural police departments, which may consist of a single officer. At last count, nearly 13,000 local police departments nationwide had an estimated 600,000 full-time employees, including about 460,000 sworn personnel.[27] Metropolitan police departments are attracting applicants who value an exciting, well-paid job that also offers them an opportunity to provide valuable community service. Salaries in municipal police agencies are becoming more competitive.

Most TV police shows feature the crime-fighting efforts of big-city police officers, but in an overwhelming majority of departments, there are fewer than 50 officers that serve a population of fewer than 25,000. Recent data reveal that nearly three-quarters of all local police departments serve populations of fewer than 10,000 people. Around 650 such agencies employ just one sworn officer.

Municipal police officers' responsibilities are immense, and they are often forced to make split-second decisions on life-and-death matters. At the same time, they must be sensitive to the needs of citizens who are often of diverse racial and ethnic backgrounds. What's more, local police perform multiple roles, including (but not limited to) investigating crimes, identifying suspects, and making arrests (see Exhibit 4.1).

Smaller agencies can have trouble carrying out many of the same functions as their big-city counterparts; the hundreds of small police agencies in each state often provide duplicate services. Whether consolidating smaller police agencies into "superagencies" would improve services is often debated among police experts. Smaller municipal agencies can provide important specialized services that might have to be relinquished if they were combined and incorporated into larger departments. Another approach has

---

EXHIBIT 4.1

Core Functions of Municipal Police

Law Enforcement Functions

- Identifying criminal suspects
- Investigating crimes
- Apprehending offenders and participating in their trials
- Deterring crime through patrol
- Enhancing public safety by maintaining a visible police presence

Order Maintenance Functions

- Resolving conflict and keeping the peace
- Maintaining a sense of community security and public order (i.e., peacekeeping) within the patrol area

- Keeping vehicular and pedestrian movement efficient
- Promoting civil order

Service Functions

- Aiding individuals in danger or in need of assistance
- Providing emergency medical services
- Providing public education and outreach
- Maintaining and administering police services
- Recruiting and training new police officers

MYTH OR REALITY?

Most metropolitan law enforcement agencies employ fewer than 50 officers.

REALITY. The overwhelming majority of metropolitan law enforcement agencies employ fewer than 50 officers.

Big-city police departments are the exception. Why do television shows and the movies seem to favor big-city police? How does this influence people's perceptions of the police in America?

been to maintain smaller departments but to link them via computerized information-sharing and resource-management networks.[28]

METROPOLITAN LAW ENFORCEMENT AND THE WAR ON TERROR Federal and county law enforcement agencies are not alone in responding to the threat of terrorism. And, of course, nowhere is the threat of terrorism being taken more seriously than in New York City—one of the main targets of the 9/11 attacks—which has undertaken a number of antiterrorism initiatives, including the formation of its Counterterrorism Bureau.[29] Teams within the Bureau have been trained to examine potential targets in the city and are now attempting to insulate those targets from possible attack. The city's bridges, the Empire State Building, Rockefeller Center, and the United Nations are viewed as prime targets. Bureau detectives are assigned overseas to work with the police in several foreign cities, including cities in Canada and Israel. Detectives have been assigned as liaisons with the FBI and with Interpol in Lyon, France. The Intelligence Division has also been revamped, and agents are examining foreign newspapers and monitoring Internet sites. The department is also setting up several backup command centers in different parts of the city in case a terror attack puts headquarters out of operation. Several backup senior command teams have been created so that if people at the highest levels of the department are killed, individuals will already have been tapped to step into their jobs.

The Counterterrorism Bureau has assigned more than 100 city police detectives to work with FBI agents as part of a Joint Terrorist Task Force. In addition, the Intelligence Division's investigators now devote a substantial percentage of their resources to counterterrorism, up from about 2 percent before January 2002. The department is also drawing on the expertise of other institutions around the city. For example, NYPD SHIELD, one of the department's latest initiatives, is a public–private security partnership geared primarily toward equipping the private sector with information and training to effectively defend against terrorism.[30]

Private Policing

Supplementing local police forces has recently become a burgeoning private security industry. Private security service is a multibillion-dollar industry with 10,000 firms and 1.5 million employees. Even federal police services have been privatized to cut expenses. Today, people employed in private policing outnumber public police by almost three to one.[31]

Some private security firms have become billion-dollar companies. For example, G4S Security Solutions is one of the world's largest providers of security services. Among its clients are a number of Fortune 500 companies. It has several subsidiaries that work for the federal government. It has also been a contractor for NASA and the US Army, and it has provided security and emergency response services to local governments—helping them guard their public transport systems, among other services. G4S has helped the US government protect nuclear reactors, and it guards the Trans-Alaska Pipeline System and maintains security in closed government facilities. It also maintains a Custom Protection Officer Division, made up of highly trained uniformed security officers assigned to critical or complex facilities or situations requiring special skills in such places as government buildings, banks, and other special situations. (The Careers in Criminal Justice feature discusses a career in the private security area.)

REASONS FOR PRIVATE POLICING Private policing is so popular for the following three reasons:

- A preference for nongovernmental provision of important services, particularly crime control. Many people feel the private sector can do a more effective job than traditional government-led policing.
- The growth of mass private property, particularly large shopping malls and other properties, that attract large numbers of consumers and have little other police protection.
- A belief that government police are not capable of providing the level of service and presence that the public desires.[32]

PRIVATE AND PUBLIC POLICE COMPARED Private policing is different from public policing. Private policing is largely "client-driven," meaning that it serves the needs of those who pay the bills. And while the public police are driven by a public mandate, their primary focus is enforcement of the criminal law. Private police, in contrast, may do almost anything on behalf of their clients, some of which may have little to do with the criminal law itself. Private police are *directly* employed by a client. In contrast, public police are *indirectly* employed by taxpayers. Four additional factors distinguish private police from public police:[33]

- *Focus on loss instead of crime.* Much of private policing is concerned with loss prevention. Loss prevention includes most notably protection from theft. Major retailers employ loss prevention specialists (see accompanying Careers in Criminal Justice box) to protect their goods from being stolen. However, goods may also be "lost" through error, unethical practices, accidents, and so on. Such behaviors do not fall within the scope of the criminal law that the public police are tasked with enforcing.

  The focus on loss also removes private police from the moral dimension of the criminal law. Instead of focusing on what is right and wrong, private police are concerned solely with what their *clients* view as priorities. As Elizabeth Joh notes, "When sanctions are imposed, there may be little or no emphasis on condemning the individual wrongdoer and 'making an example' out of him or her. A bank may require an embezzler to sign a loan guarantee to pay back stolen funds, for example, rather than choose public prosecution."[34]

- *Preventive methods.* Private police are concerned almost solely with prevention. Public police also work to prevent crime, but the usual public policing method of addressing crime is reactionary; of necessity, the police usually wait for calls for service before responding. *Surveillance* is paramount in the private policing context, whereas public policing relies more heavily on detection of criminal acts and apprehension of suspects.

  Surveillance includes the use of obvious technologies such as closed-circuit television and security cameras, but private police also employ other "embedded" techniques to guard against loss and ensure compliance with expected norms of behavior. Clifford Shearing and Philip Stenning cite the example of Disneyland.[35] Every employee—and indeed, every feature, whether it be the costumed characters or the guardrails and ropes promoting a smooth flow of patrons—is there to entertain but also subtly enforce compliance with what Disney considers appropriate behavior. People who do not comply face expulsion.

- *Private justice.* Not surprisingly, private policing often employs private justice. For example, a "card counter" may be permanently banned from a casino. Another example is termination for an employee who steals from his or her employer.

  Private companies often have an incentive to keep matters involving loss shielded from the public eye. High-profile incidents can result in negative publicity, which can in turn affect the bottom line. Similarly, cooperation with the police in an investigation takes time away from business activity, possibly eroding profits further. Interestingly, one study found that the Macy's department store in New York City reported just over half of shoplifting incidents to the police, which again underscores the reality that private companies' priorities are often different than those of the public police.[36]

- *Private property.* The public police focus their efforts on both public and private property. Whether it be burglary from a residence, assault at a bar, or vandalism on a highway overpass, the public police make few distinctions between the types of property where the crimes occur. Private property is of course protected, such as by the US Constitution's Fourth Amendment, but the point is that public police are able to enforce and focus on crime regardless of where it occurs. In contrast, private police are concerned almost exclusively with private property.

CRITICISMS OF PRIVATE POLICING Private policing is controversial for a number of reasons. First, there is some concern that privatization puts the profit motive ahead of more lofty concerns such as protection of public safety. Another concern is that private police could eventually replace government, or public, police. Fortunately, this looks unlikely. As one expert observed, "Private policing poses no risk of supplanting public law enforcement entirely, at least not in our lifetime, and it is far from clear to what extent the growing numbers of private security employees are actually performing functions previously carried out by public officers."[37]

More legal scrutiny will also likely result as the private security business blossoms. A number of questions remain to be answered. One important issue is whether security guards are subject to the same search and seizure standards as police officers. The US Supreme Court has repeatedly stated that purely private search activities do not violate the Fourth Amendment's prohibitions.

Might security guards be subject to Fourth Amendment requirements if they are performing services that are traditionally reserved for the police? The Supreme Court answered this question with a yes in the 1964 case of *Griffin v. Maryland*.[38] In that case, an amusement park security guard was "deputized" by the county sheriff. He subsequently arrested five black men and charged them with criminal trespass for violating the privately owned park's racial segregation policy, which permitted only whites to enter the premises. The Court ruled not only that the arrest was inappropriate, but that it amounted to "state action." This decision, and some others since,[39] suggests that when private police are sworn or act as *de facto* public police, they are bound by the same constitutional constraints as any police officer.

CAREERS IN CRIMINAL JUSTICE LOSS PREVENTION SPECIALIST

Duties and Characteristics of the Job Qualifications

- Loss prevention specialists primarily protect merchandise in retail businesses. These duties extend beyond the retail setting to include shippers, wholesalers, and other companies engaged in commerce and concerned with loss and/or theft of its products.

- Those in loss prevention provide surveillance (e.g., monitoring security camera displays) and, as appropriate, detention of shoplifters.

- Companies also use loss prevention specialists to protect them from theft by employees. The position may also perform regular inventory or "shrink" assessments, manage alarm systems, and control access to warehousing, distribution centers, and even manufacturing facilities.

Job Outlook

- Security is one of the fastest-growing professional careers worldwide.

- Opportunities exist at all levels within the security industry, and all businesses, no matter their size, need qualified personnel to address their security concerns, prevent theft, deter workplace violence, and otherwise protect themselves to ensure normal business operations.

- The Bureau of Labor Statistics estimates that employment of loss prevention specialists and other security/surveillance professionals will grow by 18 percent over the next decade.

Salary

- Entry-level positions in retail loss prevention are among the lowest paying security jobs, but the pay prospects improve as one ascends to a management position.

- Loss prevention managers make, on average around $24,000 per year. Moving into other industries, such as banking and financial services, entry-level and mid-level management positions carry a salary range of $35,000 to $100,000, depending on several factors.

Qualifications

- The qualifications for an entry-level loss prevention position are minimal. Usually just a high school diploma is required, but employees will, at a minimum, be expected to pass routine drug tests, have strong interpersonal and administrative skills, and be comfortable around computers.

- Qualifications may be stricter and increase depending upon the individual's position in the corporate hierarchy or level of risk and responsibility associated with the position.

Education and Training

- Managerial positions may require an associate's or bachelor's degree in criminal justice or a related discipline, sometimes combined with a certain amount of real-world experience.

- Some colleges and universities also offer dedicated security education degrees.

- The American Society for Industrial Security (ASIS) offers three certifications for security professionals, including those of the Certified Protection Professional (CPP), the Professional Certified Investigator (PCI), and the Physical Security Professional (PSP). These certifications require that certain knowledge and skills be demonstrated, but they also help differentiate applicants from one another, and they improve an applicant's professional credibility and earnings potential.

Reality Check

- Entry-level positions do not pay particularly well.

- Some of the most coveted positions will require specialized training and a willingness to be mobile (i.e., move to where the work is).

- The work can be dry and "routine" much of the time, punctuated by occasional moments of excitement.

Sources: Bureau of Labor Statistics, "Security Guards and Gaming Surveillance Officers," http://www.bls.gov/ooh/Protective-Service/Security-guards.htm (accessed February 2015); ASIS International, "Certified Protection Professional," https://www.asisonline.org/Certification/Board-Certifications/CPP/Pages/default.aspx (accessed May 2015).

States, on the other hand, have given private police much more latitude, exempting them from the Fourth Amendment,[40] the *Miranda* rule[41] (see Chapter 6), and the exclusionary rule[42] (also see Chapter 6). This does not mean, however, that private police have unbridled authority. In most instances, they have no more authority than the typical private citizen. As one expert put it, "Many private security guards ... possess no greater legal capabilities than do ordinary citizens to forcibly detain persons who are suspected of or have in fact committed a crime."[43] But as time goes on and the private policing industry continues to grow, it will be interesting to see how the courts weigh in.

Technology and Law Enforcement

Policing relies more and more frequently on modern technology to increase effectiveness, and the influence of technology on policing will certainly continue to grow. Police officers now trained to prevent burglaries may someday have to learn to create high-tech forensic labs that can identify suspects involved in theft of genetically engineered cultures from biomedical labs.[44] Criminal investigation is being enhanced by the application of all varieties of sophisticated electronic gadgetry.

Police are becoming more sophisticated in their use of computer software to identify and convict criminals. Advanced computer software has helped in both the allocation of resources and the investigation of crime.

A number of other information technology techniques are now being used to increase police effectiveness and efficiency. For example, it is now recognized that a majority of predatory crimes are concentrated in geographic "hot spots."[45] Computer mapping programs that can translate addresses into map coordinates allow departments to identify problem areas for particular crimes, such as drug dealing. Computer maps enable police to identify the location and time of day at which crimes occurred, as well as the linkage among criminal events, and to concentrate their forces accordingly.

Already in use, but not yet widespread, license plate recognition (LPR) technology employs cameras and computer software to discern the letters and numbers of vehicle license plates and then compare them with records contained in state and federal databases. New technology makes it possible to place the imaging cameras on the front or roof of a vehicle or in a patrol unit's light bar. Initially designed for use in parking lots (to record the time a vehicle entered), for access control (allowing authorized vehicles

Technology has and will continue to have a significant impact on law enforcement operations. This vehicle-mounted digital camera captures images of license plates and helps police identify suspects with outstanding warrants, stolen vehicles, and the like, all without the need to make a stop. What are the pros and cons of such devices?

SALLY RYAN/The New York Times/Redux Pictures

Police Shootings

At Officer Wnjian Liu's funeral in New York City, hundreds of police officers turned their back on Mayor Bill de Blasio, due to a perception that he had not been supportive of the agency. De Blasio came under fire for comments he made after a grand jury declined to indict an NYPD officer in the death of Eric Garner in 2014 (see Chapter 6 opening story) and for perceptions that he created a climate of distrust between community members and the police. Were the officers justified in their actions? If not, what could they have done differently? If so, why?

WEB APP 4.3 Visit the PoliceOne website, and navigate to the page about police body cameras at **http://www.policeone.com/police-products/body-cameras/**. Why is video becoming increasingly popular in policing? To what extent do police officers want body-worn cameras?

LO8 Explain the role of technology in police work

DNA profiling The identification of criminal suspects by matching DNA samples taken from their person with specimens found at the crime scene.

into a secure area), and for paying tolls, LPR technology recently has expanded into the realms of border control, identification of stolen vehicles, and traffic-fine enforcement (e.g., issuing tickets for running red lights), and vendors are marketing systems specifically for use by the law enforcement community.

Some police departments are also using computerized imaging systems for criminal identification. Several software companies have developed identification programs that help witnesses create a composite picture of the perpetrator. A vast library of photographed or drawn facial features can be stored in computer files and accessed on a terminal screen. Witnesses can scan thousands of noses, eyes, and lips until they find those that match those belonging to the perpetrator. Eyeglasses, mustaches, and beards can be added, and skin tones can be altered.

Another technique is to digitize thousands of facial images. Police can then easily create a "photo lineup" of all suspects having a particular characteristic described by a witness. New computer software allows two-dimensional mug shots to be re-created on a three-dimensional basis. Effects on the three-dimensional image such as lighting and angles can also be changed to better reproduce the conditions that prevailed in the environment where a crime took place.[46]

The use of computerized automated fingerprint identification systems (AFIS) is growing as well. Using mathematical models, AFIS can classify fingerprints and identify up to 250 characteristics (minutiae) of the print. These automated systems use high-speed computer chips to plot each point of minutiae and count the number of ridge lines between that point and its four nearest neighbors. This substantially improves the speed and accuracy of fingerprint identification.

Advanced technology is also spurring new forensic methods of identification and analysis.[47] The most prominent technique is **DNA profiling**, a procedure that allows suspects to be identified on the basis of the genetic material found in hair, blood, and

Cook County (Chicago) Sheriff Tom Dart, left, and Sheriff's Detective Jason Moran are photographed with three recently discovered vials of mass murderer John Wayne Gacy's blood. The sheriff's office is creating DNA profiles from the blood of Gacy and other executed killers and putting them in a national DNA database of profiles created from blood, semen, or strands of hair found at crime scenes and on the bodies of victims. They hope to find evidence that links the long-dead killers to the coldest of cold cases, as well as prompt authorities in other states to submit the DNA of their own executed inmates and possibly evidence from decades-old crime scenes to help them solve their own cases.

CRIMINAL JUSTICE AND TECHNOLOGY

Body Cameras

Ozier Muhammad/The New York Times

Officer Joshua Jones demonstrates the activation of a body camera being worn by New York Police Department personnel in a trial program. While body camera evidence has already played a role in the disciplining of a few officers nationally, advocates are warning that the technology will not be a magic bullet for behavior or the resolution of legal disputes.

A number of police departments around the United States are requiring their officers to carry body-worn cameras. In-car cameras came into regular use and are now ubiquitous in modern law enforcement. Body cameras are just the next logical step, as officers routinely step out of view of their in-car cameras.

A number of companies, including even TASER, manufacture body-worn cameras for use in law enforcement. They come in various shapes and sizes, with varying abilities to "see" an officer's surrounding, such as with wide-angle lenses. Some are equipped with night vision. Some are designed to be worn on an officer's chest, others on a utility belt, and still others on a pair of glasses or sunglasses. Cameras range from the size of a smartphone to smaller than a pack of gum. Agencies are faced with a wide range of choices.

All body-worn cameras have the same core purpose, which is to record and document police–citizen encounters. At a glance, this may seem desirable, but upon further investigation, there is much more to the story. Indeed, the disadvantages could even outweigh the advantages.

Advantages

Mike White, a professor of criminology at Arizona State University, has summarized the key advantages of body-worn cameras:

- They increase transparency, thereby improving perceptions of police legitimacy.
- Body cameras create a "civilizing effect." That is, they alter *both* officer and suspect behavior.
- The cameras have evidentiary value. They are useful for expeditious resolution of citizen complaints. They can also yield evidence that is useful for criminal prosecution.
- Police training can benefit with footage of actual police–citizen encounters.

Limitations

- Cameras create privacy concerns. Recordings of child victims and offenders, medical emergencies, confidential informants, and the like may create legal complications.
- Officer privacy is also an issue with cameras. A number of police unions were resistant to in-car cameras, and the same concerns have been expressed with the advent of body cameras. When, for example, can the camera be off?
- Any new technology requires policy changes and training modifications.
- Body cameras are expensive. Aside from the cost of the cameras, a number of logistical problems arise. For example, an enormous amount of video footage must be secured and stored.

CRITICAL THINKING

1. Should officers with body-worn cameras be required to announce they are wearing the devices?
2. Under what circumstances should body-worn cameras be on and off?
3. Could an officer's health or safety be put at risk with a body-worn camera? Why or why not?

Source: Michael D. White, *Police Officer Body-Worn Cameras: Assessing the Evidence* (Washington, DC: Office of Community-Oriented Policing Services, 2014).

other bodily tissues and fluids. When DNA is used as evidence in a rape trial, DNA segments are taken from the victim, the suspect, and blood and semen found on the victim. A DNA match indicates a 4 billion-to-1 likelihood that the suspect is the offender.

Many other technological advances have aided law enforcement with identifying, locating, and capturing criminals (see the Criminal Justice and Technology feature for another example). Most are beyond the scope of this text. New investigation techniques are constantly being developed, too. With each passing year, more and more high-tech devices and techniques are being added to the law enforcement toolkit.

Police departments have for several years used the Internet and particularly their websites to communicate with the public. More recently, they have jumped on the social media and social networking bandwagon. People voluntarily reveal intimate details of their lives on sites such as Facebook, something that has proven quite useful for the police. People also follow police departments on Twitter and Nixle, the latter of which is a dedicated police local alert system to which anyone can sign up for free.

Facebook has proven particularly useful. For example, the Hartselle, Alabama, police department sees its Facebook page as providing an extra 1,300 sets of eyes in the community. The department, which has around 3,000 likes, recently used the site to identify a couple who ran up over $1,500 worth of charges on a stolen credit card.[48] After the department posted surveillance photos from a local Walmart on its Facebook page, the couple was identified by a member of the community. Other departments around the country have used Facebook to capture crooks, and not just thieves. Police in one Louisiana department successfully used Facebook as part of their effort to apprehend a suspected cop-killer.[49]

Ethical Challenge: Write an essay on the ethics of using social media for law enforcement purposes. Is it a valuable asset? Or is it cause for alarm? Is it an undesirable invasion of individual privacy, or does it represent a positive advance in security measures that generates benefits for society?

Besides reading the material in the technology section of this chapter, you can also read valuable and additional information at the Center for Social Media page, sponsored by the International Association of Chiefs of Police, at **http://www.iacpsocialmedia.org/**.

SUMMARY

LO1 *Summarize characteristics of the first law enforcement agencies* The origin of US police agencies traces to early English society. Under the pledge system, people were grouped into tithings and were entrusted with policing their own minor problems. Ten tithings were grouped into a hundred, supervised by a constable. Ten hundreds were organized into shires overseen by the shire reeve, the precursor to the modern sheriff. Early thief takers were private police who apprehended criminals for reward payments. Henry Fielding's Bow Street Runners improved on the thief-taking system. The first organized police force was founded by Sir Robert Peel in London.

LO2 *Discuss the development of law enforcement in the United States* Law enforcement in colonial America paralleled the British model. In the colonies, the county sheriff became the most important law enforcement agent. The first true US police departments were formed in Boston, New York, and Philadelphia in the early nineteenth century.

LO3 *Analyze the problems of early police agencies* Early American police were viewed as being dominated by political bosses who controlled their hiring practices and policies. In the nineteenth century, big-city police were still not respected by the public, were unsuccessful in their role as crime stoppers, and were not involved in progressive activities.

LO4 *Discuss how reformers attempted to create professional police agencies* Reform movements begun in the 1920s culminated in the concept of professionalism. Police professionalism was interpreted to mean tough, rule-oriented police work featuring advanced technology and hardware. The view that these measures would quickly reduce crime proved incorrect.

LO5 *Describe the major changes in law enforcement between 1970 and today* The police experienced turmoil in the 1960s and 1970s, which led to reforms such as the hiring of women and members of minority groups. Questions about the effectiveness of law enforcement also led to the development of community policing. Police departments began to embrace new forms of policing that stressed cooperation with the community and problem solving.

LO6 *Identify the major federal law enforcement agencies* Several major law enforcement agencies are at work in the United States. At the federal level, the FBI is the largest federal agency. Other agencies include the Drug Enforcement Administration and the US Marshals Service.

LO7 *Summarize the differences among state, county, and local law enforcement* Most states maintain state police who investigate crimes and patrol the roadways. County-level law enforcement, including running jails and patrolling rural areas, is provided by sheriffs' departments. Local police agencies engage in patrol, investigative, and traffic functions, as well as many support activities.

LO8 *Explain the role of technology in police work* Most police departments rely on advanced computer-based technology to prevent and control crime, identify suspects, and collate evidence. Examples include computerized crime mapping and automated fingerprint identification systems.

KEY TERMS

tithings, p. 88

hue and cry, p. 88

hundred, p. 88

constable, p. 88

shire reeve, p. 88

sheriff, p. 88

watch system, p. 88

justice of the peace, p. 88

vigilantes, p. 89

Federal Bureau of
    Investigation (FBI), p. 94

Drug Enforcement
    Administration (DEA),
    p. 94

Bureau of Alcohol,
    Tobacco, Firearms, and
    Explosives (ATF), p. 94

US Marshals
    Service, p. 94

Department of Homeland
    Security (DHS), p. 94

Customs and Border
    Protection (CBP), p. 94

Secret Service, p. 95

DNA profiling, p. 102

REVIEW QUESTIONS

1. List the problems faced by today's police departments that were also present during the early days of policing.

2. Distinguish among the duties of the state police, sheriffs' departments, and local police departments.

3. Do you believe that the general public has greater respect for the police today than in the past? If so, why? If not, why not?

4. What are some of the technological advances that should help the police solve more crimes? What are the dangers of these advances?

5. Discuss the trends that will influence policing during the coming decade. What other social factors may affect police?

5 The Police:
ROLE AND FUNCTION

On January 4, 2015, New York City police officers issued 48 tickets for drinking in public. On the same day a year earlier, 1,061 tickets were issued.[1] Nine summonses for urinating in public were issued during the week ending January 4, 2015, compared to 160 the year before.[2] Overall, NYPD officers issued 92 percent fewer summonses and made 56 percent fewer arrests in the early days of 2015 than they did during the same time one year earlier.[3] Why the precipitous decline? Did crime all but disappear? Serious crime *did* decline in New York during 2014. Robberies were down 14 percent, for example.[4] Nevertheless, the decline in tickets and summonses for public drinking and other quality-of-life offenses did not owe to a sudden crime drop. It was due to a work slowdown.

The NYPD work slowdown, which Commissioner William Bratton publicly confirmed took place, was due to a rift that developed between the police union and the city's mayor, Bill de Blasio. According to police unions, the mayor did not show enough support for NYPD officers when protests spread throughout the city following a grand jury's decision not to indict Daniel Pantaleo, the NYPD officer who earlier in 2014 put Eric Garner into a fatal chokehold (Garner's story is featured in more detail in the next chapter's opener). The president of the city's largest police union, the Patrolmen's Benevolent Association, also blamed the December 2014 shooting deaths of NYPD officers Wenjian Liu and Rafael Ramos on people who "incited violence on the street under the guise of protest," claiming de Blasio had "blood on his hands." The slowdown primarily involved low-level offenses, and it ended rather quickly, but it sent a powerful message officials could not ignore.

The police role is extremely varied and complex. Police officers are called on to deal with increasingly difficult and unpredictable situations. The crime problem continues to evolve in response to societal developments. Whether officers engage in preventive patrol, respond to calls for service, forge relationships with citizens, or aggressively target a small list of known criminal suspects, they have to be constantly vigilant and prepared. Anything less can give criminals the upper hand, and this includes both public and political support. Without one or the other, or both, police work becomes all the more difficult.

REALITY CHECK

MYTH OR REALITY?

- Police work primarily involves crime fighting.
- Rapid response to 911 calls reporting a crime in progress increases the likelihood that the offender will be apprehended.
- The more serious the crime, the more likely it is that detectives will solve it.
- Most crimes are solved when the perpetrator is identified at the crime scene.
- Community-oriented policing can succeed in any community if the police try hard enough.

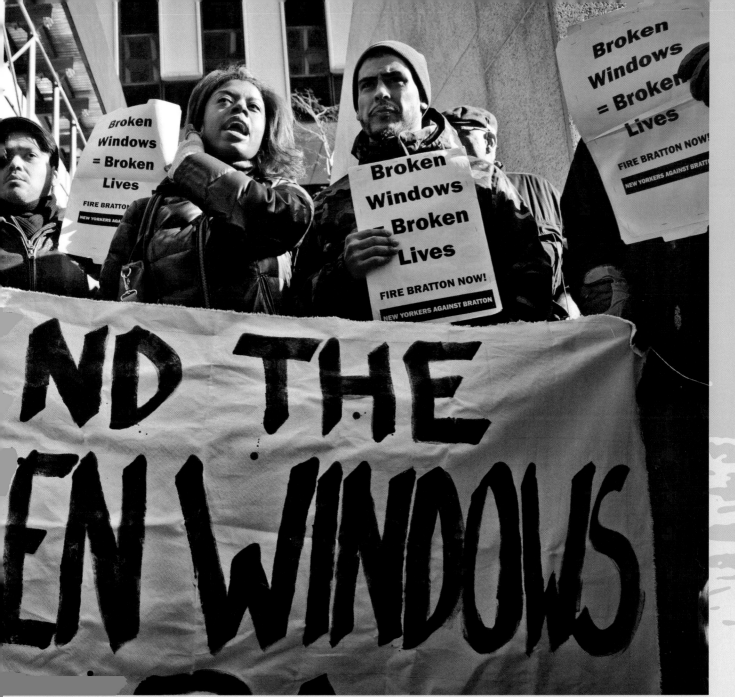

AP Images/Bebeto Matthews

LEARNING OBJECTIVES

LO1 *Explain the organization of police departments*

LO2 *Articulate the complexities of the police role*

LO3 *Explain the limitations of patrol and methods for improving it*

LO4 *Summarize the investigation function*

LO5 *Explain what forensics is and what forensics experts do for police agencies*

LO6 *Discuss the concept of community-oriented policing*

LO7 *Discuss the concept of problem-oriented policing*

LO8 *Explain intelligence-led policing and the various means by which it occurs*

LO9 *Describe the various police support functions*

This chapter describes the organization of police departments and their various operating branches: patrol, investigation, service, and administration. It discusses the realities and ambiguities of the police role and traces how the concept of the police mission has been changing radically. The chapter concludes with a brief overview of some of the most important administrative issues confronting today's US law enforcement agencies.

The Police Organization

Most municipal police departments in the United States are independent agencies within the executive branch of government, operating without specific administrative control from any higher governmental authority. Although they often cooperate and participate in mutually beneficial enterprises, such as a joint task force with state and federal law enforcement agencies, local police agencies are functionally independent organizations with unique sets of rules, policies, procedures, norms, budgets, and so on.

Most local police departments are organized in a hierarchical manner, as illustrated in Figure 5.1. Within this organizational model, each element of the department normally has its own chain of command. In a large municipal department, there may be a number of independent investigation units headed by a captain who serves as the senior administrator, a lieutenant who oversees cases and investigations and acts as liaison with other police agencies, and sergeants and inspectors who carry out fieldwork. Smaller departments may have a captain or lieutenant as head of a particular branch or unit.

Department size also affects the number of subunits. A department the size of New York's may contain several specialized investigative units, such as special victims or sex crimes, whereas many smaller departments do not employ detectives at all and rely on county or state police investigators to probe unsolved crimes. Regardless of its size, at the head of the organization is the **police chief** (sometimes called the commissioner or similar), who sets policy and has general administrative control over all the department's various operating branches.

Pros and Cons of Police Organization

The police administrative organization has both pros and cons. Because most departments are civil service organizations, administrators must rise through the ranks to get to command positions. To be promoted, they must pass a battery of tests, profiles,

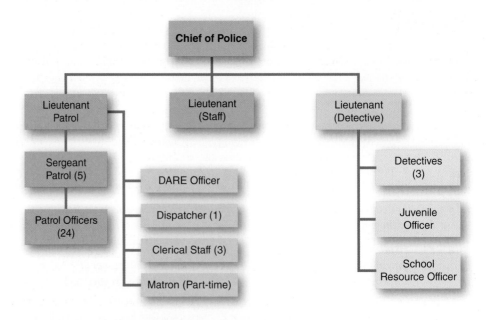

FIGURE 5.1 Vestal, New York, Police Department

Source: Town of Vestal, New York, http://www.vestalny.com/DeptPage.aspx?pID=10 (accessed February 2013).

WEB APP 5.1 Visit the website of the Chicago Police Department and examine its organizational chart at **https://portal.chicagopolice .org/portal/page/portal/ClearPath /About%20CPD/CPD%20Organization /DeptOrgChartMar12.pdf.** How does the department differ organizationally compared to the Vestal Police Department shown in Figure 5.1? How is it similar?

police chief The top administrator of the police department who sets policy and has general control over departmental practices. The chief is typically a political rather than a civil service appointee and serves at the pleasure of the mayor.

L01 Explain the organization of police departments

interviews, and so on. Most police departments employ a **time-in-rank system** for determining promotion eligibility. This means that before moving up the administrative ladder, an officer must spend a certain amount of time in the next lowest rank; a sergeant cannot become a captain without serving an appropriate amount of time as a lieutenant.

This system has both benefits and shortcomings. On the plus side, it is designed to promote stability and fairness and to limit favoritism. The chief's favorite cannot be promoted over a more experienced officer who is better qualified. Once earned, a rank can rarely be taken away or changed if new management takes over. The rank system also protects police agencies from losing talented officers trained at public expense to other departments who offer more money or other incentives.

On the downside, the rank system restricts administrative flexibility. Unlike in the private sector, where the promotion of talented people can be accelerated in the best interests of the company, the time-in-rank system prohibits rapid advancement. A police agency would probably not be able to hire a computer systems expert with a PhD and give her a command position in charge of its data-analysis section. The department would be forced to hire the expert as a civilian employee under the command of a ranking senior officer who might not be as technically proficient. Because senior administrators are promoted from within only after years of loyal service, time-in-rank may render some police agencies administratively conservative. Even when police executives adopt new programs, such as CompStat (more on this later in the chapter), they are most likely to choose those elements that confer legitimacy on existing organizations and on implementing them in ways that minimize disruption to existing organizational routines, rather than embracing truly innovative changes.[5]

The Police Role

In countless books, movies, and TV shows, the public has been presented with a view of policing that romanticizes cops as fearless crime fighters who think little of their own safety as they engage in daily high-speed chases and shootouts. How close is this portrayal of a crime fighter to real life? Not very close, according to most research. A police officer's crime-fighting efforts are only a small part of his or her overall activities. Studies of police work indicate that a significant portion of an officer's time is spent handling minor disturbances, service calls, and administrative duties. Police work, then, involves much more than catching criminals.

The most recent national survey of police contacts with civilians found that almost 44 million persons had at least one contact with police that year, and very few of them were criminals in the conventional sense of the term.[6] More than half of the contacts were for traffic-related matters, and about 30 percent were to report problems or ask for assistance, such as responding to a neighbor's complaint about music being too loud during a party or warning kids not to shoot off fireworks. These results are not surprising when Uniform Crime Report (UCR) arrest data are also considered. Each year, about 700,000 local, county, and state police officers make about 14 million arrests, or about 20 each. Of these, about 2 million (approximately three per officer) are for serious Part I crimes. Given an even distribution of arrests, it is evident that the average police officer makes fewer than two arrests per month and fewer than a single felony arrest every four months.

These figures should be interpreted with caution because not all police officers are engaged in activities that allow them to make arrests, such as patrol or detective work. About one-third of all sworn officers in the nation's largest police departments are in such units as communications, antiterrorism, administration, and personnel. Even if the number of arrests per officer were adjusted by one-third, it would still amount to only 9 or 10 serious crime arrests per officer per year. So even though police handle thousands of calls each year, relatively few result in an arrest for a serious crime such as a robbery or burglary; in suburban and rural areas, years may go by before a police officer arrests someone for a serious crime.

time-in-rank system For police officers to advance in rank, they must spend an appropriate amount of time, usually years, in the preceding rank; for example, to become a captain, an officer must first spend time as a lieutenant.

The evidence, then, shows that unlike their TV and film counterparts, the police engage in many activities that are not related to crime. Police officers function in a variety of roles ranging from dispensers of emergency medical care to keepers of the peace on school grounds. Although officers in large urban departments may be called on to handle more felony cases than those in small towns, they too will probably find that most of their daily activities are not crime related. What are some of the most important functions of police?

The Patrol Function

Regardless of the policing style, uniformed patrol officers are the backbone of the police department, usually accounting for about two-thirds of a department's personnel.[7] Patrol officers are the most highly visible components of the entire criminal justice system. Patrols serve the following major purposes:

- Deter crime by maintaining a visible police presence.
- Maintain public order (peacekeeping) within the patrol area.
- Enable the police department to respond quickly to violations of law or other emergencies.
- Identify and apprehend law violators.
- Aid individuals and care for those who cannot help themselves.
- Facilitate the movement of traffic and people.
- Create a feeling of security in the community.[8]

Patrol Activities

order maintenance (peacekeeping) The order-maintenance aspect of the police role involves peacekeeping, maintaining order and authority without the need for formal arrest, "handling the situation," and keeping things under control by using threats, persuasion, and understanding.

Most experts agree that the great bulk of patrol efforts are devoted to what has been described as order maintenance, or peacekeeping: maintaining order and civility in their assigned jurisdiction.[9] Order-maintenance functions occupy the border between criminal and noncriminal behavior. The patrol officer's discretion often determines whether a noisy neighborhood dispute involves the crime of disturbing the peace or can be controlled by exercising street-corner diplomacy and sending the combatants on their way. Similarly, teenagers milling around in the shopping center parking lot may be brought in and turned over to the juvenile authorities or dispersed in a less formal and often more efficient manner.

The primary role of police seems to be "handling the situation." Police encounter many troubling incidents that need some sort of "fixing up."[10] Enforcing the law might be one tool a patrol officer uses; threat, coercion, sympathy, and understanding might be others. Most important is keeping things under control so that there are no complaints that the officer is doing nothing at all or doing too much. The real police role, then, may be as a community problem solver.

Police officers actually practice a policy of selective enforcement, concentrating on some crimes but handling the majority in an informal manner. A police officer is supposed to know when to take action and when not to, as well as whom to arrest and whom to deal with by issuing a warning or some other informal action. If a mistake is made, the officer can come under fire from peers and superiors, as well as the media and the general public.

The effectiveness of patrol has been a topic of research for several decades. The Contemporary Issues in Criminal Justice feature summarizes the key findings in this area.

Improving Patrol

In recent years, police departments have initiated a number of programs and policies in an attempt to improve patrol effectiveness. Some have proved more successful than others. Some are also more controversial than others.

PROACTIVE POLICING AND DIRECTED PATROL Although the mere presence of police may not be sufficient to deter crime, the manner in which they approach their task may make a difference. Police departments that use a proactive, aggressive law enforcement

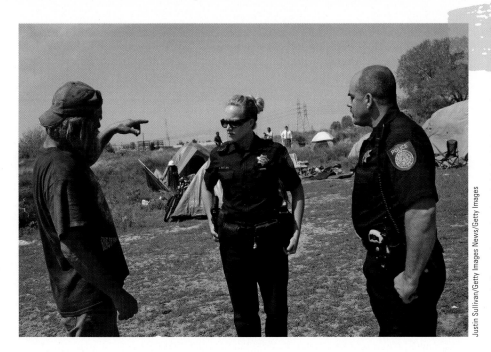

Despite what the media might lead us to believe, police work does not always involve chasing down criminals and making arrests. The great bulk of patrol efforts are devoted to order maintenance and peacekeeping rather than to shootouts with dangerous criminals. Here Sacramento police officers Sara Butler and Mike Cooper talk with a homeless man as they hand out eviction notices to residents at a homeless tent city. Hundreds of residents living in a tent city along the American River were issued notices of eviction and were told to relocate to a nearby shelter. Their tent city was located on land belonging to the Sacramento Municipal Utility District.

Justin Sullivan/Getty Images News/Getty Images

style may help reduce crime rates. Jurisdictions that encourage patrol officers to stop motor vehicles to issue citations and to aggressively arrest and detain suspicious persons also experience lower crime rates than jurisdictions that do not follow such proactive policies.[11] Departments that more actively enforce minor regulations, such as laws prohibiting disorderly conduct and traffic laws, are also more likely to experience lower felony rates.[12]

Pinpointing why **proactive policing** works so effectively is difficult. Proactive patrol efforts may help improve response time and increase the number of patrol cars

proactive policing A police department policy that emphasizes stopping crimes before they occur, rather than reacting to crimes that have already occurred.

CONTEMPORARY ISSUES IN CRIMINAL JUSTICE

Does Patrol Deter Crime? A Look at the Evidence

A primary goal of police patrol has been to deter criminal behavior. The visible presence of patrol cars on the street and the rapid deployment of police officers to the scene of a crime are viewed as effective methods of crime control. Is this view correct? The most widely heralded attempt at measuring patrol effectiveness was undertaken during the early 1970s in Kansas City, Missouri, where researchers divided 15 separate police districts into three groups: one group retained normal patrol; the second (proactive) set of districts were supplied with two to three times the normal amount of patrol forces; and the third (reactive) group had its preventive patrol eliminated, with police officers responding only when summoned by citizens to the scene of a particular crime. The Kansas City study found that these variations in patrol had little effect on the crime patterns in the 15 districts. The presence or absence of patrol officers did not seem to affect residential or business burglaries, motor vehicle thefts, larceny involving auto accessories, robberies, vandalism, or other criminal behavior, nor did their presence or absence influence citizens' attitudes toward the police, their satisfaction with police, or their fear of future criminal behavior.

Since the Kansas City study findings were published, dozens of researchers have continued to seek an answer to the question of whether adding more police helps to bring down the crime rate. At one time, reviews of the existing research found that the actual number of law enforcement

officers in a jurisdiction seemed to have little effect on area crimes. However, during the past decade, larger cities have expanded their police forces, and crime rates have plummeted—a trend which suggests that adding police may in fact reduce crime rates. The association between the number of police personnel and crime rates has also been supported by a number of recent studies. Using a variety of methodologies, these studies have found that police presence may actually reduce crime levels and that adding police may bring crime levels down.

CRITICAL THINKING

The evidence is mixed on the deterrent effects of preventive patrol. This should not be taken to mean that patrol doesn't work. What can a police agency do to improve patrol? What methods are likely the most effective and why?

Source: George Kelling, Tony Pate, Duane Dieckman, and Charles Brown, *The Kansas City Preventive Patrol Experiment: A Summary Report* (Washington, DC: Police Foundation, 1974); Thomas Marvell and Carlisle Moody, "Specification Problems, Police Levels, and Crime Rates," *Criminology* 34 (1996): 609–646; Colin Loftin and David McDowall, "The Police, Crime, and Economic Theory: An Assessment," *American Sociological Review* 47 (1982): 393–401; John L. Worrall, "The Effects of Policing on Crime: What Have We Learned?" in *Critical Issues in Policing,* 6th ed., ed. R. Dunham and G. Alpert (Long Grove, IL: Waveland, 2010).

deterrent effect Stopping or reducing crime by convincing would-be criminals that they stand a significant risk of being apprehended and punished for their crimes.

directed patrol A patrol strategy that involves concentrating police resources in areas where certain crimes are a significant problem.

that respond per crime.[13] It may have a deterrent effect as well: Aggressive policing increases community perception that police arrest many criminals and that most violators get caught. Criminals may think twice about committing crimes in a town that has such an active police force! Proactive policing may also help control crime because it results in conviction of more criminals. Because aggressive police arrest more suspects, there are fewer suspects left on the street to commit crime; fewer criminals produce lower crime rates.

Evidence also shows that targeting specific crimes through directed patrol can be successful. One aggressive patrol program, known as the Kansas City Gun Experiment, was directed at restricting the carrying of guns in high-risk places at high-risk times. Working with academics from the University of Maryland, the Kansas City Police Department focused extra patrol attention on a "hot spot" high-crime area identified by computer analysis of all gun crimes. Over a 29-week period, the gun patrol officers conducted thousands of car and pedestrian checks and traffic stops and made more than 600 arrests. Using frisks and searches, they found 29 guns; an additional 47 weapons were seized by other officers in the experimental area. In the target beat, 169 gun crimes were committed in the 29 weeks before the gun patrol but only 86 were committed while the experiment was under way, a decrease of 49 percent.[14]

Strategies such as these have been a critical success. The downturn in the violent crime rate over the past decade has been attributed to aggressive police work in large cities, such as New York, aimed at controlling or eliminating lifestyle crimes: vandalism, panhandling, and graffiti.[15] Although some commentators fear that aggressive policing will result in antagonism between proactive cops and the general public, recent research indicates that precinct-level efforts to ensure that officers are respectful of citizens helped lower the number of complaints and improved community relations.[16]

MAKING ARRESTS Can formal police action, such as an arrest, reduce crime? The evidence is mixed, but some studies suggest that contact with the police may cause some offenders to forgo repeat criminal behavior. Many first offenders will forgo criminal activity after undergoing arrest.[17] For example, an arrest for drunk driving reduces the likelihood of further driving while intoxicated.

Why do arrests deter crime? It is possible that news of increased and aggressive police arrest activity is rapidly diffused through the population and has an immediate impact on crime rates.[18] Arrests may also alter perceptions. An arrest for drunk driving may convince people that they will be rearrested if they drink and drive.[19] Consequently, as the number of arrests per capita increases, crime rates go down.

RAPID RESPONSE Improving response time may be one way of increasing police efficiency. Unfortunately, however, the research fails to support such assumptions. A National Institute of Justice study examined police response times in four cities. The authors found that rapid response had virtually no effect on crime.[20] Why? One explanation is that people tend to be slow when it comes to reporting crime. For example, a person may wake up in the morning and find that his or her car was vandalized. By then the trail has gone cold, making it nearly impossible to capture the perpetrator even if the police are summoned immediately upon discovery of the crime. On the other hand, if an in-progress burglary is called in, it seems police have a better chance of apprehending the suspect if they can get to the scene quickly.[21]

BROKEN WINDOWS POLICING A critical 1982 paper by George Kelling and James Q. Wilson advocated a new approach to improving police relations in the community, an approach that has come to be known as the broken windows model.[22] Kelling and Wilson made three points:

broken windows model A term used to describe the role of the police as maintainers of community order and safety.

REALITY CHECK

MYTH OR REALITY?

Rapid response to 911 calls reporting a crime in progress increases the likelihood that the offender will be apprehended.

MYTH. Research shows that rapid response has almost no effect on the probability of capturing the offender. This is a fairly general conclusion, however.

Are there certain types of crimes for which rapid response could work?

- *Neighborhood disorder creates fear.* Urban areas filled with street people, youth gangs, prostitutes, and the mentally disturbed are the ones most likely to maintain a high degree of crime.[23]

- *Neighborhoods give out crime-promoting signals.* A neighborhood filled with deteriorated housing, broken windows, and disorderly behavior gives out crime-promoting signals. Honest citizens live in fear in these areas, and predatory criminals are attracted to them.
- *Police need citizen cooperation.* If police are to reduce fear and successfully combat crime in these urban areas, they must have the cooperation, support, and assistance of the citizens.

According to the broken windows concept, a deteriorated neighborhood, whose residents are fearful, pessimistic, and despondent, is a magnet for crime. In contrast, neighborhoods where residents are civil to one another and where disorder is not tolerated send a different message: criminals are not wanted here, and criminal behavior will not be allowed. The broken windows approach holds that police administrators would be well advised to deploy their forces where they can encourage public confidence, strengthen feelings of safety, and elicit cooperation from citizens. Preserving the community, providing for public safety, and maintaining order—not crime fighting—should become the primary focus of patrol. Put another way, just as physicians and dentists practice preventive medicine and dentistry, police should help maintain an intact community structure rather than simply fighting crime.

Does it work? In one of the most rigorous tests of broken windows theory in recent years, researchers identified 34 crime-ridden areas in Lowell, Massachusetts. Half (the treatment group) received broken windows policing; the other half (the control group) received the same levels of patrol as before. Results revealed substantial reductions in crime, disorder, and calls for service in the treatment areas but not in the control areas.[24]

USING TECHNOLOGY Police departments have also relied on technology to help guide patrol efforts. The best-known program, CompStat, had its beginnings in New York City as a means of directing police efforts in a more productive way.[25] William Bratton,

CompStat A program originated by the New York City police that used carefully collected and analyzed crime data to shape policy and evaluate police effectiveness.

AP Photo/The Saginaw News, Jeff Schrier

A Saginaw, Michigan, police car camera shows officers approaching Milton Hall, 49, a homeless man who was wielding a knife and making aggressive movements toward them. The officers fatally shot Hall and were cleared of any allegations of wrongdoing, in part because of the camera footage. What are the pros and cons of in-car cameras?

Drones

Police departments across the country have purchased small unmanned surveillance drones, not unlike the drones used to track terrorists in Iraq and Afghanistan, for the purpose of tracking drug dealers and other persons of interest. Historically, the Federal Aviation Administration (FAA) made it very difficult for law enforcement agencies to secure approval for conducting drone patrols. In February 2012, however, President Obama signed a law requiring the FAA to write rules on how it would license police and other public safety agencies to fly drones at low altitudes, making it likely that small aircraft containing high-definition cameras, sensors, and recording equipment would soon be flying over many more American cities. Later that year, the FAA released its first list of agencies that were authorized to fly drones. That list has since expanded.

Hundreds of law enforcement agencies are now authorized to fly drones, but it is not clear that many of them are doing so. In addition, the FAA generally places limitations on drones' use, such as by limiting them to a defined block of airspace and/or daytime hours.

The Supporters

Supporters of drone use in domestic law enforcement see the technology as a valuable tool necessary for apprehending law breakers. The police cannot be everywhere, they claim, so an extra set of "eyes" in the sky could prove helpful in fighting crime. Supporters also argue that gun detectors, security cameras, tracking devices, and other technologies are already in use, so drones are just one more tool that can be added to the law enforcement arsenal. Drones are also affordable compared to new helicopters and airplanes.

The Critics

Critics claim that drone use, though perhaps useful for catching criminals, will also let "Big Brother" peer into the private lives of law-abiding citizens. The American Civil Liberties Union is one of the most vocal critics of police drones, having claimed that their use will eventually lead to "routine aerial surveillance" in all aspects of life. The ACLU cites specific examples of why we should be concerned:

> Deployed without proper regulation, drones equipped with facial recognition software, infrared technology, and speakers capable of monitoring personal conversations would cause real harms to our privacy rights. Interconnected drones could enable mass tracking of vehicles and people in wide areas. Imagine the personal information it could gather if deployed over a political rally or gun show. A tiny drone called the Hummingbird, developed for stealth surveillance, has a wingspan of only 6.5 inches and weighs less than a single AA battery. This could go completely unnoticed while peering into the window of a home or place of worship.

CRITICAL THINKING

1. What are the limitations of drones in law enforcement? What are their strengths?

2. Do the "pros" of drone use in policing outweigh the "cons?" Why or why not?

3. Drones are increasingly popular for personal use. Is this cause for alarm? Why or why not?

Sources: Huffington Post, "Drone List Released by FAA Shows Which Police Departments Want to Fly Unmanned Aerial Vehicles," http://www.huffingtonpost.com/2013/02/08/drone-list-domestic-police-law-enforcement-surveillance_n_2647530.html (accessed February 2015); Federal Aviation Administration, *Unmanned Aircraft Systems*, http://www.faa.gov/uas/ (accessed February 2015); American Civil Liberties Union, *Protecting Privacy From Aerial Surveillance* (New York: ACLU, 2011); Sandra Fulton, "Police Hunger for Drones May Be Growing, But So Are Privacy Concerns," https://www.aclu.org/blog/technology-and-liberty-national-security/police-hunger-drones-may-be-growing-so-are-privacy (accessed February 2015).

WEB APP 5.2 Read about the CompStat process at **http://www.policechiefmagazine.org/magazine/index.cfm?fuseaction=display&article_id=998.** Is the "directing and controlling" aspect of CompStat ideal? Are there any potential pitfalls associated with CompStat?

LO3 Explain the limitations of patrol and methods for improving it

who had been appointed NYC police chief, wanted to revitalize the department and break through its antiquated bureaucratic structures. He installed CompStat, a computerized system that gave local precinct commanders up-to-date information about where and when crime was occurring in their jurisdictions. Part of the CompStat program, twice-weekly "crime control strategy meetings," brought precinct commanders together with the department's top administrators who asked them to report on crime problems in their precincts and tell what they were doing to turn things around. Those involved in the strategy sessions had both detailed data and electronic pin maps that showed how crime clustered geographically in the precinct and how patrol officers were being deployed.

The CompStat program required local commanders to demonstrate their intimate knowledge of crime trends and develop strategies to address them effectively. When ideas were presented by the assembled police administrators, the local commanders were required to demonstrate, in follow-up sessions, how they had incorporated the new strategies in their patrol plan. CompStat proved extremely successful and is generally credited with making a major contribution to the dramatic drop in New York City's crime rate during the past decade. See the accompanying Criminal Justice and Technology feature for a look at another technological advancement that may assist in police patrol operations.

Images taken by the drone pictured here are simultaneously displayed on the monitor. Drones such as these are finding their way into a variety of law enforcement functions, but their use remains highly restricted. Critics fear too much drone use will raise privacy concerns.

The Investigation Function

Fictional detectives in movies and on television shoot first and ask questions later. When they do conduct an interrogation, they think nothing of beating a confession out of the suspect. How accurate are these portrayals? Not very. The modern criminal investigator is likely to be an experienced civil servant, trained in investigatory techniques, knowledgeable about legal rules of evidence and procedure, and at least somewhat cautious about the legal and administrative consequences of his or her actions.[26]

Investigative services can be organized in a variety of ways. In New York, each borough or district has its own detective division that supervises investigators assigned to neighborhood police precincts (stations). Local squad detectives work closely with patrol officers to provide an immediate investigative response to crimes and incidents. (In some TV shows and movies, New York City detectives are shown barking commands at patrol officers and even snapping orders at uniformed sergeants and lieutenants; in reality, both branches are considered equal, so that would never happen. A patrol sergeant is the superior officer of a junior grade detective.) New York City also maintains specialized borough squads—homicide, robbery, and special victims—to give aid to local squads and help identify suspects whose crimes may have occurred in multiple locations. Also, specialty squads help in areas such as forensics. In smaller cities, detective divisions may be organized into sections or bureaus, such as homicide, robbery, or rape.

How Do Detectives Detect?

Detectives investigate the causes of crime and attempt to identify the individuals or groups responsible for committing particular offenses. They may enter a case after patrol officers have made the initial contact, such as when a patrol car interrupts a crime in progress, and the offenders flee before they can be apprehended. Detectives can investigate a case entirely on their own, sometimes by following up on leads provided by informants. Sometimes detectives go undercover to investigate crime; a lone agent can infiltrate a criminal group or organization to gather information on future criminal activity. Undercover officers can also pose as victims to capture predatory criminals who have been conducting street robberies and muggings.[27]

In his study of investigation techniques, Martin Innes found that police detectives rely heavily on interviews and forensic evidence to flesh out a narrative of the crime, creating in a sense the "story" that sets out how, where, and why the incident took place.[28] To create their story, contemporary detectives typically use a three-pronged approach:[29]

- *Specific focus.* Interview witnesses, gather evidence, record events, and collect facts at the immediate crime scene.
- *General coverage.* (1) Canvass the neighborhood and make observations; (2) conduct interviews with friends, families, and associates; (3) contact coworkers or employers for information about victims and suspects; (4) construct victim/suspect time lines to outline their whereabouts prior to the incident.
- *Informative.* Use modern technology to collect records of cell phones and pagers, computer hard drives (palm devices, laptops, notebooks, desktops, and servers), diaries, notes, and documents. This approach includes data that persons of interest in the investigation use, which, in turn, tell about their lives, interactions with others, and geographic connections.

Detective work is an art as well as a science, based on experience and knowledge of human behavior gained on the job. As sociologist Robert Jackall found when he studied detectives in New York City, the investigative branch has a unique culture and operating style.

Sting Operations

Another approach to investigation, commonly referred to as a sting operation, involves organized groups of detectives or patrol officers working in plain clothes who deceive criminals into openly committing illegal acts or conspiring to engage in criminal activity.

To sting criminals, some jurisdictions maintain vice squads, patrol officers working in plain clothes who focus on crimes of public morals such as prostitution or gambling. For example, female police officers may pose as prostitutes and arrest men who solicit their services.

Sting operations can be highly successful, but they are also open to criticism.[30] Covert police activities have often been criticized as violating the personal rights of citizens, while forcing officers into demeaning roles. Ironically, Mary Dodge and her associates found that rather than considering it demeaning, female officers find their sting work as make-believe prostitutes exciting; they also consider it a stepping-stone for promotion.[31]

By its very nature, a sting involves deceit by police agents that often comes close to entrapment. Sting operations may encourage criminals to commit new crimes because they have a new source for fencing stolen goods. Innocent people may damage their reputations by buying merchandise from a sting operation when they had no idea the items had been stolen. By putting the government into the fencing business, such operations blur the line between law enforcement and criminal activity.

Evaluating Investigations

Serious criticism has been leveled at the nation's detective forces for being bogged down in paperwork and being relatively inefficient in clearing cases. One famous study of 153 detective bureaus by the RAND Corporation, a well-known think tank, found that a great deal of a detective's time was spent in unproductive work and that investigative expertise did little to solve cases; half of all detectives could be replaced without negatively influencing crime clearance rates.[32]

Although some questions remain about the effectiveness of investigations, police detectives do make a valuable contribution to police work because their skilled interrogation and case-processing techniques are essential to eventual criminal conviction.[33] Detective work may be improved if investigators are able to spend more time on each case, allowing them to carefully collect physical evidence at the scene of the crime, identify witnesses, check departmental records, and use informants. Research shows that in more serious cases, especially homicide investigations, where detectives devote a lot of attention to a single crime, the likelihood increases that they will eventually identify and arrest the culprit.[34]

sting operation An undercover police operation in which police pose as criminals to trap law violators.

vice squad Police officers assigned to enforce morality-based laws, such as those on prostitution, gambling, and pornography.

REALITY**CHECK**

MYTH OR REALITY?

The more serious the crime, the more likely it is that detectives will solve it.

REALITY. Investigations of serious criminal incidents receive more attention. Consequently, they are solved at a higher rate.

Are there any unintended side effects of concentrating resources on serious crimes at the expense of less serious ones? Or are serious crimes solved for other reasons than just prioritizing them?

An undercover Palm Beach County (Florida) Sheriff's deputy poses as a prostitute. The sting was one of several recent furtive operations by the agency intended to catch "johns" in the act. The man was not arrested and did not hire the decoy for sexual acts.

Nonetheless, a majority of cases that are solved are done so when the perpetrator is identified at the scene of the crime by patrol officers. Research shows that if a crime is reported while in progress, the police have about a 33 percent chance of making an arrest; the arrest probability declines to about 10 percent if the crime is reported 1 minute later, and to 5 percent if more than 15 minutes have elapsed. As the time between the crime and the arrest grows, the chances of a conviction are also reduced, probably because the ability to recover evidence is lost. Put another way, after a crime has been completed and the investigation is put in the hands of detectives, the chances of identifying and arresting the perpetrator diminish rapidly.[35]

One reason for investigation ineffectiveness is that detectives often lack sufficient resources to carry out a lengthy ongoing probe of any but the most serious cases. Research shows the following:

- *Unsolved cases.* Almost 50 percent of burglary cases are screened out by supervisors before assignment to a detective for a follow-up investigation. Of those assigned, 75 percent are dropped after the first day of the follow-up investigation. Although robbery cases are more likely to be assigned to detectives, 75 percent of them are also dropped after one day of investigation.
- *Length of investigation.* The vast majority of cases are investigated for no more than four hours stretching over 3 days. An average of 11 days elapses between the initial report of a crime and suspension of the investigation.
- *Sources of information.* Early in an investigation, the focus is on the victim; as the investigation is pursued, emphasis shifts to the suspect. The most critical information for determining case outcome is the name and description of the suspect and related crime information. Victims are most often the source of information; unfortunately, witnesses, informants, and members of the police department are consulted far less often. However, when these sources are tapped, they are likely to produce useful information.
- *Effectiveness.* Preliminary investigations by patrol officers are critical. In situations where the suspect's identity is not known immediately after the crime is committed, detectives make an arrest in less than 10 percent of all cases.[36]

Improving Investigation with Technology

In Chapter 4, some technological breakthroughs that have aided crime investigation were discussed in some detail. Information technology (IT) has revolutionized police work in many areas, including communications, criminal identification, and record

LO4 Summarize the investigation function

REALITY CHECK

MYTH OR REALITY?

Most crimes are solved when the perpetrator is identified at the crime scene.

REALITY. The majority of cases are solved when the perpetrator is identified early.

This is contrary to the view portrayed in the fictional media, wherein the investigators always apprehend criminals by examining trace evidence and following up on questionable leads. What other misconceptions are conveyed by programs such as *CSI* and *Law & Order*?

storage. A number of tasks that used to involve painstaking labor by individuals are now being conducted with IT. Take, for instance, searching criminal histories. Police agencies are now using a program called CopLink to facilitate this time-consuming task. CopLink integrates information from different jurisdictions into a single database that detectives can access when working on investigations.[37] The CopLink program enables investigators to search the entire database of past criminal records and computes a list of possible suspects even if only limited data are available, such as first or last name, partial license plate numbers, vehicle type, vehicle color, location of crime, and/or type of weapon used.

Another technique that is improving investigation success is the use of DNA profiling. Using DNA in support of criminal investigations has increased both in the United States and around the world. The first national DNA database—the National DNA Database of England & Wales—is regarded by many police experts as the most important development in investigative technology since the adoption of fingerprint comparison early in the previous century.[38] Still other strategies have been employed, such as the use of social networking.

Improving Investigations with Forensic Science

forensic science The use of scientific techniques to investigate questions of interest to the justice system and to solve crimes.

Investigations have improved along with advances in forensic science. The *CSI* television series and its various spin-offs have drawn attention to the developing field of forensics in police work, which uses a variety of sciences, mathematical principles, and problem-solving methods to identify perpetrators. Forensic means "pertaining to the law," and forensic scientists perform comprehensive chemical and physical analyses on evidence submitted by law enforcement agencies. Although most forensic scientists focus on criminal cases (they are sometimes referred to as criminalists), others work in the civil justice system—for example, performing handwriting comparisons to determine the validity of a signature on a will.

Today, forensic specialists can examine blood and other body fluids and tissues for the presence of alcohol, drugs, and poisons and can compare body fluids and hair for

A Utah medical examiner, relying in part on DNA and dental records, determined that the bones pictured here were those of 23-year-old Theresa Rose Greaves, who disappeared in 1983.

AP Images/Scott G Winterton

typing factors, including DNA analysis. Forensic scientists analyze trace physical evidence such as blood spatters, paint, soil, and glass to help reconstruct a crime scene and interpret how the crime was committed. In addition to forensics, investigation is being improved by information technology, which allows investigators to compare evidence found at the crime scene with material collected from similar crimes by other police agencies.

Forensic analyses involve the use of complex instruments and of chemical, physical, and microscopic examining techniques. In addition to analyzing crime scene investigations, forensic scientists provide testimony in a court of law when the case is brought to trial. Some forensic scientists are generalists, and others specialize in a particular scientific area, including toxicology, blood pattern analysis, crime scene investigation, impression evidence (e.g., footprints), trace evidence (e.g., hair left at a crime scene), and questioned documents. There is a forensics expert for nearly every conceivable type of evidence and criminal activity.

L05 Explain what forensics is and what forensics experts do for police agencies

Community-Oriented Policing

Police agencies have been trying for several decades to gain the cooperation and respect of the communities they serve. At first, efforts at improving the relationships between police departments and the public involved programs with the general title of police–community relations (PCR). Developed at the station house and departmental levels, these initial PCR programs were designed to make citizens more aware of police activities, alert them to methods of self-protection, and improve general attitudes toward policing.

Although PCR efforts demonstrated the willingness of police agencies to cooperate with the public, some experts believed that law enforcement agencies needed to undergo a significant transformation to create meaningful partnerships with the public. In their view, community relations and crime control effectiveness cannot be the province of a few specialized units housed within a traditional police department. Instead, the core police role must be altered if community involvement is to be won and maintained. This led to the development of community-oriented policing (COP), a set of programs and strategies designed to bring police and the public closer together and create a more cooperative working environment between them.

community-oriented policing (COP) Programs and strategies designed to bring police and the public closer together and create a more cooperative working environment between them.

Officer Mohamed stops by an impromptu soccer game while fulfilling his community policing duties in Mankato, Minnesota. Mohamed, originally from Somalia, is hoping to start a more organized sports program this summer as part of his community policing assignment in the city's Somali community.

NYPD Work Slowdown

Community policing emphasizes working *with* citizens, rather than against them, in the ongoing struggle against crime. Did the NYPD work slowdown in early 2015 comport with a COP philosophy? On the one hand, officers were not thinking of the community when they drastically scaled back on certain enforcement activities. On the other hand, critics of a broken windows model claim that a focus on low-level quality of life offenses threatens police–community relations. The slowdown may therefore have been a welcome change. Whose interests were served by the slowdown?

foot patrol Police patrols that take officers out of cars and put them on a walking beat to strengthen ties with the community.

neighborhood-oriented policing (NOP) Community-oriented policing efforts aimed at individual neighborhoods.

Implementing Community-Oriented Policing

The COP concept was originally implemented through a number of innovative demonstration projects.[39] Among the most publicized were experiments in **foot patrol**, which took officers out of cars and set them to walking beats in the neighborhood. Foot patrol efforts were aimed at forming a bond with community residents by acquainting them with the individual officers who patrolled their neighborhood and letting them know that police were caring and available.

The first foot patrol experiments were conducted in cities in Michigan and New Jersey. An evaluation of foot patrol indicated that although it did not bring down the crime rate, residents in areas where foot patrol was added perceived greater safety and were less afraid of crime.[40]

Since the advent of these programs, hundreds of communities have adopted innovative forms of decentralized, neighborhood-based COP models. The federal government has encouraged the growth of COP by providing billions of dollars to hire and train officers through its Office of Community Oriented Policing Services (COPS) program, which has given local departments more than $10 billion in aid since its inception.[41] Recent surveys indicate that there has been a significant increase in COP activities and that certain core programs, such as crime prevention, have become embedded in the police role.[42] COP programs have been implemented in large cities, suburban areas, and rural communities.[43]

Changing the Police Role

COP also emphasizes sharing power with local groups and individuals. A key element of the COP philosophy is that citizens must actively participate with police to fight crime. Such participation is essential because the community climate is influenced by the informal social control created by a concerned citizenry coupled with effective policing.[44] Participation might involve providing information in area-wide crime investigations or helping police reach out to troubled youths. The following are some other changes that have been linked to COP initiatives:

- *Neighborhood orientation.* To achieve the goals of COP, some police agencies have tried to decentralize, an approach sometimes referred to as **neighborhood-oriented policing (NOP)**.[45] According to this view, problem solving is best done at the neighborhood level where issues originate, not at a far-off central headquarters. Because each neighborhood has its own particular needs, police decision making must be flexible and adaptive. For example, neighborhoods undergoing change in racial composition may experience high levels of racially motivated violence and require special police initiatives to reduce tensions.[46]
- *Changing management styles.* COP also means the redesign of police departments' administration and management. Management's role must be reinterpreted to focus on the problems of the community, not on the needs of the police department. The traditional vertical police organizational chart must be altered so that top-down management gives way to bottom-up decision making. The patrol officer becomes the manager of his beat and a key decision maker.
- *Changing recruitment and training.* COP means that police departments must alter their recruitment and training requirements. Future officers must develop community-organizing and problem-solving skills, along with traditional police skills. Their training must prepare them to succeed less on their ability to make arrests or issue citations and more on their ability to solve problems effectively.

Challenges of Community-Oriented Policing

The core concepts of police work are changing as administrators recognize the limitations and realities of police work in modern society. If they are to be successful, COP strategies must be able to react effectively to some significant administrative problems.

DEFINING COMMUNITY Critics believe that COP works best in stable, affluent areas that are already characterized by a strong sense of community. The challenge of community is to reach out to all people in all neighborhoods, including young people and minorities, who may previously have been left out of the process.

DEFINING ROLES Police administrators must also establish the exact role of community police agents. How should they integrate their activities with those of regular patrol forces? For example, should foot patrols have primary responsibility for policing in an area, or should they coordinate their activities with officers assigned to patrol cars?

CHANGING SUPERVISOR ATTITUDES Some supervisors are wary of COP because it supports a decentralized command structure. Supervisors who learn to actively embrace COP concepts are the ones best able to encourage patrol officers to follow suit.[47]

REORIENTING POLICE VALUES Research shows that police officers who have a traditional crime control orientation are less satisfied with COP efforts than those who are public service oriented.[48] In some instances, officers holding traditional values may go as far as stigmatizing their own comrades assigned to COP; their targets often feel penalized by a lack of administrative support.[49] It is thus unlikely that COP activities can be successful unless police line officers make a firm commitment to the values of the program.[50]

REVISED TRAINING Because the COP model calls for an expansion of the police role from law enforcer to community organizer, police training must be revised to reflect this new mandate. If COP is to be adopted on a wide scale, a whole new type of police officer must be recruited and trained in a completely new way. Training must prepare officers to succeed less on their ability to make arrests or issue citations and more on their ability to solve problems, prevent crime effectively, and deal with neighborhood diversity and cultural values.[51]

REORIENTED RECRUITMENT To make COP successful, mid-level managers must be recruited and trained who are receptive to and can implement community-change strategies.[52] The selection of new recruits must be guided by a desire to find individuals with the skills and attitudes that support COP.

Community-Oriented Policing Effectiveness

Empirical evidence suggests that *some* COP efforts can reduce disorder and impact the crime rate.[53] The most successful programs give officers time to meet with local residents to talk about crime in the neighborhood and allow officers to use personal initiative to solve problems. Although not all programs work (police–community newsletters and cleanup campaigns do not seem to do much good), the overall impression has been that patrol officers can actually reduce the level of fear in the community. Where it is used, citizens seem to like COP, and those who volunteer and get involved in community crime-prevention programs report higher confidence in the police force and its ability to create a secure environment.[54]

On the other hand, there is no clear-cut evidence that COP is highly successful at reducing crime across the board. Crime rate reductions in cities that have used COP may be the result of an overall downturn in the nation's crime rate, rather than a result of COP efforts. Researchers have also found that it is difficult to change the traditional values and attitudes of police officers involved in the programs.[55]

L06 Discuss the concept of community-oriented policing

San Francisco police officers investigate the scene where a high-speed car chase ended with a crash and the fatal shooting of a carjacking suspect in San Francisco. Officers shot and killed a man after he led them on a lengthy high-speed chase, crashed his truck in downtown San Francisco, and then fired a gun at good Samaritans who tried to help him according to authorities.

AP Images/Eric Risberg

Problem-Oriented Policing

Closely associated with, yet independent from, the COP concept are the **problem-oriented policing (POP)** strategies. Traditional police models focus on responding to calls for help in the shortest possible time, dealing with the situation, and then getting on the street again as soon as possible. In contrast, POP is proactive.

POP requires police agencies to identify particular long-term community problems—street-level drug dealers, prostitution rings, gang hangouts—and develop strategies to eliminate them.[56] As with COP, police departments must rely on local residents and private resources to be problem solvers. This means that police managers must learn how to develop community resources, design efficient and cost-effective solutions to problems, and become advocates as well as agents of reform.[57]

A significant percentage of police departments are now using special units to confront specific social problems. POP models are supported by ample evidence that a great deal of urban crime is concentrated in a few hot spots.[58] A significant portion of all police calls in metropolitan areas typically radiate from a relatively few locations: bars, malls, bus depots, hotels, and certain apartment buildings.[59] By implication, concentrating police resources on these **hot spots of crime** could reduce crime appreciably.[60] Problem-oriented strategies are being developed that focus on specific problem areas and/or specific criminal acts. For example, a POP effort in Sarasota, Florida, which was aimed at reducing prostitution, involved intensive, focused, high-visibility patrols to discourage prostitutes and their customers; undercover work to arrest prostitutes and drug dealers; and collaboration with hotel and motel owners to identify and arrest pimps and drug dealers.[61]

Another well-known program, Operation Ceasefire, is a POP intervention aimed at reducing youth homicide and youth firearms violence in Boston. According to evaluations of the program, Ceasefire produced significant reductions in youth homicide victimization and gun assault incidents in Boston that were not experienced in other communities in New England or elsewhere in the nation.[62]

Although programs such as these seem successful, the effectiveness of any street-level problem-solving effort must be interpreted with caution.[63] It is possible that the criminals will be displaced to other, "safer" areas of the city and will return shortly after the program is declared a success and the additional police forces have been pulled from the area.[64] Nonetheless, evidence shows that whereas merely saturating an area with police may not deter crime, focusing efforts on a particular problem may indeed have a crime-reducing effect.

problem-oriented policing (POP) A style of police operations that stresses proactive problem solving, rather than reactive crime fighting.

WEB APP 5.3 Read about specific POP strategies at the website of the Center for Problem-Oriented Policing: **http://www.popcenter.org/.** What have police departments done to target difficult problems such as false burglary alarms, loud car stereos, drive-by shootings, and homeless encampments? Which of these and other problems listed under the website's "POP Guides" tab do you think is most demanding of law enforcement? Why?

hot spots of crime Places from which a significant portion of all police calls originate. These hot spots include taverns and housing projects.

LO7 Discuss the concept of problem-oriented policing

Intelligence-Led Policing

Since 9/11, policing has experienced a fundamental philosophical change by combining a homeland security focus with the many advances made in the realms of COP and POP.[65] An outgrowth of this combination is intelligence-led policing (ILP), which has been described as "the collection and analysis of information to produce an intelligence end product designed to inform police decision making at both the tactical and strategic levels."[66] More simply, ILP is intended to further shift the emphasis in police work away from reactive responses and individual case investigations. It instead emphasizes information sharing, collaboration, and strategic solutions to crime problems at various levels. ILP relies heavily on the following:

intelligence-led policing (ILP) The collection and analysis of information to generate an "intelligence end product" designed to inform police decision making at both the tactical and the strategic level.

- Confidential informants
- Offender interviews
- Careful analysis of crime reports and calls for service
- Suspect surveillance
- Community sources of information[67]

The British have a long history of sophisticated intelligence gathering and analysis. All 43 British constabularies, as well as the London Metropolitan Police, have had intelligence units for some time to deal with problems ranging from drugs to organized crime.[68] The UK's National Drugs Intelligence Unit, created in the 1980s, gathers intelligence to aid in the enforcement of laws against drug trafficking. In 1992, the National Criminal Intelligence Service (NCIS) was formed, mainly to deal with the problem of organized crime. One of its responsibilities is to work with the chemical industry in the UK to identify and disrupt the production of synthetic drugs.

In contrast, American law enforcement agencies have, until recently, had little intelligence-gathering capacity. If it occurred at all, intelligence gathering was mostly reserved for large police agencies. According to David Carter, one of the leading experts on ILP, "Early law enforcement initiatives typically had no analysis and essentially consisted of dossiers kept on individuals who were suspicious or were deemed to be threats of some sort, often based on intuitive, rather than empirical, threat criteria."[69] Current ILP initiatives attempt to compensate for this shortcoming.

ILP bears a great deal of similarity to POP. The two are somewhat different, however, in that POP puts problem identification and solution in the hands of individual street-level officers, whereas ILP emphasizes a top-down managerial approach by which administrators set priorities for crime prevention and enforcement and then pass these priorities down through the agency.[70] ILP is also similar to COP in that it relies on residents as part of the intelligence-gathering process. But it is different, too, because whereas COP emphasizes the desires of the community, ILP relies on problem identification through careful analysis of the criminal environment as a whole. ILP has even been likened to CompStat, discussed earlier in this chapter. See Table 5.1 for a summary of the differences and commonalities between CompStat and ILP.

To gain a more concrete grasp of the ILP concept, consider these examples:

- A county sheriff's office identifies narcotics control as its top priority and develops strategies accordingly. The office targets known offenders and groups, shuts down open-air drug markets and crackhouses, and participates in school-based drug awareness programs to help prevent drug use.
- A statewide agency identifies vehicle insurance fraud as a top area for enforcement. The agency targets those involved in staged accidents, identifies communities in which insurance fraud is prevalent, exposes ongoing fraudulent activity, and mounts a public education campaign.
- A police agency in a small city makes safe streets a priority. The agency focuses on directed enforcement in identified hot spots. It also targets career criminals whose apprehension will significantly reduce the number of crimes being committed. Preventive measures include enhanced patrols, improved street lighting, and crime-watch programs.[71]

LO8 Explain intelligence-led policing and the various means by which it occurs

TABLE 5.1 Comparison of CompStat and intelligence-led policing

CompStat	Commonalities	Intelligence-Led Policing
Single jurisdiction	Both have a goal of prevention.	Multiple jurisdictions
Incident-driven	Both require the following: • Organizational flexibility • Consistent information input • A significant analytic component	Threat-driven
Street crime and burglary		Criminal enterprises and terrorism
Crime mapping		Commodity flow; trafficking and transiting logistics
Time-sensitive (24-hour feedback and response)		Strategic
Disrupt crime series (e.g., burglary ring)		Disrupt enterprises
Drives operations: • Patrol • Tactical unit • Investigators		Drives operations: • Joint terrorism task forces • Organized crime investigations • Task forces
Analysis of offender MO (*modus operandi*)		Analysis of enterprise MO (*modus operandi*)

Source: Office of Community-Oriented Policing Services, *Intelligence-Led Policing: The Integration of Community Policing and Law Enforcement Intelligence, Part 4* (Washington, DC: COPS Office, n.d.), p. 43. Available at www.cops.usdoj.gov/pdf/e09042536_Chapter_04.pdf.

Fusion Centers

In the spring of 2002, law enforcement executives from around the country met at a Criminal Intelligence Sharing Summit. Summit participants called for the development of a national intelligence plan that could be used to prevent future terrorist attacks like the ones that occurred on 9/11. After this meeting, the Global Justice Information Sharing Initiative and the Intelligence Working Group were formed. These groups eventually developed the **National Criminal Intelligence Sharing Plan (NCISP)**.[72] The report outlined a number of "action steps" that could be taken to improve intelligence gathering and sharing among law enforcement agencies across the country. The NCISP sought to communicate the following:

- A model intelligence-sharing plan
- A mechanism to promote ILP
- A blueprint for law enforcement administrators to follow when enhancing or building an intelligence system
- A model for intelligence process principles and policies
- A plan that respects and protects individuals' privacy and civil rights
- A technology architecture to provide secure, seamless sharing of information among systems
- A national model for intelligence training
- An outreach plan to promote timely and credible intelligence sharing
- A plan that leverages existing systems and networks, yet allows flexibility for technology and process enhancements

As part of this process, many states and large cities have formed **fusion centers**. According to the National Fusion Center Guidelines, a fusion center is "an effective and efficient mechanism to exchange information and intelligence, maximize resources, streamline operations, and improve the ability to fight crime and terrorism by analyzing data from a variety of sources."[73] Often located in police departments, these centers are set up for the purpose of sharing information and intelligence within specific jurisdictions and across levels of government. Fusion centers often emphasize terrorism prevention and crime fighting

National Criminal Intelligence Sharing Plan (NCISP) A formal intelligence-sharing initiative that identifies the security and intelligence-sharing needs recognized in the wake of the 9/11 terrorist attacks.

fusion center A mechanism to exchange information and intelligence, maximize resources, streamline operations, and improve the ability to fight crime and terrorism by analyzing data from a variety of sources.

The Palm Beach Regional Fusion Center (PBRFC), operated by the Homeland Security Bureau of the Palm Beach County Sheriff's Office, in conjunction with other public agencies, federal authorities, and private sector representatives, is responsible for the management of real-time situational awareness and the monitoring of criminal activity. The PBRFC works to detect, deter, and prevent terrorist acts and other criminal activity, as well as prepare for and respond to natural or manmade disasters.

with extensive use of technology. They frequently resemble a department's technological "nerve center" and are usually housed in a central location where information is collected and then shared with decision makers. Fusion centers focus on four main goals:

- Provide support for a range of law enforcement activities, including anticrime operations and terrorism prevention.
- Provide help for major incident operations and support for units charged with interdiction and criminal investigations.
- Provide the means for community input, often through tip lines.
- Provide assistance to law enforcement executives so they can make informed decisions about departmental priorities.[74]

Fusion centers are intended to provide a mechanism through which government agencies, law enforcement, and the private sector can work together for the common purpose of protecting the homeland and preserving public safety. They are based on a model of collaboration. Collaboration between agencies and across levels of government has been lacking throughout history, but the events of 9/11 affirmed a need for change. The concept of fusion centers will continue to catch on, and more will probably be developed as law enforcement becomes increasingly aware of the benefits they can yield.

Support Functions

As the model of a typical police department indicates (refer to Figure 5.1), not all members of a department engage in what the general public regards as "real police work"—patrol, detection, and traffic control. Even in departments that are embracing COP and POP, many police resources are actually devoted to support and administrative functions. There are too many tasks to mention in detail, but the most important include those discussed next.

Many police departments maintain their own personnel service, which carries out such functions as recruiting new police officers, creating exams to determine the most qualified applicants, and handling promotions and transfers. Innovative selection techniques are constantly being developed and tested. For example, the Behavioral-Personnel Assessment Device (B-PAD) requires police applicants to view videotaped scenarios and respond as though they were officers handling the situation; reviews indicate that this procedure may be a reliable and unbiased method of choosing new recruits.[75]

Larger police departments often maintain an internal affairs branch charged with policing the police. Internal affairs units process citizen complaints of police corruption, investigate what may be the unnecessary use of force by police officers, and probe police participation in actual criminal activity, such as burglaries or narcotics violations. In addition, internal affairs divisions may assist police managers when disciplinary action is brought against individual officers. The internal affairs function is controversial because investigators are feared and distrusted by fellow police officers. Nonetheless, rigorous self-scrutiny is the only way police departments can earn the respect of citizens. Because of these concerns, it has become commonplace for police departments to institute citizen oversight over police practices and to establish civilian review boards that have the power to listen to complaints and conduct investigations.

Most police departments are responsible for the administration and control of their own budgets. This task includes administering payroll, purchasing equipment and services, planning budgets for future expenditures, and auditing departmental financial records.

Police departments include separate units charged with maintaining and disseminating information on wanted offenders, stolen merchandise, traffic violators, and so on. Modern data management systems enable police to use their records in a highly sophisticated fashion. For example, officers in a patrol car who spot a suspicious-looking vehicle can instantly receive a computerized rundown on whether it has been stolen. And if stolen property is recovered during an arrest, police using this sort of system can determine who reported the loss of the merchandise and arrange for its return.

Another important function of police communication is the effective and efficient dispatching of patrol cars. Again, modern computer technologies have been used to make the most of available resources.[76]

In many departments, training is continuous throughout an officer's career. Training usually begins at a police academy, which may be run exclusively for larger departments or may be part of a regional training center serving smaller and varied governmental units. More than 90 percent of all police departments require preservice training, including nearly all departments in larger cities (population over 100,000). The average officer receives more than 500 hours of preservice training, including 400 hours in the classroom and the rest in field training. Police in large cities receive more than 1,700 hours of instruction divided almost evenly between classroom and field instruction.[77] Among the topics usually covered are law and civil rights, firearms handling, emergency medical care, and restraint techniques.[78]

After assuming their police duties, new recruits are assigned to field-training officers who break them in on the job. However, training does not stop here. On-the-job training is a continuous process in the modern police department and covers such areas as weapons skills, first aid, crowd control, and community relations. Some departments use roll call training, in which superior officers or outside experts address police officers at the beginning of the workday. Other departments allow police officers time off to attend annual training sessions to sharpen their skills and learn new policing techniques.

Police departments provide emergency aid to the ill, counsel youngsters, speak to school and community agencies on safety and drug abuse, and provide countless other services designed to improve citizen–police interactions.

L09 Describe the various police support functions

Larger police departments maintain specialized units that help citizens protect themselves from criminal activity. They advise citizens on effective home security techniques or conduct Project ID campaigns—engraving valuables with an identifying number so that they can be returned if recovered after a burglary; police also work in schools teaching kids how to avoid drug use.[79] Police agencies maintain (or have access to) forensic laboratories that enable them to identify substances to be used as evidence and to classify fingerprints.

Planning and research functions include designing programs to increase police efficiency and strategies to test program effectiveness. Police planners monitor recent technological developments and institute programs to adapt them to police services. Crime analysts support the department through the compilation and analysis of statistics to help administrators make decision as to how best allocate resources. See the accompanying Careers in Criminal Justice feature for additional information.

Duties and Characteristics of the Job

- Crime analysts engage in a number of important law enforcement support functions. Foremost, they study patterns of criminal activity and profile suspects.

- They analyze crime data (calls for service, arrests made, etc.) and often use that information to forecast the days, times, and places those crimes are most likely to occur.

- They are also called upon to provide information on demand, analyze long-term programs, and develop intelligence.

Job Outlook

- The job outlook for crime analysts is quite favorable.

- According to the International Association of Crime Analysts (IACA), the demand for qualified crime analysts has increased more than tenfold in the past 15 years. It will continue to increase even more over time as law enforcement further comes to realize the potential of sophisticated data gathering and analysis.

- Some crime analysts are involved in grant writing and may earn part of their wages from "soft money," which can make the situation unpredictable for some of them.

- Less populous cities with few police officers generally do not require dedicated or full-time crime analysts. Opportunities also exist in certain task force offices.

Salary

- Specialized knowledge is required and, as such, crime analysts tend to do fairly well in terms of compensation.

- An entry-level crime analyst can make as much as $60,000 per year. Experienced and well-educated crime analysts can make $80,000 per year or more.

- A supervising crime analyst in a large city such as Los Angeles can make close to $100,000 per year, if not more.

Qualifications

- Crime analysts are often civilian employees, which may prove desirable for those who do not want to become sworn peace officers.

- Crime analysts require knowledge of techniques and methods used in data collection, statistical analysis, report preparation, and research.

- Knowledge of numerous computer applications is also required, as is a full command of the English language for report writing and communications, familiarity with law enforcement operations, and the like.

Education and Training

- Many positions require a four-year degree, often with a concentration in criminal justice, criminology, and/or policing. Some permit a combination of work experience and education short of a four-year degree.

- Positions may or may not require any particular licensing or certification, but either can make an applicant more competitive. For example, the International Association of Crime Analysts (IACA) offers a certification program. According to IACA, graduates may be more marketable and/or earn more from their employing agencies as a result of the certification.

Reality Check

- A crime analyst position requires specialized knowledge of complex computer applications and a fondness for numbers.

- Most positions are located in large police departments.

- Crime analysis is mostly a "behind the scenes" function and does not see the level of action one may encounter in a sworn position.

Sources: University of Maryland, "What Is Crime Analysis?," http://www.crimeanalysis.umd.edu/crimeanalysis.php (accessed February 2015); International Association of Crime Analysts, "Analyst Position Descriptions," http://www.iaca.net/dc_position_descriptions.asp (accessed February 2015).

ETHICAL Challenge

The Middle City police force created Crime Control Teams—decentralized units relieved of routine duties that were not crime related and given responsibility for controlling serious crime, apprehending offenders, conducting investigations, and increasing clearance rates on a neighborhood basis. Two team members, Officers Donald Libby and Karen Johnson, each with more than 15 years on the force, were part of a team assigned to displace gangs of local teenagers who were constantly causing problems in the neighborhood. After a few months on the job, Libby and Johnson were the target of numerous complaints related to their treatment of neighborhood youths. They were charged with roughing up neighborhood kids, slapping some of them around, and being disrespectful. In the most serious incident, they used a nightstick on a 15-year-old whom they claim had resisted arrest after they found him smoking marijuana in the park. The youth suffered a broken arm and concussion and required hospitalization. When interviewed by the Internal Affairs bureau, the officers admitted they scuffled with the boy but claimed they were "only doing their job." Besides, they argued, community leaders had demanded results, and their aggressive style had helped lower the crime rate in the area by more than 20 percent. The boy and his parents have also filed suit, claiming that the amount of force used was unnecessary and violated his civil rights.

Ethical Challenge: As the officers' defense attorney, write an essay outlining their defense. Don't worry about legal rules. How would you defend the two officers? Draw from this chapter's sections on community policing, problem solving, and other sections as needed. Also consider visiting and gathering additional information from the Office of Juvenile Justice and Delinquency Prevention's (OJJDP) Model Programs site at http://www.ojjdp.gov/mpg.

SUMMARY

LO1 *Explain the organization of police departments* Most municipal police departments in the United States are independent agencies within the executive branch of government. Typically, local police departments are organized in a hierarchical manner and employ a time-in-rank system for determining promotion eligibility.

LO2 *Articulate the complexities of the police role* A police officer's crime-fighting efforts are only a small part of his or her overall activities. Studies of police work indicate that a significant portion of an officer's time is spent handling minor disturbances, service calls, and administrative duties. The police role involves many activities that are not crime related. The primary role of police seems to be "handling the situation."

LO3 *Explain the limitations of patrol and methods for improving it* Most experts agree that the great bulk of patrol efforts are devoted to what has been described as order maintenance or peacekeeping: maintaining order and civility in the assigned jurisdiction. Evidence is mixed on the deterrent effect of patrol. Efforts to improve patrol have included proactive policing and directed patrol, targeting specific offenses for more arrests, rapid response, broken windows policing, and increased utilization of technology, including CompStat. Of these, rapid response has proven least effective.

LO4 *Summarize the investigation function* The first independent detective bureau was established by the London Metropolitan Police in 1841. Detectives investigate the causes of crime and attempt to identify the individuals or groups responsible for committing particular offenses. Police detectives make a valuable contribution to police work because their skilled interrogation and case-processing techniques are essential to eventual criminal conviction.

LO5 *Explain what forensics is and what forensics experts do for police agencies* Investigations have improved along with advances in forensic science. Forensic scientists perform comprehensive chemical and physical analyses on evidence submitted by law enforcement agencies.

LO6 *Discuss the concept of community-oriented policing* Hundreds of communities have adopted innovative forms of decentralized, neighborhood-based COP models. Empirical evidence suggests that some COP efforts can reduce disorder and lessen the crime rate.

LO7 *Discuss the concept of problem-oriented policing* Closely associated with, yet independent from, the COP concept are POP strategies. Proactive POP strategies require police agencies to identify particular long-term community problems (such as street-level drug dealers, prostitution rings, and gang hangouts) and develop strategies to eliminate them.

LO8 *Explain intelligence-led policing and the various means by which it occurs* ILP consists of the collection and analysis of information designed to inform police decision making at both the tactical and strategic levels. It emphasizes top-down problem solving. ILP relies on community input, but priorities are set at the department level, rather than identified by residents.

LO9 *Describe the various police support functions* Many police departments maintain their own personnel service, which carries out such functions as recruiting new police officers, creating exams to determine the most qualified applicants, and handling promotions and transfers. Larger police departments often maintain an internal affairs branch charged with "policing the police." Another important function of police communication is the effective and efficient dispatching of patrol cars. Again, modern computer technologies have been used to make the most of available resources.

KEY TERMS

police chief, p. 108

time-in-rank system, p. 109

order maintenance (peacekeeping), p. 110

proactive policing, p. 111

deterrent effect, p. 112

directed patrol, p. 112

broken windows model, p. 112

CompStat, p. 113

sting operation, p. 116

vice squad, p. 116

forensic science, p. 118

community-oriented policing (COP), p. 119

foot patrol, p. 120

neighborhood-oriented policing (NOP), p. 120

problem-oriented policing (POP), p. 122

hot spots of crime, p. 122

intelligence-led policing (ILP), p. 123

National Criminal Intelligence Sharing Plan (NCISP), p. 124

fusion center, p. 124

internal affairs, p. 126

REVIEW QUESTIONS

1. Should the primary police role be law enforcement or community service? Explain.

2. Should a police chief be permitted to promote an officer with special skills to a supervisory position, or should all officers be forced to spend "time in rank"? Explain your answer.

3. Do the advantages of proactive policing outweigh the disadvantages? Explain.

4. Explain the concept of broken windows policing. Why might it be successful?

5. What are the problems facing investigators and forensics experts today?

6. Can the police and the community ever form a partnership to fight crime? Why or why not? Does the COP model remind you of early forms of policing? Explain.

6 ISSUES IN POLICING:
PROFESSIONAL, SOCIAL, AND LEGAL

On July 17, 2014, New York City police officers moved to arrest 43-year-old Eric Garner, an African American, on suspicion that he was selling "loosies," or single cigarettes from packs without tax stamps, on the curb outside a beauty supply store.[1] Garner had previously been arrested for the same offense (and several others) and was out on bail at the time. When Officer Daniel Pantaleo approached him to make the arrest, Garner swatted his hand away, saying "Don't touch me, please." Pantaleo then put 350-pound Garner in a headlock, or "chokehold," from behind, and then pulled backwards in an effort to bring Garner to the ground. A video of the incident (available here: https://www.youtube.com/watch?v=N__5p_dNW3U) next showed Pantaleo removing his arms from around Garner's neck and then using his hands to push Garner's head onto the sidewalk. Garner was heard repeatedly saying "I can't breathe." He eventually became motionless and unresponsive. An ambulance arrived a few minutes later. Garner was pronounced dead on arrival at the hospital one hour later.[2]

Officer Pantaleo was placed on desk duty during a subsequent investigation, as was another officer involved in the arrest. On July 19, Al Sharpton organized a peaceful protest on Staten Island. A few days later, another protest was held in Times Square. On August 19, the Staten Island district attorney announced that the case against Pantaleo would go before a grand jury. Panteleo would later testify before the grand jury in November. After a two-month investigation, the grand jury announced on December 3, 2014, that it would not indict Panteleo. Protests erupted across the country (306 people were arrested in New York City alone), and as we discussed in the opening of Chapter 4, the subsequent execution-style killings of two NYPD officers occurred at least partially in retaliation for Garner's death. As of this writing, Pantaleo remains on the force, but continues on desk duty.

The police have always been put in a difficult spot when it comes to enforcing the law and, at the same time, preventing unnecessary loss of life. Many people feel the police should control and prevent crime, even if doing so requires a no-nonsense, heavy-handed approach. Supporters of "get-tough" law enforcement feel that if the greater good is served, then occasional injuries and deaths as a result of Taser use—or even gun use—go

New York Daily News/Getty Images

LEARNING OBJECTIVES

LO1 Summarize demographic trends in policing

LO2 Explain how minority and female officers act and are treated

LO3 Explain police culture and personality

LO4 Identify distinct policing styles

LO5 Describe factors that affect police discretion

LO6 Discuss four major problems of policing

LO7 Distinguish between deadly and nondeadly force—and methods for controlling each

LO8 Explain the importance of less-lethal weapons

LO9 Analyze the Supreme Court's involvement with the police through its effort to control search and seizure and interrogation, and through establishment of the exclusionary rule with the territory. On the other hand, police do not work in a vacuum. They work in a very visible, politically contentious, media-driven world. Anything that even *possibly* results in unnecessary injury or death places the police in the hot seat, forcing them to defend their public image.

The Taser and all its alternatives raise important questions about the problems that police departments face while interacting with the society they are entrusted with supervising: Are police officers too forceful and brutal, and do they discriminate in their use of deadly force? When officers need to use force, what options are available to them? Which option should they pursue and under what circumstances? Are police too quick to resort to force? How many officers are deviant, and to what extent can deviance be controlled? This chapter focuses on these and other questions facing police officers in contemporary society. First, we begin with a discussion of the makeup of the police and the police profession.

This chapter also focuses on a number of other social and professional issues facing police officers in the modern world. It begins by examining issues police face on the job, in court, and in society. Topics covered include diversity, police discretion, stress, fatigue, and use of force. This chapter concludes with a look at law enforcement's legal environment.

Who Are the Police?

The composition of the nation's police forces is changing. Less than 50 years ago, police agencies were composed primarily of white males with a high school education who viewed policing as a secure position that brought them the respect of family and friends and took them a step up the social ladder. It was not uncommon to see police families in which one member of each new generation would enter the force. This picture has been changing and will continue to change. As criminal justice programs turn out thousands of graduates every year, an increasing number of police officers have at least some college education. In addition, affirmative action programs have slowly helped change the racial and gender composition of police departments to reflect community makeup. The following sections explore these changes in detail.

Demographic Makeup

With few exceptions, the personnel in most early police departments were white and male, a condition that persisted through most of the twentieth century. However, in most regions, the image of the police department as a bastion of white male dominance is either obsolete or rapidly changing. For more than 30 years, US police departments have made a concerted effort to attract women and minority police officers, and there have been some impressive gains.[3] Today, about 13 percent of all officers are female, and about 25 percent are members of minority groups.[4]

The reasons behind this effort are varied. Viewed in its most positive light, diversity initiatives by police departments are intended to field a more balanced force that truly represents the communities they serve. A heterogeneous police force can be instrumental in gaining the confidence of the community by helping dispel the view that police departments are generally bigoted or biased organizations.[5] Furthermore, women and minority police officers possess special qualities that can serve to improve police performance. Spanish-speaking officers can facilitate investigations in Hispanic neighborhoods, and Asian officers are essential for undercover or surveillance work with Asian gangs and drug importers.

LO1 Summarize demographic trends in policing

Minority Police Officers

The earliest known date of when an African American was hired as a police officer was 1861 in Washington, DC; Chicago hired its first African American officer in 1872.[6] By 1890, an estimated 2,000 minority police officers were employed in the United States. At first, African American officers suffered a great deal of discrimination. Their work assignments were restricted, as were their chances for promotion. Minority officers were

Cleveland police chief Calvin Williams, right, is congratulated by Mayor Frank Jackson after a ceremony at City Hall. Williams succeeded Michael McGrath, who became the new public safety director.

often assigned solely to patrolling African American neighborhoods, and, in some cities, they were required to call a white officer to make an arrest. Racial prejudice was common among white officers, and as late as the 1950s, some refused to ride with African Americans in patrol cars.[7]

The experience of African American police officers has not been an easy one. In his classic 1969 book *Black in Blue,* Nicholas Alex pointed out that African American officers of the time suffered from what he called **double marginality**.[8] On the one hand, African American officers had to deal with the expectation that they would give members of their own race preferential treatment. On the other hand, black officers were the target of institutional racism. Alex found that African American officers adapted to these pressures in a range of ways, from denying that African American suspects should be treated differently from whites, to treating African American offenders more harshly than white offenders in order to prove their lack of bias.

Much has changed over the years. Minority police officers now seem as self-assured as white officers.[9] They may even be more willing than white officers to use their authority to take official action: the higher the percentage of black officers on the force, the higher the arrest rate for crimes such as assault.[10] Unfortunately, though, minority officers appear to be experiencing some of the same problems and issues encountered by white officers.[11] They report feeling similar rates of job-related stress and strain stemming from the same types of stressors, such as family conflict.[12] What is more, minority officers do report more stress when they consider themselves "tokens" or marginalized within the department.[13]

Women in Policing

In 1910, Alice Stebbins Wells became the first woman to hold the title of police officer (in Los Angeles) and to have arrest powers.[14] For more than half a century, female officers endured separate criteria for selection, were assigned menial tasks, and were denied the opportunity for advancement.[15] Some relief was gained with the passage of the 1964 Civil Rights Act and its subsequent amendments. Courts have consistently supported the addition of women to police forces by striking down entrance requirements that eliminated almost all female candidates but could not be proved to predict job performance, such as criteria involving height and upper-body strength.[16] (Women do not do as well as men on strength tests and are much more likely to fail the entrance physical than male recruits;

double marginality The social burden African American police officers carry by virtue of being both minority group members and law enforcement officers.

REALITY CHECK

MYTH OR REALITY?

Male police officers believe that female police officers can perform the job just as well as they can.

MYTH. Although there are certainly exceptions, survey research reveals that male officers tend to view policing as mainly a masculine profession.

Are these perceptions changing? What positive traits and characteristics do female officers bring to the job that male officers may not?

critics contend that many of these tests do not reflect the actual tasks of police on the job.[17]) Nonetheless, the role of women in police work is still restricted by social and administrative barriers that have been difficult to remove. According to the most recent data, as we have noted, women make up more than 11 percent of officers, up from 7.6 percent in 1987.[18]

Studies of policewomen indicate that many are still struggling for acceptance, believe that they do not receive equal credit for their job performance, and even report sexual harassment by their coworkers.[19] One reason for this may be that many male police officers tend to view policing as an overtly masculine profession that is not appropriate for women. Surveys of male officers show that many do not think women can handle the physical requirements of the job as well as men can.[20] Female police officers may also be targeted for more disciplinary action by administrators and, if cited, are more likely

CAREERS IN CRIMINAL JUSTICE POLICE OFFICER

Duties and Characteristics of the Job

- Police officers are responsible for enforcing the written laws and ordinances of their jurisdiction.

- Police officers patrol within their jurisdiction and respond to calls wherever police attention is needed.

- Duties can be routine, such as writing a speeding ticket, or more involved, such as responding to a domestic disturbance or investigating a robbery.

- Nonpatrol duties include testifying in court and writing reports of their law enforcement actions.

- Some officers will choose or be chosen to work in specialized units such as the well-known special weapons and tactics (SWAT) or canine corps (K9).

- Police officers patrol jurisdictions of various sizes and have varying duties based on the nature of their jurisdiction. For example, sheriffs and their deputies enforce the laws within a county. State police primarily patrol state highways and respond to calls for backup from police units across their respective state. Institutions such as colleges and universities often have their own police forces as well, which enforce laws and rules in this specific area.

- Police work can be an intense and stressful job; it sometimes entails encounters with hostile and potentially violent people. Police are asked to put their lives on the line to preserve order and safety. Their actions are watched closely and reflect upon their entire department.

- Because the places that police protect must be watched at all times, police work shifts that may fall on weekends and holidays. Quite often, it is the younger police officers who take these less desirable shifts. Additionally, police officers will often have to work overtime; 45-hour workweeks are common.

Job Outlook

- Government spending ultimately determines how many officers a department has.

- Overall opportunities in local police departments will be good for individuals who meet the psychological, personal, and physical qualifications. In addition to openings from employment growth, many openings will be created by the need to replace workers who retire and those who leave local agencies for federal jobs and private-sector security jobs.

- Police work is appealing to many because of the good benefits and retirement policies.

- For the better-paying positions, there may be more applicants than available positions. This competition means those with qualifications such as a college education will have better chances of being hired.

- After several years, those with a reputation for good work as well as the proper education can rise in the ranks of their department

or be assigned to other desirable positions such as detective or investigator.

Salary

- Police patrol officers have median annual wages of approximately $57,000. The lowest 10 percent earned less than $33,000, and the highest 10 percent earned $93,000 and beyond.

- The median annual wage for detectives and investigators is $74,300. Chiefs and those in administrative posts make more money, often well in excess of six figures in larger cities.

Qualifications

- To be a police officer, you must be in good shape mentally and physically, as well as meet certain education requirements and pass written tests.

- New police officers go through rigorous training and testing—normally in the form of a local police academy for 12 to 14 weeks—before they go out on the streets.

- During training, new officers learn diverse skills that will be necessary for their job, such as knowledge of laws and individual rights, self-defense, and first aid. Applicants can also expect to be asked to pass lie detector and drug tests.

- Because of the enormous responsibility associated with being a police officer, certain personal qualities are considered key for future officers, such as responsibility, good communications skills, good judgment, and the ability to make quick decisions.

Education and Training

- In most cases, a high school diploma is required to be a police officer, but more and more jurisdictions are requiring at least some college education.

- Although some college credits are enough to obtain a position on the police force, more education (generally in the form of a bachelor's degree in a relevant field, especially criminal justice) is necessary to be promoted and move up in rank.

Reality Check

- Generally more opportunities for employment are available in larger departments, usually in larger urban or suburban areas.

- Not surprisingly, most opportunities exist in areas with comparatively higher crime rates or lower salaries.

Sources: Bureau of Labor Statistics, US Department of Labor, "Police and Detectives," *Occupational Outlook Handbook*, http://www.bls.gov/ooh/protective-service/police-and-detectives.htm (accessed February 2015); *Princeton Review*, "Police Officer/Manager," http://www.princetonreview.com/Careers.aspx?cid=120 (accessed February 2015).

to receive harsher punishments than male officers—that is, a greater percentage receive punishments more severe than a reprimand.[21]Considering the sometimes-hostile reception they get from male colleagues and supervisors, it may not come as a surprise that female officers report significantly higher levels of job-related stress than male officers.[22]

Despite these problems, the future of women in policing grows brighter every year.[23] Female officers want to remain in policing because it pays a good salary, offers job security, and is a challenging and exciting occupation.[24] These factors should continue to bring women to policing for years to come, but it is doubtful that we will see gender parity any time soon.[25]

LO2 Explain how minority and female officers act and are treated

Educational Characteristics

Even though most law enforcement agencies still do not require recruits to have a college degree, the number of agencies that require advanced education in the hiring and promotion process is growing. Today, about one-third of all police departments require at least some type of college for new recruits, more than three times the number in 1990.[26]

What type of major are police departments looking for? About half the surveyed departments expressed a preference for criminal justice majors, most often because of their enhanced knowledge of the entire criminal justice system and of issues that arise in policing. What are the benefits of higher education for police officers? Better communication with the public, especially minority and ethnic groups, is believed to be one benefit. Educated officers write better and more clearly and are more likely to be promoted. Police administrators believe that education enables officers to perform more effectively, generate fewer citizen complaints, show more initiative in performing police tasks, and generally act more professionally.[27] In addition, educated officers are less likely to have disciplinary problems and are viewed as better decision makers.[28] Higher education is also associated with greater self-confidence.[29]

The Police Profession

All professions have unique characteristics that distinguish them from other occupations and institutions. Policing is no exception. Police experts have long sought to understand the unique nature of the police experience and to determine how the challenges of police work shape the field and its employees. In this section, some of the factors that make policing unique are discussed in detail.

Police Culture

Police experts have found that the experience of becoming a police officer and the nature of the job itself cause most officers to band together in a police subculture, characterized by cynicism, clannishness, secrecy, and insulation from others in society—the so-called blue curtain. Police officers tend to socialize with one another and believe that their occupation cuts them off from relationships with civilians. Joining the police subculture means always having to stick up for fellow officers against outsiders; maintaining a tough, macho exterior; and distrusting the motives and behavior of outsiders.[30] The code of silence demands that officers never turn in their peers, even if they engage in corrupt or illegal practices.[31]

Some police experts have described the following core beliefs as the heart of the police culture today:

cynicism The belief that most people's actions are motivated solely by personal needs and selfishness.

blue curtain The secretive, insulated police culture that isolates officers from the rest of society.

- *Police are the only real crime fighters.* The public wants the police officer to fight crime; other agencies, both public and private, only play at crime fighting.
- *No one else understands the real nature of police work.* Lawyers, academics, politicians, and the public in general have little concept of what it means to be a police officer.
- *Loyalty to colleagues counts above everything else.* Police officers have to stick together because everyone is out to get the police and make the job more difficult.
- *It is impossible to win the war against crime without bending the rules.* Courts have awarded criminal defendants too many civil rights.

REALITY. Many officers feel that the public neither understands nor fully appreciates what they do. There are exceptions to this view, but it remains a fairly common characteristic of police culture.

Police officers tend to move in the same circles. What are the implications of this for relations between police and the public and for policing effectiveness?

- *Members of the public are basically unsupportive and unreasonably demanding.* People are quick to criticize police unless they themselves need police help.
- *Patrol work is the pits.* Detective work is glamorous and exciting.[32]

The forces that support a police culture are generally believed to develop out of on-the-job experiences. Most officers, both male and female, originally join police forces because they want to help people, fight crime, and have an interesting, exciting, prestigious career with a high degree of job security.[33] Recruits often find that the social reality of police work does not mesh with their original career goals. They are unprepared for the emotional turmoil and conflict that accompany police work today.

Some experts fear that the police culture divides officers from the people they serve and creates an "us against the world" mentality, an independent police culture in which violations of the law may result in stigmatization of offenders and lead to a leveling of sanctions against those who occupy the "other" status.[34] Criminals are referred to as "terrorists" and "predators," terms that suggest they are evil individuals eager to prey upon the poor and vulnerable. This vision may encourage and promote violence and brutality.

At first glance, the existence of an independent police subculture seems damaging, but it may also have some benefits. Membership in the police culture helps recruits adjust to the rigors of police work and provides the emotional support needed for survival.[35] The culture encourages decisiveness in the face of uncertainty and the ability to make split-second judgments that may later be subject to extreme criticism. Officers who view themselves as crime fighters are the ones most likely to value solidarity and depend on the support and camaraderie of their fellow officers.[36] The police subculture encourages its members to draw a sharp distinction between good and evil. Officers, more than mere enforcers of the law, are warriors in the age-old battle between right and wrong.[37] Police officers perceive their working environment to be rife with danger, an outlook that reinforces cohesion among officers.[38] And because criminals—"predators"—represent a real danger, the police culture demands that its members be both competent and concerned with the safety of their peers and partners.[39]

In sum, the police culture has developed in response to the insulated, dangerous lifestyle of police officers. Policing is a dangerous occupation, and the unquestioned support and loyalty of their peers is not something officers could readily do without.[40] Although it is feared that an independent police culture may isolate police officers from the community and make them suspicious and mistrustful of the public they serve, it may also unify the police and improve the camaraderie and solidarity among fellow officers.

The Police Personality

To some commentators, the typical police personality can be described as dogmatic, authoritarian, and suspicious.[41] Cynicism has been found at all levels of policing (including chiefs of police) and throughout all stages of a police career.[42] These negative values and attitudes are believed to cause police officers to be secretive and isolated from the rest of society, weaving the blue curtain.[43]

How does cynicism develop? The police officer's working personality is shaped by constant exposure to danger and the need to use force and authority to defuse and control threatening situations.[44] Police feel suspicious of the public they serve and defensive about the actions of their fellow officers. There are two opposing viewpoints on the cause of this phenomenon. One is that police departments attract recruits who are by nature cynical, authoritarian, secretive, and so on.[45] Other experts maintain that socialization and experience on the police force itself cause these character traits to develop in officers. According to this view, as their experiences in the separate police culture develops, officers eventually embrace a unique set of personality traits that distinguishes them from the average citizen.[46]

Despite popular belief and some research support, efforts to find and identify a classic "police personality" have had mixed results. Although some research concludes that police values are different from those of the general adult population, other efforts reach an opposite conclusion: some have found that police officers are actually more psychologically healthy than the general population, less depressed and anxious, and more social and assertive.[47] Police officers have been found to value such personality traits as warmth, flexibility, and emotion; these qualities are far removed from rigidity and cynicism.[48]

LO3 Explain police culture and personality

EXHIBIT 6.1

The Four Basic Styles of Policing

The Crime Fighter To the crime fighter, the most important aspects of police work are investigating serious crimes and apprehending criminals. Crime fighters focus on the victim and view effective police work as the only force that can keep society's "dangerous classes" in check. They are the thin blue line protecting society from murderers and rapists. They consider property crimes to be less significant and believe that such matters as misdemeanors, traffic control, and social service functions would be better handled by other agencies of government. The ability to investigate criminal behavior that poses a serious threat to life and safety, combined with the power to arrest criminals, separates a police department from other municipal agencies. Crime fighters see diluting these functions with minor social service and non-enforcement duties as harmful to police efforts to create a secure society.

The Social Agent The social agent believes that police should be involved in a wide range of activities without regard for their connection to law enforcement. Rather than viewing themselves as "criminal catchers," the social agents consider themselves as community problem solvers. They are troubleshooters who patch the holes that appear where the social fabric wears thin. They are happy to work with special-needs populations, such as the homeless, school kids, and those in need of emergency services. The social agent fits well in a community policing unit.

The Law Enforcer According to this view, duty is clearly set out in law. Law enforcers stress playing it "by the book." Because the police are specifically charged with apprehending all types of lawbreakers, they see themselves as generalized law enforcement agents. Although law enforcers may prefer working on serious crimes—because they are more intriguing and rewarding in terms of achievement, prestige, and status—they see the police role as one of enforcing all statutes and ordinances. They perceive themselves neither as community social workers nor as vengeance-seeking vigilantes: quite simply, they are professional law enforcement officers who perform the functions of detecting violations, identifying culprits, and taking the lawbreakers before a court. The law enforcer is devoted to the profession of police work and is the officer most likely to aspire to command rank.

The Watchman The watchman style is characterized by an emphasis on maintaining public order as the police goal, rather than law enforcement or general service. Watchmen choose to ignore many infractions and requests for service unless they believe that the social or political order is jeopardized. Juveniles are "expected" to misbehave and are best ignored or treated informally. Motorists will often be left alone if their driving does not endanger or annoy others. Vice and gambling are problems only when the currently accepted standards of public order are violated. Like the watchman of old, this officer takes action only when and if a problem arises. The watchman is the most passive officer, more concerned with retirement benefits than crime rates.

Sources: William Muir, *Police: Streetcorner Politicians* (Chicago: University of Chicago Press, 1977); James Q. Wilson, *Varieties of Police Behavior* (Cambridge, MA: Harvard University Press, 1968).

Because research has found evidence supportive of both viewpoints, it is not possible to determine how the police personality develops—or even whether one actually exists.

Policing Style

Part of the socialization of a police officer is developing a working attitude, or style, through which to approach policing. For example, some police officers may view the job as a well-paid civil service position that emphasizes careful compliance with written departmental rules and procedures. Other officers may see themselves as part of the "thin blue line" that protects the public from wrongdoers. They will use any means to get the culprit, even if it involves planting evidence on an obviously guilty person who has so far escaped arrest.

Several studies have attempted to define and classify police styles into behavioral clusters. An examination of this literature suggests that four styles of police work seem to fit the current behavior patterns of most police agents: the crime fighter, the social agent, the law enforcer, and the watchman (all described in Exhibit 6.1). Although officers who embrace a particular style of policing may emphasize one area of law enforcement over another, their daily activities are likely to require them to engage in some police duties they consider trivial or unimportant.

LO4 Identify distinct policing styles

Police Discretion

Police have the ability to deprive people of their liberty, arrest them and take them away in handcuffs, and even use deadly force to subdue them. A critical aspect of this professional responsibility is the personal **discretion** each officer has in carrying out his or her responsibilities. Discretion can involve selective enforcement of the law—as occurs, for instance, when a vice squad plainclothes officer decides not to take action against a tavern that is serving drinks after hours. Patrol officers use discretion when they decide to arrest one suspect for disorderly conduct but to escort another home.

discretion The use of personal decision making and choice in carrying out operations in the criminal justice system. For example, police discretion can involve deciding whether to make an arrest; prosecutorial discretion can involve deciding whether to accept a plea bargain.

emotional intelligence The capability of monitoring one's own feelings and actions in order to guide action.

The majority of police officers use a high degree of personal discretion in carrying out daily tasks, sometimes referred to as "low-visibility decision making" in criminal justice.[49] This terminology suggests that, unlike members of almost every other criminal justice agency, police are neither regulated in their daily procedures by administrative scrutiny nor subject to judicial review (except when their behavior clearly violates an offender's constitutional rights). The public recognizes the right of police to exercise discretion, even if it means using force to control an unruly suspect while treating a more cooperative one with deference and respect.[50]

The concept of **emotional intelligence** has important implications for the study of police discretion. Defined as the "ability to monitor one's own and others' feelings and emotions, to discriminate among them and to use this information to guide one's thinking and actions,"[51] emotional intelligence is critically important for police officers. Being in tune with one's emotions, being able to act in an emotionally mature fashion, and managing one's own mental state during difficult encounters can make all the difference in responding to the many situations that make policing a unique profession. Only recently has emotional intelligence training begun working its way into police training curricula.[52]

Researchers have identified a number of factors that affect police decision making.[53] The following sections describe the factors that influence police discretion and review suggestions for its control.

Legal Factors

Police discretion is inversely related to the severity of the offense. This means police have far less personal discretion when they confront a suspect in a case involving murder or rape than when the offense is a simple assault or trespass.[54] For example, if a weapon is brandished or used, police are much more likely to respond with a formal arrest.[55] The likelihood of a police officer taking legal action, then, partly depends on how the individual officer views the severity of the offense.

Environmental Factors

The degree of discretion an officer will exercise is at least partially defined by the officer's living and working environment.[56] Police officers may work or dwell in a community culture that either tolerates eccentricities and personal freedoms or expects extremely conservative, professional, no-nonsense behavior on the part of its civil servants. Communities that are proactive and include progressive governmental institutions also may influence a police officer's discretion. Police officers in communities that provide training in domestic violence prevention and maintain local shelters for battered women are more likely to take action in cases involving spousal abuse.[57]

Departmental Factors

Where and how the department operates also shape police practices. For example, officers are more likely to be proactive and use their arrest powers when they work in departments that are located in high-crime areas but have relatively few personnel.[58] In these departments, individual officers may believe they have to be proactive to compensate for the lack of resources. Departments also issue directives intended to influence police conduct, such as mandatory arrest policies for certain crimes.

Peer Factors

Police discretion is also subject to peer influence.[59] Police officers turn to their peers for both on-the-job advice and off-the-job companionship, essentially forming a subculture

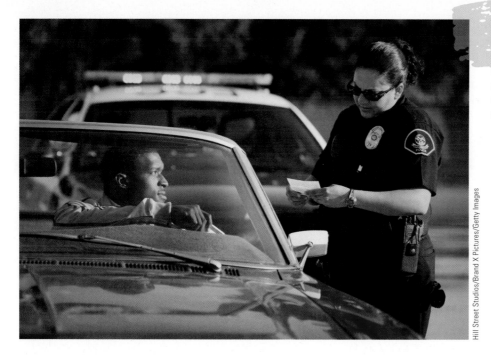

Police officers have a good deal of latitude to decide whether, as in the scenario depicted here, to issue a traffic citations. What are the benefits and drawbacks that go along with this and other forms of police discretion?

to provide a source of status, prestige, and reward. The peer group affects how police officers exercise discretion on two distinct levels. In an obvious, direct manner, other police officers dictate acceptable responses to street-level problems by providing or withholding approval in office discussions. Second, officers who take their job seriously and desire the respect and friendship of others will take their advice, abide by their norms, and seek out the most experienced and influential patrol officers on the force to adopt as behavior models.

Situational Factors

Some research efforts find that police officers rely on **demeanor** (the attitude and appearance of the offender) in making decisions.[60] That is, if an offender is surly, talks back, or otherwise challenges the officer's authority, formal action is more likely to be taken.[61] Not everyone agrees, however. David Klinger, a police officer turned criminologist, maintains that demeanor may not be as much of a factor in shaping discretion as most others believe. Klinger believes that the average officer becomes used to surly demeanor and uncivil behavior, so it takes more than that to influence discretion.[62]

The way a crime or situation is encountered may also influence discretion. When a police officer stumbles on an altercation or break-in, the discretionary response may be different from the response when the officer is summoned by police radio. If an act has received official police recognition, such as the dispatch of a patrol car, police action must be taken or an explanation made as to why it was not. If a matter is brought to an officer's attention by a citizen observer, the officer can ignore the request and risk a complaint or take discretionary action.

Extralegal Factors

One oft-debated issue is whether police take race, class, and gender into account when making arrest decisions. Research results are mixed: Some studies show that the offender's age, gender, and racial characteristics are key determinants that shape the arrest process.[63] Others find that this unequal treatment is not a serious problem. For example, the gender gap in police arrests is closing; women are getting arrested for certain offenses (such as drunk driving) more than they ever have been in the past.[64]

Victim characteristics also appear to influence police action. For example, police are more willing to make an arrest when the victim is older, white, or affluent.[65] Neighborhood

demeanor The way in which a person outwardly manifests his or her personality.

L05 Describe factors that affect police discretion

factors matter, as well. Related to this is the relationship between the parties. If the victim and the offender know one another, there is less of a chance that an arrest will be made.[66]

One significant issue is whether race plays a role in the decision to stop, question, and search motorists, a practice referred to as racial profiling. There is evidence that minorities are searched more often than whites.[67] Yet a number of researchers have found little to no evidence of racial profiling.[68] Some argue that it can even be beneficial. How could profiling be beneficial? Two Harvard scholars, Mathias Risse and Richard Zeckhauser, have argued that a significant correlation exists between membership in certain racial groups and the propensity to commit certain crimes.[69]

✓ Problems of Policing

Law enforcement is not an easy job. The role ambiguity, social isolation, and threat of danger present in "working the street" are the police officer's constant companions. What effects do these strains have on police? This section discusses four of the most significant problems: job stress, fatigue, violence, and corruption.

Job Stress

The complexity of their role, the need to exercise prudent discretion, the threat of having to use violence and of having violence used against them, and isolation from the rest of society all take a toll on law enforcement officers. It is not surprising, then, that police officers experience tremendous stress, a factor that leads some to alcoholism, depression, and even suicide. Evidence shows that police officers are all too often involved in marital disputes and even incidents of domestic violence that may be linked to stress.[70] These developments are not lost on police officers, many of whom feel significant amounts of job-related stress, a condition that may undermine their enthusiasm and commitment.[71] Stress and burnout become part of the job. Stress may not be constant, but at some time during their career (usually the middle years), most officers will feel the effects of stress.[72]

CAUSES OF STRESS A number of factors have been associated with job stress.[73] The pressure of being on duty 24 hours a day leads to stress and emotional detachment from both work and public needs. Policing is a dangerous profession, and officers are at risk for many forms of job-related accidental deaths. Stress has been related to internal conflict with administrative policies that deny officers support and a meaningful role in decision making. Some officers may become stressed when they are forced to adapt to the demands of community-oriented policing but are skeptical about the utility or effectiveness of this change in policy.[74] In addition, police suffer stress in their personal lives when they "bring the job home" or when their work hours are shifted, causing family disruptions.[75] Those who feel alienated from family and friends at home are more likely to feel stress on the job.[76]

Other stressors include poor training, substandard equipment, inadequate pay, lack of opportunity, job dissatisfaction, role conflict, exposure to brutality, and fears about competence, success, and safety.[77] Some officers may feel stress because they believe that the court system favors the rights of the criminal and handcuffs the police; others may be sensitive to a perceived lack of support from governmental officials and the general public.[78] Some officers even believe that their superiors care little about their welfare.[79]

The effects of stress can be shocking. Police work has been related to both physical and psychological ailments.[80] Police have a high rate of premature death caused by such conditions as heart disease and diabetes. They also experience a disproportionate number of divorces and other marital problems. Research indicates that police officers in some departments, but not all, have higher suicide rates than the general public.[81] Police who feel stress may not be open to adopting new ideas and programs such as community policing.[82]

COMBATING STRESS Research efforts have shown that the more support police officers get in the workplace, the lower their feelings of stress and anxiety.[83] Consequently, departments have attempted to fight job-related stress by training officers to cope with its effects. Today stress training includes diet information, biofeedback, relaxation and meditation, and exercise. Many departments include stress management as part of an overall wellness program also designed to promote physical and mental health, fitness, and good nutrition.[84] Some programs have included family members; they may be better able to help the officer cope if they fully understand the difficulties of police work. Total wellness programming enhances the physical and emotional well-being of officers by emphasizing preventive physical and psychological measures.[85] And because police are aware of the many benefits of their job and enjoy the quality of life it provides, stress-reduction programs can help officers focus on the positive aspects of police work.[86]

Fatigue

Nearly everyone has been tired at work from time to time. But whereas on-the-job sleepiness is inconsequential for many workers, it can lead to disaster for others. No one wants airline pilots to fall asleep, and the prospect of a truck driver sleeping behind the wheel is equally disturbing. What about a police officer? A police officer who is overly tired may be at a higher risk of acting inappropriately or being injured on the job.[87]

The problem of "tired cops"[88] has largely been overlooked, but it should not be.[89] Police officers often work lengthy shifts with unpredictable hours. The *Boston Globe* investigated one agency and found that 16 officers worked more than 80 hours in a week. One even worked 130 hours! Although it is difficult to fault anyone for seeking overtime pay, too much work can lead to disaster. Here are some examples:

- A Michigan police officer working nearly 24 hours straight crashes his cruiser while chasing a fleeing motorist. He is critically injured.
- In California, a sheriff's deputy working alone drifts off a deserted highway and is killed instantly when his patrol car crashes into a tree.
- An officer in Florida, who has had trouble staying awake, runs a red light in her patrol car and crashes into a van driven by a deputy sheriff, injuring him severely.
- A police officer driving home from working in Ohio nods off at the wheel, begins swerving in and out of traffic, and runs off the road, striking and killing a man jogging down the sidewalk.

CONTROLLING FATIGUE What can be done to control police fatigue? One option is for administrators to make special efforts during scheduling to ensure that officers do not work too much overtime. Another is for administrators to adopt policies that place

New York City police officers embrace outside of Christ Tabernacle Church, in the Glendale section of Queens, before funeral services for officer Rafael Ramos, in New York. Ramos and his partner, officer Wenjian Liu, were killed on December 20, 2014, as they sat in their patrol car on a Brooklyn street. The shooter, Ismaaiyl Brinsley, later killed himself.

AP Images/Julio Cortez

WEB APP 6.2 Read the report *Tired Cops: The Prevalence and Potential Consequences of Police Fatigue* at **https://www.ncjrs.gov /pdffiles1/jr000248d.pdf**. What else besides what is briefly discussed in this chapter can be done to control the problem of fatigue in law enforcement? Also visit the National Sleep Foundation site at **http:// sleepfoundation.org/sleep-topics /shift-work-and-sleep**, and research the effects of shift work on sleep-related issues and fatigue.

limitations on second jobs. Many officers moonlight as security guards, which may affect their on-the-job performance. A recent government report offered several other recommendations for limiting fatigue.

Violence and Brutality

Evidence shows that only a small proportion of officers are continually involved in use-of-force incidents. Why do these cops continually get involved in violent confrontations? Aggressive cops may overreact to the stress of police work and at the same time feel socially isolated. They believe that the true source of their frustration is beyond their reach, so they take their frustrations out on readily available targets: vulnerable people in their immediate environment.[90]

What kind of police officer gets involved in problem behavior? Are some officers "chronic offenders"? Research seems to show that a few officers are in fact chronic offenders who account for a significant portion of all citizen complaints. The officers receiving the bulk of complaints tend to be young and less experienced.[91] Efforts to deal with these "problem cops" are now being undertaken in police departments around the nation.

REALITY CHECK

MYTH OR REALITY?

Veteran police officers receive the most citizen complaints.

MYTH. Younger and less-experienced officers receive the most complaints.

Why do younger and less-experienced officers receive the most complaints? Can training solve the problem? If so, what kind of training: academy or on-the-job?

CURBING VIOLENCE Because incidents of brutality undermine efforts to build a bridge between police and the public, police departments around the United States have instituted specialized training programs to reduce them. A number of larger departments are instituting early warning systems to change the behavior of individual officers who have been identified as having performance problems. In most systems, problem officers are identified by their behavior profiles: citizen complaints, firearm discharge and use-of-force reports, civil litigation, incidents of resisting arrest, and high-speed pursuits and vehicular damage. The initial intervention generally consists of a review by the officer's immediate supervisor, who advises the officer of the sanctions he faces if problems continue; some cases are referred to counseling, training, or police psychologists. Evaluations of early warning programs indicate that they are quite successful.[92]

Some departments have developed administrative policies that emphasize limiting the use of force and containing armed offenders until specially trained backup teams are sent to take charge of the situation. Administrative policies have been found to be an effective control on use of deadly force, and their influence can be enhanced if they are clearly supported by the chief of police.[93]

Some cities are taking an aggressive, proactive stance to curb violent cops. Since 1977, the New York Police Department has been operating a Force-Related Integrity Testing program in which undercover officers pose as angry citizens in elaborate sting operations intended to weed out officers with a propensity for violence. In a typical encounter, officers responding to a radio call on a domestic dispute confront an aggressive husband who spews hatred at everyone around, including the police. The "husband" is actually an undercover officer from the internal affairs bureau, who is testing whether the officers, some of whom have a history of civilian complaints, will respond to verbal abuse with threats or violence. The NYPD along with other law enforcement agencies around the country carry out a variety of integrity tests on their officers to help promote highly professional standards of conduct.[94]

Perhaps the greatest factors in controlling the use of **police brutality** are the threat of civil judgments against individual officers who use excessive force, police chiefs who ignore or condone violent behavior, and the expectations that prevail in the cities and towns in which they are employed.

Corruption

Ever since their creation, US police departments have wrestled with the problem of controlling illegal and unprofessional behavior by their officers. **Corruption** pervaded the American police when the early departments were first formed. In the nineteenth century, police officers systematically ignored violations of laws related to drinking, gambling, and prostitution in return for regular payoffs. Some actually entered into relationships

police brutality Usually involves such actions as the use of abusive language, the unnecessary use of force or coercion, threats, prodding with nightsticks, stopping and searching people to harass them, and so on.

corruption Exercising legitimate discretion for improper reasons or using illegal means to achieve approved goals.

with professional criminals, especially pick-pockets. Illegal behavior was tolerated in return for goods or information. Police officers helped politicians gain office by allowing electoral fraud to flourish; some senior officers sold promotions to higher rank in the department. [95] Although most police officers are not corrupt, the few who are dishonest bring discredit to the entire profession.

VARIETIES OF CORRUPTION Police deviance can include a number of activities. In a general sense, it involves misuse of authority by police officers in a manner designed to yield personal gain for themselves or others. [96] However, debate continues over whether a desire for personal gain is an essential part of corruption. Some experts argue that police misconduct also involves such issues as the unnecessary use of force, unreasonable searches, or an immoral personal life and that these should be considered just as serious as corruption motivated by economic gain.

Scholars have attempted to create typologies categorizing the forms that the abuse of police powers can take. When investigating corruption among police officers in New York City, the **Knapp Commission** classified abusers into two categories: **meat eaters** and **grass eaters**. Meat eaters aggressively misuse police power for personal gain by demanding bribes, threatening legal action, or cooperating with criminals. In contrast, grass eaters accept payoffs when their everyday duties place them in a position to "look the other way."

Other police experts have attempted to create models to better understand police corruption. It may be possible to divide police corruption into four major categories, as depicted in Exhibit 6.2.

CAUSES OF CORRUPTION No single explanation satisfactorily accounts for the various forms the abuse of power takes. One view holds that policing tends to attract individuals who do not have the financial means to maintain a coveted middle-class lifestyle. As they develop the cynical, authoritarian police personality, accepting graft seems an all-too-easy method of achieving financial security. A second view is that the wide discretion police enjoy, coupled with low visibility among the public and their own supervisors, makes them likely candidates for corruption. A third perspective holds that corruption is a function of society's ambivalence toward many forms of vice-related criminal behavior that police officers are sworn to control. Unenforceable laws governing moral standards promote corruption because they create large groups with an interest in undermining law enforcement. These include consumers who do not want to be deprived of their chosen form of recreation—people who gamble, want to drink after the legal closing hour, or patronize prostitutes.

CONTROL OF CORRUPTION How can police misconduct be controlled? One approach is to strengthen the internal administrative review process in police departments. A strong and well-supported internal affairs division has been linked to lowered corruption rates. [97] Another approach, instituted by then New York Commissioner Patrick Murphy in the wake of the Knapp Commission, is the *accountability system*. This holds that supervisors at each level are directly accountable for the illegal behaviors of the officers under them. Consequently, a commander can be demoted or forced to resign if

Knapp Commission A public body that led an investigation into police corruption in New York and uncovered a widespread network of payoffs and bribes.

meat eaters A term for police officers who actively solicit bribes and vigorously engage in corrupt practices.

grass eaters A term for police officers who accept payoffs when everyday duties place them in a position to "look the other way."

Patrolman Michael Thomas Slager, pictured here, was charged with murder in the shooting death of a black motorist after a traffic stop. Slager was arrested and charged after law enforcement officials viewed a video of the shooting following a traffic stop.

Thousands of people are fatally shot by police each year.

MYTH. Fatal police shootings are very rare. On the order of 350 to 400 people are fatally shot each year.

Media portrayals in the news and on television make it seem that police shootings are more common. Why? What are the implications for police work of a view that police shootings are more common than they really are?

LO6 Discuss four major problems of policing

deadly force Force that is likely to cause death or bodily harm.

suicide by cop A form of suicide in which a person acts in an aggressive manner with police officers in order to induce them to shoot to kill.

nondeadly force Force that is unlikely to cause death or significant bodily harm.

TABLE 6.1 Police response in encounters with citizens in which use of force was reported

Type of force used or threatened by police	Percent
Pushed or grabbed	53.5
Kicked or hit	12.6
Sprayed chemical/pepper spray	4.9
Electroshock weapon (stun gun)	4.1
Pointed gun	25.6
Threatened force	76.6
Shouted at resident	75.5
Cursed at resident	39.1
Number (in thousands)	**574**

Source: Christine Eith and Matthew R. Durose, *Contacts between Police and the Public, 2008* (Bureau of Justice Statistics, 2011), p. 13, http://bjs.ojp.usdoj.gov/content/pub/pdf /cpp08.pdf. Percentages do not sum to 100 because some people reported, in cases where force was used, that officers used more than one type of force.

someone under his or her command is found guilty of corruption.[98] Close scrutiny by a department, however, can lower officer morale and create the impression that the officers' own supervisors distrust them.

Another approach is to create outside review boards or special prosecutors, such as the Mollen Commission in New York and the Christopher Commission in Los Angeles, to investigate reported incidents of corruption. However, outside investigators and special prosecutors are often limited by their lack of intimate knowledge of day-to-day operations. As a result, they depend on the testimony of a few officers who are willing to cooperate, either to save themselves from prosecution or because they have a compelling moral commitment. Outside evaluators also face the problem of the blue curtain, which is quickly drawn when police officers feel their department is under scrutiny.

Some jurisdictions have even developed review boards that monitor police behavior and tactics and investigate civilian complaints. Although police agencies in some communities have embraced citizen reviews, others find them troublesome. Departmental opposition is most likely when oversight procedures represent outside interference, oversight staff lack experience with and understanding of police work, and/or oversight processes are unfair. Despite serious reservations about citizen oversight, many law enforcement administrators have identified positive outcomes from having a review board in place. These include improving community relations, enhancing an agency's ability to police itself, and (most important) improving an agency's policies and procedures. Citizen oversight bodies can recommend changes in the way the department conducts its internal investigations into alleged misconduct and can also suggest ways to improve department policies governing officer behavior.[99]

Use of Force

How much force is being used by the police in the United States today? Despite some highly publicized incidents that get a lot of media attention, research reveals that the use of force is not very common. A national survey on police contacts with civilians, sponsored by the federal government, sheds some light on this issue.[100] The following are among the survey's most important findings:

- An estimated 17 percent of US residents age 16 or older had a face-to-face contact with a police officer.
- Contact between police and the public was more common among males, whites, and younger residents.
- Overall, about 9 out of 10 persons who had contact with police felt officers acted properly.
  - An estimated 1.4 percent of people stopped by police had force used or threatened against them during their most recent contact.
  - Blacks and Hispanics were two to three more times likely than whites to be searched during traffic stops.[101]

The data indicate that (1) relatively few contacts with police and the public involve physical force, but (2) there seem to be race and ethnic differences in the rate at which force is applied. As Table 6.1 shows, half of the force incidents involved more than scuffling or shouting. And even though African Americans (82 percent) were less likely than whites (91 percent) to feel that the police acted properly during a contact, the great majority of citizens of all races considered police behavior to be appropriate given the circumstances of the contact.

Deadly Force

As it is commonly used, the term **deadly force** refers to the actions of a police officer who shoots and kills a suspect who flees from arrest, assaults a victim, or attacks an officer.[102] The justification for the use of deadly force can be traced to English common law, in which almost every criminal offense was a felony and bore the death penalty. The use of deadly force in the course of arresting a felon was considered expedient, saving the state the trouble of conducting a trial (the "fleeing-felon rule").[103]

Although the media depict hero cops in a constant stream of deadly shootouts in which scores of bad guys are killed, the actual number of people killed by the police each year is usually between 400 and 250.[104] And some of these shootings may even be precipitated by the target as a form of suicide.[105] This tragic event has become so common that the term suicide by cop has been coined to denote victim-precipitated killings by police.[106]

CONTROLLING DEADLY FORCE Because the police use of deadly force is such a serious issue, ongoing efforts have been made to control it. One of the most difficult issues in controlling the problem was the continued use of the fleeing-felon rule in a number of states. In 1985, the Supreme Court outlawed the indiscriminate use of deadly force with its decision in *Tennessee v. Garner*. In this case, the Court ruled that the use of deadly force against apparently unarmed and nondangerous fleeing felons is an illegal seizure of their person under the Fourth Amendment. Deadly force may not be used unless it is necessary to prevent an escape, and the officer has probable cause to believe that the suspect poses a significant threat of death or serious injury to the officer or others. The majority opinion stated that where the suspect poses no immediate threat to the officer and no threat to others, the harm resulting from failing to apprehend the suspect does not justify the use of deadly force to do so: "A police officer may not seize an unarmed, nondangerous suspect by shooting him dead."[107]

Individual state jurisdictions still control police shooting policy. Some states have adopted statutory policies that restrict the police use of violence. Others have upgraded training in the use of force. So-called "force continuums" have been adopted by a number of police departments, but they are gradually giving way to an "objective reasonableness" standard, which is discussed further in the nondeadly force section below. Also see Figure 6.1 for a "ranking" of types of force, from least to most serious.

Another way to control police shootings is through internal review and policy making by police administrative review boards. For example, since 1972, the New York City Police Department has conducted an internal investigation any time an officer's weapon is discharged (within the exception of training situations). Several dispositions are possible. These can range from a conclusion that the shooting was in accordance with law and policy, all the way to termination and even criminal prosecution (if the prosecutor feels criminal charges are merited). The review board approach is controversial because it can mean that the department recommends that one of its own officers be turned over for criminal prosecution.[108]

Nondeadly Force

Nondeadly force is force that is unlikely to cause death or significant bodily harm. Nondeadly force can range from the use of handcuffs and suspect compliance techniques to rubber bullets and stun guns. Officers resort to nondeadly force in a number of circumstances. They may begin with verbal commands and then escalate the force used when confronted with a resistant suspect. Researchers have found that the crime in question is strongly linked to the type of nondeadly force used and that officers are also influenced by past experience, the presence of other officers, and the presence and behavior of bystanders.[109] And even though nondeadly force is used more often than deadly force, it is still relatively rare—and at the lower end of the

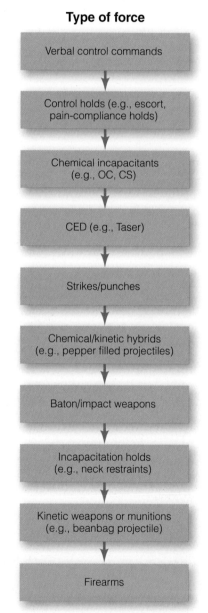

Type of force

Verbal control commands

Control holds (e.g., escort, pain-compliance holds)

Chemical incapacitants (e.g., OC, CS)

CED (e.g., Taser)

Strikes/punches

Chemical/kinetic hybrids (e.g., pepper filled projectiles)

Baton/impact weapons

Incapacitation holds (e.g., neck restraints)

Kinetic weapons or munitions (e.g., beanbag projectile)

Firearms

FIGURE 6.1 **Relative Ranking of Force Types**

Source: Adapted from Michael R. Smith, Robert J. Kaminski, Geoffrey P. Alpert, Lorie A. Fridell, John MacDonald, and Bruce Kubu, *A Multi-Method Evaluation of Police Use of Force Outcomes: Final Report to the National Institute of Justice* (Washington, DC: National Institute of Justice, 2010), Table 3-13, p. 3-22, https://www.ncjrs.gov/pdffiles1 /nij/grants/231176.pdf

Kristine Biggs Johnson breaks down as her attorney, Bob Sykes, plays a YouTube video from a law enforcement dash camera when she was shot in the eye. She filed a lawsuit against a Morgan County Sheriff's (Utah) deputy for improper use of deadly force against her. The shooting was deemed unjustified by Davis County Attorney Troy Rawlings, but no charges were filed against the deputy.

AP Images/Al Hartmann/The Salt Lake Tribune

LO7 Distinguish between deadly and nondeadly force—and methods for controlling each

severity scale (e.g., grabbed by officer instead of hit). Researchers have estimated that police use or threaten to use nondeadly force in only 1.7 percent of all contacts and 20 percent of all arrests.[110]

CONTROLLING NONDEADLY FORCE In *Graham v. Connor*, the Supreme Court ruled that issues related to nondeadly force must be judged from the standpoint of a reasonable officer (formally called "objective reasonableness").[111] For example, say an officer is approached in a threatening manner by someone wielding a knife. The assailant fails to stop when warned and is killed by the officer, but it turns out later that the shooting victim was deaf and could not hear the officer's command. The officer would not be held liable if, at the time of the incident, he had no way of knowing the person's disability.

less-lethal weapons Weapons designed to disable or immobilize rather than kill criminal suspects.

Less-Lethal Weapons

In the past few years, about a thousand local police forces have started using so-called less-lethal weapons to subdue certain suspects. Some of the most widely used less-lethal weapons are wood, rubber, or polyurethane bullets shot out of modified 37-mm pistols or 12-gauge shotguns. At short distances, officers use pepper spray and Tasers (see accompanying Contemporary Issues in Criminal Justice box), which deliver electric shocks with long wire tentacles, producing intense muscle spasms. Other technologies still in development include guns that shoot giant nets, guns that squirt sticky glue, and lights that can temporarily blind a suspect. New weapons are being developed that shoot bags filled with lead pellets; the weapons have a range of 100 feet and pack the wallop of a pro boxer's punch.[112]

LO8 Explain the importance of less-lethal weapons

Recent research efforts indicate that less-lethal weapons may help reduce police use of force.[113] Greater effort must be made to regulate these less-lethal weapons and create effective policies for their use.[114]

ETHICAL REFLECTION

Eric Garner Death

Officer Pantaleo had previously been sued, along with other officers, on three separate occasions for alleged use of excessive force. Two men received a payout of $15,000 each. The other two lawsuits were pending as of this writing. It is not uncommon for police officers to be sued, and New York City is no exception. Nevertheless, should the police department have reacted differently (e.g., dismissal instead of placement on desk duty) in light of Pantaleo's prior history? Why or why not?

Are Tasers Effective?

As Tasers have found their way into mainstream law enforcement use, researchers have been drawn to the question of whether they present an effective alternative to conventional use-of-force measures. This research has yielded a wide range of conclusions, ranging from very supportive to very critical. Staunch advocates of Tasers include the manufacturer and much of the law enforcement community. Critics include most notably Amnesty International, the human rights organization. It has been especially critical of Taser deaths. Most research findings fall somewhere between these extremes.

For example, research has shown that Tasers are more effective at incapacitating suspects than pepper spray. And as Eugene Paoline and his colleagues found, Taser use reduces officer injury compared to other force measures. Dozens of studies have also concluded that Tasers pose minimal risk of death or serious injury, but much of the research has been conducted in laboratory settings on animals and healthy human volunteers. In response to this limitation, Michael White and Justin Ready compared news reports of fatal and nonfatal Taser incidents. They found that suspect drug use, mental illness, and continued resistance were associated with Taser deaths, but they concluded that more research is necessary if we are ever to know for sure. In the meantime, they suggest the development of model policy guidelines for Taser use because the hope is that policy guidance for police can minimize any unfortunate consequences associated with Taser use. To this end, the Police Executive Research Forum has come up with several guiding principles for the proper use of Tasers and related CEDs:

1. ECWs [electronic control weapons] should be considered less-lethal weapons.

2. ECWs should be used as weapons of need, not a tool of convenience.

3. Officers should not over-rely on ECWs in situations where more effective and less risky alternatives are available.

4. ECWs are just one of a number of tools that police have available to do their jobs, and they should be considered one part of an agency's overall use-of-force policy.

5. In agencies that deploy ECWs, officers should receive comprehensive training on when and how to use ECWs.

6. Agencies should monitor their own use of ECWs and should conduct periodic analyses of practices and trends.

7. Agencies should consider the expectations of their community when developing an overall strategy for using ECWs.

A recent National Institute of Justice report on the safety of conducted energy devices (CED) concluded that use of the devices against healthy adults poses minimal risk of death or bodily injury. The report, which contained findings from a panel of experts, came to the following conclusion:

There is no conclusive medical evidence in the current body of research literature that indicates a high risk of serious injury or death to humans from the direct or indirect cardiovascular or metabolic effects of short-term CED exposure in healthy, normal, nonstressed, nonintoxicated persons. Field experience with CED use indicates that short-term exposure is safe in the vast majority of cases. The risk of death in a CED-related use-of-force incident is less than 0.25 percent, and it is reasonable to conclude that CEDs do not cause or contribute to death in the large majority of those cases.

Not everyone is convinced, however. The recent study published in the journal *Circulation*, featured at the beginning of this chapter, suggests that in certain cases, Taser use can induce cardiac arrest.

Sources: Taser International, www.taser.com/research-and-safety/field-use-and-statistics (accessed February 2015); Stricter Limits Urged as Deaths Following Police Taser Use Reach 500 (Amnesty International, 2012), www.amnesty.org/en/news/usa-stricter-limits-urged-deaths-following-police-taser-use-reach-500-2012-02-15 (accessed February 2015); Taser International, *Advanced Taser M26 Field Report Analysis* (Scottsdale, AZ: Taser International, 2002); Robert J. Kaminski, "Research on Conducted Energy Devices: Findings, Methods, and Possible Alternatives," *Criminology and Public Policy* 8 (2009): 903–913; Eugene Paoline, William Terrill, and Jason Ingram, "Police Use of Force and Officer Injuries: Comparing Conducted Energy Devices (CEDs) to Hands- and Weapons-Based Tactics," *Police Quarterly* 15 (2012): 115–136; Michael D. White and Justin Ready, "Examining Fatal and Nonfatal Incidents Involving the Taser," *Criminology and Public Policy* 8 (2009): 865–891; Police Executive Research Forum, *2011 Electronic Control Weapon Guidelines* (Washington, DC: Police Executive Research Forum, 2011), p. 11, https://www.amnesty.org/articles/news/2012/02/usa-stricter-limits-urged-deaths-following-police-taser-use-reach/ (accessed February 2015); National Institute of Justice, *Study of Deaths Following Electro-Muscular Disruption* (Washington, DC: National Institute of Justice, 2011), p. viii, www.ncjrs.gov/pdffiles1/nij/233432.pdf (accessed February 2015); Douglas Zipes, "Sudden Cardiac Arrest and Death Associated with Application of Shocks from a TASER Electronic Control Device," *Circulation*, April 30, 2012 (published online ahead of print).

Police Searches and Interrogations

The police are charged with preventing crime and, when crime does occur, with investigating the case, identifying the culprit, and making an arrest, all while gathering sufficient evidence to convict the culprit at trial. To carry out these tasks, police officers need to be able to search for evidence, to seize items such as guns and drugs, and to question suspects, witnesses, and victims, because at trial, they must provide prosecutors with sufficient evidence to prove guilt "beyond a reasonable doubt." This requirement means that soon after a crime is committed, they must make every effort to gather physical evidence, obtain confessions, and take witness statements that will stand up in court. Police officers also realize that evidence such as the testimony of a witness or a co-conspirator may evaporate before the trial begins. Then the outcome of the case may depend on some piece of physical evidence or a suspect's statement taken early during the investigation.

WEB APP 6.3 Visit the National Institute of Justice's website on the Taser at **http://www.nij.gov/topics/technology/less-lethal/conducted-energy-devices.htm**. Carefully read the section on "Safety of Conducted Energy Devices." Write an essay that answers the following question: Are Tasers safe? Be sure to explain what "weight" should be assigned to reporting from the National Institute of Justice relative to other organizations, such as Taser International, the device's manufacturer.

The need for police officers to gather evidence can conflict with the constitutional rights of citizens. For example, although police might prefer a free hand to search homes and cars for evidence, the Fourth Amendment restricts police activities by limiting searches and seizures to those deemed "reasonable." Likewise, when police want to vigorously interrogate a suspect, they must honor the Fifth Amendment's prohibition against forcing people to incriminate themselves. The following sections address some key areas in which police operations have been restricted or curtailed by the courts.

Interrogation and Confessions

After an arrest is made, police want to interrogate suspects, hoping they will confess to a crime, name co-conspirators, or make incriminating statements that can be used against them in court. But the Fifth Amendment guarantees people the right to be free from self-incrimination. The courts have used this phrase to prohibit law enforcement agents from using physical or psychological coercion while interrogating suspects to get them to confess or give information. Confessions obtained from defendants through coercion, force, trickery, or promises of leniency are inadmissible because their trustworthiness is questionable.

THE *MIRANDA* RULE In 1966, in the case of *Miranda v. Arizona*, the Supreme Court created objective standards for questioning by police after a defendant has been taken into custody.[115] Custody occurs when a person is not free to walk away, such as when an individual is arrested. The Court maintained that before the police can question a person who has been arrested or is in custody, they must inform the individual of his or her Fifth Amendment right to be free from self-incrimination. This is accomplished by the police issuing what is known as the *Miranda* warning, which informs the suspect of the following:

- He has the right to remain silent.
- If he makes a statement, it can be used against him in court.
- He has the right to consult an attorney and to have the attorney present at the time of the interrogation.
- If he cannot afford an attorney, one will be appointed by the state.

If the defendant is not given the *Miranda* warning before the investigation, the evidence obtained from the interrogation cannot be admitted at trial. An accused person can waive his or her *Miranda* rights at any time. For the waiver to be effective, however, the state must first show that the defendant was aware of all the *Miranda* rights and must then prove that the waiver was made with the full knowledge of constitutional rights. People who cannot understand the *Miranda* warning because of their age, mental handicaps, or language problems cannot be legally questioned without their attorney present; if they *can* understand their rights and then waive them, they may be questioned.[116] The Supreme Court has decided a number of *Miranda*-related cases over the years. The key cases are summarized in Exhibit 6.3.

Miranda is now a police (and a prime-time television) institution. It is not surprising that today police administrators who in the past might have been wary of the restrictions forced by *Miranda* now actually favor its use.[117] Yet in spite of its acceptance, critics have called the *Miranda* decision incomprehensible and difficult to administer. How can one tell when a confession is truly voluntary or when it has been produced by pressure and coercion? Aren't all police interrogations essentially coercive?[118] To ensure that *Miranda* rules are being followed, many departments now routinely videotape interrogations.[119] Nonetheless, the *Miranda* decision continues to be an important one.

Search and Seizure

When conducting investigations, police officers want to collect evidence, seize it, and carry it away. They may want to enter a suspect's home; look for evidence of a crime, such as bloody clothes, drugs, missing money, or a weapon; seize the evidence; and store it in the evidence room so it can later be used at trial. The manner in which police may seize

Miranda warning The requirement that police officers inform suspects subjected to custodial interrogation that they have a constitutional right to remain silent, that their statements can later be used against them in court, that they can have an attorney present to help them, and that the state will pay for an attorney if they cannot afford to hire one.

REALITY CHECK

MYTH OR REALITY?

The police are not required to advise all arrestees of their *Miranda* rights.

REALITY. *Miranda* rights need be read only when custody (such as arrest) is coupled with interrogation.

Police departments may adopt more restrictive policies, however, requiring Miranda warnings any time a person is arrested. Should the Miranda warnings be read every time a person is arrested?

At the police station of the 4th district, on Rampart Street, which separates the Red Zone of the French Quarter (New Orleans), two police officers interrogate a dealer who was arrested for drug and weapon possession. The man was facing 15 years in prison for being a repeat offender.

Patrick Chauvel/Corbis News/Corbis

EXHIBIT 6.3

Important Miranda-Related Decisions over the Years

***Fare v. Michael C.* (1978)** The *Miranda* warning applies only to the right to have an attorney present. The suspect cannot demand to speak to a priest, a probation officer, or any other official.[119]

***New York v. Quarles* (1984)** A suspect can be questioned in the field without a *Miranda* warning if the information the police seek is needed to protect public safety. For example, in an emergency, suspects can be asked where they hid their weapons.[121] This is known as the public safety doctrine.

***Oregon v. Elstad* (1985)** Admissions made in the absence of *Miranda* warnings are not admissible at trial, but post-*Miranda* voluntary statements (those made after the warnings are read) are admissible. A post-Miranda voluntary statement is admissible even if an initial incriminating statement was made in the absence of *Miranda* warnings.[122]

***Colorado v. Connelly* (1986)** The admissions of mentally impaired defendants can be admitted in evidence as long as the police acted properly, and there is a preponderance of evidence that the defendants understood the meaning of *Miranda*.[123]

***Moran v. Burbine* (1986)** An attorney's request to see the defendant does not affect the validity of the defendant's waiver of the right to counsel. Police misinformation to an attorney does not affect waiver of *Miranda* rights.[124] For example, a suspect's statements may be used if they are given voluntarily, even though his family has hired an attorney and the statements were made before the attorney arrived. Only the suspect can request an attorney, not his friends or family.

***Colorado v. Spring* (1987)** Suspects need not be aware of all the possible outcomes of waiving their rights for the *Miranda* warning to be considered properly given.[125]

***Minnick v. Mississippi* (1990)** When counsel is requested, interrogation must cease and cannot be resumed until an attorney is present.[126]

***Arizona v. Fulminante* (1991)** The erroneous admission of a coerced confession at trial can be ruled a harmless error that would not automatically result in overturning a conviction.[127]

***Davis v. United States* (1994)** A suspect who makes an ambiguous reference to an attorney during questioning, such as "Maybe I should talk to an attorney," is not protected under *Miranda*. The police may continue their questioning.[128]

***Chavez v. Martinez* (2003)** Failure to give a suspect a *Miranda* warning is not illegal unless the case becomes a criminal issue.[129]

***United States v. Patane* (2004)** A voluntary statement given in the absence of a *Miranda* warning can be used to obtain evidence that can be used at trial. Failure to give the warning does not make seizure of evidence illegal per se.[130]

***Missouri v. Seibert* (2004)** *Miranda* warnings must be given before interrogation begins. The accused in this case was interrogated and confessed in the absence of *Miranda* warnings. *Miranda* rights were then read, at which point the accused "re-confessed." The pre-*Miranda* questioning was improper.[131]

***Maryland v. Shatzer* (2010)** *Miranda* protections do not apply if a suspect is released from police custody for at least 14 days and then questioned. However, if the suspect is rearrested, then *Miranda* warnings must be read.[132]

***Florida v. Powell* (2010)** The *Miranda* warnings do not require that the suspect be advised that he or she has the right to have an attorney present during questioning. It is sufficient to advise the suspect that he or she has the right to talk with a lawyer before questioning and to consult a lawyer at any time during questioning.[133]

***Berghuis v. Thompkins* (2010)** Unless a suspect asserts his or her *Miranda* rights, any subsequent voluntary statements given after the warnings are admissible in court. Simply remaining silent does not imply that a suspect has invoked *Miranda* protection.[134]

***J.D.B. v. North Carolina* (2011)** Children may be more prone to confessing to crimes they did not commit, and this needs to be taken into consideration in deciding whether a police interrogation is also custodial. In other words, the suspect's age factors into the *Miranda* custody analysis.[135]

***Howes v. Fields* (2012)** A prisoner questioned about events that occurred prior to his or her incarceration is not considered "in custody" for *Miranda* purposes. In this case, Fields, the inmate, was free to walk away from questioning and go back to his cell.[136]

search warrant An order issued by a judge, directing officers to conduct a search of specified premises for specified objects or persons and bring them before the court.

probable cause The evidentiary criterion necessary to sustain an arrest or the issuance of an arrest or search warrant; less than absolute certainty or "beyond a reasonable doubt," but greater than mere suspicion or "hunch."

stop and frisk The situation when police officers who are suspicious of an individual run their hands lightly over the suspect's outer garments to determine whether the person is carrying a concealed weapon. Also called a patdown or threshold inquiry, a stop and frisk is intended to stop short of any activity that could be considered a violation of Fourth Amendment rights.

REALITYCHECK

MYTH OR REALITY?

Some warrantless searches are permissible as long as the police have probable cause.

REALITY. Certain types of warrantless searches are permissible, but not all of them. For example, it is never permissible for an officer, with probable cause but no warrant, to enter a private residence in the absence of exigent circumstances.

Has the Supreme Court created enough exceptions to the Fourth Amendment warrant requirement? Why or why not?

evidence is governed by the search-and-seizure requirements of the Fourth Amendment of the US Constitution, which was designed by the framers to protect a criminal suspect from unreasonable searches and seizures. Under normal circumstances, no search or seizure undertaken without a search warrant is lawful.

A **search warrant** is a court order authorizing and directing the police to search a designated place for evidence of a crime. To obtain a search warrant, the following procedural requirements must be met: (1) the police officer must request the warrant from the court; (2) the officer must submit an affidavit establishing the proper grounds for the warrant; and (3) the affidavit must state the place to be searched and the property to be seized.

A warrant cannot be issued unless the presiding magistrate is presented with sufficient evidence to conclude that an offense has been or is being committed and that the suspect is the one who committed the offense; this is referred to as the **probable cause** requirement. In other words, the presiding judge must conclude from the facts presented by the police that there is probable cause a crime has been committed and that the person or place to be searched is materially involved in that crime; there must be solid evidence of criminal involvement.

Searches must also be reasonable under the circumstances of the crime. Police would not be able to get a warrant to search a suspect's desk drawer for a missing piano! Nor could police obtain a warrant that allows them to tear down the walls of a person's house because it is suspected that they contain drugs. A search is considered unreasonable when it exceeds the scope of police authority or is highly invasive of personal privacy, even if it reveals incriminating evidence.

WARRANTLESS SEARCHES To make it easier for police to conduct investigations and to protect public safety, the Supreme Court has ruled that under certain circumstances, a valid search may be conducted without a search warrant. The six major exceptions are search incident to a valid arrest, stop and frisk, automobile search, consent search, plain-view search, and exigent circumstances, as described next.

- *Search incident to a valid arrest.* A warrantless search is valid if it is made incident to a lawful arrest. The reason for this exception is that the arresting officer must have the power to disarm the accused, protect himself or herself, preserve the evidence of the crime, and prevent the accused from escaping from custody. Because the search is lawful, the officer retains what he or she finds if it is connected with a crime. The officer is permitted to search only the defendant's person and the areas in the defendant's immediate physical surroundings that are under his or her control.[137] Interestingly, the Supreme Court recently decided that officers *cannot*, without a warrant, search digital information on a cell phone following a person's arrest.[138]

- *Stop and frisk.* In the landmark *Terry v. Ohio* decision, the Supreme Court held that police officers can perform a **stop and frisk** when they have reasonable suspicion to believe criminal activity is afoot. For example, say the individual is seen lurking outside a closed store and peering through the windows. In such a case, the officer has a right to stop and question the individual and, if the officer has reason to believe that the person is carrying a concealed weapon, may frisk the subject—that is, pat down the person's outer clothing for the purpose of finding a concealed weapon. If an illegal weapon is found, then an arrest can be made and a search incident to the arrest performed.[139] Would it be legal to pat down a person merely because that person is standing in a high-crime neighborhood? Probably not. The Supreme Court suggests that an officer would need more suspicion— for example, if the person ran away when he spotted the police approaching.[140]

- *Automobile search.* An automobile may be searched without a warrant if there is probable cause to believe the car was involved in a crime.[141] Because automobiles are inherently mobile, there is a significant chance that evidence will be lost if the search is not conducted immediately; also, people should not expect as much privacy in their cars as in their homes.[142] Police officers who have legitimately stopped an automobile and who have probable cause to believe that contraband is concealed somewhere inside it may conduct a warrantless search of the vehicle that is as thorough as a magistrate could authorize by warrant.

Because traffic stops can be dangerous, the Court has ruled that if a police officer perceives danger during a routine traffic stop, he can order the driver and passengers from the car without suspicion and conduct a limited search of their persons to ensure police officer safety.[143] Police officers can search the car and passengers after a traffic stop, as long as the search is reasonable and related to officer safety.[144] Usually, the search must be limited to the area under the driver's control or reach. Also, if someone in the vehicle is arrested, officers can only then search the vehicle for objects related to the offense of arrest, as the Supreme Court announced in *Arizona v. Gant*.[145]

- *Consent search.* In a consent search, individuals waive their constitutional rights; therefore, neither a warrant nor probable cause need exist. For a consent search to be legal, the consent must be given voluntarily; threat or compulsion invalidates the search.[146] Although it has been held that voluntary consent is required, it has also been maintained that the police are under no obligation to inform individuals of their right to refuse the search.[147]

- *Plain-view search.* Even when an object is in a house or other areas involving an expectation of privacy, the object can be freely inspected if it can be seen by the general public. If a police officer looks through a fence and sees marijuana growing in a suspect's fields, no search warrant is needed for the property to be seized. The articles are considered to be in plain view, and therefore a search warrant need not be obtained to seize them.[148]

- *Exigent circumstances.* The Supreme Court has identified a number of exigent, or emergency, circumstances in which a search warrant might normally have been required, but because of some immediate emergency, police officers can search suspects and places without benefit of a warrant. These circumstances include hot pursuit, danger of escape, threats to evidence, and threats to others. In each situation, officers must have probable cause.[149] For example, as the Supreme Court recently decided in *Kentucky v. King*, it is constitutionally permissible for officers to forcibly enter a residence if they have probable cause that evidence is being destroyed within.[150] They can also use deadly force to terminate car chases that pose grave public safety risks, as was decided in 2014.[151]

The Exclusionary Rule

The exclusionary rule provides that all evidence obtained by unreasonable searches and seizures is inadmissible in criminal trials. Similarly, it excludes the use of illegal confessions under Fifth Amendment prohibitions.

After police agencies were created in the mid-nineteenth century, evidence obtained by unreasonable searches and seizures was admitted by state and federal governments in criminal trials. The only criteria for admissibility were whether the evidence was incriminating and whether it would help the judge or jury reach a verdict. Then, in 1914, the US Supreme Court established the exclusionary rule in the case of *Weeks v. United States*, when it ruled that evidence obtained by unreasonable search and seizure must be excluded from a federal criminal trial.[152] In 1961, the Supreme Court made the exclusionary rule applicable to state courts in the landmark decision of *Mapp v. Ohio*.[153]

CONTROVERSY AND CURRENT STATUS When the exclusionary rule applies, valuable evidence may not be usable at trial because the police made an error or failed to obtain a proper warrant. This means that guilty defendants can go free when the police make mistakes, intentional or otherwise. What's more, because courts frequently decide in many types of cases (particularly those involving victimless offenses, such as gambling and drug use) that certain evidence should be excluded, the rule is believed to result in excessive court delays and to affect plea-bargaining negotiations negatively. In fact, however, the rule appears to result in relatively few case dismissals. Research efforts show that prosecutions are lost because of suppression rulings less than 1 percent of the time.[154]

Over time, the Supreme Court has been diminishing the scope of the exclusionary rule. For example, evidence is admissible in court if the police officers acted in good faith by first obtaining court approval for their search, even if the warrant they received was deficient or faulty.[155] This has come to be known as the good faith exception.

exclusionary rule Evidence seized in violation of the Fourth Amendment cannot be used in a court of law.

good faith exception The principle that evidence may be used in a criminal trial, even though the search warrant used to obtain it is technically faulty, if the police acted in good faith and to the best of their ability when they sought to obtain it from a judge.

LO9 Analyze the Supreme Court's involvement with the police through its effort to control search and seizure and interrogation, and through establishment of the exclusionary rule the exclusionary rule

REALITY**CHECK**

MYTH OR REALITY?

Legal loopholes enable guilty criminals to go free in alarming numbers.

MYTH. One of the supposed loopholes is the exclusionary rule, discussed in this section. Although it can result in the guilty going free, it is rarely invoked. Police mistakes and misconduct that lead to the exclusion of evidence are extremely rare. And many suspects in custodial interrogation situations waive their rights and agree to talk with police, contrary to movie and television depictions.

Despite the evidence, many people still feel that the exclusionary rule is a loophole. Why do such perceptions persist?

Sgt. Jennifer Dorety is an eight-year veteran of the Midcity police force. On the morning of November 5, 2012, Paul C. Bessey, a city councilman, spots Dorety leaving a local restaurant without paying. When he queries the restaurant owner, she laughingly states that "Officer Jen" had been coming there for breakfast for two years, and it's "always on the house." It is a mutual understanding they have because Dorety has been very helpful in keeping "riffraff" out of the place. In fact, she tells the councilman that she once called for her at the station house, and Officer Jen drove all the way across town to tell a troublemaker to leave.

The town has a strict policy prohibiting police officers from accepting or soliciting bribes or gratuities, so Councilman Bessey files a complaint against Dorety with the city's Civilian Review Board. There will be a hearing on the matter, and, if found liable, Dorety faces three possible penalties: suspension, suspension and loss of rank, or dismissal. Dorety asks you to act as her representative at the meeting.

Ethical Challenge: Write an essay on how you would defend her actions before the board and what you believe is a fair outcome in the case. It may be helpful to read the International Association of Chiefs of Police *Model Policy on Standards of Conduct,* which is available at http://www.theiacp.org/PoliceServices /ProfessionalAssistance/Ethics/ModelPolicyonStandard-sofConduct/tabid/196/Default.aspx#ModelPolicy. Does reading the policy change your opinion as to the proper outcome in this case? Why or why not?

SUMMARY

LO1 Summarize demographic trends in policing
US police departments have made a concerted effort to attract women and minority police officers, and today about 11 percent of all officers are female and about 23 percent are racial minorities.

LO2 Explain how minority and female officers act and are treated
Minority police officers now seem as self-assured as white officers. They may even be more willing to use their authority to take official action than white officers. Studies of policewomen indicate that they are still struggling for acceptance, believe that they do not receive equal credit for their job performance, and report that it is common for them to be sexually harassed by their coworkers. African American women, who account for less than 5 percent of police officers, occupy a unique status. They often incur the hostility of both white women and African American men, who feel threatened that these officers will take their place.

LO3 Explain police culture and personality
Experts have found that the experience of becoming a police officer and the nature of the job itself cause most officers to band together in a police subculture characterized by cynicism, clannishness, secrecy, and insulation from others in society—the blue curtain. The police officer's working personality is shaped by constant exposure to danger and the need to use force and authority to defuse and control threatening situations.

LO4 Identify distinct policing styles
Four styles of police work seem to fit the current behavior patterns of most police agents: the crime fighter, the social agent, the law enforcer, and the watchman.

LO5 Describe factors that affect police discretion
The majority of police officers use a high degree of personal discretion in carrying out daily tasks, a phenomenon sometimes referred to as "low-visibility decision making" in criminal justice. Several factors contribute to discretionary decision making: legal factors, environmental factors, departmental factors, peer factors, situational factors, and extralegal factors.

LO6 Discuss four major problems of policing
Police officers experience tremendous stress. Fatigue is also a problem in modern police agencies; officers often work long hours and can become overly tired from performance of their duties. Because incidents of brutality undermine efforts to build a bridge between police and the public, police departments around the United States have instituted specialized training programs to reduce it. Ever since their creation, US police departments have wrestled with the problem of controlling illegal and unprofessional behavior by their officers.

LO7 Distinguish between deadly and nondeadly force—and methods for controlling each
Police officers are empowered to use force in the pursuit of their daily tasks. The term "deadly force" refers to the actions of a police officer who shoots and kills a suspect who flees from arrest, assaults a victim, or attacks an officer. "Nondeadly force" is that which is unlikely to cause death or significant bodily harm. Because the police use of force is such a serious issue, ongoing efforts have been made to control its use. Methods used to control police force include adhering to important court decisions and formulating appropriate policies.

LO8 Explain the importance of less-lethal weapons
Less-lethal weapons give police officers an opportunity to subdue certain suspects without the need for lethal force. The Taser is the most popular less-lethal weapon in use today.

LO9 Analyze the Supreme Court's involvement with the police through its effort to control search

and seizure and interrogation, and through establishment of the exclusionary rule The need for police officers to gather evidence can conflict with the constitutional rights of citizens. In the 1966 case of *Miranda v. Arizona,* the Supreme Court created objective standards for questioning by police after a defendant has been taken into custody. Under normal circumstances, no search or seizure undertaken without a search warrant is lawful. The Supreme Court has also ruled that under certain circumstances, a valid search may be conducted without a search warrant. The exclusionary rule provides that all evidence obtained by unreasonable searches and seizures is inadmissible in criminal trials.

KEY TERMS

double marginality, p. 133

cynicism, p. 135

blue curtain, p. 135

discretion, p. 137

emotional intelligence, p. 138

demeanor, p. 139

racial profiling, p. 140

police brutality, p. 142

Corruption, p. 142

Knapp Commission, p. 143

meat eaters, p. 143

grass eaters, p. 143

deadly force, p. 144

suicide by cop, p. 144

nondeadly force, p. 144

less-lethal
    weapons, p. 146

Miranda warning, p. 148

search warrant, p. 150

probable cause, p. 150

stop and frisk, p. 150

exclusionary rule, p. 151

good faith
    exception, p. 151

REVIEW QUESTIONS

1. Should male and female officers have the same duties in a police department? Explain your reasoning.

2. How can education enhance the effectiveness of police officers?

3. Do you think that an officer's working the street will eventually produce a cynical personality and distrust for civilians? Explain.

4. A police officer orders an unarmed person running away from a burglary to stop; the suspect keeps running and is shot and killed by the officer. Has the officer committed murder? Explain.

5. Would you like to live in a society that abolished police discretion and used a full enforcement policy? Why or why not?

6. Should illegally seized evidence be excluded from trial, even though it is conclusive proof of a person's criminal acts? Might there be another way to deal with police violation of the Fourth Amendment—for example, making them pay a fine?

7. Have criminals been given too many rights by the courts? Should courts be more concerned with the rights of victims or the rights of offenders? Have the police been "handcuffed" and prevented from doing their job in the most efficient manner?

AP Images/Dominic Lipinski

154

PART 3

COURTS AND ADJUDICATION

St. Louis Circuit Attorney Jennifer Joyce is a force to be reckoned with on Twitter and Facebook. Unlike many of her predecessors who chose to stick to the confines of the courthouse, she has chosen to have a particularly vocal presence in social media. Some of her recent tweets include the following:

- "Bad guys take heed: Lafayette Park folks WILL catch you & they WILL go to court to get your bond raised. Saw this today!"
- "Carl Barnes and David Townes came to City to steal dumpsters. Both now charged with felony stealing. Stay out of our town!"
- "Stanley Bailey assaulted an 80 yr old lady & stole her purse. He now has 20 yrs to ask himself why he's a jerk."
- "Don't threaten police with a weapon, unless you want to be shot AND charged with a felony (unlawful use of a weapon), like Carl Evans was today."

Some would say Joyce's comments are a breath of fresh air, making it clear to all who follow her how her office will treat those who break the law. Other prosecutors take a more measured stance, refusing to publicly discuss specific offenders and/or cases.

Is there an ethical dilemma here? For example, can publicity of this sort contaminate the jury pool? Could "tweets" and Facebook status posts come back to later haunt the officials who post them? Indeed, a Florida defense attorney was fired and a mistrial was declared after she posted a picture on Facebook of her client's leopard-print underwear, apparently mocking him.[1] Another post questioned her client's innocence.[2] Arguably she went too far in this case, but where do we draw the line between proper and improper use of social media in the court context?

Part 3 of this text covers courts and adjudication. Chapter 7 provides an introduction to the court system as well as the roles of the prosecution and the defense. Chapter 8 covers pretrial and trial procedures. Pretrial topics include bail, charging the defendant, plea-bargaining, and diversion. The trial section of Chapter 8 summarizes the trial process and the legal rights defendants enjoy. Chapter 9 looks at punishment and sentencing. The chapter begins with the history and goals of punishment, and then it moves into specific types of sentences. Chapter 9 wraps up with a review of capital punishment and the controversies surrounding it.

7 Courts, Prosecution, and the Defense

REALITY CHECK

MYTH OR REALITY?

- Every state has just one court of last resort.
- There are almost no formal qualifications for federal judges.
- Elected state judges can be affiliated with a political party.
- Prosecutors base their charging decisions solely on legal factors, such as the seriousness of the offense.
- Privately retained defense attorneys are more effective than court-appointed defense attorneys.

Miriam Conrad, head of Boston's Federal Public Defender Office, was the lead defense attorney for Dzhokhar Tsarnaev, the man convicted for the Boston marathon bombing on April 15, 2013. She has been called a terrorist sympathizer, an enemy combatant, and America's "most reviled lawyer."[3] Why? In addition to defending Tsarnaev, she also represented a number of other infamous criminals, including shoe bomber Richard Reid, and Rezwan Ferdaus, who is serving 17 years in prison for plotting to bomb the Pentagon and US Capitol with remote control aircraft. Conrad, a former newspaper reporter turned attorney, takes a measure of delight in defending high-profile suspects. "There are very few clients I've had who I didn't like," she said. "If you scratch the surface, many have had difficult lives, and as their lawyer, I sort of see them whole, not just as a person charged with a crime."[4]

Judy Clarke, another lawyer on the Tsarnaev defense team, also defended *her* share of America's most despised criminals, including the Unabomber, Ted Kaczynski; Eric Rudolph, the man who detonated a bomb at the 1996 Olympics in Atlanta; and Jared Loughner, who shot former Representative Gabrielle Giffords and 18 others outside a supermarket in Arizona in 2011. All three men received life in prison rather than the death penalty. With the Tsarnaev trial, Clarke, Conrad, and the rest of the defense team had their work cut out for them.[5] In the end, though, their client was sentenced to death. Tsarnaev awaits execution in federal prison.

The criminal court is the setting in which many of the most important decisions in the criminal justice system are made. Eyewitness identification, bail, trial, plea negotiations, and sentencing all involve court decisions. The criminal court is a complex social agency with many independent but interrelated subsystems: administrator, prosecutor, defense attorney, judge, and probation department. The entire process—from filing of the initial complaint to final sentencing of the defendant—is governed by precise rules of law designed to ensure fairness. However, in today's crowded court system, such abstract goals are often impossible to achieve. The nation's court system is chronically underfunded, and recent economic downturns have not helped matters.

LEARNING OBJECTIVES

LO1 Describe the varying structures of state court systems

LO2 Describe the federal court system

LO3 Summarize the selection procedure for and duties of the trial judge

LO4 Explain the role of the prosecutor

LO5 Describe prosecutorial discretion, and summarize its pros and cons

LO6 Identify the role of the defense attorney in the justice process

LO7 Discuss the different forms of indigent defense

LO8 Summarize the pros and cons of private attorneys

LO9 Evaluate the expanding role of technology in the court process

These constraints have a significant impact on the way courts carry out justice. Quite often, the US court system is the scene of accommodation and "working things out," rather than an arena for a vigorous criminal defense. Plea negotiations and other nonjudicial alternatives, such as diversion, are far more common than the formal trial process. Consequently, US criminal justice can be selective. Discretion accompanies defendants through every step of the process, determining what will happen to them and how their cases will be resolved. "Discretion" means that two people committing similar crimes may receive highly dissimilar treatment. Most people convicted of homicide receive a prison sentence, but about 5 percent receive probation as a sole sentence; indeed, more murderers get probation than the death penalty.[6]

In this chapter, we examine the structure and function of the court system. The US court system has evolved over the years into an intricately balanced legal process. To carry out this complex process, each state maintains its own state court organization and structure, and the federal court has an independent trial court system. These are described next.

State Courts

Every state maintains its own court system. States are free to create as many courts as they wish, to name courts what they like (in New York, felony courts are known as supreme courts!), and to establish specialized courts that handle a single type of legal matter, such as drug courts and domestic courts. Consequently, no two court organizations are exactly alike. State courts handle a wide variety of cases and regulate numerous personal behaviors ranging from homicide to property maintenance.

Courts of Limited Jurisdiction

state courts of limited jurisdiction Courts that have jurisdiction over misdemeanors and conduct preliminary investigations of felony charges.

Depending on the jurisdiction in which they are located, state courts of limited jurisdiction are known by a variety of names—municipal courts, county courts, district courts, and metropolitan courts, to mention just a few. They are known as courts of limited jurisdiction because they are restricted to hearing minor or less serious civil and criminal cases.

Usually, courts of limited jurisdiction handle misdemeanor criminal infractions, violations of municipal ordinances, traffic violations, and civil suits where the damages involve less than a certain amount of money (usually $1,000 or less). In criminal matters, they hear cases involving misdemeanors such as shoplifting, disorderly conduct, and simple assault. Their sanctioning power is also limited. In criminal matters, punishments may be limited to fines, community sentencing, or incarceration in the county jail for up to a year. In addition to their trial work, limited jurisdiction courts conduct arraignments, preliminary hearings, and bail hearings in felony cases (before they are transferred to superior courts).

The nation's approximately 13,500 independent courts of limited jurisdiction are the ones most often accused of providing assembly-line justice. Because the matters they decide involve minor personal confrontations and conflicts—family disputes, divorces, landlord–tenant conflicts, barroom brawls—the rule of the day is "handling the situation" and resolving the dispute.

SPECIALIZED COURTS A growing phenomenon in the United States is the creation of specialty courts that focus on one type of criminal act, such as drug courts and mental health courts.[7] All cases within the jurisdiction that involve this particular type of crime are funneled to the specialty court, where presumably they will be resolved promptly. Examples of such courts are featured in the accompanying Contemporary Issues in Criminal Justice box.

What makes specialized courts different from traditional courts? According to the Center for Court Innovation[8], specialized courts have these six features:

- *Outcomes are elevated above process.* The main concern is reducing recidivism.
- *Judicial monitoring is critical.* Judges closely monitor offenders.

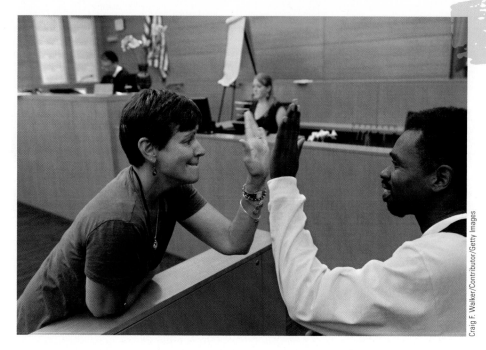

George Brady gets a high five from Shari Lewinski, program administrator of behavioral health courts, in Denver, Colorado. George, a client in Denver's Court to Community Program, was commended by Judge Johnny Barajas for keeping all his appointments for the second week in a row. The Court to Community program is a jail diversion initiative designed to help keep people with mental illness out of jail.

Craig F. Walker/Contributor/Getty Images

- *Informed decision making is necessary.* Judges hand down sentences with more information about offenders' backgrounds than may be available in traditional sentencing contexts.
- *Collaboration.* Specialized courts typically collaborate with other public and private agencies, many of which are often housed in the courthouse.
- *Nontraditional roles.* Specialized court personnel often assume different roles. For example, prosecutors in specialized courts are more interested in helping defendants than in seeing that they are convicted or punished.
- *Systemic change.* Specialized courts try to change the way the criminal justice system works.

CONTEMPORARY ISSUES IN CRIMINAL JUSTICE

Specialized Courts

Drug Courts

The drug court movement began in Florida to address the growing problem of prison overcrowding due in large part to an influx of drug-involved offenders. Drug courts were created to have primary jurisdiction over cases involving substance abuse and drug trafficking. The aim is to place nonviolent first offenders into intensive treatment programs rather than in jail or prison. Today, nearly 3,000 drug courts operate across the United States. Drug courts address the overlap between the public health threats of drug abuse and crime: Crimes are often drug-related, and drug abusers are frequently involved with the criminal justice system. Drug courts provide an ideal setting to address these problems by linking the justice system with health services and drug treatment providers, while easing the burden on the already overtaxed correctional system.

Mental Health Courts

Based largely on the organization of drug courts, mental health courts focus their attention on mental health treatment to help people with emotional problems reduce their chances of reoffending. By focusing on the need for treatment, along with providing supervision and support from the community, mental health courts provide a venue for those dealing with mental

health issues to avoid the trauma of jail or prison, where they will have little if any access to treatment.

Community Courts

Community courts are also becoming popular. Rather than targeting specific types of problems such as drugs or mental health, these courts take a more generalized focus. The main concern with community courts is providing "accessible justice" for residents who cannot easily get to downtown courthouses and focusing on quality-of-life offenses that may not be seen as top priority in traditional criminal courts. Community courts often have several on-site services available, as well. The first community court was Manhattan's Midtown Community Court.

Domestic Violence Courts

Several jurisdictions across the country have created their own domestic violence courts. Brian Ostrom described domestic violence courts in this way: They "seek to coordinate with medical, social service, and treatment providers and establish special procedures and alternative sentencing options to promote effective outcomes. Success necessitates systemwide collaboration

(Continued)

and the ongoing commitment of judges, health care professionals, the police, prosecution, and citizens who witness violent acts." Today, some 300 domestic violence courts are in operation nationwide. Given how new they are, however, not many of them have been evaluated.

Gun Courts

Rhode Island created the nation's first gun court in 1994. Unlike some of the other specialized courts, this gun court was concerned mainly with minimizing delay and ensuring that gun offenders received the toughest penalties the law allows. Other gun courts emphasize educating defendants about gun violence and safety. Many such courts have focused their efforts on juvenile gun offenders.

Other Specialized Courts

There are specialized courts for many different types of crime and social problems. In addition to targeting the preceding crimes, specialized courts have been formed to deal with everything from homelessness and sex offenses to parole reentry and teen bullying. We have moved well beyond the world of the traditional limited jurisdiction court. Limited jurisdiction courts

still exist, but these are often being supplanted by courts whose jurisdiction is not only limited but also very narrow.

CRITICAL THINKING

1. Do you believe that specialized courts are needed for other types of crimes, such as sex offenses?

2. Should a judge preside over a specialized court, or should it be administered by treatment personnel?

Sources: US Department of Justice, *Drug Courts* (Washington, DC: US Department of Justice, 2012), http://www.ncjrs.gov/pdffiles1/nij/238527.pdf (accessed April 10, 2014); Shelli Rossman et al., *Criminal Justice Interventions for Offenders with Mental Illness: Evaluation of Mental Health Courts in Bronx and Brooklyn, New York* (Washington, DC: US Department of Justice, National Institute of Justice, 2012); Brian J. Ostrom, "Domestic Violence Courts: Editorial Introduction," *Criminology and Public Policy* 3 (2003): 105–108; Office of Juvenile Justice and Delinquency Prevention, *Gun Court—Providence, RI, Profile No. 37* (Washington, DC: US Department of Justice, Office of Juvenile Justice and Delinquency Prevention, n.d.), http://www.ojjdp.gov/pubs/gun_violence/profile37.html (accessed February 2015); Greg Berman, John Feinblatt, and Sarah Glazer, *Good Courts: The Case for Problem-Solving Justice* (New York: New Press, 2005).

---

courts of general jurisdiction State or federal courts that have jurisdiction over felony offenses and more serious civil cases (i.e., cases involving more than a dollar amount set by the legislature).

appellate court A court that reconsiders a case that has already been tried to determine whether the measures used complied with accepted rules of criminal procedure and were in accordance with constitutional doctrines.

REALITY CHECK

MYTH OR REALITY?

Every state has just one court of last resort.

MYTH. Most states have just one, but Oklahoma and Texas have two courts of last resort.

In Texas, the Court of Criminal Appeals is the highest court for criminal cases. The Texas Supreme Court is the court of last resort for juvenile and civil cases. Is this a favorable arrangement? Why do Texas and Oklahoma's courts of last resort differ in their structure from the rest of the nation?

Courts of General Jurisdiction

Approximately 2,000 courts of general jurisdiction exist in the United States; they are variously called felony, superior, supreme, county, and circuit courts. Courts of general jurisdiction handle the more serious felony cases, such as murder, rape, and robbery, and civil cases where damages are over a specified amount, such as $10,000. Courts of general jurisdiction may also be responsible for reviewing cases on appeal from courts of limited jurisdiction.

Courts of general jurisdiction are typically organized in judicial districts or circuits, based on a political division such as a county or a group of counties. They then receive cases from the various limited courts located within the county or jurisdiction. Some general courts separate criminal and civil cases so that some specialize in civil matters while others maintain a caseload that is exclusively criminal.

State court systems now handle about 100 million new cases each year, a number that has increased more than 10 percent in the past decade. The great majority of these cases are traffic related, and about 20 million of these cases involve some form of criminal conduct.[9]

Appellate Courts

If defendants believe that the procedures used were in violation of their constitutional rights, they may ask an appellate court to review the trial process. Appellate courts do not try cases; they review the procedures of the case to determine whether an error was made by judicial authorities. In some instances, defendants can file an appeal if they believe that the law they were tried under was in violation of constitutional standards (e.g., the crime they were charged with—say, "being a public nuisance"—was vague and ill defined) or if the procedures used in the case contravened principles of due process and equal protection or were in direct opposition to a constitutional guarantee (e.g., they were denied the right to have competent legal representation).

It is the role of the appellate court to decide whether the trial judge made a legal error that influenced the outcome of the case, thereby denying the defendant a fair trial. Judicial error can include admitting into evidence illegally seized material, improperly charging a jury, allowing a prosecutor to ask witnesses improper questions, and so on. If, upon review, the appellate court decides that an error has been made, it can order a new trial or even allow the defendant to go free.

State criminal appeals are heard in one of the appellate courts in the 50 states and the District of Columbia. Each state has at least one court of last resort, usually called a state supreme court, which reviews issues of law and fact appealed from the trial courts; a few states have two high courts, one for civil appeals and the other for criminal cases.

Many people believe that criminal appeals clog the nation's court system because so many convicted criminals try to "beat the rap" on a technicality. Actually, criminal appeals represent a small percentage of the total number of cases processed by the nation's appellate courts. All types of appeals, including criminal ones, continue to inundate the courts, so most courts are having problems processing cases expeditiously.

Figure 7.1 illustrates the interrelationship of appellate and trial courts in a model state court structure. Each state's court organization, of course, may vary from this standard pattern. Although most states have a tiered court organization (lower, upper, and appellate courts), all vary in the way they delegate responsibility to a particular court system, and some have consolidated their courts into a single, unified system.

court of last resort A court that handles the final appeal on a matter. The US Supreme Court is the official court of last resort for criminal matters.

LO1 Describe the varying structures of state court systems

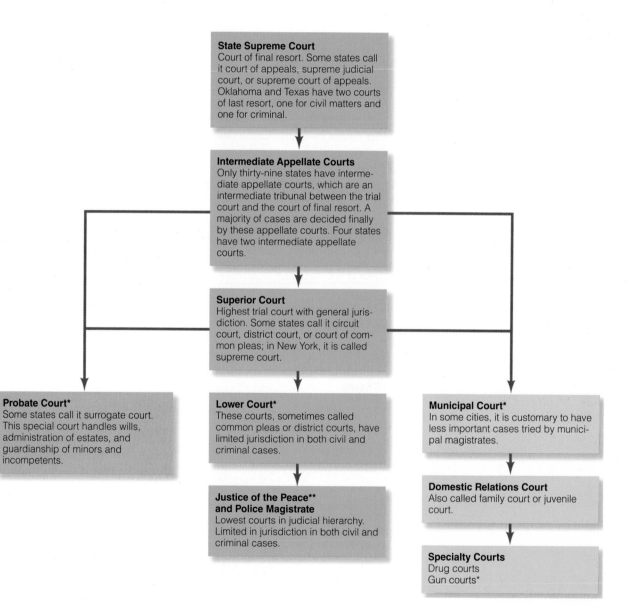

FIGURE 7.1 Model of a State Judicial System

*Courts of special jurisdiction, such as probate, family, and juvenile courts, and the so-called inferior courts, such as common pleas and municipal courts, may be separate courts or part of the trial court of general jurisdiction.

**Justices of the peace do not exist in all states. Where they do exist, their jurisdictions vary greatly from state to state.

Source: American Bar Association, *Law and the Courts* (Chicago: ABA, 1974), p. 20; Bureau of Justice Statistics, State Court Organization–1998 (Washington, DC: Department of Justice, 2000).

WEB APP 7.1 Visit the Court Statistics Project website and examine the court system structure in the state in which you reside at **http://www.courtstatistics.org/Other-Pages/State_Court_Structure_Charts.aspx**. Compare and contrast your state's court system structure with that of a neighboring state.

Federal Courts

The legal basis for an independent federal court system is contained in Article 3, Section 1, of the US Constitution, which provides that "the judicial power of the United States shall be vested in one Supreme Court, and in such inferior courts as Congress may from time to time ordain and establish." The important clauses in Article 3 indicate that the federal courts have jurisdiction over the laws of the United States and over treaties and cases involving admiralty and maritime jurisdiction, as well as over controversies between two or more states and citizens of different states.[10] This complex language generally means that state courts have jurisdiction over most common-law crimes but that the federal system maintains jurisdiction over violations of federal criminal statutes, civil suits between citizens of different states, and suits between a citizen and an agency of the federal government.

Within this authority, the federal government has established a three-tiered hierarchy of court jurisdiction that, in order of ascendancy, consists of the (1) US district courts, (2) US courts of appeals (circuit courts), and (3) the US Supreme Court (see Figure 7.2).

US District Courts

The US district courts serve as the trial courts of the federal system and were organized by Congress in the Judicial Act of 1789. Today, 94 independent courts are in operation. Originally, each state was allowed one court; as the population grew, however, so did the need for courts, so now some states have multiple jurisdictions.

US district courts have jurisdiction over cases involving violations of federal laws, including civil rights abuses, interstate transportation of stolen vehicles, and kidnappings. They may also hear cases on questions involving citizenship and the rights of aliens. The jurisdiction of the US district court will occasionally overlap that of state

Supreme Court — United States Supreme Court

Appellate Courts — U.S. Courts of Appeals / 12 Regional Circuit Courts of Appeals / 1 U.S. Court of Appeals for the Federal Circuit

Trial Courts — U.S. District Courts / 94 judicial districts / U.S. Bankruptcy Courts / U.S. Court of International Trade / U.S. Court of Federal Claims

Federal Courts and other entities outside the Judicial Branch — Military Courts (trial and appellate) / Court of Veterans Appeals / U.S. Tax Court / Federal administrative agencies and boards

FIGURE 7.2 The Federal Judicial System

Source: Administrative Office of the U.S. Courts, The United States Federal Courts, www.uscourts.gov/EducationalResources/FederalCourtBasics/CourtStructure/StructureOfFederalCourts.aspx (accessed June 2014).

courts. Citizens who reside in separate states and are involved in litigation of an amount in excess of $10,000 may choose to have their cases heard in either of the states or in the federal district court. Finally, federal district courts hear cases where one state sues a resident (or firm) in another state, where one state sues another, or where the federal government is a party in a suit.

US Courts of Appeals

There are 13 judicial circuits, each with a court of appeals. Each circuit's court of appeals (formally called the "Court of Appeals for the [number] Circuit") is empowered to review federal and state appellate court cases on substantive and procedural issues involving rights guaranteed by the Constitution. Circuit courts do not actually retry cases, nor do they determine whether the facts brought out during trial support conviction or dismissal. Instead, they analyze judicial interpretations of the law, such as the charge (or instructions) to the jury, and reflect on the constitutional issues involved in each case they hear.

Although federal court criminal cases make up only a small percentage of appellate cases, they are still of concern to the judiciary. Steps have been taken to make appealing more difficult. The US Supreme Court has tried to limit the number of appeals being filed by prison inmates, which often represent a significant number of cases appealed in the federal criminal justice system.

LO2 Describe the federal court system

The US Supreme Court

The Supreme Court is the nation's highest appellate body and the court of last resort for all cases tried in the various federal and state courts. The Court is composed of nine members appointed for lifetime terms by the president, with the approval of Congress. The Court has discretion over most of the cases it will consider and may choose to hear only those it deems important, appropriate, and worthy of its attention. The Court chooses some 300 of the 5,000 cases appealed each year, and only about 100 of these receive full opinions.

When the Supreme Court decides to hear a case, it grants a writ of certiorari, requesting a transcript of the proceedings of the case for review. At least four of the nine justices sitting on the Court must vote to grant the writ of certiorari even before the case can be considered for review. More than 90 percent of the cases heard by the Court are brought by petition for a writ of certiorari. The Court has original jurisdiction for the remaining cases (e.g., those involving disputes between the states).

When the Supreme Court rules on a case, usually by majority decision (at least five votes), its rule becomes a precedent, or landmark decision, that must be honored by all lower courts. If, for example, the Court grants a particular litigant the right to counsel at a police lineup, all similarly situated clients must be given the same right.

writ of certiorari An order of a superior court requesting that the record of an inferior court (or administrative body) be brought forward for review or inspection.

landmark decision A decision handed down by the US Supreme Court that becomes the law of the land and serves as a precedent for resolving similar legal issues.

SUPREME COURT PROCEDURE After the Supreme Court decides to hear a case, it reviews written arguments (referred to as legal briefs) outlining the case and the points of law to be considered. After the written material is reviewed, attorneys for each side in the case are allowed 30 minutes to present an oral argument before the court members. Then the justices normally meet in what is known as a "case conference" to discuss the case and vote to reach a decision.

In reaching a decision, the Supreme Court reevaluates and reinterprets state statutes, the US Constitution, and previous case decisions. On the basis of its review of the case, the Court either affirms or reverses the decision of the lower court. When the justices reach a decision, and in the event that the Court's decision is split, the chief justice of the Court assigns a member of the majority group to write the opinion. Another justice normally writes a dissent, or minority, opinion; a single opinion may be written if the decision is unanimous. When the case is finished, it is submitted to the public and becomes the law of the land. The decision represents the legal precedents that add to the existing body of law on a given subject, change it, and guide its future development.

Katherine Struck and Aman Ardalan shout support for gay marriage rights in front of the U.S. Supreme Court on April 28, 2015. The Court was hearing arguments in a case that would decide whether gay and lesbian people have a constitutional right to same-sex marriage. In a decision that combined cases from Michigan, Ohio, Kentucky, and Tennessee, the highest US court ruled that states must allow same-sex couples to marry. They must also recognize same-sex marriages from other states.

John boal/EPA /Landov

The Judiciary

The judge is the senior officer in a court of criminal law. Judges' duties are quite varied and far more extensive than might be expected:

- Their primary duty is to oversee the trial process. This means that during trials, judges control the appropriateness of conduct, settle questions of evidence and procedure, and guide the questioning of witnesses.

- In a **jury trial**, the judge must instruct jurors on which evidence it is proper to examine and which should be ignored. The judge also formally charges the jury by instructing its members on what points of law and evidence they must consider to reach a decision of either guilty or not guilty.

jury trial The process of deciding a case by a group of persons selected and sworn in to serve as jurors at a criminal trial, often as a 6- or 12-person jury.

- When a jury trial is waived, in a bench trial, the judge must decide whether the defendant is guilty as charged. If a defendant is found guilty, the judge must decide on the sentence (in some cases, this is legislatively determined), which includes choosing the type of sentence, its length, and, in the case of probation, the conditions under which it may be revoked.

- The judge controls and influences court agencies: probation, the court clerk, the police, and the district attorney's office. Probation and the clerk may be under the judge's explicit control. In some courts, the operations, philosophy, and procedures of these agencies are within the magistrate's administrative domain. In others—where a state agency controls the probation department—the attitudes of the county or district court judge greatly influence the way a probation department is run and how its decisions are made.

While carrying out their duties, judges must be wary of the legal controls placed on the trial process by the appellate court system. If an error is made, the judge's decision may be reversed, causing (at the very least) personal embarrassment. Some experts believe that fear of reversal may shape judicial decision making, but research shows that judges may be more independent than previously believed. Judges relish using their judicial power as a policy-making tool to influence important social policies such as affirmative action or privacy.[11]

Of course, judges do not wield their power in isolation. They work together with prosecutors and defense attorneys, whose work is featured shortly. They are also assisted by a number of courtroom personnel, including clerks, court administrators, security personnel, court reporters, and other support staff. See Exhibit 7.1 for additional details.

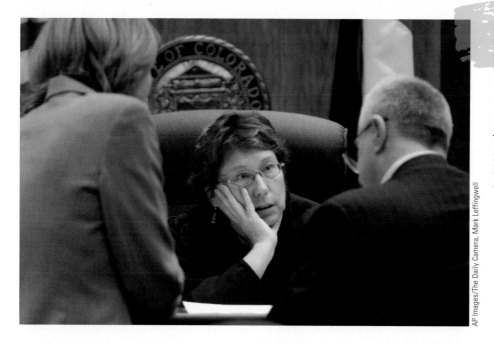

Judge Lael Montgomery, center, talks with attorneys at the bench during a trial at the Boulder County Justice Center in Boulder, Colorado. Colorado and other states are increasingly using performance reviews to hold judges more accountable without resorting to term limits or taking other measures that some fear would threaten the judiciary's independence.

AP Images/The Daily Camera, Mark Leffingwell

EXHIBIT 7.1

Court Staff

The most visible courtroom personnel include the judge, the prosecutor, and the defense attorney. However, many other important court personnel and staff persons are involved as well. The typical large jurisdiction probably has a mix of the following personnel working in the courtroom or courthouse at any given time.

Clerk Court clerks are responsible for a wide range of duties. Their main responsibilities include maintaining court records; receiving, processing, and maintaining judgments; issuing process, such as summonses, subpoenas, and wage garnishments; preserving the court seal; swearing in witnesses, jurors, and grand jurors; collecting fees and fines; handling inquiries from attorneys and other parties; and printing and distributing opinions of the court.

Court Administrator There are two general types of court administrators. The first is a state employee. In each state, these individuals are part of the state administrative office of the court, which is usually under the direction of the state supreme court. Court administrators help develop and implement policies and services for the judicial branch throughout the state. They also conduct research and determine whether judicial needs are identified and incorporated into long-term plans. They establish priorities for the courts, address financial problems and budgeting issues, and manage the use of technology within a state's judicial branch. The second type of court administrator is a local court administrator. These individuals manage the daily operations of the court, usually under the direction of the presiding judge. They provide administrative support for court programs, help the court establish new programs and evaluate them, and manage purchasing and accounts payable, among other responsibilities.

Court Security The marshal or bailiff for the court is responsible for courthouse security. In some states, such as California, court security is provided by sheriff's deputies who screen people entering the building, provide security during trials, and transport suspects to court from jail. Depending on the jurisdiction, court security personnel may take on additional responsibilities, including some investigation, bond supervising, community service monitoring, and making arrests as needed.

Legal Staff The larger and more powerful the court, the more likely it will have a variety of legal staff. These personnel can include legal counsel (prosecutors and defense attorneys), staff attorneys, research attorneys, and law clerks. Law clerks are not to be confused with court clerks. Unlike court clerks, law clerks are often recent law school graduates who assist judges with researching issues before the courts and with writing opinions. US Supreme Court law clerks are the cream of the crop, having graduated from many of the nation's top law schools.

Judicial Support Staff A judge's support staff may include executive assistants, administrative assistants, secretaries, or a mix of all three. Support staff members edit and type judicial opinions, create and arrange files, coordinate meetings, coordinate travel arrangements, answer telephone and e-mail inquiries, mail correspondence, and serve as an intermediary between the judge and other outside parties.

Court Reporter The court reporter records judicial proceedings word for word. See the Careers in Criminal Justice feature in Chapter 8 for more on court reporters.

Jury Staff Many courts have dedicated jury personnel who maintain and review lists of prospective jurors. They may also determine who is eligible to serve, determine the number of jurors needed, issue summonses for jury service, and handle requests by jurors for dismissal, exemption, or disqualification. These individuals may also meet with prospective jurors to explain the process, tell them where to go, and dismiss them from service at the end of the day.

Other Officers Many courts have representatives on site from other criminal justice agencies. Juvenile court officers may be present who are vested with the authority to take charge of children who come under the jurisdiction of the juvenile or family court. Representatives from probation may assist judges by performing presentence investigations that can be used during sentencing. In some states, the probation department is part of the judiciary and is thus more closely connected with the court than probation departments in other states.

Dzhokhar Tsarnaev Trial

Tsarnaev's defense attorneys asked Judge George O'Toole for a change of venue, arguing that Tsarnaev could not receive a fair trial in eastern Massachusetts. Their argument did not succeed, but should it have? Why?

The Judge and the Justice System

Judicial attitudes and philosophy have a major impact on how the justice system operates. Judicial attitudes may extend way beyond the courtroom. Police policies may be directly influenced by the judge, whose sentencing discretion affects the arrest process. If a local judge usually imposes minimal sentences—such as a fine—for a particular offense, the police may be reluctant to arrest offenders for that crime, knowing that doing so will basically be a waste of time. Similarly, if a judge is known to have a liberal attitude toward police discretion, the local department may be more inclined to engage in practices that border on entrapment or to pursue cases through easily obtained wiretaps. However, a magistrate oriented toward strict use of due process guarantees would stifle such activities by dismissing all cases involving apparent police abuses of personal freedoms.

The district attorney's office may also be sensitive to judicial attitudes. The district attorney might forgo indictments in cases that the presiding magistrate expressly considers trivial or quasi-criminal and in which the judge has been known to take only token action, such as the prosecution of pornographers.

Finally, the judge considers requests by prosecutors for leniency (or severity) in sentencing. The judge's reaction to these requests is important if the police and the district attorney are to honor the bargains they may have made with defendants to secure information, cooperation, or guilty pleas. When police tell informers that they will try to convince the judge to go easy on them to secure required information, they will often discuss the terms of the promised leniency with representatives of the court. If a judge ignores police demands, the department's bargaining power is severely diminished, and communication within the criminal justice system is impaired.

Judicial Qualifications and Selection

Judicial qualifications and selection vary between the federal and state levels. In general, the federal level has fewer formal qualifications and more *informal* qualifications. The opposite is often true at the state level.

FEDERAL LEVEL Federal judges are appointed by the president with the advice and consent of the Senate. Senate confirmation of federal judiciary appointees, especially those chosen to serve on the US Supreme Court, can be a contentious process. One exception to this process exists for the appointment of a US magistrate judge. Magistrate judges are federal trial judges appointed by district court judges who preside over various civil cases with the consent of the parties and over certain misdemeanor cases.

Interestingly, there are almost no formal qualifications for federal judges. The Constitution and federal law are silent on judicial qualifications. Potential federal judges do not have to pass any exams or even be a lawyer for that matter. Even so, positions in the federal judiciary are very prestigious and sought after. They thus attract highly qualified, seasoned attorneys.

STATE LEVEL The qualifications for appointment to one of the existing 30,000 judgeships vary from state to state and court to court. Most often, the potential judge must be a resident of the state, licensed to practice law, a member of the state bar association, and at least 25 years and less than 70 years of age. However, a significant degree of diversity exists in the basic qualifications, depending on the level of court jurisdiction. Although almost every state requires judges to have a law degree if they are to serve on appellate courts or courts of general jurisdiction, it is not uncommon for municipal or town court judges to lack a legal background, even though they have the power to incarcerate criminal defendants for petty crimes such as vandalism.

US magistrate judge A federal trial judge who is appointed by a district court judge and who presides over various civil cases with the consent of the parties and over certain misdemeanor cases.

Many methods are used to select judges, depending on the level of court jurisdiction. In some jurisdictions, judges are appointed officials, most often appointed by the state governor. In some states, in an effort to remove politics from judicial appointments, the governor's recommendations must be confirmed by the state senate, the governor's council, a special confirmation committee, an executive council elected by the state assembly, or an elected review board. Some states employ a judicial nominating commission that submits names to the governor for approval.

Another form of judicial selection is popular election. Judges may run as members of the Republican, Democratic, or other parties, or without party affiliation. Although this practice is used in a majority of states, each state sets its own terms of appointment. In some states, judges are elected to 15-year terms and in others to 4-year terms.[12] See Figure 7.3 for a map of judicial selection methods by state.

The state of Missouri pioneered a nonpartisan method of selecting judges. This Missouri Plan is now used in some manner in the majority of states. The plan consists of three parts:

1. A judicial nominating commission selects and nominates potential candidates for the bench. In Missouri, the judicial commission is composed of the chief justice of the state supreme court, three lawyers elected by the Missouri bar (the organization of all lawyers licensed in this state), and three citizens selected by the governor.
2. An elected official (usually from the executive branch, such as the governor) makes appointments from the list submitted by the commission.
3. Subsequent nonpartisan and noncompetitive elections take place, in which incumbent judges run on their records and voters can choose either to retain or to dismiss them.[13]

The quality of the judiciary is a concern. Although merit plans, screening committees, and popular elections are designed to ensure a competent judiciary, it has often been charged that many judicial appointments are made to pay off political debts or to reward cronies and loyal friends. Also not uncommon are charges that those who want to be nominated for judgeships are required to make significant political contributions.

Missouri Plan A method of picking judges through nonpartisan elections as a way to ensure that judges adhere to high standards of judicial performance.

 WEB APP 7.2 Visit the website of the Center for American Progress, an independent and nonpartisan educational institute, and read its article on partisan judicial elections at **http://www.americanprogress.org/issues/civil-liberties/report/2012/10/25/42895/partisan-judicial-elections-and-the-istorting-influence-of-campaign-cash.**
Do you agree with the article's viewpoint? Why or why not? For a contrasting viewpoint, read the article "The Case for Partisan Judicial Elections," available at the Federalist Society's website: **http://www.fed-soc.org/publications/detail/the-case-for-partisan-judicial-elections.**

LO3 Summarize the selection procedure for and duties of the trial judge

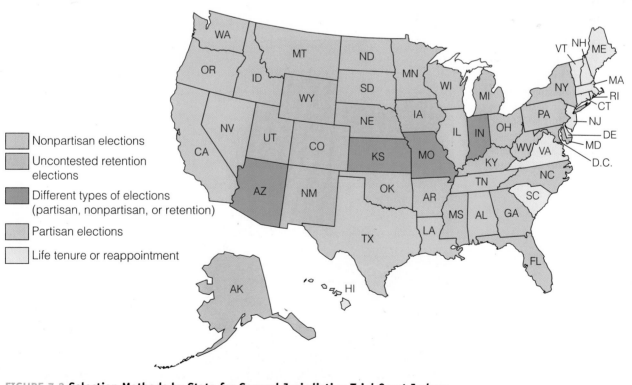

FIGURE 7.3 Selection Methods by State for General Jurisdiction Trial Court Judges

Source: American Bar Association, http://www.americanbar.org/content/dam/aba/migrated/leadership/fact_sheet.authcheckdam.pdf

REALITY**CHECK**

MYTH OR REALITY?

Elected state judges can be affiliated with a political party.

REALITY. This is not true in all states, but some states permit partisan judicial elections. This means a judge can run as a Democrat, a Republican, an independent, or a member of any other political party.

Should judges be allowed to run on political platforms? Why or why not?

The Prosecutor

Depending on the level of government and the jurisdiction in which he or she functions, the prosecutor may be known as a district attorney, county attorney, state's attorney, or US attorney. Whatever the title, the prosecutor is the people's attorney, who is responsible for representing the public in criminal matters.

Because they are the chief law enforcement officers of a particular jurisdiction, their jurisdiction spans the entire justice system process from the time when search and arrest warrants are issued or a grand jury is impaneled to the final sentencing decision and appeal. Following are some of the general duties of a prosecutor:

- Provides advice to law enforcement officers during investigation to determine whether criminal charges should be filed
- Represents the state in plea negotiations, pretrial motions, and bail hearings during the pretrial stage
- Represents the state at hearings, criminal trials, and appeals
- Acts as legal advisor to county commissioners and other elected officials

In addition to these duties, local jurisdictions may create specific programs directed by local prosecutors. One example is career-criminal prosecution programs, which involve identifying dangerous adult and juvenile offenders who commit a high number of crimes, so that prosecutors can target them for swift prosecution. Many jurisdictions have developed protection programs so that victims of domestic violence can obtain temporary court orders (and, after a hearing, more long-term court orders) protecting them from an abusive spouse; research indicates that protection orders can reduce the incidence of repeat violence.[14]

Types of Prosecutors

In the federal system, prosecutors are known as US attorneys and are appointed by the president. They are responsible for representing the government in federal district courts. The chief prosecutor is usually an administrator, and assistants normally handle

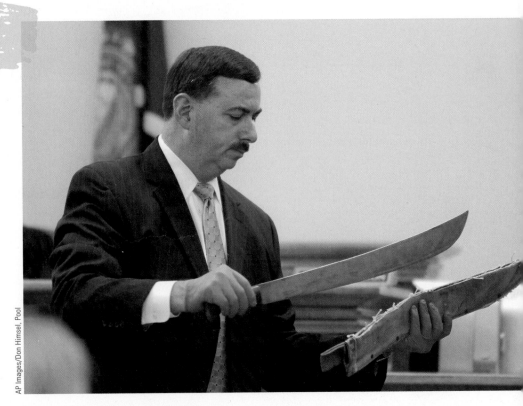

New Hampshire State Police investigator Steve Puckett shows the machete presented as evidence during testimony in Steve Spader's trial in Nashua, New Hampshire. Prosecutors say Spader wielded a machete during a home invasion, killing 42-year-old Kimberly Cates and maiming her 11-year-old daughter.

AP Images/Don Himsel, Pool

the actual preparation and trial work. Federal prosecutors are professional civil service employees with reasonable salaries and job security.

On the state and county levels, the attorney general and the district attorney, respectively, are the chief prosecutorial officers. Again, the bulk of the criminal prosecution and staff work is performed by scores of full- and part-time attorneys, police investigators, and clerical personnel. Most attorneys who work for prosecutors at the state and county levels are political appointees who earn low salaries, handle many cases, and (in some jurisdictions) maintain private law practices. Many young lawyers take these staff positions to gain the trial experience that will qualify them for better opportunities.

In urban jurisdictions, the structure of the district attorney's office is often specialized, with separate divisions for felonies, misdemeanors, and trial and appeal assignments. In rural offices, chief prosecutors handle many of the criminal cases themselves. Where assistant prosecutors are employed, they often work part time, have limited professional opportunities, and depend on the political patronage of chief prosecutors for their positions.

The personnel practices, organizational structures, and political atmosphere of many prosecutors' offices often restrict their effectiveness in investigating and prosecuting criminal offenses. For many years, prosecutors have been criticized for bargaining justice away, using their positions as stepping-stones to higher political office, and often failing to investigate or simply dismissing criminal cases. Lately, however, the prosecutor's public image has improved. Violations of federal laws, such as

CAREERS IN CRIMINAL JUSTICE PARALEGAL

Duties and Characteristics of the Job

- Paralegals assist lawyers by conducting much of the preparation for trials.

- A paralegal's exact duties vary according to the needs of the office for which he or she works. However, a paralegal's work typically includes assisting with or carrying out client interviews, drafting legal documents, reviewing pertinent case law, summarizing legal proceedings, and doing some standard office work.

- Paralegals do much of the same work as a lawyer, but within definite limits. For example, paralegals cannot advise on legal issues.

- Although most paralegals have general legal knowledge, it is becoming more common, especially for long-term or career paralegals, to choose a field of specialization.

Job Outlook

- The paralegal profession is expected to grow rapidly in the near future for several reasons, most prominently the fact that some organizations need legal expertise but do not want the extra expense of hiring a lawyer.

- Opportunities for advancement are available in larger offices, especially in urban areas.

- Ultimately, many paralegals use their knowledge and skills to earn a law degree and become a lawyer or judge. They can also move on to better-paying careers where legal experience is useful, such as insurance claims adjuster.

Salary

- The median (half earn above the amount, half earn below it) annual salary for paralegals is $47,000

- The lowest 10 percent earned less than $29,420, but the top 10 percent earned more than $75,410.

Qualifications

- Much of a paralegal's work is focused on conducting legal research, so skills that aid this process are critical.

- There is something of a political aspect to gaining this position because in some areas, one must be elected or appointed to it.

Education and Training

- A bachelor's degree with an emphasis on writing, analytical, and research skills is necessary.

- Because much of this research can now be done using computer programs, databases, and the Internet, up-to-date computer skills confer a distinct advantage.

- Most paralegals enter their profession with training from a two-year paralegal program approved by the American Bar Association. However, it is possible for people with a liberal arts degree to enter the field by working in legal offices and learning skills on the job.

Reality Check

- Relevant educational experience and certification are useful for gaining employment.

- Paralegal work involves a great deal of behind-the-scenes office work and research, so applicants need to be comfortable with both.

- Jobs with the most potential for upward mobility will be found in urban settings.

- Paralegals must always keep up with changes in the law in their areas of specialization.

Sources: Bureau of Labor Statistics, US Department of Labor, "Paralegals and Legal Assistants," *Occupational Outlook Handbook*, http://www.bls.gov/ooh/Legal/Paralegals-and-legal-assistants.htm (accessed February 2015); Princeton Review, *Careers: Paralegal*, http://www.princetonreview.com/careers/105/paralegal (accessed February 2015).

white-collar crime, drug peddling, and corruption, are being more aggressively investigated by the 94 US attorneys and the nearly 2,000 assistant US attorneys. Aggressive federal prosecutors have also made extraordinary progress in the war against insider trading and securities fraud on Wall Street. There have been a number of highly publicized indictments alleging that some corporate managers abused their power to loot company assets.

Today, about 2,400 state court prosecutors' offices are in operation, which employ about 79,000 attorneys, investigators, and support staff to handle felony cases in the state trial courts.[15] Usually, the most active prosecutors are employed in larger counties with populations of more than 500,000.

Prosecutors, like other justice system professionals, are now confronting issues related to cyber crime and terrorism and the use of technology both to commit crimes and to solve them after they occur. According to the most recent federal survey of prosecutors:

- At least two-thirds of state court prosecutors had litigated a computer-related crime such as credit card fraud (80 percent), identity theft (69 percent), or transmission of child pornography (67 percent).
- About one-quarter (24 percent) of the offices participated in a state or local task force for homeland security; one-third reported that an office member attended training on homeland security issues.
- Most prosecutors (95 percent) relied on state-operated forensic laboratories to perform DNA analysis, with about a third (34 percent) also using privately operated DNA labs.[16]

Prosecutorial Discretion

The prosecutor decides whether to bring a case to trial or to dismiss it outright. Even if the prosecutor decides to pursue a case, the charges may later be dropped if conditions are not favorable for a conviction; this is referred to as *nolle prosequi*.

The courts have protected the prosecutor's right to exercise discretion over processing of legal cases, maintaining that prosecutorial decision making can be controlled or overturned only if a defendant can prove that the prosecutor let discrimination guide his or her decision making.[17] Even in felony cases, the prosecutor ordinarily exercises much discretion in deciding whether to charge the accused with a crime.[18] After a police investigation, the prosecutor may be asked to review the sufficiency of the evidence to determine whether a criminal complaint should be filed. In some jurisdictions, this may involve presenting the evidence at a preliminary hearing. In other cases, the prosecutor may decide to seek a criminal complaint through the grand jury or other information procedure.

Without question, prosecutors exercise a great deal of discretion in even the most serious cases. In a now classic study, Barbara Boland examined the flow of felony cases through three jurisdictions in the United States: Golden, Colorado; the borough of Manhattan in New York City; and Salt Lake City, Utah.[19] Although procedures were different in the three districts, prosecutors used their discretion to dismiss a high percentage of the cases before trial. When cases were forwarded for trial, very few defendants were actually acquitted, indicating that the prosecutorial discretion was exercised to screen out the weakest cases. In addition, of those cases accepted for prosecution, a high percentage ended with the defendant pleading guilty. All the evidence here points to the conclusion that prosecutorial discretion is used to reduce potential trial cases to a minimum.

The prosecutor may also play a limited role in exercising discretion in minor offenses. This role may consist of simply consulting with the police after their investigation results in a complaint being filed against the accused. In such instances, the decision to charge a person with a crime may be left primarily to the discretion of the law enforcement agency. The prosecutor may decide to enter this type of case after an arrest has been made and a complaint filed with the court, and then subsequently determine whether to adjust the matter or proceed to trial.

LO4 Explain the role of the prosecutor

Factors Influencing Prosecutorial Discretion

Research indicates that a wide variety of factors influence prosecutorial discretion in invoking criminal sanction. These include legal issues, victim issues, extralegal issues, and resource issues.

LEGAL ISSUES Legal issues can include the characteristics of the justice system, the crime, the criminal, and the victim. The quality of police work and the amount and relevance of the evidence the police gather are critical legal variables that a prosecutor considers in deciding whether to bring a case forward to trial. [20] A defendant who is a known drug user, has a long history of criminal offending, and caused the victim extensive physical injuries is more likely to be prosecuted than one who is a first offender, does not use drugs, and did not seriously injure a victim. [21] Crime seriousness certainly influences discretion, too. As might be expected, prosecutors are much more likely to use their discretion in minor incidents than in more serious ones.

VICTIM ISSUES In some instances, the victim's behavior may influence charging decisions. Some victims may become reluctant to press charges, especially if the offender is a parent or spouse. Domestic violence cases are often difficult to prosecute. Some victims are unlikely to encourage or work with prosecutors even after the police get involved. Victim cooperation is a key factor in the decision to prosecute cases: the odds of a case being prosecuted are seven times greater when victims are considered cooperative. [22]

EXTRALEGAL ISSUES Extralegal factors include the offender's race, gender, and ethnic background. Of course, due process considerations demand that these personal characteristics have no bearing on the use of prosecutorial discretion. Nonetheless, some research efforts have found that the race of the offender or victim influences prosecutorial discretion, but others show that decisions are relatively unbiased. [23] Proving racial influence is difficult. To establish bias, a defendant must produce credible evidence that similarly situated defendants of other races could have been prosecuted but were not.

RESOURCE ISSUES Resource issues that influence prosecutorial discretion include the availability of treatment and detention facilities, the size of caseloads, and the number of prosecutors available. In some drug cases, prosecutors may decline to bring the case to trial because preparing it for prosecution would demand costly forensic analysis, expert witnesses, and forensic accountants. [24] Some research efforts have concluded that the availability of resources may be a more critical factor in shaping prosecutorial discretion than either legal or extralegal factors. In a world of tight government budgets, a prosecutor's office may be forced to accept plea bargains simply because it lacks the resources and personnel to bring many cases to trial. [25]

The Pros and Cons of Prosecutorial Discretion

Regardless of its source, the proper exercise of prosecutorial discretion can improve the criminal justice process by preventing the rigid implementation of criminal law. Discretion allows the prosecutor to consider alternative decisions and humanize the operation of the criminal justice system. If prosecutors had little or no discretion, they would be forced to prosecute all cases brought to their attention. As Judge Charles Breitel put it, "If every policeman, every prosecutor, every court, and every postsentence agency performed his or its responsibility in strict accordance with rules of law, precisely and narrowly laid down, the criminal law would be ordered but intolerable." [26]

On the other side, too much discretion can lead to abuses that result in the abandonment of law. Prosecutors are political creatures. Although they are charged with serving the people, they also must keep their reputations in mind; losing too many high-profile cases may jeopardize their chances of reelection. They therefore may be unwilling to prosecute cases where the odds of conviction are low; they are worried about convictability. [27]

LO5 Describe prosecutorial discretion, and summarize its pros and cons

Prosecutorial Ethics

Although the prosecutor's primary duty is to enforce criminal law, the fundamental obligation is to seek justice. If the prosecutor discovers facts suggesting that the accused is innocent, he or she must bring this information to the attention of the court.

In carrying out their stated duties, prosecutors are sometimes caught in an ethical conundrum. They are compelled by their supervisors to do everything possible to obtain a guilty verdict, while acting as public officials concerned to ensure that justice is done. Sometimes this conflict can lead to prosecutorial misconduct. According to some legal authorities, unethical prosecutorial behavior is often motivated by the desire to obtain a conviction and by the fact that such misbehavior is rarely punished by the courts.[28] Some prosecutors may conceal evidence, misrepresent evidence, or influence juries by impugning the character of opposing witnesses. Even where a court may instruct a jury to ignore certain evidence, a prosecutor may attempt to sway the jury or the judge by simply mentioning the tainted evidence.

Prosecutorial Misconduct

Because prosecutorial misconduct is a serious matter, the courts have reviewed such prosecutorial behavior as making disruptive statements in court, failing to adhere to sentence recommendations pursuant to a plea bargain, making public statements harmful to the state's case that are not constitutionally protected under the First Amendment, and withholding evidence that might exonerate a defendant.

Courts have also been more concerned about prosecutors who use their discretion in a vindictive manner to punish defendants who exercise their legal rights. Three cases illustrate controls placed on "vindictive" prosecutors:

- *North Carolina v. Pearce.* In this case, the US Supreme Court held that a judge in a retrial cannot impose a sentence more severe than that originally imposed. In other words, a prosecutor cannot seek a stricter sentence for a defendant who succeeds in getting her first conviction set aside.[29]
- *Blackledge v. Perry.* The US Supreme Court found that imposing a penalty on a defendant for having successfully pursued a statutory right of appeal is a violation of due process of law and amounts to prosecutorial vindictiveness.[30]
- *Bordenkircher v. Hayes.* In this case, the Court allowed the prosecutor to carry out threats of increased charges made during plea negotiations when the defendant refused to plead guilty to the original charge.[31]

These decisions provide the framework for the "prosecutorial vindictiveness" doctrine: due process of law may be violated if the prosecutor retaliates against a defendant, and there is proof of actual vindictiveness. The prosecutor's legitimate exercise of discretion must be balanced against the defendant's legal rights.

The Defense Attorney

The defense attorney is the counterpart of the prosecuting attorney in the criminal process. The accused has a constitutional right to counsel, and when the defendant cannot afford an attorney, the state must provide one. The accused may obtain counsel from the private bar if he can afford to do so; if the defendant is indigent, private counsel or a public defender may be assigned by the court (see the discussion on the defense of the indigent later in this chapter).

public defender An attorney usually employed (at no cost to the accused) by the government to represent poor persons accused of a crime.

The Role of the Criminal Defense Attorney

The defense counsel is an attorney as well as an officer of the court. As an attorney, the defense counsel is obligated to uphold the integrity of the legal profession and to observe the requirements of the American Bar Association's Code of Professional Responsibility in the defense of a client.

Defense attorneys are viewed as the prime movers in what is essentially an adversarial procedure: the procedure used to determine truth in the adjudication of guilt, in which the defense (advocate for the accused) is pitted against the prosecution (advocate for the state), with the judge acting as arbiter of the legal rules. Under the adversary system, the burden is on the state to prove the charges beyond a reasonable doubt. The defense uses all means at its disposal to refute the state's case. This system of having the two parties publicly debate, though imperfect, is thought to be the most effective method of arriving at the truth in a criminal case.

As a member of the legal profession, however, the defense counsel must be aware of his or her role as an officer of the court. The defense counsel is obligated to uphold the integrity of the legal profession and to rely on constitutional ideals of fair play and professional ethics to provide adequate representation for a client.

adversarial procedure The process of publicly pitting the prosecution and the defense against one another in pursuit of the truth.

LO6 Identify the role of the defense attorney in the justice process

The Right to Counsel

The Sixth Amendment to the US Constitution allows for provision of counsel at trial. But what about the indigent criminal defendant who cannot afford to retain an attorney?

In the 1963 landmark case of *Gideon v. Wainwright*, the US Supreme Court took the first major step on the issue of right to counsel by holding that state courts must provide counsel to indigent defendants in felony prosecutions.[32] Almost 10 years later, in the 1972 case of *Argersinger v. Hamlin,* the Court extended the obligation to provide counsel to all criminal cases where the penalty includes imprisonment—regardless of whether the offense is a felony or a misdemeanor.[33] These two major decisions are related to the Sixth Amendment right to counsel as it applies to the presentation of a defense at the trial stages of the criminal justice system.

In numerous Supreme Court decisions since *Gideon v. Wainwright* (see Exhibit 7.2), the states have been required to provide counsel for indigent defendants at virtually all other stages of the criminal justice process, beginning with arrest and concluding with the defendant's release from the system. Today, the Sixth Amendment right to counsel and the Fifth and Fourteenth Amendments' guarantee of due process of law have been judicially interpreted together to provide the defendant with counsel by the state in all types of criminal proceedings.

Sixth Amendment The US constitutional amendment containing various criminal trial rights, such as the right to public trial, the right to trial by jury, and the right to confrontation of witnesses.

Gideon v. Wainwright The 1963 US Supreme Court case that granted counsel to indigent defendants in felony prosecutions.

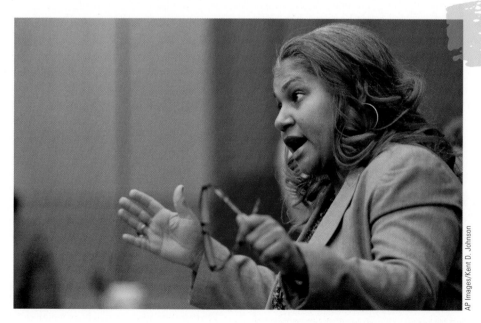

Defense attorney Teresa Mann presents an argument to Fulton County Superior Court Judge Jerry Baxter during the Atlanta Public Schools test-cheating trial in Fulton County Superior Court. Several educators were convicted on April 1, 2015, of racketeering and other lesser offenses for inflating test scores of children in struggling schools. Nine of them were sentenced to prison.

AP Images/Kent D. Johnson

EXHIBIT 7.2

Important *Gideon*-Related Decisions over the Years

Douglas v. California (1963) The Fourteenth Amendment guarantees the defendant the right to counsel during his or her first mandatory appeal.[34]

In re Gault (1967) Juveniles enjoy the right to counsel in adjudicatory hearings.[35]

Coleman v. Alabama (1970) The preliminary hearing is a "critical stage," meaning that the defendant enjoys the right to counsel at it.[36]

Argersinger v. Hamlin (1972) The Sixth Amendment right to counsel extends to those accused of committing misdemeanors.[37]

Morrissey v. Brewer (1972) There is no right to counsel in parole revocation hearings.[38]

Gagnon v. Scarpelli (1973) There is no right to counsel in probation revocation hearings.[39]

Ross v. Moffitt (1974) There is no right to counsel provided for the second, discretionary appeal.[40]

Scott v. Illinois (1979) If there is no possibility of confinement, the Sixth Amendment right to counsel does not apply.[41]

Morris v. Slappy (1983) The Sixth Amendment does not require a "meaningful" relationship between the defendant and his or her attorney.[42]

Wheat v. United States (1988) A trial court can deny the defendant's choice of counsel if the attorney's representation carries with it the strong possibility of a conflict of interest.[43]

United States v. Monsanto (1989) It is not unconstitutional for a court to seize a defendant's assets such that it forces him or her to rely on a public defender.[44]

United States v. Gonzalez-Lopez (2006) A convicted defendant has the automatic right to a new trial when a trial judge mistakenly refuses to allow the defendant's paid attorney to represent him.[45]

Rothgery v. Gillespie County (2008) The right to counsel attaches at the initial appearance, shortly after arrest.[46]

Areas remain in the criminal justice system where the courts have not required that the assistance of counsel be provided for the accused. These include pre-indictment lineups; booking procedures, including the taking of fingerprints and other forms of identification; grand jury investigations; appeals beyond the first review; disciplinary proceedings in correctional institutions; and revocation hearings after release. Nevertheless, the general rule of thumb is that no person can be deprived of freedom or lose a "liberty interest" without representation by counsel.

Legal Services for the Indigent

To satisfy the constitutional requirements that indigent defendants be provided with the assistance of counsel at various stages of the criminal process, the federal government and the states have had to evaluate and expand criminal defense services. Today, about 3,000 state and local agencies are providing indigent legal services in the United States.

Providing legal services for the indigent offender is a huge and costly undertaking. And although most states have a formal set of rules to signify who is an indigent, and many require indigents to repay the state for at least part of their legal services (known as "recoupment"), indigent legal services still cost over $1.5 billion annually.

Programs providing counsel assistance to indigent defendants can be divided into three major categories: public defender systems, assigned counsel systems, and contract systems (see Exhibit 7.3). Other approaches to the delivery of legal services include the use of mixed systems, such as representation by both the public defender and the private bar, law school clinical programs, and prepaid legal services. Although many jurisdictions have a combination of these programs, statewide public defender programs seem to be on the increase.[47]

In general, the attorney list/assigned counsel system is used in less populated areas, where case flow is minimal, and a full-time public defender is not needed. Public defenders are usually found in larger urban areas with high case flow rates. So although a proportionately larger area of the country is served by the assigned counsel system, a significant proportion of criminal defendants are represented by public defenders.

assigned counsel A lawyer appointed by the court to represent a defendant in a criminal case because the person is too poor to hire counsel.

contract system (attorney) Providing counsel to indigent offenders by having attorneys under contract to the county handle all (or some) such cases.

ETHICAL REFLECTION

Dzhokhar Tsarnaev Trial

At one time or another, all defense attorneys have to represent unsavory characters. At the same time, though, some defense attorneys actively *seek* to defend the worst of the worst. Some even do it for free. Is this ethical? Why or why not?

The Private Bar

Although most criminal defendants are represented by publicly supported lawyers, there are also private attorneys who specialize in

The Forms of Indigent Defense

Public Defender A salaried staff of full-time or part-time attorneys render indigent criminal defense services through a public or private nonprofit organization, or as direct government-paid employees. The first public defender program in the United States opened in 1913 in Los Angeles. Public defenders can be part of a statewide agency, county government, the judiciary, or an independent nonprofit organization or other institution.

Assigned Counsel The appointment is from a list of private bar members who accept cases on a judge-by-judge, court-by-court, or case-by-case basis. This may include an administrative component and a set of rules and guidelines governing the appointment and processing of cases handled by the private bar members. There are two main types of assigned counsel systems. In the first, which makes up about 75 percent of all assigned counsel systems, the presiding judge appoints attorneys on a case-by-case basis; this is referred to as an ad hoc assigned counsel system. The second type is referred to as a coordinated assigned counsel system, in which an administrator oversees the appointment of counsel and sets up guidelines for the administration of indigent legal services. The fees awarded to assigned counsels can vary widely, depending on the nature of the case. Restructuring the attorney fee system is undoubtedly needed to maintain fair standards for the payment of such legal services.

Contract Nonsalaried private attorneys, bar associations, law firms, consortiums or groups of attorneys, or nonprofit corporations contract with a funding source to provide court-appointed representation in a jurisdiction. In some instances, an attorney is given a set amount of money and is required to handle all cases assigned. In other jurisdictions, contract lawyers agree to provide legal representation for a set number of cases at a fixed fee. A third system involves representation at an estimated cost per case until the dollar amount of the contract is reached. At that point, the contract may be renegotiated, but the lawyers are not obligated to take new cases.

Sources: Carol J. DeFrances, *State-Funded Indigent Defense Services, 1999* (Washington, DC: Bureau of Justice Statistics, 2001).

criminal practice. Because most lawyers are not prepared in law school for criminal work, their skill often results from their experience in the trial courts. Some nationally known criminal defense attorneys represent defendants for large fees in celebrated and widely publicized cases, but this occurs rather infrequently.

Besides this limited group of well-known criminal lawyers, some lawyers and law firms serve as house counsel for such professional criminals as narcotics dealers, gamblers, prostitutes, and even big-time burglars. These lawyers, however, constitute a very small percentage of the private bar practicing criminal law.

A large number of criminal defendants are represented by lawyers who often accept many cases for small fees. These lawyers may belong to small law firms or work alone, but a sizable portion of their practice involves representing those accused of crime. Other private practitioners occasionally take on criminal matters as part of their general practice. A lawyer whose practice involves a substantial proportion of criminal cases is often considered a specialist in the field. And there is little question that having a preeminent private attorney can help clients achieve a favorable outcome ("not guilty" verdict).

LO7 Discuss the different forms of indigent defense

Does the Type of Lawyer Matter?

Do criminal defendants who hire their own private lawyers do better in court than those who depend on legal representatives provided by the state? Is one type of defense attorney for the indigent better than another?

Public vs. Private Attorneys Although there are some advantages to private counsel, national surveys indicate that state-appointed attorneys do quite well in court. According to data compiled by the federal government:

- Conviction rates for indigent defendants and for those with their own lawyers were about the same in federal and state courts. About 90 percent of the federal defendants and 75 percent of the defendants in the most populous counties were found guilty regardless of which type of attorneys represented them.
- Of those found guilty, however, those represented by publicly financed attorneys were incarcerated at a higher rate than those defendants who paid for their own legal representation.
- On average, sentence lengths for defendants sent to jail or prison were shorter for those with publicly financed attorneys than for those who hired counsel. In federal district court, those with publicly financed attorneys were given just under five years on average, and those with private attorneys just over five years. In large state courts, those with publicly financed attorneys were sentenced to an average of two and a half years, and those with private attorneys to three years.[48]

LO8 Summarize the pros and cons of private attorneys

Disgraced and disbarred Fort Lauderdale (Florida) attorney Scott Rothstein shows off part of his watch collection before he was sentenced to prison for 50 years, having funded his extravagant lifestyle with money from a $1.2 billion Ponzi scheme. While he remains in prison, he is also under witness protection. His cooperation with authorities led to convictions and prison sentences for more than two-dozen acquaintances, former co-workers, and family members.

MCT/Landov

WEB APP 7.3 Visit the American Bar Association Journal's Legal Ethics website at **http://www .abajournal.com/topic/legal+ethics**. Find and report on a recent example of an attorney's ethical violation and the sanction imposed. Was the sanction fair? Why or why not? If no sanction was imposed, why was that? If the sanction was self-imposed (e.g., a resignation), do you agree with it? Explain.

REALITY CHECK

MYTH OR REALITY?

Privately retained defense attorneys are more effective than court-appointed defense attorneys.

MYTH. Research reveals that public defenders and court-appointed attorneys perform similarly on average.

No clear evidence exists that having an expensive, privately retained attorney markedly increases one's chance of acquittal. What does this say about privately retained defense attorneys? What about court-appointed attorneys?

The Competence of Defense Attorneys

Inadequacy of counsel may occur in a variety of instances. The attorney may refuse to meet regularly with the client, fail to cross-examine key government witnesses, or fail to investigate the case properly. A defendant's plea of guilty may be based on poor advice, where the attorney may misjudge the admissibility of evidence. When co-defendants have separate counsel, conflicts of interest between the defense attorneys may arise. On an appellate level, the lawyer may decline to file a brief, instead relying on a brief submitted for one of the co-appellants.

The US Supreme Court defined the concept of attorney competence in the 1984 case of *Strickland v. Washington*.[49] The case established the two-pronged test for determining effectiveness of counsel:

1. The defendant must show that the counsel's performance was deficient and that such serious errors were made as to essentially eliminate the presence of counsel guaranteed by the Sixth Amendment.
2. The defendant must also show that the deficient performance prejudiced the case to such an extent that the defendant was deprived of a fair trial.

Determining whether defense counsel is ineffective is a subjective decision. The Supreme Court has ruled that an attorney can be effective even when he admits a client's guilt before the trial is over, as long as doing so is part of a reasonable defense strategy, such as gaining sympathy from the jury.[50] For a defense attorney to be considered incompetent, he or she would have to miss filings, fail to follow normal trial procedure, and/or fail to use defense tactics that the average attorney would be sure to follow, such as using expert witnesses or mentioning past behaviors that might mitigate guilt.

Court Administration

In addition to qualified personnel, there is a need for efficient management of the judiciary system. The need for efficient management techniques in an ever-expanding criminal court system has led to the recognition that improving court administration is one way to relieve court congestion. Management goals include improving the organization and scheduling of cases, devising methods to allocate court resources efficiently, administering fines and monies due to the court, preparing budgets, and overseeing personnel.

The federal courts have led the way in creating and organizing court administration. In 1939, Congress passed the Administrative Office Act, which established the Administrative Office of the United States Courts. Its director was charged with gathering statistics on the work of the federal courts and preparing the judicial budget for approval by the Conference of Senior Circuit Judges. One clause of the act created a judicial council with general supervisory responsibilities for the district and circuit courts.

Unlike the federal government, the states have experienced slow and uneven growth in the development and application of court management principles. The first state to establish an administrative office was North Dakota in 1927. Today, all states employ some form of central administration.

Using Technology in Court Management

In most jurisdictions today, centralized court administrative services perform numerous functions with the help of computers that free the judiciary to fulfill their roles as arbiters of justice. Rapid retrieval and organization of data are now being used for such functions as these:

- Maintaining case histories and statistical reporting
- Monitoring and scheduling cases
- Preparing documents
- Indexing cases
- Issuing summonses
- Notifying witnesses, attorneys, and others of required appearances
- Selecting and notifying jurors
- Preparing and administering budgets and payrolls

Computer technology is also being applied in the courts in such areas as videotaped testimonies, new court reporting devices, information systems, and data processing systems to handle such functions as court docketing and jury management. In 1968, only 10 states had state-level automated information systems; today, all states employ such systems for a variety of tasks and duties. Other developing areas of court technology include the following.[51]

COMMUNICATIONS Court jurisdictions are cooperating with police departments in the installation of communications gear that makes it possible to arraign defendants over closed-circuit television while they are in police custody. Closed-circuit television

Technology will become ever more present in the courtrooms of the future.
The courtroom featured here contains flat screen televisions throughout, including one in front of each juror. Courts like this one rely on computer technology and the Internet to bring together witnesses, lawyers, judges, and the jury.

LO9 Evaluate the expanding role of technology in the court process

has been used for judicial conferences and scheduling meetings. Some courts are using voice-activated cameras to record all testimony during trials; these are the sole means of keeping trial records.

VIDEOCONFERENCING About 400 courts across the country have videoconferencing capabilities. It is now being employed for juvenile detention hearings, expert witness testimony at trial, oral arguments on appeal, and parole hearings. More than 150 courts use two-way live, televised remote link-ups for first appearance and arraignment. Defendants typically appear from a special location in the jail where they can see and hear, and be seen and heard by, the presiding magistrate.

EVIDENCE PRESENTATION High-tech courtrooms are now equipped for real-time transcription and translation, audio-video preservation of the court record, remote witness participation, computer graphics displays, television monitors for jurors, and computers for counsel and judge.

CASE MANAGEMENT In the 1970s, municipal courts installed tracking systems, which used databases to manage court data. These older systems were limited and could not process the complex interrelationships that pervade information about persons, cases, time, and financial matters in court cases. Contemporary relational databases now provide the flexibility to handle complex case management.

INTERNET UTILIZATION The Internet has found its way into the court system. In the federal system, J-Net is the judiciary's intranet website. J-Net makes it easier for judges and court personnel to find important information in a timely fashion. The federal court's Administrative Office also sends official correspondence by e-mail, which provides instantaneous communication of important information.

INFORMATION SHARING Technology has been harnessed to make it easier for courts to share information within and between states. This helps cut down on costs and accelerates the criminal justice process.

The computer cannot replace the judge, but it can be used to help speed up the trial process by identifying backlogs and bottlenecks that can be eradicated with intelligent managerial techniques. Just as a manager must know the type and quantity of goods on hand in a warehouse, so an administrative judge must have available information about those entering the judge's domain, what happens to them after they are in it, and how they fare after judgment has been rendered.

SUMMARY

LO1 *Describe the varying structures of state court systems* State courts handle a wide variety of cases and regulate numerous personal behaviors ranging from homicide to property maintenance. Courts of limited jurisdiction are restricted in the types of cases they may hear. Courts of general jurisdiction handle the more serious felony cases (such as murder, rape, and robbery) and civil cases in which damages are over a specified amount, such as $10,000. Appellate courts

do not try cases; they review the procedures of the case to determine whether an error was made by judicial authorities.

LO2 *Describe the federal court system* The federal government has established a three-tiered hierarchy of court jurisdiction that, in order of ascendancy, consists of the US district courts, the US courts of appeals (circuit courts), and the US Supreme Court.

L03 *Summarize the selection procedure for and duties of the trial judge* The judge is the senior officer in a court of criminal law. His or her primary duty is to oversee the trial process. The qualifications for appointment to one of the existing 30,000 judgeships vary between the federal and state level—and from state to state. Most typically, the potential judge must be a resident of the state, must be licensed to practice law, must be a member of the state bar association, and must be at least 25 years of age and less than 70 years of age. Selection methods vary, too, and include election, appointment, and combinations of each.

L04 *Explain the role of the prosecutor* In the federal system, prosecutors are known as US attorneys and are appointed by the president. On the state and county levels, the attorney general and the district attorney, respectively, are the chief prosecutorial officers. Whatever the title, the prosecutor is the people's attorney, who is responsible for representing the public in criminal matters. Even if the prosecutor decides to pursue a case, the charges may later be dropped if conditions are not favorable for a conviction, in a process called *nolle prosequi.*

L05 *Describe prosecutorial discretion, and summarize its pros and cons* Regardless of its source, the proper exercise of prosecutorial discretion can improve the criminal justice process by preventing the rigid implementation of criminal law. Although the prosecutor's primary duty is to enforce criminal law, his or her fundamental obligation as an attorney is to seek justice, as well as to convict those who are guilty.

L06 *Identify the role of the defense attorney in the justice process* The defense attorney is the counterpart of the prosecuting attorney in the criminal justice process. In the 1963 landmark case of *Gideon v. Wainwright,* the Supreme Court took the first major step on the issue of right to counsel by holding that state courts must provide indigent defendants in felony prosecutions with private counsel or a public defender.

L07 *Discuss the different forms of indigent defense* To satisfy the constitutional requirements that indigent defendants be provided with the assistance of counsel at various stages of the criminal process, the federal government and the states have had to provide indigent defense services. Most criminal defendants are represented by publicly supported lawyers (e.g., public defenders), but many private attorneys also specialize in criminal practice.

L08 *Summarize the pros and cons of private attorneys* Even though there are some advantages to private counsel, national surveys indicate that state-appointed attorneys do quite well in court. The *Strickland v. Washington* case established the two-pronged test for determining effectiveness of counsel.

L09 *Evaluate the expanding role of technology in the court process* Technology is important to the administration and management of courts. High-tech courtrooms are equipped for real-time transcription and translation, audio-video preservation of the court record, remote witness participation, computer graphics displays, television monitors for jurors, and computers for counsel and judge. Contemporary relational databases provide the flexibility to handle complex case management.

KEY TERMS

state courts of limited jurisdiction, p. 158

courts of general jurisdiction, p. 160

appellate court, p. 160

court of last resort, p. 161

writ of certiorari, p. 163

landmark decision, p. 163

jury trial, p. 164

US magistrate judge, p. 166

Missouri Plan, p. 167

prosecutor, p. 168

public defender, p. 172

adversarial procedure, p. 173

Sixth Amendment, p. 173

Gideon v. Wainwright, p. 173

assigned counsel, p. 174

contract system (attorney), p. 174

REVIEW QUESTIONS

1. Specialized courts (such as drug courts) are popping up all over the country. What is your assessment of this trend? Why do you feel this way?

2. Should defense attorneys cooperate with a prosecutor if it means their clients will go to jail?

3. Should a prosecutor have absolute discretion over which cases to proceed on and which to drop?

4. Should clients be made aware of an attorney's track record in court?

5. Does the assigned counsel system present an inherent conflict of interest, inasmuch as attorneys are hired and paid by the institution they are to oppose?

6. Should victims play a role in the application of prosecutorial discretion? Before you answer, consider how that system might harm some defendants and benefit others.

8 Pretrial and Trial Procedures

On November 6, 2012, Washington and Colorado voted to legalize possession of marijuana, up to a certain quantity. On December 5, one day before Washington's "Initiative 502" went into effect, the Seattle Police Department's "SPD Blotter" website informed city residents that people were now free to consume marijuana in the privacy of their own homes. The site also noted that for the time being, officers would only issue warnings to those caught smoking weed in public. The site went on to say:

> Does this mean you should flagrantly roll up a mega-spliff and light up in the middle of the street? No. If you're smoking pot in public, officers will be giving helpful reminders to folks about the rules and regulations under I-502 (like not smoking pot in public). But the police department believes that, under state law, you may responsibly get baked, order some pizzas, and enjoy a *Lord of the Rings* marathon in the privacy of your own home, if you want to.[1]

Straightforward enough, right? Perhaps it is, but there are complications. Marijuana remains illegal under federal law. What's more, Washington's and Colorado's neighboring states continue to criminalize marijuana. So what happens, for example, if a Utah resident drives into Colorado and legally purchases an ounce of marijuana, drives back home, and gets caught with the drug? The easy answer is that the person will be prosecuted under Utah law. But will a prosecution actually occur? Utah, like other states neighboring Washington and Colorado, has plenty of other problems. Will so-called "marijuana tourists" create new headaches for officials in the states where marijuana is still illegal? How will police—and particularly prosecutors— adjust to the possible increase in their workload? "It would be like a place people go to get cheap beer. We're not talking about medical marijuana. We're talking about people who just want to get high," said a district attorney in Oregon.[2]

Some states are already fed up. As of this writing, two neighboring states are suing Colorado, arguing that the legalization experiment is undermining their enforcement efforts. According to Nebraska Attorney General Jon Bruning, "While Colorado reaps millions from the sale of pot, [our] taxpayers have to bear the cost."[3] Oklahoma Attorney General Scott Pruitt said this in a statement: "As the state's chief legal officer, the attorney general's office is taking this step to protect the health and safety of Oklahomans."

Didier Ruef/Cosmos/Redux

LEARNING OBJECTIVES

L01 Summarize the bail process

L02 Discuss the main issues associated with bail

L03 Differentiate between the two main mechanisms for charging defendants (grand jury indictment and prosecutor's information)

L04 Summarize the pleas available to a criminal defendant

L05 Explain the issues involved in plea bargaining

L06 Describe the plea-bargaining process

L07 Explain the purpose of pretrial diversion

L08 Describe the goals and purpose of the trial process

L09 Explain the legal rights of the accused at trial

L10 Summarize the trial process

pretrial procedures Critical pretrial processes and decisions, including bail, arraignment, and plea negotiation.

This chapter reviews the pretrial and trial process, beginning with the pretrial procedures. Pretrial procedures are important components of the justice process because the vast majority of criminal cases are resolved informally at this stage and never come before the courts. Although the media like to focus on the elaborate jury trial with its dramatic elements and impressive setting, formal criminal trials are relatively infrequent. Consequently, understanding the events that take place during the pretrial period is essential to grasping the reality of the criminal justice process.

Bail

bail The monetary amount for or condition of pretrial release, normally set by a judge at the initial appearance. The purpose of bail is to ensure the return of the accused at subsequent proceedings.

A cash bond or some other security provided to the court to ensure the appearance of the defendant at every subsequent stage of the criminal justice process, especially trial, is known as bail. Its purpose is to obtain the release from custody of a person charged with a crime. After the amount of bail is set by the court, the defendant is required to deposit all or a percentage of the entire amount in cash or security (or to pay a professional bonding agent to submit a bond). If the defendant is released on bail but fails to appear in court at the stipulated time, the bail deposit is forfeited. A defendant who fails to make bail is confined in jail until the court appearance.

Right to Bail

pretrial detention Holding an offender in secure confinement before trial.

The Eighth Amendment to the US Constitution does not guarantee a right to bail but rather prohibits "excessive bail." Because many state statutes place no precise limit on the amount of bail a judge may impose, many defendants who cannot make bail are placed in detention while awaiting trial. It has become apparent over the years that the bail system is discriminatory because defendants who are financially well off can make bail, whereas indigent defendants languish in pretrial detention in the county jail. In addition, keeping a person in jail imposes serious financial burdens on local and state governments—and, in turn, on taxpayers—who must pay for the cost of confinement. These factors have given rise to bail reform programs that depend on the defendant's personal promise ("recognizance") to appear in court for trial, rather than on her or his financial ability to make bail.

The Eighth Amendment restriction on excessive bail may also be interpreted to mean that the sole purpose of bail is to ensure that the defendant returns for trial; bail may not be used as a form of punishment, nor may it be used to coerce or threaten a defendant. In most cases, a defendant has the right to be released on reasonable bail. Many jurisdictions also require a bail review hearing by a higher court when the initial judge has set what might be considered excessive bail.

In *Stack v. Boyle,* the Supreme Court found bail to be a traditional right to freedom before trial that permits unhampered preparation of a defense and prevents the criminal defendant from being punished prior to conviction.[4] The Court held that bail is excessive when it exceeds an amount reasonably calculated to ensure that the defendant will return for trial. To meet this criterion, bail should be in the amount that is generally set for similar offenses. Higher bail can be imposed when evidence supporting the increase is presented at a hearing at which the defendant's constitutional rights can be protected. Although *Stack* did not mandate an absolute right to bail, it did set guidelines for state courts to follow: if a crime is bailable, the amount set should not be frivolous, unusual, or beyond a person's ability to pay.

REALITY CHECK

MYTH OR REALITY?

There is no constitutional right to bail.

REALITY. The Eighth Amendment only prohibits excessive bail (and cruel and unusual punishment).

The prohibition against excessive bail does not extend to everyone because the Supreme Court has not required that the states honor this part of the Eighth Amendment. Nearly every state constitution has some sort of prohibition against excessive bail, but there can still be considerable variability in what is considered "excessive."

Bail Release Mechanisms

When and how are bail decisions made? Bail in a felony case is typically considered at a court hearing conducted shortly after a person has been taken into custody. At the hearing, such issues as type of crime, flight risk, and dangerousness are considered before a bail amount is set. In jurisdictions with pretrial release programs, program staff often interview arrestees detained at the jail before the first hearing, verify their background information, and present recommendations to the court at arraignment. Prior record is

Marion "Suge" Knight, right, appears in court for a bail review hearing in Los Angeles on March 20, 2015. Knight, a former record producer and CEO of Black Kapital Records, was charged with murder following a hit-and-run crash in Compton, California. Partly due to his earlier legal troubles, bail was set at $10 million. As of this writing, Knight awaits his trial in jail.

an important factor: less than half of defendants with an active criminal justice status (such as parole or probation) at the time of arrest are released, compared to more than two-thirds of those with no active status. Some jurisdictions have developed bail schedules to make amounts uniform based on crime and criminal history.

Bail is typically granted during a court hearing in felony cases, but in less serious cases, bail may be handled in a variety of ways:

- *Police field citation release.* An arresting officer releases the arrestee on a written promise to appear in court, at or near the actual time and location of the arrest. This procedure is commonly used for misdemeanor charges and is similar to the issuance of a traffic ticket.
- *Police station house citation release.* The determination of an arrestee's eligibility and suitability for release and the actual release of the arrestee are deferred until after he or she has been removed from the scene of an arrest and brought to the station house or police headquarters.
- *Police/pretrial jail citation release.* The determination of an arrestee's eligibility and suitability for citation release and the actual release of the arrestee are deferred until after he or she has been delivered by the arresting department to a jail or other pretrial detention facility for screening, booking, and admission.
- *Direct release programs.* To streamline release processes and reduce the length of stay in detention, pretrial program courts may authorize pretrial programs to release defendants without direct judicial involvement.
- *Police/court bail schedule.* An arrestee can post bail at the station house or jail according to amounts specified in a bail schedule. The schedule is a list of all bailable charges and a corresponding dollar amount for each. Schedules vary widely from jurisdiction to jurisdiction.

In practice, a significant majority of criminal defendants are released on bail prior to trial.[5] The most recent surveys of pretrial release practices show that about 60 percent of felony defendants were released before the final disposition of their case. Defendants charged with the most serious violent offenses were less likely to be released than those charged with less serious public-order or drug offenses. Nonetheless, more than half of all violent criminals are released before trial. As might be expected, defendants charged with murder are the least likely to be released prior to case disposition (about 8 percent are released on pretrial bail), followed by defendants whose most serious arrest charge was robbery (about 39 percent are released on bail).

Types of Bail

A variety of ways or mechanisms are available to secure bail, depending on the jurisdiction, the crime, and the defendant:

- *Full cash bail.* The defendant pays the full bail amount out of pocket. In some jurisdictions, property can be pledged instead of cash.
- *Deposit bail.* The defendant deposits a percentage of the bail amount, typically 10 percent, with the court. When the defendant appears in court, the deposit is returned, sometimes minus an administrative fee. If the defendant fails to appear, he or she is liable for the full amount of the bail.
- *Surety bail.* The defendant pays a percentage of the bond, usually 10 percent, to a bonding agent who posts the full bail. The fee paid to the bonding agent is not returned to the defendant if he or she appears in court. The bonding agent is liable for the full amount of the bond should the defendant fail to appear. Bonding agents often require posting collateral to cover the full bail amount. This is the most common form of bail.
- *Conditional bail.* The defendant is released after promising to obey some specified conditions in lieu of cash, such as attending a treatment program before trial.
- *Unsecured bond.* The defendant is released with no immediate requirement of payment. However, if the defendant fails to appear, he or she is liable for the full amount.
- *Release on recognizance.* According to the **release on recognizance (ROR)** concept, eligible defendants are released without bail upon their promise to return for trial.

Bail Issues

Whether a defendant can be expected to appear for his or her trial is a key issue in determining bail. Bail cannot be used to punish an accused, nor can it be denied or revoked at the whim of the court. Nonetheless, for the following reasons, critics argue that monetary bail is one of the most objectionable aspects of the criminal justice system:

- It is discriminatory because it works against the poor.
- It is costly because the government must pay to detain those offenders who cannot make bail but who would otherwise remain in the community.
- It is unfair because a higher proportion of detainees receive longer sentences than people released on bail.
- It is dehumanizing because innocent people who cannot make bail suffer in the nation's deteriorated jail system.

There is also the problem of racial and ethnic disparity in the bail process. Some research efforts show that the decision whether to grant bail may be racially or ethnically biased; black and Latino defendants receive less favorable treatment than whites charged with similar offenses.[6] Although these results are troubling, it is often difficult to gauge racial/ethnic disparity in the bail process because differences in income, community ties, family support, and criminal record, rather than judicial bias, may account for any observed differences in the bail process. Despite these drawbacks, the bail system remains in place to ensure that defendants return for trial and that the truly dangerous can be kept in secure confinement pending their court proceedings.

BONDSMEN AND BOUNTY HUNTERS When bailees abscond before trial, bondsmen routinely hire skip tracers, enforcement agents, or bounty hunters to track them down. Each year an estimated 400 full-time bail enforcement agents catch some 25,000 fugitives in the United States.[7] Although organizations such as the National Institute of Bail Enforcement attempt to provide training, some untrained and/or unprofessional bounty hunters may use brutal tactics that can end in tragedy. Consequently, efforts have been made to reform and even eliminate money bail and reduce the importance of bonding agents.

LO1 Summarize the bail process

release on recognizance (ROR)
A nonmonetary condition for the pretrial release of an accused individual; an alternative to monetary bail that is granted after the court determines that the accused has ties in the community, has no prior record of default, and is likely to appear at subsequent proceedings.

WEB APP 8.1 Visit the website of the Fugitive Recovery Network, an organization devoted to supporting the bail bond industry, at **http://fugitiverecovery.com/.** From there click on "Bail Bond Laws," click on the map of the United States, then click on your state, and read the law(s) in the state where you reside (not all states may be available). What are the limits on fugitive recovery, according to state law?

Aaron Kennedy, left, and Jim Elliott, bail enforcement agents from Salt Lake City, look over paperwork while trying to track down a man who jumped bail and had a warrant out for his arrest. Kennedy and Elliott were contracted by a bail bond company.

PRETRIAL DETENTION CONDITIONS The criminal defendant who is not eligible for bail or ROR is subject to pretrial detention in the local county jail. The jail has long been a trouble spot for the criminal justice system. Conditions tend to be poor, and rehabilitation is a low priority. Hundreds of jails are overcrowded, and many are under court orders to reduce their populations and improve conditions.

What happens to people who do not get bail or who cannot afford to put up bail money? Traditionally, these individuals are more likely to be convicted and then to get longer prison sentences than those who commit similar crimes but who were released on bail. A federally sponsored study of case processing in the nation's largest counties found that about 63 percent of all defendants granted bail were convicted; in contrast, 78 percent of detainees were convicted.[8] Detainees are also more likely than releasees to be convicted of a felony offense and, therefore, are eligible for a long prison sentence instead of the much shorter term of incarceration given misdemeanants.

BAIL REFORM Critics believe that the bail system is discriminatory because defendants who are financially well off can make bail, whereas indigent defendants languish in pretrial detention in the county jail—and then get convicted at higher rates. This has led to a number of bail-related reforms. The first such reform program was pioneered by the Vera Institute of Justice in an experiment called the Manhattan Bail Project, which began in 1961 with the cooperation of the New York City criminal courts and local law students.[9] The project found that if the court had sufficient background information about the defendant, it could make a reasonably good judgment about whether the accused would return to court. When release decisions were based on such information as the nature of the offense, family ties, and employment record, most defendants who were released on their own recognizance returned to court. The results of the Vera Institute's initial operation showed a default rate of less than 0.7 percent.

The success of ROR programs in the early 1960s resulted in bail reforms that culminated with the enactment of the federal Bail Reform Act of 1966, the first change in federal bail laws since 1789.[10] This legislation sought to ensure that release would be granted in all noncapital cases in which there was sufficient reason to believe that the defendant would return to court. The law clearly established the presumption of ROR that must be overcome before money bail is required, authorized 10 percent deposit bail, introduced the concept of conditional release, and stressed the philosophy that release should be under the least restrictive conditions necessary to ensure court appearance.

MYTH OR REALITY?

A significant percentage of those released on bail never show up for their scheduled court dates.

MYTH. Research suggests otherwise. The Manhattan Bail Project found that less than 1 percent of those released default.

Official statistics tell a similar story; relatively few people released before their trial dates reoffend, get arrested, or fail to show up when they are required to do so. Could the same be expected with ROR programs?

Manhattan Bail Project The innovative experiment in bail reform that introduced and successfully tested the concept of release on recognizance.

deposit bail The monetary amount set by a judge at a hearing as a condition of pretrial release; the percentage of the total bond required to be paid by the defendant.

During the 1970s and early 1980s, the pretrial release movement was hampered by public pressure over pretrial increases in crime. As a result, the more recent federal legislation, the **Bail Reform Act of 1984**, mandated that no defendants will be kept in pretrial detention simply because they cannot afford money bail, established the presumption for ROR in all cases in which a person is bailable, and formalized restrictive preventive detention provisions (explained later in this chapter). The 1984 act required that community safety, as well as the risk of flight, be considered in the release decision. Consequently, such criminal justice factors as the seriousness of the charged offense, the weight of the evidence, the sentence that may be imposed upon conviction, court appearance history, and prior convictions are likely to influence the release decisions of the federal court.

PREVENTIVE DETENTION Bail reform acts have made it easier for some people to secure pretrial release, but they have also helped keep defendants who are considered dangerous behind bars before trial without the possibility of bail—a practice known as **preventive detention**. These laws require that certain dangerous defendants be confined before trial for their own protection and that of the community. Preventive detention is an important manifestation of the crime control perspective on justice because it favors the use of incapacitation to control the future behavior of suspected criminals. Critics, however, are concerned that preventive detention amounts to punishment before trial.

The most striking use of preventive detention can be found in the federal Bail Reform Act of 1984.[11] Although the act does contain provisions for ROR, it also allows judges to order preventive detention if they determine "that no condition or combination of conditions will reasonably assure the appearance of the person as required and the safety of any other person and the community."[12]

A number of state jurisdictions have incorporated elements of preventive detention into their bail systems. Although most of the restrictions do not constitute outright preventive detention, they serve to narrow the scope of bail eligibility. These provisions include three main features: (1) exclusion of certain crimes from bail eligibility, (2) definition of bail to include appearance in court and community safety, and (3) the limitations on right to bail for those previously convicted.

PRETRIAL SERVICES In our overburdened court system, determining which defendants can safely be released on bail pending trial is critical.[13] In many jurisdictions, specialized pretrial services help courts deal with this problem. Hundreds of pretrial bail programs have been established in rural, suburban, and urban jurisdictions; they are typically operated in probation departments, court offices, and local jails, and through independent county contractors. These programs provide a number of critical services:

- Gathering and verifying information about arrestees—including criminal history, current status in the criminal justice system, address, employment, and drug and alcohol use history—which judicial officers can then take into account in making release/detention decisions.
- Assessing each arrestee's likelihood of failure to appear and chances of being rearrested.
- Monitoring released defendants' compliance with conditions of release designed to minimize pretrial crime, including curfews, orders restricting contact with alleged victims and possible witnesses, home confinement, and drug and alcohol testing.
- Providing direct "intensive" supervision for some categories of defendants by using program staff and collaborating with the police, other agencies, and community organizations.

Some pretrial services programs are now being aimed at special needs. One type focuses on defendants suffering from mental illness; almost three-quarters of pretrial services programs now inquire about mental health status and treatment as a regular part of their interview, and about one-quarter report having implemented special supervision procedures for defendants with mental illness. Another area of concern is domestic violence. About one-quarter of all pretrial programs have developed special risk-assessment procedures for defendants charged with domestic violence offenses, and about one-third have implemented special procedures to supervise defendants charged with domestic violence offenses.

LO2 Discuss the main issues associated with bail

Charging the Defendant

Charging a defendant with a crime is a process that varies somewhat, depending on whether it occurs via a grand jury or a preliminary hearing.

The Indictment Process and the Grand Jury

The grand jury was an early development of the English common law. Under the Magna Carta (1215), no freeman could be seized and imprisoned unless he had been judged by his peers. To determine fairly who was eligible to be tried, a group of freemen from the district where the crime was committed would be brought together to examine the facts of the case and determine whether the charges had merit. Thus, the grand jury was created as a check against arbitrary prosecution by a judge who might be a puppet of the government.

The concept of the grand jury was brought to the American colonies by early settlers and later incorporated into the Fifth Amendment of the US Constitution, which states that "no person shall be held to answer for a capital, or otherwise infamous crime, unless on presentment or indictment of a grand jury." What is the role of the grand jury today? First, the grand jury has the power to act as an independent investigating body. In this capacity, it examines the possibility of criminal activity within its jurisdiction. These investigative efforts may be directed toward general rather than individual criminal conduct, for example, organized crime or insider trading. After an investigation is completed, a report called a **presentment** is issued. The presentment contains not only information concerning the findings of the grand jury but also, usually, a recommendation of indictment.

The grand jury's second and better-known role is to act as the community's conscience in determining whether the accusation of the state (the prosecution) justifies a trial. The grand jury relies on the testimony of witnesses called by the prosecution through its subpoena power. After examining the evidence and the testimony of witnesses, the grand jury decides whether probable cause exists for prosecution. If it does, an **indictment**, or true bill, is affirmed. If the grand jury fails to find probable cause, a **no bill** (meaning that the indictment is ignored) is passed. In some states, a prosecutor can present evidence to a different grand jury if a no bill is returned; in other states, this action is prohibited by statute.

CRITIQUING THE GRAND JURY The grand jury usually meets at the request of the prosecution, and hearings are closed and secret. Neither the defense attorney nor the defendant is allowed to attend, and grand jury hearings are not open to the public. The prosecuting attorney presents the charges and calls witnesses who testify under oath to support the indictment. This process has been criticized as being a "rubber stamp" for the prosecution because the presentation of evidence is shaped by the district attorney, who is not required by law to reveal information that might exonerate the accused.[14] An alternative is to open the grand jury room to the defense and hold the government to the same types of constitutional safeguards to protect defendants that are now used at trial.[15]

The Information Process and the Preliminary Hearing

In about half the states, a prosecutor's **information** is the charging mechanism of choice. When a person is charged in this fashion, a **preliminary hearing** is necessary. The purposes of the preliminary hearing and the grand jury hearing are the same—to establish whether probable cause is sufficient to merit a trial. The procedures differ between the two, however.

WEB APP 8.2 Visit Professor Susan Brenner's grand jury website at **http://campus.udayton.edu/~grandjur.** Click on the "State Grand Jury Info" tab, and answer these questions about your state: What is the size of the grand jury? What is the quorum of jurors necessary to conduct business? Back up and answer the same questions for federal grand juries. Compare and contrast the roles of federal and state grand juries.

presentment The report of a grand jury investigation, which usually includes a recommendation of indictment.

indictment The action by a grand jury when it finds that probable cause exists for prosecution of an accused suspect.

no bill The action by a grand jury when it votes not to indict an accused suspect.

information Charging document filed by the prosecution that forms the basis of the preliminary hearing.

preliminary hearing A hearing that occurs in lieu of a grand jury hearing, when the prosecutor charges via information. Three issues are decided: whether a crime was committed, whether the court has jurisdiction over the case, and whether there is sufficient probable cause to believe the defendant committed the alleged crime.

This photo provided by the Baltimore Police Department shows, top row from left, Caesar R. Goodson Jr., Garrett E. Miller, and Edward M. Nero, and bottom row from left, William G. Porter, Brian W. Rice, and Alicia D. White, the six police officers charged with felonies ranging from assault to murder in the death of Freddie Gray on April 12, 2015.

AP Images/Baltimore Police Department

The preliminary hearing is conducted before a magistrate or lower-court judge and, unlike the grand jury hearing, is open to the public unless the defendant requests otherwise. Present at the preliminary hearing are the prosecuting attorney, the defendant, and the defendant's counsel, if one has already been retained. The prosecution presents its evidence and witnesses to the judge. The defendant or the defense counsel then has the right to cross-examine witnesses and to challenge the prosecutor's evidence.

After hearing the evidence, the judge decides whether there is sufficient probable cause to believe that the defendant committed the alleged crime. If so, the defendant is bound over for trial, and the prosecuting attorney's information (described earlier; it is similar to an indictment) is filed with the superior court, usually within 15 days. If the judge does not find sufficient probable cause, the charges are dismissed, and the defendant is released from custody.

A unique aspect of the preliminary hearing is the defendant's right to waive the proceeding, a procedure that has advantages (and disadvantages) for both the prosecutor and the defendant. For the prosecutor, waiver helps avoid the need to reveal evidence to the defense before trial. Defense attorneys may waive the preliminary hearing for three possible reasons: (1) when the defendant has already decided to plead guilty, (2) to speed the criminal justice process, and/or (3) to avoid the negative publicity that might result from the hearing. On the other hand, a preliminary hearing may have some advantage for the defendant who believes that it will result in a dismissal of the charges. In addition, the preliminary hearing gives the defense an opportunity to learn what evidence the prosecution has.

Figure 8.1 outlines the significant differences between the grand jury and the preliminary hearing processes.

LO3 Differentiate between the two main mechanisms for charging defendants (grand jury indictment and prosecutor's information)

ETHICAL REFLECTION

Marijuana Legalization

Should a person who purchases marijuana legally in Washington or Colorado be charged with a crime if he or she is not a resident of either state and is caught in his or her home state? Why or why not? Would your answer change if marijuana remained criminal in Washington and Colorado? Why or why not? To what extent and how could ethical considerations creep into a prosecutor's decision regarding whether to press charges in cases like these?

Arraignment

After an indictment or information is filed following a grand jury or preliminary hearing, an arraignment takes place before the court that will try the case. At the arraignment, the judge informs the defendant of the charges against him or her and appoints

FIGURE 8.1 Charging the Defendant with a Crime
Note the difference between the grand jury and the preliminary hearing.

counsel if one has not yet been retained. According to the Sixth Amendment of the US Constitution, the accused has the right to be informed of the nature and cause of the accusation; thus, the judge at the arraignment must make sure that the defendant clearly understands the charges.

After the charges are read and explained, the defendant is asked to enter a plea. If a plea of not guilty or not guilty by reason of insanity is entered, a trial date is set. When the defendant pleads guilty or *nolo contendere,* a date for sentencing is arranged. The magistrate then either sets bail or releases the defendant on personal recognizance.

The Plea

Ordinarily, a defendant in a criminal trial will enter one of three pleas: guilty, not guilty, or *nolo contendere.*

GUILTY Most defendants appearing before the courts plead guilty prior to the trial stage. A guilty plea has several consequences. It functions not only as an admission of guilt but also as a surrender of the entire array of constitutional rights designed to protect a criminal defendant against unjustified conviction, including the right to remain silent, the right to confront witnesses against him or her, the right to a trial by jury, and the right to have an alleged offense proven beyond a reasonable doubt. After a plea is made, it cannot be rescinded or withdrawn after sentencing, even if there is a change in the law that might have made conviction more problematic.[16]

As a result, judges must follow certain procedures when accepting a plea of guilty. First, the judge must clearly state to the defendant the constitutional guarantees that he or she automatically waives by entering this plea. Second, the judge must believe that the facts of the case establish a basis for the plea and that the plea is made voluntarily. Third, the defendant must be informed of the right to counsel during the pleading process. In many felony cases, the judge will insist on the presence of defense counsel. Finally, the judge must inform the defendant of the possible sentencing outcomes, including the maximum sentence that can be imposed.

A person arraigned on criminal charges must plead either guilty or innocent.

MYTH. The media routinely get it wrong, claiming that so-and-so pleaded innocent. There is no such plea!

What is the difference between "not guilty" and "innocent"?

LO4 Summarize the pleas available to a criminal defendant

plea bargaining Nonjudicial settlement of a case in which the defendant exchanges a guilty plea for some consideration, such as a reduced sentence.

After a guilty plea has been entered, a sentencing date is arranged. In a majority of states, a guilty plea may be withdrawn and replaced with a not-guilty plea at any time prior to sentencing, if good cause is shown.

NOT GUILTY At the arraignment or before the trial, a not-guilty plea is entered in one of two ways: (1) it is verbally stated by the defendant or the defense counsel, or (2) it is entered for the defendant by the court while the defendant stands mute before the bench.

After a plea of not guilty is recorded, a trial date is set. In misdemeanor cases, trials take place in the lower-court system, whereas felony cases are normally transferred to the superior court. At this time, a continuance or issuance of bail is once again considered.

NOLO CONTENDERE With this plea (which means "no contest"), the defendant does not accept or deny responsibility for the crime(s) charged but agrees to accept punishment. Even though *nolo contendere* is essentially a plea of guilty, it may not be held against the defendant as proof in a subsequent legal matter, such as a civil lawsuit, because technically there has been no admission of guilt. This plea is accepted at the discretion of the trial court and must be voluntarily and intelligently made by the defendant.

Plea Bargaining

Plea bargaining is the exchange of prosecutorial and judicial concessions for pleas of guilty. Normally, a bargain can be made between the prosecutor and the defense attorney in one of four ways:

- The initial charges may be reduced to those of a lesser offense, thus automatically reducing the sentence imposed.
- In cases where many counts are charged, the prosecutor may reduce the number of counts.
- The prosecutor may promise to recommend a lenient sentence, such as probation.
- When the charge imposed has a negative label attached (e.g., child molester), the prosecutor may alter the charge to a more "socially acceptable" one (such as assault) in exchange for a plea of guilty.

There is little question that these methods result in lesser sentences, especially when defendants are in states whose sentencing policies limit judicial discretion. Pleading guilty to reduced charges may help replace the absence of judicial leniency.[17]

Plea bargaining is one of the most common practices in the criminal justice system and a cornerstone of the informal justice system. Today more than 90 percent of criminal convictions are the result of negotiated pleas of guilty. Even in serious felony cases, plea bargaining can be an option. See the accompanying Contemporary Issues in Criminal Justice box for more on some interesting plea agreements.

Plea bargaining is actually a relatively recent development, which took hold late in the nineteenth century. During the first 125 years after the nation's birth, the trial by jury was viewed as the fairest and most reliable method of determining the truth in a criminal matter. However, plea bargaining became more attractive at the turn of the twentieth century, when the mechanization of manufacture and transportation prompted a flood of complex civil cases; this event persuaded judges that criminal cases had to be settled quickly lest the court system break down.[18]

Pros and Cons of Plea Negotiation

Because of excessive criminal court caseloads and the personal and professional needs of the prosecution and the defense (to reach disposition of the case in the least possible time), plea bargaining has become an essential yet controversial part of the administration of justice. Proponents contend that plea bargaining actually benefits both the state and the defendant in the following ways:

- The overall costs of the criminal prosecution are reduced.
- The administrative efficiency of the courts is greatly improved.

Strange Plea Agreements

The typical plea agreement results in a reduced charge or a favorable sentencing recommendation by the prosecutor, but some agreements can only be described as strange or at least unusual. What follows are some examples identified by law professor and former judge Joseph Colquitt. In exchange for leniency, the defendant agrees to do the following:

- Make a charitable contribution
- Relinquish property ownership
- Surrender a professional license
- Undergo sterilization
- Undergo surgical castration
- Enter the military
- Not pursue appeals
- Undertake a shaming punishment, such as carrying a sign that says "I stole from this store"
- Seal the records of a case
- Surrender profits from crime, such as from books written about the crime
- Be banished to another location

These are examples of what Colquitt calls "ad hoc plea bargaining." In his view, ad hoc plea bargaining takes these forms:

(1) the court may impose an extraordinary condition of probation following a guilty plea, (2) the defendant may offer or be required to perform some act as a quid pro quo for a dismissal or more lenient sentence, (3) the court may impose an unauthorized form of punishment as a substitute for a statutorily established method of punishment, (4) the state may offer some unauthorized benefit in return for a plea of guilty, or (5) the defendant may be permitted to plead guilty to an unauthorized offense, such as a "hypothetical" or nonexistent charge, a nonapplicable lesser-included offense, or a nonrelated charge.

Ad hoc plea bargaining is controversial not just because it is unusual. In some cases, it can border on unethical. In one case, the prosecutor offered leniency to a drug defendant if he would surrender several thousand dollars in cash that was found during a search of his property. In another case, a defendant was afforded leniency for agreeing to forfeit interest in his vehicle.

CRITICAL THINKING

1. Are ad hoc plea bargains reasonable? Are they fair?

2. What if the tables were turned and, say, a speeding motorist offered $100 to the officer who stopped her in exchange for leniency? What would happen then?

Sources: Joseph A. Colquitt, "Ad Hoc Plea Bargaining," *Tulane Law Review* 75 (2001): 695–776; Timothy Lynch, *The Case against Plea Bargaining,* http://heartland.org/sites/all/modules/custom/heartland_migration/files/pdfs/13561.pdf (accessed February 2015).

- The prosecution can devote more time to more serious cases.
- The defendant avoids possible detention and an extended trial and may receive a reduced sentence.
- Resources can be devoted more efficiently to cases that need greater attention.[19]

Those who favor plea bargaining believe it is appropriate to enter into plea discussions when the interests of the state in the effective administration of justice will be

Attorney Alan Zegas reads a statement to the media as David Wildstein listens after his first federal court appearance in Newark, New Jersey, on May 1, 2015. Wildstein, a former ally of Governor Chris Christie, pleaded guilty to helping engineer traffic jams at the George Washington Bridge in a political payback scheme he said also involved two other Christie loyalists.

AP Images/Rich Schultz

served. Opponents of the plea-bargaining process believe that the negotiated plea should be eliminated for the following reasons:

- It encourages defendants to waive their constitutional right to trial.
- Plea bargains allow dangerous offenders to receive lenient sentences. Jesse Timmendequas, a previously convicted sex offender, was given a 10-year plea-bargained sentence for child rape. Upon his release, he raped and killed 7-year-old Megan Kanka in one of the nation's most notorious crimes.[20]
- Plea bargaining also raises the danger that an innocent person will be convicted of a crime if he or she is convinced that the lighter treatment ensured by a guilty plea is preferable to the risk of conviction and a harsher sentence following a formal trial.
- Prosecutors are given a free hand to induce or compel defendants to plea-bargain, thus circumventing the law.[21]
- It is possible that innocent persons will admit guilt if they believe that the system is biased and that they have little chance of being acquitted.
- A guilty-plea culture has developed among defense lawyers. Elements of this attitude include the belief that most of their clients are dishonest people who committed the crime with which they have been charged and that getting a "sentence discount" for them is the best and only way to go.[22]

Legal Issues in Plea Bargaining

The Supreme Court has reviewed the propriety of plea bargaining in several decisions and, while imposing limits on the practice, has upheld its continued use. The Court has ruled in several key cases that:

- Defendants are entitled to the effective assistance of counsel to protect them from pressure and influence.[23]
- Pleas must be made voluntarily and without pressure. However, a prosecutor can tell defendants that they may be facing the death penalty if they go to trial.[24]
- Any promise made by the prosecutor during the plea negotiations must be kept after the defendant admits guilt in open court. A prosecutor who promises leniency in private negotiations must stick to that position in court.[25]
- Defendants must also keep their side of the bargain to receive the promised offer of leniency.[26] For example, if they agree to testify against a co-defendant, they must give evidence at trial or forfeit the bargain.
- A defendant's due process rights are not violated when a prosecutor threatens to reindict the accused on more serious charges—for example, as a habitual offender—if the defendant does not plead guilty to a lesser offense.[27]
- Accepting a guilty plea from a defendant who maintains his or her innocence is valid.[28]
- Statements made during a plea bargain may be used under some circumstances at trial if the negotiations break down. Statements made during a plea negotiation can be used if the defendant (1) admits to a crime during the bargaining process but then (2) later testifies in open court that he or she did not do the act and (3) is innocent of the charges.[29]

LO5 Explain the issues involved in plea bargaining

Plea-Bargaining Decision Making

The plea-bargaining process is largely informal, lacking in guidelines, and discretionary. Research shows that prosecutorial discretion rather than defendant characteristics controls plea negotiations.[30] Yet studies also show that plea bargaining reflects a degree of cooperation between prosecutors and defense attorneys; in the vast majority of cases, they work together to achieve a favorable outcome.[31]

Research on plea negotiation indicates that the process is rather complex. Offender, case, and community characteristics also weigh heavily on the negotiation process.[32] Such factors as the offense, the defendant's prior record and age, and the type, strength, and admissibility of evidence are important in the plea-bargaining decision as well. The attitude of the complainant is also an important factor in the decision-making process. In victimless cases, such as heroin possession, the attitude of the police is most often considered, whereas in victim-related crimes, such as rape, the victim's attitude is a primary concern. Even the prosecutor's ego or political objectives can factor in. The list of factors that can affect plea agreements is practically endless.

THE ROLE OF THE DEFENSE COUNSEL Although the prosecutor formulates and offers the deal, the defense counsel—a public defender or a private attorney—is required to play an advisory role in plea negotiations. The defendant's counsel is expected to be aware of the facts of the case and familiar with the law and to advise the defendant of the alternatives available. The defense attorney is basically responsible for making certain that the accused understands the nature of the plea-bargaining process and the guilty plea. This means that the defense counsel should explain to the defendant that by pleading guilty, he is waiving certain rights that would be available if he were to go to trial. In addition, the defense attorney has the duty to keep the defendant informed of developments and discussions with the prosecutor regarding plea bargaining. While doing so, the attorney for the accused cannot misrepresent evidence or mislead the client into making a detrimental agreement. The defense counsel is not just ethically but also constitutionally required to communicate all plea-bargaining offers to a client, even if counsel believes the offers to be unacceptable.[33]

THE ROLE OF THE JUDGE The leading national legal organization, the ABA, is opposed to judicial participation in plea negotiations.[34] According to ABA standards, judges should not be a party to arrangements for the determination of a sentence, whether as a result of a guilty plea or a finding of guilty based on proof. According to this view, judicial participation in plea negotiations (1) creates the impression in the mind of defendants that they cannot receive a fair trial, (2) lessens the ability of the judge to make an objective determination of the voluntary nature of the plea, (3) is inconsistent with the theory behind the use of presentence investigation reports, and (4) may induce innocent defendants to plead guilty because they are afraid to reject the disposition desired by the judge.[35] How, then, are judges involved in plea bargaining? Judges must approve plea agreements.

THE ROLE OF THE VICTIM What role should victims play in plea bargaining? Some suggest that the system today is too "victim driven" and that prosecutors too often seek approval for the plea from a victim or family member. Others maintain that the victim plays an almost secondary role in the process. In reality, the victim is not "empowered" at the pretrial stage of the criminal process. Statutes do not require that the prosecutor defer to the victim's wishes, and there are no legal consequences of ignoring the victim in a plea-bargaining decision.

LO6 Describe the plea-bargaining process

Plea-Bargaining Reform

In recent years, efforts have been made to convert plea bargaining into a more visible, understandable, and fair dispositional process. Safeguards and guidelines have been developed to ensure that innocent defendants do not plead guilty under coercion. For example, the judge questions the defendant about the facts of the guilty plea before accepting the plea; the defense counsel is present and can advise the defendant of his or her rights; the prosecutor and the defense attorney openly discuss the plea; and full and frank information about the defendant and the offenses is made available at this stage of the process. In addition, judicial supervision ensures that plea bargaining is conducted in a fair manner.

NEGOTIATION OVERSIGHT Some jurisdictions have established guidelines to provide consistency in plea-bargaining cases. Guidelines define the kinds and types of cases and offenders that may be suitable for plea bargaining. Guidelines cover such aspects as avoiding overindictment and controlling unprovable indictments, reducing felonies to misdemeanors, and bargaining with defendants.[36]

BANNING PLEA BARGAINING What would happen if plea bargaining were banned outright, as its critics advocate? Numerous jurisdictions throughout the United States have experimented with bans on plea bargaining. In 1975, Alaska eliminated the practice. Honolulu has also attempted to abolish plea bargaining. Other jurisdictions, including Iowa, Arizona, Delaware, and the District of Columbia, have sought to limit the use of plea bargaining.[37] In theory, eliminating plea bargains means that prosecutors in these jurisdictions make no concessions to a defendant in exchange for a guilty plea.

In reality, however, in these and most jurisdictions, sentence-related concessions, charge-reduction concessions, and alternative methods for prosecution continue to be used in one way or another.[38] Where plea bargaining is limited or abolished, the number of trials may increase, the sentence severity may change, and more questions about the right to a speedy trial may arise. Discretion may also be shifted further up the system. Instead of spending countless hours preparing for and conducting a trial, prosecutors may dismiss more cases outright or decide not to prosecute them after initial action has been taken.

Pretrial Diversion

diversion A noncriminal alternative to trial, usually featuring counseling, job training, and educational opportunities.

Another important feature in the early court process is placing offenders into noncriminal **diversion** programs before their formal trial or conviction. The first pretrial diversion programs were established more than 40 years ago to reduce the stigma created by the formal trial process. To avoid stigma and labeling, diversion programs suspend criminal proceedings so that the accused can participate in a community treatment program under court supervision. Diversion programs give the client an opportunity to do the following:

- Avoid the stigma of a criminal record.
- Continue to work and support his or her family.
- Continue pursuing educational goals.
- Access rehabilitation services, such as anger management, while remaining in the community.
- When needed, make restitution to the victim of crime or pay back the community through volunteer services.

WEB APP 8.3 Visit the San Francisco Pretrial Diversion Project website at **http://sfpretrial.com.** What programs and services are available to certain defendants in lieu of trial? What defendants are eligible? Which program do you feel is most effective and why?

Diversion also enables the justice system to reduce costs and alleviate prison crowding. Diversion programs can take many forms. Some are run by separate, independent agencies that were originally set up with federal funds but are now being continued with county or state assistance. Others are organized as part of a police, prosecutor, or probation department's internal structure. Still others represent a joint venture between the county government and a private, nonprofit organization that carries out the treatment process.

First viewed as a panacea that could reduce court congestion and help treat minor offenders, diversion programs soon came under fire when national evaluations concluded that they are no more successful at avoiding stigma and reducing recidivism than traditional justice processing.[39] There was also the suspicion that diversion might "widen the net" of the justice system. By this, critics meant that the people placed in diversion programs were the ones most likely to have otherwise been dismissed after a brief hearing with a warning or small fine.[40] Now they were receiving more treatment than they would have if the program had not been in place. Those who would ordinarily have received a more serious sentence were not eligible for diversion anyway. Thus, rather than limiting contact with the system, the diversion programs actually increase its grasp.

Of course, not all justice experts agree with this charge, and some programs have shown great promise. Recent evaluations indicate that given the proper treatment, some types of offenders, such as drug offenders, who are offered a place in pretrial programs can significantly lower their rates of recidivism.[41]

L07 Explain the purpose of pretrial diversion

The Trial

The criminal trial is an open and public hearing designed to examine the facts of the case brought by the state against the accused. Criminal trials are relatively rare events (most cases are settled by a plea bargain during the pretrial stage), but they are an important and enduring fixture in the criminal justice system. By its very nature, the criminal trial is a symbol of the moral authority of the state and of the administration of objective and impartial justice.

Most formal trials are heard by a jury, although some defendants waive their constitutional right to a jury trial and request a **bench trial**, in which the judge alone renders a verdict. In this situation, which occurs daily in the lower criminal courts, the judge may initiate a number of formal or informal dispositions, including dismissing the case, finding the defendant not guilty, finding the defendant guilty and imposing a sentence, or even continuing the case indefinitely. The decision the judge makes often depends on the seriousness of the offense, the background and previous record of the defendant, and the judgment of the court about whether the case can be properly dealt with in the criminal process. The judge may simply continue the case without a finding, in which case the verdict is withheld without a finding of guilt to induce the accused to improve her behavior in the community; if the defendant's behavior does improve, the case is ordinarily closed within a specific amount of time.

This section reviews some of the institutions and processes involved in **adjudication** and trial. We begin with a discussion of the legal rights that structure the trial process.

bench trial The trial of a criminal matter by a judge only. The accused waives any constitutional right to trial by jury.

adjudication The determination of guilt or innocence; a judgment concerning criminal charges. The majority of offenders charged plead guilty; of the remainder, some cases are adjudicated by a judge and a jury, some are adjudicated by a judge without a jury, and others are dismissed.

LO8 Describe the goals and purpose of the trial process

Legal Rights during Trial

Underlying every trial are constitutional principles, complex legal procedures, rules of court, and interpretations of statutes—all designed to ensure that the accused will receive a fair trial.

THE RIGHT TO AN IMPARTIAL JUDGE Even though the Constitution does not say so, every criminal defendant enjoys the right to a trial by an impartial judge. The Supreme Court ruled as much way back in the 1927 case of *Tumey v. Ohio.* In that case, a municipal court judge was also the mayor, an executive official. What's more, he received fines and fees that he ordered against defendants who were convicted in his courtroom. The Supreme Court held that it is a violation of due process when a judge "has a direct, personal, substantial pecuniary interest in reaching a conclusion against [a defendant] in his case."[42]

What if a judge is not impartial? How can such a judge be removed? Generally, the judge will excuse himself or herself if there is a conflict of interest. Judicial codes of ethics provide the guidelines judges need to make such decisions. Some jurisdictions, however, permit peremptory removal of judges.[43] These are like the peremptory challenges used in jury selection (covered later in this chapter). When this occurs, one of the attorneys can move to have the judge removed, and another judge will come on board. Usually the peremptory removal can occur only once.

THE RIGHT TO BE COMPETENT AT TRIAL To stand trial, a criminal defendant must be considered mentally competent to understand the nature and extent of the legal proceedings. If a defendant is considered mentally incompetent, his trial must be postponed until treatment renders him capable of participating in his own defense.

Can state authorities force a mentally unfit defendant to be treated so that he can be tried? In *Riggins v. Nevada* (1992), the US Supreme Court ruled that forced treatment does not violate a defendant's due process rights if it was medically appropriate and, considering less intrusive alternatives, was essential for the defendant's own safety or the safety of others.[44]

THE RIGHT TO CONFRONT WITNESSES The Sixth Amendment states that "In all criminal prosecutions, the accused shall enjoy the right ... to be confronted with the witnesses against him." The accused enjoys this right not just by being able to confront

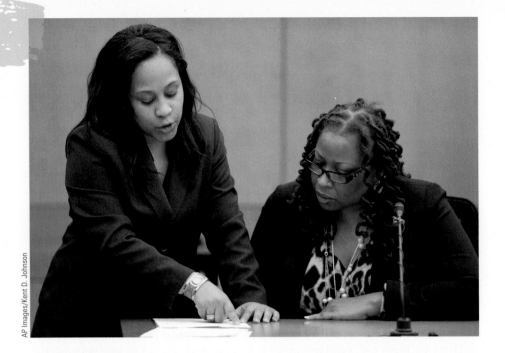

Fulton County Assistant District Attorney Fani Willis questions Shawnna Hayes-Tavares as she testified in the Atlanta Public Schools test-cheating trial before Judge Jerry Baxter in Fulton County Superior Court on February 10, 2015. The trial lasted five months and resulted in convictions and prison sentences for several area school officials. Ms. Hayes-Tavares was one of several parents called to testify in connection with the case.

AP Images/Kent D. Johnson

confrontation clause A part of the Sixth Amendment that establishes the right of a criminal defendant to see and cross-examine all the witnesses against him or her.

hearsay evidence Testimony that is not firsthand but, rather, relates information told by a second party.

compulsory process Compelling the production of witnesses via a subpoena.

witnesses in person, but by being allowed to participate in his or her trial. That is, trials cannot be conducted without the accused being afforded the right to appear in person. This right can be waived or forfeited through misconduct. The accused may choose not to show up,[45] which is constitutionally permissible, and he or she may forfeit the right to appear by acting out and causing a significant distraction in the courtroom.[46] There are also some exceptions, such as in child abuse cases, where it is felt that child victims would suffer irreparable harm by being forced to appear before their abusers.[47]

The **confrontation clause** is essential to a fair criminal trial because it restricts and controls the admissibility of **hearsay evidence**. Hearsay evidence is akin to secondhand evidence; rather than being told firsthand, it consists of information related by a second party (it is what one person hears and then says—hence the term "hearsay"). The framers of the Constitution sought face-to-face accusations in which the defendant has a right to see and cross-examine all witnesses. The idea that it is always more difficult to tell lies about people to their face than behind their back underlies the confrontation clause.

THE RIGHT TO COMPULSORY PROCESS The Sixth Amendment says, in part, that the accused shall "have compulsory process for obtaining witnesses in his favor." **Compulsory process** means to compel the production of witnesses via a subpoena. A subpoena is an order requiring a witness to appear in court at a specified time and place. The Supreme Court decided that compulsory process is a fundamental right in the case of *Washington v. Texas* (1967).[48]

THE RIGHT TO AN IMPARTIAL JURY It is no accident that of all the rights guaranteed to the people by the Constitution, only the right to a jury trial in criminal cases appears in both the original Constitution (Article III, Section 2) and the Bill of Rights (the Sixth Amendment). Although they may have disagreed on many points, the framers did not question the wisdom of the jury trial.

Today, the criminal defendant has the right to choose whether the trial will be before a judge or a jury. Although the Sixth Amendment guarantees the defendant the right to a jury trial, the defendant can and often does waive this right. A substantial proportion of defendants, particularly those charged with misdemeanors, are tried before the court without a jury.

The major legal issue surrounding jury trial has been whether all defendants—those accused of misdemeanors as well as those accused of felonies—have an absolute right to a jury trial. Although the Constitution says that the right to a jury trial exists in *"all criminal prosecutions,"* the US Supreme Court has restricted this right. In *Baldwin v. New York* (1970), the Supreme Court decided that a defendant has a constitutional right to a jury trial when facing a possible prison sentence of six months or more, regardless of whether the crime committed was a felony or a misdemeanor.[49] When the possible sentence is six months or less, the accused is not entitled to a jury trial unless it is authorized by state statute. In most jurisdictions, the more serious the charge, the greater the likelihood of trial—and by jury.

THE RIGHT TO COUNSEL AT TRIAL Recall from previous chapters that the defendant has a right to counsel at numerous points in the criminal justice process. Today, state courts must provide counsel at trial to indigent defendants who face even the possibility of incarceration.[50] The threat of incarceration need not be immediate. Even if the defendant might be sentenced to probation in which a prison or jail term is suspended, or might receive any other type of sentence containing a threat of future incarceration, he or she is afforded the right to counsel at trial.[51]

What if a defendant wants to serve as his or her own attorney? As a result of a 1975 Supreme Court decision, defendants are now permitted to proceed *pro se*, or for themselves.[52] Today, when defendants ask to be permitted to represent themselves and are found competent to do so, the court normally approves their requests. However, these defendants are nearly always cautioned by the court against self-representation. When *pro se* defendants' actions are disorderly and disruptive, the court can terminate their right to represent themselves.

THE RIGHT TO A SPEEDY TRIAL The tactics employed by wary defense attorneys (pretrial motions, complex plea negotiations, delay tactics during trial), along with inefficiencies in the court process (such as the frequent granting of continuances, poor scheduling procedures, and the abuse of time by court personnel), have made delays in criminal cases a serious and constitutional issue. As the American Bar Association states in the *Standards Relating to Speedy Trial,* "Congestion in the trial courts of this country, particularly in urban centers, is currently one of the major problems of judicial administration."[53] Delays in the trial process conflict with the Sixth Amendment's guarantee of a right to a speedy trial.[54]

THE RIGHT TO A PUBLIC TRIAL The Sixth Amendment refers to a "public trial." This simply means that all trials must be open to the public. The right to a public trial is generally unrestricted. Anyone who wants to see a criminal trial can do so.

Sometimes having a trial open to the public can cause problems. In the 1966 case of *Sheppard v. Maxwell,* the courtroom was packed with people, including members of the media, for all nine weeks of the trial. Reporters handled evidence and took pictures throughout the trial. The Supreme Court eventually reversed the defendant's conviction, citing the "carnival atmosphere." The case did not lead to the exclusion of cameras from the courtroom, but some judges require that they be kept out. This is why one sometimes sees sketches of a case instead of actual photos.

Adverse pretrial publicity can prevent a defendant from getting a fair trial. The release of premature evidence by the prosecutor, extensive and critical reporting by the news media, and vivid and uncalled-for details in indictments can all prejudice a defendant's case. Press coverage can begin early in a criminal case and can even affect the outcome.

As a general rule, pretrial publicity and reporting cannot be controlled. However, judges may bar the press from some pretrial legal proceedings and hearings, such as preliminary hearings, when police officers make an arrest, or when a warrant is being served, if their presence will infringe on the defendant's right to a fair trial.[55] Other steps can be taken as well. These include changes of venue (moving the trial to another jurisdiction, where there is less press coverage and hence less contamination of the pool of potential jurors) and gag orders (restrictions on what the parties or the media can report), among others.

LO9 Explain the legal rights of the accused at trial

THE RIGHT TO BE CONVICTED BY PROOF BEYOND A REASONABLE DOUBT The standard required to convict a defendant charged with a crime at the adjudicatory stage of the criminal process is proof beyond a reasonable doubt. This requirement dates back to early American history, and over the years has become the accepted measure of persuasion needed by the prosecutor to convince the judge or jury of the defendant's guilt. Many twentieth-century US Supreme Court decisions have reinforced this standard by making "beyond a reasonable doubt a due process and constitutional requirement."[56] In *Brinegar v. United States* (1949), for instance, the Supreme Court stated:

> Guilt in a criminal case must be proven beyond a reasonable doubt and by evidence confined to that which long experience in the common-law tradition, to some extent embodied in the Constitution, has crystallized into rules of evidence consistent with that standard. These rules are historically grounded rights of our system, developed to safeguard men from dubious and unjust convictions with resulting forfeitures of life, liberty, and property.[57]

The reasonable doubt standard is an essential ingredient of the criminal justice process. It is the prime instrument for reducing the risk of convictions based on factual errors.[58] The underlying premise of this standard is that it is better to release a guilty person than to convict someone who is innocent. Because the defendant is presumed innocent until proven guilty, this standard forces the prosecution to overcome this presumption with the highest standard of proof. Unlike the civil law, where a mere preponderance of the evidence is the standard, the criminal process requires proof beyond a reasonable doubt for each element of the offense.[59] The various evidentiary standards of proof are analyzed and compared in Exhibit 8.1.

The Trial Process

The trial of a criminal case is a formal process conducted in a specific and orderly fashion in accordance with rules of criminal law, procedure, and evidence. Unlike what transpires in popular TV programs involving lawyers—where witnesses are often asked leading and prejudicial questions and where judges go far beyond their supervisory role—the modern criminal trial is a complicated and often time-consuming, technical affair. It is a structured adversarial proceeding in which both prosecution and defense follow specific procedures and argue the merits of their cases before the judge and jury. Each side seeks to present its case in the most favorable light.

EXHIBIT 8.1

Evidentiary Standards of Proof: Degrees of Certainty

Standard	Definition	Ruling
Absolute certainty	No possibility of error; 100 percent certainty	Not used in civil or criminal law
Beyond reasonable doubt; moral certainty	Conclusive and complete proof, without leaving any reasonable doubt about the innocence or guilt of the defendant; allows the defendant the benefit of any possibility of innocence	Criminal trial
Clear and convincing	Prevailing and persuasive to the trier of fact	Civil commitments, insanity defense evidence
Preponderance of the evidence	Greater weight of evidence in terms of credibility; more convincing than an opposite point of view	Civil trial
Probable cause	US constitutional standard for arrest and search warrants, requiring existence of facts sufficient to warrant that a crime has been committed	Arrest, preliminary hearing, motions
Sufficient evidence	Adequate evidence to reverse a trial court	Appellate review
Reasonable suspicion	Rational, reasonable belief that facts warrant investigation of a crime on less than probable cause	Police investigations
Less than probable cause	Mere suspicion; less than reasonable belief to conclude criminal activity exists	Prudent police investigation where safety of an officer or others is endangered

Although each jurisdiction in the United States has its own trial procedures, all jurisdictions conduct criminal trials in a generally similar fashion. The basic steps of the criminal trial, which proceed in an established order, are described in this section and outlined in Figure 8.2.

JURY SELECTION In both civil and criminal cases, jurors are selected randomly from licensing or voter registration lists within each court's jurisdiction. Few states impose qualifications on those called for jury service, although most mandate a residency requirement.[60] There is also little uniformity in the amount of time served by jurors; the term ranges from one day to months, depending on the nature of the trial. In addition, most jurisdictions prohibit convicted felons from serving on juries, as well as others exempted by statute, such as public officials, physicians, and attorneys.

The initial list of persons chosen, which is called a *venire*, or jury array, provides the state with a group of potentially capable citizens able to serve on a jury. Many states, by rule of law, review the venire to eliminate unqualified persons and to exempt those who, by reason of their professions, are not allowed to be jurors. The actual jury selection process begins with those remaining on the list.

The court clerk, who handles the administrative affairs of the court—including the processing of the complaint and other documents—randomly selects what he or she believes will be enough names to fill the required number of places on the jury. After reporting to a courtroom, the prospective jurors are first required to swear that they will truthfully answer all questions asked about their qualifications to serve. A group of 12 will be asked to sit in the jury box while the remaining group stands by.

After prospective jurors are chosen, the lengthy process of *voir dire* (from the Old French for "to tell the truth") starts. To determine their appropriateness to sit on the jury, prospective jurors are examined under oath by the government, the defense, and sometimes the judge about their backgrounds, occupations, residences, and possible knowledge of or interest in the case. A juror who acknowledges any bias for or prejudice against the defendant—if the defendant is a friend or relative, or if the juror has already formed an opinion about the case—may be removed by either the prosecution or the

AP Images/Texas Department of Criminal Justice

Eddie Ray Routh, the former Marine found guilty in the shooting deaths of "American Sniper" author Chris Kyle and Chad Littlefield, is processed at an intake center in the Texas prison system.

venire The group called for jury duty from which jury panels are selected.

voir dire The process in which a potential jury panel is questioned by the prosecution and the defense to select jurors who are unbiased and objective.

Voir dire → Prosecutor's opening statement to the jury → Defense attorney's opening statement to the jury → Prosecutor's presentation of evidence and direct examination → Defense attorney's cross-examination → Defense attorney's presentation of evidence and direct examination → Prosecutor's cross-examination →

Defense attorney's closing statements to the jury → Prosecutor's closing statements to the jury (summation) → Judge's instructions to the jury on the law, evidence, and standards of proof → Jury deliberation and voting → Pronouncement of the verdict → Judicial sentencing

FIGURE 8.2 The Steps in a Jury Trial

Source: Marvin Zalman and Larry Siegel, *Criminal Procedure: Constitution and Society* (St. Paul, MN: West, 1991), p. 655.

challenge for cause A request that a prospective juror be removed because he or she is biased or has prior knowledge about a case, or for other reasons that demonstrate the individual's inability to render a fair and impartial judgment in a particular case.

peremptory challenge The dismissal of a potential juror by either the prosecution or the defense for unexplained, discretionary reasons.

REALITY CHECK

MYTH OR REALITY?

There is nothing inherently wrong with a black jury deciding the fate of a white defendant.

REALITY. The Sixth Amendment requires an "impartial jury of the state." If a black jury can be impartial with respect to a white defendant, there is no problem. The reverse is also true.

The problem is one of appearances. Also, and very important, if it can be shown that prospective jurors were excluded because of race, then the resulting jury will not conform to Sixth Amendment requirements.

defense with a challenge for cause asking the judge to dismiss the biased juror. If the judge accepts the challenge, the juror is removed for cause and replaced with another juror from the remaining panel. Because normally no limit is placed on the number of challenges for cause that can be exercised, it often takes considerable time to select a jury, especially for controversial and highly publicized criminal cases.

Besides challenges for cause, both the prosecution and the defense are allowed peremptory challenges, which enable the attorneys to excuse jurors for no particular reason or for undisclosed reasons. A prosecutor might not want a bartender as a juror in a drunk-driving case, believing that a person with that occupation would be sympathetic to the accused. Or the defense attorney might excuse a male prospective juror because the attorney prefers to have a predominantly female jury. The number of peremptory challenges given to the prosecution and defense is limited by state statute and often varies by case and jurisdiction.

The peremptory challenge has been criticized by legal experts who question the fairness and propriety with which it has been used.[61] Historically, the most significant criticism was that it was used by the prosecution to exclude African Americans from serving on juries in which the defendant was also African American—a policy that seemed to allow legally condoned discrimination against minority group members. In the landmark 1986 case *Batson v. Kentucky,* the Supreme Court held that the use of peremptory challenges against potential jurors by prosecutors in criminal cases violated the US Constitution if the challenges were based solely on race.[62] Since that decision, the issue of race discrimination in the use of peremptory challenges has been raised by defendants in numerous cases.

It is becoming increasingly difficult to find impartial jurors, especially in this technological age. Heinous crimes have always been broadcast all over the news, and the result has sometimes been to contaminate the pool of prospective jurors. This still happens, of course, but such crimes are the exception rather than the rule. But now jurors are able to turn to their smartphones and seek information about *any* case. By searching the Internet and sharing information (such as on Facebook), they often learn more about cases than is presented in court, which they are expressly forbidden to do. As one article noted, this practice is "wreaking havoc on trials around the country, upending deliberations and infuriating judges."[63] Although there is no official tally of the number of cases compromised by jurors' Internet research, the number is certainly growing. For example, a Florida case involving a man accused of illegally selling prescription drugs was upended because one juror researched the case on her own and was able to discover information not presented at trial. After her actions came to light, the judge had no choice but to declare a mistrial.

OPENING STATEMENTS After the jury has been selected, and the criminal complaint has been read to the jurors by the court clerk, the prosecutor and the defense attorney may each make an opening statement about the case. The purpose of the prosecutor's statement is to acquaint the judge and jury with the particular criminal charges, to outline the facts, and to describe how the government will prove the defendant guilty beyond a reasonable doubt. The defense attorney reviews the case and indicates how the defense intends to show that the accused is not guilty.

Both sides use the opening statement to give the jury a concise overview of the evidence that is to follow. Neither attorney is allowed to make prejudicial remarks or inflammatory statements or to mention irrelevant facts. Both are free, however, to identify what they will eventually prove by way of evidence, which includes witnesses, physical evidence, and the use of expert testimony. The opening statements are important because they give both sides an opportunity to sway the jury before the trial begins.

PROSECUTION'S CASE Following the opening statements, the government begins its case by presenting evidence to the court through its witnesses. Numerous types of evidence are presented at trial (see Exhibit 8.2). Those called as witnesses—such as police officers, victims, or experts—provide testimony via direct examination. During direct examination, the prosecutor questions the witness to reveal the facts believed pertinent

direct examination The questioning of one's own (prosecution or defense) witness during a trial.

EXHIBIT 8.2

Types of Evidence Presented at Trial

In general, the primary test for the admissibility of evidence in a criminal proceeding is its relevance; that is, the court must consider whether the gun, tool, or bottle has relevant evidentiary value in determining the issues in the case. Ordinarily, evidence that establishes an element of the crime is acceptable to the court. In a prosecution for possession of drugs, evidence that shows the defendant to be a known drug user might be relevant. In a prosecution for bribery, photos of the defendant receiving a package from a co-conspirator would clearly be found relevant to the case. The following are the four main types of evidence:

- *Testimonial evidence.* Given by police officers, citizens, and experts, this is the most basic form of evidence. The witness must state, under oath, what he or she heard, saw, or experienced.

- *Real evidence.* Exhibits that can be taken into the jury room for review by the jury constitute real evidence. A revolver that may have been in

the defendant's control at the time of a murder, tools in the possession of a suspect charged with a burglary, and a bottle allegedly holding narcotics are examples of real, or physical, evidence. Photographs, maps, diagrams, and crime scene displays are other types of real evidence.

- *Documentary evidence.* This type of evidence includes writings, government reports, public records, business or hospital records, fingerprint identification, and DNA profiling.

- *Circumstantial evidence.* In trial proceedings, circumstantial (indirect) evidence is often inferred or indirectly used to prove a fact in question. For example, in a murder case, evidence that carpet fibers found on the body match the carpet in the defendant's home may be used at trial to link the two, even though they do not provide direct evidence that the suspect actually killed the victim.

---

to the government's case. Testimony involves what the witness actually saw, heard, or touched; it does not include opinions. However, a witness's opinion can be given in certain situations, such as when describing the motion of a vehicle or indicating whether a defendant appeared to act intoxicated or insane. Witnesses may also qualify to give opinions because they are experts on a particular subject relevant to the case. For example, a psychiatrist may testify about a defendant's mental capacity at the time of the crime.

Upon completion of the prosecutor's questioning, the defense usually conducts a **cross-examination** of the witness. During this exchange, the defense attorney may challenge elements of the testimony, such as the witness's accuracy in reporting what was seen or heard. The right to cross-examine witnesses is an essential part of a trial, and unless extremely unusual circumstances exist (such as a person's being hospitalized), witness statements will not be considered unless they are made in court and are open for question. If desired, the prosecutor may seek a second direct examination after the defense attorney has completed cross-examination; this allows the prosecutor to ask additional questions about information brought out during cross-examination. Finally, the defense attorney may then question, or re-cross-examine, the witness once again. All witnesses for the trial are sworn in and questioned in the same basic manner.

cross-examination The process in which the defense and the prosecution interrogate witnesses for the other side during a trial.

THE CRIMINAL DEFENSE After the prosecutor has provided all the government's evidence against a defendant, he will inform the court that he rests the people's case. The defense attorney at this point may enter a motion for a **directed verdict**. This is a procedural device in which the defense attorney asks the judge to order the jury to return a verdict of not guilty. Depending on the weight of the prosecution's case, the judge may either sustain or overrule this motion. In essence, the defense attorney argues in the directed verdict that the prosecutor's case against the defendant is insufficient to support the legal elements needed to prove the defendant guilty beyond a reasonable doubt. If the court sustains the motion, the trial is terminated. If it rejects the motion, the defense begins to legally rebut the prosecution's case.

directed verdict The right of a judge to direct a jury to acquit a defendant because the state has not proved the elements of the crime or otherwise has not established guilt according to law.

The defense attorney has the option of presenting many, some, or no witnesses on behalf of the defendant. The burden of proving guilt is on the prosecution, and if the defense team believes that the burden has not been met, they may feel there is no need to present witnesses of their own. In addition, the defense attorney must decide whether the defendant should take the stand and testify in his own behalf. In a criminal trial, the defendant is protected by the Fifth Amendment right to be free from self-incrimination, which means that a person cannot be forced by the state to testify against himself. However, defendants who choose voluntarily to tell their side of the story can be subject to cross-examination by the prosecutor.

The defense attorney is charged with putting on a vigorous defense in the adversary system of justice. She presents her own witnesses and introduces evidence to refute the prosecution's allegations. After the defense concludes its case, the government may then present rebuttal evidence. If the judge grants permission, this involves bringing forward evidence to refute, counteract, or disprove evidence introduced by the defense. A prosecutor may not go into new matters or present evidence that further supports or reinforces his own case. At the end of rebuttal, the defense may be allowed surrebuttal—presenting witnesses to respond to issues that were raised for the first time in the prosecutor's rebuttal case. The defense cannot restate its case or introduce new issues during surrebuttal evidence.

CLOSING ARGUMENTS In closing arguments, the attorneys review the facts and evidence of the case in a manner favorable to their respective positions. At this stage of the trial, both prosecution and defense are permitted to draw reasonable inferences and to show how the facts prove or refute the defendant's guilt. Often both attorneys have a free hand in arguing about the facts, issues, and evidence, including the applicable law. They cannot comment on matters not in evidence, however, or on the defendant's failure to testify in a criminal case. Normally, the prosecutor makes a closing statement first, followed by the defense, and many jurisdictions allow the prosecution an opportunity for rebuttal. Either party can elect to forgo the right to make a final summation to the jury.

INSTRUCTIONS TO THE JURY In a criminal trial, the judge will instruct, or charge, the jury members on the principles of law that ought to guide and control their decision on the defendant's innocence or guilt. The charge includes information about the elements of the alleged offense, the type of evidence needed to prove each element, and the burden of proof that must be met to obtain a guilty verdict. Although the judge commonly provides this instruction, he or she may ask the prosecutor and the defense attorney to submit instructions for consideration; the judge will then exercise discretion in determining whether to use any of their instructions. The instructions that cover the law applicable to the case are extremely important because they may serve as the basis for a subsequent appeal.

DELIBERATION AND VERDICT After the charge is given to the jury members, they retire to deliberate on a verdict. In highly publicized and celebrated cases, the judge may sequester the jury, preventing them from having contact with the outside world. This process is discretionary, and most judges believe that sequestering or "locking up a jury" is needed only in sensational cases.

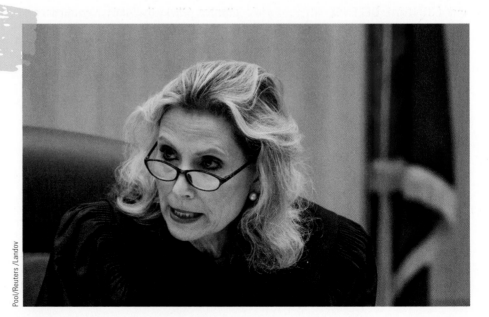

Judge Sherry Stephens gives instructions to the jury during a second sentencing hearing for Jodi Arias in Phoenix on March 3, 2015. Two years before, the first jury could not reach a unanimous decision as to whether Arias should be sentenced to death in connection with the 2008 murder of her husband. Ultimately, the jury in the second hearing was unable to reach consensus, forcing Judge Stephens to declare yet another mistrial and sentence Arias to life in prison.

Pool/Reuters /Landov

A review of the case by the jury may take hours or even days. The jurors always meet privately during their deliberations, and in certain lengthy and highly publicized cases, they are kept overnight in a hotel until the verdict is reached. In less sensational cases, the jurors may be allowed to go home, but they are cautioned not to discuss the case with anyone.

If a verdict cannot be reached, the trial may result in a hung jury, after which the prosecutor must bring the defendant to trial again if the prosecution desires a conviction. If found not guilty, the defendant is released from the criminal process. If the defendant is convicted, the judge will normally order a presentence investigation by the probation department before imposing a sentence. Before sentencing, the defense attorney will probably submit a motion for a new trial, alleging that legal errors occurred in the trial proceedings. The judge may deny the motion and impose a sentence immediately, a practice quite common in most misdemeanor offenses. In felony cases, however, the judge will set a date for sentencing, and the defendant will either be placed on bail or held in custody until that time.

Although jurors are required by law to base their decision on the facts of the case and on the judge's legal instructions, they are sometimes asked by the defense to ignore both and render decisions based on emotion and personal preference.[64] This strategy, called jury nullification, has been in practice since 1735 when John Peter Zenger, editor of the *New York Weekly Journal,* was charged with printing libelous statements about the governor of the Colony of New York, William Cosby. Despite the fact that Zenger clearly printed the alleged libels, and the trial judge gave the jury clear instructions for a finding of guilt, the jury found Zenger not guilty on all charges. The Zenger case remains one of the most famous examples of jury nullification in the nation's history.

Supporters of jury nullification argue that it is an important safeguard against government oppression and that the function of the jury is to serve as a safety valve against the unjust application of the law. Critics, however, see jury nullification as an abuse of power. Would it be fair if jurors, motivated by racial bias, found a person accused of a hate crime not guilty despite overwhelming evidence of guilt?[66]

THE SENTENCE Imposing the criminal sentence is normally the responsibility of the trial judge. In some jurisdictions, the jury may determine the sentence or make recommendations involving leniency for certain offenses. Often, the sentencing decision is based on information and recommendations given to the court by the probation department after a presentence investigation of the defendant. The sentence itself is determined by the statutory requirements for the particular crime as established by the legislature; in addition, the judge ordinarily has a great deal of discretion in reaching a sentencing decision. The different criminal sanctions available include fines, probation, imprisonment, and even commitment to a state hospital. The sentence may be a combination of all these.

APPEALS After a verdict has been rendered and a defendant found guilty, the defense may petition an appellate court to review the procedures used during trial. Defendants have two main avenues to challenge such procedures: appeals and *habeas corpus*. These both give the convicted person an opportunity to appeal to a higher state or federal court on the basis of an error that affected the conviction in the trial court. Extraordinary trial court errors, such as denial of the right to counsel or inability to provide a fair trial, are subject to the plain error rule of the federal courts.[67] Harmless errors, such as the use of innocuous identification procedures or the denial of counsel at a noncritical stage of the proceeding, would not necessarily result in the overturning of a criminal conviction.

jury nullification A defense tactic that consists of suggesting that the jury acquit a defendant, despite evidence that he actually violated the law, by maintaining that the law was unjust or not applicable to the case.

REALITY CHECK

MYTH OR REALITY?

Appellate court judges are partially responsible for the number of appeals filed by convicted individuals.

REALITY. Appellate judges decide whether they want to hear certain appeals. If they refused to hear all such discretionary appeals, there would be no incentive to appeal. Word would get around that appeals are a waste of time.

Thinking about the lengthy death penalty appeals process, then, who is most responsible for the delay between the crime and the execution? Do appellate court judges share some of the blame?

A postconviction **appeal** is a request for an appellate court to examine a lower court's decision to determine whether proper procedures were followed. It is important to note that appeals do not give the convicted an opportunity to try the case a second time, only to challenge procedural matters (such as a judge's decision to exclude a witness's testimony). Most defendants benefit from at least one direct appeal. Direct appeals are guaranteed by law; the result is that most defendants get to appeal at least once, even if they cannot afford it.[68] Discretionary appeals are also possible. The appellate court decides whether it will hear a discretionary appeal. There is no restriction on the number of discretionary appeals that can be filed.

Through objections made at the pretrial and trial stages of the criminal process, the defense counsel will reserve specific legal issues on the record as the basis for appeal. A copy of the transcript of these proceedings will serve as the basis on which the appellate court will review any errors that may have occurred during the lower-court proceedings. The Careers in Criminal Justice feature describes the work of the court reporter, the person who prepares these transcripts.

A **writ of *habeas corpus*** is the primary means by which state prisoners have their convictions or sentences reviewed in the federal court. A writ of *habeas corpus* (which means "you may have the body") seeks to determine the validity of a detention by asking the court to release the person or give legal reasons for the incarceration.

LO10 Summarize the trial process

CAREERS IN CRIMINAL JUSTICE COURT REPORTER

Duties and Characteristics of the Job

- Court reporters create the official transcripts of legal proceedings such as trials and depositions.

- These transcripts include all the dialogue as well as other important details, such as emotional reactions.

- Court reporters use voice writers that make an audio record of the proceedings.

- Some use audio equipment to tape an event and then supplement this recording later with notes taken during the proceedings.

- The commonly used recording method in legal and courtroom settings is the stenographic machine, which court reporters use to transcribe spoken words. A court reporter can press multiple keys simultaneously to represent words, sounds, or even phrases.

- Although the primary responsibility of court reporters is to record courtroom legal proceedings, they also provide this information from the official record when requested.

- Court reporters can advise lawyers on legal procedure when necessary.

Job Outlook

- The number of jobs available for court reporters is greater than the number of trained professionals entering the field.

- The job outlook is favorable for entry-level court reporters, especially those who are certified.

- Court reporters are always needed in courtrooms and lawyers' offices across the country, although jobs may be more plentiful in urban areas.

- They often freelance for extra income at attorneys' offices or as closed-captioners and/or real-time translators.

- Other court reporters work for court reporting agencies or freelance full time.

- Agency workers and freelancers enjoy the flexibility of setting their own schedules.

Salary

- Pay will depend on several factors, including method of transcription, region of the United States, type of employer, amount of previous work experience, and level of certification.

- The median annual salary for court reporters is around $50,000. The majority of court reporters earn between $35,390 and $67,430. At the extremes, a small percentage of court reporters earn $24,790 and the highest paid earn $90,530 or more.

Qualifications

- The qualifications to be a practicing court reporter vary by state.

- In some states, court reporters are required to be notary publics; in others, an individual must become a certified court reporter (CCR) by passing a state certification test.

- Court reporters must continually study and practice their skills.

Education and Training

- At minimum, a court reporter needs an associate's degree, although requiring a bachelor's degree is more common.

- In addition to general education, training programs are available at vocational or technical schools.

- Currently, 70 programs are approved by the National Court Reporters Association in the United States and Canada.

Reality Check

- Because a court reporter must create a record of events as they occur, the ability to listen carefully and work quickly is key. Familiarity with legal terms and practices is necessary, as is a thorough knowledge of grammar, spelling, and vocabulary.

- Court reporters must become intimately familiar with stenotype machines. As one reporter said, "Your wrists will become your worst enemy if you don't show them some love."

(Continued)

- Despite the seemingly simple training requirements, many people drop out, partly as a consequence of the high speed required (around 225 words per minute, far in excess of the speed at which skilled typists can type).

- The constant pressure to be fast and accurate can cause considerable stress.

- The future is somewhat uncertain; digital audio recorders could well replace court reporters someday.

Sources: S. E. Lambert and D. Regan, "Court Reporter," *Great Jobs for Criminal Justice Majors* (New York: McGraw-Hill, 2001), pp. 159–161; Bureau of Labor Statistics, US Department of Labor, "Court Reporters," *Occupational Outlook Handbook,* http://www.bls.gov/ooh/legal/court-reporters.htm (accessed February 2015).

ETHICAL Challenge

Shantel is an unemployed former crack addict with an extensive criminal record. When she was actively using, she gave birth to six children, each of whom was taken away by Child Protective Services. She has since put her life back on track, secured a job, stopped using drugs, and given birth to her seventh child, Keisha, who lives with her. When Keisha was 2 years old, Shantel moved back in with her estranged boyfriend, Deshaun, whom she thought had also stopped using. Unbeknownst to Shantel, although Deshaun had stopped using crack, he had become hooked on OxyContin and was using the drug on a regular basis. Not long after they moved in together, the police served a search warrant on their property and found a stash of the drug. Both Shantel and Deshaun were charged with drug possession. Shantel's extensive criminal record would probably result in a long-term prison sentence, not to mention the possible loss of Keisha, if she were found guilty at a trial. Surprisingly, during Shantel's pretrial negotiations, the district attorney offered a plea bargain to give Shantel three years *or* probation and no jail time if she agreed to sterilization. Shantel did not want to take the chance of going to trial and getting a long-term prison sentence. She knew she would not have any chance of getting Keisha back if she got a long-term prison sentence. She felt her only option was to agree to the plea negotiation of probation and sterilization.

Ethical Challenge: Write an essay on the ethical issues raised in this plea-bargaining scenario. In doing so, answer these questions: Should Shantel plead guilty to a crime she did not commit? Should she subject herself to sterilization for a crime she did not commit? How many other defendants plead guilty to crimes they have not committed? Is it even possible to know? One of the main criticisms of plea bargaining is just this; a guilty plea does not always mean the offender is guilty. What other criticisms of plea bargaining have been raised? Consult this chapter's "Plea Bargaining" section as you answer the questions.

SUMMARY

LO1 ***Summarize the bail process*** The purpose of bail is to obtain the release from custody of a person charged with a crime. The Eighth Amendment to the US Constitution does not guarantee a right to bail but, rather, prohibits "excessive bail." Bail is typically granted during a court hearing, but bail may be granted at other stages in the system as well, depending on the jurisdiction, the crime, and the defendant. In practice, a majority of criminal defendants are released on bail prior to trial.

LO2 ***Discuss the main issues associated with bail*** Bail is a controversial practice, but it serves a valuable function. Bonding agents are available to assist defendants who do not have sufficient resources with pretrial release. Those who cannot make bail often wait in jail until trial. Jail conditions are often unpleasant and crowded. Jailed defendants are also convicted at higher rates than those released on bail. In light of these issues, various bail reforms have been enacted over the years, ranging from release on recognizance to preventive detention. Pretrial services are also provided for certain defendants.

LO3 ***Differentiate between the two main mechanisms for charging defendants (grand jury indictment and prosecutor's information)*** The grand jury's role is to act as the community's conscience in determining whether the accusation of the state (the prosecution) justifies a trial. If the grand jury believes charges are merited, an indictment will be issued. If not, a "no bill" is passed. The charging mechanism used in about half the states, as an alternative to the grand jury, is a prosecutor's information. An information is a written accusation submitted to the court by a prosecutor, alleging that a particular individual committed the offense in question.

LO4 ***Summarize the pleas available to a criminal defendant*** The defendant in a criminal trial will enter one of three pleas: guilty, not guilty, or *nolo contendere*. The pleas of guilty and not guilty are self-explanatory. *Nolo contendere* is essentially a plea of guilty, but it may not be held against the defendant as proof in a subsequent legal matter, such as a civil lawsuit.

L05 ***Explain the issues involved in plea bargaining*** Plea bargaining is one of the most common practices in the criminal justice system and is a cornerstone of the informal justice system. Today, more than 90 percent of criminal convictions are estimated to result from negotiated pleas of guilty. Some critics of plea bargaining believe that defendants are treated with leniency as a result of the practice. Supporters of plea bargaining point out that all parties benefit from the practice (the prosecutor gets a conviction, the defense gets leniency, and the court saves the costs of a trial). Various Supreme Court decisions place constraints on plea bargaining.

L06 ***Describe the plea-bargaining process*** The plea-bargaining process is largely informal, lacking in guidelines, and discretionary. The prosecutor typically presents the defendant with an offer of a reduced charge or favorable sentencing recommendation. Defense counsel is required to play an advisory role in plea negotiations. Judges should not be a party to arrangements for the determination of a sentence, whether as a result of a guilty plea or as a result of a finding of guilty based on proof. The victim is not empowered at the pretrial stage of the criminal process to influence a plea-bargaining decision. Recently, efforts have been made to convert plea bargaining into a more visible, understandable, and fair process.

L07 ***Explain the purpose of pretrial diversion*** Another important feature in the early court process is placing offenders into noncriminal diversion programs before their formal trial or conviction. Pretrial diversion helps the accused avoid the stigma of a criminal conviction.

L08 ***Describe the goals and purpose of the trial process*** The criminal trial is an open and public hearing designed to examine the facts of the case brought by the state against the accused. The trial is an important and enduring fixture in the criminal justice system. By its very nature, it is a symbol of the moral authority of the state and impartial justice. Most formal trials are heard by a jury, although some defendants waive their constitutional right to a jury trial and request a bench trial, in which the judge alone renders a verdict.

L09 ***Explain the legal rights of the accused at trial*** Legal rights at trial include the right to an impartial judge, the right to be competent at trial, the right to confront witnesses, the right to compulsory process, the right to an impartial jury, the right to counsel, the right to a speedy trial, the right to a public trial, and the right to be convicted by proof beyond a reasonable doubt.

L010 ***Summarize the trial process*** The criminal trial is a formal process conducted in a specific and orderly fashion in accordance with rules of criminal law, procedure, and evidence. After the jury has been selected, the prosecutor and the defense attorney may each make an opening statement about the case. Following the opening statements, the government begins its case by presenting evidence to the court through its witnesses. After the prosecution has provided all the government's evidence against a defendant, it will inform the court that it rests the people's case. Next, the defense will present its case. After that, closing arguments are used by the attorneys to review the facts and evidence of the case in a manner favorable to their respective positions. The judge will then instruct, or charge, the jury members on the principles of law that ought to guide and control their decision on the defendant's innocence or guilt. Imposing the criminal sentence (if a "guilty" verdict is reached) is normally the responsibility of the trial judge.

KEY TERMS

pretrial procedures, p. 182

bail, p. 182

pretrial detention, p. 182

release on recognizance (ROR), p. 184

Manhattan Bail Project, p. 185

deposit bail, p. 185

Bail Reform Act of 1984, p. 186

preventive detention, p. 186

presentment, p. 187

indictment, p. 187

no bill, p. 187

information, p. 187

preliminary hearing, p. 187

plea bargaining, p. 190

diversion, p. 194

bench trial, p. 195

adjudication, p. 195

confrontation clause, p. 196

hearsay evidence, p. 196

compulsory process, p. 196

pro se, p. 197

proof beyond a reasonable doubt, p. 198

preponderance of the evidence, p. 198

venire, p. 199

voir dire, p. 199

challenge for cause, p. 200

peremptory challenge, p. 200

direct examination, p. 200

cross-examination, p. 201

directed verdict, p. 201

jury nullification, p. 203

appeal, p. 204

writ of *habeas corpus*, p. 204

REVIEW QUESTIONS

1. Should those accused of violent acts be subjected to preventive detention instead of bail, even though they have not been convicted of a crime? Is it fair to the victim to have the alleged attacker running around loose?

2. Should criminal defendants be allowed to bargain for a reduced sentence in exchange for a guilty plea? Should the victim always be included in the plea-bargaining process?

3. What purpose does a grand jury or preliminary hearing serve in adjudicating felony offenses? Should one of these methods be abandoned, and if so, which one?

4. Do criminal defendants enjoy too many rights at trial? Why or why not?

5. Should people be denied the right to serve as jurors without explanation or cause? In other words, should the peremptory challenge be maintained?

6. "In the adversary system of criminal justice, the burden of proof in a criminal trial to show that the defendant is guilty beyond a reasonable doubt is on the government." Explain the meaning of this statement.

9 Punishment and Sentencing

In 2012, one day after Thanksgiving, Jordan Davis, 17, a passenger in an SUV with three of his friends, pulled into a gas station in Jacksonville, Florida. The music was blaring—loudly. As the driver, Tommie Stornes, was inside buying gum and cigarettes, Michael Dunn (pictured), a 45-year-old software developer, pulled into the parking spot next to the SUV. After his girlfriend went into the store, Dunn exited his vehicle and asked the men in the SUV to turn the music down. The front passenger, Tevin Thompson, complied, but Davis, who was seated in the back, objected and turned the music back up. According to Dunn, Davis then went further, threatening to kill him and brandishing a gun. Dunn, who had a concealed weapons permit, went to his car, removed a handgun from the glove compartment, and began firing at Davis. As the SUV sped off, Dunn continued firing at it, a total of 10 times. Davis was killed. Dunn did not call the police. Instead, he left the scene with his girlfriend, went back to his hotel, made a drink, ordered a pizza, took his dog for a walk, and went to bed. Investigators were unable to find any weapons during a subsequent search of the SUV.

Dunn was put on trial for murder, but in February 2014, the trial jury became hopelessly deadlocked, and a mistrial was declared.[1] Prosecutors retried the case, and in the fall of 2014, Dunn was found guilty of first-degree murder.[2] He was subsequently sentenced to life in prison. "Mr. Dunn, your life is effectively over," said Circuit Judge Russell Healey during the sentencing hearing. "What is sad is that this case exemplifies that our society seems to have lost its way."[3] Was Dunn's punishment appropriate? Or was it too harsh? Will society be safer as a result of the verdict and the sentence?

This chapter first examines the history of punishment and then focuses on incarceration and capital punishment, the two most traditional and punitive forms of criminal sanctions used today. Chapter 10 reviews alternative sentences that have been developed to reduce the strain on the overburdened correctional system; these sentences provide intermediate sanctions designed to control people whose behavior and personality make incarceration unnecessary. Such sanctions include probation and other forms of community correction.

LEARNING OBJECTIVES

LO1 *Outline the historical development of punishment*

LO2 *Explain the major goals of contemporary sentencing*

LO3 *Identify various sentencing models*

LO4 *Explain how sentences are imposed*

LO5 *Summarize factors associated with sentencing decisions*

LO6 *List the arguments for and against capital punishment*

LO7 *Articulate the legal issues associated with capital punishment*

The History of Punishment

The punishment and correction of criminals has changed considerably through the ages, reflecting customs, economic conditions, and religious and political ideals.[4]

From Exile to Fines, Torture to Forfeiture

In early Greece and Rome, the most common state-administered punishment was banishment or exile. Only slaves were commonly subjected to harsh physical punishment for their misdeeds. Interpersonal violence, even attacks that resulted in death, were viewed as a private matter. These ancient peoples typically used economic punishments, such as fines, for such crimes as assault on a slave, arson, and housebreaking.

During the Middle Ages (the fifth to fifteenth centuries), there was little law or governmental control. Offenses often sparked blood feuds carried out by the families of the injured parties. When possible, the Roman custom of settling disputes by fine or an exchange of property was adopted as a means of resolving interpersonal conflicts with a minimum of bloodshed. After the eleventh century, during the feudal period, forfeiture of land and property was common punishment for persons who violated law and custom or who failed to fulfill their feudal obligations to their lord. The word "felony" has its origins in the twelfth century, when the term "felonia" referred to a breach of faith with one's feudal lord.

During this period, the main emphasis of criminal law and punishment was on maintaining public order. If in the heat of passion or while intoxicated a person severely injured or killed his neighbor, freemen in the area would gather to pronounce a judgment and make the culprit do penance or pay compensation called *wergild* (literally, "man payment"). The purpose of the fine was to pacify the injured party and ensure that the conflict would not develop into a blood feud and anarchy. The inability of the peasantry to pay a fine led to the use of corporal punishment, such as whipping or branding, as a substitute penalty.

The development of the common law in the eleventh century brought some standardization to penal practices. However, corrections remained an amalgam of fines and brutal physical punishments. The criminal wealthy could buy their way

In earlier times, punishment was often quite severe. Even kings, such as Charles I of England, were not immune to death by beheading.

out of punishment and into exile, but capital and corporal punishment were used to control the criminal poor, who were executed and mutilated at ever-increasing rates. Execution, banishment, mutilation, branding, and flogging were inflicted on a whole range of offenders, from murderers and robbers to vagrants and Gypsies. Punishments became unmatched in their cruelty, featuring a gruesome variety of physical tortures, often administered as part of a public spectacle, presumably so that the horrific sanctions would act as deterrents. But the variety and imagination of the tortures inflicted on even minor criminals before their death suggest that retribution, sadism, and spectacle were more important than any presumed deterrent effect.

Public Work and Transportation to the Colonies

By the end of the sixteenth century, the rise of the city and overseas colonization provided tremendous markets for manufactured goods and spurred the need for labor. Punishment of criminals changed to meet the demands created by these social conditions. Instead of being tortured or executed, many offenders were made to do hard labor for their crimes. "Poor laws," developed at the end of the sixteenth century, required that the poor, vagrants, and vagabonds be put to work in public or private enterprises. Houses of correction were developed to make it convenient to assign petty law violators to work details. In London, a workhouse was developed at Brideswell in 1557; its use became so popular that by 1576, Parliament ordered a Brideswell-type workhouse to be built in every county in England. Many convicted offenders were pressed into sea duty as galley slaves. Galley slavery was considered so loathsome a fate that many convicts mutilated themselves rather than submit to servitude on the high seas.

The constant shortage of labor in the European colonies also prompted authorities to transport convicts overseas. In England, an Order in Council of 1617 granted a reprieve and stay of execution to people convicted of robbery and other felonies who were strong enough to be employed overseas. Similar measures were used in France and Italy to recruit galley slaves and workers.

Transporting convicts to the colonies became popular: it supplied labor, cost little, and was actually profitable for the government because manufacturers and plantation owners paid for the convicts' services. The Old Bailey Court in London supplied at least 10,000 convicts between 1717 and 1775. Convicts would serve a period as workers and then become free again.

The American Revolution ended the transportation of felons to North America, but it continued in Australia and New Zealand. Between 1787 and 1875, when the practice was finally abandoned, more than 135,000 felons were transported to Australia.

Although transportation in lieu of a death sentence might at first glance seem merciful, transported prisoners endured terrible hardships. Those who were sent to Australia suffered incredible physical abuse, including severe whippings and mutilation. Many of the British prison officials placed in charge of the Australian penal colonies could best be described as sociopaths or sadists.

The Rise of the Prison

Between the American Revolution in 1776 and the first decades of the nineteenth century, the European and US populations increased rapidly. Transportation of convicts to North America was no longer an option. The increased use of machinery made industry capital intensive, not labor intensive. As a result, there was less need for unskilled laborers in England, and many workers could not find suitable employment.

The gulf between poor workers and wealthy landowners and merchants widened. The crime rate rose significantly, prompting a return to physical punishment and increased use of the death penalty. In England during the latter part of the eighteenth century, 350 types of crimes were punishable by death. Although many people sentenced to death for trivial offenses were spared the gallows, the use of capital punishment was common in England during the mid-eighteenth century. Prompted by the excessive use of physical and capital punishment, legal philosophers argued that physical punishment should be replaced by periods of confinement and incapacitation. Jails and workhouses were thus used to hold petty offenders, vagabonds, the homeless, and debtors. However, these institutions were not meant for hard-core criminals. One solution to imprisoning a growing criminal population was to keep prisoners in abandoned ships anchored in rivers and harbors throughout England. In 1777, the degrading conditions under which prisoners lived in these ships inspired John Howard, the sheriff of Bedfordshire, to write *The State of the Prisons in England and Wales*, which led to Parliament's passage of legislation mandating the construction of secure and sanitary structures to house prisoners.

By 1820, long periods of incarceration in walled institutions called reformatories, or **penitentiaries**, began to replace physical punishment in England and the United States. These institutions were considered to represent liberal reform at a time when harsh physical punishment and incarceration in filthy holding facilities were the norm. The history of correctional institutions will be discussed further in Chapter 11. Incarceration has remained the primary mode of punishment for serious offenses in the United States since it was introduced in the early nineteenth century. Ironically, in our high-tech society, some of the institutions developed soon after the Revolutionary War are still in use today. In contemporary society, prison as a method of punishment has been supplemented by a sentence to community supervision for less serious offenders, and the death penalty is reserved for those considered the most serious and dangerous.

The Goals of Modern Sentencing

When we hear about a notorious criminal receiving a long prison sentence or the death penalty for a particularly heinous crime, each of us has a distinct reaction. Some of us are gratified that a truly evil person "got just what he deserved"; many people feel safer because a dangerous person is now "where he can't harm any other innocent victims"; others hope the punishment serves as a warning to potential criminals that "everyone gets caught in the end"; some may actually feel sorry for the defendant—"he got a raw deal, he needs help, not punishment"; and still others hope that "when he gets out, he'll have learned his lesson." And when an offender is forced to pay a large fine, we say, "What goes around comes around."

Each of these sentiments may be at work when criminal sentences are formulated. After all, sentences are devised and implemented by judges, many of whom are elected officials and share the general public's sentiments and fears. The objectives of criminal sentencing today can usually be grouped into five distinct areas: deterrence (both general and specific), incapacitation, retribution/just desert, rehabilitation, and equity/restitution.

Deterrence

Deterrence is one of the most popular goals of sentencing. There are two types of deterrence: general and specific. According to the concept of **general deterrence**, people will be too afraid to break the law if they believe that they will be caught and punished severely. The more certain and severe the punishment is, the greater the deterrent effect. However, punishment cannot be so harsh that it seems disproportionate and unfair. If it were, people would believe they had nothing to lose, and their crimes might escalate in frequency and severity. Thus, if the crime of rape were punished by death, rapists might be encouraged to kill their victims to dispose of the one person who could identify them at trial. Because they would already be facing the death penalty for rape, they would have nothing more to lose by committing murder as well.

Some justice experts believe that the recent decline in the crime rate is a result of increasing criminal penalties. Once arrested, people have a greater chance of being convicted today than they did in the past. This phenomenon is referred to as "expected punishment," defined as the number of days in prison a typical criminal

penitentiary A state or federal correctional institution for the incarceration of felony offenders for terms of one year or more.

LO1 Outline the historical development of punishment

LO2 Explain the major goals of contemporary sentencing

general deterrence The theory that crime rates are influenced and controlled by the threat of criminal punishment. If people fear being apprehended and punished, they will not risk breaking the law.

can expect to serve per crime.[5] Despite rising recently, expected punishment rates are actually still quite low because (1) crime clearance rates remain well under 50 percent, (2) many cases are dropped at the pretrial and trial stages (*nolle prosequi*), and (3) about one-third of convicted felons are given probationary sentences rather than prison sentences.

Take the crime of burglary. In the 2 million burglaries reported to the police each year, about 200,000 burglars are arrested, 100,000 are convicted, and about 40,000 are sent to prison. Therefore, for every 50 reported burglaries, only 1 burglar is incarcerated. (Keep in mind that some burglars commit many crimes per year, so we are not talking about 2 million individual burglars but 2 million burglaries!) Such inefficiency limits the deterrent effect of punishment.

Because the justice system is still inefficient, the general deterrent effect of punishment is less than desired. The percentage of convicted offenders who receive a prison sentence has actually declined during the past decade, and the estimated average prison sentence received by violent felony offenders in state courts decreased from nearly 10 years in 1994 to about 8 years today.[6] If this trend continues, the deterrent effect of punishments may decline, and crime rates may increase as a result. Note, however, that the actual time served per sentence has increased somewhat, meaning that inmates are spending more of their sentence behind bars before they are released. This may help neutralize the effect of lighter sentences.

In contrast to general deterrence, the goal of **specific deterrence** is to convince offenders that the pains of punishment are greater than the benefits of crime; hence, they will not repeat their criminal offending. The experience of suffering punishment should inhibit future law violations.

Claims for a specific deterrent effect are weakened by data showing that most inmates (more than 80 percent) who are released from prison have had prior convictions, and the great majority (68 percent) will reoffend soon after their release. A prison stay seems to have little effect on reoffending.[7] Despite these sketchy results, the goal of specific deterrence remains a fundamental part of sentencing. Some judges and policy makers maintain that a "taste of the bars" should reduce the desire for repeat offending.[8]

specific deterrence A crime control policy suggesting that punishment should be severe enough to convince convicted offenders never to repeat their criminal activity.

Incapacitation

Because criminals will not be able to repeat their criminal acts while they are under state control, **incapacitation** of criminals is another goal of sentencing. For some offenders, this means a period in a high-security state prison where behavior is closely monitored. Keeping dangerous criminals behind bars prevents them, during this period of incapacitation, from repeating their illegal activities.

incapacitation The policy of keeping dangerous criminals in confinement to eliminate the risk of their repeating their offense in society.

Does incapacitating criminals help reduce the crime rate? The evidence is mixed. Between 1990 and the present, the prison population more than doubled (from 700,000 to almost 1.6 million[9]), and the crime rate dropped dramatically, indicating a significant incarceration effect. However, there have been periods, such as between 1980 and 1990, when the prison population increased and so did the crime rate. This indicates that incarceration trends may influence crime rates but that reductions in crime may also be related to other factors, such as population makeup, police effectiveness, declining drug use, and the economy.[10]

Incarceration may also have a short-term effect that diminishes as more and more people are put in prison, and the incarceration benefit of incarcerating each new inmate decreases. Think of it this way: If the country had only a single prison cell and only one person could be locked up at a time, chances are that person would be the nation's most dangerous, violent chronic offender. The crime reduction benefit of locking up just that single person would be significant. If we could incarcerate only two, the second inmate would be slightly less dangerous. Each time a person is added to the prison population, the crime reduction benefit is somewhat less than that achieved by imprisoning the inmate who came before. We now have approximately 1.6 million people behind bars. The millionth-plus inmate is far less dangerous than

blameworthy Culpable or guilty of participating in a particular criminal offense.

just desert The philosophy of justice asserting that those who violate the rights of others deserve to be punished. The severity of punishment should be commensurate with the seriousness of the crime.

rehabilitation The strategy of applying proper treatment so an offender will present no further threat to society.

equity The action or practice of awarding each person what is due him or her; sanctions based on equity seek to compensate individual victims and society in general for their losses due to crime.

the first, and the incarceration benefits of locking him up are significantly less, yet the *cost* of incarcerating each new inmate remains the same as that of locking up the first![11] Thus, by definition, using incapacitation to reduce crime rates always yields diminishing returns.[12]

Retribution/Just Desert

According to the retributive goal of sentencing, the essential purpose of the criminal process is to punish offenders—fairly and justly—in a manner that is proportionate to the gravity of their crimes.[13] Offenders are punished simply and solely because they *deserve* to be disciplined for what they have done: "the punishment should fit the crime."[14] It would be wrong to punish people to set an example for others or to deter would-be criminals, as the general deterrence goal demands. Punishment should be no more or less than the offender's actions deserve; it must be based on how **blameworthy** the person is. This is referred to as the concept of **just desert**.[15]

According to this view, punishments must be equally and fairly distributed to all people who commit similar illegal acts. However, determining just punishments can be difficult because there is generally little consensus about the treatment of criminals, the seriousness of crimes, and the proper response to criminal acts. Consequently, there has been an ongoing effort to calculate fair and just sentences and to apply them in an equitable way.

Rehabilitation

Some sentences are based on the need to treat and/or rehabilitate criminal offenders. Because society has failed them, many offenders have been forced to grow up in disorganized neighborhoods, have been the target of biased police officers, and are disadvantaged at home, at school, and in the job market. To compensate for these deprivations, the justice system is obligated to help these unfortunate people and not simply punish them for their misdeeds.[16] Advocates of **rehabilitation** believe that if the proper treatment is applied, an offender will present no further threat to society.[17] It is not surprising, then, that the general public supports the treatment goal of sentencing and prefers it to policies based on punishment and incarceration.[18]

Equity/Restitution

Because criminals benefit from their misdeeds, it seems both fair and just to demand that they reimburse society for the losses their crimes have caused. In the early common law, *wergild* and fines represented the concept of creating an equitable solution to crime by requiring the convicted offender to make restitution to both the victim and the state. Today, judges continue to require that offenders compensate victims for their losses.

The **equity** goal of punishment means that convicted criminals should pay back their victims for their loss, the justice system for the costs of processing their case, and society for any disruption they may have caused. In a so-called victimless crime such as drug trafficking, the social costs might include the expense of drug enforcement efforts, drug treatment centers, and care for infants born to drug-addicted mothers. The costs of violent crimes might include the services of emergency room doctors, lost workdays and productivity, and treatment for long-term psychological problems. To help defray these costs, convicted offenders might be required to pay a fine, forfeit the property they acquired through illegal gain, do community service work, make financial restitution to their victim, and reimburse the state for the costs of the criminal process. And because the criminals' actions helped expand their personal gains, rights, and privileges at society's expense, justice demands that they lose rights and privileges to restore the social balance.

Sentencing Models

When a convicted offender is sentenced to prison, the statutes of the jurisdiction in which the crime was committed determine what penalties the court may impose. Over the years, a variety of sentencing structures have been used in the United States. They include indeterminate sentences, determinate sentences, and mandatory sentences.

Indeterminate Sentences

In the 1870s, prison reformers Enoch Wines and Zebulon Brockway and others called for creation of indeterminate sentences tailored to fit individual needs. Offenders, the argument went, should be placed in confinement only until they are rehabilitated and then released on parole. Criminals were believed to be "sick" rather than bad; they could be successfully treated in prison. Rather than holding that "the punishment should fit the crime," reformers believed that "the treatment should fit the offender."

Under indeterminate sentencing, convicted offenders are typically given a "light" minimum sentence that must be served and a lengthy maximum sentence that is the outer boundary of the time that can be served. For example, the legislature might set a sentence of a minimum of 2 years and a maximum of 20 years for burglary; the convicted offender must be sentenced to no less than 2 years but no more than 20 years in prison. Under this scheme, the actual length of time served by the offender is controlled by both the judge and the correctional agency. A judge could sentence a burglar to 5–15 years; the inmate then may be paroled from confinement soon after serving the minimum sentence *if* the correctional authorities believe that she is ready to live in the community. If the inmate accumulates good time, she could be released in as little as 30 months; a troublesome inmate, however, would be forced to do all 15 years.

The basic purpose of the indeterminate sentence is to individualize each sentence in the interests of rehabilitating the offender. This type of sentencing allows for flexibility not only in the type of sentence to be imposed but also in the length of time to be served.

Most jurisdictions that use indeterminate sentences employ statutes that specify minimum and maximum terms but allow judicial discretion to fix the actual sentence within those limits. The typical minimum sentence is at least one year; a few state jurisdictions require at least a two-year minimum sentence for felons.[19]

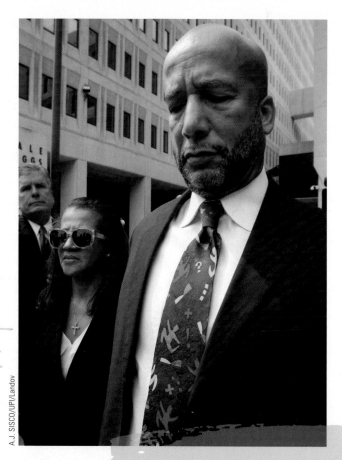

A.J. SISCO/UPI/Landov

Former New Orleans mayor Ray Nagin leaves the federal courthouse with his wife, Seletha, after he was sentenced to 10 years in prison. Nagin was found guilty of fraud, bribery, and related charges involving crimes that took place before and after Hurricane Katrina devastated the city in August of 2005. He was ordered to report to federal prison and also to pay restitution of $82,000.

indeterminate sentence A term of incarceration with a stated minimum and maximum length, such as a sentence to prison for a period of 3 to 10 years. The prisoner would be eligible for parole after the minimum sentence has been served. Based on the belief that sentences should fit the crime, indeterminate sentences allow individualized sentences and provide for sentencing flexibility. Judges can set a high minimum to override the purpose of the indeterminate sentence.

Determinate Sentences

Dissatisfaction with the disparities and uncertainty of indeterminate sentencing has prompted some states and the federal government to abandon it in favor of determinate sentencing models or structured sentencing models, aimed at curbing judicial discretion.

ETHICAL REFLECTION

Jordan Davis Shooting

Prosecutors are afforded discretion in deciding whether to pursue charges against suspected criminals. Return to the Jordan Davis/Michael Dunn case featured at the outset of this chapter. The first time Dunn was tried, the judge declared a mistrial, as jurors could not agree on the murder charge. The jurors did, however, find Dunn guilty on lesser charges than murder, namely three counts of attempted second-degree murder. In light of the jury's findings, should the judge have declared a mistrial? And should prosecutors have pursued the second trial? Why or why not?

Determinate sentences offer a fixed term of years, the maximum set in law by the legislature, to be served by the offender sentenced to prison for a particular crime. If the law provides for a sentence of up to 20 years for robbery, the judge might sentence a repeat offender to a 15-year term; another, less-experienced felon might receive a more lenient sentence of 5 years.

To regulate the length of determinate sentences and curb judicial discretion, most jurisdictions that employ them have developed methods to structure and control the sentencing process and make it more rational. To accomplish this task, sentencing guidelines have been implemented by determinate-sentencing states and the federal government. Guidelines give judges a recommended sentence based on the seriousness of a crime and the background of an offender—the more serious the crime and the more extensive the offender's criminal background, the longer the prison term recommended by the guidelines. For example, guidelines might recommend a sentence of five years for robbery if the offender had no prior offense record and did not use excessive force or violence. For a second offense, the recommended sentence would increase to seven years; those who used force and had a prior record would have three years added to their sentence, and so on. Guidelines are designed to reduce racial and gender disparity by eliminating judicial discretion.[20]

THE FUTURE OF GUIDELINES Several states use some form of structured sentencing. Until recently, some states used voluntary/advisory sentencing guidelines (sometimes called descriptive guidelines), which merely suggest rather than mandate sentences, whereas others used presumptive sentencing guidelines (sometimes called prescriptive guidelines), which required judges to use the guidelines to shape their sentencing decisions.[21]

Two Supreme Court cases have placed a moratorium on the use of presumptive guidelines and put their future in doubt. First, in *Blakely v. Washington,* the Court found that Washington State's sentencing guidelines were a violation of a defendant's Sixth Amendment rights because they allowed a judge to consider aggravating factors that would enhance the sentence.[22] The Court ruled that this amounts to a finding of fact without the benefit of a jury trial or personal admission. In *Blakely,* the sentencing judge, acting alone, had decided that the offense involved "deliberate cruelty" and enhanced Blakely's sentence. Proving a state of mind such as "deliberate cruelty" must be determined by a jury "beyond a reasonable doubt" and not by a judge applying guidelines. Then, in *United States v. Booker,* the Court ruled that the federal guidelines were unconstitutional, allowing that judges should consider the guideline ranges but must also be permitted to alter sentences in consideration of other factors; sentences could then be subject to appellate review if they were unreasonable.[23] Since these cases were decided, guidelines have been used in an advisory capacity alone.

Even before *Blakely* and *Booker* limited their use, presumptive guidelines had been criticized as being rigid, harsh, overly complex, and disliked by the judiciary.[24] They substantially increased correctional populations, especially when they were used in a haphazard fashion and were not tied to the availability of correctional resources.[25]

These cases did not in essence outlaw guidelines but, rather, ruled that changes were needed in the way they are administered. State and federal courts are now addressing these issues and creating mechanisms for proper administration of the guidelines, especially if the case involves sentencing enhancement. Since these cases were decided, the future of guidelines seems hazy. However, a report by the Federal Sentencing Commission found that even though federal courts interpreted the *Booker* decision in different ways, the majority of cases continue to be sentenced within the range of existing sentencing guidelines. So even though the guidelines are now advisory rather than mandatory, they still have a great deal of impact on sentencing decisions.[26] Sentencing guidelines are still being used in this new advisory fashion in Minnesota and other states.

Mandatory Sentences

Another effort to limit judicial discretion and at the same time get tough on crime has been development of the mandatory sentence. Some states have passed legislation prohibiting people convicted of certain offenses, such as violent crimes or drug trafficking, from being placed on probation; they must serve at least some time in prison. Other statutes are aimed at chronic recidivists. Mandatory-sentencing legislation may impose minimum and maximum terms, but usually it requires a fixed prison sentence.

Mandatory sentencing generally limits the judge's discretionary power to impose any disposition but that authorized by the legislature. On the one hand, it limits individualized sentencing and restricts sentencing disparity. On the other hand, the discretion taken from judges does not disappear. Studies show that mandatory-sentencing laws give prosecutors considerable power because they can decide whether or not a particular defendant should be charged under a mandatory-sentencing statute.[27]

The majority of states have already replaced discretionary sentencing with fixed-term mandatory sentences for such crimes as the sale of hard drugs, kidnapping, gun possession, and arson. The results have been mixed. Mandatory sentences have helped increase the size of the correctional population to record levels. Because of mandatory sentences, many offenders who in the past might have received probation are being incarcerated. Mandatory sentences have also failed to eliminate racial disparity from the sentencing process.[28]

THREE-STRIKES LAWS Three-strikes (and you're out) laws are perhaps the most widely known form of determinate sentencing. They provide lengthy prison terms, usually 25 years to life, for any person convicted of three felony offenses. Approximately half the states have three-strikes laws, but nearly all of them require that the third felony be a serious one.

Three-strikes laws have undeniable political appeal to legislators being pressured by their constituents to "do something about crime." Yet even if they may possibly be effective against crime, any effort to deter criminal behavior through tough laws is not without costs. Criminologist Marc Mauer, a leading opponent of the three-strikes law, finds that the approach may satisfy the public's hunger for retribution but that it makes little practical sense.[29] First, many "three-time losers" are on the brink of aging out of crime; locking them up for life should have little effect on the crime rate. In addition, current sentences for chronic violent offenders are already severe, and yet their punishment seems to have had little efficacy in reducing national violence rates. A three-strikes policy also suffers because criminals typically underestimate their risk of apprehension while overestimating the rewards of crime.

WEB APP 9.1 Visit the Families Against Mandatory Minimums website at **http://www.famm.org**. Click on the "Prisoner Profiles" link, and read some of the profiles of federal and state inmates featured on the site. Are their cases extreme? Or are these individuals truly the "face" of mandatory minimums? Why or why not?

Emmanuel Dunand/Getty Images

Computer hacker Hector Xavier Monsegur, better known by his screen name "Sabu," walks out of federal court in New York after his sentencing. The hacker, who directed hundreds of cyber attacks on corporations and foreign governments before becoming an FBI informant, walked free after being handed a symbolic seven-month sentence. Monsegur was first arrested in 2011 and had already served seven months in jail before being released on bail in December, 2012. The original charges could have landed him in prison for decades, but the government asked for him to be exempt from even a mandatory minimum sentence given his "extraordinary cooperation."

Theft can result in life in prison.

MYTH. It used to be that if you had two felony convictions in the state of California, grand theft could result in life in prison. In November 2012, however, Californians voted to restrict its three-strikes law to only "serious or violent" third-time felonies.

Do you agree with California's decision to change its three-strikes law? Why or why not?

LO3 Identify various sentencing models

concurrent sentences Prison sentences for two or more criminal acts, served simultaneously and run together.

consecutive sentences Prison sentences for two or more criminal acts, served one after the other.

Three-strikes laws, particularly California's (before changes approved in 2012), have prompted a number of studies seeking to determine whether they deter crime. Although a handful of studies report a deterrent effect, the vast majority show that three-strikes laws have little or no effect on crime.[30] The authors of two studies even found that there is more homicide in three-strikes states, which suggests that those who face life in prison have a powerful incentive not to go down without a fight.[31]

Three-strikes laws have also been challenged on constitutional grounds. For example, on March 6, 2003, the Supreme Court upheld the three-strikes sentence of Leandro Andrade, a man sentenced to prison in California for 50 years for stealing $153 worth of videotapes.[32] It also upheld the conviction of Gary Ewing, who appealed a prior 25-year sentence for stealing a set of golf clubs.[33] In both cases, the Court ruled that the challenged sentences were not so grossly disproportionate as to violate the Eighth Amendment's prohibition against cruel and unusual punishment.

Truth in Sentencing

As you may recall, although criminal sentences are getting shorter, people are spending more of their sentence behind bars. One reason is the "get tough" measure known as *truth in sentencing*, which is designed to fight a rising crime rate. These laws require offenders to serve a substantial portion of their prison sentence behind bars.[34] Parole eligibility and good-time credits are restricted or eliminated. The movement was encouraged by the Violent Offender Incarceration and Truth-in-Sentencing Incentive Grants Program, part of the federal government's 1994 crime act, which offered funds to help offset the state costs involved with creating longer sentences. To qualify for federal funds, states must require persons convicted of a violent felony crime to serve not less than 85 percent of their prison sentence. The provision is already having an effect: violent offenders released from prison in 1996 served slightly more than half of their prison sentence, or 45 months. Under truth-in-sentencing laws, violent inmates entering prison today will serve an average of 88 months behind bars. Today, more than half the states and the District of Columbia have met the federal Truth-in-Sentencing Incentive Grants Program eligibility criteria, and another 13 have adopted some form of truth-in-sentencing program.

Imposing the Sentence

In most felony cases, except where the law provides for mandatory prison terms, sentencing is usually based on a variety of information available to the judge. Some jurisdictions allow victims to make impact statements that are considered at sentencing hearings. Most judges also consider a presentence investigation report by the probation department as they make a sentencing decision. This report is a social and personal history, as well as an evaluation of the defendant's chances for rehabilitation within the community. Judges may also issue credit for time already served, such as during pretrial detention.

Concurrent versus Consecutive Sentences

In some instances, when an accused is convicted of two or more charges, the judge must decide whether to impose consecutive or concurrent sentences. If the sentences are concurrent, they begin the same day and are completed when the longest term has been served. For example, say a defendant is convicted of burglarizing an apartment and assaulting its occupant. He is sentenced to 3 years on a charge of assault and 10 years for burglary, with the sentences to be served concurrently. After 10 years in prison, the sentences would be completed.

In contrast, receiving a consecutive sentence means that upon completion of the sentence for one crime, the offender begins serving time for the second of multiple crimes. If the defendant in the previous example had been sentenced consecutively, he would serve 3 years on the assault charge and then 10 years for the burglary, for a total term on the two charges of 13 years. Concurrent sentences are the norm; consecutive

Example: In state X
1. Rape is punishable by 10 years in prison
2. Possession of a handgun by 3 years
3. Possession of heroin by 4 years

Consecutive sentence
Rape + possession of a handgun + possession of heroin

10 + 3 + 4 = 17 years

(each sentence must be served individually)

Concurrent sentence
Rape + possession of a handgun + possession of heroin

10 years

(all sentences served simultaneously)

© Cengage Learning

FIGURE 9.1 Consecutive vs. Concurrent Sentences

sentences are requested for the most serious criminals and for those who are unwilling to cooperate with authorities. Figure 9.1 shows the difference between a consecutive and a concurrent sentence.

The Effect of Good Time

When judges impose an incarceration sentence, they know and take into account the fact that the amount of time spent in prison is reduced by the implementation of "time off for good behavior." This concept was first used in 1817 in New York, and it was quickly adopted in most other jurisdictions. Good time is still in use today; inmates can accrue standard good time at a rate ranging from 10 to 15 days per month. In addition, some correctional authorities grant earned sentence reductions to inmates who participate in treatment programs, such as educational and vocational training, or who volunteer for experimental medical testing programs. In some jurisdictions, more than half of a determinate sentence can be erased by accumulating both standard and earned good time.

Good-time laws enable inmates to calculate their release date at the time they enter prison by subtracting the expected good time from their sentence. However, good time can be lost if inmates break prison rules, get into fights, or disobey correctional officers. In some jurisdictions, former inmates can be returned to prison to serve the balance of their unexpired sentence when their good time is revoked for failing to conform to conditions set down for their release (e.g., by not reporting to a postrelease supervisor or by abusing drugs).

How People Are Sentenced

The federal government conducts surveys on sentencing practices in state and federal courts.[35] The most recent survey found that more than 1 million adults are convicted of felonies in a single year. What happens after convictions? About 70 percent of all felons convicted in state courts were sentenced to a period of confinement—40 percent to state prisons and 30 percent to local jails.[36] The remaining 30 percent were sentenced to straight probation with no jail or prison time to serve. Felons sentenced to a state prison had an average sentence of four and a half years but were likely to serve only half of that sentence before release. Besides being sentenced to incarceration or probation, about one-third of all sentenced offenders are typically expected to pay a fine, pay victim restitution, receive treatment, perform community service, or comply with some other additional penalty. As Table 9.1 shows (most recent data available as of this writing), violent offenders who are given a prison sentence average about eight years, whereas property offenders are

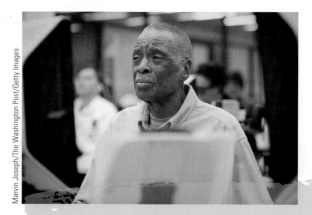

Marvin Joseph/The Washington Post/Getty Images

Since being released from prison, David Belton takes advantage of free education programs, including this introduction to personal computers class. Belton spent over forty years in prison for murdering a man. His service as a mentor in prison and good behavior eventually helped get him an early release.

TABLE 9.1 Lengths of felony sentences imposed by state courts

Most serious conviction offense	Mean Sentence Length in State Courts for Felons Sentenced to Incarceration or Probation			
	Total prison (months)	Jail (months)	Straight probation (months)
All offenses	38	59	6	38
Violent offenses	71	96	7	44
Property offenses	30	47	6	38
Drug offenses	31	50	5	37
Weapon offenses	32	48	6	37
Other offenses	24	41	5	36

Note: Means exclude life sentences and death sentences.

Source: Sean Rosenmerkel and Matthew Durose, *Felony Sentences in State Courts, 2006* (Washington, DC: Bureau of Justice Statistics, 2009), http://bjs.ojp.usdoj.gov/content/pub/pdf/fssc06st.pdf.

LO4 Explain how sentences are imposed

typically sentenced to about four years. If they receive a jail sentence, their period of confinement is considerably less.

The number of convicted offenders being sent to prison today is actually lower than a decade ago, illustrating the increasing popularity of cost-effective community sentencing. However, because of tough sentencing laws requiring people to spend more time behind bars, the average time served per offense has not decreased substantially.

What Factors Affect Sentencing?

What factors influence judges when they decide on criminal sentences? As already mentioned, crime seriousness and the offender's prior record are certainly considered. State sentencing codes usually include various factors that can legitimately influence the length of prison sentences, including the following:

- The severity of the offense
- The offender's prior criminal record
- Whether the offender used violence
- Whether the offender used weapons
- Whether the crime was committed for money

Research does in fact show a strong correlation between these legal variables and the type and length of sentence received. Judges sentence more severely in cases involving the most serious criminal charges, such as terrorism, while tempering the severity of sentencing in less egregious offenses.[37] As Figure 9.2 shows, people with prior felony convictions are much more likely to receive prison time than those convicted of misdemeanors and those who have no prior convictions.

Besides these legally appropriate factors, sentencing experts suspect that judges may also be influenced by the defendant's social class, gender, age, and race—and even by victim characteristics. Consideration of such variables would be a direct violation of constitutional due process and equal protection, as well as of federal statutes, such as the Civil Rights Act. Limiting judicial bias is one reason why states have adopted determinate and mandatory sentencing statutes.

SOCIAL CLASS Evidence supports an association between social class and sentencing outcomes: members of the lower class may expect to get longer prison sentences than more affluent defendants. Not all research efforts have found a consistent relationship between social class and sentence length.

ETHICAL REFLECTION

Jordan Davis Shooting

Michael Dunn's sentence of life in prison for killing Jordan Davis occurred amidst a backdrop of what seems like all-too-frequent shootings of unarmed black men (e.g., Trayvon Martin, Michael Brown). To what extent should this affect sentencing? Crime seriousness and the offender's prior record are the most important sentencing considerations, but for better or worse, community sentiments are difficult to ignore, even for nonelected judges.

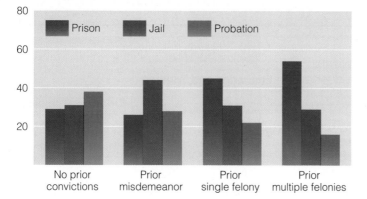

Percent of defendants convicted of a violent felony

Percent of defendants convicted of a nonviolent felony

FIGURE 9.2 Sentence by Prior Record

Source: Thomas H. Cohen and Tracey Kyckelhahn, *Felony Defendants in Large Urban Counties*, 2006 (Washington, DC: Bureau of Justice Statistics, 2010), p. 14, http://bjs.ojp.usdoj.gov/content/pub/pdf/fdluc06.pdf

The relationship may be more robust for some crime patterns than for others. Nonetheless, the consensus is that affluent defendants are more likely than the indigent to receive lenient sentences.[38]

GENDER Does a defendant's gender influence how he or she is sentenced? Some theorists believe that women benefit from sentence disparity because the criminal justice system is dominated by men who have a paternalistic or protective attitude toward women; this is referred to as the chivalry hypothesis. In contrast, others argue that female criminals can be the victim of bias because their law breaking violates what men view as "proper" female behavior.[39]

Which position is true? Most research indicates that women receive more favorable outcomes the further they go in the criminal justice system: they are more likely to receive preferential treatment from a judge at sentencing than they are from the police officer making the arrest or the prosecutor seeking the indictment.[40] This favoritism crosses both racial and ethnic lines, benefiting African American, white, and Hispanic women.[41] Gender bias may be present because judges perceive women as better risks than men. Women have been granted more lenient pretrial release conditions and lower bail amounts than men; women are also more likely to spend less time in pretrial detention.[42] Ironically, mandatory and structured sentences, designed originally to limit bias and discretion, have resulted in harsher sentences for women. Because these methods are "gender neutral," they reverse any advantage women may have had in sentencing decisions. Some women who were peripherally involved in drug trafficking through association with boyfriends and husbands have received very long sentences.[43]

chivalry hypothesis The view that the low rates of female crime and delinquency are a reflection of the leniency with which police and judges treat female offenders.

AGE Another extralegal factor that may play a role in sentencing is age. It should be expected that older people will be punished more harshly than younger ones because they have had a greater opportunity to accumulate a criminal record, and most state laws increase penalties for multiple offenders. Of course, this creates a dilemma: because of crimes he might have committed years ago, an older offender may be punished more severely than a younger offender who is actually more dangerous or is committing more crimes in the present.[44] This association of more severe punishment with older offenders does not always hold, however. Some judges may instead be more lenient with older defendants and more punitive toward younger ones.[45] Although sentencing leniency may be a result of judges' perception that the elderly pose little risk to society, such practices are a violation of the civil rights of younger defendants.[46] On the other hand, some judges may want to protect the youngest defendants, sparing them the pains of a prison experience.[47]

WEB APP 9.2 Go to the Sentencing Project's website at **http://www .sentencingproject.org** and click on the "Racial Disparity" tab. Read an article under the "Racial Disparity News" section, and summarize the issue at stake. How does the article align with what you have read in this section of Chapter 9?

RACE No issue concerning personal factors in sentencing is more important than the suspicion that race influences sentencing outcomes. Racial disparity in sentencing has been suspected because a disproportionate number of African American inmates are in state prisons and on death row. Minorities—especially those who are indigent or unemployed—seem to receive longer sentences than Caucasians.[48] Shawn Bushway and Anne Morrison Piehl studied sentencing outcomes in Maryland and found that, on average, African Americans have 20 percent longer sentences than whites, even when age, gender, and recommended sentence length are held constant.[49] Young black men are more likely to be imprisoned for drug offenses, a practice (says sentencing expert Michael Tonry) that places the entire cohort of young African American males in jeopardy.[50]

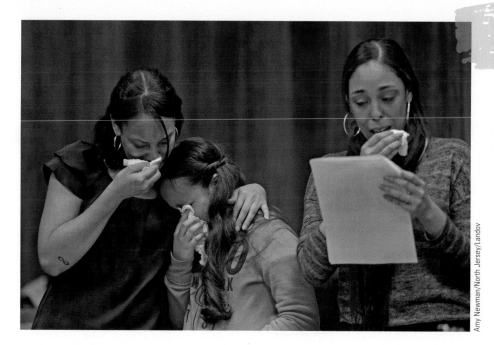

Family members read a victim impact statement prior to the sentencing of Edwin Jimenez in Passaic County (New Jersey) Superior Court. Jimenez was sentenced to 35 years in prison for a shooting that claimed the lives of Ishmael Pena and Stevenson Matos and wounded a third man outside a Passaic bodega in 2012.

Although some research does indicate that a defendant's race has a direct effect on sentencing outcomes, other efforts show that the influence of race on sentencing is less clear-cut than anticipated. As John Wooldredge found, in some contexts, minority group members actually get more lenient sentences than whites.[51] It is possible, the counter-argument goes, that the disproportionate number of minority group members in prison is not a function of racial bias by judges but, rather, reflects actual racial and ethnic differences in the crime rate: minority group members go to prison more often simply because they commit more crime.

Race may also affect sentencing in other ways. Research indicates that it is the victim's race, rather than the offender's, that structures sentencing outcomes.[52] Minority defendants are sanctioned more severely if their victim is white than if their target is a fellow minority group member; minority defendants who kill whites are more likely to get the death penalty than are those who kill other minorities.[53]

In sum, although the true association between race and sentencing is complex, there is little question that the defendant's race helps shape the contours of justice. Whatever the cause, the effects can be devastating. As Bruce Western warns, whole communities are being destabilized by the marginalizing and incarcerating of so many African American men. And doing prison time can turn minor offenders into hardened criminals, which removes any chance of rehabilitation. Indeed, the prison boom "may be a self-defeating strategy for crime control."[54]

VICTIM CHARACTERISTICS Victim characteristics may also influence sentencing. Victims may be asked or allowed to make a **victim impact statement** before the sentencing judge, which gives them the opportunity to tell their experiences and describe their ordeal. In a murder case, the surviving family can recount the effect the crime has had on their lives and well-being.[55] The effect of victim and witness statements on sentencing has been the subject of some debate. Some research suggests that victim statements result in a higher rate of incarceration, but other efforts find that the effects of victim and witness statements are insignificant.[56]

A victim's personal characteristics may influence sentencing. Sentences may be reduced when victims have "negative" personal characteristics or qualities. For example, people convicted of raping prostitutes or substance abusers receive much shorter sentences than those who assault women without these negative characteristics.[57]

victim impact statement A post-conviction statement by the victim of crime that may be used to guide sentencing decisions.

L05 Summarize factors associated with sentencing decisions

Capital Punishment

The most severe sentence used in the United States is capital punishment, or execution. Approximately 15,000 confirmed executions have been carried out in America under civil authority, starting with the execution of Captain George Kendall in 1608. Most of these executions have been for murder and rape. However, federal, state, and military laws have conferred the death penalty for other crimes, including robbery, kidnapping, treason (offenses against the federal government), espionage, and desertion from military service.

In recent years, the Supreme Court has limited the death penalty to first-degree murder and then only when aggravating circumstances, such as murder for profit or murder using extreme cruelty, are present.[58] The federal government still has provisions for imposing the death penalty for espionage by a member of the armed forces, treason, and killing during a criminal conspiracy, such as drug trafficking. Some states have laws permitting capital punishment for crimes besides first-degree murder, but those laws continue to come under scrutiny. Figure 9.3 provides a perspective on executions from 1930 to the present. Figure 9.4 presents a map of the death-penalty states and non-death-penalty states.

No issue in the criminal justice system is more controversial or emotional than implementation of the death penalty. Opponents and proponents have formulated a number of powerful arguments in support of their positions; these arguments are reviewed in the following sections.

Arguments for the Death Penalty

The death penalty has long been one of the most controversial aspects of the justice system, and it will probably continue to be a source of significant debate.[59] Let's first consider the views supporting availability of the death penalty.

DETERRENCE Proponents of capital punishment argue that executions serve as a strong deterrent for serious crimes. From a specific deterrent standpoint, an offender who is dead can no longer commit crime! From a general deterrent standpoint, proponents maintain that an execution can produce a substantial decline in the murder rate.[60] They argue, for example, that homicide rates increased dramatically in the 1960s and 1970s, when executions were halted by the courts, and death penalty laws were subsequently

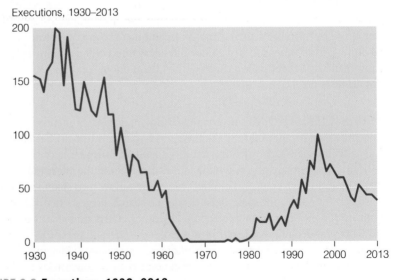

FIGURE 9.3 **Executions, 1930–2012**

Source: Tracy L. Snell, Capital Punishment, 2013—Statistical Tables (Washington, DC: Bureau of Justice Statistics, 2014).

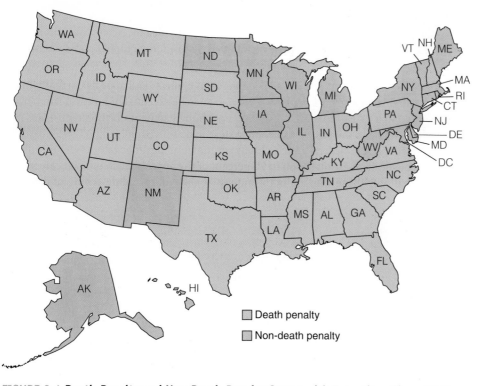

FIGURE 9.4 **Death-Penalty and Non-Death-Penalty States with Executions Since 1976**

Source: Death Penalty Information Center, http://www.deathpenaltyinfo.org/states-and-without-death-penalty

abolished. It is not a coincidence, they argue, that murder rates have dropped since the death penalty was reinstated; murder rates would actually be much higher if capital punishment were not being used.[61] The death penalty scares would-be criminals, and, not surprisingly, homicide rates drop after a well-publicized execution.[62]

MORALLY CORRECT Death penalty supporters often argue that such a harsh punishment is morally correct. After all, it is mentioned in the Bible and other religious works. And although the US Constitution forbids "cruel and unusual punishment," it does not prohibit the death penalty, as it was widely used at the time the Constitution was drafted. The "original intent" of the founding fathers was to allow the states to use the death penalty. Supporters also argue that the death penalty is morally correct because it provides the greatest justice for the victim and helps alleviate the psychic pain of the victim's family and friends. In sum, the death penalty makes a moral statement: there is behavior that is so unacceptable to a community of human beings that one who engages in such behavior forfeits his right to live.[63]

PROPORTIONAL TO THE CRIME Putting dangerous criminals to death also conforms to the requirement that the punishment must be proportional to the seriousness of the crime. We use a system of escalating punishments, so it follows that the most serious punishment should be used to sanction the most serious crime. Before the brutality of the death penalty is considered, the cruelty with which the victim was treated should not be forgotten.

REFLECTS PUBLIC OPINION Supporters also argue that the death penalty is justified because it represents the will of the people. A majority of the general public believe that criminals who kill innocent victims should forfeit their own lives. Public opinion polls show that Americans favor the use of the death penalty by a wide majority.[64] Public approval rests on the belief that the death penalty is an important instrument of social control, can deter crime, and is less costly than maintaining a murderer in prison for life.

REALITYCHECK

MYTH OR REALITY?

The United States is one of the few countries that still retains the death penalty.

REALITY. According to Amnesty International, 139 countries have abolished the death penalty in law or practice, or for certain crimes, leaving 58 "retentionist countries."

Few of the retentionist countries are what we would call industrialized, advanced, or close allies of the United States. Why does the United States retain the death penalty when the majority of the industrialized countries in the world have abolished it?

Research by Alexis Durham and his associates found that almost everyone (95 percent) would give criminals the death penalty under some circumstances, and the most heinous crimes are those for which the public is most likely to approve capital punishment.[65]

UNLIKELY CHANCE OF ERROR The many legal controls and appeals currently in use make it almost impossible for an innocent person to be executed or for the death penalty to be used in a racist or capricious manner. Although some unfortunate mistakes may have been made in the past, the current system makes it virtually impossible to execute an innocent person. Federal courts closely scrutinize all death penalty cases and rule for the defendant in an estimated 60 to 70 percent of the appeals. Such judicial care should ensure that only those who are both unquestionably guilty and deserving of death are executed.

Arguments against the Death Penalty

Arguments for the death penalty are countered as follows by those who support its abolition.

POSSIBILITY OF ERROR Researchers have estimated that on the order of 2,000 innocent defendants go to prison every year.[66] Thanks to the advent of DNA evidence, hundreds of wrongfully convicted individuals have been exonerated in recent years, but the wrongful conviction problem persists. This raises several questions. Why are these cases coming to light? How often are innocent people imprisoned? Has an innocent person been executed in the past 40 years? Why do wrongful convictions occur? What can be done to reduce justice system errors?

In the early 1990s, only two organizations existed to take on cases of prisoners claiming to be factually innocent. Today, more than 50 innocence projects exist. Collectively, as an Innocence Network, they screen claims of innocence, work to exonerate the factually innocent, promote policies to reduce errors of justice, and provide support for exonerees.

According to the Innocence Project,[67] more than 325 DNA exonerees have been released after being convicted of crimes they did not commit. Almost all of these exonerations were for the crimes of murder and rape. Experts and criminal justice officials estimate that at least one-half of 1 percent of all types of felony convictions are "wrong-person convictions." This would mean that of the 1.1 million convictions each year, at least 5,500 people suffer the humiliation of being wrongly convicted, and 3,800 of them the anguish of being jailed or imprisoned for a crime they did not commit. Recent research by Samuel Gross and his colleagues estimates that 1 in 25 death row inmates is innocent.[68]

The pressures to ensure convictions in homicide cases may lead to a higher rate of wrongful convictions in murder cases. There have been no official exonerations of an innocent person executed since 1973, but intensive investigations provide strong evidence that at least some people have been executed for murders they did not commit. See the accompanying Contemporary Issues in Criminal Justice box for more on the causes of wrongful convictions—and a summary of recent reform efforts.

WEAK PUBLIC SUPPORT Although the majority of Americans approve of the death penalty, evidence suggests that their approval has declined over the past decade.[69] Also, when surveys give respondents a choice of punishments, such as life without parole, support for the death penalty declines to approximately 50 percent.[70] Well-publicized cases of innocent people being sentenced to death have also helped erode support for capital punishment.[71] So although a majority of the public still support the death penalty in principle, a substantial proportion of the public lack confidence in its use and believe that executions should be halted until the justice system can be made foolproof.[72]

Evidence also suggests that support for the death penalty is influenced by such factors as the personal characteristics of the offender and the circumstances of the offense.[73] People who generally support the death penalty may not want to see it used

Reducing Wrongful Convictions

The criminal justice system produces a steady stream of such serious errors for several reasons. As many as 25 percent of all eyewitness identifications may be wrong; many of these errors are caused by suggestive police line-ups. After a person is misidentified, police may develop "tunnel vision"—an unshakeable belief that the suspect is the real criminal. Tunnel vision can lead police to become overly aggressive during interrogations, causing innocent persons to confess to escape the enormous psychological strain of high-pressure interrogation. This is a special problem with suspects who are more easily manipulated, such as teenagers and mentally challenged suspects. Police often rely on informants, especially jailhouse snitches claiming that a suspect confessed. These snitches may be pathological liars willing to say anything to get a break in their cases.

Police are also not required to include exculpatory evidence—evidence that favors innocence—in their investigative reports. Even if they do, many prosecutors fail to turn over exculpatory evidence to defense lawyers, although required to do so by law. Overworked or incompetent defense attorneys often fail to provide a competent defense. Judges and appellate courts tend to favor the prosecution and, in a large proportion of cases, simply overlook serious errors. In a number of cases, junk science, substandard forensic laboratories, or fraudulent forensic scientists have presented juries with completely erroneous conclusions.

Reform Efforts

In the past few years, a number of reform efforts have begun to percolate through several cities and states in response to the crisis of convicting the innocent. In 2006, North Carolina became the first state to establish an Innocence Inquiry Commission to review and investigate prisoners' claims that they were wrongly convicted. Several states and a large number of police departments have started videotaping the entire interrogation of suspects, not just the confession. Police strongly support this reform because confessions by guilty suspects provide strong proof at trial, and the videotape can be used to confirm that they used proper procedures.

A number of lineup reforms are shown by psychological experiments to reduce eyewitness errors. The most important include "double-blind" lineup administration, where the officer running the lineup does not know the identity of the suspect. Other procedures to ensure lineup accuracy include carefully documenting the identification, telling eyewitnesses that the perpetrator may or may not be included in the lineup, and picking "fillers" from witnesses' verbal descriptions and not the likeness of the suspect (who might be innocent). Somewhat more controversial is the recommendation to replace the traditional side-by-side live or photographic simultaneous lineups with a one-at-a-time, or sequential, lineup.

In addition to these and many other suggested reforms, there has been a call for all states to provide monetary compensation and psychological and other support for the wrongly convicted, many of whom suffer serious psychological damage from their ordeals. The conviction of a factually innocent person creates multiple victims: the wrongly convicted person who does time for another person's crime; the original crime victims, who later learn that instead of providing closure, the criminal justice system compounded their woes; and those people later victimized by the real criminal who was not caught in the first place. Knowledge about wrongful convictions should be viewed as an important topic in criminal justice and an opportunity to create a more professional criminal justice system.

CRITICAL THINKING

1. Describe how the conviction of an innocent person actually creates multiple victims, and cite other people or institutions that are damaged by a wrongful conviction.

2. Apply what you know about criminal justice to create an innovative approach that might help reduce wrongful convictions. What role, if any, does technology play in your plan to reduce wrongful convictions?

Sources: D. Michael Risinger, "Innocents Convicted: An Empirically Justified Factual Wrongful Conviction Rate," *Journal of Criminal Law and Criminology* 97 (2007): 761–806; Barry Scheck, Peter Neufeld, and Jim Dwyer, *Actual Innocence: When Justice Goes Wrong and How to Make It Right* (New York: Penguin/New American Library, 2003); The Justice Project, "Eyewitness Identification: A Policy Review," http://www.psychology. iastate.edu/~glwells/The_Justice%20Project_Eyewitness_Identification_%20A_Policy _Review.pdf (accessed February 2015); Samuel R. Gross, Kristen Jacoby, Daniel J. Matheson, Nicholas Montgomery, and Sujata Patil, "Exonerations in the United States, 1989 through 2003," *Journal of Criminal Law and Criminology* 95 (2005): 523–560.

with juveniles, the mentally challenged, or the mentally ill.[74] And even if a majority support capital punishment, their motives must be closely examined: Is it possible that support for the death penalty is a function of racist attitudes and the belief that capital punishment helps control and restrain the minority population?[75]

LITTLE DETERRENT EFFECT The general consensus among death penalty researchers today is that the threat of capital punishment has little effect on murder rates. Indeed, a report released by the prestigious National Research Council of the National Academies reviewed more than three decades of death penalty research and concluded, "...the research to date on the effect of capital punishment on homicide is not informative about whether capital punishment decreases, increases, or has no effect on homicide rates. ...Nothing is known about how potential murderers actually perceive their risk of punishment."[76]

A few studies have found that the long-term application of capital punishment may actually reduce the murder rate.[77] However, these studies have been disputed by researchers who questioned the methodology used and maintain that the deterrent effects the studies uncovered are an artifact of the statistical techniques used in the research.[78]

MYTH OR REALITY?

The death penalty deters homicide.

MYTH. Most research on this subject has shown that the death penalty does little, if anything, to deter homicide.

Why are most researchers convinced the death penalty fails to deter homicide? Clearly it is effective from a specific deterrent standpoint, but why might would-be killers not be deterred by the threat of capital punishment?

Despite the less-than-conclusive empirical evidence, many people still insist on the efficacy of the death penalty as a crime deterrent, and recent Supreme Court decisions seem to justify its use. Some researchers continue to find that the death penalty can deter crime, although their findings are the exception.[79] Of course, even if the death penalty were no greater a deterrent than a life sentence, some people would still advocate its use on the grounds that it is the only way to permanently rid society of particular dangerous criminals who deserve to die.

RACE, GENDER, AND OTHER BIAS Capital punishment may be tarnished by gender, racial, ethnic, and other biases. More people are sentenced to death, and the death penalty is used more often, in nations with a large minority population. This phenomenon has led to formulation of what is referred to as the "minority-group-threat hypothesis," which states that the use of extreme punishment is related to the regulation of groups that are racially, culturally, or ethnically different.[80] Let's look at some of the evidence:

- Homicides with male offenders and female victims are more likely to result in a death sentence than homicides involving female offenders and male victims.[81]
- Homicides involving strangers are more likely to result in a death sentence than homicides involving nonstrangers or acquaintances.
- Prosecutors are more likely to recommend the death sentence for people who kill white victims than they are in any other racial combination of victim and criminal.[82] Prosecutors are less likely to seek the death penalty if the victim is a minority group member.[83] A male minority group member killing a white female is more likely to result in the death penalty than any other race/gender combination.[84]

Ever since the death penalty was first instituted in the United States, disproportionate numbers of minorities have been executed. Charges of racial bias are supported by the disproportionate numbers of African Americans who have received the death sentence, who are currently on death row, and who have been executed (53.5 percent of all executions). Racism was particularly blatant when the death penalty was invoked in rape cases: of those receiving the death penalty for rape, 90 percent in the South and 63 percent in the North and West were African American.[85] Today, about 40 percent of inmates on death row are African American, a number disproportionate to the minority representation in the population. When a black criminal kills a white victim, the likelihood of the death penalty being invoked is far greater than when a white criminal kills a black victim.[86]

CAUSES MORE CRIME THAN IT DETERS Some critics fear that the introduction of capital punishment will encourage criminals to escalate their violent behavior, consequently putting police officers at risk. A suspect who kills someone during a botched robbery may be inclined to "fire away" upon encountering police rather than to surrender peacefully. The killer faces the death penalty already, so what does he have to lose? Geoffrey Rapp studied the effect of capital punishment on the killings of police and found that, all other things being equal, the greater the number of new inmates on death row, the greater the number of police officers killed by citizens.[87] Rapp concluded that what the death penalty seems to do is create an extremely dangerous environment for law enforcement officers because it does not deter criminals and may lull officers into a false sense of security, leading them to believe that the death penalty will deter violence directed against them and causing them to let their guard down.

The death penalty may also produce more violence than it prevents—the so-called **brutalization effect**.[88] Executions may increase murder rates because they raise the general violence level in society and because people prone to violence actually identify with the executioner, not with the target of the death penalty. When someone gets in a conflict with such violence-prone individuals or challenges their authority, these individuals may "execute" them, just as the state executes people who violate its rules.[89] Evidence shows that the brutalization effect does influence murder rates: stranger homicides increase after an execution.[90] People may be more inclined to settle conflicts with violence after a state executes a criminal—"If they can do it, why can't I?"[91]

brutalization effect An outcome of capital punishment that enhances, rather than deters, the level of violence in society. The death penalty reinforces the view that violence is an appropriate response to provocation.

CRUEL AND INHUMAN Abolitionists believe that executions are unnecessarily cruel and inhuman and come at a high moral and social cost. Even death by lethal injection, which is considered relatively humane by advocates, has been challenged because it may cause extreme pain and can take much longer to cause death than was originally believed.[92] Our society does not punish criminals by subjecting them to the same acts they themselves committed. Rapists are not sexually assaulted, and arsonists do not have their houses burned down. Why, then, should murderers be killed?

Robert Johnson has described the execution process as a form of torture in which the condemned are first tormented psychologically by being made to feel powerless and alone while on death row; suicide is a constant problem among those awaiting death.[93] The execution itself is a barbaric affair marked by the smell of burning flesh and stiffened bodies. The executioners suffer from delayed stress reactions, including anxiety and a dehumanized personal identity.

MOST DEVELOPED COUNTRIES HAVE ABANDONED IT According to the Death Penalty Information Center, over half the countries in the world have abolished the death penalty in law or in practice. Just since 1990, more than 45 countries have abolished the death penalty for all crimes. Even China has recently revised its criminal law to eliminate the death penalty for certain crimes. According to LiYing Li, "This signifies a leap forward in China's legal reforms and an effort by China to move closer to the international norms."[94]

IT IS EXPENSIVE Some people complain that they do not want to support "some killer in prison for 30 years." Abolitionists counter that legal appeals drive the cost of executions far higher than the cost of years of incarceration. If the money spent on the judicial process were invested, the interest would more than pay for the lifetime upkeep of death row inmates. Because of numerous appeals, the median time between conviction by a jury, sentencing by a judge, and execution can be rather lengthy. For example, recent data show that the average inmate sentenced to death has been on death row for almost 12 years.[95] Several states have begun to explore abolishing the death penalty to save money in light of the recession.

MORALLY WRONG The death penalty is brutal and demeaning, according to critics. They argue that even if the general public voices approval of the death penalty, "social vengeance by death is a primitive way of revenge which stands in the way of moral progress."[96] And although early religious leaders accepted the death penalty, today many (such as the Catholic Church) condemn the practice of execution.[97]

In his book *The Contradictions of American Capital Punishment,* Franklin Zimring links America's obsession with the death penalty—unique among developed nations—with its vigilante tradition, in which people on the frontier took justice into their own hands, assuming that their targets were always guilty as charged.[98] The death penalty was widely practiced against slaves, and, at one time, mass executions were a brutal and common practice to stifle any thought of escapes and/or revolts.[99]

While the debate continues, there seems to be little question that the public's support for the death penalty has weakened, and concomitantly, the number of death sentences being handed down is in sharp decline (see Figure 9.5).[100] Whether these developments portend the demise of capital punishment remains to be seen.

Legal Issues in Capital Punishment

The constitutionality of the death penalty has been a major concern to both the nation's courts and its social scientists. In 1972, the Supreme Court in *Furman v. Georgia* decided that the discretionary imposition of the death penalty was cruel and unusual punishment under the Eighth and Fourteenth Amendments of the US Constitution.[101] The Supreme Court did not completely rule out the use of capital punishment as a penalty; rather, it objected to the arbitrary and capricious manner in which it was

WEB APP 9.3 Take the Death Penalty Quiz on the Death Penalty Information Center's (DPIC) website at **http://www .deathpenaltyinfo.org/node/183.** Also visit Amnesty International's website for a list of countries that have abolished (called abolitionists) and retained (called retentionists) capital punishment at **http://www.amnesty .org/en/death-penalty/abolitionist -and-retentionist-countries.** Is the United States in good company with countries that have retained the death penalty? Why or why not?

LO6 List the arguments for and against capital punishment

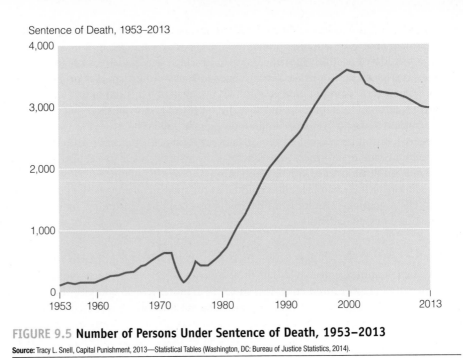

Sentence of Death, 1953–2013

FIGURE 9.5 Number of Persons Under Sentence of Death, 1953–2013

Source: Tracy L. Snell, Capital Punishment, 2013—Statistical Tables (Washington, DC: Bureau of Justice Statistics, 2014).

imposed. After *Furman*, many states changed statutes that had allowed jury discretion in imposing the death penalty. Then, in July 1976, the Supreme Court ruled on the constitutionality of five state death penalty statutes. In the first case, *Gregg v. Georgia*, the Court found valid the Georgia statute holding that a finding by the jury of at least 1 "aggravating circumstance" out of 10 is required in pronouncing the death penalty in murder cases.[102] In the *Gregg* case, the jury imposed the death penalty after finding beyond a reasonable doubt two aggravating circumstances: (1) the offender was engaged in the commission of two other capital felonies, and (2) the offender committed the offense of murder for the purpose of receiving money and other financial gains

Anthony Sowell, left, stands with his attorney, Rufus Sims, as the jury recommends the death penalty following Sowell's conviction for the murder of 11 women in Cleveland. Sowell, a registered sex offender, was required to check in regularly with authorities. However, because he was not on probation or parole at the time, police did not have authority to search his house. That was until a woman went to the police, claiming Sowell raped her. After obtaining an arrest warrant, police entered Sowell's house and eventually located the 11 victims' remains.

(specifically, an automobile).[103] The *Gregg* decision signaled the return of capital punishment as a sentencing option.

Although the Court has supported the legality of the death penalty, it has also placed significant limitations on its use. Rulings have promoted procedural fairness in the capital sentencing process. For example, in *Ring v. Arizona,* the Court found that juries, not judges, must make the critical findings that send convicted killers to death row. The Court reasoned that the Sixth Amendment's right to a jury trial would be "senselessly diminished" if it did not allow jurors to decide whether a person deserves the death penalty.[104] A number of other legal restrictions have also been put in place. For an overview, see Exhibit 9.1.

LO7 Articulate the legal issues associated with capital punishment

EXHIBIT 9.1

Important Death Penalty Decisions over the Years

***Furman v. Georgia* (1972)** The death penalty (in three Georgia cases) amounts to cruel and unusual punishment in violation of the Eighth Amendment. *Furman* led to a de facto moratorium on capital punishment.[105]

***Gregg v. Georgia* (1976)** The punishment of death for the crime of murder does not violate the Eighth Amendment under all circumstances.[106]

***Woodson v. North Carolina* (1976)** Mandatory death penalty laws (those that do not take into account aggravating and mitigating circumstances) violate the Eighth Amendment and are thus unconstitutional.[107]

***Coker v. Georgia* (1977)** Rapists cannot be sentenced to death.[108]

***Lockett v. Ohio* (1978)** The defendant must be allowed to present all mitigating evidence pertaining to his or her "character, record, and circumstances of the crime."[109]

***Enmund v. Florida* (1982)** It is a violation of the Eighth Amendment to impose the death penalty on a person who commits a felony that results in murder without considering the person's level of intent.[110]

***Glass v. Louisiana* (1985)** Death by electrocution is not cruel and unusual punishment.[111]

***Cabana v. Bullock* (1986)** The death penalty cannot be imposed on an accomplice unless it is proved that the accomplice killed, attempted to kill, or intended to kill.[112]

***Ford v. Wainwright* (1986)** It is a violation of the Eighth Amendment to execute a person who is insane (or was insane at the time of the crime).[113]

***Atkins v. Virginia* (2002)** The execution of a mentally retarded individual violates the Eighth Amendment.[114]

***Ring v. Arizona* (2002)** It is a violation of the Sixth Amendment's jury trial provision to allow a judge, rather than a jury, to find aggravating circumstances necessary for imposition of the death penalty.[115]

***Roper v. Simmons* (2005)** It is a violation of the Eighth Amendment to sentence to death a defendant who committed his or her capital crime under the age of 18.[116]

***Deck v. Missouri* (2005)** It is unconstitutional to force the defendant to wear visible shackles during the sentencing phase of a capital trial.[117]

***Oregon v. Guzek* (2006)** Death penalty defendants may not present new evidence during the sentencing phase of the criminal process.[118]

***Baze v. Rees* (2008)** A three-drug lethal injection procedure does not violate the Eighth Amendment.[119]

***Kennedy v. Louisiana* (2008)** A child rapist cannot be sentenced to death if the crime did not result in (or was not intended to result in) the child's death.[120]

ETHICAL Challenge

Carla is a 36-year-old white female convicted of killing her husband of 12 years, Jack, a wealthy and prominent attorney. The police report shows that to inherit his substantial trust fund, Carla gave her husband a large dose of a sleeping sedative, and, when he felt uncomfortable and dizzy, offered to take him to the emergency room at the local hospital. After he passed out in the car, she slid the comatose man into the driver's seat and then rolled the vehicle down an embankment. After watching the car burst into flames, she walked to her own car, which she had hidden earlier, and drove home. When police came to report the accident, she told the officers that Jack had gone to get some groceries and she was wondering why he had taken so long. At first she expressed shock over his death and burst into tears. Later, forensic evidence and an eyewitness to the event helped investigators unravel her plot.

This is Carla's first conviction. She is a highly educated woman with a degree in French literature from an Ivy League university. She comes from a loving and devoted family. Her parents and sisters, though in shock, are willing to stand beside her. She has two young children who are currently living with relatives; they also seem devoted to their mother. She has done charitable work and is well liked. She has no prior history of violence, mental instability, or the like. Psychiatric reports show that she is unlikely to commit further crimes.

At the sentencing hearing, Carla is filled with remorse and states that her greed overcame her reasoning. She is currently on a suicide watch at the county jail because she has told her counselor that she "does not deserve to live"; her anguish seems genuine.

Ethical Challenge: As a member of the jury during the capital sentencing stage, you hold Carla's fate in your hands. You can recommend death, life in prison, a prison sentence, or even probation. State law requires that each jury member provide a written document stating the reasons for his or her sentencing decision. What are the reasons for your decision?

SUMMARY

LO1 *Outline the historical development of punishment* Historically, people who violated the law were considered morally corrupt and in need of strong discipline. In early Greece and Rome, the most common state-administered punishment was banishment or exile. During the Middle Ages, people found guilty of crime faced a wide range of punishments, including physical torture, branding, whipping, and, for most felony offenses, death. The development of the common law in the eleventh century brought some standardization to penal practices. By the end of the sixteenth century, many offenders were made to do hard labor for their crimes. In England, transporting convicts to the colonies became popular.

LO2 *Explain the major goals of contemporary sentencing* The goals of criminal sentencing today can be grouped into six distinct areas: general deterrence, incapacitation, specific deterrence, retribution/just desert, rehabilitation, and equity/restitution. According to the concept of general deterrence, people will be too afraid to break the law if they believe that they will be caught and punished severely. The purpose of specific deterrence, another goal of punishment, is to convince offenders that the pains of punishment are greater than the potential benefits of crime. Because criminals will not be able to repeat their criminal acts while they are under state control, incapacitation of criminals is another goal of sentencing. According to the retributive goal of sentencing, the essential purpose of the criminal process is to punish offenders—fairly and justly—in a manner that is proportionate to the gravity of their crimes. Some sentences are based on the need to treat and/or rehabilitate criminal offenders. Because criminals profit from their misdeeds, it seems both fair and just to demand that they reimburse society for losses it has sustained because of their crimes.

LO3 *Identify various sentencing models* Indeterminate sentences are tailored to fit individual needs. Convicted offenders are typically given a "light" minimum sentence that must be served and a lengthy maximum sentence that is the outer boundary of the time that can be served. Determinate sentences offer a fixed term of years, the maximum set in law by the legislature, to be served by the offender sentenced to prison for a particular crime. Sentencing guidelines have been implemented to provide judges with a recommended sentence based on the seriousness of a crime and the background of an offender. Some states have passed mandatory sentence legislation (e.g., three-strikes) prohibiting people convicted of certain offenses, such as violent crimes or drug trafficking, from being placed on probation; they must serve at least some time in prison.

LO4 *Explain how sentences are imposed* In some instances, when an accused is convicted of two or more charges, the judge must decide whether to impose consecutive or concurrent sentences. When judges impose an incarceration sentence, they know and take into account the fact that the amount of time spent in prison is reduced by the implementation of "time off for good behavior."

LO5 *Summarize factors associated with sentencing decisions* State sentencing codes usually include various factors that can legitimately influence the length of prison sentences, including the severity of the offense, the offender's prior criminal record, whether the offender used violence, whether the offender used weapons, and whether the crime was committed for money. Evidence supports an association between social class and sentencing outcomes: members of the lower class may expect to get longer prison sentences than more affluent defendants. Most research indicates that women receive more favorable outcomes the further they go in the criminal justice system. The same is often true with the elderly. Minorities also seem to receive longer sentences than Caucasians, especially those who are indigent or unemployed.

LO6 *List the arguments for and against capital punishment* Proponents of capital punishment feel that executions serve as a strong deterrent for serious crimes. They also argue that capital punishment is morally correct, is proportional to the crime, reflects public opinion, and can be implemented with little to no chance of error. Critics of capital punishment cite the potential for error and the supposed unfair use of discretion in sentencing people to death (some offenders get death sentences while others do not). They also claim that capital punishment represents misplaced vengeance and that there is not enough public support for the death penalty. Finally, critics argue the death penalty does not deter crime; that it abandons all hope for offender rehabilitation; is biased against certain demographics; amounts to immoral, cruel, and inhuman punishment; may cause crime to increase; is expensive; and has been abandoned in most developed nations.

LO7 *Articulate the legal issues associated with capital punishment* The constitutionality of the death penalty has been a major concern to both the nation's courts and its social scientists. Although the Supreme Court has upheld the death penalty for the most serious offenders, it has prohibited it as a sentence for certain crimes, notably rape—even child rape. Juveniles cannot be sentenced to death, nor can the mentally retarded.

KEY TERMS

penitentiary, p. 212

general deterrence, p. 212

specific deterrence, p. 213

incapacitation, p. 213

blameworthy, p. 214

just desert, p. 214

rehabilitation, p. 214

equity, p. 214

indeterminate
    sentence, p. 215

determinate
    sentence, p. 216

sentencing guidelines, p. 216

mandatory sentence, p. 216

concurrent sentences, p. 218

consecutive sentences, p. 218

chivalry hypothesis, p. 221

victim impact
    statement, p. 223

brutalization effect, p. 228

REVIEW QUESTIONS

1. Discuss the sentencing dispositions in your jurisdiction. What are the pros and cons of each?

2. Compare the various types of incarceration sentences. What are the similarities and differences? Why are many jurisdictions considering the passage of mandatory sentencing laws?

3. Discuss the issue of capital punishment. In your opinion, does it serve as a deterrent? What new rulings has the Supreme Court made on the legality of the death penalty?

4. Why does the problem of sentencing disparity exist? Do programs exist that can reduce the disparity of sentences? If so, what are they? Should all people who commit the same crime receive the same sentence? Explain.

5. Should convicted criminals be released from prison when correctional authorities are convinced they are rehabilitated? Why or why not?

PART 4

CORRECTIONS AND ALTERNATIVE SANCTIONS

Evan Ebel (pictured in inset photo) made national headlines in 2013 when he killed Tom Clements, the director of the Colorado Prison System. Ebel also killed a Domino's deliveryman, Nathan Leon, simply because he wanted his uniform to use as a disguise. Some believe that Clements's death was ordered by members of Ebel's white supremacist prison gang, 211 Crew, as revenge for putting some of them in solitary confinement. Before his death, Leon was forced to read a statement about Clements that said in part:

You treated us inhumanely, and so we simply seek to do the same. . . . For twenty years, we've been subject to your faddism not witness ours, you didn't give two (expletive) about us or our families, and you ensured that we were locked behind a door, to disrespect us at every opportunity, so why should we care about you and yours."

After the murders, Ebel fled to Texas where he was eventually pulled over by Texas authorities two days later and engaged in a high-speed chase and gun battle with them during which he was shot and killed.

Some terrible mistakes were made in the case. Ebel was serving an eight-year prison term but was released on parole four years early because of a clerical error. Before he went on his murderous spree,

Ebel tore off his electronic monitoring device, but it took five days for corrections officers to become aware of the disconnect because they were inundated with alerts, and some went unnoticed.

The Ebel case illustrates the many problems faced by the American correctional system. Due to overcrowding, mistakes are made, and people may be released who present a risk to society. At the same time, many people are being held behind bars who might be better served in the community. Ebel was placed on electronic monitoring, a device that some experts view as an important technological innovation. Yet Ebel was able to simply cut off his monitor, an act that escaped detection because correctional systems were overwhelmed.

Part 4 contains three chapters that cover the current correctional process in all its various forms. Chapter 10 surveys community-based corrections, including probation, and alternative sanctions ranging from fines to electronic monitoring and home confinement. Chapter 11 introduces the history of corrections and also reviews the various forms of secure corrections being used today. Finally, Chapter 12 looks at the prison experience, covering such topics as prison culture, sexual assault, treatment programs, and prisoners' rights. Leaving prison, parole, and the reentry process are also discussed.

10 Community Sentences:

PROBATION, INTERMEDIATE SANCTIONS, AND RESTORATIVE JUSTICE

In 2014, "Real Housewives of New Jersey" stars Teresa and Joe Giudice pleaded guilty in a Newark Federal Court on 41 counts, including conspiracy to commit wire fraud and failing to file income tax returns. It seems that facing financial difficulties, the Giudices applied for $5 million in bank loans and used fraudulent and falsified claims in their application. Teresa, one of the highest paid reality stars, pleaded guilty to the fraud charges, while Joe pleaded guilty to the same counts as Teresa, plus one count of failure to file tax returns. Because they are the parents of four girls under age 14, Joe will be allowed to serve his 40-month sentence after Teresa completes her 15 months behind bars.[1]

The Giudices' downfall is particularly shocking because they were financially successful with Teresa pulling down a salary of more than $650,000 per year from her "Real Housewife" gig alone, not to mention the royalties from her best-selling cookbooks. While they made a lot of money, they spent even more on their 10,000-square-foot home, beach getaway, and other expensive toys.[2] Even though they engaged in fraudulent activity to keep the party going, should they both have been given prison terms? On one hand, they did break the law, and not punishing them severely might send the unwanted message that severe criminal punishments can be avoided, especially if you are a celebrity. Would that encourage others to engage in similar fraudulent transactions? Do the Giudices deserve to be punished severely for their crimes?

On the other hand, the Giudices are not a danger to society; now that their fraud has been exposed, it is unlikely that anyone would consider lending them large amounts of money again. Incarcerating them costs thousands of dollars each month, paid for by taxes that could otherwise be used to support education and medical care. Would it not have been better for them to remain in the community under close supervision so they can pay off their debts, rather than behind bars wasting taxpayer money? And what about the long-term social costs they face, and the costs to their children?

If you agree that the Giudices would have been better served by being monitored in the community, you are not alone. For the past 200 years, offenders who are considered good risks have been placed in community-based sentencing alternatives, most commonly probation, which has become

REALITYCHECK

MYTH OR REALITY?

- Violent offenders who commit murder, rape, or assault are barred from probation.
- Probation officers can search a probationer's home without a warrant if they suspect foul play or criminal activity.
- Married probationers are more likely to succeed than their single or divorced peers.
- Convicted criminals can be forced to forfeit their homes and cars.

Mike Coppola/Getty Images Entertainment/Getty Images

LEARNING OBJECTIVES

LO1 *Explain the concept of community sentencing*

LO2 *Describe the history of community sentences*

LO3 *Recognize the different types of probation sentences*

LO4 *Recall the rules of probation*

LO5 *Explain the organization and administration of probation services*

LO6 *List and discuss the elements of a probation department's duties*

LO7 *Recall the legal rights of probationers*

LO8 *Debate the effectiveness of probation*

LO9 *Explain what is meant by intermediate sanctions*

LO10 *Define restorative justice, and discuss its merits*

237

the most widely used means of correction today. Millions of people are now being treated in the community for crimes ranging from fraud to rape and even homicide. Those who support community corrections believe that offenders are much more likely to be successfully rehabilitated if they can avoid the pains of incarceration.

This chapter reviews community-based criminal sanctions. It begins with a brief history of community sentencing and then discusses the role of traditional probation as a community-based correctional practice. Next, it focuses on so-called alternative or intermediate sanctions such as intensive supervision, house arrest, and electronic monitoring. Finally, the chapter turns to a discussion of the concept of restorative justice and programs based on its principles.

What is Probation?

probation A sentence entailing the conditional release of a convicted offender into the community under the supervision of the court (in the person of a probation officer), subject to certain conditions for a specified time.

As the term is used today, **probation** is a criminal sentence that suspends or delays a correctional term in a prison or jail so that, instead of being incarcerated, offenders are returned to the community for a period in which they must (1) abide by certain conditions set forth by the court, and (2) be supervised by a probation officer. It is the most commonly used means of dispensing correctional treatment to convicted offenders.

The fact that probation is used so often rests on the belief that most convicted criminals are neither dangerous nor a menace to society and can be reformed if given a second chance. Probation provides offenders the opportunity to prove themselves while being closely supervised in the community by trained personnel who can help them reestablish proper forms of behavior. Even felony offenders can be successfully rehabilitated if given the proper balance of community supervision, treatment, and control. And importantly, during tough economic times, probation is a cost-effective alternative to incarceration. So it's not just petty offenders who get probation: an overwhelming majority of convicted offenders including felons also get a "second chance" via probation.[3]

LO1 Explain the concept of community sentencing

The History of Probation and Community Sentencing

judicial reprieve The common-law practice that allowed judges to suspend punishment so that convicted offenders could seek a pardon, gather new evidence, or demonstrate that they had reformed their behavior.

recognizance The medieval practice of allowing convicted offenders to go unpunished if they agreed to refrain from any further criminal behavior.

sureties During the Middle Ages, people responsible for the behavior of an offender released before trial.

Where did the idea of community supervision and control begin? During medieval times, the practice of **judicial reprieve** allowed judges to suspend punishment so that convicted offenders could seek a pardon, gather new evidence, or demonstrate that they had reformed their behavior. Another practice, called **recognizance**, enabled convicted offenders to go unpunished if they agreed to refrain from further criminal behavior. Sometimes **sureties** were required—these were people who made themselves responsible for the behavior of an offender after the offender's release.

John Augustus and the Creation of Probation

John Augustus of Boston is usually credited with originating community sentencing.[4] As a private citizen, Augustus began in 1841 to supervise offenders released to his custody by a Boston judge. Over an 18-year period, Augustus supervised close to 2,000 convicted offenders and helped them get jobs and establish themselves in the community. Augustus had an amazingly high success rate, and few of his charges ever became involved in crime again.

In 1878, Augustus's work inspired the Massachusetts legislature to pass a law authorizing the appointment of a paid probation officer for the city of Boston. In 1880, probation was extended to other jurisdictions in Massachusetts, and by 1898, the probation movement had spread to the superior (felony) courts.[5] The Massachusetts experience was copied by Missouri (1887) and Vermont (1898) and, soon after, by most other states. In 1925, the federal government established a probation system for the US district courts. The probation concept soon became the most widely used correctional mechanism in the United States.[6]

Probation Today

Approximately 2,000 adult probation agencies are currently in operation in the United States. Slightly more than half are associated with a state-level agency, whereas the remaining agencies are organized at the county or municipal level of government. About 30 states combine probation and parole supervision into a single agency; in some jurisdictions, probation supervision is carried out by private contractors.

As Figure 10.1 shows, the adult probation population grew between 2000 and 2008 until more than 4 million people were on probation. Then, in 2009, the number of people on probation slowly began to decline, a trend that has continued until today.[7]

While growth in the probation population has ended for now, there are still almost 4 million people on probation, and more than 2 million people are placed on probation annually.

Who is on probation? Males make up three-quarters of the adult probation population. More than half of probationers are white non-Hispanic, and nearly a third are African Americans. Nearly 20 percent, or one in five, probationers are being supervised for a violent offense; little more than half of probationers are being supervised for a felony offense. Without probation, the correctional system would rapidly become even more overcrowded, overly expensive, and unmanageable.

Awarding Probation

Most probation orders involve a contract between the court and the offender in which a prison or jail term is suspended, and the probationer promises to obey a set of **probation rules**, or conditions mandated by the court. If the rules are violated, or if the probationer commits another criminal offense, probation may be revoked: the community sentence is terminated, and the original sentence of incarceration is enforced. **Revocation** is not automatic, and the presiding judge can decide to let the offender remain in the community. If an offender on probation commits a second offense that is more serious than the first, he or she may also be indicted, tried, and sentenced to a longer prison sentence based on the second offense.

Today, probationary sentences may be granted by state and federal district courts and state superior (felony) courts. In most jurisdictions, although juries can recommend probation, the presiding judge makes the final sentencing decision. Most states have attempted to shape judicial discretion by creating guidelines for granting probation, directing them to look at such factors as the manner in which the crime was carried out or whether pain was inflicted on a vulnerable victim such as a child. In contrast, probation may be recommended when defendants are youthful or when they were pressured by a co-defendant into committing the crime. A recent Supreme Court case, *Gall v. United States,* held that granting a probationary sentence to a deserving defendant was not unreasonable even though the Federal Sentencing Guidelines called for a prison sentence. Gall had voluntarily withdrawn from a drug ring three years before indictments were handed down. He moved to another state, opened a business, and started a new life. The judge decided to give him a break and handed down a

probation rules Conditions or restrictions mandated by the court that must be obeyed by a probationer.

revocation An administrative act performed by a parole authority that removes a person from parole, or a judicial order by a court removing a person from parole or probation, in response to a violation on the part of the parolee or probationer.

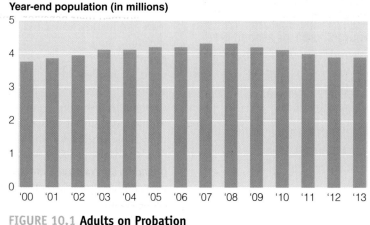

Year-end population (in millions)

FIGURE 10.1 Adults on Probation

Source: Laura M. Maruschak and Erika Parks, *Probation and Parole in the United States, 2013* (Washington, DC: Bureau of Justice Statistics, 2014).

Probation Eligibility

Does it violate your sense of justice that some people who commit multiple felonies, including violent crimes such as rape and assault, receive probation sentences? What about the rights of potential victims who may be injured by someone who should have been behind bars but was granted a probation sentence (referred to as an avertable recidivist)?

suspended sentence A prison term that is delayed while the defendant undergoes a period of community treatment. If the treatment is successful, the prison sentence is terminated.

LO3 Recognize the different types of probation sentences

LO4 Recall the rules of probation

probation-only sentence. When the prosecution appealed, the Court held that it is appropriate for the sentencing judge to consider all the elements in the case when deciding whether a probation sentence is appropriate.[8]

More than half of all cases involve a direct sentence to probation for a fixed period of time. In many cases, the judge will formulate a prison sentence and then suspend it if the offender agrees to obey the rules of probation while living in the community (a suspended sentence). If the offender completes the probation term without further trouble, his or her sentence is considered served. Some offenders receive a split sentence in which they must first serve a jail term before being released on probation. In the remaining cases, the imposition of the sentence is suspended and the case continued without a finding until further notice.

For misdemeanors, probation usually extends for the entire period of the jail sentence, whereas felonies are more likely to warrant probationary periods that are actually shorter than the suspended prison sentences. The typical felony probation sentence is a little more than three years.[9]

Probation Eligibility

Although originally conceived as a way to provide a second chance for young offenders who committed nonserious crimes, probation today is also a means of reducing the population overload in an overcrowded and underfunded correctional system. Many serious criminal offenders are therefore given probation sentences, including people with prior felony convictions; many repeat felony offenders are given community sentences!

This means that criminal defendants may receive probation even though the current offense was at least their second conviction for a felony offense. Nor are violent criminals exempt from receiving a community sentence: about 20 percent of all people convicted of violent felonies receive probation.[10] So there are two distinct sides to probation: (1) the treatment and rehabilitation of nondangerous offenders deserving of a second chance, and (2) the supervision and control of criminals who might otherwise be incarcerated if probation were not available.

Conditions of Probation

When granting probation, the court sets down certain conditions or rules of behavior that the probationer is bound to obey. Although probation officers themselves can later set some conditions, courts have typically ruled that the most restrictive ones must be approved by the sentencing judge and that probation officers cannot require the defendant to adhere to new requirements of supervision about which he or she did not have reasonable notice.[11]

Some conditions are standard and are applied in every probation case (e.g., "Do not leave the jurisdiction"), but the sentencing judge usually has broad discretion to set specific conditions on a case-by-case basis. Sometimes an individual probationer is given specific rules related to his or her particular circumstances, such as the requirement to enroll in an anger management or drug treatment program, make a personal apology to the victim, or have no contact with his or her ex-spouse.[12] A presiding judge may not impose capricious or cruel conditions, of course, such as requiring an offender to make restitution out of proportion to the seriousness of the criminal act.[13] Judges may, however, legally impose restrictions tailored to fit the probationer's individual needs and/or to protect society from additional harm. For example, they can force sex offenders to register with state authorities and require probationers to take periodic polygraph tests to determine whether they have engaged in illegal behavior.[14] Community supervision may be revoked if probationers fail to comply with the conditions of their probation and do not obey the reasonable requests of the probation staff to meet their treatment obligations.[15]

Administration of Probation Services

Probation services are organized in a variety of ways, depending on the state and the jurisdiction in which they are located. Some states have an independent state-wide probation service, and, in others, probation is controlled by local courts. Some states bifurcate the process, for example, by having a state agency monitor felony probationers and local courts supervise misdemeanants. Thirty-five states combine probation and parole supervision services in a single unit situated within the department of corrections or organized as an independent agency; about one-quarter of probationers are supervised in these joint operations. Some departments combine juvenile and adult probation departments, whereas others maintain these departments separately.

Regardless of how probation services are organized, probation officers (POs) are typically assigned to a department situated in a single court district, such as a juvenile, superior, district, or municipal court. The relationship between the department and court personnel (especially the judge) is extremely close.

In the typical department, the chief probation officer (CPO) sets policy, supervises hiring, determines training needs, and may personally discuss with or recommend sentencing to the judge. The probation staff carries out the actual monitoring and treatment of offenders.

An officer's working style is influenced by both personal values and the department's general policies and orientation toward the goals of probation.[16] Traditionally, probation officers were placed along a continuum. At one extreme, officers considered themselves "social workers" who maintained a treatment orientation with the goal of helping offenders adjust in the community, whereas at the other extreme, they considered themselves "law enforcers" who were more concerned with supervision, control, and public safety. Another group took a more balanced approach to their work, employing a blend of social work and law enforcement that is neither indulgent of antisocial attitudes and noncompliance nor authoritative and heavy-handed toward their clients.[17]

Recently, Joel Miller surveyed thousands of active probation officers and found that they can be grouped around their engagement with clients, ranging from those most involved to those least involved.[18] Those who were most involved were concerned with emphasizing consequences of behaviors and risks of detention, monitoring behaviors, and fully enforcing rules when transgressions occur. The highly involved officers want to engage probationers with therapeutic services, family-based services, and skill-building programs, while helping them avoid risky places and activities. High engagers are willing to work with family members to help the client. In contrast, low engagers often have minimal or sporadic contact with clients and almost none with family members. They are the officers least able to help clients navigate the path to successful completion of probation orders and rules.

For more on a career as a probation officer, see the Careers in Criminal Justice feature.

L05 Explain the organization and administration of probation services

Elements of Probation

Probation officers engage in five primary tasks: presentence investigation, intake, diagnosis/risk classification, supervision, and treatment.

PRESENTENCE INVESTIGATION In the investigative stage, the supervising probation officer accumulates important information on the background and activities of the offender being considered for probation. This presentence investigation serves as the basis for sentencing and controls whether the convicted defendant will be granted community release or be sentenced to secure confinement. In the event that the offender is placed on probation, the investigation becomes useful as a tool to shape treatment and supervision efforts.

presentence investigation An investigation performed by a probation officer attached to a trial court after the conviction of a defendant.

WEB APP 10.1 To learn more about the administration of probation services and a variety of probation issues and programs, go to the American Probation and Parole Association website at **http://www .appa-net.org.**

Duties and Characteristics of the Job

- Probation officers monitor offenders' behavior through personal contact with the offenders and their families.

- Another part of the probation officer's job involves working in the courts.

- The number of cases a probation officer has depends on both the counseling needs of offenders and the risks they pose to society.

- Probation officers may find their jobs stressful because they work with convicted criminals and interact with many other individuals who may be angry, upset, or uncooperative, including family members and friends of their clients.

- Although stress makes these jobs difficult at times, the work also can be rewarding. Many probation officers gain personal satisfaction from counseling members of their community and helping them become productive citizens.

Job Outlook

- Jobs for probation officers are more plentiful in urban areas.

- There are also more jobs in states that have numerous men and women on probation.

- Employment of probation officers is projected to grow during the next few years.

- Overcrowding in prisons also has swelled the probation population as judges and prosecutors search for alternative forms of punishment, such as electronic monitoring and day reporting centers.

- Other openings will result from the need to replace workers who leave the occupation permanently, including the large number expected to retire over the next several years.

Salary

- The 90,000 probation officers in the United States earn a median annual salary of about $48,000, or about $23 per hour.

- Officers and specialists who work in urban areas usually have higher earnings than those working in rural areas.

Qualifications

- Prospective probation officers must be in good physical condition and must be emotionally stable.

- Most agencies require applicants to be at least 21 years old and, for federal employment, not older than 37.

- Those convicted of felonies may not be eligible for employment in these occupations.

- Probation officers need strong writing skills due to the large number of reports they must prepare.

- Familiarity with computers is often required.

- Job candidates also should be knowledgeable about laws and regulations pertaining to corrections.

Education and Training

- Educational requirements for probation officers vary by state, but a bachelor's degree in social work or criminal justice is usually required.

- Some states require probation officers to have one year of work experience in a related field or one year of graduate study in criminal justice, social work, or psychology.

- Most probation officers must complete a training program and work as trainees for about six months. Candidates who successfully complete the training period obtain a permanent position after which they may have to pass a certification test. In addition, they may be required to work as trainees for up to one year before being offered a permanent position.

- Some probation officers specialize in a certain type of casework. For example, an officer may work only with domestic violence offenders or deal only with substance-abuse cases. Officers receive training specific to the group that they are working with so that they are better prepared to help that type of offender.

- Applicants usually must also pass written, oral, psychological, and physical examinations.

Reality Check

- Probation can be challenging, but it is also quite rewarding.

- Although an advanced degree is not a requirement, it may be the key to advancement in larger departments.

- Budget cutbacks may mean tougher cases entering community corrections rather than more expensive custodial placements.

Source: US Dept. of Labor, "Probation Officers and Correctional Treatment Specialists," 2015, http://www.bls.gov/ooh/community-and-social-service/probation-officers-and-correctional-treatment-specialists.htm (accessed March 2015).

The style and content of presentence investigations may vary among jurisdictions and also among individual POs within the same jurisdiction. Some departments require voluminous reports covering every aspect of the defendant's life. Other departments require that officers stick to the basic facts, such as the defendant's age, race, sex, and previous offense record.

At the conclusion of most presentence investigations, a recommendation is made to the presiding judge that reflects the department's sentencing posture on the case at hand. This is a crucial aspect of the report because the sentencing judge usually follows the probation department's recommendation. Numerous factors may contribute to a recommendation of community treatment; among the most critical are the investigator's conclusion that the defendant is someone probation officers can work with and effectively treat. Equally important is the belief that the perspective probationer will be able to abide by both legal and institutional rules.[19]

Probation supervision can involve going into the field and engaging in such activities as searching probationers residence for contraband or conducting drug testing. Here the Orange County California Deputy Probation Officer Erin Merritt searches one of her client's homes for illegal substances.

INTAKE Probation officers who conduct **intake** interviews may be looking to settle the case without the necessity of a court hearing. The probation officer will work with all parties involved in the case—offender, victim, police officer, and so on—to design an equitable resolution of the case. If the intake process is successful, the probation officer may settle the case without further court action, recommend restitution or other compensation, or recommend unofficial or informal probation. If an equitable solution cannot be found, the case is filed for a court hearing.

intake The process in which a probation officer settles cases at the initial appearance before the onset of formal criminal proceedings; also, the process in which a juvenile referral is received and a decision is made to file a petition in the juvenile court, release the juvenile, or refer the juvenile elsewhere.

DIAGNOSIS/RISK CLASSIFICATION To select appropriate treatment modes, probation officers analyze the client's character, attitudes, and behavior at various points in the probation process, from the assignment of cases to selection of treatment modalities.[20] An effective diagnosis integrates all that has been learned about the individual, organized in such a way as to facilitate the establishment of future treatment goals. Based on the risk level diagnosis, some clients may receive frequent (intensive) supervision in which they are contacted by their supervising probation officer almost every day, whereas those considered low risk are assigned to minimum monitoring.

Developing effective risk assessment has taken on greater importance because probation is now routinely employed with felons who have been convicted of violent crimes such as rape and murder.[21] A number of **risk classification** approaches are now used, but most employ such objective measures as the offender's age, employment status, drug abuse history, prior felony convictions, and number of address changes in the year prior to sentencing. Some departments are using standardized tests to predict failure and assign treatment such as the Level of Service Inventory-Revised (LSI-R).[22] Another approach, the Post-Conviction Risk Assessment (PCRA) scale, is widely used to classify probationers in the federal system and is now being evaluated to determine whether it can be employed to pinpoint risk factors that interfere with supervision of probationers and undermine effectiveness.[23]

risk classification Classifying probationers so that they may receive an appropriate level of treatment and control.

Some critics have complained that the emergence of standardized diagnostic tools and tests has diminished the probationer officer's individual role in classification, thereby eliminating the human element from diagnosis and treatment.[24] To counter this argument, a number of jurisdictions are testing or have implemented advanced classification systems based on highly sophisticated methodologies. Philadelphia is now using *random forest modeling* to assess each new case and then assign the probationer to a high-, moderate-, or low-risk category. The tool is a sophisticated

Probation Eligibility

A probation department has been sued by a rape victim when she found out that her attacker was a probationer with a history sexual assault and was still on the street despite repeatedly violating his probation orders. Is it ethical to award her damages, or should probation officers and departments be exempt from litigation because no one can accurately predict the future behavior of probationers?

statistical approach that considers the effects of a large number of personal, social, and legal variables with complex interactions. In 10–15 seconds, the tool assigns a new probationer to one of three categories. The lowest level of risk is assigned to those who are predicted to not commit any new offense in the next two years. The moderate-risk level identifies those who are likely to commit a crime, but not a serious one. The high-risk level is for those who are most likely to commit a serious crime such as murder, attempted murder, aggravated assault, rape, and arson.

Community supervision is based on the determined risk level. Probation officers who are supervising high-risk individuals are given the smallest caseloads.[25]

SUPERVISION An important part of the probation officer's duties is monitoring clients in the community, making sure they obey their probation orders, and helping them to stay out of trouble. In some cases, this can mean giving random drug tests, monitoring the family situation, and keeping in touch with employers. Some officers have a control orientation, believe in strict supervision, and are quick to sanction offenders who violate rules. Others are more treatment oriented and question the effectiveness of punitive sanctions and strict supervision. Recent research has identified a new breed of younger probation officers who are actually more inclined to control and punish rule violators than their older counterparts. One reason for this turn to closer and more punitive supervision is the threat of litigation. Failure to supervise probationers adequately can result in the officer and the department being held legally liable for civil damages.[26]

Several newly developed technologies are now being used to aid supervision, and some can provide probation officers with tools to better manage their caseloads. For example, sleep pattern analysis technology, already used by some jurisdictions, provides preliminary indications of substance abuse that creates identifiable sleep disruption patterns. The technology consists of a small device, secured to an offender's wrist with a tamper-evident band, that measures sleep quality by recording gross motor activity. Some departments are now monitoring probationers forbidden to drive with ankle bracelets that collect data on the unique patterns of movement associated with foot-to-brake, foot-to-gas pedal, and acceleration and deceleration of a motor vehicle.[27]

TREATMENT Probation staff are assigned to carry out a program of therapy designed to help the client deal with the problems that are suspected of being the cause of her or his antisocial behavior. In years past, the probation staff had primary responsibility for supervision and treatment, but today's large caseloads limit opportunities for hands-on treatment; most probation treatment efforts rely on community resources.

Treatment protocols may vary according to client needs. Some of those who have a drinking problem may be asked to participate in a community-based 12-step program; others might spend time in a residential detoxification center. A spousal abuser may be required to enroll in an anger management program. A probation officer may work with teachers and other school officials to develop a program designed to help a young probationer reduce his or her truancy and avoid becoming a dropout.

A number of innovative techniques are now being used with probationers. One popular technique, motivational interviewing, assumes that disinterested probationers forced into treatment will lack the will to change. Motivational interviewing therefore attempts to increase probationers' awareness of their potential problems and to help them acknowledge the risks they face if they fail to change their behavior. Clients are asked to visualize a better future and learn strategies to reach their goals.[28] Another popular client-centered approach, cognitive behavioral therapy, is discussed in the Contemporary Issues in Criminal Justice feature.

motivational interviewing
A technique that increases the probationers' awareness of their potential problems by asking them to visualize a better future and learn strategies to reach their goals.

LO6 List and discuss the elements of a probation department's duties

Legal Rights of Probationers

What are the legal rights of probationers? How has the US Supreme Court set limits on the probation process? A number of important legal issues surround probation, one set involving the civil rights of probationers and another involving the rights of probationers during the revocation process.

CIVIL RIGHTS The Court has ruled that probationers have a unique status and therefore are entitled to fewer constitutional protections than other citizens.

- *Minnesota v. Murphy (1984).*[29] The probation officer-client relationship is not confidential, as are physician-patient and attorney-client relationships. If a probationer admits to committing a crime to his or her probation supervisor, the information can be passed on to the police or district attorney. The *Murphy* decision held that a probation officer could even use trickery or psychological pressure to get information and turn it over to the police.
- *Griffin v. Wisconsin (1987).*[30] *Griffin* held that a probationer's home may be searched without a warrant because probation departments "have

AP Images/Timothy D. Easley

Probation departments are constantly trying out new treatment techniques. On April 9, 2015, Judge David A. Tapp, right, addresses members of the Supervision Motivation Accountable Responsibility and Treatment program, also known as SMART probation, at the Pulaski County Courthouse in Somerset, Kentucky. This group is among a handful of addicts that are participating in a special probation program overseen by Judge Tapp. The program provides medication under the brand name Vivitrol that blocks the opioid receptors in the brain. This means that opioids like prescription painkillers and heroin would have no effect on addicts, which would help them stop using the drugs.

CONTEMPORARY ISSUES IN CRIMINAL JUSTICE

Treating Probationers with Cognitive Behavioral Therapy

Cognitive behavioral therapy (CBT) is a correctional treatment approach that focuses on patterns of thinking and the beliefs, attitudes, and values that underlie thinking. The therapy assumes that most people can become conscious of their own thoughts and behaviors and then make positive changes. A person's thoughts are often the result of experience, and behavior is often influenced and prompted by these thoughts. In addition, thoughts may sometimes become distorted and fail to reflect reality accurately.

When a probationer is placed in a CBT program, the goal is to restructure distorted thinking and perception, which in turn changes a person's behavior for the better. Characteristics of distorted thinking may include immature or developmentally arrested thoughts; poor problem solving and decision making; an inability to consider the effects of one's behavior; a hampered ability to reason and accept blame for wrongdoing; or an inability to manage feelings of anger. These distorted thinking patterns can lead to making poor decisions and engaging in antisocial behavior to solve problems.

A number of reviews have found that the approach can be effective with both juvenile and adult offenders. The present study evaluated the long-term effectiveness of a cognitive behavioral group therapy program called Community Opportunity Growth. This study monitored juvenile delinquents' recidivism across a 7-year time period, with the average length to follow-up being 39 months. It was hypothesized that program graduates (N = 178) would have a significantly lower recidivism rate than a control

group (program nonstarters; N = 66) and program dropouts (whose predisposing factors may have influenced their program participation; N = 150). Analyses controlled for sex, ethnicity, age, prior petitions, highest class of prior petition, and months to follow-up. Results show a general trend indicating the long-term effectiveness of the program as graduates had a lower incidence of petitions at follow-up compared with dropouts and fewer petitions compared with the other two groups.

Patrick Clark reviewed the existing literature on cognitive behavior and found that, unlike other approaches, CBT places responsibility in the hands of clients while supplying them with the tools to solve their problems, that is, focusing on the present rather than the past. People taking part in CBT learn specific skills that can be used to solve the problems they confront all the time as well as skills they can use to achieve legitimate goals and objectives. CBT first concentrates on developing skills to recognize distorted or unrealistic thinking when it happens, and then on changing that thinking or belief to mollify or eliminate problematic behavior.

Program Effectiveness

CBT is one of the few treatment approaches that has been broadly validated with research. Unlike other traditional and popular therapies, CBT has been the subject of more than 400 clinical trials involving a broad range of conditions and populations. For example, a number of research studies have found CBT to be reliably effective with a wide variety of personal problems and behaviors, including substance abuse, antisocial

(Continued)

and aggressive behavior, and mood disorders, all of which have been linked to criminality. Jeremy Jewell and his associates found evidence that youth who complete the program have lower recidivism rates than control group members.

Evidence of the treatment's effectiveness has been produced by Mark Lipsey, who examined the effectiveness of various approaches to intervention with offenders. His review analyzed the results of 548 studies from 1958 to 2002 that assessed intervention policies, practices, and programs. Lipsey found that interventions based on punishment and deterrence actually increased recidivism. On the other hand, therapeutic approaches based on counseling, skill building, and multiple services had the greatest impact in reducing further problem behavior. In a recent review of correctional treatment, Lipsey, along with Nana Landenberger, found that CBT significantly reduced recidivism. The greatest effects were found among more serious offenders, perhaps because CBT's enabling, self-help approach increases program participation and is therefore most effective with clients who shun or resist other approaches. The therapy is also more effective in reducing further criminal behavior when clients simultaneously receive other support, such as supervision, employment, education and training, and other mental health counseling.

CRITICAL THINKING

If changing or altering disruptive thinking patterns is key to changing behavior, does that mean that crime is more of an individual problem than a result of poverty, social inequality, and disorganization? Is the logical conclusion, then, that if crime is more common in poor neighborhoods and communities, affluent people have better cognitive skills than the poor?

Sources: Jeremy Jewell, Michael Malone, Paul Rose, Dennis Sturgeon, and Sarah Owens, "Multiyear Follow-Up Study Examining the Effectiveness of a Cognitive Behavioral Group Therapy Program on the Recidivism of Juveniles on Probation," *International Journal of Offender Therapy & Comparative Criminology* 59 (2015): 259–272; Sesha Kethineni and Jeremy Braithwaite, "The Effects of a Cognitive-Behavioral Program for At-Risk Youth: Changes in Attitudes, Social Skills, Family, and Community and Peer Relationships," *Victims and Offenders* 6 (2011): 93–116; Patrick Clark, "Preventing Future Crime with Cognitive Behavioral Therapy," *National Institute of Justice Journal* 265 (2010), http://www.ojp.usdoj.gov/nij/journals/265/therapy.htm (accessed March 2015); Martin Lipsey, "The Primary Factors that Characterize Effective Interventions with Juvenile Offenders: A Meta-Analytic Overview," *Victims and Offenders* 4 (2009): 124–147; Nana Landenberger and Martin Lipsey, "The Positive Effects of Cognitive-Behavioral Programs for Offenders: A Meta-Analysis of Factors Associated with Effective Treatment," *Journal of Experimental Criminology* 1 (2005): 451–476.

---

in mind the welfare of the probationer" and must "respond quickly to evidence of misconduct."

- *United States v. Knights (2001).*[31] The warrantless search of a probationer's home for the purposes of gathering criminal evidence is legal under some circumstances—for example, if (1) the search was based on a reasonable suspicion that the probationer had committed another crime while on probation, and (2) submitting to searches was part of the probation order. The government's interest in preventing crime, combined with *Knights*'s diminished expectation of privacy, required only a *reasonable suspicion* to make the search fit within the protections of the Fourth Amendment.

REVOCATION RIGHTS During the course of a probationary term, violating the rules or terms of probation or committing a new crime can result in probation being revoked, at which time the offender may be placed in an institution. Revocation is not often an easy decision because it conflicts with the treatment philosophy of many probation departments.

If revocation is a possibility, the offender is notified, and a formal hearing is scheduled to look into the matter. If the charges against the probationer are upheld, the offender can either be maintained on probation or have his probation revoked and be forced to serve the remainder of his sentence behind bars.

In some significant decisions, the US Supreme Court provided procedural safeguards to apply at proceedings to revoke probation (and parole):

- *Mempa v. Rhay (1967).* A probationer is constitutionally entitled to counsel in a revocation-of-probation proceeding where the imposition of sentence had been suspended.[32]
- *Morrissey v. Brewer (1972). Morrissey,* a parole case, established that an informal inquiry must be held to determine whether there is probable cause that a parolee has violated the conditions of parole. If so, a formal revocation hearing is required before parole can be revoked. Because the revocation of probation and that of parole are similar, the standards in *Morrissey* are applied to the probation process as well.[33]
- *Gagnon v. Scarpelli (1973). Gagnon* established that both probationers and parolees have a constitutionally limited right to legal counsel in revocation proceedings.[34] A judge may deny counsel under some circumstances, such as when probation will be continued despite the violation.

REALITYCHECK

MYTH OR REALITY?

Probation officers can search a probationer's home without a warrant if they suspect foul play or criminal activity.

REALITY. Probationers have fewer expectations of privacy than the average citizen, and their home can be searched without a warrant if there is cause.

Do you think that probationers should have the same civil rights as anyone else living in the community?

- *Beardon v. Georgia (1983).* In *Beardon,* the US Supreme Court ruled that a judge cannot revoke a defendant's probation for failure to pay a fine and/or make restitution. The state may not thereafter imprison a defendant solely because he or she lacks the resources to pay because this would be a violation of a probationer's right to equal protection.[35]
- *United States v. Granderson (1994).* The *Granderson* ruling helped clarify what can happen to a probationer whose community sentence is revoked. Granderson was eligible for a 6-month prison sentence but instead was given 60 months of probation. When he tested positive for drugs, his probation was revoked. The statute he was sentenced under required that he serve one-third of his original sentence in prison. When the trial court sentenced him to 20 months, he appealed. Was his original sentence 6 months or 60 months? The Supreme Court found that it would be unfair to force a probationer to serve more time in prison than he would have served if originally incarcerated and ruled that the proper term should have been one-third of the 6 months, or 2 months.[36]

L07 Recall the legal rights of probationers

How Successful Is Probation?

Probation is the most commonly used alternative sentence for a number of reasons: it is humane, it helps offenders maintain community and family ties, and it is cost effective. Incarcerating an inmate typically costs over $25,000 per year, whereas probation costs about $2,000 per year.

Although unquestionably inexpensive, is probation successful? If most probation orders fail, the costs of repeated criminality would certainly outweigh the cost savings of a probation sentence. National data indicate that about 60 percent of probationers successfully complete their probationary sentence, whereas about 40 percent are rearrested, violate probation rules, or abscond. Of those who leave probation, about 15 percent find themselves behind bars.

Most revocations occur for technical violations during the first three months of the probation sentence.[37] Typically, many revocations stem from failure to attend required treatment programs that were originally created to help probationers kick their drug habits, stay out of trouble, and succeed on probation; others are absconders who leave the jurisdiction without notice.[38]

Probation may work because it is easier to treat offenders in their home environment than in a closed institution. When Christopher Krebs and his associates carefully compared treatment outcomes of large groups of drug-involved offenders in the state of Florida, they found that institutional treatment in jail or prison cost three times as much as community-based treatment but was actually less successful; inmates showed no particular improvement after attending institutional drug treatment programs, while those on probation achieved positive results. They concluded that the use of community-based treatment can increase public safety while costing a lot less than locking up offenders.[39] Even clients with the most serious personal problems, such as mental illness, seem to do better on probation than in closed institutions.[40]

How Successful Is Felony Probation?

Are probationers convicted of serious felonies more likely to recidivate than minor offenders who receive probation? Is it possible that the success of probation reflects the fact that probationers are far less dangerous and incorrigible than offenders sentenced to prison? One way to determine the real success of probation is to disaggregate felons from misdemeanants and see how the former group does on community sentencing. In a classic study, Joan Petersilia and her colleagues at the RAND Corporation, a private think tank, traced the outcomes of 1,672 men convicted of felonies who had been granted probation in Los Angeles and Alameda counties in California.[41] The crimes these probationers committed were indistinguishable from those of offenders sentenced to prison.

Petersilia found that 1,087 (65 percent) of the felony probationers were soon rearrested; of those rearrested, 853 (51 percent) were convicted; and of those convicted, 568 (34 percent) were sentenced to jail or prison. Of the probationers who had new charges filed against them, 75 percent were charged with burglary, theft, robbery, and other predatory crimes; 18 percent were convicted of serious, violent crimes.

Although the failure rate found by Petersilia seems disturbingly high, her findings still support the continued use of probation, given the fact that felons who receive probation are less likely to recidivate than felons who are sent to prison for committing similar crimes.[42] Incarcerating offenders increases the likelihood of recidivism.[43] Granting felons probation may actually produce more favorable outcomes at a much lower cost than an incarceration sentence.

LO8 Debate the effectiveness of probation

Who Fails on Probation and Who Succeeds?

Who is most likely to fail on probation? Many probationers have grown up in troubled households in which family members are or have been incarcerated and/or drug abusers. Others have lived part of their lives in foster homes or state institutions and have suffered high rates of physical and sexual abuse. This sort of deprived background often makes it difficult for probationers to comply with the rules of probation and forgo criminal activity. Surveys indicate that almost 20 percent of probationers suffer from mental illness and that those with a history of instability are most likely to be rearrested.[44]

Prior record is also related to probation success: clients who have a history of criminal behavior, prior probation, and previous incarceration are the most likely to fail.[45] Also, as probation sentences have become more common, caseloads now contain significant numbers of serious repeat offenders, a group that is difficult to treat and control.[46]

In contrast, probationers who are married with children, have lived in the area for two or more years, and are adequately employed are the most likely to be successful on probation.[47] Among female probationers, those who have stable marriages, are better educated, and are employed are more likely to complete probation orders successfully than male or female probationers who are single, less educated, and unemployed.

The Future of Probation

Some critics are worried that probation is now undergoing a shift from traditional casework methods that featured diagnosis and treatment to an emphasis on risk assessment and control.[48] To improve the effectiveness of probation even more, in a process that leading expert Joan Petersilia calls "reforming, reinvesting, and restructuring," several steps appear to be necessary, including providing more financial resources and implementing quality programming for appropriate probation target groups.[49] A number of initiatives that are now ongoing or being suggested may help shape the future of probation:

day fees A program requiring probationers to pay some of the costs of their treatment.

- *Making probationers pay.* At least 25 states now impose some form of fee on probationers to defray the cost of community corrections. Massachusetts initiated day fees, which are based on the probationer's wages (the usual fee is between one and three days' wages each month).[50] Texas requires judges to impose supervision fees unless the offender is truly unable to pay; fees make up more than half the probation department's annual budget.[51]
- *Making probation more effective.* Legislatures are instituting policies that reward the most effective and efficient local departments. In 2008, the Arizona legislature established an incentive system that rewards departments with up to 40 percent of any cost savings in each county resulting from a reduction in probation revocations. The money can then be used to fund substance abuse treatment, community supervision services, and victim services.[52]
- *HotSpot probation.* HotSpot probation initiatives involve police officers, probation agents, neighbors, and social service professionals in community supervision teams. Using a team approach, they provide increased monitoring of offenders through home visits and drug testing. They also work with the offenders to ease reentry through offender creation of work crews that participate in community cleanups, work on vacant houses, and participate in other projects.[53]
- *Area needs.* Some experts suggest that probation caseloads be organized around area needs rather than client needs. Research shows that probationers' residences are

REALITYCHECK

MYTH OR REALITY?

Married probationers are more likely to succeed than their single or divorced peers.

REALITY. Getting and staying married seems to help probationers succeed. Marriage seems to bring stability into people's lives and helps law violators go straight.

What is it about marriage that helps people succeed on probation? Is it the fact that a romantic relationship helps probationers avoid a life of crime? Or is it possible that people who have decided to go straight seek out a stable partner?

concentrated in certain locations. In the future, probation officers may be assigned cases on the basis of where they live so that they can acquire a working knowledge of community issues and develop expertise on how best to serve their clients' interests and needs.[54]

- *Specialized probation.* Some probation departments are experimenting with focused or specialized probation, in which teams of probation officers take on clients convicted of one specific type of crime, such as drug offenses or domestic violence, rather than treating a mixed bag of offenders. Focusing on specialized caseloads enables probation officers to develop specific treatment and control skills.[55] In some instances, probation officers collaborate with other social service agencies such as public health to provide a range of services to treat special needs clients.[56]

- *Private probation.* Used in at least 10 states, including Florida, Georgia, Colorado, and Missouri, private probation involves contracting with companies that, for a fee, engage in many typical probation activities from supervision to giving periodic breathalyzer tests.[57] By utilizing private probation for low-risk offenders, state probation departments can commit more resources to high-risk offenders.[58]

- *Swift and sure punishment.* The threat of swift and sure punishment that is somewhat less than a full revocation may help reduce rule violations. Hawaii has been experimenting with a system that provides immediate punishment for any probationers found in violation of their court orders; Hawaii's HOPE program is described in the accompanying Contemporary Issues feature.[59] Delaware's Step'n Out program is designed for offenders who fail drug tests. Participants are then given drug tests once or twice a week. Continued drug use progressively leads to mandated treatment, more frequent testing, curfew, and incarceration sanctions. Those who are drug free are reclassified and move to standard community supervision.[60]

Probation is unquestionably undergoing dramatic changes. In many jurisdictions, traditional probation is being supplemented by **intermediate sanctions**, which are penalties that fall between traditional community supervision and confinement in jail or prison. These new correctional services are discussed in the following sections.

intermediate sanctions Punishments that fall between probation and prison ("probation plus"). Community-based sanctions, including house arrest and intensive supervision, serve as alternatives to incarceration.

CONTEMPORARY ISSUES IN CRIMINAL JUSTICE

Hawaii Hope?

Hawaii's HOPE program is designed to keep people on probation by threatening them at a formal warning hearing with "swift and certain" punishment, rather than severe sanctions, for violating terms of probation. The program is geared to drug-involved offenders.

HOPE begins with a "warning hearing," sometimes called an "orientation hearing" in which the judge clearly lays out the program's rules and structure, and probationers are put on notice that they will be punished for violations and that a probationer's success is entirely within his or her own control.

The program requires probationers with drug conditions to undergo regular random drug tests (six times a month during the first few months) to insure that there is a zero-tolerance approach to drug usage; those who fail a drug test are arrested immediately. Typically, the term is several days, servable on the weekend if the probationer is employed; sentences increase for successive violations.

HOPE differs from other programs by:

- Focusing on reducing drug use and missed appointments rather than on drug treatment and imposing drug treatment on every participant.

- Mandating drug treatment for probationers only if they continue to test positive for drug use or if they request a treatment referral. A HOPE probationer who has a third or fourth missed or "dirty" drug test may be mandated into residential treatment as an alternative to probation revocation.

- Requiring probationers to appear before a judge only when a violation is detected—in this respect, HOPE requires less treatment and fewer court resources than drug courts.

- Having probationers who are employed serve any jail time, at least initially, on a weekend so they do not jeopardize their employment.

Because only a small fraction of HOPE probationers receive mandated treatment, the program can afford to use intensive, long-term residential treatment, rather than relying primarily on outpatient drug-free counseling as do most diversion programs and drug courts.

Careful evidence-based evaluations of the HOPE program have found the following:

- It is cost-efficient because it covers a large number of clients while delivering intensive treatment to only those in need.

- It puts a smaller strain on treatment capacity by avoiding the situation in which clients for whom treatment is mandated crowd out clients who voluntarily seek treatment.

- Because the treatment mandate follows repeated failures, it helps break through denial; an offender who has spent three brief spells in jail for dirty drug tests may find it hard to keep telling himself that he is in control of his drug use.

(Continued)

Is Hope a Panacea?

Currently, at least 40 replications of HOPE-style models are being tested around the nation, and many correctional experts see its swift and sure punishment approach as a correctional panacea. But some respected correctional experts caution that what worked in Hawaii may have limited effect elsewhere. Some critics, such as Stephanie Duriez and her colleagues are concerned because there have been few evaluations of HOPE, and the existing ones have produced mixed results. One problem they find is that the program relies on swift-and-certain sanctions and that alone may not be enough to reduce recidivism and improve people's lives

While questions about HOPE still remain, supporters outnumber skeptics, and it is now being employed around the nation.

CRITICAL THINKING

Do you agree with the Hawaii HOPE model? Can warning people and punishing them be enough to turn their lives around? Does it just seem too easy to be true?

Sources: Stephanie Duriez, Francis Cullen, and Sarah Manchak, "Is Project HOPE Creating a False Sense of Hope? A Case Study in Correctional Popularity," *Federal Probation* 78 (2014), http://www.uscourts.gov/statistics-reports/publications/federal-probation-journal (accessed, May 2015); Beth Pearsall, "Replicating HOPE: Can Others Do It as Well as Hawaii?" *NIJ Journal* 273 (2014): 36–42, http://www.nij.gov/journals/273/pages/replicating-hope.aspx; National Institute of Justice, "'Swift and Certain'" Sanctions in Probation Are Highly Effective: Evaluation of the HOPE Program," http://www.nij.gov/topics/corrections/community/drug-offenders/hawaii-hope.htm (accessed April 2013).

FIGURE 10.1 **Punishment Ladder**

(ladder rungs, top to bottom: Death penalty; Prison; Shock probation; Residential community center; Electronic monitoring; House arrest; Intensive probation; Restitution; Probation; Forfeiture; Fines; Pretrial release; Restorative justice)

© Cengage Learning

Intermediate Sanctions

He may be willing to take a grenade for us, do the halftime show at the Super Bowl, and give us uptown funk, but will he do community service? Just a few days after winning the Grammy for "Best Male Pop Vocal Performance," Bruno Mars pleaded guilty to cocaine possession at a court in Las Vegas but was spared going to jail. His punishment was probation, a $2,000 fine, 200 hours of community service at a nonprofit organization, and 8 hours with a drug counselor in Los Angeles.

Bruno Mars's sentence reflects the growing trend to add additional sanctions to traditional probation sentences; in his case, the sanctions were monetary fines and community service. These programs can be viewed as "probation plus" because they add restrictive penalties and conditions to traditional community service orders, which feature treatment and rehabilitation over control and restraint.[61] Here are some of the advantages of intermediate sanctions:

- They are less costly than jail or prison sentences.
- They help the offender maintain family and community ties.
- They can be structured to maximize security and maintain public safety.
- They can be scaled in severity to correspond to the seriousness of the crime.
- They can feature restoration and reintegration rather than punishment and ostracism.
- By siphoning off offenders from the secure correctional system, they reduce the need for future prison and jail construction.
- Intermediate sanctions help meet the need to develop community sentences that are fair, equitable, and proportional.[62]
- They can be designed to increase control over probationers whose serious or repeat crimes make a straight probation sentence inappropriate, yet for whom a prison sentence would be unduly harsh and counterproductive.[63]
- Intermediate sanctions can potentially be used as halfway-back strategies for offenders who violate the conditions of their community release. Rule violators can be placed under increasingly more intensive supervision before actual incarceration is required.

Intermediate sanctions include programs that are usually administered by probation departments: intensive probation supervision, house arrest, electronic monitoring, restitution orders, shock probation or split sentences, and residential community corrections.[64] Intermediate sanctions also involve sentences that may be administered independently of probation: fines and forfeiture, pretrial programs, and pretrial and post-trial residential programs. Intermediate sanctions therefore range from the barely intrusive, such as restitution orders, to the highly restrictive, such as house arrest accompanied by electronic monitoring and a stay in a community correctional center.

As Figure 10.2 illustrates, intermediate sanctions can form the successive steps of a meaningful "ladder" of scaled punishments outside of prison, thereby restoring fairness

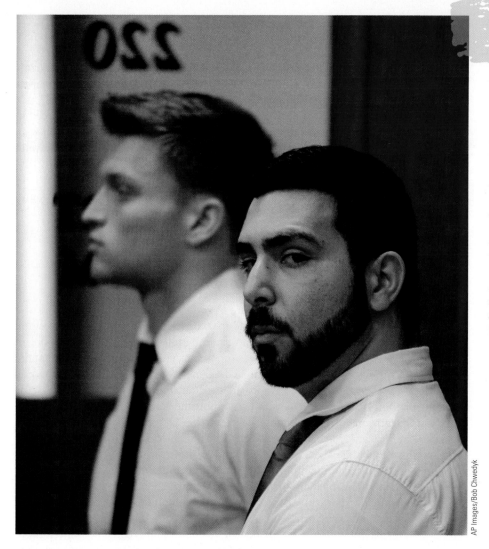

Probation can be used as a sentence even in cases involving serious crimes. Steven A. Libert of Naperville, left, and Mar Salameh of DeKalb are two of 22 former Northern Illinois University fraternity members found guilty of reckless conduct charges and sentenced to community service and fines for the 2012 death of David Bogenberger, a frat pledge. On the night he died, Bogenberger, 19, was taking part in a pledge initiation activity at the Pi Kappa Alpha house on the NIU campus. He and other pledges were required to go room to room in the house, answering questions posed by fraternity members, and downing shots of alcohol. The amount of alcohol he consumed caused his heart to stop during the night.

and equity to nonincarceration sentences.[65] Forgers may be ordered to make restitution to their victims, and rapists can be placed in a community facility and receive counseling at a local clinic. This feature of intermediate sanctions enables judges to fit the punishment to the crime without resorting to a prison sentence.

The forms of intermediate sanctions currently in use are more thoroughly discussed in the following sections.

Fines

Monetary payments, or **fines**, can be imposed on offenders as an intermediate punishment for their criminal acts. They are a direct offshoot of the early medieval practice of requiring that compensation (*wergild*) be paid to the victim and the state for criminal acts. Fines are still commonly used in Europe, where they are often the sole penalty, even in cases involving chronic offenders who commit fairly serious crimes.[66]

In the United States, fines are most commonly used in cases involving misdemeanors and lesser offenses. Fines are also frequently used in felony cases where the offender benefited financially.

Fines may be used as a sole sanction but are typically combined with other punishments, such as probation. Judges commonly levy other monetary sanctions along with fines, such as court costs, public defender fees, probation and treatment fees, and victim restitution, to increase the force of the financial punishment. However, evidence shows that many offenders fail to pay fines and that courts are negligent in their efforts to collect unpaid fees.[67]

fine A money payment levied on offenders to compensate society for their misdeeds.

In most jurisdictions, little guidance is given to the sentencing judge directing the imposition of the fine. Judges often have inadequate information on the offender's ability to pay, and this results in defaults and contempt charges. Because the standard sanction for nonpayment is incarceration, many offenders held in local jails are confined for nonpayment of criminal fines. Even though the US Supreme Court in *Tate v. Short* (1971) recognized that incarcerating a person who is financially unable to pay a fine discriminates against the poor, many judges continue to incarcerate offenders for noncompliance with financial orders.[68] To compensate for this disparity, some jurisdictions have experimented with **day fines** geared to an offender's net daily income. Used in Europe, day fines are designed to be equitable and fairly distributed, by being weighted by a daily-income value taken from a chart similar to an income tax table; the number of the offender's dependents is also taken into account. The day fine concept means that the severity of punishment is geared to the offender's ability to pay.[69]

Forfeiture

Another intermediate sanction with a financial basis is criminal (*in personam*) and civil (in rem) **forfeiture**. Both involve the seizure of goods and instrumentalities related to the commission or outcome of a criminal act. The difference is that criminal forfeiture proceedings target criminal defendants and can only follow a criminal conviction. In contrast, civil forfeiture proceedings target property used in a crime and do not require that formal criminal proceedings be initiated against a person or that the person be proved guilty of a crime.[70] Federal law provides that after arresting drug traffickers, the government may seize the boats they used to import the narcotics, the cars they used to carry the drugs overland, the warehouses in which the drugs were stored, and the homes paid for with the drug profits; on conviction, the drug dealers lose permanent ownership of these "instrumentalities" of crime.

Forfeiture is not a new sanction. During the Middle Ages, "forfeiture of estate" was a mandatory result of most felony convictions. The Crown could seize all of a felon's real and personal property. Forfeiture derived from the common-law concept of "corruption of blood," or "attaint," which prohibited a felon's family from inheriting or receiving his property or estate. The common law mandated that descendants could not inherit property from a relative who might have obtained the property illegally: "[T]he Corruption of Blood stops the Course of Regular Descent, as to Estates, over which the Criminal could have no Power, because he never enjoyed them."[71]

Forfeiture gained momentum in US law with the passage of the Racketeer Influenced and Corrupt Organization (RICO) Act and the Continuing Criminal Enterprises Act, both of which allow the seizure of any property derived from illegal enterprises or conspiracies. Although these acts were designed to apply to ongoing criminal conspiracies, such as drug or pornography rings, they are now being applied to a far-ranging series of criminal acts, including white-collar crimes. More than 100 federal statutes use forfeiture of property as a punishment.

Although law enforcement officials at first applauded the use of forfeiture as a hard-hitting way of seizing the illegal profits of drug law violators, the practice has been criticized because the government has often been overzealous in its application. For example, million-dollar yachts have been seized because someone aboard possessed a small amount of marijuana; this confiscatory practice is referred to as **zero tolerance**. This strict interpretation of the forfeiture statutes has come under fire because it is often used capriciously, the penalty is sometimes disproportionate to the crime involved, and it makes the government a "partner in crime."[72] It is also alleged that forfeiture unfairly targets a narrow range of offenders. For example, it is common for government employees involved in corruption to forfeit their pensions, but employees of public companies are exempt from such punishment.[73] There is also the issue of conflict of interest: because law enforcement agencies can use forfeited assets to supplement their budgets, they may direct their efforts to cases that promise the greatest "payoff" rather than to cases that have the highest law enforcement priority.[74]

day fine A fine geared to the average daily income of the convicted offender in an effort to bring equity to the sentencing process.

forfeiture The seizure of personal property by the state as a civil or criminal penalty.

REALITY CHECK

MYTH OR REALITY?

Convicted criminals can be forced to surrender their homes and cars.

REALITY. Under forfeiture programs, people can be forced to surrender the instrumentalities of their criminal behavior.

Should someone convicted of DWI for the third time forfeit his or her vehicle?

zero tolerance The practice of seizing all instrumentalities of a crime, including homes, boats, and cars. It is an extreme example of the law of forfeiture.

Restitution

Another popular intermediate sanction is restitution, which can take the form of requiring offenders either to pay back the victims of crime (monetary restitution) or to serve the community to compensate for their criminal acts (community service restitution).[75] Restitution programs offer offenders a chance to avoid a jail or prison sentence or a lengthier probation period. The programs may help them develop a sense of allegiance to society, better work habits, and some degree of gratitude for being given a second chance. Restitution serves many other purposes, including giving the community something of value without asking it to foot the bill for an incarceration, and helping victims regain lost property and income.

If a defendant is sentenced to pay monetary restitution as part of her probation order, victim loss is determined, and a plan is developed for paying fair compensation. To avoid the situation in which a wealthy offender can fill a restitution order by merely writing a check, judges will sometimes order that compensation be paid out of income derived from a low-paid social service or public works job.

Community service orders usually require duty in a public nursing home, shelter, hospital, drug treatment unit, or works program; some young vandals may find that they must clean up the damage they caused to the school or the park. Judges and probation officers have embraced the concept of restitution because it appears to benefit the victim, the offender, the criminal justice system, and society.[76] Financial restitution is inexpensive to administer, helps avoid stigma, and provides some compensation for victims of crime. Helping them avoid a jail sentence can mean saving the public thousands of dollars that would have gone to maintaining them in a secure institution, frees up needed resources, and gives the community the feeling that equity has been restored to the justice system.

Does restitution work? Most reviews rate it as a qualified success. One evaluation of community service in Texas found that nearly three-fourths of offenders with community service orders met their obligations and completed community service work.[77] The Texas experience is not atypical; most restitution clients successfully complete their orders and have no subsequent contact with the justice system.[78]

Shock Probation and Split Sentencing

Shock probation and split sentences are alternative sanctions designed to allow judges to grant offenders community release only after they have sampled prison life. These sanctions are based on the premise that if offenders get a taste of incarceration sufficient to shock them into law-abiding behavior, they will be reluctant to violate the rules of probation or commit another crime.

In a number of states and in the Federal Criminal Code, a jail term can actually be a condition of probation, an arrangement known as split sentencing. About 10 percent of probationers are now given split sentences. The shock probation approach involves resentencing an offender to probation after a short prison stay. The shock comes because the offender originally received a long maximum sentence but is then eligible for release to community supervision at the discretion of the judge (usually within 90 days of incarceration).

Shock probation and split sentencing have been praised as ways to limit prison time, reintegrate the client quickly into the community, maintain family ties, and reduce prison populations and the costs of corrections.[79] An initial jail sentence probably makes offenders more receptive to the conditions of probation because it amply illustrates the problems they will face if probation is violated.

But split sentences and shock probation programs have been criticized by those who believe that even a brief period of incarceration can interfere with the purpose of probation, which is to provide the offender with nonstigmatizing, community-based treatment. Even a short-term commitment subjects probationers to the destructive effects of institutionalization, disrupts their life in the community, and stigmatizes them for having been in jail.

restitution A condition of probation in which the offender repays society or the victim of crime for the trouble and expense the offender caused.

monetary restitution A sanction requiring that convicted offenders compensate crime victims by reimbursing them for out-of-pocket losses caused by the crime. Losses can include property damage, lost wages, and medical costs.

community service restitution An alternative sanction that requires an offender to work in the community at such tasks as cleaning public parks or working with disabled children in lieu of an incarceration sentence.

shock probation A sentence in which offenders serve a short prison term before they begin probation to impress them with the pains of imprisonment.

split sentence A practice that requires convicted criminals to spend a portion of their sentence behind bars and the remainder in the community.

AP Images/Max Faulkner

The swift and sure approach to probation mandates the quick application of sanctions for rule violations. Daniel Black stands in front of his home in Burleson, Texas, after he was released from SWIFT probation, an intensive probation court program that deals with high-risk offenders. SWIFT, or Supervision with Intensive enForcemenT, has become the last stop for many offenders in danger of being sent to prison. Unlike traditional probation, in which offenders are often allowed to let violations stack up before having their probation revoked, SWIFT uses immediate sanctions.

Intensive Probation Supervision

intensive probation supervision (IPS) A type of intermediate sanction involving small probation caseloads and strict monitoring on a daily or weekly basis.

Intensive probation supervision (IPS) programs, also referred to as intensive supervision probation, have been implemented in some form in about 40 states. IPS programs involve small caseloads of 15 to 40 clients who are kept under close watch by probation officers. IPS programs typically have three primary goals:

- *Decarceration*. Without intensive supervision, clients would normally be sent to already overcrowded prisons or jails.
- *Control*. High-risk offenders can be maintained in the community under much closer security than traditional probation efforts can provide.
- *Reintegration*. Offenders can maintain community ties and be reoriented toward a more productive life, while avoiding the pains of imprisonment.

In general, IPS programs rely on a great degree of client contact to achieve the goals of decarceration, control, and reintegration. Most programs have admissions criteria based on the nature of the offense and the offender's criminal background. Some programs exclude violent offenders; others will not take substance abusers. In contrast, some jurisdictions do not exclude offenders based on their prior criminal history.

IPS programs are used in several ways. In some states, IPS is a direct sentence imposed by a judge; in others, it is a postsentencing alternative used to divert offenders from the correctional system. A third practice is to use IPS as a case management tool to give the local probation staff flexibility in dealing with clients. Other jurisdictions use IPS in all three ways, in addition to applying it to probation violators to bring them halfway back into the community without resorting to a prison term.

EVALUATIONS OF IPS IPS programs are a mixed bag. IPS clients have a higher rearrest rate than other probationers. IPS clients may be perceived as more serious criminals who might otherwise have been incarcerated. Probation officers may also be more willing to revoke the probation of IPS clients because they believe these clients pose a greater risk to the community. Why risk the program to save a few "bad apples"?

Although these results are discouraging, other efforts do show more positive outcomes.[80] One recent evaluation conducted in probation departments in Iowa, Oklahoma, and Colorado found that reducing probation officer caseloads can reduce criminal recidivism. Reduced caseloads can lead to improved recidivism outcomes because officers are better able to identify treatment needs among their clientele, and thus better able to direct resources to those most in need.[81] Research also has found that IPS clients have better records than similar offenders who suffer incarceration.[82]

IPS seems to work better for some offenders than for others. Those with good employment records seem to do better than the underemployed or unemployed.[83] Younger offenders who commit petty crimes are the most likely to fail on IPS; ironically, people with these characteristics are the ones most likely to be included in IPS programs.[84]

IPS may also be more effective when it is combined with particular treatment modalities such as cognitive-behavioral treatment, which stresses such life skills as problem solving, social skills, negotiation skills, management of emotion, and values enhancement.[85]

House Arrest

When design guru and television personality Martha Stewart was released from prison in 2005 after serving time in an insider trading case, she was required to serve a five-month term of house arrest in which she could not leave home for more than 48 hours at a time and had to wear an electronic tracking device. Her sentence was not unique—except for the fact that her estate is so big that walking to the edges of the property put her out of range of her tracking device.

house arrest A form of intermediate sanction that requires the convicted offender to spend a designated amount of time per week in his or her own home—such as from 5 P.M. Friday until 8 A.M. Monday.

House arrest requires convicted offenders to spend extended periods of time in their own home as an alternative to an incarceration sentence. For example, persons convicted on a drunk-driving charge might be sentenced to spend between 6 P.M. Friday and 8 A.M. Monday and every weekday after 5:30 P.M. in their home for six months. According to current estimates, more than 10,000 people are under house arrest.

As with IPS programs, house arrest initiatives vary a great deal. Some are administered by probation departments, and others are simply judicial sentences monitored by surveillance officers. Some check clients 20 or more times a month, whereas others do only a few curfew checks. Some use 24-hour confinement; others allow offenders to attend work or school.

No definitive data indicate that house arrest is an effective crime deterrent, nor is there sufficient evidence to conclude that it has utility as a device to lower the recidivism rate. Existing data show that IPS recidivism rates are almost identical to a matched sample of inmates.[86] Although these findings are troublesome, the advantages of house arrest in reducing costs and overcrowding in the correctional system probably make further experimentation inevitable.

Electronic Monitoring

For house arrest to work, sentencing authorities must be assured that arrestees are actually at home during their assigned times. Random calls and visits are one way to check on compliance with house arrest orders. However, one of the more interesting developments in the criminal justice system has been the introduction of electronic monitoring (EM) devices to manage offender obedience to home-confinement orders.[87] Some use continuous signaling devices that are battery powered and transmit a radio signal two or more times per minute. They are placed on the offender's wrist or ankle with a tamper-resistant strap and must be worn at all times. A receiver detects the transmitter's signals and conveys a message via telephone report to a central computer when either it stops receiving the radio frequency or the signal resumes. When installed in a typical home environment, receivers can detect transmitter signals from a distance of 150 feet or more.

Electronic monitoring supporters claim EM has the benefits of relatively low cost and high security, while helping offenders avoid the pains of imprisonment in overcrowded, dangerous state facilities. Because offenders are monitored by computers, an initial investment in hardware eliminates the need for hiring many more supervisory officers to handle large numbers of clients. Due to its low cost and assumed effectiveness, EM is now being used with a wide variety of offenders, even those who have committed serious felony sex offenses.[88]

Another innovation is the field monitoring device, or "drive-by" units: probation officers use a portable device that can be handheld or used in a vehicle with a roof-mounted antenna. When within 200 to 800 feet of an offender's ankle or wrist transmitter, the portable device can detect the radio signals of the offender's transmitter.[89] These services are particularly important in domestic violence cases, where victims may not feel safe in their own home and are forced to flee to shelters.[90]

There is evidence that EM can be effective. Studies conducted in California and Florida show very positive results.[91] For example, when Kathy Padget and her associates evaluated data on more than 75,000 offenders placed on home confinement in Florida, they found that EM significantly reduces the likelihood of technical violations, reoffending, and absconding.[92] William Bales and his associates found strong empirical evidence that EM is an effective correctional strategy to divert offenders from prison and can also be used effectively as a form of postprison supervision. They conclude that the recent growth in the use of EM is beneficial and reduces threats to public safety, especially when combined with GPS tracking technology.[93] However, other studies found little evidence that EM can reduce recidivism, and, in some instances, it may have a negative effect.[94]

Global Positioning System (GPS)

Effectively managing offenders within the community requires knowing what inmates are doing at all times and making sure they are not placing themselves in risky situations. GPS technology now enables authorities to monitor the geographic locale and conditions

electronic monitoring (EM)
Requiring convicted offenders to wear a monitoring device as part of their community sentence. Typically part of a house arrest order, this enables the probation department to ensure that offenders are complying with court-ordered limitations on their freedom.

of release. For example, the system can be programmed to indicate a violation whenever a known sex offender approaches a school or a day care center.[95] Some GPS technology employs victim notification systems that alert the victim when the offender is approaching that person's residence. A transmitter is worn by both the offender and the victim, and a receiver is placed at both residences.

The Oklahoma Department of Corrections is now testing a GPS-based monitoring system called GeoShadow that uses GIS (geographic information system) to analyze patterns of movement of both individuals and groups within the community. GeoShadow is designed to let probation officers better assess an offender's location in the community, identify patterns that lead to problem behavior as it unfolds, and improve corrections-based GPS monitoring systems. Knowing an offender's movement patterns also helps assess treatment issues and make decisions about early intervention.[96]

Residential Community Corrections

residential community corrections (RCC) A nonsecure facility, located in the community, that houses probationers who need a more secure environment. Typically, residents are free during the day to go to work, school, or treatment, and they return in the evening for counseling sessions and meals.

The most secure intermediate sanction is a sentence to a **residential community corrections (RCC)** facility. Such a facility has been defined as "a freestanding nonsecure building that is not part of a prison or jail and houses pretrial and adjudicated adults. The residents regularly depart to work, to attend school, and/or [to] participate in treatment activities and programs."[97]

Traditionally, the role of community corrections was played by the nonsecure halfway house, which was designed to reintegrate soon-to-be-paroled prison inmates into the community. Inmates spend the last few months of their sentence in the halfway house, acquiring suitable employment, building up cash reserves, obtaining an apartment, and developing a job-related wardrobe.

The traditional concept of community corrections has expanded. Today, the community correctional facility is a vehicle to provide intermediate sanctions as well as a prerelease center for those about to be paroled from the prison system. RCC has been used as a direct sentencing option for judges who believe particular offenders need a correctional alternative halfway between traditional probation and a stay in prison. Placement in an RCC center can be used as a condition of probation for offenders who need a nonsecure community facility that provides a more structured treatment environment than traditional probation. It is commonly used in the juvenile justice system for youths who need a more secure environment than can be provided by traditional probation yet are not deemed a threat to the community and do not require a secure placement.

More than 2,000 state-run community-based facilities are in use today. In addition, up to 2,500 private, nonprofit RCC programs operate in the United States. About half also house inmates who have been released from prison and use the RCC placement as a way to ease back into society. The remainder are true intermediate sanctions, including about 400 federally sponsored programs.

day reporting center (DRC) A nonresidential community-based treatment program.

DAY REPORTING CENTERS One recent development in community corrections has been the use of RCC facilities as **day reporting centers (DRCs)**.[98] These provide a single location to which a variety of clients can report for supervision and treatment. They can be used as a step up in security for probationers who have failed in the community and as a step down in security for jail or prison inmates.[99]

Evaluations show that DRCs can be successful at reducing recidivism.[100] DRCs seem to work better with certain types of offenders, such as those who are older and more experienced, than with others, such as younger offenders.[101] DRC participants with alcohol problems, criminal companions, and poor living situations are also more likely to fail. In contrast, those who receive counseling seem to do better.[102]

Concept Summary 10.1 sets out the goals and problems of the various forms of intermediate sanctions.

LO9 Explain what is meant by intermediate sanctions

Sanction	Goal	Problems
Fines	Monetary sanction	Overburdens the poor
Forfeiture	Monetary sanction, equity	Can be overreaching
Restitution	Pay back victim	Does not reduce recidivism
Shock incarceration and split sentence	"Taste of bars" as a deterrent	Can cause labeling and stigma
Intensive probation	Small caseloads, more supervision	High failure rate
House arrest	Avoids jail	Lacks treatment possibility
Electronic monitoring	Supervision by computer	Technology-dependent, no treatment
Residential community	Less secure than prison	Expensive, high failure rate

© Cengage Learning

Restorative Justice Programs

Some critics and specialists in criminal justice believe that the new alternative and intermediate sanctions add a punitive aspect to community sentencing that can hinder rehabilitation efforts. Instead, the advocates of restorative justice suggest a policy based on restoring the damage caused by crime and creating a system of justice that includes all the parties harmed by the criminal act: the victim, the offender, the community, and society.[103]

Restorative justice models are consistent with the thought of Australian justice expert John Braithwaite, who argues that crime control today involves shaming and stigmatizing offenders. This helps set them apart from normative society and undermines their potential for change. Instead, he calls for a policy of "reintegrative shaming." Here disapproval is limited to the offender's evil deeds. Law violators must be brought to realize that although their actions have caused harm, they are still valuable people—people who can be reaccepted by society. A critical element of reintegrative shaming occurs when the offenders themselves begin to understand and recognize their wrongdoing and shame. To be reintegrative, shaming must be brief and controlled, and it must be followed by ceremonies of forgiveness, apology, and repentance.[104] Braithwaite's work is at the core of the restorative justice movement.

restorative justice A view of criminal justice that advocates peaceful solutions and mediation rather than coercive punishments.

The Concept of Restoration

According to the restorative view, crimes bring harm to the community in which they occur. The traditional justice system has done little to involve the community in the justice process. What has developed is a system of coercive punishments administered by bureaucrats that is inherently harmful to offenders and reduces the likelihood that they will ever again become productive members of society. This system relies on punishment, stigma, and disgrace. What is needed instead is a justice policy that repairs the harm caused by crime and involves all parties that have suffered from that harm, including the victim, the community, and the offender. Exhibit 10.1 sets out the principles of the restorative justice approach.

An important aspect of achieving these goals is that offenders must accept accountability for their actions and responsibility for the harm their actions caused. Only then can

---

EXHIBIT 10.1

Basic Principles of Restorative Justice

- Crime is an offense against human relationships.
- Victims and the community are central to justice processes.
- The first priority of justice processes is to assist victims.
- The second priority is to restore the community, to the greatest degree possible.
- The offender has a personal responsibility to victims and to the community for crimes committed.
- The offender will develop improved competency and understanding as a result of the restorative justice experience.
- Stakeholders share responsibilities for restorative justice through partnerships for action.

Source: Anne Seymour, "Restorative Justice/Community Justice," in the *National Victim Assistance Academy Textbook* (Washington, DC: National Victim Assistance Academy, 2001), updated June 2015.

Restorative justice programs can be aimed at the front end of the system as an alternative to incarceration, but can also be aimed at people already in the system. Here Manuel Zarate hugs his daughter Brittany and grandson Andrew Almodovar at the end of a "Get On the Bus" visiting day to Folsom State Prison arranged by the California Department of Corrections and Rehabilitation (CDCR) and the Center for Restorative Justice Works (CRJW) in Folsom, California. Buses with children and their caregivers traveled free of charge to two prisons, as part of an outreach program to reunite children with their incarcerated fathers.

Elijah Nouvelage/Reuters /Landov

they be restored as productive members of their community. Restoration involves turning the justice system into a "healing" process rather than a distributor of retribution and revenge.

Most people involved in offender-victim relationships actually know one another or were related in some way before the criminal incident took place. Instead of treating one of the involved parties as a victim deserving sympathy and the other as a criminal deserving punishment, it is more productive to address the issues that produced the conflict between these people. Rather than taking sides and choosing whom to isolate and punish, society should try to reconcile the parties involved in conflict.[105] The effectiveness of justice ultimately depends on the stake a person has in the community (or a particular social group). If a person does not value her membership in the group, she will be unlikely to accept responsibility, show remorse, or repair the injuries caused by her actions.

Restoration Programs

Restoration programs try to include all the parties involved in a criminal act: the victim, the offender, and the community. Although processes differ in structure and style, they generally include the following:

- Recognition by offenders that they have caused injury to personal and social relations, and a determination and acceptance of responsibility (ideally accompanied by a statement of remorse)
- A commitment to both material reparation (e.g., monetary restitution) and symbolic reparation (e.g., an apology)
- A determination of community support and assistance for both victim and offender

The intended result of the process is to repair injuries suffered by the victim and the community, while ensuring reintegration of the offender.

Negotiation, mediation, consensus building, and peacemaking have been part of the dispute resolution process in European and Asian communities for centuries.[106] Native American people and members of Canada's First Nations have long used the type of community participation in the adjudication process (in sentencing circles, sentencing panels, and panels of elders) that restorative justice advocates are now embracing.[107]

In some Native American communities, people accused of breaking the law meet with community members, victims (if any), village elders, and agents of the justice system in a **sentencing circle**. All members of the circle express their feelings about the

WEB APP 10.2 There are many sources detailing restorative justice. A few sites that can help you learn more about this approach include the following:
Restorative Justice Online, **http://www.restorativejustice.org/**
Eastern Mennonite University, Center for Justice and Peacebuilding, **http://www.emu.edu/cjp/restorative-justice/**

sentencing circle A type of sentencing in which victims, family members, community members, and the offender participate in an effort to devise fair and reasonable sanctions that are ultimately aimed at reintegrating the offender into the community.

act that was committed and raise questions or concerns. The accused can express regret about his or her actions and a desire to change the harmful behavior. People may suggest ways in which the offender can make things up to the community and those who were harmed. A treatment program, such as Alcoholics Anonymous, may be suggested, if appropriate.

Restoration in Practice

Restorative justice policies and practices are now being adapted around the world. Restorative justice is being embraced on many levels in the justice system.

SCHOOLS Some schools have employed restorative justice practices to avoid more punitive measures such as expulsion in dealing with students involved in drug and alcohol abuse. Schools in Minnesota, Colorado, and elsewhere are trying to involve students in "relational rehabilitation" programs, which strive to improve offenders' relationships with key figures in the community who may have been harmed by their actions.[108]

POLICE PROGRAMS Restorative justice has also been implemented when police first encounter crime. The new community policing models can be viewed as an attempt to incorporate restorative concepts into law enforcement. Restorative justice relies on criminal justice policy makers listening to and responding to the needs of those who will be affected by their actions, and community policing relies on policies established with input and exchanges between officers and citizens.[109] The technique is also being used by police around the world. In England, police are using a format called restorative cautioning. After an arrest was made, police in England and Wales traditionally had four alternative procedures they could follow: (1) take no further action, (2) give an informal warning, (3) administer a formal police caution, or (4) decide to prosecute by sending the case to the Crown Prosecution Service. In the new restorative cautioning approach, a trained police facilitator uses a script to encourage an offender to take responsibility for repairing the harm caused by the offense. Sometimes the victim is present, in which case the meeting is called a restorative conference; usually, however, the victim is not present. Traditional cautioning, by contrast, lasts only a few minutes, requires no special training, and focuses on the officer explaining the possible consequences of future offending.[110]

PRETRIAL PROGRAMS Some jurisdictions have instituted restorative justice programs as a form of diversion from the court process. A popular restorative justice method is the family group conference, made up of the person who has committed the offense (usually a young first-time offender), members of his or her family and whomever the family invites, the victim(s) or their representative, a support person for the victim(s), a representative of the police, the mediator or manager of the process, and sometimes a social worker and/or a lawyer. The main goal of a conference is to formulate a plan about how best to deal with the offending. There are three principal components to this process:

- Ascertain whether or not the young person admits the offense; conferences only proceed if the young person does so or if the offense has been proved in the Youth Court.
- Share information among all the parties at the conference about the nature of the offense, the effects of the offense on the victims, the reasons for the offending, any prior offending by the young person, and so on.
- Decide the outcome or recommendation.

The family group conference is a meeting between those entitled to attend in a relatively informal setting. The room is usually arranged with comfortable chairs in a circle. When all are present, the meeting may open with a prayer or a blessing, depending on the customs of those involved. The coordinator then welcomes the participants, introduces each of them, and describes the purposes of the meeting. What happens next can vary, but usually the police representative then reads out the summary of the offense. The young person is asked if he or she agrees that this is what happened, and any variation is noted. If he or she does not agree, the meeting progresses no further, and the police may consider referring the case to the Youth Court for a hearing. Assuming the young person agrees, the victim or a spokesperson for the victim is then usually asked to describe what the events meant for them. Next, a general discussion of the offense and the circumstances underlying it occurs. There can be a lot of emotion expressed at this point. It is at this point, too, that the young person and his or her family may express their remorse for what has happened and make an apology to the victim, although more often this occurs later on. After everybody has discussed what the offending has meant and options for making good the damage, the professionals and the victim leave the family and the young person to meet privately to discuss what plans and recommendation they want to make to repair the damage and to prevent reoffending. The private family time can take as little as half an hour or much longer. When the family is ready, the others return, and the meeting is reconvened. This is the point at which the young person and the family usually apologize to the victim. A spokesperson for the family outlines what they propose, and all discuss the proposal. When there is agreement among all present, the details are formally recorded, and the conference concludes with the sharing of food.[111]

COURT PROGRAMS In the court system, restorative programs usually involve diverting the offender from the formal court process. Instead, these programs encourage meeting and reconciling the conflicts between offenders and victims via victim advocacy, mediation programs, and sentencing circles, in which crime victims and their families are brought together with offenders and their families in an effort to formulate a sanction that addresses the needs of each party. Victims are given a chance to tell their stories, and offenders can help compensate them financially or provide some service (such as repairing damaged property).[112] Again, the goal is to enable offenders to appreciate the damage they have caused, to make amends, and to be reintegrated into society. Restorative justice has found a niche all over the world. It is even being used to resolve cases in the Middle East involving Arabs and Israelis![113]

The Challenge of Restorative Justice

Although restorative justice holds great promise, there are also some concerns.[114] One issue is whether programs reach out to all members of the community. Research indicates that entry into these programs may be tilted toward white offenders and more restrictive to minorities, a condition that negates the purpose of the restorative movement.[115]

Restorative justice programs must be especially aware of cultural and social differences, which can be found throughout America's heterogeneous society.[116] What may be considered restorative in one subculture may be considered insulting and damaging in another.[117] Similarly, so many diverse programs call themselves restorative that evaluating them is difficult. Each one may be pursuing a unique objective. In other words, no single definition of restorative justice has been arrived at.[118]

Possibly the greatest challenge to restorative justice is the difficult task of balancing the needs of offenders with those of their victims. If programs focus solely on responding to the victim's needs, they may risk ignoring the offender's needs and increasing the likelihood of reoffending. Advocates of restorative justice may falsely assume that relatively brief interludes of public shaming will change deeply rooted criminal predispositions.[119] But is it reasonable to include any form of punishment or sanction in a restorative-based program?[120]

In contrast, programs focusing on the offender may turn off victims and their advocates. Many victims do want an apology, if it is heartfelt and easy to get. But some want, even more urgently, to put the traumatic incident behind them, to retrieve stolen property being held for use at trial, and to be assured that the offender will receive treatment he is thought to need if he is not to victimize someone else. For victims such as these, restorative justice processes can seem unnecessary at best.[121]

LO10 Define restorative justice, and discuss its merits

Frank Fellman, the first-round draft choice of the local NFL team, has been convicted for reckless endangerment. He was driving at 2 a.m. when he struck a young woman who was crossing an intersection; she suffered a broken leg. At trial, the evidence showed that the woman was legally drunk and had entered the intersection against the light. Fellman, who has had a long history of battles with the law, was already under a probation order forbidding any misbehavior and imposing an 11 p.m. curfew. At a hearing, the presiding judge reminded him that he had been warned against any further violations and it had been made clear that violating the conditions of probation would not be tolerated. During the presentencing investigation, the probation department concluded that Fellman was not a danger, and his scores on the risk assessment scale used by the department found that minimum supervision probation would work in his case. Based on this evidence, the judge chose not to revoke his probation if he made restitution to the victim, surrendered his license, and wore an ankle bracelet tracking device. Because his probation was continued, Fellman would be able to attend training camp and not miss the season.

The news media got hold of the story and claimed that Fellman was being given an unfair advantage because he was an athlete. As a result of the public outcry, the judge reversed his decision and ordered Fellman to serve six months in jail. Fellman's lawyers have filed an emergency appeal, asking you, the appellate court judge, to grant him relief and suggesting (1) that the original sentence was overly harsh, and (2) the withdrawal of the house arrest order solely because of media attention was a violation of his due process rights.

Ethical Challenge: Write an essay on how you would deal with the case. In your paper, address whether you think Fellman should be jailed for his behavior even though his scores on a risk classification scale say otherwise. Should we trust these scales, or do they conflict with the ethical treatment of people convicted of crime? You may also want to address these issues: Is he being punished because of his status? How would the public be served by putting Fellman in jail and jeopardizing his career?

SUMMARY

LO1 *Explain the concept of community sentencing* Community sentencing relies on the belief that the typical offender can be successfully treated while remaining in the community and, given the proper care and services, is unlikely to recidivate. A great variety of community sentences are in use now, ranging from traditional probation to house arrest and placement in community correctional centers.

LO2 *Describe the history of community sentences* The roots of community sentencing can be traced to the English common law practice of judicial reprieve, which allowed judges to suspend punishment so that convicted offenders could seek a pardon, gather new evidence, or demonstrate that they had reformed their behavior. John Augustus of Boston is usually credited with pioneering community sentencing in the United States when he voluntarily supervised young people convicted of crime, a practice that led to the modern probation concept.

LO3 *Recognize the different types of probation sentences* Probationary sentences may be granted by state and federal district courts and state superior (felony) courts. Some are to a straight term of probation, while others involve a suspended sentence, a delayed sentence, or a mixed sentence involving a jail or prison stay.

LO4 *Recall the rules of probation* When granting probation, the court sets down certain conditions or rules of behavior that the probationer is bound to obey. Rules can set curfews, prohibit behaviors such as drinking and owning a gun, and/or mandate that the probationer hold a job and not leave the jurisdiction without permission. Probation may be revoked if clients fail to comply with rules and disobey reasonable requests to meet their treatment obligations.

LO5 *Explain the organization and administration of probation services* Some states have a statewide probation service, but each court jurisdiction controls its local department. Other states maintain a strong statewide authority with centralized control and administration.

LO6 *List and discuss the elements of a probation department's duties* Staff officers in probation departments are usually charged with five primary tasks: investigation, intake, diagnosis/risk classification, supervision, and treatment. As part of clients' entry into probation, an assessment is made about how much risk they pose to the community and themselves. On the basis of this assessment, offenders are assigned to a specific supervision level.

LO7 *Recall with the legal rights of probationers* The US Supreme Court has ruled that probationers have a unique status and therefore are entitled to fewer constitutional protections than other citizens. During the course of a probationary term, violating the rules or terms of probation or committing a new crime can result in probation being revoked.

LO8 *Debate the effectiveness of probation* Probation is cost-effective. Although the failure rate seems disturbingly high, even the most serious criminals who receive probation are less likely to recidivate than those who are sent to prison for committing similar crimes. Young males who are unemployed or who have a very low income, a prior criminal record, and a history of instability are most likely to be rearrested.

LO9 *Explain what is meant by intermediate sanctions* Intermediate sanctions add some other community sanction to a probation sentence, such as a fine, electronic monitoring, or house arrest. They offer effective alternatives to prisons and jails. They also have the potential to save money; although they are more expensive than traditional probation, they are far less costly than incarceration.

LO10 *Define restorative justice, and discuss its merits* Restorative programs stress healing and redemption rather than punishment and deterrence. Restoration means that offenders accept accountability for their actions and responsibility for the harm their actions caused. Restoration programs are now being used around the nation and involve mediation, sentencing circles, and similar nonpunitive treatment efforts.

KEY TERMS

probation, p. 238

judicial reprieve, p. 238

recognizance, p. 238

sureties, p. 238

probation rules, p. 239

revocation, p. 239

suspended sentence, p. 240

presentence investigation, p. 241

intake, p. 243

risk classification, p. 243

motivational interviewing, p. 244

day fees, p. 248

intermediate sanctions, p. 249

fine, p. 251

day fine, p. 252

forfeiture, p. 252

zero tolerance, p. 252

restitution, p. 253

monetary restitution, p. 253

community service restitution, p. 253

shock probation, p. 253

split sentence, p. 253

intensive probation supervision (IPS), p. 254

house arrest, p. 254

electronic monitoring (EM), p. 255

residential community corrections (RCC), p. 256

day reporting center (DRC), p. 256

restorative justice, p. 257

sentencing circle, p. 258

REVIEW QUESTIONS

1. What is the purpose of probation? Identify some conditions of probation, and discuss the responsibilities of the probation officer.

2. Discuss the procedures involved in probation revocation. What are the rights of the probationer? Is probation a privilege or a right?

3. Should a convicted criminal make restitution to the victim? When is restitution inappropriate? Could it be considered a bribe?

4. Should offenders be fined on the basis of the seriousness of what they did or in terms of their ability to pay? Is it fair to base day fines on wages? Should offenders be punished more severely because they are financially successful?

5. Does house arrest involve a violation of personal freedom? Does wearing an ankle bracelet smack of "Big Brother"? Would you want the government monitoring your daily activities?

6. Do you agree that criminals can be restored through community interaction? Considering the fact that recidivism rates are so high, are traditional sanctions a waste of time, and are restorative methods the wave of the future?

11 Corrections:
HISTORY, INSTITUTIONS, AND POPULATIONS

In 2011, a correctional officer in New York's Attica prison was distributing mail to inmates in C Block when he became fazed by all the noise and disorder and he ordered the inmates to quiet down. The inmates ignored the order, and one had the temerity to shout back "You shut up!" while taunting the officer with an obscene suggestion. After calm was restored and the inmates locked down, three officers went to the cell of George Williams whom they suspected as being disrespectful. Williams, a 29-year-old African American, was serving a sentence of two to four years for robbing two jewelry stores in Manhattan and had just been transferred to Attica. He had only four months to go on his sentence and was trying to stay out of trouble; he was not even aware of what had gone on earlier. The guards ordered him to strip for a search and then marched him down the hall to an empty room where he assumed he would be asked to give a urine test. Instead, after they entered the room, the three of the guards began pummeling Williams so severely that he suffered broken bones in his legs and face. Witnesses said he had been kicked up to 50 times, and struck with a dozen more blows from nightsticks. Mr. Williams begged for his life, and cried loud enough that prisoners two floors below could hear his screams. Other guards were called in to join the beating.

Williams was brought to the prison infirmary, but because his injuries were so serious, he was taken to two local Buffalo hospitals. All told, Williams suffered a broken shoulder, several cracked ribs and two broken legs, a severe fracture of the orbit surrounding his left eye, a large amount of blood lodged in his left maxillary sinus, and multiple cuts and bruises.

When medical personnel alerted state authorities, an investigation was conducted that led to charges of gang assault and evidence tampering against three corrections officers—Keith Swack, Sean Warner, and Matthew Rademacherbeing. Hoping to avoid a jail sentence, on March 5, 2015, the three pleaded guilty to misdemeanor charges of official misconduct.[1]

The Williams case aptly illustrates the brutality of prison life and the violence that is a routine occurrence in large maximum-security prisons. George Williams was just one of the more than 1.5 million inmates in a vast correctional system that has branches in the federal, state, and county levels of government.[2] Felons may be placed in state or federal penitentiaries

LEARNING OBJECTIVES

LO1 *Discuss the meaning of the term* new penology

LO2 *Explain how the first penal institutions developed in Europe*

LO3 *Explain how William Penn revolutionized corrections*

LO4 *Compare the New York and Pennsylvania prison models*

LO5 *Chart the development of penal reform*

LO6 *Discuss how parole developed*

LO7 *Explain the purposes of jails and the makeup of jail populations*

LO8 *Define the term new-generation jail*

LO9 *Classify the different types of federal and state penal institutions*

LO10 *Discuss prison population trends*

265

(prisons), which are usually isolated, high-security structures. Misdemeanants are housed in local county jails, reformatories, or houses of correction. Juvenile offenders have their own institutions called schools, camps, ranches, or homes; these are typically nonsecure facilities that provide both confinement and rehabilitative services for young offenders and will be discussed further in Chapter 13.

The contemporary correctional system, then, encompasses a wide range of institutions ranging from nonsecure camps that house white-collar criminals to super-maximum-security institutions, such as the federal prison in Florence, Colorado, where the nation's most dangerous felons are confined.

One of the great tragedies of our time is that "correctional" institutions—whatever form they may take—do not seem to "correct," and many former inmates recidivate soon after reentering society. It can be reasonably estimated that more than half of all inmates will be back in prison within six years of their release; this means that each year, many thousands of former inmates return to prison because they failed on parole. Despite this failure, we are still locking up more than 2 million people in state and federal prisons and local jails in what has become called a prison boom.

A debate has been ongoing regarding the true role of secure corrections. Some penal experts maintain that prisons and jails should be used to keep dangerous offenders apart from society, dispensing "just deserts" for their crimes.[3] Under this model, correctional effectiveness is measured in terms of such outcomes as physical security, length of incapacitation, and inmates who return to society fearing criminal sanctions. An opposing view is that the purpose of corrections is treatment and that, when properly funded and effectively directed, correctional facilities can provide successful offender rehabilitation.[4] Numerous examples of successful treatment programs flourish in prisons. Educational programs enable inmates to get college credits, vocational training has become more sophisticated, counseling and substance abuse programs are almost universal, and every state maintains early-release and community correctional programs of some sort.

Today, the desert/incapacitation model, sometimes called the *new penology*, holds sway. Rather than administer individualized treatment, decision makers rely on actuarial tables and tests to make decisions; indeed, they seem more concerned with security and "managing" large inmate populations than with treating individual offenders.[5] Critics charge that this policy has resulted in a rapidly increasing prison population that is bereft of the human touch; defenders counter that it is effective because the crime rate declined at the same time that the number of people under lock and key began to significantly increase. Although the prison population has begun to decline, as a result of this 20-year prison boom, the United States today has the highest percentage of the population behind prison bars of any country in the Western world (478 per 100,000); in comparison, Germany has about 79 prisoners per 100,000 population, France 98, Japan 51, and India 30.[6]

Is there any point to this creation of mass incarceration in the United States? Although some experts believe it is responsible for the crime rate drop in America, others are still unsure. Police effectiveness and improving social conditions may be more important factors in lowering crime rates than the current prison boom.[7] Some such as Ernest Drucker go as far as to treat it as a plague on society, whose root can be traced back to the war on drugs and the unconscious desire to control the behavior of young minority males, who make up a disproportionate number of the drug offenders put behind bars.[8] In a widely read book, *The New Jim Crow*, Michelle Alexander also links the rise in the prison population to efforts by the government to marginalize young people of color at every stage of the justice system and then make it almost impossible for them to reform after their release.[9] She believes strong parallels can be drawn between what is being done today and the Jim Crow laws that created a racial caste systems of the past: racial stigma, shame, disenfranchisement, and legalized discrimination.

Even though the new penology dominates, correctional rehabilitation is still an important element of the justice system, and there are numerous opportunities for careers in such positions as corrections counselor, described in the Careers in Criminal Justice feature.

prison A state or federal correctional institution for incarceration of felony offenders for terms of one year or more.

jail A place to detain people awaiting trial, to serve as a lockup for drunks and disorderly individuals, and to confine convicted misdemeanants serving sentences of less than one year.

In this chapter, we explore the correctional system, beginning with the history and nature of correctional institutions. Then, in Chapter 12, we will examine institutional life in some detail.

LO1 Discuss the meaning of the term *new penology*

The History of Correctional Institutions

The original legal punishments were typically banishment or slavery, restitution, corporal punishment, and execution. The concept of incarcerating convicted offenders for long periods of time as a punishment for their misdeeds did not become the norm of corrections until the nineteenth century.[10]

Although the use of incarceration as a routine punishment began much later, some early European institutions were created specifically to detain and punish criminal offenders. Penal institutions were constructed in England during the tenth century to hold pretrial detainees and those waiting for their sentence to be carried out.[11] During the twelfth century, King Henry II constructed a series of county jails to hold thieves and vagrants before the disposition of their sentence. In 1557, the workhouse in Brideswell was built to hold people convicted of relatively minor offenses who would work to pay off their debt to society. Those who had committed more serious offenses were held there pending execution.

Le Stinche, a prison in Florence, Italy, was used to punish offenders as early as 1301.[12] Prisoners were enclosed in separate cells, classified on the basis of gender, age, mental state, and seriousness of their crime. Furloughs and conditional release were permitted, and—perhaps for the first time—a period of incarceration replaced corporal punishment for some offenses. Although Le Stinche existed for 500 years, relatively little is known about its administration or whether this early example of incarceration was unique to Florence.

Jail conditions were deplorable because jailers ran them for personal gain. The fewer services provided, the greater their profit. Early jails were catchall institutions that held not only criminal offenders awaiting trial but also vagabonds, debtors, the mentally ill, and assorted others.

From 1776 to 1785, a growing inmate population that could no longer be transported to North America forced the English to house prisoners on hulks—abandoned ships anchored in harbors.

hulks Abandoned ships anchored in harbors and used in eighteenth-century England to house prisoners.

The hulks became infamous for their degrading conditions and brutal punishments but were not abandoned until 1858. The writings of John Howard, the reform-oriented sheriff of Bedfordshire, drew attention to the squalid conditions in British penal institutions. His famous book, *The State of the Prisons* (1777), condemned the lack of basic care given to English inmates awaiting trial or serving sentences.[13] Howard's efforts to create humane standards in the British penal system resulted in the Penitentiary Act, by which Parliament established a more orderly penal system, with periodic inspections, elimination of the fee system, and greater consideration for inmates.

LO2 Explain how the first penal institutions developed in Europe

The Origin of Corrections in the United States

Although Europe had jails and a variety of other penal facilities, correctional reform was first instituted in the United States. The first American jail was built in James City in the Virginia colony in the early seventeenth century. However, the modern American correctional system had its origin in Pennsylvania under the leadership of William Penn.

At the end of the seventeenth century, Penn revised Pennsylvania's criminal code to forbid torture and the capricious use of mutilation and physical punishment. These penalties were replaced with imprisonment at hard labor, moderate flogging, fines, and forfeiture of property. All lands and goods belonging to felons were to be used to make restitution to the victims of their crimes, with restitution being limited to twice the value of the damages. Felons who owned no property were assigned by law to the prison workhouse until the victim was compensated.

Penn ordered that a new type of institution be built to replace the widely used public forms of punishment—stocks, pillories, gallows, and branding irons. Each county was instructed to build a house of corrections similar to today's jails. County trustees or commissioners were responsible for raising money to build the jails and providing for their maintenance, although they were operated by the local sheriff. Penn's reforms remained in effect until his death in 1718, at which time the criminal penal code was changed back to open public punishment and harsh brutality.

One of the first American penal institutions was Newgate Prison, which opened in 1773 in Connecticut on the site of an abandoned copper mine and was in use until the 1820s.[14] In 1785, Castle Island prison was opened in Massachusetts and operated for about 15 years. The origin of the modern correctional system is usually traced to eighteenth-century developments.

The Development of Prisons

Why did prisons develop at this time? One reason was that during this period of enlightenment, a concerted effort was made to alleviate the harsh punishments and torture that had been the norm. The interest of religious groups, such as the Quakers, in prison reform was prompted in part by humanitarian ideals. Another factor was the economic potential of prison industry, which was viewed as a valuable economic asset in times of short labor supply.[15]

In 1776, these trends led Pennsylvania once again to adopt William Penn's code, and, in 1787, a group of Quakers led by Benjamin Rush formed the Philadelphia Society for Alleviating the Miseries of Public Prisons. The aim of the society was to bring some degree of humane and orderly treatment to the growing penal system. The Quakers' influence on the legislature resulted in limiting the use of the death penalty to cases involving treason, murder, rape, or arson. Their next step was to reform the institutional system so that the prison could serve as a suitable alternative to physical punishment.

The only models of custodial institutions at that time were the local county jails that Penn had established. These facilities were designed to detain offenders, to securely incarcerate convicts awaiting other punishment, or to hold offenders who were working off their crimes. The Pennsylvania jails placed men, women, and children of all ages indiscriminately in one room. Liquor was often freely sold.

Under pressure from the Quakers to improve these conditions, the Pennsylvania legislature in 1790 called for the renovation of the prison system. The eventual result was the creation of a separate wing of Philadelphia's Walnut Street Jail to house convicted felons (except those sentenced to death). Prisoners were placed in solitary cells, where they remained in isolation and did not have the right to work.[16] Quarters that contained the solitary or separate cells were called the penitentiary house, as was already the custom in England.

Pictured is 'Death Row' at the Eastern State Penitentiary in Philadelphia, Pennsylvania. The prison was operational from 1829 until 1971 and used a "revolutionary" system of separate incarceration cells. When it was built, it was the largest and most expensive public structure in the world.

Walnut Street Jail An eighteenth-century institution that housed convicted criminals in Philadelphia.

penitentiary house Term used for early prisons, so named because inmates were supposed to do penitence for their sins.

LO3 Explain how William Penn revolutionized corrections

The New York and Pennsylvania Systems

As the nineteenth century got under way, both the Pennsylvania and the New York prison systems were experiencing difficulties maintaining the ever-increasing numbers of convicted criminals. Initially, administrators dealt with the problem by increasing the use of pardons, relaxing prison discipline, and limiting supervision.

In 1816, New York built a new prison at Auburn, hoping to alleviate some of the overcrowding at Newgate. The Auburn Prison design became known as the congregate system because most prisoners ate and worked in groups. In 1819, construction began on a wing of solitary cells to house unruly prisoners. Three classes of prisoners were then created. One group remained continually in solitary confinement as a result of breaches of prison discipline, the second group was allowed labor as an occasional form of recreation, and the third and largest class worked together during the day and was separated only at night.

The philosophy of the Auburn prison system was crime prevention through fear of punishment and silent confinement. The worst felons were to be cut off from all contact with other prisoners, and although they were treated and fed relatively well, they had no hope of pardon to relieve their solitude or isolation. For a time, some of the worst convicts were forced to remain alone and silent during the entire day. This practice, which led to mental breakdowns, suicides, and self-mutilations, was abolished in 1823. The solution adopted at Auburn was to keep convicts in separate cells at night but allow them to work together during the day under enforced silence.

Regimentation became the standard mode of prison life. Convicts did not simply walk from place to place; instead, they went in close order and single file, each looking over the shoulder of the preceding person, faces inclined to the right, feet moving in unison. The lockstep prison shuffle was developed at Auburn and is still used in some institutions today.[17] The inmates' time was regulated by bells telling them when to wake up, sleep, and work. The system was so like the military that many of its early administrators were recruited from the armed services.

congregate system Prison system first used in New York that allowed inmates to engage in group activities such as work, meals, and recreation.

REALITY**CHECK**

MYTH OR REALITY?

The first correctional institutions were actually considered a "liberal" reform.

REALITY. Although they might be considered a harsh form of punishment today, prisons were originally considered a humanitarian reform sponsored by religious groups.

Considering that recidivism rates are so high, should we embrace the treatment and rehabilitation elements of incarceration rather than focusing on prison as a means of dispensing punishment?

In 1818, Pennsylvania took the radical step of establishing a prison that placed each inmate in a single cell for the duration of his sentence. Classifications were abolished because each cell was intended as a miniature prison that would prevent the inmates from contaminating one another. The new Pennsylvania state prison, called the Western Penitentiary, had an unusual architectural design. It was built in a semicircle, with the cells positioned along its circumference. Built back to back, some cells faced the boundary wall, and others faced the internal area of the circle. Its inmates were kept in solitary confinement almost constantly, being allowed out for about an hour a day for exercise. In 1829, a second, similar penitentiary using the isolate system was built in Philadelphia and was called the Eastern Penitentiary.

Pennsylvania system The correctional model used in Pennsylvania that isolated inmates from one another to prevent them from planning escapes, to make them easy to manage, and to give them time to experience penitence.

Supporters of the Pennsylvania system believed that the penitentiary was truly a place to do penance. By removing the sinner from society and allowing the prisoner a period of isolation in which to consider the evils of crime, the Pennsylvania system reflected the influence of religion and religious philosophy on corrections. Its supporters believed that solitary confinement with in-cell labor would make work so attractive that upon release, the inmate would be well suited to resume a productive existence in society.

The Pennsylvania system eliminated the need for large numbers of guards or disciplinary measures. Isolated from one another, inmates could not plan escapes or collectively break rules. When discipline was a problem, however, the whip and the iron gag were used.

Advocates of the Auburn system believed that theirs was the cheapest and most productive way to reform prisoners and that solitary confinement as practiced in Pennsylvania was cruel and inhumane. In contrast, advocates of Pennsylvania's isolation model argued that their system was quiet, efficient, humane, and well ordered, yielding the ultimate correctional facility.[18] They considered the Auburn system a breeding place for criminal associations because it allowed inmates to get to know one another.

LO4 Compare the New York and Pennsylvania prison models

New York's congregate model eventually prevailed and spread throughout the United States. Many of its features are still used today. Its innovations included congregate working conditions, the use of solitary confinement to punish unruly inmates, military regimentation, and discipline. Concept Summary 11.1 describes the differences between these two prison systems.

Corrections in the Nineteenth Century

The prison of the nineteenth century was remarkably similar to that of today. The congregate system was adopted in all states except Pennsylvania. Prisons were overcrowded, and the single-cell principle was often ignored. Although the prison was viewed as an improvement over capital and corporal punishment, it quickly became the scene of depressed conditions. Inmates were treated harshly and routinely whipped and tortured. Prison brutality flourished in these institutions, which had originally been devised as a more humane correctional alternative. In these early penal institutions, brutal corporal punishment was doled out indoors where, hidden from public view, it could become even more savage.[19]

Prison industry developed and became the predominant theme around which institutions were organized. Some prisons used the contract system, in which officials sold the labor of inmates to private businesses. Sometimes the contractor supervised the inmates inside the prison itself. Under the convict-lease system, the state leased its prisoners to a business for a fixed annual fee and gave up supervision and control. Finally, some institutions had prisoners produce goods for the prison's own use.[20]

contract system The practice of correctional officials selling the labor of inmates to private businesses.

convict-lease system The practice of leasing inmates to a business for a fixed annual fee.

CONCEPT SUMMARY 11.1 Early Correctional Systems				
Prison	**Structure**	**Living Conditions**	**Activities**	**Discipline**
Auburn system	Tiered cells	Congregate	Group work	Silence, harsh punishment
Pennsylvania system	Single cells set in semicircle	Isolated	In-cell work, Bible study	Silence, harsh punishment

© Cengage Learning

The development of prison industry quickly led to the abuse of inmates, who were forced to work for almost no wages, and to profiteering by dishonest administrators and business owners. During the Civil War era, prisons were major manufacturers of clothes, shoes, boots, furniture, and the like. Beginning in the 1870s, opposition by trade unions sparked restrictions on interstate commerce in prison goods. The prison, like the police department, became the scene of political intrigue and of efforts by political administrators to control the hiring of personnel and dispensing of patronage.

REFORM EFFORTS The National Congress of Penitentiary and Reformatory Discipline, held in Cincinnati in 1870, heralded a new era of prison reform. Organized by penologists Enoch Wines and Theodore Dwight, the congress provided a forum for corrections experts from around the nation to call for the treatment, education, and training of inmates. By 1870, Zebulon Brockway, warden of the Elmira Reformatory in New York, advocated individualized treatment, the indeterminate sentence, and parole. The reformatory program initiated by Brockway included elementary education for illiterates, designated library hours, lectures by faculty members of the local Elmira College, and a group of vocational training shops. From 1888 to 1920, Elmira administrators used military-like training to discipline the inmates and organize the institution. The military organization could be seen in every aspect of the institution: schooling, manual training, sports, supervision of inmates, and even parole decisions.[21] The cost to the state of the institution's operations was to be held to a minimum.

THE DEVELOPMENT OF PAROLE In the early seventeenth century, English judges began to spare the lives of offenders by banishing them to the newly formed overseas colonies. In 1617, the Privy Counsel of the British Parliament standardized this practice by passing an order granting reprieves and stays of execution to convicts willing to be transported to the colonies. Transportation was viewed as an answer to labor shortages caused by war, disease, and the opening of new commercial markets.

In 1717, the British Parliament passed legislation embodying the concept of *property in service,* which transferred control of prisoners to a contractor or shipmaster until the expiration of their sentences. When the prisoners arrived in the colonies, their services could be resold to the highest bidder. After sale, an offender's status changed from convict to indentured servant.

Transportation quickly became the most common sentence for theft offenders. In the American colonies, property in service had to be abandoned after the revolution. Thereafter, Australia, claimed as a British colony in 1770, became the destination for most transported felons. From 1815 to 1850, large numbers of inmates were shipped to Australia to serve as indentured servants working for plantation owners, in mines, or on sheep stations.

The English Penal Servitude Act of 1853 all but ended transportation and substituted imprisonment as a punishment. Part of this act made it possible to grant a *ticket-of-leave* to those who had served a sufficient portion of their prison sentence. This form of conditional release permitted former prisoners to be at large in specified areas. The conditions of their release were written on a license that the former inmates were required to carry with them at all times. Conditions usually included sobriety, lawful behavior, and hard work. Many releasees violated these provisions, prompting criticism of the system. Eventually, members of prisoner aid societies helped supervise and care for releasees.

The concept of parole spread to the United States. As early as 1822, volunteers from the Philadelphia-based Society for Alleviating the Miseries of Public Prisons began to

Apic/Hulton Archive/Getty Images

This image shows the execution of a woman by electrocution in Sing Sing prison in Newburgh, New York, on April 9, 1899.

L05 Chart the development of penal reform

help offenders after they were released from prison. In 1851, the society appointed two agents to work with inmates discharged from Pennsylvania penal institutions. Massachusetts appointed an agent in 1845 to help released inmates obtain jobs, clothing, and transportation.

In the 1870s, using a carefully weighted screening procedure, Zebulon Brockway selected rehabilitated offenders from Elmira Reformatory for early release under the supervision of citizen volunteers known as *guardians*. The guardians met with the parolees at least once a month and submitted written reports on their progress. The parole concept spread rapidly. Ohio created the first parole agency in 1884. By 1901, as many as 20 states had created some type of parole agency. By 1927, only Florida, Mississippi, and Virginia had not established some sort of parole release. Parole had become institutionalized as the primary method of release for prison inmates, and half of all inmates released in the United States were paroled.[22]

LO6 Discuss how parole developed

Prisons in the Twentieth Century

The early twentieth century was a time of contrasts in the US prison system.[23] At one extreme were those who advocated reform, such as the Mutual Welfare League, led by Thomas Mott Osborne. Prison reform groups proposed better treatment for inmates, an end to harsh corporal punishment, the creation of meaningful prison industries, and educational programs. Reformers argued that prisoners should not be isolated from society and that the best elements of society—education, religion, meaningful work, and self-governance—should be brought to the prison. Osborne went so far as to spend a week in New York's notorious Sing Sing Prison to learn firsthand about its conditions.

In time, some of the more rigid prison rules gave way to liberal reform. By the mid-1930s, few prisons required inmates to wear the red-and-white-striped convict suit; nondescript gray uniforms were substituted. The code of silence ended, as did the lockstep shuffle. Prisoners were allowed "the freedom of the yard" to mingle and exercise an hour or two each day.[24] Movies and radio appeared in the 1930s. Visiting policies and mail privileges were liberalized.

A more important trend was the development of specialized prisons designed to treat particular types of offenders. In New York, for example, the prisons at Clinton and Auburn were viewed as industrial facilities for hard-core inmates, Great Meadow was an agricultural center for nondangerous offenders, and Dannemora was a facility for the criminally insane. In California, San Quentin housed inmates considered salvageable by correctional authorities, and Folsom was reserved for hard-core offenders.[25]

Prison industry also evolved. Opposition by organized labor helped put an end to the convict-lease system and forced inmate labor. By 1900, a number of states had restricted the sale of prisoner-made goods on the open market. The worldwide Great Depression, which began in 1929, prompted industry and union leaders to further pressure state legislators to reduce competition from prison industries. A series of ever more restrictive federal legislative initiatives led to the Sumners-Ashurst Act (1940), which made it a federal offense to transport interstate commerce goods made in prison for private use, regardless of the laws of the state receiving the goods.[26] The restrictions imposed by the federal government helped to severely curtail prison industry for 40 years. Private entrepreneurs shunned prison investments because they were no longer profitable. The result was inmate idleness and make-work jobs.[27]

Despite some changes and reforms, the prison in the mid-twentieth century remained a destructive total institution. Although some aspects of inmate life improved, severe discipline, harsh rules, and solitary confinement were the way of life in prison.

State Library and Archives of Florida

Under the lease system, private companies would pay corrections officials for the services of inmates for farming, road construction and other labor-intensive projects. This 1915 photo on the right shows inmates who had been leased out to harvest timber in Florida.

Contemporary Correctional Institutions

The modern era has been a period of change and turmoil in the nation's correctional system. Three trends stand out. First, the prisoners' rights movement occurred between 1960 and 1980. After many years of indifference (the so-called "hands-off" doctrine), state and federal courts ruled in case after case that institutionalized inmates had rights to freedom of religion and speech, medical care, procedural due process, and proper living conditions. Inmates won rights unheard of in the nineteenth and early twentieth centuries. Since 1980, however, an increasingly conservative judiciary has curtailed the growth of inmate rights.

Second, violence within the correctional system became a national concern. Well-publicized riots at New York's Attica Prison and the New Mexico State Penitentiary drew attention to the potential for death and destruction that lurks in every prison. Prison rapes and killings have become commonplace. The locus of control in many prisons has shifted from the correctional staff to violent inmate gangs. In reaction, some administrators have tried to improve conditions and provide innovative programs that give inmates a voice in running the institution. Another reaction has been to tighten discipline and build new super-maximum-security prisons to control the most dangerous offenders. The problem of prison overcrowding has made efforts to improve conditions extremely difficult.

Third, the view that traditional correctional rehabilitation efforts have failed prompted many penologists to reconsider the purpose of incarcerating criminals. Between 1960 and 1980, it was common for correctional administrators to cling to the **medical model**, which viewed inmates as sick people who were suffering from some social malady that prevented them from adjusting to society. Correctional treatment could help cure them and enable them to live productive lives after they returned to the community. In the 1970s, efforts were also made to help offenders become reintegrated into society by providing them with new career opportunities that relied on work-release programs. Inmates were allowed to work outside the institution during the day and return in the evening. Some were given extended furloughs in the community. Work-release programs became a political issue when, in a famous incident, Willie Horton, a furloughed inmate from Massachusetts, raped a young woman. Criticism of the state's "liberal" furlough program helped Vice President George H. W. Bush defeat Massachusetts Governor Michael S. Dukakis for the US presidency in 1988. In the aftermath of the Horton case, a number of states, including Massachusetts, restricted their furlough policies.

medical model A correctional philosophy grounded on the belief that inmates are sick people who need treatment rather than punishment to help them reform.

AP Images/Elaine Thompson

Prison security is always a problem, especially those measures designed to reduce sexual assaults. A convex mirror helps to prevent hidden space at the Washington Corrections Center For Women in Gig Harbor, Washington. A 2003 federal law was meant to put a stop to sexual assault in the nation's prisons, jails, and juvenile detention centers, and more than $110 million in state and federal money has been spent to help states tackle the problem. Every state is now required to have standards in place, ranging from increased training of staff about sex abuse policies to procedures meant to help inmates safely report attacks.

George Williams

The penal harm movement suggests that inmates be treated harshly to convince them never to return to a life of crime. Can this attitude help explain the development of brutal and callous behavior by correctional officers who hope to teach inmates like George Williams a lesson they won't forget? Is it ethical for correctional officers to use harsh tactics and a no frills approach?

penal harm A philosophy based on the belief that harsh treatment while serving a correctional sentence will convince offenders that crime does not pay, thereby lowering the chances of recidivism

Prisons have come to be viewed as places for control, incapacitation, and punishment, instead of sites for rehabilitation and reform. Advocates of the "no-frills," or **penal harm** movement believe that if prison is a punishing experience, would-be criminals will be deterred from committing crimes, and current inmates will be encouraged to go straight. Nonetheless, efforts to use correctional institutions as treatment facilities have not ended, and such innovations as the development of private industries on prison grounds have kept the rehabilitative ideal alive.

The pressure on correctional institutions caused by overpopulation and the burden of constantly increasing correctional costs have prompted the development of alternatives to incarceration, such as intensive probation supervision, house arrest, and electronic monitoring (refer to Chapter 10). What has developed is a dual correctional policy: keep as many nonviolent offenders out of the correctional system as possible by means of community-based programs, and incarcerate dangerous, violent offenders for long periods of time.[28] These efforts have been compromised by a growing get-tough stance in judicial and legislative sentencing policy, accented by mandatory minimum sentences for gun crimes and drug trafficking. More than 2 million people are still behind bars in prisons and jails despite the development of alternatives to incarceration and a two-decade-long decline in the crime rate.

The following sections review the most prominent types of correctional facilities in operation today.

Jails

The nation's jails are institutional facilities with five primary purposes:

- Detain accused offenders who cannot make or are not eligible for bail prior to trial
- Hold convicted offenders who are awaiting sentence
- Serve as the principal institution of secure confinement for offenders convicted of misdemeanors
- Hold probationers and parolees picked up for violations and waiting for a hearing
- House felons when state prisons are overcrowded

A number of formats are used to jail offenders. About 15,000 local jurisdictions maintain short-term police or municipal lockups that house offenders for no more than 48 hours before a bail hearing can be held; thereafter, detainees are kept in the county jail.

TABLE 11.1 Gender trends in local jail populations

| | Local jail | |
	Males	Females
2000	550,200	71,000
2010	656,400	92,400
2013	628,900	102,400
Percent change, 2000–2010		
Total	19.3%	30.1%
Average annual	1.8	2.6
Percent change, 2010–2013		
Total	−4.2%	10.8%
Average annual	−1.4	3.4

Source: Lauren Glaze and Danielle Kaeble, *Correctional Populations in the United States, 2013* (Washington, DC: US Department of Justice, 2014).

Jail Populations and Trends

After rising for more than a decade, the number of people being held in jail began to decline in 2009, and there were about 730,000 jail inmates by 2013.[29] The jail incarceration rate—the confined population per 100,000 US residents—is now about 231 per 100,000, down from a 2007 high of 259 jail inmates per 100,000 residents. This recent downward trend in jail population may be a reflection of a declining US crime rate and greater reliance on alternatives to incarceration such as probation, electronic monitoring, and house arrest.

Who goes to jail? Although males outnumber females by a significant margin, the gap is narrowing. While the male population actually declined between 2010 and 2013, the female population increased more than 10 percent (see Table 11.1).

European Americans make up about 47 percent of the jail population, meaning that a disproportionate number of jail inmates are minority group members. Over their lifetime, African Americans are nearly five times more likely than whites, nearly three times more likely than Hispanics, and over nine times more likely than persons of other races to have been in jail; this pattern has not changed for the past decade. Disproportionate minority representation in jail may be caused, in part, by race-based disparity in sentencing practices. Research shows that black men have an increased likelihood of receiving jail sentences (as opposed to probation) compared to white men and women who commit similar crimes.[30]

Another reason may be linked to racial differences in the economy, which translates into racial differences in the ability to both personally meet bail and qualify for third-party loans (from bondsmen) to qualify for bail. The inability to obtain bail can have long-term consequences: pretrial detainees tend to get longer prison sentences and are more likely to be incarcerated than those released on bail. The failure by minority group members to obtain bail may be the first step to subsequent overrepresentation in jail and prison.

At one time, many thousands of minor children were held in jails as runaways, truants, and so on. The number of juveniles held in adult jails has been in decline since 1995, a result of ongoing government initiatives to remove juveniles from adult facilities; nonetheless, about 4,600 minors are still being held in adult jails each day.

Jail Conditions

Jails are usually a low-priority item in the criminal justice system. Because they are often administered on a county level, jail services have not been sufficiently regulated, nor has a unified national policy been developed to mandate what constitutes adequate jail conditions. Consequently, jails in some counties are physically deteriorated, holding dangerous and troubled people, many of whom suffer emotional problems that remain untreated.

Suicide

Considering the fact that jails hold troubled people with substance abuse and mental health issues, it should come as no surprise that the percentage of jail inmates who take their own lives is still higher than that of the general population. However, while jail conditions and jail suicides remain an important problem, a national survey conducted by the National Center on Institutions and Alternatives (NCIA) found a dramatic decrease in the rate of suicide in county jails during the past 20 years. The suicide rate in county jails was calculated to be 38 deaths per 100,000 inmates, which was approximately three times greater than that in the general population of the United States (at 11 deaths per 100,000 citizens), but about a 70 percent decrease from the 107 suicides per 100,000 inmates 20 years ago.[31] Why have jail suicides declined? One reason may be greater recognition of the problem and efforts to provide services to the jail population, a significant portion of whom have psychological and substance abuse problems and a history of past suicide attempts. Another possible answer may be found in the development of new-generation jails, discussed next.

LO7 Explain the purposes of jails and be familiar with the makeup of jail populations

New-Generation Jails

To relieve overcrowding and improve effectiveness, a jail-building boom has been under way. Many of the new jails are using modern designs referred to as "new-generation jails."[32] Traditional jails are constructed in what is referred to as the linear/intermittent surveillance model. Jails using this design are rectangular, with corridors leading to either single- or multiple-occupancy cells arranged at right angles to the corridor. Correctional officers must patrol to see into cells or housing areas, and when they are in a position to observe one cell, they cannot observe others; unobserved inmates are essentially unsupervised.

In contrast, new-generation jails allow for continuous observation of residents. There are two types: direct-supervision and indirect-supervision jails. Direct-supervision jails contain a cluster of cells surrounding a living area or "pod," which has tables, chairs,

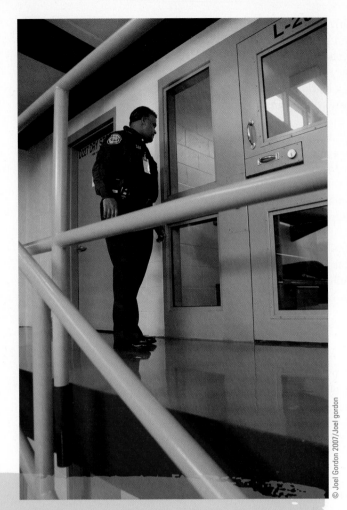

© Joel Gordon 2007/Joel gordon

New generation jails are designed to increase and improve security measures while giving inmates a sense of respect and privacy. Here Major Raul Banasco is conducting a weekend tour at a new generation jail cellblock.

LO8 Define the term
new-generation jail

maximum-security prison A correctional institution that houses dangerous felons and maintains strict security measures, high walls, and limited contact with the outside world.

televisions, and other material. A correctional officer is stationed within the pod. The officer can observe the inmates continuously and is able to relate to them on a personal level. Placing the officer in the pod achieves an increased awareness of the behaviors and needs of the inmates. This results in a safer environment for both staff and inmates. Because interaction between inmates is constantly and closely monitored, dissension can be quickly detected before it escalates. During the day, inmates stay in the open area (dayroom) and typically are not permitted to go into their rooms except with permission of the officer in charge. The officer controls door locks to cells from the control panel. In case of trouble or if the officer leaves the station for an extended period of time, command of this panel can be switched to a panel at a remote location, known as central control. The officer usually wears a device that permits immediate communication with central control, and the area is also covered by a video camera monitored by an officer in the central control room. Indirect-supervision jails are similar in construction, but the correctional officer's station is located inside a secure room. Microphones and speakers inside the living unit permit the officer to hear and communicate with inmates.

Prisons

The state and federal governments maintain secure correctional facilities, also called prisons, penitentiaries, or reformatories. The most recent government figures show that federal and state governments now spend about $60 billion on these secure correctional facilities each year, up from about $12 billion in 1986.[33]

The prison is the final repository for the most troubled criminal offenders. Many come from distressed backgrounds and have little hope or opportunity; all too many have emotional problems and grew up in abusive households. A majority are alcohol and drug dependent at the time of their arrest. Those considered both dangerous and incorrigible may find themselves in super-maximum-security prisons, where they spend most of their days confined to their cells.

Types of Prisons

More than 1,700 public adult correctional facilities are currently housing state prisoners. In addition, there are about 100 federal prisons and more than 250 privately run institutions. Usually, prisons are organized or classified on three levels—maximum-, medium-, and minimum security—and each has distinct characteristics.

MAXIMUM-SECURITY PRISONS Housing the most notorious criminals, and often the subject of films and stories, maximum-security prisons are probably the institutions most familiar to the public. Famous "max prisons" have included Sing Sing, Joliet, Attica, Walpole, and the most fearsome prison of all, the now-closed federal facility on Alcatraz Island known as the Rock.

A typical maximum-security facility is fortress-like, surrounded by stone walls with guard towers at strategic places. These walls may be 25 feet high, and sometimes inner and outer walls divide the prison into courtyards. Barbed wire or electrified fences are used to discourage escape. High security, armed guards, and stone walls give the inmate the sense that the facility is impregnable and reassure the citizens outside that convicts will be completely incapacitated. Because they fear that violence may flair up at any minute, prison administrators have been quick to adapt the latest high-tech measures to help them maintain security, a topic covered in the Criminal Justice and Technology feature.

Technocorrections: Contemporary Correctional Technology

Technical experts have identified numerous areas of correctional management that can be aided by information technology (IT), including reception and commitment; sentence and time accounting; classification; caseload management; security; discipline; housing/bed management; medical services; grievances; programs; scheduling; investigations/gang management; property; trust accounting; visitation; release and discharge; and community supervision. Because IT can be applied in so many areas within correctional establishments, prison administrators have begun to take advantage of the potential offered by the new technologies. Following are a few examples of IT being used in prisons today.

All-In-One Drug Detection Spray

Mistral sprays are now being used and have proven effective at identifying drugs without adverse impact on the safe operation of the prison. Mistral's drug detection and identification system consists of four types of aerosol sprays and three types of test papers. Used in different combinations, the sprays and test papers can detect trace quantities of marijuana, methamphetamines, heroin, or cocaine.

Ground-Penetrating Radar

Ground-penetrating radar (GPR) can locate tunnels that inmates use to escape. GPR works almost like an old-fashioned Geiger counter, but instead of detecting metal, the system detects changes in ground composition, including voids such as those created by a tunnel.

Heartbeat Monitoring

Now it is possible to prevent escapes by monitoring inmates' heartbeats! The Advanced Vehicle Interrogation and Notification System (AVIAN) detects the presence of persons trying to escape by hiding in vehicles. Using the data from seismic sensors that are placed on the vehicle, the AVIAN reads the shock wave generated by the beating heart, which couples to any surface or object with which the body is in contact. It collects the data and analyzes it using advanced signal-processing algorithms in less than two minutes to detect a person hiding in a vehicle such as a large truck. The system works by accounting for all the frequencies of movement in the vehicle, such as the expansion and contraction of an engine or rain hitting the roof.

Backscatter Imaging System for Concealed Weapons

This system uses a backscatter imager to detect weapons and contraband. The primary advantage of this device over current walk-through portals is that it can detect nonmetallic as well as metallic weapons. It uses low-power x-rays equal to about five minutes of exposure to the sun at sea level. Although these x-rays penetrate clothing, they do not penetrate the body.

Body-Scanning Screening System

This is a stationary screening system to detect nonmetallic weapons and contraband in the lower body cavities. It uses simplified magnetic resonance imaging (MRI) as a noninvasive alternative to x-ray and physical body cavity searches. The stationary screening system makes use of first-generation medical MRI.

Personal Alarm Location System

It is now possible for prison employees to carry a tiny transmitter linking them with a computer in a central control room. In an emergency, they can hit an alarm button and transmit to a computer that automatically records whose distress button has been pushed. An architectural map of the facility instantly appears on screen, showing the exact location of the staff member in need of assistance.

Biometric Recognition

A new biometric system uses facial recognition by matching more than 200 individual points on the human face with a digitally stored image. The system is used to control access in buildings and rooms inside buildings. It is now available and will become much more common in the near future.

Monitoring Trouble Spots

The Correctional Operational Trend Analysis System (COTAS) is used to monitor places by predicting potential trouble spots within prisons. Knowing ahead of time where trouble might arise lets managers assign extra staff or take other actions that can prevent violence and other problems. The system manages information that lets all levels of managers monitor cross-functional operations quickly. COTAS can identify trends, patterns, and areas of concerns within specific individual institutions and statewide.

Suicide Warning System

An automated suicide warning system has been developed as a cost-effective, noninvasive approach to behavior monitoring. This radar-based system can measure an inmate's heart rate, breathing rate, and body motions without being attached to the individual. The system consists of the following:

- "Personal health status" sensors that can be enclosed in a box on the ceiling to remotely and noninvasively monitor inmates' pulse and breathing
- Network connections to remote monitors
- Software designed to interpret motion data and create a decision tree for when to notify officers

A wall-mounted range controlled radar (RCR) system—originally designed for home security motion detectors—measures subtle motions on the body's surface caused by heart and lung activity. Alarms are activated when the system detects suspicious changes in heart rate, breathing rate, or body motion. A key feature of the device is that it is less obtrusive. Inmates are prone to tamper with or destroy monitoring devices, but a device that does not require physical contact with the prisoner could make tampering or destruction less likely. Automated monitoring technology provides continuous surveillance to supplement the visual inspections and alert officers quickly to any attempt. By installing these devices, prisons are able to reduce the number of officers needed to monitor prisoners, freeing staff for other corrections tasks.

CRITICAL THINKING

1. Some elements of technocorrections intrude on the privacy of inmates. Should the need for security outweigh an inmate's right to privacy?

2. Should probationers and parolees be monitored with modern technology? Do they deserve more privacy than incarcerated inmates?

Sources: National Institute of Justice, "Predicting Trouble Spots within Prisons," 2012, http://www.nij.gov/nij/topics/corrections/institutional/monitoring-inmates/predicting-trouble.htm (accessed March 2015); National Institute of Justice, "Suicide Watch Technologies Could Improve Monitoring, Reduce Staff Time," 2012, http://nij.gov/topics/corrections/institutional/monitoring-inmates/pages/suicide-watch.aspx (accessed March 2015); National Institute of Justice, "Detecting Drugs on Surfaces Quickly and Easily," 2012, http://nij.gov/topics/corrections/institutional/contraband/Pages/drug-detection.aspx (accessed March 2015).

Inmates live in interior, metal-barred cells that contain their own plumbing and sanitary facilities and are locked securely either by key or by electronic device. Cells are organized in sections called blocks, and, in large prisons, a number of cell blocks make up a wing. During the day, the inmates engage in closely controlled activities: meals, workshops, education, and so on. Rule violators may be confined to their cells or spend time in solitary confinement; and working and other shared recreational activities are viewed as privileges.

The byword of the maximum-security prison is "security." Correctional workers are made aware that each inmate may be a dangerous criminal or violent, and, as a result, the utmost security must be maintained. These prisons are designed to eliminate hidden corners where people can congregate, and passages are constructed so that they can be easily blocked off to quell disturbances.

SUPER-MAXIMUM-SECURITY PRISONS Some states have constructed super-maximum-security prisons (supermax prisons) to house the most predatory criminals. These high-security institutions can be independent correctional centers or locked wings of existing prisons.[34] Some supermax prisons lock inmates in their cells 22 to 24 hours a day, never allowing them out unless they are shackled.[35]

The 490-bed facility in Florence, Colorado, has the most sophisticated security measures in the United States, including 168 video cameras and 1,400 electronically controlled gates. Inside the cells, all furniture is unmovable; the desk, bed, and TV stand are made of cement. All potential weapons, including soap dishes, toilet seats, and toilet handles, have been removed. The cement walls are 5,000-pound quality, and steel bars crisscross every eight inches inside the walls. Cells are angled so that inmates can see neither each other nor the outside. This cuts down on communication and denies inmates a sense of location to prevent escapes.

Despite the fact that supermax prisons such as Florence have gotten mixed reviews, they are now being used around the world.[36] Some critics believe that they infringe directly on the right of inmates because they deprive them of such basic rights such as human contact; they also eliminate any opportunity for rehabilitation.[37] Others claim that a disproportionate number of minority group members are being held in these institutions under extremely harsh conditions.[38] Keramet Reiter argues that while supermaxes are technologically advanced, they are intentionally designed to limit all physical, human contact because they contain "the worst of the worst prisoners"—those too violent and dangerous to live in a general prison population. The unintended consequence of this draconian regime is the creation of violence. Supermaxes, she concludes, are a novel and uniquely modern form of state violence, and their legal and ethical implications should be reconsidered.[39]

Some of the most important research on supermax prisons has been conducted by Daniel Mears and his colleagues. In one study, Mears, along with Jamie Watson, found that supermax prisons may actually enhance the quality of life of inmates and consequently improve their mental health. They increase privacy, reduce danger, and even provide creature comforts (such as TV sets) that are unavailable in general-population prisons. Staff report less stress and fear because they have to contend with fewer disruptive inmates.

On the other hand, Mears has found that supermax prisons also have some unintended negative consequences. Staff may have too much control over inmates—a condition that damages staff–inmate relationships. Long hours of isolation may be associated with mental illness and psychological disturbances. Supermax inmates seem to have a more difficult time readjusting upon release. A stay in a supermax prison inhibits reintegration into other prisons, communities, and families. In one study that examined data from the Florida Department of Corrections, Mears, along with William Bales, found that supermax incarceration may increase violent

WEB APP 11.2 To read about the harsh life in a supermax prison, go to http://www.npr.org/2012/06/21/155513749/the-grim-realities-of-life-in-supermax-prisons. Are supermax prisons essentially damaging to inmates, and should they be abolished?

ETHICAL REFLECTION

George Williams

Let's say an inmate was highly disruptive and potentially violent. Would he not be better off in a supermax prison than in a maximum-security facility where the guards may want to take matters into their own hands? Might a stay in a supermax prison be the ethical choice for some inmates?

recidivism.[40] Mears and colleague Jennifer Castro also surveyed wardens and found that even though they seem to favor supermax prisons, they also expressed concern that the general public consider supermax institutions inhumane, that they drain limited funds from state budgets, and that they produce increases in litigation and court interventions, as well as increased recidivism and reentry failure among released inmates.[41]

MEDIUM-SECURITY PRISONS Although they are similar in appearance to maximum-security prisons, in medium-security prisons, the security and atmosphere are neither so tense nor so vigilant. Medium-security prisons are also surrounded by walls, but there may be fewer guard towers or other security precautions; visitations with personal contact may be allowed. Although most prisoners are housed in cells, individual honor rooms in medium-security prisons are used to reward those who make exemplary rehabilitation efforts. Finally, medium-security prisons promote greater treatment efforts, and the relaxed atmosphere allows freedom of movement for rehabilitation workers and other therapeutic personnel.

MINIMUM-SECURITY PRISONS Operating without armed guards or perimeter walls, minimum-security prisons usually house the most trustworthy and least violent offenders; white-collar criminals may be the most common occupants. Inmates are allowed a great deal of personal freedom. Instead of being marched to activities by guards, they are summoned by bells or loudspeaker announcements, and they assemble on their own. Work furloughs and educational releases are encouraged, and vocational training is of the highest level. Dress codes are lax, and inmates are allowed to grow beards or mustaches and to demonstrate other individual characteristics.

Minimum-security facilities may have dormitories or small private rooms for inmates. Prisoners are allowed to own personal possessions that might be deemed dangerous in a maximum-security prison, such as radios.

Minimum-security prisons have been criticized for being like "country clubs"; some federal facilities for white-collar criminals even have tennis courts and pools (they are derisively called "Club Fed"). Yet they remain prisons, and the isolation and loneliness of prison life deeply affects the inmates.

Alternative Correctional Institutions

In addition to prisons and jails, a number of other correctional institutions are operating within the United States. Some have been in use for quite some time, whereas others have been developed more recently as part of innovative or experimental programs.

Prison Farms and Camps

Prison farms and camps are used to detain offenders. These types of facilities are found primarily in the South and the West and have been in operation since the nineteenth century. Today, more than 100 facilities (vocational training centers, ranches, and so on) exist in the nation. Prisoners on farms produce dairy products, grain, and vegetable crops that are used in the state correctional system and other governmental facilities, such as hospitals and schools. Forestry camp inmates maintain state parks, fight forest fires, and do reforestation work. Ranches, primarily a western phenomenon, employ inmates in cattle raising and horse breeding, among other activities. Road gangs repair roads and state highways.

Shock Incarceration in Boot Camps

Another correctional innovation that gained popularity in the 1980s and 1990s, the boot camp, housed youthful, first-time offenders in military discipline and physical training. The concept is that short periods (90 to 180 days) of high-intensity exercise and work will "shock" the inmate into going straight. Tough physical training is designed to

medium-security prison A less secure institution that houses nonviolent offenders and provides more opportunities for contact with the outside world.

minimum-security prison The least secure institution, which houses white-collar and nonviolent offenders, maintains few security measures, and has liberal furlough and visitation policies.

boot camp A short-term militaristic correctional facility in which inmates undergo intensive physical conditioning and discipline.

Evelyn Cole, 23, scratches Shake You Down, a 16-year-old retired racehorse at Second Chance Farm, at the Lowell Correctional Institution in Lowell, Florida. Cole worked with Shake You Down and other horses at the prison's farm when she was an inmate doing time for stabbing another girl when she had a fight at the age of 16. She claims that working with horses while she was in prison helped her immensely. She is married now and has a 6-year-old son. The farm recently celebrated 15 years and has graduated dozens of prisoners, the vast majority, like Evelyn, have been able to turn their life around upon release.

WEB APP 11.3 Although boot camps have been closing around the nation, some states still maintain the practice. You can read about one at **http://www.dcor.state .ga.us/Divisions/Corrections /BootCamps.html.**

Do you believe boot camps serve a purpose?

halfway house A community-based correctional facility that houses inmates before their outright release so they can become gradually acclimated to conventional society.

promote responsibility and improve decision-making skills, build self-confidence, and teach socialization skills. Inmates are treated with rough intensity by drillmasters who may call them names and punish the entire group for the failure of one member.[42]

Some programs also include educational and training components, counseling sessions, and treatment for special-needs populations, whereas others devote little or no time to therapeutic activities. Some allow voluntary participation, and others allow voluntary termination.[43]

Empirical research has not supported boot camp effectiveness.[44] There is little evidence that boot camps can significantly lower recidivism rates. Because of these sketchy results, the federal government and most state correctional authorities have closed their boot camp programs, and relatively few remain in operation.[45]

Community Correctional Facilities

Community correctional facilities called **halfway houses** hold inmates just before their release. These facilities are designed to bridge the gap between institutional living and the community. Specialized treatment may be offered, and the residents use the experience to cushion the shock of reentering society.

Halfway houses can look like residential homes and, in many instances, were originally residences; in urban centers, older apartment buildings can be adapted for the purpose. Usually, these facilities have a central treatment theme—such as group therapy or reality therapy—that is used to rehabilitate and reintegrate clients.

Despite the encouraging philosophical concept presented by the halfway house, evaluation of specific programs has not led to a definite endorsement of this type of treatment.[46] One significant problem has been a lack of support from community residents, who fear the establishment of an institution housing "dangerous offenders" in their neighborhood. Court actions have been brought and zoning restrictions imposed

Bruce ackerman/Ocala Star-Banner/Landov

in some areas to foil efforts to create halfway houses. As a result, many halfway houses are located in decrepit neighborhoods in the worst areas of town—certainly a condition that must influence the attitudes and behavior of the inmates. Furthermore, the climate of control exercised in most halfway houses, where rule violation can be met with a quick return to the institution, may not be one that the average inmate can distinguish from his former high-security penal institution.

Private Prisons

On January 6, 1986, the Corrections Corporation of America opened the first private state prison in Marion, Kentucky—a 300-bed minimum-security facility for inmates who were within three years of parole. Today, CCA houses nearly 70,000 inmates in more than 60 facilities, the majority of which are company-owned, with a total bed capacity of more than 80,000. CCA currently partners with all three federal corrections agencies (the Federal Bureau of Prisons, the US Marshals Service, and Immigration and Customs Enforcement), 16 states, more than a dozen local municipalities, and Puerto Rico and the US Virgin Islands.[47]

A competitor, the GEO Group has 106 facilities with approximately 85,500 beds, and 19,000 employees around the globe, including facilities located in the United States, United Kingdom, Australia, and South Africa. GEO maintains a wide range of facilities, including state and federal prisons, detention centers, community reentry facilities, and other special needs institutions, and it provides community supervision services, including electronic monitoring technologies.[48] Private prisons are not a uniquely American institution: they also play an important correctional role in Australia and the United Kingdom.[49]

In some instances, a private corporation will finance and build an institution and then contract with correctional authorities to provide services for convicted criminals. Sometimes the private concern will finance and build the institution and then lease it outright to the government. This model has the advantage of allowing the government to circumvent the usually difficult process of getting voters to approve a bond issue and raising funds for prison construction. Another common form of private involvement is specific service contracts; for example, a private concern might be hired to manage the prison health-care system, food services, or staff training.

In all, private prisons now hold about 137,000 inmates in the United States or about 7 percent of the total state prison population and 19 percent of the federal prison population.[50] However, as the total inmate population has declined, the number of those being held in private institutions has declined as well. Some states, including Kentucky and Wisconsin, that employed private prisons in the past reported having no prisoners housed in private prison facilities as of 2014.

DO PRIVATE PRISONS WORK? The most thorough evaluations of differences in recidivism rates between private and public facilities find little difference between the recidivism rates of inmates released from the two different types of institutions.[51] There is

AP Images/Patrick Semansky

Halfway houses help former inmates adjust back into society. Most utilize treatment programs and drug monitoring. On March 26, 2015, Former U.S. Representative Jesse Jackson Jr. is administered a breathalyzer test as he checks in at a Baltimore halfway house after being released from a minimum security federal prison camp at Maxwell Air Force Base in Alabama. Jackson served the remainder of his term (two years) at the halfway house after pleading guilty to spending $750,000 in campaign money on personal items.

some evidence that inmates released from private prisons who do reoffend may commit less serious offenses than those released from public institutions, and although private and state institutions cost about the same to operate, private prisons seem cheaper to construct.[52]

Although these findings help support the concept of the private correctional institution, some experts question reliance on private prisons, believing that their use raises a number of vexing problems. Will private providers be able to evaluate programs effectively, knowing that a negative evaluation might cause them to lose their contract? Will they skimp on services and programs to reduce costs? Might they not skim off the "easy" cases and leave hard-core inmates to the state's care? And will the need to keep business booming require widening the net to fill empty cells?

Private corrections firms also run into opposition from existing state correctional staff and management, who fear the loss of jobs and autonomy. Moreover, the public may be skeptical about an untested private concern's ability to provide security and protection. Private correction firms also face administrative problems. How will program quality be controlled? To compete on price, a private facility may have to cut corners to beat the competition. Determining accountability for problems and mishaps will be difficult when dealing with a corporation whose managers and officers are protected legally from personal responsibility for their actions.

SUING PRIVATE PRISONS Must private providers maintain state-mandated liability insurance to cover inmate claims? Some private service providers have been sued because their services were inadequate, causing harm to inmates.

Recently the Supreme Court reviewed an important legal issue: Can private prisons be sued in federal court by inmates charging that their constitutional rights had been violated? Richard Lee Pollard, an inmate at a federal prison run by the GEO Group, slipped on a cart left in a doorway and injured both elbows. As GEO employees were preparing to transport him to an outside orthopedic clinic, he said they made him wear a jumpsuit and a "black box" wrist restraint, despite his claim that both would cause him excruciating pain. Pollard sued GEO and its employees for allegedly violating his Eighth Amendment protection against cruel and unusual punishment. In *Minneci v. Pollard*, the Court ruled that an inmate could not sue for damages against employees of a privately operated federal prison based on constitutional principles such as the Eighth Amendment's ban on cruel and unusual punishment. In the circumstances of this case, Pollard should have sued for damages in state court.[53] This ruling limits the exposure private prison companies have to inmate lawsuits.

Inmate Populations

LO9 Classify the different types of federal and state penal institutions

This vast correctional system, with more than 2,000 public and private institutions, now contains more than 1.6 million inmates in the state and federal prison systems.[54]

As Figure 11. 1 shows, after decades of sharp increases, the imprisonment rate peaked in 2007, at 506 inmates per 100,000 residents. Since then, the prison population has finally leveled off and the rate of imprisonment has declined. While the number of inmates actually rose between 2012 and 2013, the US population grew at a faster rate in 2013 so that the imprisonment rate actually declined despite an increase in the number of sentenced prisoners. In 2014, the imprisonment rate for US residents of all ages was 478 sentenced prisoners per 100,000.

Although any decline in the prison population is welcome, a disconnect remains between the significant drop in the crime rate and the more modest reduction in the imprisonment rate. What are the causes of this disjunction?

- Many people who are released from prison soon return after failing on parole and other forms of early release. Hence, a significant portion of the prison population is made up of reentries. About 250,000 new inmates, or one-third of the people now entering prison, are parole violators.[55]

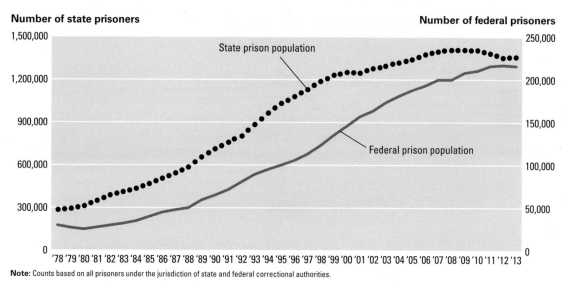

Number of state prisoners — **Number of federal prisoners**

State prison population

Federal prison population

Note: Counts based on all prisoners under the jurisdiction of state and federal correctional authorities.

FIGURE 11.1 Total State and Federal Prison Populations

Source: E. Ann Carson, *Prisoners, 2013* (Washington, DC: Bureau of Justice Statistics, 2014).

- Criminal legislation, including guideline-based mandatory-minimum sentencing laws, increases the chances that a convicted offender will be incarcerated and limits the availability of early release via parole.[56]
- The amount of time served in prison has increased because of such developments as truth-in-sentencing laws that require inmates to serve at least 85 percent of their sentences behind bars. Although truth in sentencing funding has ended, its effects are still being felt. Between 1990 and 2012, the number of inmates who maxed out their sentences in prison grew 119 percent, from fewer than 50,000 to more than 100,000. More than 40 percent of inmates maxed out their prison terms and left without supervision in Florida, Maine, Massachusetts, New Jersey, North Carolina, Ohio, Oklahoma, South Carolina, and Utah.[57]
- There is a significant association among drug use, drug arrests, and prison overcrowding.[58] The drug epidemic in the 1980s and 1990s helped swell prison populations with people serving very long sentences.

While the prison inmate population has stabilized, there are still far too many people in prison. In Exhibit 11.1, legal scholar Michael Tonry sets out a 10-point plan to reduce the prison population over the next five years.

LO10 Discuss prison population trends

EXHIBIT 11.1

What Can Be Done to Reduce the Inmate Population?

1. Three-strikes, mandatory minimum sentence, and similar sentencing enhancement laws should be abolished.

2. Sentencing enhancement laws that are not repealed should be significantly narrowed in range and severity.

3. Sentencing enhancement laws that are not repealed should authorize judges to grant another lesser sentence when it's "in the interest of justice."

4. Life-without-possibility-of-parole laws should be rescinded or considerably narrowed.

5. The use of truth-in-sentencing laws should be ended.

6. Criminal codes should be changed to set considerably lower maximum sentences that correspond more closely to the seriousness of crimes.

7. Every state that does not already have one should establish a sentencing commission and promulgate presumptive sentencing guidelines.

8. All states should establish a parole board and employ a parole guidelines system.

9. The combined rate of federal and state jail and prison populations should be cut in half by 2020.

10. Every state should enable all prisoners serving fixed terms longer than 5 years, or indeterminate terms, to be eligible for early release at the end of 5 years, and making all prisoners 35 years of age or older eligible for parole after serving 3 years.

Source: Michael Tonry, "Remodeling American Sentencing: A Ten-Step Blueprint for Moving Past Mass Incarceration," *Criminology and Public Policy* 13 (2014): 503–533.

The inmate population is now decreasing because the crime rate is down.

REALITY. The prison population has finally started to stabilize and even decline in some states.

Tougher prison sentences, coupled with longer stays before release, have resulted in a growing prison population. Nonetheless, the rate of growth seems finally to be slowing. Why?

Profile of the Prison Inmate

Who makes up this population? Prison inmates are disproportionately young, male, minority group members, and poor.

RACE. African Americans (37 percent) make up the largest portion of male inmates compared to European Americans (32 percent) and Hispanics (22 percent). White European American females comprised almost half of the female prison population, and African American females accounted for 22 percent. However, the imprisonment rate for black females (113 per 100,000) was twice the rate of white females (51 per 100,000). Almost 3 percent of black male US residents of all ages were imprisoned as 2014 began, (2,805 inmates per 100,000 black male US residents), compared to 1 percent of Hispanic males (1,134 per 100,000) and 0.5 percent of white males (466 per 100,000). Clearly, the racial disparity in the sentencing process results in similar disparity in the prison population.

AGE AND GENDER. As of 2014, there were about 104,000 female inmates, or 7 percent of the total. However, average annual increases in the female inmate population (1.2 percent per year) have been greater than increases in the male population (.7 percent).

Inmates tend to be relatively young. About 12 percent were under 24 years or age, and another 17 percent were aged 30 to 34; in contrast, 2 percent were aged 65 or older. Although the inmate population is generally young, long prison sentences for some crimes have created an ongoing problem of the elderly inmate, which is discussed in the Contemporary Issues in Criminal Justice feature.

OFFENSE. About half of all inmates in state prisons were serving sentences for violent offenses, and about 20 percent for property offenses. Robbery was the most common violent offense among state prisoners, followed by murder and nonnegligent manslaughter and rape or sexual assault. A higher percentage of males (55 percent) were imprisoned for violent offenses than females (37 percent).

SOCIAL PROBLEMS. Many inmates suffer from multiple social problems: they are undereducated, underemployed, and come from abusive homes. A significant number experienced homelessness (living on the street or in a homeless shelter) and other related social problems, including mental illness, substance abuse, and unemployment just before their incarceration.[59] For these reasons, it is not surprising when surveys show that inmates suffer from serious psychological and emotional problems, including psychosis and major depression.[60]

CONTEMPORARY ISSUES IN CRIMINAL JUSTICE

Elderly Inmates

The population of elderly prisoners in the United States has increased by more than 1,400 percent since 1981. Three decades ago, American prisons housed fewer than 9,000 prisoners age 55 and older; today, that number stands at 145,000. By 2040, the elderly prisoner population may top 400,000.

The care of the elderly is extremely expensive. Inmates over 50 are more likely to have health and mental health problems than noninstitutionalized Americans because they often come from poor backgrounds, have a greater likelihood of drug and alcohol abuse, and have more restricted access to health care. Many suffer from chronic illnesses such as hypertension, asthma or other lung disease, and arthritis. National studies find that nearly 40 percent of state inmates 55 and older have a recent history of mental health problems or disorders. It is not surprising then that the average cost of housing an inmate over 60 is $70,000 a year, which is about three times the average cost for other prisoners. More than $16 billion is now being spent annually caring for these aging inmates, and this amount is expected to grow dramatically as their numbers rise.

The aging of the prison population has come about from longer sentences resulting from the get-tough-on-crime measures that impose truth-in-sentencing, mandatory sentences, and three-strikes laws, as well as an increasing number of older people convicted of sex crimes and murder.

There are different adjustment rates for elderly prisoners. The longer the amount of time remaining to be served, the harder it usually is for the elderly person to deal with confinement. Background factors, such as level of education and marital status, can also affect the adjustment of the elderly. Some inmates, especially those imprisoned early in life, are more institutionally dependent than others. Some have higher morale and are more involved in programs and prison life than others. In many prisons, however, there is little programming or specialized treatment geared for elderly inmates. The elderly prisoner is vulnerable to victimization and requires special attention when it comes to medical treatment, housing, nutrition, and institutional activities.

(Continued)

What Can Be Done?

Some states are now contracting with private nursing homes to care for some of their elderly and disabled inmates under so-called "medical parole" programs. However, there has been resistance to this form of early release, and not all private facilities have been willing to accept elderly inmates. Connecticut has asked the commercial nursing home industry to create unique, nonsecure facilities that hold prison inmates and patients from the state mental hospital who require long-term nursing care. This way, the inmates are not sharing a room with noncriminals. Other states, including Michigan, Kentucky, and Wisconsin, are considering this approach.

CRITICAL THINKING

Older prisoners need more orderly conditions, safety precautions, emotional feedback, and familial support than younger prisoners. They are particularly uncomfortable in crowded conditions, tend to prefer small groups, and want

time alone. Should they be housed in traditional prisons, no matter what they have done in the past? Would community-based institutions be a more suitable alternative?

Sources: Christine Vestal, "For Aging Inmates, Care Outside Prison Walls," *Kaiser Health News* (August 12, 2014), http://kaiserhealthnews.org/news/for-aging-inmates -care-outside-prison-walls/ (accessed March 2015); American Civil Liberties Union, "At America's Expense: The Mass Incarceration of the Elderly," 2012, http://www.aclu .org/criminal-law-reform/americas-expense-mass-incarceration-elderly (accessed March 2013); B. Williams, M. Stern, J. Mellow, M. Safer, and R. B. Greifinger, "Aging in Correctional Custody: Setting a Policy Agenda for Older Prisoner Health Care," *American of Journal Public Health* 102 (2012): 1475–1481; D. J. James and L. E. Glaze, *Mental Health Problems of Prison and Jail Inmates* (Washington, DC: Bureau of Justice Statistics, 2006); Anthony A. Sterns and Greta Lax, "The Growing Wave of Older Prisoners: A National Survey of Older Prisoner Health, Mental Health and Programming," *Corrections Today* 70 (August 2008): 70–76.

ETHICAL Challenge

Legal scholar Alexander Volokh has proposed a novel approach to improve prisons: create a voucher system. School vouchers have been used to allow parents to choose which school to send their children, with the aim of improving school quality by transforming students and parents into consumers. Volokh asks, what if we did the same for prisons? What if convicted criminals could choose their prison rather than being assigned by a correctional authority? Under his voucher system, prisons would compete for prisoners, with the result that prisons would adopt policies prisoners value. Prisons would become more constitutionally flexible—for example, allowing for more faith-based programs—and would also have increased freedom to offer valued benefits in exchange for the waiver of constitutional rights. As far as prison quality goes, the advantages of vouchers would plausibly include greater security, higher-quality health care, and better educational opportunities—features that prison reformers favor for their rehabilitative value. The counterarguments are threefold: (1) allowing inmates to choose their prison is either impossible or morally undesirable; (2) due to informational or other problems, prisoner choice would not succeed in improving overall prison quality; (3) prison quality might improve too much, diluting the deterrent value of prison. Although Volokh believes these counterarguments have substantial force, he believes they do not foreclose the possibility that prison choice could result in socially desirable improvements that could outweigh these disadvantages.

Ethical Challenge: Write an essay discussing the ethics of a prison voucher system. Are they really similar to school vouchers? If the purpose of prisons is to dispense punishment, is it ethical to allow people to choose their own penalty?

Source: Alexander Volokh, "Prison Vouchers," *University of Pennsylvania Law Review* 160 (2012): 779–863.

SUMMARY

LO1 *Discuss the meaning of the term* new penology
The new penology refers to the fact that today's correctional system relies on the use of actuarial tables and tests in decision making. Administrators seem more concerned with security and "managing" large inmate populations than with treating individual offenders.

LO2 *Explain how the first penal institutions developed in Europe* Although the routine use of incarceration as a criminal punishment began in the late eighteenth and early nineteenth centuries, some early

European institutions were created specifically to detain and punish criminal offenders.

LO3 *Explain how William Penn revolutionized corrections* The "modern" American correctional system had its origins in Pennsylvania under the leadership of William Penn. Penn created Philadelphia's Walnut Street Jail, which was used to house convicted felons, except those sentenced to death. He believed inmates could be reformed through work and religious training.

LO4 *Compare the New York and Pennsylvania prison models* In 1816, New York built a new prison at Auburn that used the congregate system, in which most prisoners ate and worked in groups. In contrast, Pennsylvania established a prison that placed each inmate in a single cell for the duration of his sentence. By the late nineteenth century, the congregate system was adopted in all states except Pennsylvania.

LO5 *Chart the development of penal reform* The National Congress of Penitentiary and Reformatory Discipline, held in Cincinnati in 1870, heralded a new era of prison reform. Another important trend was the development of specialized prisons designed to treat particular types of offenders.

LO6 *Discuss how parole developed* The forerunner of parole began in Ireland in the 1850s, when penitentiary inmates spent the last portion of their sentences living in an intermediate institution and working in the outside community. In 1822, volunteers from the Philadelphia-based Society for Alleviating the Miseries of Public Prisons began to help offenders after they were released from prison. In 1851, the society appointed two agents to work with inmates discharged from Pennsylvania penal institutions. Massachusetts appointed an agent in 1845 to help released inmates obtain jobs, clothing, and transportation.

LO7 *Explain the purposes of jails and the makeup of jail populations* The nation's jails are institutional facilities used to detain accused offenders who cannot make or are not eligible for bail prior to trial and to hold convicted offenders awaiting sentence. They serve as the principal institution of secure confinement for offenders convicted of misdemeanors.

LO8 *Define the term* **new-generation jail** New-generation jails allow for continuous observation of residents. In the direct supervision version, officers are stationed within pods and get to interact with and monitor inmates. Indirect-supervision jails have correctional officers stationed inside a secure room. Microphones and speakers inside the living unit permit the officer to hear and communicate with inmates.

LO9 *Classify the different types of federal and state penal institutions* Maximum-security prisons housing the most notorious criminals are fortress-like, surrounded by stone walls with guard towers at strategic places. Some states have constructed super-maximum-security prisons (supermax prisons) to house the most predatory criminals. Similar in appearance to maximum-security prisons, medium-security prisons are characterized by less vigilant security provisions and a less tense atmosphere. Operating without armed guards or perimeter walls, minimum-security prisons usually house the most trustworthy and least violent offenders.

LO10 *Discuss prison population trends* After years of rapid growth, the inmate population has finally stabilized. The population is still high despite the nation's crime drop, most likely because tough new criminal legislation, including mandatory sentencing laws, increased the chances that a convicted offender will be incarcerated and limited the availability for early release via parole. The recent stabilization in the prison population may be temporary; if the crime rate increases, so too will the number of inmates.

KEY TERMS

prison, p. 266

jail, p. 266

hulks, p. 268

Walnut Street Jail, p. 269

penitentiary house, p. 269

congregate system, p. 269

Pennsylvania system, p. 270

contract system, p. 270

convict-lease system, p. 270

medical model, p. 273

penal harm, p. 274

maximum-security prison, p. 276

super-maximum-security prison, p. 278

medium-security prison, p. 279

minimum-security prison, p. 279

boot camp, p. 279

halfway house, p. 280

REVIEW QUESTIONS

1. Would you allow a community correctional center to be built in your neighborhood?

2. Should pretrial detainees and convicted offenders be kept in the same institution?

3. Should inmates be allowed to choose the type of prison in which they serve their sentence?

4. Should private companies be allowed to run correctional institutions?

5. What are the drawbacks to shock incarceration?

6. Should the elderly be housed in the same institutions as younger inmates?

12 Prison Life:
LIVING IN AND LEAVING PRISON

ocked up at the high-security prison in Florence, Colorado, Tommy Silverstein has been held in solitary confinement for the past 27 years.[1] His days are all the same: The lights are always on, and guards slip him food through a slot in his cell door. A few times a week, he is permitted to exercise in the recreation room, and visits with his family and his lawyers are conducted through Plexiglas.

What did Silverstein do to deserve this harsh treatment? Silverstein's life behind bars began in 1978 when as a 26-year-old heroin addict, he was given a 15-year sentence for robbery, crimes he committed with his father. Two years later, Silverstein was convicted of murdering a fellow inmate in a Kansas prison. Moved to a maximum-security prison in Marion, Illinois, he was convicted of murdering two inmates in that prison. But he did not stop there: in 1983, he fatally stabbed 51-year-old prison guard Merle Clutts. This killing prompted a judge to issue a no-contact order, preventing him from being in the room with another human being.

Silverstein, now 58, practices yoga and meditates in his cell, watches TV, crochets, and spends much of his time writing letters. While he does not deny his crimes, he believes his treatment is inhumane and cruel. He says about his treatment:

My experience of extreme seclusion with no human contact or meaningful interpersonal socialization for three decades, I believe, is just one of those things that only I will ever fully comprehend. It has been something so horrifying to the human mind that the only even remote comparable parallel I can imagine is to be literally buried alive, not for a day or a year, but for an entire lifetime.[2]

Inmates like Tommy Silverstein are not unique. There are all too many dangerous people in prison, and their treatment can be harsh and demeaning. Many are being housed in state and federal maximum-security institutions that feature round-the-clock electronic surveillance with little human contact.

REALITY CHECK

MYTH OR REALITY?

- Prison rapes are common, and most inmates are sexually assaulted soon after they arrive in prison.
- Despite negative publicity that "nothing works," many prison rehabilitation efforts are actually effective.
- Inmates lose all civil rights after they enter a high-security correctional facility.

Lizzie Himmel/Sygma/Corbis

Federal Bureau of Prisons

LEARNING OBJECTIVES

L01 Discuss the problems of the adult correctional system

L02 Explain the term *total* institution

L03 Discuss the problem of sexual coercion in prison and what is being done to help

L04 Chart the prisonization process and the development of the inmate social code

L05 Compare the lives and cultures of male and female inmates

L06 Discuss the different forms of correctional treatment

L07 Describe the world of correctional officers

L08 Discuss the causes of prison violence

L09 Explain what is meant by prisoners' rights, and discuss some key privileges that have been granted to inmates

L010 Discuss the parole process and the problems of prisoner reentry

289

Tommy Silverstein

Should inmates who kill guards be given harsher treatment and punishment than those who kill a fellow inmate? Is one life worth more than another? And even if harsh punishment is warranted, is there a tipping point? Is 27 years in solitary confinement overly cruel, even for a multiple murderer?

WEB APP 12.1 You can visit Silverstein's website at **https:// thomassilverstein .wordpress.com/**.

LO1 Discuss the problems of the adult correctional system

total institution A regimented, dehumanizing institution such as a prison, in which inmates are kept in social isolation, cut off from the world at large.

The sad truth is that a majority of inmates return to prison soon after their release. But despite such stories, mass incarceration is still a prominent feature of American corrections. Although the inmate population seems to have stabilized, there are still about 1.6 million people behind bars. As a result of this policy of mass incarceration, the nation has undergone a prison building boom: during the past two decades, the number of state facilities increased from just under 600 to more than 1,000.[3] These facilities take on a variety of forms, including prisons, prison hospitals, prison farms, and boot camps; centers for reception, classification, or alcohol and drug treatment; and work release centers.[4] Not all prisons are brand new: 25 were built before 1875, 79 between 1875 and 1924, and 141 between 1925 and 1949. In fact, some of the first prisons ever constructed, such as the Concord Reformatory in Massachusetts, are still in operation.

More than half of all inmates are held in large, fortress-like maximum-security institutions where overcrowding can be a significant problem. Despite the stabilization of the inmate population, many institutions are operating above stated capacity. Meaningful treatment efforts are often wishful thinking, and recidivism rates are shockingly high; about half of all inmates return within three years of being released on parole.[5] It is not surprising that many inmates are resentful of the deteriorated conditions or that correctional officers fear the consequences of inmate unrest. Rather than deterring people from future criminality, a prison stay may actually reinforce and/or encourage their criminal offending.[6] The typical prison has been described as a "school for crime" in which young offenders are taught by older cons to become sophisticated criminals.

This chapter presents a review of some of the most important issues confronting the nation's correctional system, including inmate life, treatment strategies, inmate legal rights, and release from prison.

Men Imprisoned

Prisons in the United States are **total institutions**. This means that inmates locked within their walls are segregated from the outside world, kept under constant surveillance, and forced to obey strict official rules to avoid facing formal sanctions. Their personal possessions are taken from them, and they must conform to institutional norms of dress and personal appearance. Many human functions are strictly curtailed; heterosexual sex, friendships, family relationships, education, and participation in group activities become privileges of the past.

An inmate's first experience most often occurs in a classification or reception center, where inmates are given a series of psychological and other tests and evaluated on the basis of their personality, background, offense history, and treatment needs. On the basis of the classification they are given, they are assigned to a permanent facility. Hard-core, repeat, and violent offenders will go to the maximum-security unit; white-collar, nondangerous offenders may qualify for a minimum-security facility; mentally disordered offenders will be held in a facility that can provide psychiatric care; and so on. Today, sophisticated classification instruments are being used to maximize the effectiveness of placements, thereby cutting down on the cost of incarceration.[7]

When they arrive at prison, inmates are stripped, searched, shorn, and assigned living quarters. They quickly learn what the term *total institution* really means. Inmate turned author James A. Paluch, Jr., calls his cell a "cold coffin ... leaving a chilling effect on anyone forced to live inside them."[8] Those with extremely long prison sentences—for example, life without parole—may lose hope and develop significant psychological disorders.[9]

Newcomers swiftly discover that all previous concepts of personal privacy and dignity are soon forgotten. Inmates in large, inaccessible prisons may find themselves physically cut off from families, friends, and associates. Visitors may find it difficult to travel great distances to see them; mail is censored and sometimes destroyed. And while incarcerated, inmates are forced to associate with a peer group afflicted with a disproportionate share of mental and physical problems. Various communicable diseases are commonly found, such as hepatitis C virus, HIV, and syphilis. Not surprisingly, inmate health is significantly worse than that of the general population.[10] Personal losses include the deprivation of liberty, goods and services, heterosexual relationships, autonomy, and security.[11] Inmates, even tough guys like Tommy Silverstein, may be subject to verbal and physical attack and threats, with little chance of legal redress. Overcrowded prisons are filled with young, aggressive men who are responsible for the majority of inmate-on-inmate assaults.[12]

Inmates may find that some prisoners have formed cliques, or groups, based on ethnic backgrounds or personal interests; they are also likely to encounter Mafia-like or racial terror groups that must be dealt with. Inmates may find that power in the prison is shared by correctional officers and inmate gangs; the only way to avoid being beaten and raped may be to learn how to beat and rape.

Some prisoners, especially the most vulnerable, become the target of charismatic leaders seeking to recruit them to some cause or group. Angry and embittered by their circumstances and separated from their families, these vulnerable inmates are looking for meaning and identity. Some inmates are so alienated from social life that they fall prey to radical antigovernment groups that have their own hierarchy, code of conduct, secret communication system, and collective identity.

But not all inmates are radicalized or have what it take to join radical cells. If they are weak and unable to defend themselves, new inmates may find that they are considered "punks"; if they ask a guard for help, they are labeled a "snitch." Those most likely to be targets of sexual assaults may spend their sentence in protective custody, sacrificing the "freedom of the yard" and rehabilitation services for personal protection.[13]

LO2 Explain the term *total institution*

Coping in Prison

Despite all these hardships, many inmates learn to adapt to the prison routine. Each prisoner has his own method of coping. He may stay alone, become friends with another inmate, join a group, or seek the advice of treatment personnel. Inmates soon learn that their lifestyle and activities can contribute to their being victimized by more aggressive inmates. The more time they spend in closely guarded activities, the less likely they are to become the victims of violence. The more they isolate themselves from others who might protect them, the greater their vulnerability to attack. The more visitors they receive, the more likely they are to be attacked by fellow inmates jealous of their relationships with the outside world.[14]

Some learn how to fight back to prove they are not people who can be bullied. Older, more experienced men are better able to cope with the prison experience; younger inmates, especially juveniles sent to adult prisons, are more likely to participate in violent episodes.[15]

Men who viewed violence as an acceptable method of settling disputes before entering prison are the ones most likely to use violence while they are inmates.[16] Inmates who have a history of prearrest drug use and have been incarcerated for violent crimes are the ones most likely to get involved in assaults and drug/alcohol offenses while they are incarcerated.[17] Survival in prison may depend on one's ability to identify troubled inmates and avoid contact.

Sexual Coercion

Scott Howard, a 39-year-old federal prisoner, went to Washington to testify before a Congressional committee about his experiences behind bars. During the three years he had spent in Colorado, he was repeatedly raped, assaulted, and extorted by members of a large, notorious gang. The gang was the 211 Crew, a white supremacist group whose leaders pressured him for money and demanded that he help them in an ambitious $300,000 fraud scheme; their threats soon turned into physical attacks, then sexual assaults. He was forced to perform oral sex on gang members and raped repeatedly. Having been housed in other facilities, Howard thought he knew how to keep out of trouble. He'd seen plenty

WEB APP
12.2 To read more about Scott Howard's case, go to **http://www.westword .com/2011-02-03/news/211 -crew-rapes-extorts-scott-howard -colorado-prison/**. Would you advocate a policy of isolating gay men from the general prison population?

of intimidation and gang-related fights at other lockups, but nothing like the atmosphere in Colorado's Fremont Prison where he had been assigned. Prisoners sporting black eyes in the lunch line were a common sight. Members of the 211 Crew commanded their own set of tables in the dining hall, known as the Four Corners, and charged weaker white inmates tribute for the privilege of living in one of "their" units. Howard told the committee, "My efforts to report were mostly fruitless—and often put me at greater risk. I spent well over a year trying to get protection by writing to officials. Because I am openly gay, officials blamed me for the attacks. They said as a homosexual I should expect to be targeted by one gang or another." On his last day as a Colorado prisoner before going to federal prison, he was put in a cell with one of the gang leaders and sexually assaulted. He eventually settled a civil-rights lawsuit against several corrections officials for $165,000.[18] Is it ethical and fair to house a vulnerable inmate such as Scott Howard in the general prison population? But then again, should someone get special housing based on their sexual orientation? If so, should there be a separate wing for gay inmates? Following this logic, should prisons be racially or ethnically segregated?

Scott Howard's experience is certainly not unique: rape and sexual coercion are customary prison behavior. Some inmates will demand regular sexual access in exchange for protection from even more violent rape and beatings. In his shocking memoir, *Fish,* T. J. Parsell writes about how he was sent to prison at age 17 for a robbery (with a toy gun). Parsell was raped on his first night by four older inmates, who then flipped a coin to decide who would "own" him for the rest of his sentence.[19]

Who are the targets of prison sexual violence? Younger inmates, gay men, and bisexual men are selected most often to be targets of sexual assaults.[20] Young males may be raped and kept as sexual slaves by older, more aggressive inmates. When these "slave holders" are released, they often sell their "prison wives" to other inmates.[21] Some inmates will request that regular sexual payments be made to them in exchange for protection from even more violent inmates who threaten rape and beatings.[22] These weaker inmates are called "punks" and put at the bottom of the inmate sexual hierarchy. Straight inmates are more likely to respect "true" homosexuals because they were gay before entering prison and are therefore "true to themselves," while punks are despised because they are weak: they did not want to have sex with other men, but were too weak to resist or not brave enough to stand up to sexual predators. Even "queens," inmates who look and act like women, get more respect than punks because they chose their lifestyle and did not have it forced upon them by others.[23]

HOW COMMON IS PRISON RAPE? While stories of prison rape abound, it has proven difficult to gain an accurate picture of the frequency and prevalence of sexual assault in prison. The most recent national survey employed a sample of about 100,000 inmates, ages 16 and older asking them about nonconsensual sexual acts, abusive sexual contacts, inmate-on-inmate and staff-on-inmate victimization, and level of coercion. The survey found the following:

- An estimated 4.0 percent of state and federal prison inmates and 3 percent of jail inmates reported experiencing one or more incidents of sexual victimization by another inmate or facility staff in the past 12 months or since admission to the facility, if less than 12 months.
- Sexual assault rates reported by prison and jail inmates were higher among females than males, higher among whites than blacks, and higher among inmates with a college degree than those who had not completed high school.
- Some institutions had much higher rates of victimization than others.
- An estimated 1.8 percent of juveniles ages 16 to 17 held in prisons and jails reported being victimized by another inmate, compared to 2.0 percent of adults in prisons and 1.6 percent of adults in jails.
- Among state and federal prison inmates, an estimated 6.3 percent of those identified with serious psychological distress reported that they were sexually victimized by another inmate. In comparison, among prisoners with no indication of mental illness, 0.7 percent reported being victimized by another inmate.[24]

If 4 percent of all inmates were sexually assaulted in the past year, it means that at least 60,000 inmates were victimized. However, this data must be interpreted with caution because many victims may be reluctant to admit to being raped. Some are either too embarrassed to tell anyone or fear harassment by other inmates and further retaliation by their attackers.[25] Others may misunderstand what constitutes a "rape," not considering verbal coercion a form of sexual assault. Some refuse to report rape because they believe nothing can be done. It is not surprising that there is little consistency in estimates of inmate assault: some research efforts indicate that rape is very rare, whereas others find that nearly half of all inmates experience some form of sexual coercion.[26]

One way to avoid these problems is by surveying inmates *after* they are released from prison, thereby removing the threat of coercion that occurs while they are still behind bars. A national survey of released inmates found evidence that prison rape is still a significant problem: about 10 percent former state or local prisoners in America reported being sexually victimized at least once by an inmate or staff member in prison. Just about the same number of former inmates were victimized by staff members as they were by other inmates; any sexual contact between staff and inmate is considered nonconsensual and illegal. About half who reported sexual involvement with a prison staff member said they were offered favors or privileges in exchange, while a third said they were verbally coerced. Gay and bisexual men seemed to be by far the most frequently targeted in prison; 39 percent of gay men and 34 percent of bisexual men reported being sexually victimized by another inmate, while only 3.5 percent of heterosexual men reported incidents.[27]

It is disturbing, to say the least, that inmates are more likely to experience sexual coercion from staff than other inmates.[28] If anything, these data may underreport the problem: most inmates say they are aware of sexual coercion in prison and at least know an inmate who had been raped.[29]

To help correctional administrators better cope with this problem, Congress enacted the Prison Rape Reduction Act of 2003, which established three programs in the Department of Justice:

- A program dedicated to collecting national prison rape statistics, interpreting data, and conducting research
- A program dedicated to the dissemination of information and procedures for combating prison rape
- A program to assist in funding state programs[30]

The Inmate Social Code

For many years, criminal justice experts maintained that inmates formed their own world with a unique set of norms and rules, known as the inmate subculture.[31] A significant aspect of the inmate subculture was a unique inmate social code—unwritten guidelines that expressed the values, attitudes, and type of behavior that older inmates demanded of younger ones. Passed on from one generation of inmates to another, the inmate social code represented the values of interpersonal relations in the prison.

National attention was first drawn to the inmate social code and subculture by Donald Clemmer's classic book *The Prison Community*, in which he presented a detailed sociological study of life in a maximum-security prison.[32] Clemmer was able to identify a unique language, or argot, that prisoners use. He found that prisoners tend to group themselves into cliques on the basis of such personal criteria as sexual preference, political beliefs, and offense history. He found complex sexual relationships in prison and concluded that many heterosexual men turn to homosexual relationships when faced with long sentences and the loneliness of prison life.

Clemmer's most important contribution may have been his identification of the prisonization process. This he defined as the inmate's assimilation into the existing prison culture through acceptance of its language, sexual code, and norms of behavior. Those who become the most "prisonized" are the least likely to reform on the outside.

Using Clemmer's work as a jumping-off point, a number of prominent sociologists have set out to explore more fully the various roles in the prison community. The most important principles of the dominant inmate culture are listed in Exhibit 12.1.

LO3 Discuss the problem of sexual coercion in prison and what is being done to help

inmate subculture The loosely defined culture that pervades prisons and has its own norms, rules, and language.

inmate social code An unwritten code of behavior, passed from older inmates to younger ones, that serves as a guideline to appropriate inmate behavior within the correctional institution.

prisonization Assimilation into the separate culture in the prison that has its own set of rewards and behaviors, as well as its own norms, rules, and language. The traditional prison culture is now being replaced by a violent gang culture.

LO4 Chart the prisonization process and the development of the inmate social code

Although some inmates violate the code and exploit their peers, the "right guy" is someone who uses the inmate social code as his personal behavior guide. He is always loyal to his fellow prisoners, keeps his promises, is dependable and trustworthy, and never interferes with inmates who are conniving against the officials.[33] The right guy does not go around looking for a fight, but he never runs away from one; he acts "like a man."

The effects of prisonization may be long-term and destructive. Many inmates become hostile to the legal system, learning to use violence as a means of solving problems and to value criminal peers.[34] For some, this change may be permanent; for others, it is temporary, and they may revert to their "normal" life after release.

The New Inmate Culture

The importation of outside values into the inmate culture has had a dramatic effect on prison life. Although the old inmate subculture may have been harmful because its norms and values insulated the inmate from change efforts, it also helped create order in the institution and prevented violence among the inmates. People who violated the code and victimized others were sanctioned by their peers. An understanding developed between guards and inmate leaders: the guards would let the inmates have things their own way, and the inmates would not let things get out of hand and draw the attention of the administration.

The old system may be dying or already dead in most institutions. The change seems to have been precipitated by the black power movement in the 1960s and 1970s. Black inmates were no longer content to play a subservient role and challenged the power of established white inmates. As the black power movement gained prominence, racial tension in prisons created divisions that severely altered the inmate subculture. Older, respected inmates could no longer cross racial lines to mediate disputes. Predatory inmates could victimize others without fear of retaliation. Consequently, more inmates than ever are now assigned to protective custody for their own safety.

In the new culture, African American and Latino inmates are much more cohesively organized than whites.[35] Inmates with long histories of delinquent and antisocial behaviors imported their cultural values into prison.[36]

New prison groups formed out of religious or political affiliations, such as the Black Muslims; others out of efforts to combat discrimination in prison, such as the Latino group La Nuestra Familia; or from street gangs, such as the Vice Lords or Gangster Disciples in the Illinois prison system and the Crips in California. Where white inmates have successfully organized, it is in the form of a neo-Nazi groups such as Aryan Brotherhood. Racially homogeneous gangs are so cohesive and powerful that they are able to replace the original inmate code with one of their own.

Women Imprisoned

At the turn of the twentieth century, female inmates were viewed as morally depraved people who flouted conventional rules of female behavior. The treatment of white and African American women differed significantly. In some states, white women were placed in female-only reformatories designed to improve their deportment; black women were placed in male prisons, where they were put on chain gangs and were subject to beatings.[37]

Female Institutions

Women's prisons tend to be smaller than those housing male inmates. Although some female institutions are strictly penal, with steel bars, concrete floors, and other security measures, the majority are nonsecure institutions similar to college dormitories and group homes in the community. Women's facilities, especially those in the community, commonly offer inmates a great deal of autonomy and allow them to make decisions affecting their daily lives.

However, like men's prisons, women's prisons suffer from a lack of adequate training and of health, treatment, and educational facilities. Psychological counseling often takes the form of group sessions conducted by laypeople, such as correctional officers. Many female inmates are mothers and had custody of their children before incarceration, but little effort is made to help them develop better parenting skills. Although most female (and male) inmates have at least one child, less than a quarter actually get an annual visit. Who takes care of these children while their mothers are incarcerated? Most children of incarcerated women are placed with their father, a grandparent, another relative, or a family friend. About 10 percent wind up in foster homes or state facilities.[38]

Job-training opportunities are also a problem. Where vocational training exists, it is in areas that offer limited financial reward, which hinders adjustment upon release. Female inmates, many of whom were on the economic margin before their incarceration began, find little opportunity for improvement during their prison experience.[39] Surveys also indicate that the prison experience does little to prepare women to reenter the workforce after they complete their sentence. Gender stereotypes still shape vocational opportunities.[40] Female inmates are still being trained for "women's roles," such as child-rearing, and are not given the preparation they need to make successful adjustments in the community.[41]

Female Inmates

Like their male counterparts, female inmates are young (most are under age 30), minority group members, unmarried, undereducated (more than half are high school dropouts), and either unemployed or underemployed. The typical woman behind bars is a poor, unskilled woman of color who has small children, has health problems, has a history of abuse, and is incarcerated for low-level drug or property offenses.[42] Recent research shows a high correlation between early experience of abuse and serving a life sentence and that women serving time are much more likely to experience abuse than male inmates.[43] It is not surprising that these conditions also produce high suicide rates in the female prison population.[44] They lack a solid employment history, are in poor physical health, and have a history of financial problems.[45]

Incarcerated women also have had a troubled family life. Significant numbers were at-risk children, products of broken homes and the welfare system; over half have received welfare at some time during their adult lives. Many have been physically or sexually abused at some point in their lives. This pattern continued in adult life: many female inmates were victims of domestic violence. It is not surprising that many display psychological problems.[46]

A significant number of female inmates report having substance abuse problems. About three-fourths have used drugs at some time in their lives, and almost half were involved with addictive drugs, such as cocaine, heroin, or PCP. The incarceration of so many women who are low criminal risks yet face a high risk of exposure to HIV (human immunodeficiency virus, which causes AIDS) and other health threats because of their prior history of drug abuse presents a significant problem. One study of incarcerated women found that one-third of the sample reported that before their arrest, they had traded sex for money or drugs; 24 percent of the women reported trading sex for money or drugs "weekly or more often."[47] Such risky behavior significantly increases the likelihood of their carrying the AIDS virus or other sexually transmitted diseases.

WEB APP 12.3 To read about the problems faced by women in prison, go to the ACLU website at **https://www.aclu.org/prisoners-rights/women-prison.** Should there be a difference in the way men and women are treated in prisons?

Tiffany Schipitz, center, sits with other female inmates during a Prostitution Anonymous meeting at Chicago's Cook County Jail. Schipitz, 35, says she was coerced into prostitution and stayed because of a drug addiction.

AP Images/Martha Irvine

Prison life may be particularly harsh on African American female inmates, who suffer discrimination within the prison setting itself.[48] As Donna Hubbard Spearman, who spent 24 years in prison on drug-related offences, writes:

> African American women are already subjected by a society that places us at the bottom of the totem pole. Within the prison system, not only are we placed at the bottom of the totem pole, but we are considered less than the average inmate. We have a stigma of going back into a community where African American men are almost made martyrs and heroes when they come out of prison ... but when we go back into our communities, we are not only unfit people, now we're unfit mothers, and it's hard to trust us.[49]

The picture that emerges of the female inmate is troubling. After a lifetime of emotional turmoil, physical and sexual abuse, and drug use, it seems improbable that overcrowded, underfunded correctional institutions can forge a dramatic turnaround in the behavior of at-risk female inmates. Many have lost custody of their children, a trauma that is more likely to afflict those who are already substance abusers and suffer from depression.[50] It should come as no surprise that many female inmates feel strain and conflict, which are psychological conditions related to violent episodes.[51]

SEXUAL VIOLENCE IN WOMEN'S PRISONS There are also numerous reports of female prisoners being sexually abused and exploited by male correctional workers who either use brute force or psychological coercion to gain sexual control over inmates. The national survey on sexual abuse found that almost 7 percent of female inmates report being abused by another inmate and 2 percent by a staff member.[52] Staff-on-inmate sexual misconduct covers a wide range of behaviors, from lewd remarks to voyeurism, to assault and rape. Few if any of these incidents are reported, and perpetrators rarely go to trial. Institutional workers cover for each other, and women who file complaints are offered little protection from vengeful guards.[53] Because the situation persists, more than 40 states and the District of Columbia have been forced to pass laws criminalizing some types of staff sexual misconduct in prisons. However, not all sexual liaisons in women's prisons are unwanted, and when Rebecca Trammell conducted interviews with former female inmates, she found that some inmates fight over correctional officers as the only men in their lives. The "relational violence" which may occur is similar to what is commonly described as adolescent behavior.[54]

Adapting to the Female Institution

Many of you have seen the TV series, Orange Is the New Black, that tells the tale of Piper Chapman, a 30-something public relations executive who is sentenced to a year in a minimum-security women's prison in Connecticut for a crime she committed 10 years earlier. Chapman learns how to adjust to life behind bars and actually makes her friends with her fellow inmates, some of whom are street-tough drug users with little education when compared to her own experience at Smith College. Kerman has to endure senseless rules, frequent strip searches and head counts, and boring days. She works as an electrician and starts running on the track. Not the typical prisoner (she is white, educated, and gets family support), she nonetheless finds prison to be not as bad as she at first feared.

Orange Is the new Black may be accurate in that daily life in women's prisons differs somewhat from that in male institutions. As Piper Chapman finds, women usually do not present an immediate physical danger to staff and fellow inmates. Relatively few engage in violent behavior, and incidents of inmate-initiated sexual aggression, so common in male institutions, are rare in women's prisons.[55] Few female inmates experience the violent atmosphere common in male institutions or suffer the same racial and ethnic conflict and divisiveness.[56] However, even though female inmates may not experience the same level of violence as do male inmates, that does not mean their experience is a bed of roses. Many are forced to undergo a process of prison socialization fraught with danger and volatile situations.[57] However, female inmates seem to receive more social support from both internal sources (e.g., inmate peers, correctional staff) and external sources (e.g., families, peers)—a factor that may lessen the pains of prison life, help them adjust, and improve the social climate within female institutions.[58]

The rigid, anti-authority inmate social code found in many male institutions does not exist in female institutions.[59] Confinement for women, however, may produce severe anxiety and anger because of separation from families and loved ones and the inability to function in normal female roles. Unlike men, who direct their anger outward, female prisoners may turn to more self-destructive acts to cope with their problems. Female inmates are more likely than males to mutilate their own bodies and to attempt suicide. For example, one common practice among female inmates is self-mutilation, or "carving." This ranges from simple scratches to carving on their body the name of their boyfriend or even complex statements or sentences ("To mother, with hate").[60]

Another form of adaptation to prison used by women is the make-believe family. This group contains masculine and feminine figures acting as fathers and mothers; some even act as children and take on the role of brother or sister. Formalized marriages and divorces may be conducted. Sometimes one inmate plays multiple roles, such that a "sister" in one family may "marry" and become the "wife" of another inmate. It is estimated that about half of all female inmates are members of make-believe families.

make-believe family In female institutions, the substitute family group—including faux father, mother, and siblings—created by some inmates.

LO5 Compare the lives and cultures of male and female inmates

Correctional Treatment

Almost every prison facility uses some mode of treatment for inmates. This may come in the form of individual or group therapy programs or educational or vocational training. Some inmates are in significant need of services, and it is often difficult to match inmates with the correct treatment assistance.[61] This section presents a number of therapeutic methods that have been used nationally in correctional settings and identifies some of their more salient features.

Individual and Group Treatment

Prison inmates typically suffer from a variety of cognitive and psychosocial deficits, such as poor emotional control, social skills, and interpersonal problem solving; these deficits are often linked to long-term substance abuse. Modern counseling programs help inmates control emotions (e.g., understanding why they feel the way they do, dealing with nervousness or anxiety, solving their problems creatively); communicate with others (e.g., understanding what people tell them, communicating clearly when they write);

deal with legal concerns (e.g., keeping out of legal trouble, avoiding breaking laws); manage general life issues (e.g., finding a job, dealing with difficult coworkers, being a good parent); and develop and maintain social relationships (e.g., having good relations with others, making others happy, making others proud).[62]

To achieve these goals, correctional systems use a variety of intensive individual and group techniques, including behavior modification, aversive therapy, milieu therapy, reality therapy, transactional analysis, and responsibility therapy. Some programs use traditional techniques such as group therapy while others employ nontraditional artistic and spiritual activities, such as visual and performance arts, meditation, and yoga.[63]

ANGER MANAGEMENT Anger and lack of self-control have been linked to violent criminal behavior both in the institution and, upon release, in the community. As a result, anger management programs may be the form of group therapy most frequently offered within prison settings.[64] Anger management is often combined with other group techniques as part of drug treatment and sex offender treatment programs. Cognitive-behavioral approaches are frequently used as a means of helping inmates find ways to control their anger. Anger management or violence management programs have also been implemented in other countries; for example, violence management programs are widely used in Australia.[65]

COGNITIVE BEHAVIORAL THERAPY (CBT) A very popular treatment approach in the correctional setting,[66] cognitive behavioral therapy (CBT) focuses on patterns of thinking and the beliefs, attitudes, and values that underlie thinking. The therapy assumes that most people can become conscious of their own thoughts and behaviors and then make positive changes. A person's thoughts are often the result of experience, and behavior is often influenced and prompted by these thoughts. In addition, thoughts may sometimes become distorted and fail to reflect reality accurately. When used in a correctional setting, the goal of CBT is to restructure distorted thinking and perception, which in turn changes a person's behavior for the better. Characteristics of distorted thinking may include immature or developmentally arrested thoughts; poor problem solving and decision making; an inability to consider the effects of one's behavior; a hampered ability to reason and accept blame for wrongdoing; or an inability to manage feelings of anger. These distorted thinking patterns can lead to making poor decisions and engaging in antisocial behavior to solve problems. People taking part in CBT learn specific skills that can be used to solve the problems they confront all the time as well as skills they can use to achieve legitimate goals and objectives. CBT first concentrates on developing skills to recognize distorted or unrealistic thinking when it happens, and then on changing that thinking or belief to mollify or eliminate problematic behavior.

National evaluations of CBT programs in the prison setting find them highly successful. Cognitive behavioral therapy seems to be more effective with more dangerous, hard-core offenders than with less dangerous clients. The best results occur when higher-risk offenders receive more intensive services that target criminogenic characteristics such as criminal thinking patterns, using cognitive behavioral and social learning approaches.[67]

FAITH-BASED PROGRAMS Research has shown that inmates involved in religious programs and education do better following release than those in comparison groups but that the differences quickly erode.[68] Nonetheless, under the George W. Bush administration, faith-based rehabilitation efforts flourished.[69] In 2003, then-governor Jeb Bush dedicated the first faith-based prison in the United States, a 750-bed medium-security facility for men in Lawtey, Florida.[70] Missouri and Florida also opened facilities for youthful offenders based on faith-based principles.[71] Private institutions are also getting into the mix. In 2014, Corrections Corporation of America (CCA) announced that it now employs chaplains and program facilitators, who offer inmate residents a variety of worship services, faith-based counseling, and religious resources to address practical

cognitive behavioral therapy (CBT) A treatment approach that focuses on patterns of thinking and beliefs to help people become conscious of their own thoughts and behaviors so they can make positive changes.

and spiritual needs. These professionals design and deliver a continuum of care that approaches and treats the inmate as "the total person." By addressing such social problems as addiction, education, and faith in integrative programs and therapeutic living communities, CCA clients are provided with a variety of rehabilitative opportunities.[72]

Although these programs are based on faith or spiritual principles, the study of religious texts or materials and participation in religious services or rituals are not viewed as their central focus. Instead, faith-based programs are more often involved in secular activities such as helping clients gain skills or training, building support networks, and creating a supportive relationship among staff, volunteers, and clients.[73]

Faith-based programs seem to work better with some inmates than others, and those who enter such programs with feelings of self-worth are more likely to complete the course than those with less confidence.[74]

DRUG TREATMENT Many prisons have programs designed to help inmates suffering from alcohol and substance abuse. However, the need for services is overwhelming because about 85 percent of the entire inmate population are addicted to drugs and alcohol, have a history of substance abuse, were under the influence of alcohol or other drugs at the time of their crime, committed their offense to get money to buy drugs, were incarcerated for an alcohol or drug law violation, or shared some combination of these characteristics. Despite this overwhelming need, only about 11 percent of inmates are provided with some form of services.[75]

In the face of this apparent lack of adequate substance abuse treatment, there have been efforts to aid inmates suffering from addiction. One of the first institutions to develop drug treatment, the Federal Bureau of Prisons uses cognitive-behavioral treatment as its centerpiece. This extensive program includes drug abuse education, non-residential drug abuse treatment for short-term offenders, and the Residential Drug Abuse Program (RDAP), in which inmates live in a unit separate from the general population and experience living in a prosocial community. They participate in half-day programming and half-day work, school, or vocational activities. RDAP is typically nine months long. After they leave the institution, drug-involved inmates participate in community treatment services (CTS), which provide continuity of care for offenders placed in Residential Reentry Centers (RRCs) and on home confinement. CTS provides a comprehensive network of contracted community-based treatment providers in all 50 states that provide treatment services to RDAP participants, including treatment for mentally ill offenders and sex offenders, and crisis intervention counseling for situational depression, grief/loss, adjustment issues, and anxiety.[76]

In addition to this federal program, state institutions provide drug programs that sometimes rely on inmate self-help through 12-step groups such as Narcotics Anonymous or Alcoholics Anonymous. Others rely on traditional counseling programs such as cognitive-behavioral counseling. Another approach is to provide abusers with methadone as a substitute for heroin; some evaluations have shown this method to be effective.[77] Because substance abuse is so prevalent among correctional clients, some correctional facilities have been reformulated into **therapeutic communities** (TC) that apply a psychosocial, experiential learning process and rely on positive peer pressure within a highly structured social environment. The community itself, including staff and program participants, becomes the primary method of change. They work together as members of a "family" to create a culture where community members confront each other's negative behavior and attitudes and establish an open, trusting, and safe environment. The TC approach, then, relies on mutual self-help. It also encourages personal disclosure rather than the isolation of the general prison culture.[78]

Treating substance-abusing offenders has proven difficult. Even such highly touted programs as CBT and the TC approach have yielded mixed results: some evaluations have found clients in these programs are just as likely to recidivate as those in the general population.[79] Nonetheless, success rates may be masked by the way individual programs are administered and the effectiveness of treatment delivery. For example, evidence suggests that those inmates who successfully complete TC programs have significantly

therapeutic communities Institutions that rely on positive peer pressure within a highly structured social environment to create positive inmate change.

lower recidivism rates than nonattendees and are more likely to seek treatment after they return to the community. In addition, when run correctly, TC programs seem effective in reducing rearrest and reincarceration rates.[80]

HIV/AIDS TREATMENT The AIDS-infected inmate has been the subject of great concern. Two groups of people at high risk of contracting HIV are intravenous drug users who share needles and males who engage in same-sex relations—two behaviors common in prison. Because drug use is common and syringes scarce, many high-risk inmates share drug paraphernalia, increasing the danger of HIV infection.[81] Although the numbers are constantly changing, the rate of HIV infection among state and federal prisoners has stabilized at around 2 percent, and there are about 25,000 HIV-infected inmates.

Correctional administrators have found it difficult to arrive at effective policies to confront AIDS. Although all state and federal jurisdictions do some AIDS testing, only the Federal Bureau of Prisons and relatively few states conduct mass screenings of all inmates. Most states test inmates only if there are significant indications that they are HIV-positive.

Most correctional systems are now training staff about AIDS. Educational programs for inmates are often inadequate because administrators are reluctant to give them information on safe sex and the proper cleaning of drug paraphernalia (both sexual relations and drug use are forbidden in prison).

Educational Programs

Besides programs stressing personal growth through individual analysis or group therapy, inmate rehabilitation is also pursued through vocational and educational training. Although these two kinds of training sometimes differ in style and content, they can also overlap when, for example, education involves practical, job-related study.

The first prison treatment programs were in fact educational. A prison school was opened at the Walnut Street Jail in 1784. Elementary courses were offered in New York's prison system in 1801 and in Pennsylvania's in 1844. An actual school system was established in Detroit's House of Corrections in 1870, and the Elmira Reformatory opened a vocational trade school in 1876. Today, most institutions provide some type of educational program. At some prisons, inmates can obtain a high school diploma or a general educational development (GED) certificate through equivalency exams. Other institutions provide an actual classroom education, usually staffed by certified teachers employed full time at the prison or by part-time teachers who also teach full time at nearby public schools.

Educational programs vary in quality and intensity. Some are full-time programs employing highly qualified and concerned educators, whereas others are part-time programs without any real goals or objectives. In some institutions, programs have been designed to circumvent the difficulties inherent in the prison structure. They encourage volunteers from the community and local schools to tutor willing and motivated inmates. Some prison administrators have arranged flexible schedules for inmate students and actively encourage their participation in these programs. In several states, statewide school districts serving prisons have been created. Forming such districts can make better-qualified staff available and provide the materials and resources necessary for meaningful educational programs.

Most research indicates that participation in correctional education programs has benefits both in and out of prisons. Karen Lahm found that inmates who take part in GED, high school, vocational, and/or college programs report much fewer rule violations while incarcerated than those who ignore educational opportunities.[82] Participation in prison-based education produces higher postrelease earnings and employment rates, especially for minority inmates.[83] However, the results of prison education on recidivism are a mixed bag: some studies show a positive effect, while others find little or no relationship.[84]

Educational programs are offered in most correctional facilities. Here Simone Taylor, 25, receives her high school diploma from School Board Vice President Linda Young during a graduation ceremony at Nevada's Florence McClure Women's Correctional Center. More than 70 female inmates at Nevada's only women's prison earn their high school diplomas, GEDs, and vocational certificates each year from the Clark County School District's adult education program.

Vocational Programs

Every state correctional system also has some job-related services for inmates. Some have elaborate training programs inside the institution, whereas others have instituted prerelease and postrelease employment services. Inmates who hope to obtain parole need to participate in prison industry. Documenting a history of stable employment in prison is essential if parole agents are to convince prospective employers that the ex-offender is a good risk, and postrelease employment is usually required for parole eligibility.[85]

A few of the more important work-related services are discussed in the following sections.

VOCATIONAL TRAINING Most institutions provide vocational training programs. On the federal level, the Federal Prison Industries, which is more commonly known as UNICOR, teaches inmates to produce goods and services for government use such as clothing and textiles, industrial products, and office furniture. UNICOR sales average about $800 million a year and yield a profit of $120 million a year—making UNICOR the most profitable line of business in the United States.[86]

Despite the promising aspects of such programs, they have also been seriously criticized. Inmates often have trouble finding skill-related, high-paying jobs upon their release. Equipment in prisons is often secondhand, obsolete, and hard to come by. Some programs are thinly disguised excuses for prison upkeep and maintenance, and unions and other groups resent the intrusion of prison labor into their markets.

WORK RELEASE To supplement programs stressing rehabilitation via in-house job training or education, more than 40 states have attempted to implement work release or furlough programs. These allow deserving inmates to leave the institution and hold regular jobs in the community.

Inmates enrolled in work release may live at the institutions at night while working in the community during the day. However, security problems (e.g., contraband may be brought in) and the usual remoteness of prisons often make this arrangement difficult. More typical is the extended work release, where prisoners are allowed to remain in the community for significant periods of time. To help inmates adjust, some states operate community-based prerelease centers where inmates live while working. Some inmates may work at their previous jobs, whereas others seek new employment.

work release A prison treatment program that allows inmates to be released during the day to work in the community and then return to prison at night.

furlough A correctional policy that allows inmates to leave the institution for vocational or educational training, for employment, or to maintain family ties.

Work release programs have proven to be a mixed bag as well. On the one hand, inmates are sometimes reluctantly received in the community and find that certain areas of employment are closed to them. Citizens are often concerned about prisoners "stealing" jobs or working for lower than normal wages; consequently, such practices are prohibited by Public Law 89-176, which controls the federal work release program. On the other hand, inmates gain many benefits from work release, including the ability to maintain work skills, maintain community ties, and make an easier transition from prison to the outside world. For those who have learned a skill in the institution, work release offers an excellent opportunity to try out a new occupation. For others, the job may be a training situation in which new skills are acquired. A number of states have reported that few work release inmates abscond while in the community.

PRIVATE PRISON ENTERPRISE The federal government helped put private industry into prisons when it approved the Free Venture Program in 1976. Seven states, including Connecticut, South Carolina, and Minnesota, were given grants to implement private industries inside prison walls.

Today, private prison industries use a number of models. One approach, the state-use model, makes the correctional system a supplier of goods and services that serves state-run institutions.[87] In another approach, the free-enterprise model, private companies set up manufacturing units on prison grounds or purchase goods made by inmates in shops owned and operated by the corrections department. In the corporate model, a semi-independent business is created on prison grounds, and its profits go to the state government and inmate laborers.

POSTRELEASE PROGRAMS Vocational programming also involves helping inmates obtain jobs before they are released and keep them after they are on the outside. A number of correctional departments have set up employment services designed to ease the transition between institution and community. Employment program staff assess inmates' backgrounds to determine their abilities, interests, goals, and capabilities. They also help them create job plans essential to receiving early release (parole) and successfully reintegrating into the community. Some programs maintain community correctional placements in sheltered environments that help inmates bridge the gap between institutions and the outside world. Services include job placement, skill development, family counseling, and legal and medical assistance.

Can Rehabilitation Work?

Despite the variety and number of treatment programs in operation, questions remain about their effectiveness. In an oft-cited research effort, Robert Martinson and his associates (1975) found that a majority of treatment programs were failures, giving birth to the cry that "nothing works" in prison rehabilitation.[88] Martinson's work created considerable debate over the effectiveness of correctional treatment. Even some of the most carefully crafted treatment efforts, using the most up-to-date rehabilitation modalities (such as CBT), failed to have a positive impact on inmates returning to the community, a finding that supports the "nothing works" mantra.[89]

Treatment proponents have dismissed the "nothing works" philosophy as exaggerated and, using sophisticated data analysis techniques, have found evidence that correctional rehabilitation can be effective.[90] When Paul Gendreau and Robert Ross reviewed the published work on correctional rehabilitation programs, they found that many intervention programs reported success.[91] More recently, Mark Lipsey and Francis Cullen's comprehensive review of the studies of correctional rehabilitation found consistently positive effects on reducing recidivism. Success seems to rely on the type of treatment, its implementation, and the nature of the offenders to whom it is applied.[92]

Correctional Officers

Controlling a prison is a complex task. On the one hand, a tough, high-security environment may meet the goals of punishment and control but fail to reinforce positive behavior changes. On the other hand, too liberal an administrative stance can lower staff morale and place inmates in charge of the institution. For many years, prison guards were viewed as ruthless people who enjoyed their power over inmates, fought rehabilitation efforts, were racist, and had a "lock psychosis" developed from years of counting, numbering, and checking on inmates. This view has changed in recent years. Correctional officers are now viewed as public servants who are seeking the security and financial rewards of a civil service position.[93] Most are in favor of rehabilitation efforts and do not harbor any particular animosity toward the inmates.[94] The correctional officer has been characterized as a "people worker" who must be prepared to deal with the problems of inmates on a personal level and also as a member of a complex bureaucracy who must be able to cope with the demands of an evolving inmate population. For example, with the increasing population of older inmates, correctional officers must now be able to recognize impairment in prison, assess the effects of dementia, recognize the special needs of older prisoners, and work in geriatric housing units.[95]

What are the most significant problems faced by correctional workers today? Those forced to work in facilities that are underfunded, understaffed, and crowded report high levels of stress and impaired job performance due to understaffing and overwork. Research shows that officers at the most crowded prisons are most stressed and fearful of inmates.[96]

Another problem faced by correctional officers is probably the stress created by the duality of their role: maintainers of order and security *and* advocates of treatment and rehabilitation.[97] Eric Lambert and his associates found that the stress of the prison experience can lead to emotional exhaustion, a powerful dimension of job burnout, which if left unchecked is associated with high levels of turnover, absenteeism, and general job dissatisfaction.[98]

Although these problems are significant, correctional officers who have high levels of job satisfaction, good relations with their coworkers, and high levels of social support seem to be better able to deal with the stress of the correctional setting.[99] The most successful officers can have a sizable impact on a prisoner's ability to adjust to prison life. Correctional staff members who conduct themselves professionally and gain the respect and cooperation of the inmates are able to have a very positive influence on their later readjustment to society.[100]

CAREERS IN CRIMINAL JUSTICE CORRECTIONAL OFFICER

Duties and Characteristics of the Job

- The primary job of a correctional officer is to supervise individuals who are serving time in prison after being convicted.

- Their duties include supervising and submitting reports on inmate behavior, maintaining order within the population by enforcing institutional rules and policies, and ensuring order in the institution by searching for contraband or settling disputes between inmates.

- Although correctional officers tend to work a standard 5-day, 40-hour work week, odds are they will work overtime on weekends, holidays, and nights as well, because jails and prisons must be staffed at all hours.

Job Outlook

- Opportunities exist for employment at the local level, but a majority of correctional officer positions are at state and federal prisons. A smaller number of jobs are available with private institutions.

- Thanks to a growing demand for correctional officers, combined with high rates of turnover within the field, prospects for employment are very good.

- A good correctional officer with the proper education and training has the potential to be promoted to correctional sergeant and to other administrative and supervisory positions.

Salary

- Median annual salary for a correctional officer is about $39,000 per year or about $19 per hour.

- Median annual earnings in the public sector were recently $47,750 in the federal government, $36,140 in state government, and $34,820 in local government.

- Correctional officers usually are provided with uniforms or a clothing allowance to purchase their own uniforms. Their retirement coverage entitles correctional officers to retire at age 50 after 20 years of service or at any age with 25 years of service.

Qualifications

- Exact qualifications vary depending on what level of government and what type of setting the position is in.

(Continued)

- A majority of correctional institutions look for several characteristics in potential employees: correctional officers should be US citizens, be at least 18 to 21 years old, and be able to pass a background check and a drug test.

- Correctional officers must also be in good physical and mental health, meet education requirements, and be able to work in a challenging environment where good judgment and quick thinking are necessary.

- Tests may be administered to judge whether an applicant meets these qualifications.

Education and Training

- Although only a high school diploma may be necessary to become a correctional officer, a bachelor's degree (especially in a field such as criminology, sociology, or criminal justice) will make career advancement easier and can greatly increase annual salary.

- After hiring and training, there may be a period of on-the-job training with an experienced officer.

- At the federal level, a bachelor's degree or three years of experience in a related occupation is necessary for employment.

- Federal corrections officers will have at least 200 hours of on-the-job training and a period of training at the Federal Bureau of Prisons.

Reality Check

- Correctional officers are forced to routinely deal with, and sometimes restrain, people who suffer from HIV, hepatitis B and C, tuberculosis, and other contagious diseases.

- Officers are in danger of physical harm from prison-made weapons.

- When conducting body or cell searches, correction officers are in danger of being jabbed or cut by a piece of contraband.

- Officers must control mentally ill inmates.

- Officers are subject to taunts and verbal harassment.

Source: Bureau of Labor Statistics, *Correctional Officers*, 2013, http://www.bls.gov/ooh /Protective-Service/Correctional-officers.htm (accessed March 2013).

For more on the work of a correctional officer, read the Careers in Criminal Justice feature.

Female Correctional Officers

Women now work side by side with male guards in almost every state, performing the same duties. Research indicates that discipline has not suffered because of the inclusion of women in the guard force. Sexual assaults have been rare, and more negative attitudes have been expressed by the female guards' male peers than by inmates. Most commentators believe that the presence of female guards can have an important beneficial effect on the self-image of inmates and can improve the guard–inmate working relationship.

Ironically, female correctional officers may find that an assignment to a male institution can boost their career. Recent restrictions on male staff in female institutions, in the

A cell extraction team prepares to enter a prisoner's cell where a prisoner is not obeying orders. All prisons have special units of correction officers who enter cells and use physical force to subdue prisoners who do not obey verbal commands.

Andrew Lichtenstein/Corbis News/Corbis

wake of well-publicized sex scandals, have forced administrators to assign women officers to the dormitory areas, the least desirable areas in which to work. Women officers are not similarly restricted in male-only facilities.[101]

L07 Describe the world of correctional officers

Prison Violence

Conflict, violence, and brutality are sad but ever-present facts of institutional life. Violence can involve individual conflict: inmate versus inmate, inmate versus staff, and staff versus inmate. Nonsexual assaults may stem from an aggressor's desire to shake down the victim for money and personal favors, may be motivated by racial conflict, or may simply be used to establish power within the institution. For example, a riot on May 20, 2012, at the Adams County Correctional Center in southwest Mississippi led to the death of one correctional officer and injuries to five other officers and three inmates.[102] The suspected cause was gang conflict.

Violence can also involve large groups of inmates, such as the infamous Attica riot in 1971, which claimed 39 lives, or the New Mexico State Penitentiary riot of February 1980, in which the death toll was 33. More than 300 prison riots have occurred since the first one in 1774; 90 percent have occurred since 1952.[103]

What Causes Violence?

What are the causes of prison violence? There is no single explanation for either collective or individual violence, although theories abound.[104] However, research by Benjamin Steiner shows that factors related to prison administration, inmate population characteristics, and the racial makeup of inmates and staff can influence violence levels.[105] Some of the factors related to individual and collective violence, respectively, are discussed in some detail next.

INDIVIDUAL VIOLENCE

- *History of prior violence.* Before they were incarcerated, many inmates were violence-prone individuals who always used force to get their own way. Some are former gang members who join inmate gangs as soon as they enter the institution.[106] In many instances, street gangs maintain prison branches that unite the inmate with his former violence-prone peers.[107] Although the association between a history of violence and aggression behind bars is significant, some recent research by Jon Sorenson and Mark Cunningham found that people convicted of murder are no more violent than other members of the inmate population. Their finding is important because it runs counter to the argument that murderers are dangerous people with a "propensity for murder." Sorenson and Cunningham's conclusion that a murder conviction is not any greater predictor of prison violence than a conviction for some other offense counters an important argument for the use of capital punishment.[108]

- *Age.* Younger inmates, those with a record of prior incarceration, and those who have suffered prearrest drug use are the ones most likely to engage in disruptive behavior in prison, especially if they are not active participants in institutional treatment programs.[109] Sadly, juvenile offenders who are sentenced to adult institutions have significantly higher violence rates than the adult inmate population.[110] Although it may be puzzling to some that inmates convicted of murder seem no more violent behind bars than the next inmate, it is possible that these may be older inmates who have learned from experience to "do their own time."[111]

- *Psychological factors.* Many inmates suffer from personality disorders. Research shows that among institutionalized offenders, psychopathy is the strongest predictor of violent recidivism and indifferent response to treatment.[112] In the crowded, dehumanizing world of the prison, it is not surprising that people with extreme psychological distress may resort to violence to dominate others.[113]

- *Prison conditions.* The prison experience itself causes people to become violent. Inhuman conditions, including overcrowding, depersonalization, and the threat of sexual assault, are violence-producing conditions.[114] Research shows that violence rates may be higher in the most run-down and unwholesome prisons.[115] Even in the most humane prisons, life is a constant put-down, and prison conditions are a threat to the inmates' sense of self-worth; violence is an expected consequence of these conditions. Violence levels are not much different between high-security and low-security prisons, suggesting that the prison experience itself, and not the level of control, produces violence.[116] The converse is also true: effective interventions can help reduce violence in even the most disruptive inmates, especially those who begin to realize that repeat violent incidents are punished by long-term stays in segregation and other negative consequences.[117]

- *Lack of dispute-resolution mechanisms.* Many prisons lack effective mechanisms for handling inmate grievances against either prison officials or other inmates fairly and equitably. Prisoners who complain about other inmates are viewed as "rats" or "snitches" and are marked for death by their enemies. Similarly, inmates' complaints or lawsuits filed against the prison administration may result in their being placed in solitary confinement—"the hole."

- *Basic survival.* Inmates resort to violence to survive. The lack of physical security, the dearth of adequate mechanisms for resolving complaints, and the code of silence promote individual violence by inmates who might otherwise be effectively controlled.

COLLECTIVE VIOLENCE

- *Inmate-balance theory.* Riots and other forms of collective violence occur when prison officials make an abrupt effort to take control of the prison and limit freedoms. Crackdowns occur when officials perceive that inmate leaders have too much power and take measures to control their illicit privileges, such as gambling or stealing food.[118]

- *Administrative-control theory.* Collective violence is caused by prison mismanagement, lack of strong security, and inadequate control by prison officials. Poor management may inhibit conflict management and set the stage for violence. Repressive administrations give inmates the feeling that nothing will ever change, that they have nothing to lose, and that violence is the only means for change.

Despite these problems, both the suicide rate and the homicide rate in prisons have been in sharp decline. Although it is difficult to determine the cause of this drop in violence directed at self and others, more advanced security measures coupled with improved prison administration may be responsible.

L08 Discuss the causes of prison violence

In 2015, correction officers work in the Enhanced Supervision Housing Unit at Manhattan's Rikers Island Correctional Facility. The jail has been the scene of considerable violence so the New York City correctional department is implementing a plan to reduce violence among inmates by limiting visitors, adding security cameras, and separating rival gangs.

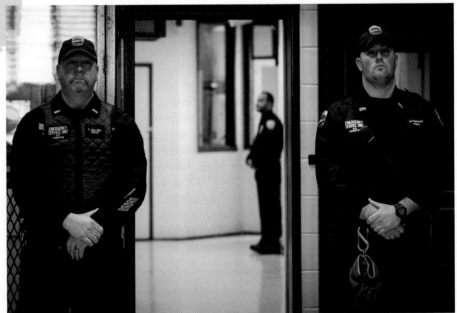

Brendan Mcdermid/Reuters /Landov

Prisoners' Rights

Before the early 1960s, it was accepted that upon conviction, an individual forfeited all rights not expressly granted by statutory law or correctional policy; in other words, inmates were civilly dead. The US Supreme Court held that convicted offenders should expect to be penalized for their misdeeds and that part of their punishment was the loss of freedoms that law-abiding citizens take for granted.

One reason why inmates lacked rights was that state and federal courts were reluctant to intervene in the administration of prisons unless the circumstances of a case clearly indicated a serious breach of the Eighth Amendment protection against cruel and unusual punishment. This judicial policy is referred to as the hands-off doctrine.

As the 1960s drew to a close, the hands-off doctrine was eroded. Federal district courts began seriously considering prisoners' claims about conditions in the various state and federal institutions and used their power to intervene on behalf of the inmates. In some ways, this concern reflected the spirit of the times, which saw the onset of the civil rights movement, and subsequently emerged in the areas of student rights, public welfare, mental institutions, juvenile court systems, and military justice.

Beginning in the late 1960s, such activist groups as the NAACP Legal Defense Fund and the ACLU's National Prison Project began to search for appropriate legal vehicles to bring prisoners' complaints before state and federal courts. The most widely used device was the federal Civil Rights Act, 42 U.S.C. 1983:

> Every person who, under color of any statute, ordinance, regulation, custom, or usage of any State or Territory subjects, or causes to be subjected, any citizen of the United States or other person within the jurisdiction thereof to the deprivation of any rights, privileges, or immunities secured by the Constitution and laws shall be liable to the party injured in an action at law, suit in equity, or other proper proceeding for redress.

The legal argument went that, as US citizens, prison inmates could sue state officials if their civil rights were violated—for example, if they were the victims of racial or religious discrimination.

The subsequent prisoners' rights crusade, stretching from 1964 to 1980, paralleled the civil rights and women's movements. Battle lines were drawn between prison officials, who hoped to maintain their power and resented interference by the courts, and inmate groups and their sympathizers, who used state and federal courts as a forum for demanding better living conditions and personal rights.

To slow down prison litigation, which had been clogging the federal courts, Congress passed the Prison Litigation Reform Act in 1996.[119] The most important provision of the act requires prisoners to exhaust all internal administrative grievance procedures before they can file a civil rights case in federal court. It also bars litigation if a prisoner has not suffered a physical injury in addition to a violation of his or her constitutional rights. There is a limitation on the number of times an appeal can be filed: If a judge decides that it is frivolous, malicious, or does not state a proper claim, it counts as a "strike." After you get three strikes, another lawsuit cannot be filed unless the inmate is willing to pay the entire court filing fee up-front. The US Supreme Court has upheld the provisions of the act in two cases—one dealing with a request for monetary relief and the other with allegations of excessive use of force—*Booth v. Churner* (2001) and *Porter v. Nussle* (2002), respectively, in which the Court ruled that it is constitutional to require that an inmate go through all administrative processes before a case can be brought to the courts.[120] Civil rights groups believe that these cases have a chilling effect on inmate litigation.[121]

Although the prisoners' rights movement may have slowed, it has not ended. Some of the most important substantive and procedural rights of inmates are discussed next.

Substantive Rights

Through a slow process of legal review, the courts have granted inmates a number of substantive rights that have significantly influenced the entire correctional system. The most important of these rights are discussed in the following sections.

hands-off doctrine The legal practice of allowing prison administrators a free hand to run the institution, even if correctional practices violate inmates' constitutional rights; ended with the onset of the prisoners' rights movement in the 1960s.

substantive rights A number of civil rights that the courts, through a slow process of legal review, have established for inmates, including the rights to receive mail and medical benefits and to practice their religion.

ACCESS TO COURTS, LEGAL SERVICES, AND MATERIALS Courts have held that inmates are entitled to have legal materials available and must be provided with assistance in drawing up and filing complaints. Inmates who help others, so-called jailhouse lawyers, cannot be interfered with or harassed by prison administrators.

FREEDOM OF THE PRESS AND OF EXPRESSION Courts have consistently ruled that only when a compelling state interest exists can prisoners' First Amendment rights be modified; correctional authorities must justify the limiting of free speech by showing that granting it would threaten institutional security. If prison administrators believe that correspondence undermines prison security, the First Amendment rights of inmates can be curtailed.[122]

FREEDOM OF RELIGION The Supreme Court has ruled that inmates have the right to assemble and pray in the religion of their choice, even if the religions are not mainstream such as Wiccan or Satanism.[123] There are some exceptions, for example, if religious prisoners receive favored treatment, or if religious exercise and security concerns are not properly balanced. Therefore, religious symbols and practices that interfere with institutional security can be restricted. Administrators can draw the line if responding to religious needs becomes cumbersome or impossible for reasons of cost or security.

The 2015 case of *Holt v. Hobbs* illustrates how the line between religious and institutional security can become blurred. Gregory Holt, an Arkansas inmate who had converted to the Muslim religion and changed his name to Abdul Muhammad, was denied the ability to grow the half-inch beard that his Muslim faith commanded because prison officials were afraid that contraband such as razor blades, drugs, homemade darts, and SIM cards for cell phones could be hidden in beards. After numerous appeals in lower courts, the Supreme Court took the case. Writing for the majority, Justice Alito found that Muhammad had "easily satisfied" the requirement of showing that the ban on beards burdened his religious practices. He discounted the allegation that security "would be seriously compromised by allowing an inmate to grow a half-inch beard is hard to take seriously." He went on to say "An item of contraband would have to be very small indeed to be concealed by a half-inch beard," he wrote, "and a prisoner seeking to hide an item in such a short beard would have to find a way to prevent the item from falling out." In this case the right to religious freedom won out over the need for prison security.

MEDICAL RIGHTS In early prisons, inmates' right to medical treatment was restricted through the "exceptional circumstances doctrine." Using this policy, the courts would hear only those cases in which the circumstances revealed utter disregard for human dignity, while denying hearings to less serious cases. The cases that were allowed access to the courts usually entailed total denial of medical care.

To gain their medical rights, prisoners have resorted to class-action suits (suits brought on behalf of all individuals affected by similar circumstances—in this case, poor medical attention). In the most significant case, *Newman v. Alabama* (1972), the entire Alabama prison system's medical facilities were declared inadequate.[124] The Supreme Court cited the following factors as contributing to inadequate care: insufficient physician and nurse resources, reliance on untrained inmates for paramedical work, intentional failure in treating the sick and injured, and failure to conform to proper medical standards. The *Newman* case forced corrections departments to upgrade prison medical facilities.

It was not until 1976, in *Estelle v. Gamble,* that the Supreme Court clearly affirmed inmates' right to medical care.[125] Gamble had hurt his back in a Texas prison and filed suit because he contested the type of treatment he had received and questioned the lack of interest that prison guards had shown in his case. The Supreme Court said, "Deliberate indifference to serious medical needs of prisoners constitutes the 'unnecessary and wanton infliction of pain,' proscribed by the Eighth Amendment."[126] The *Gamble* ruling mandated that inmate health care reflect what is available to citizens in the general community. Consequently, correctional administrators must consider access, quality, and cost of health care as part of the prison regime.[127]

CRUEL AND UNUSUAL PUNISHMENT The concept of cruel and unusual punishment is founded in the Eighth Amendment of the Constitution. The term itself has not been specifically defined by the Supreme Court, but the Court has held that treatment constitutes cruel and unusual punishment when it does the following:

- Degrades the dignity of human beings[128]
- Is more severe than (is disproportional to) the offense for which it has been given[129]
- Shocks the general conscience and is fundamentally unfair[130]
- Is deliberately indifferent to a person's safety and well-being[131]
- Punishes people because of their status, such as race, religion, and mental state[132]
- Is in flagrant disregard of due process of law, such as punishment that is capriciously applied[133]

State and federal courts have placed strict limits on disciplinary methods that may be considered inhumane. Corporal punishment all but ended after the practice was condemned in *Jackson v. Bishop* (1968).[134] Although the solitary confinement of disruptive inmates continues, its prolonged use under barbaric conditions has been held to be in violation of the Eighth Amendment. Courts have found that inmates placed in solitary have the right to adequate personal hygiene; to exercise, mattresses, and ventilation; and to rules specifying how they can earn their release.

RACIAL SEGREGATION In the 2005 case *Johnson v. California,* the Supreme Court ruled that the segregation of prison inmates based on race, in their cells or anywhere on prison grounds, is an inappropriate form of racial classification.[135] However, it left it open for lower courts to decide, using a standard of *strict scrutiny,* when segregation is inappropriate and unconstitutional. *Johnson* focused on the policy of segregating inmates upon their arrival at a prison. However, the Court's ruling seemed to suggest that if racial segregation was allowed for incoming inmates, there is a danger that it might also be used "in the dining halls, yards, and general housing areas." Segregation should only be allowed, the judges reasoned, if a prison administrator could prove that it served a compelling interest to promote prison safety. The Court recognized that "prisons are dangerous places, and the special circumstances they present may justify racial classifications in some contexts."

ETHICAL REFLECTION

Tommy Silverstein

Is it ethical for someone like Tommy Silverstein to sue the state for cruel and unusual punishment because he is being held in long-term isolation? Shouldn't the state maintain the right to protect personnel and inmates from someone who is a multiple murderer? Does a court have the right to overrule administrative decision making when safety is the issue?

cruel and unusual punishment
Physical punishment or punishment that is far in excess of that given to people under similar circumstances and is therefore banned by the Eighth Amendment. The death penalty has so far not been considered cruel and unusual if it is administered in a fair and nondiscriminatory fashion.

REALITY CHECK

MYTH OR REALITY?

Inmates lose all civil rights after they enter a high-security correctional facility.

MYTH. Inmates retain many civil rights, even behind prison walls.

Should inmates maintain all civil rights, including the right to vote or to give press interviews, while in prison? Is it ethical to allow nonlawyers to help inmates prepare cases?

Inmates have the right to bring their legal issues to court. Here Rene Lima-Marin stands in a room waiting to be searched by a guard as per procedure before returning to his cell following an interview with The Associated Press about the circumstances of his sentencing and incarceration, inside Kit Carson Correctional Center, a privately operated prison in Burlington, Colorado. Lima-Marin, who was sent back to prison after being mistakenly released six years earlier, says it was cruel and unusual punishment to put him back behind bars after he reformed his life. An appeal filed in his case also states that his constitutional rights were violated when a judge ordered him to finish his sentence after he started a family during nearly six years of freedom. A judge in 2000 sentenced Lima-Marin to a total of 98 years in prison for multiple counts stemming from the robbery of two video stores when Lima-Marin was 20. Should someone like Lima-Marin be forced back into prison despite the fact that he appears to be rehabilitated?

AP Images/Brennan Linsley

Because a riot occurred in Chino prison after California began to integrate prison entry centers, it is possible that future efforts to racially integrate prisons will be frustrated. State courts, even when using a strict scrutiny standard, may conclude that racial integration is just too dangerous in some instances.

OVERALL PRISON CONDITIONS Prisoners have long had the right to the minimal conditions necessary for human survival, such as food, clothing, shelter, and medical care. A number of attempts have been made to articulate reasonable standards of prison care and to make sure that officials adhere to them. Courts have held that although people are sent to prison for punishment, it does not mean that prison should be a punishing experience.[136] In the 1994 case of *Farmer v. Brennan,* the court ruled that prison officials are legally liable if, knowing that an inmate faces a serious risk of harm, they disregard that risk by failing to take measures to avoid or reduce it. Furthermore, prison officials should be able to infer the risk from the evidence at hand; they need not be warned or told.[137]

Although inmates retain the right to reasonable care, if there is a legitimate purpose for the use of governmental restrictions, those restrictions may be considered constitutional. Thus, it might be possible to restrict reading material, allow strip searches, and prohibit inmates from receiving packages from the outside if the restrictions are legitimate security measures. If overcrowded conditions require it, inmates may be double-bunked in cells designed for a single inmate.[138]

parole The early release of a prisoner from imprisonment, subject to conditions set by a parole board.

Parole board A panel of people who decide whether an offender should be released from prison on **parole** after serving the minimum portion of their sentence ordered by the sentencing judge.

Leaving Prison: Parole

At the expiration of their prison term, most inmates return to society and try to resume their lives. For some inmates, their reintegration into society comes by way of parole—the planned community release and supervision of incarcerated offenders before the expiration of their full prison sentences. Once on parole, former inmates have to live by a strict set of rules that mandate they stay out of trouble, stay drug and alcohol free, be employed, and attend counseling. Parolees are monitored by their case officers, who may administer random drug tests and use GPS tracking devices to keep tabs on their whereabouts.[139]

In some states, parole is granted by a parole board, a duly constituted body of men and women who review inmate cases and determine whether offenders have reached a rehabilitative level sufficient to deal with the outside world. The board also dictates what specific parole rules parolees must obey. Most boards are independent agencies that consist of members appointed by the governor; the rest are affiliated with the Department of Corrections. A majority have the authority to make final release decisions; most require interviews with parole-eligible offenders prior to release. A majority of parole boards also set the rules of parole and are given the power to revoke parole when these rules are violated or the parolee commits another crime.[140]

In a number of jurisdictions, discretionary parole has been abandoned, and the amount of time a person must remain in prison is a predetermined percentage of the sentence, assuming there are no infractions or escape attempts. In this "mandatory parole release" approach, the inmate is released when the unserved portion of the maximum prison term equals his or her earned good time (minus time served in jail awaiting trial). In some states, sentences can be reduced by more than half with a combination of statutory and earned good time. If the conditions of their release are violated, mandatory releasees can have their good time revoked and be returned to the institution to serve the remainder of their unexpired term. The remaining inmates are released for a variety of reasons, including expiration of their term, commutation of their sentence, and court orders to relieve overcrowded prisons. The use of discretionary parole has been in steep decline, while the number of inmates released on mandatory parole has increased significantly. More than 850,000 people are currently on parole. However, like the prison population itself, the number of people on parole has finally stabilized, reversing years of increases upward.[141]

Is There a Legal Right to Parole?

What happens if the parole authority denies early release, but the inmate believes he is deserving of parole? Perhaps he has witnessed other inmates receiving parole who have similar institutional records. Can he question the parole board's decision via the courts? The Supreme Court answered this question in 2011 when it ruled in the consolidated cases of *Swarthout v. Cooke* and *Cate v. Clay* that there is in essence no absolute or legal right to receive parole. The Court held that while the due process clause requires fair procedures in parole hearing, both Cooke and Clay received adequate process because they were allowed an opportunity to be heard and were provided a statement of the reasons why parole was denied. However, the courts do not have the right to step in and conclude the parole board's (and governor's) decisions were faulty. If the process is fair, then the inmate must live with the outcome.[142]

Parole Effectiveness

Despite all efforts to treat, correct, and rehabilitate incarcerated offenders, many return to prison shortly after their release. Persons released from prison face a multitude of difficulties. They remain largely uneducated, unskilled, and usually without solid family support systems—then add to this the burdens of a prison record. Not surprisingly, most parolees fail, and rather quickly; rearrests are most common in the first six months after release. The latest government data on parole failure indicate the following:

- About two-thirds (68 percent) of released prisoners were arrested for a new crime within three years, and three-quarters (77 percent) were arrested within five years.
- Within five years of release, 82 percent of property offenders were arrested for a new crime, compared to 77 percent of drug offenders, 74 percent of public order offenders, and 71 percent of violent offenders.
- More than a third (37 percent) of all prisoners who were arrested within five years of release were arrested within the first six months after release, with more than half (57 percent) arrested by the end of the first year.
- A sixth (16 percent) of released prisoners were responsible for almost half (48 percent) of the nearly 1.2 million arrests that occurred in the five-year follow-up period.
- Within five years of release, 84 percent of inmates who were age 24 or younger at release were arrested, compared to 79 percent of inmates ages 25 to 39 and 69 percent of those age 40 or older.[143]

Figure 12.1 shows how a majority of inmates fail on parole and fail quickly.

A report by the influential Pew Foundation also found high recidivism rates but that not all states had the same failure rates. The more successful ones made important correctional decisions—such as the types of offenders sentenced to prison, how inmates are selected for release, how long they are under supervision—using carefully drawn empirical evidence. Which strategies were the most successful? States that made extensive use of probation for petty offenders had relatively higher inmate recidivism rates because only the most hard-core inmates were actually sent to prison. Parole was more successful in states that employed programs that target motivated offenders to stay crime- and drug-free through a combination of swift and certain sanctions for prison violations and rewards for obeying correctional rules.[144]

Supervision on the Outside

After they are on the outside, parolees are supervised and monitored by parole officers, some of whom maintain a social work, treatment orientation, while

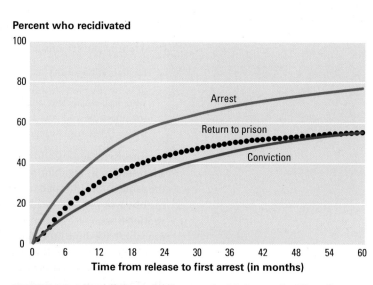

Percent who recidivated

FIGURE 12.1 Recidivism of Prisoners in 30 States by Time from Release to First Arrest That Led to Recidivating Event

Source: Alexia Cooper, Matthew Durose, and Howard Snyder, *Recidivism of Prisoners Released in 30 States in 2005: Patterns from 2005 to 2010* (Washington, DC: Bureau of Justice Statistics, 2014), http://www.bjs.gov/index.cfm?ty=pbdetail&iid=4986.

others are more authoritative and rule oriented. Even though the difference in style and attitude may not determine parolee success, research does show that parole officers who held more authoritative attitudes were more likely to pursue revocation hearings for offender noncompliance.[145] The following Criminal Justice Technology feature reviews new measures being used to monitor parolees in the community.

The Problem of Reentry

Parole failure is a significant problem, and a growing portion of the correctional population consists of parolees who failed on the outside. Why has the phenomenon of parole failure remained so stubborn and hard to control? Why is it so difficult to reenter society?

One reason may be the very nature of the prison experience itself. Being separated from family and friends takes a steep toll. As one inmate puts it:

> Incarceration didn't teach me nothing except how to do some bad things better; only thing prison did, they separated me from my family for a long time; you miss your kids' birthdays and their basketball games; you miss family weddings, family members die and you don't get to say goodbye to them; you can't help your mother, it hurts. (Male inmate, aged 60 years)[146]

The psychological and economic problems that lead offenders to recidivism are rarely addressed by a stay in prison. Despite rehabilitation efforts, the typical ex-convict is still the same undereducated, unemployed, substance-abusing, lower-socioeconomic-status male he was when arrested. Being separated from friends and family, not sharing in conventional society, associating with dangerous people, and adapting to a volatile lifestyle probably have done little to improve the offender's personality or behavior. It seems naïve to think that incarceration alone can help someone overcome these lifelong disabilities. By their very nature, prisons seek to impose and maintain order and conformity rather than to help inmates develop skills such as independence and critical thinking—factors that may be essential after the inmate is forced to cope outside the prison walls.[147] Once outside, the ex-inmate faces a series of barriers that inhibits his adjustment to society; some of these are discussed next.

Why Do People Fail on Parole?

Why do so many inmates fail in the community? A number of social, economic, and personal factors interfere with reentry success. Reentry risks can be tied to legal changes in how people are released from prison. Changes in sentencing laws have resulted in the growth of mandatory release and limits on discretionary parole. Inmates may be discouraged from seeking involvement in rehabilitation programs because they no longer affect the chance of parole. The lack of incentive means that fewer inmates leaving prison have participated in programs to address deficiencies in the areas of employment, education, and substance use. Many of those being released have therefore not received adequate treatment and are unprepared for life in conventional society.[148]

Nor does the situation improve upon release. Many inmates are not assigned to supervision caseloads after they are back in the community. About 200,000 released inmates go unsupervised each year, three-quarters of whom have been released after completing their maximum sentence and are therefore not required to be supervised. A number of research efforts indicate that supervision can be valuable. When Michael Osterman looked at the records of those released from prison in New Jersey, he found that after three years, those released with parole supervision were generally less involved in new crimes when compared with those who were released unconditionally.[149] Of course, inmates who "max out" or otherwise go unsupervised may be the more serious offenders whose survival in the community would be lower even if they were supervised. If these differences are controlled, the effect of supervision is neutralized.[150] So the actual effect of supervision after release is still open to debate.[151]

Regardless of how they are released, the risks the flood of newly released inmates present to the community include increases in child abuse, family violence, the spread of infectious diseases, homelessness, and community disorganization. Many have no way to cope and wind up in homeless shelters.[152] These problems take a heavy toll on communities and also limit reentry success.

PERSONAL PROBLEMS Reentry problems are related to the releasee's own lifelong personal deficits. Many have a long history of drug abuse and criminal behavior in a short time.[153] They may have an antisocial personality and childhood experiences with family dysfunction; many have suffered from a lifetime of substance abuse or dependence disorder.[154] It is not surprising that releasees who maintain criminal peer associations, carry weapons, abuse alcohol, and harbor aggressive feelings are the most likely to fail upon reentry.[155]

Once outside, those who return to reoffending often suffer stigmatizing labels from both official (e.g., police) and nonofficial (e.g., neighbors, employers) sources that may reinforce their belief that they are outside the mainstream and that a criminal way of life is the only path left open. Stigma is especially hard on former sex offenders, who must register upon release so any efforts to remain anonymous are thwarted. As one parolee put it:

> You do your time (in prison) and don't want no more trouble in your life, but people look at you like you are a constant danger. They harassed me, followed me around and pinned stuff on my car with nasty words; one time guys followed me from a store and screamed "sex offender." I told the police, but they say there's nothing they can do. I've been chased and almost beaten; even cops follow me sometimes. I can't go anywhere without people that I know. I can't talk to kids; even if they ask me something, I'm supposed to walk away, and it makes you look mean always.[156]

ECONOMIC PROBLEMS Prison takes a heavy economic toll on former inmates. Most people leave prison with no savings, no immediate entitlement to unemployment benefits, and few employment prospects, especially in this era of high unemployment.[157] The Pew Foundation found that serving time significantly reduces economic status and prospects:

- Serving time reduces hourly wages for men by approximately 11 percent, annual employment by 9 weeks, and annual earnings by 40 percent.
- By age 48, the typical former inmate will have earned $179,000 less than if he had never been incarcerated.

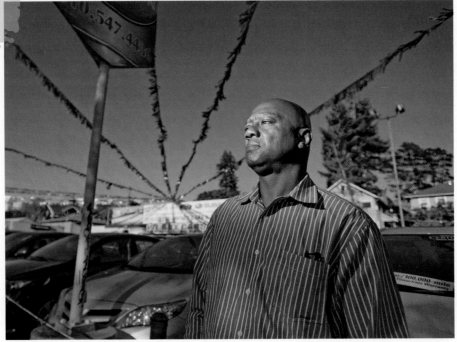

Inmates can be paroled despite multiple failures. Arthur Scott, who was paroled in March 2014, after serving time on his 22nd auto theft conviction, stands in front of an Oakland, California, Toyota dealership on Tuesday, June 24, 2014. Scott, determined to stay out of jail and currently working while taking vocational classes, says he had stolen more than five cars from the dealership. For him, stable housing was critical. Each time he was released, he found himself homeless or in a halfway house with other men who did drugs and he would get re-arrested within days.

A prison experience locks people onto the lowest rung of the economic ladder and significantly reduces their chances for upward economic mobility. A year after release, as many as 60 percent of former inmates are not employed in the regular labor market, and employers are increasingly reluctant to hire ex-offenders. Ex-offenders are commonly barred from working in the fields in which most jobs are being created, such as child care, education, security, nursing, and home health care. More jobs are also now unionized, and many unions exclude ex-offenders. Parolees who had a good employment record before their incarceration and who are able to find jobs after their release are the ones most likely to avoid recidivating. Another bit of good news comes from a four-state survey conducted by Paul Hirschfield and Alex Piquero, which found that though some people regard ex-offenders as dangerous and dishonest, many reject these stereotypes, and a majority say that they would be willing to work and associate with people who were previously incarcerated. Even people who believe in harsh punishment may be willing to work alongside people who paid their debt to society. If more people were acquainted with ex-offenders, the more willing they would be to hire them and give them the economic opportunities to succeed.[158]

FAMILY PROBLEMS Inmates with strong social support and close family ties have a better chance of making it on the outside.[159] But prison can take its toll on social relationships, and being a former inmate can devastate the economic and social functioning of a family. Poor inmates and their families may be no longer welcome in subsidized public housing complexes. This is a consequence of the US Department of Housing and Urban Development's "one strike and you're out" policy, whereby all members of the household are evicted if one member is involved in crime.[160] Without government subsidies, former inmates' families may not have the economic means to find affordable housing. The Pew Foundation found that family income averaged over the years a father is incarcerated is 22 percent lower than family income was the year before the father was incarcerated. Even in the year after the father is released, family income remains 15 percent lower than it was the year before incarceration.[161]

Kids are hurt educationally, socially, and financially if a parent is a former inmate. The Pew Foundation found that children with fathers who have been incarcerated are significantly more likely than other children to be expelled or suspended from school (23 percent compared with 4 percent). Children of incarcerated and released parents may suffer confusion, sadness, and social stigma, and these feelings often result in difficulties in school, low self-esteem, aggressive behavior, and general emotional dysfunction. One reason is that mothers released from prison have difficulty finding services such as housing, employment, and child care, and this causes stress for them and their children.

Another problem is that if the parents are negative role models, children fail to develop positive attitudes about work and responsibility. Children of incarcerated parents are five times more likely to serve time in prison than children whose parents are not incarcerated.

COMMUNITY PROBLEMS Parole expert Richard Seiter notes that when there were only a few hundred thousand prisoners and a few thousand releasees per year, the issues surrounding the release of offenders did not overwhelm communities.[162] Families could house ex-inmates, job-search organizations could find them jobs, and community social service agencies could respond to their individual needs for mental health or substance abuse treatment. Today, the sheer number of reentering inmates has taxed the communities to which they are returning.[163]

Community characteristics can also influence the way parole violations are handled. Parolees returning to communities with high unemployment rates—a factor considered by parole board members to be an unstable environment—are more likely to have their parole revoked.[164] Similarly, parolees living in areas with concentrated disadvantage and social disorder, where bars are plentiful and liquor stores abundant, also suffer higher rates of recidivism. Clearly, the neighborhood plays a significant role in parole success. Communities that can provide social and mental health services also influence parole success. For example, many former inmates need mental and psychological services that some communities simply cannot provide. Even when public mental health services are available, many mentally ill individuals fail to use them because they fear institutionalization, deny they are mentally ill, or distrust the mental health system. The situation will become more serious as more and more parolees are released into the same disorganized communities where deteriorated conditions may have motivated their original crimes. Having mental health services nearby seems to have a significant effect on parole board decision making.[165] The further parolees live from social service providers, the more likely they will be returned to prison.

Recognizing that some communities experience high rates of incarceration and reentry, some have created coalitions of community organizations to interact with every person returning home from prison. In New York City, the NYC Justice Corps provides transitional employment for young adults returning home from prison and jail in two neighborhoods most impacted by incarceration and reentry. In each location, a local organization brings together young people with their community to identify community improvement projects that the NYC Justice Corps members can execute while developing hard skills that ready them for the labor market.[166]

LEGAL PROBLEMS Ex-inmates may also find that going straight is an economic impossibility. Many employers are reluctant to hire people who have served time. Even if a criminal record does not automatically prohibit employment, why would an employer hire an ex-con when other applicants are available? If ex-offenders lie about their prison experience and are later found out, they will be dismissed for misrepresentation. Research shows that former inmates who gain and keep meaningful employment are more likely to succeed on parole than those who are unemployed or underemployed.[167] One reason why ex-inmates find it so difficult to make it on the outside is the legal restrictions they are forced to endure. These may include prohibitions on certain kinds of employment, limits on obtaining licenses, and restrictions on their freedom of movement (see the Contemporary Issues in Criminal Justice box).[168]

Improving Chances on Reentry

Can something be done to ease reentry? Now that the scope of the problem has been recognized, both the federal and state governments have devoted energy to improving success at reentry. On April 9, 2008, the Second Chance Act was signed into law.

Criminal Records and Reentry Success

I am writing this letter … out of desperation and to tell you a little about the struggles of reentering society as a convicted felon. I have worked hard to turn my life around. I have remained clean for nearly eight years, I am succeeding in college, and I continue to share my story in schools, treatment facilities, and correctional institutions, yet I have nothing to show for it…. I have had numerous interviews and sent out more than 200 résumés for jobs for which I am more than qualified. I have had denial after denial because of my felony. I do understand that you are not responsible for the choices that have brought me to this point. Furthermore, I recognize that if I was not abiding by the law, if I was not clean, and if I was not focusing my efforts toward a successful future, I would have no claim to make.

So writes Jay, a man convicted of involuntary vehicular manslaughter and sentenced to 38 months in state prison nine years before. He is not alone: a criminal label can haunt people for the rest of their life, well beyond their offending years and despite the fact that they have stayed "clean" for quite some time.

Many people with records suffer stigma that prevents them from getting jobs. A recent study shows that nearly one-third of American adults have been arrested by age 23. This record will keep many people from obtaining employment, even if they have paid their dues, are qualified for the job, and are unlikely to reoffend.

Criminal records run the gamut from one-time arrests where charges are dropped, to lengthy, serious, and violent criminal histories. Many people who have been arrested—and, therefore, technically have a criminal record that shows up on a background check—were never convicted of a crime. This is true not only among those charged with minor crimes but also for many individuals arrested for serious offenses.

The impact of having a criminal record is most often felt among African Americans, who may already experience racial discrimination in the labor market and are more likely than whites to have a criminal record. Research shows that a criminal record reduces the likelihood of a job callback or offer by approximately 50 percent. This criminal record "penalty" is substantially greater for African Americans than for white applicants. Latinos suffer similar penalties in the employment market.

In addition to these significant and often overlapping challenges, an extra set of punishments, or "collateral consequences," is imposed on individuals as a direct result of their criminal convictions. These legal restrictions create barriers to jobs, housing, benefits, and voting. More than 80 percent of the statutes that place restrictions on people convicted of crime operate as denial of employment opportunities. Although some of these consequences serve important public safety purposes, others may be antiquated and create unnecessary barriers to legitimate work opportunities. A commonly cited example is that, in some states, formerly incarcerated people who were trained as barbers cannot hold those jobs after release because state laws prohibit felons from practicing the trade, presumably because their access to sharp objects makes them a threat to the public.

Regardless of the legal restrictions, the majority of employers indicate they would "probably" or "definitely" not be willing to hire an applicant with a criminal record. A recent report by the National Employment Law Project found frequent use of blanket "no-hire" policies among major corporations. Employers do not want to hire individuals who might commit future crimes and who may be a risk to their employees' and customers' safety. The assumption, of course, is that a prior record signals higher odds that the individual will commit more crimes in the future.

CRITICAL THINKING

1. What can be done to reduce the effect of labels and stigma placed on people who have paid their debt?

2. Should records be expunged within a certain time frame if a person does not reoffend? Or should knowledge of a prior criminal record be available because employers have a right to know about the background of the people they are considering hiring?

Source: Amy Solomon, "In Search of a Job: Criminal Records as Barriers to Employment," *NIJ Journal* 270 (2012), http://www.nij.gov/nij/journals/270/criminal-records.htm (accessed June 2015).

This federal legislation authorized various grants to government agencies and nonprofit groups to provide a variety of services (including employment assistance, housing, substance abuse treatment, and family programming) that can help to reduce reoffending and decrease violations of probation and parole. A number of correctional authorities have created reentry programs, some of which start preparing inmates for release almost as soon as their sentence begins. For example, Arizona's Getting Ready program begins on day one of incarceration and continues to the conclusion of every inmate's sentence. Getting Ready redefines the officer-offender relationship, shifting many responsibilities from the staff to the inmates. For example, officers do not tell inmates when to get up and when to go to sleep. Getting Ready brings the real world—a "parallel universe"—into prison so that inmates in every custody level acquire and practice basic life skills from the first to the last day of their incarceration. An inmate is not required to complete or further his education, but until he earns a GED, he can be employed only in entry-level jobs, earning entry-level wages. However, as in the real world, after he earns a GED, many other employment opportunities open up. In Getting Ready, a GED becomes a prerequisite to job training, better work assignments, and higher wages.

Since it was implemented in 2004, Getting Ready has produced some significant improvement in Arizona's corrections system. Prison violence has been reduced, with inmate-on-inmate assaults decreasing 46 percent, inmate-on-staff assaults down 33 percent, suicides down 67 percent, and sexual assaults down 61 percent. Inmate problem solving is demonstrably better, with grievances falling 27 percent and inmate lawsuits over conditions of confinement down 63 percent. The program seems to have a positive impact on recidivism and community safety.[169]

In addition, some programs provide postrelease counseling and support. One promising Virginia program, Women Inspired to Transform (WIT), uses volunteers to teach female returnees about anger management, job interviewing, communication, relationships, and parenting.[170] Some programs enroll inmates in education, substance abuse, and other institutional programs that are customized to address their individual needs and ease their reentry, while providing follow-up postrelease treatment programming, including social service assistance (such as substance abuse and mental health treatment) and vocational development (such as training, education, and résumé development).[171]

Reentry courts are a new addition to the specialty court spectrum and are now being tested in more than 10 sites around the country. Unlike other alternative court-based programs, reentry courts serve individuals who have already been convicted and incarcerated. In general, reentry courts enroll parolees who have been screened and selected for participation and who have consented to the jurisdiction of the reentry court. Participants are typically selected based on the nature of their offense, their criminal history, and their assessed likelihood of recidivism. Most courts aim to serve nonviolent offenders at a high risk for recidivism. The goal of the program is to establish a system of offender accountability and support services throughout the reentry process. Reentry courts make use of graduated sanctions and rewards that can be used to influence parolee conduct without automatically resorting to incarceration, the most expensive and extreme sanction. They require that participants appear before the court on a regular basis for review and create a personalized program plan for each participant to follow. Most programs require between six months and one year of reentry court participation. While evaluations of the program have just become available, recent research on one program by Caitlin Taylor found that participation was associated with a significant reduction in the likelihood of supervision revocation.[172]

Lucy Nicholson/Reuters/Corbis

Vanessa Moreno, 24, holds her two-month-old baby, Makayla, at Prototypes residential treatment program in Pomona, California. Prototypes is part of the Second Chance Women's Re-entry Court program, one of the first in the United States to focus on women. It offers a cost-saving alternative to prison for women who plead guilty to nonviolent crimes and volunteer for treatment. It claims a success rate of about 90 percent.

L010 Discuss the parole process and the problems of prisoner reentry

ETHICAL Challenge

A New Jersey state trooper pulled over Albert Florence's pregnant wife as she was driving with him and their 4-year-old son in the car. Because Albert Florence owned the vehicle, the officer ran his license and discovered an outstanding warrant for a noncriminal traffic fine. Despite the fact that Florence had already paid the fine and carried an official letter proving it, the police officer arrested him and placed him in a local jail where he was incarcerated for six days and subjected to two invasive strip searches. A judge then freed Florence, confirming that he had in fact paid his fine. Florence filed suit, claiming the degrading searches violated his Fourth Amendment rights. In a 5-4 opinion, *Albert W. Florence, Petitioner v. Board of Chosen Freeholders of the County of Burlington et al.* (2012), the Supreme Court held that county jails can routinely strip search all new detainees, including those, like Albert Florence, who had been arrested for minor offenses and were unlikely to spend more than one night in jail. The Court concluded that a prisoner's likelihood of possessing contraband based on the severity of the current offense or an arrestee's criminal history is too difficult to determine effectively. The Court pointed out instances, such as the arrest of Timothy McVeigh, in which an individual who commits a minor traffic offense is capable of extreme violence. Correctional facilities have a strong interest in keeping their employees and inmates safe. A general strip search policy adequately and effectively protects that interest. The Court did note that there may be an exception to this rule when the arrestees are not entering the general population and will not have substantial contact with other inmates. In his dissent, Justice Stephen G. Breyer along with Justice Ruth Bader Ginsburg, Justice Sonia Sotomayor, and Justice Elena Kagan, opined that strip searches of individuals arrested for minor offenses are unreasonable unless the prison official has a reasonable suspicion that the individual possesses drugs or contraband.

Ethical Challenge: Write an essay addressing the ethics of correctional authorities having the right to strip search all people entering a detention facility, whether it be jail or prison. Is it fair to subject people to this indignity, as the Supreme Court suggests, to maintain security? Would it be unethical to spare some but not others this indignity? Before you answer, remember to consider whether people should be spared such treatment merely because of their age, status, religion, or gender. For example, should an elderly nun, arrested at an anti-war demonstration, be stripped searched if she is to be held in detention?

SUMMARY

LO1 *Discuss the problems of the adult correctional system* A significant number of facilities are old and in ill repair. Institutions are overcrowded, and meaningful treatment efforts are often a matter of wishful thinking. The typical prison is often described as a "school for crime." Recidivism rates are shockingly high.

LO2 *Explain what is meant by the term total institution* Prisons in the United States are total institutions that limit individuality and demand obedience. Inmates locked within their walls are segregated from the outside world. They have to learn to cope with their new environment or risk injury or even death.

LO3 *Discuss the problem of sexual coercion in prison and what is being done to help* Young males may be raped and kept as sexual slaves by older, more aggressive inmates. However, many inmates refuse to report rape, and others may misunderstand what constitutes a rape, so the true extent of prison rape may never be known. To help with the problem, the Prison Rape Reduction Act of 2003 established three programs to reduce rape in prison. However, surveys report that many inmates are still being raped and sexually assaulted.

LO4 *Chart the prisonization process and the development of the inmate social code* Part of living in prison involves learning to protect oneself and developing survival instincts. Inmates form their own world, with a unique set of norms and rules, known as the inmate subculture. Those who become the most "prisonized" will be the least likely to avoid criminal activity on the outside.

LO5 *Compare the lives and cultures of male and female inmates* Women's prisons tend to be smaller than those housing male inmates, but female inmates may suffer from a lack of adequate job training and from inferior health, treatment, and educational facilities. Unlike male inmates, women usually do not present an immediate physical danger to staff and fellow inmates. Make-believe family groups contain masculine and feminine figures acting as fathers and mothers; some even act as children and take on the role of brother or sister.

LO6 *Discuss the different forms of correctional treatment* Counseling programs help inmates control their emotions, communicate with others, deal with legal concerns, manage general life issues, control substance abuse, and develop and maintain social relationships. Inmate rehabilitation is also pursued through vocational and educational training.

LO7 *Describe the world of correctional officers* Correctional officers are now viewed as dedicated public servants. Most are in favor of rehabilitation efforts, so that the typical correctional officer has been characterized as a "people worker." There are few gender differences in the behavior of correctional officers.

LO8 *Discuss the causes of prison violence* Violence can involve individual conflict: inmate versus inmate, inmate versus staff, or staff versus inmate. Prison violence is associated with overcrowding, lack of effective dispute-resolution mechanisms, individual history of violence, and poor prison conditions.

LO9 *Explain what is meant by prisoners' rights, and discuss some key privileges that have been granted to inmates* Today, inmates have the right to medical care, freedom from cruel and unusual treatment, the right to an attorney, and the right to practice their religion. Inmates can sue the prison administration if their rights have been violated—for example, if they are denied proper medical care.

LO10 *Discuss the parole process and the problems of prisoner reentry* Most inmates are paroled either by mandatory release or parole board vote. Parole is generally viewed as a privilege granted to deserving inmates on the basis of their good behavior while in prison. More than half of all parolees return to prison shortly after their release. Recidivism may be a by-product of the disruptive effect a prison experience has on personal relationships.

KEY TERMS

total institution, p. 290

inmate subculture, p. 293

inmate social code, p. 293

prisonization, p. 293

make-believe family, p. 297

cognitive behavioral therapy (CBT), p. 298

therapeutic communities, p. 299

work release, p. 301

furlough, p. 301

hands-off doctrine, p. 307

substantive rights, p. 307

jailhouse lawyer, p. 308

cruel and unusual punishment, p. 309

parole, p. 310

REVIEW QUESTIONS

1. Considering the dangers that men face during their prison stay, should nonviolent inmates be placed in separate institutions to protect them from harm?

2. Should women be allowed to work as guards in men's prisons? What about male guards in women's prisons?

3. Should prison inmates be allowed a free college education while noncriminals are forced to pay tuition?

4. Which would be more effective: telling inmates that they have to earn the right to be paroled, or giving inmates their parole date in advance and telling them they will lose it for misbehavior?

5. What is the role of the parole board?

6. Should a former prisoner enjoy all the civil rights afforded to the average citizen?

7. Should former inmates lose their right to vote?

CONTEMPORARY ISSUES IN AMERICAN CRIMINAL JUSTICE

The US military's most accomplished sniper, Chris Kyle, a veteran of four tours in Iraq and veritable celebrity because of his book, *American Sniper* (and an eventual movie of the same title starring Bradley Cooper), was in 2013 tragically shot dead at a gun range in Glen Rose, Texas, southwest of Fort Worth, along with one of his old friends, Chad Littlefield. Eddie Ray Routh, 25, another veteran, was arrested and charged with two counts of murder. Ironically, Kyle and Littlefield reportedly took Routh to the gun range to help him cope with his apparent post-traumatic stress disorder. Routh had been in and out of mental hospitals over the preceding two years, having been diagnosed with schizophrenia.

Routh's trial kicked off in early 2015, in Stephenville, Texas, just west of Glen Rose. One of the core issues in the trial concerned the motive for the killings. What prompted Routh to allegedly kill Kyle and Littlefield? One of the prosecution's experts claimed Routh's heavy marijuana use caused a "substance-induced psychotic disorder."[1] Dash cam video of Routh's arrest showed him telling a police officer, "I've been so paranoid-schizophrenic all day, I don't know what to even think of the world right now."[2] He was also overheard in a later conversation saying, "I shot them because they wouldn't talk to me."[3] Routh's attorneys argued it was the arsenal of firearms at the shooting range that triggered his psychosis. Routh pleaded not guilty by reason of insanity,[4] but the jury was not convinced, finding him guilty, which led to an automatic life sentence with no possibility of parole. Tragic cases like this blur the lines between the war on terror and mainstream criminal justice.

Part 5 contains two chapters that cover special issues in criminal justice. Chapter 13 looks at the history of juvenile justice and current issues such as transfer to the adult court and juvenile sentencing issues. Chapter 14 looks at emerging issues the justice system must learn to confront: cyber crime, global crime, green crime, and corporate crime.

Chapter 13   **Juvenile Justice in the Twenty-First Century**

Chapter 14   **Crime and Justice in the New Millennium**

13 Juvenile Justice in the Twenty-First Century

While they were together in his bedroom, Steven Miles, a 16-year-old British boy, stabbed his girlfriend, Elizabeth Thomas, in the back of her head, killing her.[5] He then used tools from his father's tree business to dismember her corpse and stuffed the parts into trash bags. He was arrested the same day and, at his trial, admitted to jurors that he killed his girlfriend because he wanted to emulate the lead character in the Showtime series, *Dexter*.

Miles had earlier told his family that a voice in his head, from someone named "Ed," had told him to kill someone. An hour after killing Thomas, Miles told his sister, "Ed made me do something bad." According to experts, Miles displayed some narcissistic personality traits and showed some signs of autism. Nevertheless, Miles was sentenced, at age 17, to a life term in prison.[6] Lewis Power, part of Miles's defense team said:

> This was a truly gruesome killing ripped from the pages of a hit TV script . . . The case is a sad testament to the perils of how young people can become entrenched in modern TV blockbusters involving violence which, shockingly, led to a copycat killing in real life.[7]

Independent of (yet interrelated with) the adult criminal justice system, the juvenile justice system is primarily responsible for dealing with juvenile and youth crime, as well as with incorrigible and truant children and runaways. Conceived at the turn of the twentieth century, the juvenile justice system was viewed as a quasi-social welfare agency that was to act as a surrogate parent in the interests of the child; this is referred to as the *parens patriae* philosophy. Many people who work in the system still hold to the original social welfare principles of the juvenile justice system. In contrast, those who adopt a crime control orientation suggest that the juvenile justice system's *parens patriae* philosophy is outdated. They point to nationally publicized incidents of juvenile violence, such as the shootings at Columbine High School in Colorado, as indicators that serious juvenile offenders should be punished and disciplined rather than treated and rehabilitated. "Why should we give special treatment to violent young juveniles?" they ask.

parens patriae Latin term meaning "father of his country." According to this legal philosophy, the government is the guardian of everyone who has a disability, especially children, and has a legal duty to act in their best interests until they reach the age of majority.

REALITY CHECK

MYTH OR REALITY?

- *Parens patriae* is the guiding philosophy of juvenile justice today.
- All juveniles fall under the jurisdiction of the adult court at age 18.
- Juveniles enjoy different rights than adults.
- Juvenile trials are different from adult trials.
- Youths are more violent and criminally dangerous today than they were in the past.

www.surrey.police.uk

Randy Tepper/© Showtime/Courtesy Everett Collection

LEARNING OBJECTIVES

L01 Describe the history of juvenile justice

L02 Discuss the establishment of the juvenile court

L03 Describe the changes in juvenile justice that began in the 1960s and continue today

L04 Summarize police processing of juvenile offenders

L05 Describe the juvenile court process

L06 Explain the concept of waiver

L07 Explain the importance of In re Gault

L08 Describe the juvenile correctional process

323

It remains to be seen whether the juvenile justice system will continue on its path toward deterrence, punishment, and control or return to its former role as a treatment-dispensing agency. This chapter reviews the history of juvenile justice and discusses the justice system's processing of youthful offenders.

The History of Juvenile Justice

The modern practice of legally separating adult criminals and juvenile offenders can be traced back to two developments in English custom and law that occurred centuries ago: the development of Elizabethan-era poor laws and the creation of the English chancery court. Both of these innovations were designed to allow the state to take control of the lives of needy but not necessarily criminal children.[8]

- *Poor laws.* As early as 1535, the English passed statutes known as poor laws, which (among other things) mandated the appointment of overseers who placed destitute or neglected children with families who then trained them in agricultural, trade, or domestic services; this practice was referred to as *indenture*. The Elizabethan poor laws of 1601 created a system of churchwardens and overseers who, with the consent of the justices of the peace, identified vagrant, delinquent, and neglected children and took measures to put them to work. Often this meant placing them in poorhouses or workhouses or, more commonly, apprenticing them until their adulthood.
- *Chancery courts.* English chancery courts provided judicial relief to those who had no legal standing or could expect no legal relief because of the corruption and inadequacy of other common-law courts. People who felt their rights were being violated could take their cases to the chancery court for review. In this capacity, the chancery court protected the property rights and welfare of more minor children who could not care for themselves—children whose position and property were of direct concern to the monarch. The courts dealt with issues of guardianship and the use and control of property. Thus, if the guardian of an orphaned child wanted to sell off his ward's inheritance, the chancery court might be asked to review the proceedings and determine whether the sale was in the child's best interest.

Care of Children in Early America

Poor laws and chancery courts were brought from England to colonial America. Poor laws were passed in Virginia in 1646 and in Connecticut and Massachusetts in 1678, and they continued in force until the early nineteenth century. They mandated care for wayward and destitute children. However, those youths who committed serious criminal offenses continued to be tried in the same courts as adults.

To accommodate dependent youths, local jurisdictions developed almshouses, poorhouses, and workhouses. Crowded and unhealthy, these shelters accepted the poor, the insane, the diseased, and vagrant and destitute children. Middle-class civic leaders, who referred to themselves as child savers, began to develop organizations and groups to help alleviate the burdens of the poor and immigrants by sponsoring shelter care for youths, educational and social activities, and the development of settlement houses. In retrospect, their main focus seems to have been on extending governmental control over a whole range of youthful activities that previously had been left to private or family control, including idleness, drinking, vagrancy, and delinquency.[9]

The Child-Saving Movement

The child savers were responsible for creating a number of programs for indigent youths, including the New York House of Refuge, which began operations in 1825.[10] Its charter was to protect indigent youths who were at risk of crime by taking them off the streets and reforming them in a family-like environment.[11]

The New York House of Refuge, actually a reformatory, opened on January 1, 1825, with only six boys and three girls, but within the first decade of its operation, 1,678 children

Boys on the steps of an abandoned tenement building in New York City, about 1889. The child savers were concerned that, if left alone, children like these would enter a life of crime. They created the House of Refuge to care for poor and neglected kids. Critics accused them of class and race bias.

were sent there because of vagrancy and petty crimes. As a resident, an adolescent's daily schedule was devoted for the most part to supervised labor, which was regarded as beneficial to education and discipline. Male inmates worked in shops that produced brushes, cane chairs, brass nails, and shoes. The female inmates sewed uniforms, did laundry, and carried out other domestic work. The reformatory had the authority to bind out inmates through indenture agreements to private employers; most males so bound out were farm workers, and most females were domestic laborers.

The Refuge Movement Spreads

When the House of Refuge opened, critics complained that the institution was run like a prison, with strict discipline and absolute separation of the sexes. Such a harsh program drove many children to run away, and the House of Refuge was forced to take a more lenient approach. Despite criticism, the concept enjoyed expanding popularity. In 1826, for example, the Boston City Council founded the House of Reformation for juvenile offenders.[12]

The child savers also influenced state and local governments to create independent correctional institutions to house minors. The first of these reform schools opened in Westboro, Massachusetts, in 1848 and in Rochester, New York, in 1849. Children lived in congregate conditions and spent their days working at institutional jobs, learning a trade where possible, and receiving some basic education. They were racially and sexually segregated, discipline was harsh and often involved whipping and isolation, and the physical care was of poor quality.

In 1853, New York philanthropist Charles Loring Brace helped develop the **Children's Aid Society** as an alternative for dealing with neglected and delinquent youths. Brace proposed rescuing wayward youths from the harsh environment of the city and providing them with temporary shelter and care. He then sought to place them in private homes in rural communities where they could engage in farming and agricultural work beyond the influence of the city. Although some placements proved successful, others resulted in the exploitation of children in a strange environment with few avenues of escape.

Children's Aid Society A child-saving organization begun by Charles Loring Brace; it took children from the streets in large cities and placed them with farm families on the prairie.

L01 Describe the history of juvenile justice

Establishment of the Juvenile Court

juvenile court A court that has original jurisdiction over persons defined by statute as juveniles and alleged to be delinquents or status offenders.

As the nation expanded, it became evident that private charities and public organizations were not caring adequately for the growing number of troubled youths. The child savers lobbied for an independent, state-supported juvenile court, and their efforts prompted the development of the first comprehensive juvenile court in Illinois in 1899. The Illinois Juvenile Court Act set up an independent court to handle criminal law violations by children under 16 years of age, as well as to care for neglected, dependent, and wayward youths. The act also created a probation department to monitor youths in the community and to direct juvenile court judges to place serious offenders in secure schools for boys and industrial schools for girls. The ostensible purpose of the act was to separate juveniles from adult offenders and to provide a legal framework in which juveniles could get adequate care and custody. By 1925, most states had developed juvenile courts.

The Development of Juvenile Justice

The juvenile court movement quickly spread across the United States. In its early form, it provided youths with quasi-legal, quasi-therapeutic, personalized justice. The main concern was the "best interests of the child," not strict adherence to legal doctrine, constitutional rights, or due process of law. The court was paternalistic, rather than adversarial. Attorneys were not required; hearsay evidence, inadmissible in criminal trials, was commonly employed in the adjudication of juvenile offenders. Children were encouraged to admit their "guilt" in open court (in violation of their Fifth Amendment rights).

Verdicts were based on a "preponderance of the evidence," instead of being "beyond a reasonable doubt." Juvenile courts then functioned as quasi-social service agencies.

REFORM SCHOOLS Youngsters who were found delinquent in juvenile court could spend years in a state training school. Although they prided themselves on being non-punitive, these early reform schools attempted to exercise control based on the concept of reform through hard work and discipline. In the second half of the nineteenth century, the emphasis shifted from massive industrial schools to the cottage system. Juvenile offenders were housed in a series of small cabins, each one holding 20 to 40 children, run by "cottage parents," who attempted to create a homelike atmosphere. The first cottage system was established in Massachusetts, the second in Ohio. The system was generally applauded for being a great improvement over the industrial training schools.[13] By the 1950s, psychological treatment was introduced in juvenile corrections. Group counseling techniques became standard procedure in most juvenile institutions.

LO2 Discuss the establishment of the juvenile court

LEGAL CHANGE In the 1960s and 1970s, the US Supreme Court radically altered the juvenile justice system when it issued a series of decisions that established the right of juveniles to due process of law. The Court established that juveniles had the same rights as adults in important areas of trial process, including the right to confront witnesses, notice of charges, and the right to counsel. Exhibit 13.1 lists some of the legal cases that were most important in bringing procedural due process to the juvenile justice process.

Besides the legal revolution brought about by the Supreme Court, Congress passed the Juvenile Justice and Delinquency Prevention Act of 1974 (JJDP Act) and established the federal Office of Juvenile Justice and Delinquency Prevention (OJJDP).[26] This legislation was enacted to identify the needs of youths and to fund programs in the juvenile justice system. Its main goal was to separate wayward, nondangerous youths from institutions housing delinquents and to remove adolescents from institutions housing adult offenders. In 1988, the act was amended to address the issue of minority overrepresentation in the juvenile justice system, and, in 1996, in a move reflecting the growing national frustration with serious delinquent offenders, the act was again amended to make it easier to hold delinquents in adult penal institutions. The various stages in the history of juvenile justice are set out in Concept Summary 13.1.

WEB APP 13.1 Visit the website of the Office of Juvenile Justice and Delinquency Prevention in the US Justice Department at **http://www.ojjdp.gov.** Follow the "Statistics" link, and answer this question: Was juvenile delinquency more of a problem in years past? Why or why not?

EXHIBIT 13.1

Important Juvenile Justice Cases

- *Kent v. United States* (1966) determined that a child has the right to an attorney at any hearing to decide whether his or her case should be transferred to juvenile court (waiver hearings).[14]

- *In re Gault* (1967) ruled that a minor has basic due process rights at trial, including the following: (1) notice of the charges, (2) right to counsel, (3) right to confront and cross-examine witnesses, (4) privilege against self-incrimination, and (5) the right to a transcript of the trial record.[15]

- *In re Winship* (1970) determined that the level of evidence for a finding of "juvenile delinquency" is proof beyond a reasonable doubt.[16]

- *McKeiver v. Pennsylvania* (1971) held that trial by jury in a juvenile court's adjudicative stage is not a constitutional requirement.[17]

- *Breed v. Jones* (1975) ruled that a child has the protection of the double-jeopardy clause of the Fifth Amendment and cannot be tried twice for the same crime.[18]

- *Fare v. Michael C.* (1979) held that a child has the protection of the *Miranda* decision: the right to remain silent during a police interrogation and to request that a lawyer be provided to protect his or her interests.[19]

- *Schall v. Martin* (1984) allowed for the placement of children in preventive detention before their adjudication.[20]

- *New Jersey v. T.L.O.* (1985) determined that although the Fourth Amendment protection against unreasonable search and seizure applies to children, school officials can legally search kids who violate school rules (e.g., smoking on campus), even when there is no evidence that the student violated the law.[21]

- *Vernonia School District v. Acton* (1995) held that the Fourth Amendment's guarantee against unreasonable searches is not violated by drug testing all students choosing to participate in interscholastic athletics.[22]

- *Roper v. Simmons* (2005) determined that juveniles who commit murder before they turn 18 cannot be sentenced to death.[23]

- *Graham v. Florida* (2010) prohibited life imprisonment for juveniles convicted for nonhomicide offenses.[24]

- *Miller v. Alabama* (2012) held that mandatory sentences of life without parole are unconstitutional for juveniles regardless of the underlying offense.[25]

WEB APP 13.2 Visit the website of the Center for Court Innovation at **http://www.courtinnovation.org.** Follow the link to "Youth Court." What is a youth court? How does it differ from traditional court? Are youth courts more effective than traditional courts? Why or why not?

juvenile delinquency Participation in illegal behavior by a minor who falls under a statutory age limit.

status offender A juvenile who engages in behavior legally forbidden to minors, such as running away, truancy, or incorrigibility.

CONCEPT SUMMARY 13.1 Shifting Philosophies of Juvenile Justice

- **Before 1899:** Juveniles treated similarly to adult offenders. No distinction by age or capacity to commit criminal acts.
- **1899–1950s:** Children treated differently beginning with the Illinois Juvenile Court Act of 1899. By 1925, juvenile court acts had been established in virtually every state. *Parens patriae* philosophy dominates.
- **1950–1970:** Recognition by experts that the rehabilitation model and the protective nature of *parens patriae* had failed to prevent delinquency.
- **1970–1980:** Introduction of constitutional due process into the juvenile justice system. Experimentation with diversion and concern about stigma and labeling. Juvenile Justice and Delinquency Prevention Act of 1974 enacted.
- **1980–2000:** Rising juvenile crime rates, coupled with the perceived failure of rehabilitation to control delinquency, lead to a shift to a crime control and punishment philosophy similar to that of the adult criminal justice system. Focus on expanding the crime control capabilities of the juvenile justice system so that it resembles the adult system.
- **2000–today:** Balanced approach. Attempt to provide treatment to needy youths and get tough with dangerous repeat offenders.

Juvenile Justice Today

Today, the juvenile justice system has jurisdiction over two distinct categories of offenders: delinquents and status offenders.[27] **Juvenile delinquency** is a term applied to children who fall under a jurisdictional age limit, which varies from state to state, and who commit an act in violation of the penal code. **Status offenders** commit acts forbidden to minors, which include truancy and being a habitually disobedient and ungovernable child (see Figure 13.1). They are commonly characterized in state

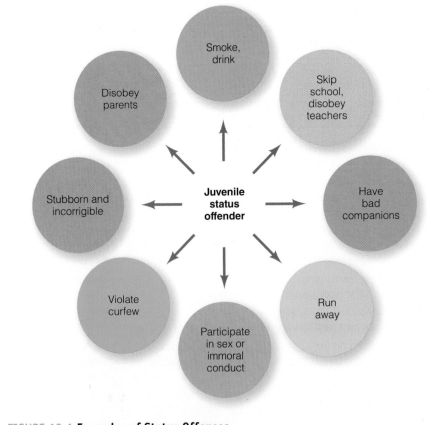

FIGURE 13.1 **Examples of Status Offenses**

statutes as persons or children in need of supervision (PINS or CHINS). Most states distinguish such behavior from delinquent conduct to reduce the effect of any stigma on children, although in most jurisdictions, status offenders can be placed on probation much as delinquent offenders can. They are, however, in most instances barred from being placed in secure facilities that hold delinquent offenders. In addition, juvenile courts generally have jurisdiction over situations involving conduct directed at (rather than committed by) juveniles, such as parental neglect, deprivation, abandonment, and abuse.

The states have also set different maximum ages below which children fall under the jurisdiction of the juvenile court. Many states include all children under 18, others set the limit at 17, and still others at 16.

Some states exclude certain classes of offenders or offenses from the juvenile justice system. Those youths who commit serious violent offenses such as rape or murder may be automatically excluded from the juvenile justice system and treated as adults on the premise that they stand little chance of rehabilitation within the confines of the juvenile system. Juvenile court judges may also transfer, or waive, to adult court repeat offenders whom they deem untreatable by the juvenile authorities.

Another trend has been to create family courts, which include a broad range of family- and child-related issues within their jurisdictions. Family courts are in use or are being considered in more than half of all states. They are designed to provide more individualized, client-focused treatment than traditional juvenile courts and to bring a holistic approach to helping kids and their families, rather than focusing on punishing and/or controlling delinquency.[28]

The juvenile justice system has evolved into a parallel yet independent system of justice with its own terminology and rules of procedure. Exhibit 13.2 describes the basic similarities and differences between the juvenile and adult justice systems. Exhibit 13.3 points out how the language used in the juvenile court differs from that used in the adult system.

EXHIBIT 13.2

Similarities and Differences between Juvenile and Adult Justice Systems

Similarities	Differences
Discretion used by police officers, judges, and correctional personnel	The primary purpose of juvenile procedures is protection and treatment; with adults, the aim is to punish the guilty.
Right to receive *Miranda* warning	Jurisdiction is determined by age in the juvenile system, but by the nature of the offense in the adult system.
Protection from prejudicial lineups or other identification procedures	Juveniles can be apprehended for acts that would not be criminal if committed by an adult (status offenses).
Procedural safeguards when making an admission of guilt	Juvenile proceedings are not considered criminal; adult proceedings are.
Advocacy roles of prosecutors and defense attorneys	Juvenile court proceedings are generally informal and private; adult court proceedings are more formal and are open to the public.
Right to counsel at most key stages of the court process	Courts cannot release to the press identifying information about a juvenile, but they must release information about an adult.
Availability of pretrial motions	Parents are highly involved in the juvenile process but not in the adult process.
Plea negotiation/plea bargaining	The standard of arrest is more stringent for adults than for juveniles.
Right to a hearing and an appeal	Juveniles are released into parental custody; adults are generally given bail.
Standard of proof beyond a reasonable doubt	Juveniles have no constitutional right to a jury trial; adults do. Some states extend this right to juveniles by statute.
Pretrial detention possible	Juveniles can be searched in school without probable cause or a warrant.
Detention without bail if considered dangerous	A juvenile's record is generally sealed when the age of majority is reached; an adult's record is permanent.
Probation as a sentencing option	A juvenile court cannot sentence juveniles to county jails or state prisons, which are reserved for adults.
Community treatment as a sentencing option	The US Supreme Court has declared that the Eighth Amendment prohibits the death penalty for juveniles under age 18.

EXHIBIT 13.3

Comparison of Terms Used in Adult and Juvenile Justice Systems

	Juvenile Terms	Adult Terms
The person and the act	Delinquent child	Criminal
	Delinquent act	Crime
Preadjudicatory stage	Take into custody	Arrest
	Petition	Indictment
	Agree to a finding	Plead guilty
	Deny the petition	Plead not guilty
	Adjustment	Plea bargain
	Detention facility; child-care shelter	Jail
Adjudicatory stage	Substitution	Reduction of charges
	Adjudicatory or fact-finding hearing	Trial
	Adjudication	
Postadjudicatory stage	Dispositional hearing	Sentencing hearing
	Disposition	Sentence
	Commitment	Incarceration
	Youth development center; treatment center; training school	Prison
	Residential child-care facility	Halfway house
	Aftercare	Parole

© Cengage Learning

LO3 Describe the changes in juvenile justice that began in the 1960s and continue today

Today, the juvenile justice system is responsible for processing and treating almost 2 million cases of youthful misbehavior annually. Each state's system is unique, so it is difficult to give a precise accounting of the justice process. Moreover, depending on local practice and tradition, case processing often varies from community to community within a single state. Keeping this in mind, the following sections provide a general description of some key processes and decision points in juvenile justice. Figure 13.2 presents a model of the juvenile justice process.

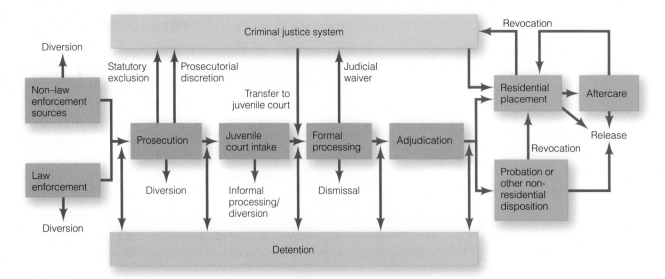

FIGURE 13.2 Case Flow Through the Juvenile Justice System

Source: Office of Juvenile Justice and Delinquency Prevention, http://www.ojjdp.gov/ojstatbb/structure_process/case.html, accessed in February 2015.

Police Processing of the Juvenile Offender

According to the Uniform Crime Reports, police officers arrested 666,263 juveniles in 2013 (most recent numbers as of this writing), down from a high of over 1.2 million in 2004.[29] Most large police departments have detectives who handle only juvenile delinquency cases and focus their attention on the problems of youth (such as youth gangs—see accompanying Contemporary Issues in Criminal Justice box). In addition to conducting their own investigations, they typically take control of cases after an arrest is made by a uniformed officer.

Most states do not have specific statutory provisions distinguishing the arrest process for children from that for adults. Some jurisdictions, however, give broad arrest powers to the police in juvenile cases by authorizing the officer to make an arrest whenever he or she believes the child's behavior falls within the jurisdiction of the juvenile court. Consequently, police may arrest youths for behavior considered legal for adults, including running away, curfew violations, and being in possession of alcohol.

Use of Discretion

When a juvenile is found to have engaged in delinquent or incorrigible behavior, police agencies are charged with the decision to release or to detain the child and refer her to juvenile court. Because of the state's interest in the child, the police generally have more discretion in the investigatory and arrest stages of the juvenile process than they do when dealing with adult offenders.

This discretionary decision—to release or to detain—is based not only on the nature of the offense but also on police attitudes and the child's social and personal conditions at the time of the arrest. The following is a partial list of factors believed to be significant in police decision making about juvenile offenders:

- The type and seriousness of the child's offense
- The ability of the parents to be of assistance in disciplining the child
- The child's past contacts with police

CONTEMPORARY ISSUES IN CRIMINAL JUSTICE

Juvenile Gangs

Since 1996, the National Youth Gang Center (NYGS) has surveyed local law enforcement agencies to gain a sense of the youth gang problem in the United States. A total of 2,199 agencies responded to the survey in 2012, which is the most recent year of data as of this writing. What did the surveys reveal? Here is a short summary of the findings:

- Youth gangs are active in about 3,000 jurisdictions across the United States.

- Youth gangs are overwhelmingly concentrated in larger urban areas, but 15 percent of rural jurisdictions reported gang problems.

- Youth gang-related homicides have increased in recent years (2,363 homicides in 2012, according to the FBI).

- In 2012, there were 30,700 youth gangs operating in the United States, with a total membership (estimated) of 850,000.

How do law enforcement agencies distinguish between gang members and nongang members? Six common practices are employed. The most successful and common strategy is to focus on specific displays and symbols (colors, tattoos, etc.). Otherwise, police may classify someone as being affiliated with a gang if he or she is arrested with known gang members, is designated as such by other police departments, or is identified by informants. A number, surprisingly, willingly identify themselves as gang members, in both custodial and noncustodial settings.

CRITICAL THINKING

1. According to recent data, gang homicides are on the rise. What can be done?

2. Why do you think so many young people join gangs?

Source: Arlen Egley, Jr., James C. Howell, and Meena Harris, *Highlights of the 2012 National Youth Gang Survey* (Washington, DC: Office of Juvenile Justice and Delinquency Prevention, 2014), http://www.ojjdp.gov/pubs/248025.pdf (accessed February 2015).

Kharey Wise arrives at Pace University to testify against the death penalty at a hearing before the New York State Assembly. Wise, who was wrongfully convicted of beating and raping a female jogger in Central Park in 1989, spent 15 years in prison. He was released when the real assailant confessed to the crime.

LO4 Summarize police processing of juvenile offenders

detention The temporary care of a child alleged to be a delinquent or status offender who requires secure custody, pending court disposition.

- The degree of cooperation obtained from the child and parents, along with their demeanor, attitude, and personal characteristics
- Whether the child denies the allegations in the petition and insists on a court hearing[30]

Legal Rights

After a juvenile has been taken into custody, the child has the same right to be free from unreasonable searches and seizures as an adult does. Children in police custody can be detained prior to trial, interrogated, and placed in lineups. However, because of their youth and inexperience, children are generally afforded more protections than adults. Even though the Supreme Court has given juveniles the same *Miranda* rights as adults, police must ensure that the juvenile suspect understands his constitutional rights and, if there is some question, must provide access to a parent or guardian to protect the child's legal interests. Police should interrogate a juvenile without an adult present only if they are sure that the youth is unquestionably mature and experienced enough to understand his legal rights.[31]

The Juvenile Court Process

After the police have determined that a case warrants further attention, they will bind it over to the prosecutor's office, which then has the responsibility for channeling the case through the juvenile court. In addition, cases may be petitioned to the court from nonlaw enforcement sources, such as when educational authorities ask the court to intervene in cases of truancy or when parents directly petition the court asking that their child be considered a status offender. The juvenile court plays a major role in controlling juvenile behavior and delivering social services to children in need.

US juvenile courts process an estimated 1.6 million delinquency cases each year. The juvenile court delinquency caseload today is four times as large as it was in 1960.

The Intake Process

After police processing, the juvenile offender is usually remanded to the local juvenile court's intake division. At this juncture, court intake officers or probation personnel review and initially screen the child and the family to determine whether the child needs to be handled formally or the case can be settled without the need for costly and intrusive official intervention. Their report helps the prosecutor decide whether to handle the case informally or bind it over for trial. The intake stage represents an opportunity to place a child in informal programs both within the court and in the community. The intake process also is critically important because more than half of the referrals to the juvenile courts never go beyond this stage.

The Detention Process

After a juvenile is formally taken into custody, either as a delinquent or as a status offender, the prosecutor usually makes a decision to release the child to the parent or guardian or to detain the child in a secure shelter pending trial.

Detention has always been a controversial area of juvenile justice. Far too many children have been routinely placed in detention while awaiting court appearances. Status offenders and delinquents have been held in the same facility, and in many parts of the country, adult county jails were used to detain juvenile offenders. The Juvenile Justice Act of 1974 emphasized reducing the number of children placed in inappropriate detention facilities. Although the act was largely effective, the practice continues in some places.

Despite such measures, hundreds of thousands of youths, most of whom are already living under difficult circumstances, are placed in pretrial detention each year. Many have suffered long histories of abuse and mental health problems.[32] The detention decision may reflect a child's personal characteristics and the quality of his or her home life rather than dangerousness or flight risk.[33] Detention is widely misapplied, according to the report by the Justice Policy Institute, a Washington, DC–based group, because even though detention facilities are meant to temporarily house those youths who are likely to reoffend before their trial or who are unlikely to appear for their court date, many of the youths in this country's detention centers do not meet these criteria. Of youths in detention, 70 percent are held for nonviolent charges. More than two-thirds are charged with property offenses, public order offenses, technical probation violations, or status offenses (such as running away or breaking curfew).[34]

LEGAL ISSUES Most state statutes ordinarily require a hearing on the appropriateness of detention if the initial decision is to keep the child in custody. At this hearing, the child has a right to counsel and may be given other procedural due process safeguards, notably the privilege against self-incrimination and the right to confront and cross-examine witnesses. Most state juvenile court acts provide criteria to support a decision to detain the child. These include (1) the need to protect the child, (2) whether the child presents a serious danger to the public, and (3) the likelihood that the juvenile will return to court for adjudication. Whereas in adult cases, most offenders are released if they can afford bail, juveniles may be detained for a variety of reasons, including their own protection. Normally, the finding of the judge that the child should be detained must be supported by factual evidence. In the 1984 case of *Schall v. Martin,* the Supreme Court upheld the right of the states to detain a child before trial to protect that child's welfare and the public safety.[35]

REFORMING DETENTION There has been an ongoing effort to reform detention. The most important reform has been the successful effort to remove status offenders from lockups containing delinquents. After decades of effort, nearly all states have passed laws

Participants in the Orange County (Florida) Youthful Offenders Program receive individualized instruction, eventually leading to a high school diploma or GED. Graduates receive recognition for their accomplishments, as shown here.

© Joel Gordon 2005

requiring that status offenders be placed in nonsecure shelters, rather than secure detention facilities, thereby reducing their contact with more dangerous delinquent youths.

Another serious problem is the detention of youths in adult jails. This practice is common in rural areas where there are relatively few separate facilities for young offenders.[36] The OJJDP has given millions of dollars in aid to encourage the removal of juveniles from adult lockups. These grants have helped jurisdictions develop intake screening procedures, specific release or detention criteria, and alternative residential and nonresidential programs for juveniles awaiting trial. By 1980, amendments to the act mandating the absolute removal of juveniles from jails had been adopted. Despite such efforts, many states are not complying with the removal provisions and still detain juveniles in adult jails. Adding to their numbers are youths who commit nonserious acts—such as running away—but are apprehended in rural areas where there are no juvenile facilities. Some states also define the age limit for delinquency as 16 or 17 and therefore treat minors of that age as legal adults.

Placing young offenders in adult jails continues to be a significant problem in the juvenile justice system. Juveniles detained in adult jails often live in squalid conditions and are subject to physical and sexual abuse. The practice is widely condemned, but eliminating the confinement of juveniles in adult institutions remains a difficult task.

Bail

If a child is not detained, the question of bail arises. Federal courts have not found it necessary to rule on the issue of a juvenile's constitutional right to bail because liberal statutory release provisions act as appropriate alternatives. Although only a few state statutes allow release on money bail, many others have juvenile code provisions that emphasize the release of the child to the parents as an acceptable substitute. A constitutional right to bail that on its face seems to benefit a child may have unforeseen results. The imposition of money bail might create a serious economic strain on the child's family, while conflicting with the protective and social concerns of the juvenile court. Considerations of economic liabilities and other procedural inequities have influenced the majority of courts that have confronted this question to hold that juveniles do not have a right to bail.

Meagan Grunwald reacts as the guilty verdict is read at 4th District Court Saturday May 9, 2015, in Provo, Utah. A jury found Grunwald, a Utah teenager, guilty Saturday for a 50-mile crime spree that left one sheriff's deputy dead and another wounded. Grunwald, 18, faces up to life in prison when she is sentenced July 18 for the January 2014 chase that also included a carjacking. Her boyfriend, 27-year-old Jose Angel Garcia-Jauregui, was killed in a shootout with police.

AP Images/Chris Detrick

LO5 Describe the juvenile court process

Plea Bargaining

Before trial, prosecutors in the juvenile courts may attempt to negotiate a settlement to the case. For example, if the offender admits to the facts of the petition, he may be offered placement in a special community-based treatment program in lieu of a term in a secure state facility. Or a status offense petition may be substituted for one of delinquency so that the adolescent can avoid being housed in a state training school and instead be placed in a more treatment-oriented facility.

If a bargain can be reached, the child will be asked to admit in open court that he did in fact commit the act of which he stands accused. State juvenile courts tend to minimize the stigma associated with the use of adult criminal standards by using other terminology, such as "agree to a finding" or "accept the petition" rather than "admit guilt." When the child makes an admission, juvenile courts require the following procedural safeguards: the child knows of the right to a trial, the plea or admission is made voluntarily, and the child understands the charges and consequences of the plea.

Waiver of Jurisdiction

Before development of the first modern juvenile court in Illinois in 1899, juveniles were tried for violations of the law in adult criminal courts. The consequences were devastating; many children were treated as criminal offenders and often sentenced to adult prisons. Although the subsequent passage of state legislation creating juvenile courts eliminated this problem, the juvenile justice system did recognize that certain forms of conduct require that children be tried as adults. Today, most American jurisdictions provide by statute for **waiver**, or transfer, of juvenile offenders to the criminal courts. Waiver is also widely used in juvenile courts in Europe and Great Britain.[37]

In its most basic form, the decision of whether to waive a juvenile to the adult, or criminal, court is made in a **transfer hearing**. The decision to transfer a juvenile to the criminal court is often based on statutory criteria established by the state's juvenile court act, so waiver provisions vary considerably among jurisdictions. Most commonly considered are the child's age and the nature of the offense alleged in the petition. Some jurisdictions require that children be over a certain age (typically, 14) before they can be waived. Others mandate that the youth be charged with a felony before being tried as an adult, whereas others permit waiver of jurisdiction to the criminal court regardless of the seriousness of the offense when a child is a chronic offender. In about 30 states, certain offenses, such as murder, have been excluded from juvenile court jurisdiction, creating a mandatory waiver provision for children who have committed those crimes.

LEGAL CONTROLS Because of the nature of the waiver decision and its effect on the child in terms of status and disposition, the Supreme Court has imposed procedural protections for juveniles in the waiver process. In *Kent v. United States* (1966), the Court held that the waiver proceeding is a critically important stage in the juvenile justice process and that juveniles must be afforded minimum requirements of due process of law at such proceedings, including the right to legal counsel.[38] Then in *Breed v. Jones* (1975), the Court held that the prosecution of juveniles as adults in the California Superior Court violated the double jeopardy clause of the Fifth Amendment if they had previously been tried on the same charge in juvenile court.[39] The Court concluded that jeopardy attaches when the juvenile court begins to hear evidence at the adjudicatory hearing; this requires that the waiver hearing take place before any adjudication.

YOUTH IN ADULT COURTS Today, all states allow juveniles to be tried as adults in criminal courts in one of four ways:

- *Direct file waiver.* The prosecutor has the discretion of filing charges for certain legislatively designated offenses in either juvenile or criminal court. About 15 states have this provision.
- *Excluded offense waiver.* State laws exclude from juvenile court jurisdiction certain offenses that are either very minor, such as traffic or fishing violations, or very serious, such as murder. About 29 states now have such laws for certain crimes.
- *Judicial waiver.* After a formal hearing at which both prosecutor and defense attorney present evidence, a juvenile court judge may decide to waive jurisdiction and transfer the case to criminal court. This procedure is also known as "binding over" or "certifying" juvenile cases to criminal court. (Nearly all states permit judicial waiver.)
- *Reverse waiver.* State laws mandate that certain offenses be tried in adult court. After the case is heard in the adult court, the trial judge may decide that the offender would be better served by the juvenile court and order a reverse waiver. About 25 states have this provision for certain circumstances.[40]

Every state has provisions for handling juveniles in adult criminal courts, and the trend is to make the waiver broader.[41] In 31 states, after a juvenile is tried in adult court, she is no longer eligible for juvenile justice on any subsequent offense.

ETHICAL REFLECTION

Elizabeth Williams Case

Reread this chapter's opening vignette. Steven Miles was sentenced to life in prison for a heinous murder. He was 16 at the time of his crime. Prior to the murder, his family signed him up for mental health services because he had heard "voices." He was released from treatment in 2013, three months before he killed his girlfriend. In light of this information, was the sentence just? Was it fair? Why or why not?

waiver (juvenile) A practice in which the juvenile court waives its jurisdiction over a juvenile and transfers the case to adult criminal court for trial. In some states, a waiver hearing is held to determine jurisdiction, whereas in others, juveniles may be automatically waived if they are accused of committing a serious crime such as murder.

transfer hearing The hearing in which a decision is made to waive a juvenile to the criminal court. Waiver decisions are based on such criteria as the child's age, her or his prior offense history, and the nature of the offense.

From left, Santa Clara County (California) District Attorney Jeff Rosen talks about the provisions of Audrie's Law, as Attorney Robert Allard, Sheila Pott, mother of Audrie Pott, and State Senator Jim Beall, listen. The law is aimed at deterring the bullying, cyberbullying, and sexual assault that played roles in the suicide of Audrie Pott, a 15-year-old Saratoga High School student.

THE EFFECT OF WAIVER The problem of youths processed in adult courts is a serious one. About 5,400 juvenile delinquency cases are now being transferred to the adult courts each year.[42] Supporters view the waiver process as a sound method of getting the most serious juvenile offenders off the streets. Kids are most likely to be transferred to criminal court if they have injured someone with a weapon or if they have a long juvenile court record.[43]

Waiver has its advocates, but many experts question its utility, arguing that it does more harm than good. One great fear is that juveniles will be forced to serve time in adult prisons, where they will be exposed to experienced criminals in what are essentially "schools for crime." In addition, children may be targets of adult predators if they are confined to adult institutions:

- Youths held in adult prisons and jails are five times more likely to be victims of attempted sexual attacks or rapes than those held in juvenile institutions.
- The suicide rate for juveniles in adult prisons and jails is nearly eight times higher than that for juveniles in youth detention centers.[44]

Although some youths who are transferred to adult court never spend a day in an adult prison, thousands do, and many of them become enmeshed in the daily life of an adult correctional facility. They miss out on being housed in juvenile facilities that are smaller, have much lower inmate-to-staff ratios, and place greater emphasis on treatment, counseling, education, and mentoring of inmates. Although some adult facilities do provide easy access to education and treatment, young inmates lose out on developing the relatively more supportive, mentoring-focused style of staff–inmate interactions that a juvenile facility provides.[45]

What is accomplished by treating juveniles as adults? Studies of the impact of the recent waiver statutes have yielded several interesting—and conflicting—results. For example, research by Benjamin Steiner and Emily Wright on the effect of direct waiver laws found that they have little effect on juvenile violent crime rates in the states that have adopted them.[46] Other studies have found that juveniles waived to adult court receive harsher punishment and may be viewed as dangerous and incapable of being rehabilitated.[47] Waived juveniles may also spend more time in juvenile detention awaiting trial. In the end, what began as a get-tough measure has had the opposite effect, while costing taxpayers more money.[48]

Transfer decisions are not always carried out fairly or equitably, and evidence indicates that minorities are waived to adult court at a rate that is greater than their representation in the population.[49] Some evidence supports a change in that trend, however. Recent data suggest that the percentage of cases judicially waived to the criminal court is roughly similar for blacks and whites.[50] This is especially true in the case of drug-related offenses.

LO6 Explain the concept of waiver

initial appearance A juvenile's first appearance before the juvenile court judge, in which the charges are reviewed and an effort is made to settle the case without a trial. If the child does not have legal counsel, an attorney is appointed.

LO7 Explain the importance of *In re Gault*

The Adjudication

There are often three judicial hearings in the juvenile court process. The first, typically called an **initial appearance**, is similar to the arraignment in the adult system. The child is informed of the charges against him, attorneys are appointed, bail is reviewed, and, in many instances, cases are settled with an admission of the facts, followed by a community sentence. If the case cannot be settled at this initial stage, it is bound over for trial.

The second is the adjudicatory hearing (often called the fact-finding hearing in juvenile proceedings). In it, the court hears evidence on the allegations stated in the delinquency petition. In its early development, the juvenile court did not emphasize judicial rule making similar to that of the criminal trial process. Absent were such basic requirements as the standard of proof, rules of evidence, and similar adjudicatory formalities. Proceedings were to be nonadversarial, informal, and noncriminal. Gradually, however, the juvenile trial process became a target of criticism because judges were handing out punishments to children without affording them legal rights. This changed in 1967 when the Supreme Court's landmark *In re Gault* decision radically altered the juvenile justice system.[51] In *Gault*, the Court ruled that the concept of fundamental fairness is applicable to juvenile delinquency proceedings. The Court granted critical rights to juvenile defendants, most important among them the notice of the charges, the right to counsel, the right to confront and cross-examine witnesses, the privilege against self-incrimination, and the right to a transcript of the trial record.

The *Gault* decision completely altered the juvenile trial process. Instead of dealing with children in a benign and paternalistic fashion, the courts were forced to process juvenile offenders within the framework of appropriate constitutional procedures. And although *Gault* was technically limited to the adjudicatory stage, it has spurred further legal reform throughout the juvenile system. Today, the right to counsel, the privilege against self-incrimination, the right to treatment in detention and correctional facilities, and other constitutional protections are applied at all stages of the juvenile process, from investigation through adjudication to parole. *Gault* ushered in an era of legal rights for juveniles.

After an adjudicatory hearing has been completed, the court is normally required to enter a judgment against the child. This may take the form of declaring the child delinquent or a ward of the court or possibly even suspending judgment to avoid the stigma of a juvenile record. After a judgment is entered, the court can begin its determination of possible dispositions for the child.

Disposition and Treatment

At the dispositional hearing, the third step in juvenile adjudication, the judge imposes a sentence on the juvenile offender based on her offense, prior record, and family background. Normally, the judge has broad discretionary power to issue a range of dispositions from dismissal to institutional commitment. In theory, the dispositional decision is an effort by the court to serve the best interests of the child, the family, and the community. In many respects, this postadjudicative process is the most important stage in the juvenile court system because it represents the last opportunity for the court to influence the child and control her behavior.

To ensure that only relevant and appropriate evidence is considered by the court during adjudication, most jurisdictions require a separate hearing to formulate an appropriate disposition. The bifurcated hearing process ensures that the adjudicatory hearing is used solely to determine the merits of the allegations, whereas the dispositional hearing determines whether the child is in need of rehabilitation.

In theory, the juvenile court seeks to provide a disposition that represents an individualized treatment plan for the child. This decision is normally based on the presentence investigation of the probation department, reports from social agencies, and possibly a psychiatric evaluation. The judge generally has broad discretion in dispositional matters but is limited by the provisions of the state's juvenile court act. The following are typical juvenile court dispositions:

- Suspended judgment
- Probation
- Placement in a community treatment program
- Commitment to the state agency responsible for juvenile institutional care

In addition, the court may place the child with parents or relatives, make dispositional arrangements with private youth-serving agencies, or order the child committed to a mental institution.

DISPOSITION OUTCOMES In dispositional hearings, juvenile court judges must determine the most appropriate sanction for delinquent youths. Disposition options include commitment to an institution or another residential facility; probation; and a

disposition For juvenile offenders, the equivalent of sentencing for adult offenders. The theory is that disposition is more rehabilitative than retributive. Possible dispositions include dismissing the case, releasing the youth to the custody of his or her parents, placing the offender on probation, or sending him or her to a state correctional institution.

commitment Decision of judge ordering an adjudicated and sentenced juvenile offender to be placed in a correctional facility.

treatment The rehabilitative method used to effect a change of behavior in the juvenile offender, in the form of therapy, or educational or vocational programs.

variety of other dispositions, such as referral to an outside agency or treatment program, community service, fines, or restitution. Very often, the court imposes some combination of these sanctions. What have been the trends in juvenile disposition? The number of adjudicated delinquency cases resulting in residential placement has increased significantly during the past decade, and today about 25 percent of all juveniles who are adjudicated delinquent get some form of residential treatment.[52] Approximately 60 percent of those adjudicated delinquent receive probation.[53]

WEB APP 13.3 Visit the Sentencing Project's Juvenile Justice page at **http://www.sentencingproject.org/template/page.cfm?id=184.** Select an article under the "Juvenile Justice News" heading, and determine whether sentencing reforms for juveniles would have made a difference. What sentencing reforms in particular would have had the greatest impact, if any? Why?

Juvenile Sentencing Reform

Over the past decade, juvenile justice experts and the general public have become aroused about the serious juvenile crime rate in general and about violent acts committed by children in particular. As a result, some law enforcement officials and conservative legislators have demanded that the juvenile justice system take a more serious stand with dangerous juvenile offenders. Many state legislatures have responded by toughening their juvenile codes. Some jurisdictions have passed mandatory or determinate incarceration sentences for juveniles convicted of serious felonies. Not all jurisdictions have abandoned rehabilitation as a primary dispositional goal, however, and some still hold to the philosophy that placements should be based on the least detrimental alternative. This view requires that judges employ the least intrusive measures possible to safeguard a child's growth and development.[54]

A second reform has been the concerted effort to remove status offenders from the juvenile justice system and restrict their entry into institutional programs. Because of the development of numerous diversion programs, many children involved in truancy and incorrigible behavior who ordinarily would have been sent to a closed institution are now being placed in community programs. There are far fewer status offenders in detention or institutions than ever before.

A third reform effort has been to standardize dispositions in juvenile court. As early as 1977, Washington passed one of the first determinate sentencing laws for juvenile offenders, resulting in other states adopting similar statutes.[55] All children found to be delinquent are evaluated on a point system based on their age, prior juvenile record, and type of crime committed. Minor offenders are handled in the community. Those committing more serious offenses are placed on probation. Children who commit the most serious offenses are subject to standardized institutional penalties. As a result, juvenile offenders who commit such crimes as rape or armed robbery are being sentenced to institutionalization for two, three, and four years. This approach is different from indeterminate sentencing, under which children who have committed a serious crime might be released from institutions in less than a year if correctional authorities believe they have been rehabilitated.

REALITY CHECK

MYTH OR REALITY?

Youths are more violent and criminally dangerous today than they were in the past.

MYTH. Highly publicized juvenile crimes may give this impression, but the data tell a different story: juvenile crime (and arrests) peaked in the early to mid-1990s.

During the latter part of the 1990s and into the early twenty-first century, juvenile crime declined. In 2004, the arrest rate for violent crimes committed by juveniles dropped to historic lows. Recently, juvenile crime and arrests have fluctuated, but they have yet to come close to their historic highs. What fuels the perception that juvenile crime is more serious and extensive than at any point in the past?

The Juvenile Correctional Process

After disposition in juvenile court, delinquent offenders may be placed in some form of correctional treatment. Although many are placed in the community, more than 100,000 are now in secure facilities.

Probation

The most commonly used formal sentence for juvenile offenders is probation, and many states require that a youth fail on probation before being sent to an institution (unless the criminal act is quite serious). Probation involves placing the child under the supervision of the juvenile probation department for the purpose of community treatment. A juvenile may also be required to follow special rules, such as maintaining a curfew or attending substance abuse meetings. Alternative sanctions such as community service or monetary restitution may be ordered. Serious offenders can be placed in intensive supervision or under house arrest. Just as in the adult system, probation can be revoked if the rules are not followed, and the court may impose stricter sanctions.

Juvenile probation is an important component of the juvenile justice system. It is the most widely used method of community treatment in juvenile court. Similar in form and function to adult probation, supervising juveniles in the community combines elements of treatment and control. Some probation officers maintain a social work orientation and want to provide needy kids with an effective treatment plan; however, others maintain a law enforcement orientation, believing that their clients are offenders who need close monitoring.[56]

Institutionalization

The most severe of the statutory dispositions available to the juvenile court involves commitment of the child to an institution. The committed child may be sent to a state training school or private residential treatment facility. These are usually minimum-security facilities with small populations and an emphasis on treatment and education. Some states, however, maintain facilities with populations of more than 1,000.

State statutes vary in terms of the length of the child's commitment. Traditionally, many jurisdictions committed the child up to majority, which usually meant 21 years of age. This normally deprived the child of freedom for an extensive period of time—sometimes longer than an adult sentenced for the same offense would be confined. As a result, some states have passed legislation under which children are committed for periods ranging from one to three years.

To better handle violent juvenile offenders, some states have created separate or intermediate juvenile systems. Under such statutes, 14- to 17-year-olds charged with certain violent felonies are treated as adults and, if convicted, are sentenced to new intermediate prisons, separated from both adult and regular juvenile offenders, for terms of two to five years.

Today about 60,000 juveniles are being held in either privately run or publicly managed residential juvenile correctional facilities.[57] That number is down significantly from years past (it was almost 100,000 in 2003, by comparison). The typical resident of a juvenile facility is a 15- to 16-year-old white male incarcerated for an average stay of five months in a public facility or six months in a private facility. Private facilities tend to house younger teens, whereas public institutions provide custodial care for older youths, including a small percentage of youths between 18 and 21 years of age.

Deinstitutionalization

Some experts in delinquency and juvenile law question the policy of institutionalizing juvenile offenders. Many believe that large institutions are too costly to operate and only produce more sophisticated criminals. This dilemma has produced a number of efforts to remove youths from juvenile facilities and replace large institutions with smaller, community-based facilities. The Commonwealth of Massachusetts closed all of its state training schools more than 20 years ago (subsequently, however, public pressure caused a few secure facilities to be reopened). Many other states have established small residential facilities operated by juvenile-care agencies to replace larger units.

Despite the daily rhetoric on crime control, public support for community-based programs for juveniles still exists. Although such programs are not panaceas, many experts still recommend more treatment and less incarceration for juvenile offenders. Utah, Maryland, Vermont, and Pennsylvania, for example, have dramatically reduced their reform school populations while setting up a wide range of intensive treatment programs for juveniles. Many large, impersonal, and expensive state institutions with unqualified staff and ineffective treatment programs have been eliminated.

Aftercare

Aftercare marks the final stage of the formal juvenile justice process. Its purpose is to help youths make the transition from residential or institutional settings back into the community. Effective aftercare programs provide adequate supervision and support services to help juvenile offenders avoid criminal activity. Examples of programs include electronic monitoring, counseling, treatment and community service referrals, education, work training, and intensive parole supervision.

Most juvenile aftercare involves parole. A juvenile parole officer provides the child with counseling, school referral, vocational training, and other services. Children who violate the conditions of parole may have their parole revoked and be returned to the institution. Unlike the adult postconviction process, where the Supreme Court has imposed procedural protections in probation and parole revocations, juveniles do not have such due process rights. State courts have also been reluctant to grant juveniles rights in this area, and those that have granted them generally refuse to require that the whole array of rights be made available, as they are to adult offenders. Since the *Gault* decision, however, many states have adopted administrative regulations requiring juvenile agencies to incorporate due process, such as proper notice of the hearing and the right to counsel in postconviction proceedings.

LO8 Describe the juvenile correctional process

Problems of Juvenile Justice

Even those experts who want to retain an independent juvenile court have called for its restructuring.[58] Crime control advocates want to reduce the court's jurisdiction over juveniles charged with serious crimes and liberalize the prosecutor's ability to try them in adult courts. Opponents feel that the traditional *parens patriae* philosophy of juvenile justice ought to prevail.

In *Bad Kids: Race and the Transformation of the Juvenile Court,* legal expert Barry Feld makes the rather controversial suggestion that the juvenile court system should be discontinued and replaced by an alternative method of justice.[59] In Feld's words, the juvenile court has become a "deficient second-rate criminal court." The welfare and rehabilitative purposes of the juvenile court have been subordinated to its role as law enforcement agent, so there is little purpose for retaining it in its current state. Feld's beliefs have been substantiated by research showing that at least in some jurisdictions, the focus of juvenile justice has shifted from individual needs to the seriousness of the crime, enhancing the prosecution's power to make decisions and the system's reliance on the adversarial process at the expense of *parens patriae*.[60]

Not all experts agree with Feld that the juvenile court has become redundant. Some, such as John Kerbs, believe that the get-tough approach will force the criminal courts to provide harsher sentences and tougher treatment—and that the brunt of these draconian sentences will fall squarely on the shoulders of minority youths. Research efforts routinely show that African American adults are unduly punished in adult courts. Sending juvenile offenders to these venues is likely to enmesh them further in a system that is already unfair.[61]

Minority Overrepresentation in Juvenile Justice

In addition to controversies over its goals and values, another significant and enduring problem in juvenile justice is the overrepresentation of minority youths in the system and the inequitable treatment they receive. Minority youths accused of delinquent acts are less likely than white youths to be diverted from the court system into informal sanctions and are more likely to receive sentences involving incarceration. Nationally, the ratio of minority custody to white custody is 2.6 to 1, meaning that there are 2.6 members of minority groups in custody for every white juvenile in custody.[62] In some states, the ratio is greater than 4 to 1.[63]

Not only is the disproportionate minority representation in juvenile correctional facilities a very serious matter, but it also reflects the racial disparity that occurs at every

Minorities are overrepresented in both the adult criminal justice system and the juvenile justice system. Why is this the case?

stage of the juvenile justice process. A disproportionate number of minority youths suffer arrest, detention, waivers, and so on. A report by the National Council on Crime and Delinquency highlights this problem. The council's "Treatment of Youth of Color in the Justice System" describes how minority youths receive differential treatment at every stage of the justice process.[64] Among the findings from the council's report are these:

- Although African American youths are 16 percent of the adolescent population in the United States, they are 38 percent of the almost 100,000 youths confined in local detention and state correctional systems. They were overrepresented in all offense categories.
- Youths of color make up the majority of young people held in both public and private facilities.
- Youths of color, especially Latino youths, are a much larger proportion of the young in public facilities than in private facilities, which tend to be less harsh environments.
- Although they represent just 34 percent of the US population, youths of color represent 62 percent of young people in detention, 66 percent of those committed to public facilities, and 55 percent of those committed to private facilities.
- Nationwide, youths of color were overrepresented in the detained population at 3.1 times the rate of white youths, among commitments to public facilities at 2.9 times the rate of white youths, and among private commitments at 2 times the rate of white youths.
- Overall, custody rates were four times greater for African American youths than for white youths. Custody rates for Latino and Native American youths were 1.8 and 2.6 times the custody rate for white youths, respectively.

Preventing Delinquency

Although the juvenile justice system has been concerned with controlling delinquent behavior, important efforts are now being made to prevent delinquency before it occurs. "Delinquency prevention" refers to intervening in young people's lives before they engage in delinquency in the first place—that is, preventing any involvement in delinquency at all. In the past, delinquency prevention was the responsibility of treatment-oriented agencies such as day care providers, YMCA and YWCA, Boys and Girls Clubs of America, and other private and public agencies. Today, there are many community-based treatment programs involving a combination of juvenile justice and treatment agencies. Some programs focus on the educational experience and attempt to help kids maintain their bond to society by strengthening their attachments to school. Much of these efforts are conducted by social workers whose specialty is working with troubled youths.

Comprehensive community-based, delinquency-prevention programs are taking a systematic approach or using a comprehensive planning model to develop preventive interventions. This includes analyzing the delinquency problem, identifying resources available in the community, prioritizing delinquency problems, and identifying successful programs in other communities and tailoring them to local conditions and needs.[65] Not all comprehensive community-based prevention programs follow this model, but evidence suggests that this approach will produce the greatest reductions in juvenile delinquency.[66]

ETHICAL Challenge

You are a juvenile court judge. John has been arrested for robbery and rape. His victim, a young neighborhood girl, was seriously injured in the attack and needed extensive hospitalization; she is now in counseling. Because the charges are serious, John can be waived to the adult court and tried as an adult even though he is only 14 years old. Under existing state law, a hearing must be held to determine whether there is sufficient evidence that John cannot be successfully treated in the juvenile justice system and therefore warrants transfer to the adult system. The final decision on the matter is yours alone.

At the waiver hearing, you discover that John is the oldest of three siblings living in a single-parent home. He has had no contact with his father for more than 10 years. His psychological evaluations show hostility, anger toward females, and great feelings of frustration. His intelligence is above average, but his behavioral and academic records are poor. John is a loner with few friends. This is his first formal involvement with the juvenile court. Previous contact was limited to an informal complaint for disorderly conduct at age 13, which was dismissed by the court's intake department. During the hearing, John verbalizes what you interpret to be superficial remorse for his offenses.

Ethical Challenge: Write an essay discussing whether you would waive John to the adult court or treat him as a juvenile. Give the reasons for your decision. Besides reading this chapter, you may want to visit the OJJDP's website and follow the topics link for "waiver/transfer" under the "Courts" heading (http://www.ojjdp.gov/search/topiclist.asp). You may also want to read this report regarding delinquency cases in juvenile court: http://www.ojjdp.gov/pubs/239081.pdf.

SUMMARY

LO1 *Describe the history of juvenile justice* The modern practice of legally separating adult and juvenile offenders can be traced back to the development of Elizabethan-era poor laws and the creation of the English chancery court. Poor laws mandated care for wayward and destitute children. Chancery courts protected the rights and welfare of children who could not care for themselves. Juvenile justice was also influenced by the child-saving movement. The child savers were responsible for creating a number of programs for indigent youths, including the New York House of Refuge, which began operations in 1825. The child savers also influenced state and local governments to create independent correctional institutions to house minors.

LO2 *Discuss the establishment of the juvenile court* The child savers lobbied for an independent, state-supported juvenile court. Their efforts prompted the development of the first comprehensive juvenile court in Illinois in 1899. The main concern was the "best interests of the child," not strict adherence to legal doctrine, constitutional rights, or due process of law. Youngsters who were found delinquent in juvenile court could spend years in a state training school.

LO3 *Describe the changes in juvenile justice that began in the 1960s and continue today* In the 1960s and 1970s, the US Supreme Court radically altered the juvenile justice system when it rendered a series of decisions that established the right of juveniles to due process of law. The term *juvenile delinquency* now refers to children who fall under a jurisdictional age limit, which varies from state to state, and who commit an act in violation of the penal code. Status offenders commit acts forbidden to minors, which include truancy, running away, and being a habitually disobedient and ungovernable child. Another trend has been to create family courts, which include a broad range of family- and child-related issues within their jurisdictions.

LO4 *Summarize police processing of juvenile offenders* Most states do not have specific statutory provisions distinguishing the arrest process for children from that for adults. Some jurisdictions give broad arrest powers to the police in juvenile cases by authorizing the officer to make an arrest whenever she or he believes that the child's behavior falls within the jurisdiction of the juvenile court. Police may arrest youths for behavior considered legal for adults, including running away, violating curfew, and being in possession of alcohol. When a juvenile is found to have engaged in delinquent or incorrigible behavior, police agencies are charged with the decision to release or to detain the child and refer her to juvenile court.

L05 *Describe the juvenile court process* After a juvenile is formally taken into custody, either as a delinquent or as a status offender, the prosecutor usually decides whether to release the child to the parent or guardian or to detain the child in a secure shelter pending trial. There are often three judicial hearings in the juvenile court process. The first, typically called an initial appearance, is similar to the arraignment in the adult system. The adjudicatory hearing (often called the fact-finding hearing) is the second. In it, the court hears evidence on the allegations stated in the delinquency petition. At a later dispositional hearing, the juvenile court judge imposes a sentence on the juvenile offender based on the offense, the youth's prior record, and his or her family background.

L06 *Explain the concept of waiver* Today, most US jurisdictions provide by statute for waiver, or transfer, of juvenile offenders to the criminal courts. In *Kent v. United States* (1966), the Supreme Court held that the waiver proceeding is a critically important stage in the juvenile justice process and that juveniles must be afforded minimum requirements of due process of law at such proceedings, including the right to legal counsel. Waiver does not seem to influence crime rates or recidivism rates; one reason may be that juveniles whose cases are waived to criminal court are sentenced more leniently than they would have been in juvenile court.

L07 *Explain the importance of In re Gault* *In re Gault* granted critical rights to juvenile defendants, the most important of these rights being notice of the charges, the right to counsel, the right to confront and cross-examine witnesses, the privilege against self-incrimination, and the right to a transcript of the trial record.

L08 *Describe the juvenile correctional process* Probation is the most commonly used formal sentence for juvenile offenders, and many states require that a youth fail on probation before being sent to an institution (unless the criminal act is quite serious). The most severe of the statutory dispositions available to the juvenile court involves commitment of the child to an institution. Some experts in delinquency and juvenile law question the policy of institutionalizing juvenile offenders.

KEY TERMS

parens patriae, p. 322	juvenile court, p. 326	waiver (juvenile), p. 335	commitment, p. 337
poor laws, p. 324	juvenile delinquency, p. 328	transfer hearing, p. 335	treatment, p. 337
child savers, p. 324	status offender, p. 328	initial appearance, p. 336	
Children's Aid Society, p. 325	detention, p. 332	disposition, p. 337	

REVIEW QUESTIONS

1. Should status offenders be treated by the juvenile court? Explain. Should they be placed in confinement for such acts as running away or cutting school? Why or why not?

2. Should a juvenile ever be waived to adult court with the possible risk that the child will be incarcerated with adult felons? Why or why not?

3. Do you support the death penalty for children? Explain.

4. Should juveniles be given mandatory incarceration sentences for serious crimes, as adults are? Explain.

5. Is it fair to deny juveniles a jury trial? Why or why not?

6. Do you think the trend toward treating juveniles like adult offenders is desirable? Explain.

14 Crime and Justice in the New Millennium

Charles Ponzi, the architect of the scheme that bears his name, promised clients a 50 percent profit within 45 days, or 100 percent profit within 90 days, while swindling them out of their money.

REALITY CHECK

MYTH OR REALITY?

- Corporate criminals rarely go to jail.
- Worries about illegal logging are the overblown fantasies of a group of troublemaking tree huggers.
- A cyber attack against Iran derailed its nuclear program.
- There are more drug users in the world than the populations of England, Italy, and France combined.

In 2015, federal agents uncovered a $40 million Ponzi scheme, and the principals were sentenced to very long prison sentences. How did this scheme unfold? It seems that in 2007, Keith Franklin Simmons, a North Carolina businessman looking for a way to make easy money—formulated an investment scheme called "Black Diamond," which he promoted as a legitimate hedge fund involved in foreign currency trading. Black Diamond, Simmons told investors, was highly safe, independently audited, and had steady rates of return. To help solicit investors from around the country, Simmons and his co-conspirators recruited "regional managers" to get investors involved, including friends, family, and acquaintances. These early investors were promised financial compensation for bringing new investors on board, so they in turn praised Black Diamond and its high rate of return to their friends, family, and acquaintances. Unfortunately, not a single dollar of investor funds was actually invested. While the fund claimed that investor accounts amounted to more than $120 million, in reality, all of the accounts combined totaled less than $1 million. What happened to the money? As long as new money was coming in, Simmons and his partners were able to keep making some payments to their early investors while at the same time continuing to fund their lavish lifestyles, which included mansions, luxury vehicles, and expensive trips. When Black Diamond began to collapse in on itself—there was not enough new money coming in to keep the old investors satisfied or to continue lining the pockets of the criminals running the fraud—Simmons began a new Ponzi scheme, and used the money from investors in the new scheme to make payments to the investors of the old scheme, keeping the rest for himself and his partners in crime. Simmons received a 40-year prison sentence, one year for each million he stole![1]

Pyramid: Selensergen/Dreamstime.com; Images of people: olly/Shutterstock.com

LEARNING OBJECTIVES

LO1 List the various forms of terrorism and their goals

LO2 Demonstrate how the USA Patriot Act is designed to combat terrorists

LO3 Evaluate the various forms of green crime

LO4 Comprehend the meaning of the term "cyber crime"

LO5 Classify the methods now being used to thwart cyber criminals

LO6 Explain the influence of globalization on crime

LO7 Interpret the concept of transnational crime

LO8 List some of the most important transnational crime groups

LO9 Explain the methods law enforcement is now using to thwart transnational criminal syndicates

It is now routine for offenders such as Keith Simmons to use complex and technologically sophisticated methods to secure illegal profits and provide criminal services. Criminal conspiracies are not only national in scope but also can be transnational enterprises that involve gangs whose activities cross nations and continents. Not only has the tech revolution spawned wide-ranging criminal conspiracies, it has also enabled law enforcement agencies to apprehend and prosecute the new breed of highly sophisticated criminals by eavesdropping on their conversations, monitoring their phone calls, and tracking suspects—advances that frighten civil libertarians concerned about the expansion of governmental interference with citizens' private lives.

In some instances, high-tech crimes can involve a single individual who engages in a complex criminal enterprise, such as a multimillion-dollar fraud. It can also involve traditional crime that spans the globe, including trafficking in contraband, such as narcotics and weapons, and even humans who are kidnapped to become sex slaves and unpaid laborers.

In this chapter, we review five independent yet interrelated emerging criminal activities that are presenting challenges for the criminal justice system: terrorism, corporate enterprise crime, green crime, cyber crime, and transnational organized crime. Although distinct and independent, these emerging crime types often overlap. Terrorists may use the Internet to plan attacks, gain recruits, and solicit operational funds. Transnational criminals may use cyberspace to conduct fraud schemes and then seek legitimate enterprises to launder money, diversify their sources of income, increase their power and influence, and gain and enhance respectability.[2] Transnational criminal gangs may appropriate marketing concepts from legitimate business enterprises. Otherwise legitimate corporate enterprise executives may turn to green crimes such as illegally dumping hazardous waste products to get around government regulations and increase their profits.[3]

terrorism Politically motivated violence designed to intimidate governmental or civilian opponents to attain political or social objectives.

corporate enterprise crime Conspiracies that involve bending the rules of legitimate business and commerce to make illegal profits in the marketplace. Enterprise crimes involve the violation of law in the course of an otherwise legitimate occupation.

green crime Criminal activity that involves violation of rules and laws designed to protect the environment, including illegal dumping, polluting, fishing, logging and so on.

cyber crime Any criminal activity that employs the Internet or other computer-based systems for illegal gain.

transnational organized crime Global criminal conspiracies designed to obtain power and influence or monetary gains that cross nation states and legal jurisdictions.

Terrorism

On May 1, 2011, Osama bin Laden—head of the al-Qaeda terror network and the world's most wanted man—was killed by members of Seal Team 6 in his secret compound located in Abbottabad, Pakistan. His burial at sea marked the end of the turbulent career of this terrorist mastermind, but it certainly did not end the threat of terror. Cells and groups have now been dispersed around the world, helping to offset this loss in leadership. The murder of US Ambassador Christopher Stevens on September 11, 2012, in Benghazi, Libya, by a local militia organization was a potent reminder that the threat of terror did not die with Osama bin Laden.

Terrorism has become a major concern of the criminal justice system, and for good reason. Since 9/11, terror attacks and plots have become so common here and abroad that the media routinely ignore bombings and shootings unless it involves a shocking murder such as that of Ambassador Stevens. So many thousands of incidents occur each year that the landscape can change at a moment's notice. Some of the latest data finds that the toll of terrorism has escalated:

- In a single year, about 18,000 people were killed in terrorist attacks, 61 percent more than the previous year.
- About 82 percent of all deaths from terrorist attack occur in just five countries: Iraq, Afghanistan, Pakistan, Nigeria, and Syria.

- Since 2000, the number of deaths from terrorism has increased 500 percent, rising from 3,361 in 2000 to 18,000 today.
- The latest jump in terrorist activity has coincided with the start of the Syrian civil war in 2011 and the resulting chaos in the area that has spilled over to neighboring states.
- Today terrorism is dominated by four groups: the Taliban, Boko Haram, ISIL, and al Qa'ida.[4]

Defining Terrorism

What exactly is terrorism? Definitions abound, but the US State Department defines terrorism (from the Latin *terrere*, to frighten) as "the premeditated, politically motivated violence perpetrated against noncombatant targets by subnational groups or clandestine agents, usually intended to influence an audience."[5] Terrorists typically emphasize violence as a mechanism to promote change and to force individuals, groups, communities, or governments into conceding to the terrorists' political demands.[6] Because the terrorist lacks large armies and formidable weapons, their use of subterfuge, secrecy, and hit-and-run tactics is designed to give them a psychological advantage and the power to neutralize the physical superiority of their opponents.

Although many terrorists have political goals, not all do, and some groups use terror tactics to bring about what they consider to be social reform—for example, by attacking women wearing fur coats or sabotaging property during a labor dispute.[7] Therefore, terrorist activities may be aimed at promoting an ideology rather than political change.

Terrorist Goals and Objectives

Terrorism has accelerated its development into a major component of contemporary conflict. In the service of various ideologies and aspirations, terrorism has become a far-reaching weapon aimed at achieving a variety of goals and objectives. Some of the more common aims of terror groups are described in the following sections.

REVOLUTIONARY TERRORISTS Revolutionary terrorists use violence to frighten those in power and their supporters to replace the existing government with a regime that holds acceptable political or religious views. Terrorist actions such as kidnapping, assassination, and bombing are designed to draw repressive responses from governments helping revolutionaries to expose, through the skilled use of media coverage, the government's inhumane nature. The original reason for the government's harsh response may be lost as the effect of counterterrorist activities is felt by uninvolved people. Recent conflict (2014–2015) in the Ukraine between the Russian-backed separatists and government forces illustrates this type of revolutionary terrorist activity.

POLITICAL TERRORISTS Political terrorism is directed at people or groups who oppose the terrorists' political ideology or whom the terrorists define as "outsiders" who must be destroyed or convinced to leave the country. Political terrorists may not want to replace the existing government but to shape public sentiment so that it reflects the terrorists' views. Domestic terrorists in the United States are often lone wolves who are acting on their own. For example, on August 5, 2012, a mass shooting took place at a Sikh temple in Oak Creek, Wisconsin, when Wade Michael Page, a white supremacist associated with the Hammerskin Nation, killed six people before taking his own life after being surrounded and wounded by police.[8] Lone wolves are not unique to the United States. On July 22, 2011, Norwegian Anders Behring Breivik, a right wing extremist whose objective was to rid the country of Muslims by replacing the liberal government, first set off a car bomb explosion at the executive government quarter of Oslo that killed eight people and wounded many others. Then dressed as a police officer, he proceeded to a youth camp organized by the liberal Norwegian Labour Party on the island of Utøya where he mercilessly gunned down 69 people, mostly young teens.[9]

NATIONALIST TERRORISM Nationalist terrorism promotes the interests of a minority ethnic or religious group that believes it has been persecuted under majority or colonial rule and wants to carve out its own independent homeland. Of course, most nations oppose loss of territory and will use violence to suppress nationalist movements. In the Middle East, Israel has long clashed with groups such as Hamas, whose aim is creating an independent Palestinian state. In Nigeria, the militant Islamist group Boko Haram is fighting to overthrow the government and create an Islamic state based on Sharia law. That terrorist group's most important objective is to rid the area of Western influence, which they consider "haram," or forbidden. They believe Muslims are forbidden from voting in elections, wearing shirts, or receiving a Western style education.

RETRIBUTIVE TERRORISM Retributive terrorists use violence as a method of influence, persuasion, or intimidation to get people to accept their social, religious, or political views.[10] Victims are usually selected for their maximum propaganda value, ensuring a high degree of media coverage. The message is that the target population had better comply with their demands because the terrorists are desperate enough to "do anything." Sometimes this may backfire if the attack results in the death of innocents, especially children, along with the symbolic targets.

Unconventional military tactics are used, especially secrecy and surprise, as well as targeting civilians, including women and children. Because the goal is to inflict maximum horror, it makes sense to choose targets that contain the largest number of victims from all walks of life. The message is that everyone is a target, and no one is safe.

The most visible retributive terrorist groups today—the Islamic State of Iraq and the Levant (ISIL)—which in its attempt to set up a caliphate in areas of Iraq and Syria has undertaken gross abuses of human rights, including indiscriminate killing and deliberate targeting of civilians, mass executions, persecution of individuals, kidnapping civilians, forced displacement of minority groups, killing and maiming of children, rape, and other forms of sexual violence. ISIL's use of beheadings and burnings to execute captured soldiers has shocked the world. At the same time, ISIL has recruited thousands of foreign fighters to Iraq and Syria from across the globe, eager to join the band. The group has made use of Internet technology to publicize its ultra-violent acts that have spurred the recruitment of violent jihadists from around the world.

STATE-SPONSORED TERRORISM State-sponsored terrorism involves the use of force by a repressive government regime that forces its citizens into obedience, oppresses minorities, and stifles political dissent. Death squads and the use of government troops to destroy political opposition parties are often associated with political terrorism. Tens of thousands of people continue to become victims of security operations that result in disappearances and executions. Political prisoners are now being tortured in about 100 countries, people have disappeared or are being held in secret detention in about 20 countries, and government-sponsored death squads have been operating in more than 35 countries. Countries known for encouraging violent control of dissidents include Brazil, Colombia, Guatemala, Honduras, Peru, Iran, and Sudan.[11] As might be expected, governments claim that repressive measures are needed to control revolutionary groups that routinely use violence. Thus the use of terror is sometimes a way of defending the nation against violence, a conundrum that supports the idea that a state is both protective and destructive.[12]

LO1 List the various forms of terrorism and their goals

Fighting Terrorism

Soon after the September 11 terrorist attacks, law enforcement agencies of both the federal and local governments switched their priorities to combat the threat of terrorism. Counterterror became a top priority of the FBI and various other state and local authorities. In addition, the Department of Homeland Security was created to coordinate the nation's antiterror activities. Local and state police agencies have developed counterterror units, especially in big cities that may be prime targets such as New York. New schemes are constantly being implemented, including using community policing tactics to reach out to the Muslim community and neutralize the appeal of jihadist groups.[13]

While most terror attacks have occurred overseas, local law enforcement agencies in larger cities are now developing anti-terror tactics. Here on New Year's Eve 2014, counterterrorism officers in New York City, armed with an explosives detection device, inspect revelers entering a cordoned off area in Times Square.

THE PATRIOT ACT Several laws were enacted to help prevent further acts of violence against the United States and create greater flexibility in the fight to control terrorist activity. Most important, Congress passed the **USA Patriot Act (USAPA)** on October 26, 2001. More than 342 pages long at the time of its passage, the Patriot Act created new laws and made changes to more than 15 different existing statutes. Its aim was to give sweeping new powers to domestic law enforcement and international intelligence agencies in an effort to fight terrorism, to expand the definition of terrorist activities, and to alter sanctions for violent terrorism. USAPA expanded all four traditional tools of surveillance—wiretaps, search warrants, pen/trap orders (installing devices that record phone calls), and subpoenas. The Foreign Intelligence Surveillance Act (FISA), which governs domestic operations by intelligence agencies, was also expanded.

USAPA gave the FBI and other intelligence agencies greater power to check and monitor phone, Internet, and computer records without first having to demonstrate that they were being used by a suspect or the target of a court order. The act also expanded the definition of "terrorism" and enabled the government to monitor more closely those people suspected of "harboring" and giving "material support" to terrorists (Sections 803, 805). It increased the authority of the US attorney general to detain and deport noncitizens with little or no judicial review. The attorney general may now certify that he has "reasonable grounds to believe" that a noncitizen endangers national security and is therefore eligible for deportation. The attorney general and secretary of state were also given the authority to designate domestic groups as terrorist organizations and to deport any noncitizen who is a member of such an organization.

On May 26, 2011, three key provisions in the USA Patriot Act were extended through 2015, including roving wiretaps, searches of business records, and conducting surveillance of "lone wolves"—individuals suspected of terrorist-related activities not linked to terrorist groups.

REFORMING THE ACT While the USAPA makes it easier for law enforcement agencies to investigate, convict, and incarcerate terror suspects, civil libertarians have been troubled by some provisions of the act that erode civil rights. For example, the Patriot Act permits the government to share information from grand jury proceedings and from criminal wiretaps with intelligence agencies. There has also been concern that the Patriot Act authority is not limited to true terrorism but that investigations cover a much broader range of activity involving reasonable political dissent. The fear of governmental intrusion into the lives of private citizens was aggravated when National Security Agency

USA Patriot Act (USAPA) A law designed to grant new powers to domestic law enforcement and international intelligence agencies in an effort to fight terrorism.

Controlling Terrorism

A device has been developed that can be implanted in every new computer to constantly monitor every web page visited on the Internet. This device can record every transaction and activity and automatically send the data to government computers programmed to look for suspicious web activity. The surveillance device would enable the government to keep tabs on what people are doing, what they buy, what they download, and so on. This new system could help track people logging on to terrorist sites or purchasing dangerous bomb-making chemicals online. After a person becomes a suspect in a crime, that person can be easily monitored from a distance without danger to any government agent. They cannot hide or escape detection.

Write an essay discussing the ethical issues that surround the employment of such a device. Even if you approve of the device, what questions might you want answered before it becomes standard equipment on home computers? You might want to refer to sections on e-tailing crimes and copyright infringement for inspiration.

LO2 Demonstrate how the USA Patriot Act is designed to combat terrorists

(NSA) employee Edward Snowden revealed that the agency was conducting widespread surveillance of the general public; Snowden fled to Russia rather than face criminal prosecution for his leak.

In the aftermath of the Snowden case, there was significant national discussion about allowing the NSA to continue to collect phone records of private citizens. Due to fears that the Patriot Act gave the government too much power to eavesdrop, Congress created a new law, the USA Freedom Act, which restored the Patriot Act's expiring provisions except for the NSA's monitoring of all phone conversations.[14] The NSA will still be able to access phone records for counterterrorism efforts, but they will need to go through phone providers to do so and will be prohibited from collecting conversations of nonterror suspects. The roving wiretaps, searches of business records, and conducting surveillance of "lone wolves" provisions are now back in effect.[15] President Obama signed the USA Freedom Act into law on June 2, 2015.

There has also been significant controversy over the long-term detention of suspected terrorists without trial at the Guantánamo camp in Cuba. Although this complex issue is far from resolved, in *Boumediene v. Bush*, the Supreme Court held that the Guantánamo prisoners had a right to *habeas corpus* protection under the US Constitution.[16] *Boumediene*, along with similar cases, indicates that terror suspects are not denied the protection of the US Constitution and that their indefinite detention without trial is not legally permissible. On January 7, 2011, President Obama signed the 2011 Defense Authorization Bill, which contains provisions preventing the transfer of Guantánamo prisoners to the mainland or to other foreign countries, a measure that continues the use of this overseas detention facility. While efforts have been made to close the base, it remains in operation at this time.

Corporate Enterprise Crime

Terrorism is not the only new problem facing the justice system. Others involve large-scale corporate enterprise crimes. Although they may get less press than terrorism, these white-collar crimes amount to hundreds of billions of dollars in losses each year, far outstripping the cost of any other type of crime. Businesspeople such as Bernard Madoff and Robert Allen Stanford, owner of Stanford Financial Group and other affiliated companies, have been convicted on charges of scamming people out of their life savings.[17] These financial crimes caused the financial collapse of 2008, during which several prominent companies (such as Bear Stearns and Lehman Brothers) went out of business, banks failed, and the federal government was forced to provide more than a trillion dollars in relief to keep other companies from failing (American Insurance Group, General Motors, and Citigroup).[18] Government enforcement agencies such as the FBI and the New York State Attorney General's office became involved in investigating accounting schemes designed to deceive both investors and government auditors about the true financial condition of a corporation in an attempt to inflate share prices based on fictitious performance indicators. This practice not only can result in financial losses to investors but has done immeasurable damage to both the states and US economy.[19]

Fraud on Wall Street

The creation of global capital markets has created unprecedented opportunities for US businesses to access capital and investors to diversify their portfolios. This large-scale investment growth, however, has also led to significant growth in the amount of fraud and misconduct on Wall Street. Investment firms have engaged in deceptive schemes to defraud clients. Investment counselors and insurance agents use their positions to cheat individual clients by misleading them on the quality of their investments. Financial organizations have cheated their clients by promoting risky investments as being iron-clad safe.

Perhaps the greatest of these crimes was pulled off by financier Bernard Madoff, His firm, Madoff Investments, became one of Wall Street's largest "specialist" trading firms, dedicated to investment management and advice. Managing billions in assets, Madoff was a member of the jet set and a trusted advisor to many wealthy people, including director Steven Spielberg, as well as sophisticated financial managers and investors. At first, Madoff promised and delivered healthy returns, helping to draw in a constant flow of investors. Things went south when the market crashed and people wanted their money back, only to find there was none available. It turns out that Madoff's asset management firm was a giant Ponzi scheme (discussed earlier). Madoff had not invested any of the money he had taken in from investors but instead deposited it in various banks, using the interest and principal to pay off investors when they wanted to take money out of their accounts. At first, few did because they were making such fantastic paper profits that they kept reinvesting dividends and capital gains. Madoff, of course, convinced them to keep their profits in the account rather than ask for a distribution. When the market turned and people began asking for their principal, his house of cards fell apart.

Madoff's Ponzi scheme has been estimated to cost clients an estimated $65 billion, maybe the largest criminal conspiracy in history. On March 12, 2009, he pleaded guilty to an 11-count criminal complaint, charged with violations of the antifraud provisions of the Securities Act of 1933, the Securities Exchange Act of 1934, and the Investment Advisers Act of 1940.[20] On June 29, 2009, Madoff was sentenced to 150 years in prison, a life sentence.[21]

Ponzi scheme An investment fraud that involves the payment of purported returns to existing investors from funds contributed by new investors.

Criminalizing Corporate Enterprise Crime

What efforts have been made to bring violators of the public trust to justice? Though law enforcement agencies and the courts have traditionally been reluctant to throw corporate executives in jail, a number of well-publicized cases (such as Bernard Madoff) indicate that the gloves are off, and the government is willing to punish high-profile corporate criminals with long prison sentences. Because the Madoff, Enron, and other scandals have deprived so many people of their life savings and caused such disruptions in the financial markets, both justice system personnel and the general public now consider corporate crimes as more serious offenses than common-law theft offenses and

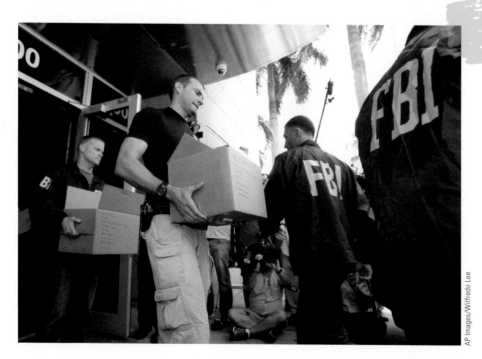

AP Images/Wilfredo Lee

Fraud may occur in both public and private organizations. Here Federal agents load a van with boxes of evidence taken from the headquarters of the Confederation of North, Central American and Caribbean Association Football (CONCACAF) in Miami Beach, Florida. Swiss prosecutors opened criminal proceedings into FIFA's awarding of the 2018 and 2022 World Cups, after seven soccer officials were arrested after probe of "rampant, systemic, and deep-rooted" corruption in the organization.

MYTH OR REALITY?

Corporate criminals rarely go to jail.

MYTH. Maybe in the past, but it is common today for corporate criminals to do time.

Is there any point in putting middle-aged corporate executives behind bars? Can you think of a better punishment for this type of crime?

their perpetrators deserving of severe punishment.[22] Penalties have been increasing, and long prison sentences are being routinely handed out for corporate crimes.[23] In fact, punishing corporate criminals with prison terms has become so routine and punishments so severe, that some commentators now argue that the government may actually be going overboard.[24]

CORPORATE CRIME LAW ENFORCEMENT The detection and enforcement of large-scale corporate crime are primarily in the hands of administrative departments and agencies with investigation arms to police the areas of commerce that are their responsibility. The Securities and Exchange Commission (SEC) has been given the responsibility for overseeing the nation's capital markets. It is assigned the task of protecting investors, facilitating capital formation, and maintaining fair, orderly, and efficient markets.

If SEC investigators detect inappropriate behavior in the financial system, they may decide either to bring a case in federal court or before an administrative law judge, depending on the type of sanction or relief that is being sought. For example, if the commission seeks to bar or remove someone from acting as a corporate officer, they must take the case to a federal district court. During the proceeding, the SEC will ask the judge to issue a court order, called an injunction, prohibiting any further acts or practices that violate the law or commission rules. An injunction can also require audits and accounting for frauds. In addition to barring or suspending the individual from serving as a corporate officer or director, the SEC can seek civil monetary penalties or the return of illegal profits (called disgorgement). A person who violates the court's order may be found in contempt and be subject to additional fines or imprisonment.

The decision to pursue criminal rather than civil violations usually is based on both the seriousness of the case and the perpetrator's intent, actions to conceal the violation, and prior record. Any evidence of criminal activity is then sent to the Department of Justice or the FBI for investigation. Some other federal agencies, such as the Environmental Protection Agency (EPA) and the US Postal Service, have their own investigative arms. Enforcement generally is reactive (generated by complaints) rather than proactive (involving ongoing investigations or the monitoring of activities). Investigations are carried out by the various federal agencies and the FBI. If criminal prosecution is called for, the case will be handled by attorneys from the criminal, tax, antitrust, and civil rights divisions of the Justice Department. If insufficient evidence is available to warrant a criminal prosecution, the case will be handled civilly or administratively by some other federal agency. For example, the Federal Trade Commission can issue a cease and desist order in antitrust or merchandising fraud cases.

STATE LEVEL ENFORCEMENT Responding to the threat of large-scale corporate fraud, a number of states have created special task forces and prosecution teams to crack down on fraudulent schemes and bring perpetrators to justice. In addition, state legislatures have passed a spate of new laws aimed directly at easing prosecution for corporate crimes. For example, the Mortgage Fraud Task Force in Dade County Florida (Miami) was created to address the issues of mortgage and foreclosure rescue fraud. The task force investigates cases in which false or misleading documents are filed to fool lenders into making mortgage loans to people who cannot hope to pay them back or on properties whose values have been grossly inflated.[25]

Green Crime

On April 20, 2010, an explosion occurred on the *Deepwater Horizon* oil rig, killing 11 platform workers and injuring 17 others.[26] The rig was built by Hyundai Heavy Industries of Korea, owned by the Transocean Drilling Corporation, the drilling overseen by Halliburton, and leased by BP (formerly British Petroleum), to drill a deep water (5,000 feet below the surface) rig in the Gulf of Mexico. At first, estimates of the spill were 5,000 barrels a day, but they quickly rose to 60,000. While company officials frantically tried to stem the flow with a variety of failed schemes, millions of barrels of escaping oil created a slick that covered thousands of square miles, devastating wildlife, and causing one of the greatest natural disasters in the nation's history. BP, facing civil fines, offered to place $20 billion in an escrow account to cover damages. The leak was finally stopped in August 2010.

On June 1, 2010, the Obama administration announced that it had launched a criminal probe to "prosecute to the fullest extent of the law" any persons or companies that broke the law in the time leading up to the spill.[27] Under federal environmental laws, a company may be charged with a misdemeanor for negligent conduct or a felony if there is evidence that company personnel knowingly engaged in conduct risking injury. It would be a criminal act if, for example, employees of BP or its subcontractors, Transocean and Halliburton did any of the following:

- Lied in the permit process for obtaining a drilling license
- Tried to cover up the severity of the spill
- Knowing of negligence in construction, chose to ignore the danger it imposed
- Engaged in or approved of unsafe, risky, or dangerous methods to remove the drill, knowing that such methods could injure those on board

In the aftermath of the case, BP agreed to pay $4.5 billion in fines and other penalties and to plead guilty to 14 criminal charges related to the rig explosion. Then, on January 3, 2013, Transocean agreed to plead guilty to violating the Clean Water Act (CWA) and to pay a total of $1.4 billion in civil and criminal fines and penalties for its conduct in relation to the *Deepwater Horizon* disaster.[28]

Oil spills are just part of the growing green crime problem that is facing the justice system. Green crimes are violations of existing criminal laws designed to protect people, the environment, or both. They include crimes against workers such as occupational health and safety crimes, as well as laws designed to protect nature and the environment (the Clean Air Act, Clean Water Act, etc.). Green crimes involve a wide range of actions and outcomes that harm the environment and that stem from decisions about what is produced, where it is produced, and how it is produced.[29] Global warming, overdevelopment, population growth, and other changes will continue to bring these issues front and center, and they will soon become a major focus of the criminal justice system.[30]

Forms of Green Crime

Green crime can take many different forms, ranging from deforestation and illegal logging to violations of worker safety. A few of the most damaging green crimes are set out next.

ILLEGAL LOGGING Illegal logging involves harvesting, processing, and transporting timber or wood products in violation of existing laws and treaties.[31] It is a universal phenomenon, occurring in major timber-producing countries, especially in the third world where enforcement is lax. Logging violations include taking trees in protected areas such as national parks, going over legally prescribed logging quotas, processing logs without acquiring licenses, and exporting logs without paying export duties. By sidestepping the law, loggers can create greater profits than those generated through legal methods. The situation is serious because illegal logging can have severe environmental and social impact: illegal logging exhausts forests, destroys wildlife, and damages its habitats. It causes ruinous damage to the forests, including deforestation and forest degradation worldwide. The destruction of forest cover can cause flash floods and landslides that have killed thousands of people.[32]

While the scale of illegal logging is difficult to estimate, it is believed that more than half of all logging activities in the most vulnerable forest regions—Southeast Asia, Central Africa, South America, and Russia—may be conducted illegally. Worldwide estimates suggest that illegal activities may account for over a tenth of the total global timber trade, representing products worth at least $15 billion per year.

REALITY CHECK

MYTH OR REALITY?

Worries about illegal logging are the overblown fantasies of a group of troublemaking tree huggers.

MYTH. Illegal logging is a $15 billion industry that is threatening the ecological balance in many areas around the globe.

If the flow of illegal drugs cannot be contained, how can we control the illegal harvesting of trees?

ILLEGAL FISHING Unlicensed and illegal fishing practices are another billion-dollar green crime. It can take on many forms and involve highly different parties, ranging from huge factory ships operating on the high seas that catch thousands of tons of fish on each voyage, to smaller, locally operating ships that confine themselves to national waters. Illegal fishing occurs when these ships sign on to their home nation's rules but then choose to ignore their scope and boundary, or operate in a country's waters without permission or on the high seas without a flag. Because catches remain clandestine and are not reported, their illegal fishing can have a detrimental effect on some species as government regulators have no idea how many are being caught. As a result, stocks become depleted and species endangered. Illegal fishing reduces the number of new adults that can replace those lost from fishing, and the ability of populations to replenish themselves is quickly lost.[33]

ILLEGAL POLLUTING Some green-criminals want to skirt local, state, and federal restrictions on dumping dangerous substances in the environment. Rather than pay expensive processing fees, they may secretly dispose of hazardous wastes in illegal dump sites. Illegally dumped wastes can be hazardous or nonhazardous materials that are discarded in an effort to avoid disposal fees or the time and effort required for proper disposal. Materials dumped range from used motor oil to waste from construction sites.

Criminal environmental pollution is defined as the intentional or negligent discharge of a toxic or contaminating substance into the biosystem that is known to have an adverse effect on the natural environment or life. Individuals and companies may commit this crime to save processing and dumping fees, thereby adding to profits. Illegal pollution schemes may involve the ground release of toxic chemicals such as Kepone, vinyl chloride, mercury, PCBs, and asbestos. Illegal and/or controlled air pollutants include hydrochlorofluorocarbons (HCFCs), aerosols, asbestos, carbon monoxide, chlorofluorocarbons (CFCs), criteria air pollutants, lead, mercury, methane, nitrogen oxides (NO_x), radon, refrigerants, and sulfur oxides (SO_2). Water pollution is defined as the dumping of a substance that degrades or alters the quality of the waters to an extent that is detrimental to their use by humans or by an animal or a plant that is useful to humans. This includes the disposal into rivers, lakes, and streams of toxic chemicals.[34]

LO3 Evaluate the various forms of green crime

Environmental crimes can range from widespread pollution caused by industrial waste to individuals illegally dumping in a neighborhood environment. Denver City Councilman Paul Lopez examines an illegal dumpsite where a fence had been torched, in an alley in the Westwood neighborhood of Denver, Colorado. Lopez was touring alleys and said he is concerned about illegal dumping in the area and is pushing for a tougher ordinance in the city. "We have to get people to realize this neighborhood is not a dumping ground. We refuse to be treated like this," Lopez said.

Craig F. Walker/Getty Images

Enforcing Environmental Laws

The United States and most sovereign nations have passed laws making it a crime to pollute or damage the environment. For example, among environmental laws in the United States are the following:

- *Clean Water Act (1972)*. Establishes and maintains goals and standards for US water quality and purity. It was amended in 1987 to increase controls on toxic pollutants, and in 1990 to more effectively address the hazard of oil spills.
- *Emergency Planning and Community Right-to-Know Act (1986)*. Requires companies to disclose information about toxic chemicals they release into the air and water and dispose of on land.
- *Endangered Species Act (1973)*. Designed to protect and recover endangered and threatened species of fish, wildlife, and plants in the United States and beyond. The law works in part by protecting species habitats.
- *Oil Pollution Act (1990)*. Enacted in the aftermath of the *Exxon Valdez* oil spill in Alaska's Prince William Sound, this law streamlines federal response to oil spills by requiring oil storage facilities and vessels to prepare spill-response plans and provide for their rapid implementation. The law also increases polluters' liability for cleanup costs and damage to natural resources.

The major enforcement arm against environmental crimes is the Environmental Protection Agency, which was given full law enforcement authority in 1988. The EPA has successfully prosecuted significant violations across all major environmental statutes, including data fraud cases (e.g., private laboratories submitting false environmental data to state and federal environmental agencies); indiscriminate hazardous waste dumping that resulted in serious injuries and death; industry-wide ocean dumping by cruise ships; oil spills that caused significant damage to waterways, wetlands, and beaches; international smuggling of CFC refrigerants that damage the ozone layer and increase skin cancer risk; and illegal handling of hazardous substances such as pesticides and asbestos that exposed children, the poor, and other especially vulnerable groups to potentially serious illness.[35] Its Criminal Investigation Division (EPA CID) investigates allegations of criminal wrongdoing prohibited by various environmental statutes.

Cyber Crime

Cyber crime, another challenge for the contemporary justice system, typically involves the theft and/or destruction of information, resources, or funds via computer networks and/or the Internet. This relatively new category of crimes presents a compelling challenge for the justice system and the law enforcement community because (1) it is rapidly evolving, with new schemes being created daily; (2) it is difficult to detect through traditional law enforcement channels; and (3) to control it, agents of the justice system must develop technical skills that match those of the perpetrators.[36] It is even possible that the recent decline in crime is actually a result of cyber crime replacing traditional street crime. Instead of robbing a bank at gunpoint, a new group of contemporary thieves finds it easier to hack into accounts and transfer funds to offshore banks. Instead of shoplifting from a brick-and-mortar store, the contemporary cyber thief devises clever schemes to steal from e-tailers.

There are actually three forms of cyber crime (summarized in Concept Summary 14.1). Some cyber criminals use modern technology to accumulate goods and services. Cyber theft schemes range from illegally copying material under copyright protection to using technology to commit traditional theft-based offenses such as larceny and fraud. Other cyber criminals are motivated less by profit and more by the urge to commit cyber vandalism, or technological destruction. They aim their malicious attacks at disrupting, defacing, and destroying technology they find offensive. Finally, cyber war consists of acts aimed at undermining the social, economic, and political system of an enemy nation by destroying its electronic infrastructure and disrupting its economy. This can range from stealing secrets from foreign nations (cyber espionage) to destroying an enemy's Web-based infrastructure.

cyber theft The use of computer networks for criminal profits. Illegal copyright infringement, identity theft, and Internet securities fraud are examples of cyber theft.

cyber vandalism Malicious attacks aimed at disrupting, defacing, and destroying technology.

cyber war Politically motivated attacks designed to compromise the electronic infrastructure of the enemy and to disrupt its economy.

WEB APP 14.1 The FBI maintains a comprehensive site that has a lot of information and stories on cyber crime: at **http://www.fbi.gov/about-us/investigate/cyber/**. Do you think a separate federal agency should be created to enforce cyber laws?

A specialist works at the Defense Computer Forensics Laboratory (DCFL) in Linthicum, Maryland. The lab is ground zero in the nation's fight against cybercrime. Government computer scientists work to combat cyber attacks by thieves, hostile states, and hackers. Since its creation in 1998, the DCFL has provided the Defense Department with investigative services, digital search assistance, and expert testimony in court.

AP Images/Manuel Balce Ceneta

CONCEPT SUMMARY 14.1 Typology of Cyber Crimes

Crime	Definition	Examples
Cyber theft	Use of cyberspace to distribute illegal goods and services or to defraud people for quick profits	Illegal copyright infringement, identity theft, Internet securities fraud, warez
Cyber vandalism	Use of cyberspace for revenge, for destruction, or to achieve malicious ends	Website defacement, worms, viruses, cyber stalking, cyber bullying
Cyber war	An effort by enemy forces to disrupt the intersection where the virtual electronic reality of computers meets the physical world	Use of logic bombs to disrupt or destroy "secure" systems or networks, use of the Internet to communicate covertly with agents around the world

Cyber Theft: Cyber Crimes for Profit

The Internet enables criminals to operate in a more efficient and effective manner. Cyber thieves now have the luxury of remaining anonymous, living almost anywhere on the planet, conducting their business during the day or at night, and working alone or in a group, while at the same time reaching a much greater number of potential victims than ever before. No longer are con artists and criminal entrepreneurs limited to fleecing victims in a particular geographic locale; the whole world can be their target. And the technology revolution has opened up novel avenues of attack for cyber theft—ranging from the unlawful distribution of computer software to Internet security fraud—that heretofore were nonexistent.

Cyber thieves conspire to use cyberspace either to distribute illegal goods and services or to defraud people for quick profits. Some of the most common methods are described next.

COMPUTER FRAUD Computer fraud is not a unique offense but rather a common-law crime committed using contemporary technology. Consequently, many computer crimes are prosecuted under such traditional criminal statutes as those prohibiting larceny and fraud. However, not all computer crimes fall under common-law statutes because the property stolen may be intangible—that is, electronic and/or magnetic impulse. Such crimes include the following:

- *Theft of information.* This is the unauthorized obtaining of information from a computer (e.g., hacking), including software that is copied for profit.
- *The "salami slice" fraud.* The perpetrator carefully "slices" small sums from the balances of a large number of accounts to bypass internal controls and escape detection.
- *Software theft.* The comparative ease of making copies of computer software has led to a huge illegal market, depriving authors of very significant revenues.[37]

INTERNET PORNOGRAPHY The IT revolution has revitalized the porn industry. The Internet is an ideal venue for selling and distributing adult material; the computer is an ideal device for storing and viewing it. Although it is difficult to estimate the extent of the industry, it is estimated that the revenue generated from adult sites each year is greater than all movie box office sales. The number of visits to pornographic sites (mostly by men, though women make up about 30 percent of the viewers) surpasses those made to Internet search engines; some individual sites report as many as 50 million hits per year.[38] Revenue from Internet porn comes from a number of sources: paid subscriptions, advertisements for other porn sites, fees for diverting web traffic to other sites, sale of sex-related products, and providing auxiliary services such as age verification services. Nonetheless, industry sales are in decline: free Internet content has cut into paid services. As a result, producers, actors, and actresses in the domestic adult film industry have found their income substantially declining.[39]

Because many porn sites are located in foreign lands, enforcement has proven difficult. However, law enforcement agencies here and abroad are now cracking down on the distribution of sexual material involving juveniles (kiddie porn).

DENIAL-OF-SERVICE ATTACK A denial-of-service attack is an attempt to extort money from legitimate users of an Internet service by threatening to interfere with the user's access to that service.[40] Examples include attempts to "flood" a computer network, thereby preventing access by legitimate network traffic; attempts to disrupt connections within a computer network, thereby interrupting access to a service; attempts to prevent a particular individual from accessing a service; and attempts to disrupt service to a specific system or person.

denial-of-service attack Extorting money from an Internet service user by threatening to prevent the user having access to the service.

COPYRIGHT INFRINGEMENT It is now common for groups of individuals to plan and work together to obtain software illegally and then "crack" or "rip" its copyright protections before posting it on the Internet for use by other members of the group. Its criminal purveyors refer to this pirated material as warez (pronounced like "wares," as in "software"). Frequently, these new pirated copies reach the Internet days or weeks before the legitimate product is commercially available.

warez Copyrighted software illegally downloaded and sold by organized groups without license to do so.

INTERNET SECURITIES FRAUD Internet securities fraud involves using the Internet to intentionally manipulate the securities marketplace for profit. Three major types of Internet securities fraud are common today:

- *Market manipulation.* Stock market manipulation occurs when an individual tries to control the price of stock by interfering with the natural forces of supply and demand. There are two principal forms of this crime: the "pump and dump" and the "cyber smear." In a pump and dump scheme, erroneous and deceptive information is posted online to get unsuspecting investors interested in a stock while those spreading the information sell previously purchased stock at an inflated price. The cyber smear is a reverse pump and dump: negative information is spread online about a stock, driving down its price and enabling people to buy it at an artificially low price before rebuttals by the company's officers reestablish the legitimate price.

- *Fraudulent offerings of securities.* Some cyber criminals create websites specifically designed to sell securities fraudulently. To make the offerings look more attractive than they are, assets may be inflated, expected returns overstated, and risks understated. In these schemes, investors are promised abnormally high profits on their investments. No investment is actually made. Early investors are paid returns with the investment money received from the later investors. The system usually collapses, and the later investors do not receive dividends and lose their initial investment.
- *Illegal touting.* This crime occurs when individuals make securities recommendations and fail to disclose that they are being paid to disseminate their favorable opinions.

IDENTITY THEFT These thieves use the Internet to steal someone's identity and/ or impersonate the victim to open a new credit card account or conduct some other financial transaction.[41] Identity theft can destroy a person's life by manipulating credit records or depleting bank accounts. Some identity thieves create false e-mails and/or websites that look legitimate but are designed to gain illegal access to a victims' personal information; this is known as phishing (and also as *carding* and *spoofing*).

Phishing e-mails and websites have become even more of a problem now that cyber criminals can easily copy brand names, the names of corporate personnel, and their insignia directly into the e-mail. The look is so authentic that victims believe the e-mail comes from the advertised company. Most phishers send out spam e-mails to a large number of recipients, knowing that some of those recipients will have accounts with the company they are impersonating. Some phishing schemes involve job offers. After the unsuspecting victims fill out the "application," answering personal questions and including their Social Security number, the phisher has them in his grasp.[42]

E-TAILING FRAUD New fraud schemes are evolving to exploit the fact that billions of dollars of goods are sold on the Internet each year. E-tailing fraud can involve both illegally buying and selling merchandise on the Internet. Some e-tailing scams involve failure to deliver on promised purchases or services, and others involve the substitution of cheaper or used material for higher-quality purchases.

ILLEGAL DRUG DISTRIBUTION The Internet has become a prime purveyor of prescription drugs, some of which can be quite dangerous when they are used to excess or fall into the hands of minors. Thousands of websites advertise or offer controlled prescription drugs for sale. Many require no prescription from a patient's physician, while others simply ask that the prescription be faxed—increasing the risk of multiple use of one prescription or other fraud.[43]

Cyber Vandalism: Cyber Crime with Malicious Intent

Some cyber criminals may be motivated not by greed or profit but by the desire for revenge, to inflict wanton destruction, and/or to achieve a malicious intent. Cyber vandalism involves such crimes as sending destructive viruses and worms to attack important computer networks. Cyber vandals are motivated more by malice than by greed:

- Some cyber vandals target computers and networks, seeking revenge for some perceived wrong.
- Some desire to exhibit their technical prowess and superiority.
- Some want to highlight the vulnerability of computer security systems.
- Some want to spy on other people's private financial and personal information ("computer voyeurism").
- Some want to destroy computer security because they believe in open access to all systems and programs.[44]

Some of the most common forms of cyber vandalism are discussed in detail next.

identity theft Using the Internet to steal someone's identity and/or impersonate the victim to conduct illicit transactions, such as committing fraud using the victim's name and identity.

phishing Also known as carding and spoofing, phishing consists of illegally acquiring personal information, such as bank passwords and credit card numbers, by masquerading as a trustworthy person or business in what appears to be an official electronic communication, such as an e-mail or an instant message. The term *phishing* comes from the lures used to "fish" for financial information and passwords.

e-tailing fraud Using the Internet to illegally buy or sell merchandise.

VIRUSES AND WORMS A computer virus is one type of malicious software program (also called *malware*) that disrupts or destroys existing programs and networks, causing them to perform the task for which the virus was designed.[45] The virus is then spread from one computer to another when a user sends out an infected file through e-mail or may even hack into a network. Computer worms are similar to viruses, but they use computer networks or the Internet to self-replicate and "send themselves" to other users, generally via e-mail without the aid of the operator.

TROJAN HORSES Some hackers may introduce a Trojan horse program into a computer system. The Trojan horse looks like a benign application, but it contains illicit codes that can damage the system operations. Sometimes hackers with a sense of irony will install a Trojan horse and claim that it is an antivirus program. When it is opened, it spreads viruses in the computer system. Trojan horses do not replicate themselves as viruses do, but they can be just as destructive.

WEB DEFACEMENT Cyber vandals may target the websites of their victims. Web defacement is a type of cyber vandalism that occurs when a computer hacker intrudes on another person's website by inserting or substituting codes that expose visitors to the site to misleading or provocative information.

CYBER STALKING AND CYBER HARASSMENT Traditional stalking involves repeated harassing or threatening behavior, such as following a person, appearing at a person's home or place of business, making harassing phone calls, leaving written messages or objects, or vandalizing a person's property. Cyber stalking is the use of the Internet, e-mail, or other electronic communications to stalk, and it generally refers to a pattern of threatening or malicious behaviors. Cyber harassment usually pertains to threatening or harassing e-mail messages, instant messages, or to blog entries or websites dedicated solely to tormenting an individual. It typically involves less threat of force and violence than cyber stalking.[46] Some cyber stalkers pursue minors through online chat rooms, establish a relationship with a child, and later ask to make contact. Today, Internet predators are more likely to meet, develop relationships with, and beguile at-risk adolescents and underage teenagers, rather than using coercion and violence.[47]

cyber stalking Using the Internet, e-mail, or other electronic communications devices to stalk or harass another person.

CYBER BULLYING In cyberspace, physical distance is no longer a refuge from the frequency and depth of harm doled out by a bully to his or her victim.[48] Cyber bullying is willful and repeated harm inflicted through the medium of electronic text. Like their real-world counterparts, cyber bullies are malicious and cowardly aggressors who seek pleasure or profit through the mistreatment of other individuals. Although power in traditional bullying might be physical (stature) or social (competency or popularity), online power may simply stem from net proficiency. Cyber bullies who are able to navigate the Web and use technology in a way that enables them to harass others are in a position of power relative to a victim.[49]

Cyber War

In 2010, Iran announced that the computers at its nuclear facility in Natanz were under attack by an outside enemy, presumably the United States. It turned out to be the Stuxnet computer worm, a destructive program that wiped out roughly a fifth of Iran's nuclear centrifuges and helped delay for years—though not destroy—Tehran's ability to make its first nuclear arms. It was the most effective use of cyber war to date.

Cyber war has been defined as "the premeditated, politically motivated attack against information, computer systems, computer programs, and data which result in violence against noncombatant targets by sub-national groups or clandestine agents."[50] It involves an effort by covert forces to disrupt the intersection where the virtual electronic reality of computers intersects with the physical world.[51] Cyber war may involve the use of computer network tools to shut down critical national infrastructures or to coerce or intimidate a government or civilian population.[52]

REALITY CHECK

MYTH OR REALITY?

A cyber attack against Iran derailed its nuclear program.

REALITY. The Stuxnet worm wiped out a fifth of the centrifuges Iran was using to make fissionable material.

Think of ways cyber war can be waged against a nation's infrastructure.

Even though they may come from a region where computer databases and the Internet are not widely used, terrorist organizations are beginning to understand the damage that cyber crime can inflict on their enemies. Terrorist organizations are now adapting IT into their arsenal, and agencies of the US justice system have to be ready for a sustained attack on the nation's electronic infrastructure.

One form of attack is cyber espionage. This involves hacking secure computer networks at the enemy's most sensitive military bases, defense contractors, and aerospace companies to steal important data or to assess their defenses. Infrastructure attacks can also be aimed at water treatment plants, electric plants, dams, oil refineries, and nuclear power plants. These industries all provide vital services to society by allowing people to go about their daily lives. Terrorist computer hackers could make a dam overflow or cause real property damage to oil refineries or nuclear plants by shutting down safeguards in the system to prevent catastrophic accidents.[53]

LO4 Comprehend the meaning of the term "cyber crime"

Controlling Cyber Crime

The proliferation of cyber crime has created the need for new laws and enforcement processes. Because technology evolves so rapidly, enforcement presents challenges that are particularly vexing. Numerous organizations have been set up to provide training and support for law enforcement agents. In addition, federal and state laws have been aimed at particular areas of high-tech crimes.[54] What are some of the legislative initiatives designed to limit or control cyber crime?

SOFTWARE PIRACY The government has actively pursued members of the warez community, and some have been charged and convicted under the Computer Fraud and Abuse Act (CFAA), which criminalizes accessing computer systems without authorization to obtain information.[55] The Digital Millennium Copyright Act (DMCA) makes it a crime to circumvent antipiracy measures built into most commercial software and also outlaws the manufacture, sale, or distribution of code-cracking devices used to copy software illegally.[56]

COPYRIGHT INFRINGEMENT The US Criminal Code provides penalties for a first-time illegal copyright offender of five years of incarceration and a fine of $250,000.[57] Infringing copies and all equipment used to make those copies are also subject to forfeiture and destruction.[58]

IDENTITY THEFT To meet this increasing threat, Congress passed the Identity Theft and Assumption Deterrence Act of 1998 (the Identity Theft Act) to make it a federal crime when anyone knowingly transfers or uses, without lawful authority, a means of identification of another person with the intent to commit, or to aid or abet, any unlawful activity that constitutes a violation of federal law, or that constitutes a felony under any applicable state or local law.[59] Violations of the act are investigated by federal investigative agencies such as the US Secret Service, the FBI, and the US Postal Inspection Service.

In 2004, the Identity Theft Penalty Enhancement Act was signed into law. The act increases existing penalties for the crime of identity theft, establishes aggravated identity theft as a criminal offense, and establishes mandatory penalties for aggravated identity theft. According to this law, anyone who knowingly "transfers, possesses, or uses, without lawful authority" someone else's identification will be sentenced to an extra prison term of two years with no possibility of parole. Individuals committing identity fraud while engaged in crimes associated with terrorism—such as aircraft destruction, arson, airport violence, or kidnapping top government officials—will receive a mandatory sentence enhancement of five years.

INTERNET PORNOGRAPHY It is difficult to detect and control Internet pornography. Opponents of any controls warn that the right of free speech may be violated. Congress has struggled to create legislation that will restrict objectionable use without violating

First Amendment freedoms. Fearing the proliferation of kiddie porn over the Internet, Congress enacted the Child Pornography Prevention Act of 1996 (CPPA), which outlawed sexually related material that used or *appeared to use* children under 18 engaging in sexual conduct. In *Ashcroft v. The Free Speech Coalition*, the Supreme Court ruled that sexually related material in which an actual child appears is illegal, but possessing "virtual" pornography is legal. The Court reasoned that real children are not harmed by pornography that depicts a virtual child.[60] In response to the Court's decision, Congress passed the PROTECT (Prosecutorial Remedies and Other Tools to end the Exploitation of Children Today) Act of 2003, which outlawed virtual kiddie porn that makes it almost impossible to distinguish the difference between a real child and a morphed or created image.[61] The Supreme Court reviewed this law in a 2009 case, *United States v. Williams*, which held that the government can legitimately outlaw the sale of child pornography even if the images are computer generated, if those purchasing the images *thought they were buying images of real children*. The Court noted that offers to engage in illegal transactions are excluded from First Amendment protection, so that the "speech" of an individual claiming to be in possession of child pornography is therefore not protected by the First Amendment.[62] So possessing virtual child pornography may be legal, but selling it may be a crime.

COMPUTER CRIMES Congress has treated computer-related crimes as distinct federal offenses since passage of the Counterfeit Access Device and Computer Fraud and Abuse Law in 1984.[63] The 1984 act protected classified US defense and foreign relations information, financial institution and consumer reporting agency files, and access to computers operated for the government. The act was supplemented in 1996 by the National Information Infrastructure Protection Act (NIIPA), which significantly broadens the scope of the law.

Enforcing Cyber Laws

How has the justice system responded to cyber crime? Most of the efforts are being made at the federal level. The government is now operating a number of organizations that are coordinating efforts to control cyber fraud. One approach is to create working groups that coordinate the activities of numerous agencies involved in investigating cyber crime. The Interagency Telemarketing and Internet Fraud Working Group brings together representatives of numerous US Attorneys' offices, the FBI, the Secret Service, the Postal Inspection Service, the Federal Trade Commission, the Securities and Exchange Commission, and other law enforcement and regulatory agencies to share information about trends and patterns in Internet fraud schemes. One of the most successful federal efforts is the New York Electronic Crimes Task Force (NYECTF), a partnership between the US Secret Service and a host of other public safety agencies and private corporations. Its success has prompted Boston, Miami, Charlotte, Chicago, Las Vegas, San Francisco, Los Angeles, and Washington, DC, to set up similar task forces.[64]

LO5 Classify the methods now in use to thwart cyber criminals

Transnational Crime

The new global economy is a particular vexing development for agents of the criminal justice system because it vastly expands the reach of criminal organizations while at the same time creating new opportunities for criminal conspiracies. Globalization refers to the process of creating transnational markets and political and legal systems and has shifted the focus of crime from a local to a world perspective.

Globalization began when large companies decided to establish themselves in foreign markets by adapting their products or services to the local culture. The process took off with the fall of the Soviet Union, which opened new European markets. The development of China into a super industrial power encouraged foreign investors to take advantage of China's huge supply of workers. As the Internet and communication revolution unfolded, companies were able to establish instant communications with their

globalization The process of creating a global economy through transnational markets and political and legal systems.

Transnational crime can involve highly complex billion dollar schemes.
On February 22, 2014, Joaquin "El Chapo" Guzman, the head of Mexico's Sinaloa Cartel is escorted to a helicopter in Mexico City following his capture in Mazatlan, Mexico. Guzman trafficked more than a billion dollars worth of drugs to the United States. Before his capture he ran a well-organized network relying on a variety of transportation methods including trains and submarines. On July 11, 2015, Guzman made a daring escape from a maximum security Mexican prison utilizing a tunnel dug by confederates. He remains at large despite a massive manhunt.

AP Images/Eduardo Verdugo

WEB APP 14.2 The International Monetary Fund has a site that contains information of globalization and its effects at **http://www.imf.org /external/np/exr/key/global.htm**.

far-flung corporate empires, a technological breakthrough that further aided trade and foreign investments.

While globalization can improve the standard of living in third-world nations by providing jobs and training, it can also be a device for criminal cartels to avoid prosecution and regulation, while expanding their markets and profits.[65]

It is not surprising that globalization has created a fertile ground for contemporary criminal organizations. By expanding the reach of both criminal and noncriminal organizations, globalization also increases the vulnerability of indigenous people with a traditional way of life.[66] With money and power to spare, criminal enterprise groups can recruit new members, bribe government officials, and even fund private armies. Transnational organized crime has globalized its activities for the same reasons as legitimate multinational corporations have expanded around the world: new markets bring new sources of profits. Illicit enterprises are able to expand to take advantage of these new economic circumstances thanks to the communications and international transportation revolution.[67] Technological advances such as efficient and widespread commercial airline traffic, improvements in telecommunications (ranging from global cell phone connectivity to the Internet), and the growth of international trade have all aided the growth in illicit transnational activities. These changes have facilitated the cross-border movement of goods and people, conditions exploited by criminals who now use Internet chat rooms to plan their activities. On a cultural level, globalization brings with it an ideology of free markets and free trade. Local officials may exploit their position and demand bribes from multinational companies to do business in their country. To limit bribing of foreign officials, Congress in 1977 passed the Foreign Corrupt Practices Act (FCPA), which made it a criminal offense to bribe foreign officials or to make other questionable overseas payments.[68]

Despite the penalties imposed by the FCPA, corporations that deal in global trade are still being forced to give bribes to secure favorable trade agreements. For example, Pfizer, one of the world's largest drug companies, paid a $60 million fine to settle a government probe of the use of illegal payments to win business in China. Pfizer is not alone. Rival Johnson & Johnson agreed to pay $70 million to settle charges that it paid bribes and kickbacks to win business in Greece, Iraq, Poland, and Romania.[69]

The cultural shift produced by globalization often means less local government intervention and regulation, conditions exploited by crime groups to cross unpatrolled borders and to expand their activities to new regions of the world. Transnational crime groups freely exploit this new freedom to travel to regions where they cannot be extradited, base their operations in countries with ineffective or corrupt law enforcement, and launder their money in countries with bank secrecy or few effective controls. Globalization has allowed both individual offenders and criminal gangs to gain tremendous operational benefits while reducing risks of apprehension and punishment. In other words, crime has gone global.

LO6 Explain the influence of globalization on crime

Types of Transnational Crimes

The globalization of crime involves traditional crimes such as the distribution of pornography and developing criminal activities such as cyber crime. Other criminal activities with a global reach include human trafficking, migrant smuggling, drug smuggling, arms dealing, maritime piracy, and trafficking in environmental resources and counterfeit goods.[70]

The global gangs exploit instability to set up operations in areas that are beyond the reach of the law. Criminal gangs then create even more instability so that the local population becomes dependent on criminal activity for their economic survival. Would a local farmer involved in drug production in a rural area of Bolivia dare to take on the criminal gang—which he not only depends on for his livelihood but which promises deadly reprisals for disloyalty—knowing that he is beyond the protection of the law?

Global gangs take advantage of the latest technological developments to distribute illegal materials. An example of a traditional crime that has been revolutionized by global communications is child pornography. The Internet has enabled cheap and instant global distribution to millions of customers from concealed origins, usually situated in countries where prosecution is unlikely. In the past, the images would have had to be processed, printed, and the hard copies distributed via mail or retail outlets.[71]

The trade in human organs—especially kidneys—is substantial, and demand appears to be growing. Desperate victims in developing countries are exploited as their kidneys are purchased for low prices; others sell their body parts when traffickers use coercive means, such as force or threats of force to secure the removal of the victim's organs. These crimes would not be possible without global transportation means available today.[72]

The profits from transnational criminal enterprise can be immense. The United Nations estimates that immigrant smugglers earn about $7 billion per year smuggling an estimated 3 million people (though some may be smuggled more than once). Of the between 170 and 250 million drug users in the world, up to 38 million may be routine or problem users, and more than 4 million are in treatment. The illegal drug trade brings in about $350 billion per year. Human trafficking, another activity of transnational gangs, is discussed in the Contemporary Issues in Criminal Justice feature.

REALITYCHECK

MYTH OR REALITY?

There are more drug users in the world than the populations of England, Italy, and France combined.

REALITY. And you can throw in Spain and Holland as well.

With an estimated 250 million users, the profits from illegal drug trafficking are immense.

LO7 Interpret the concept of transnational crime

CONTEMPORARY ISSUES IN CRIMINAL JUSTICE

Global Trafficking in Persons

Human trafficking has become a global problem. How great a problem? The United Nations estimates that at least 12 million adults and children are in forced labor, bonded labor, and commercial sexual servitude at any given time. Of these victims, more than half are female, many forced into sexual slavery. A disturbing trend is an increase in the share of children among the victims. Globally, children now comprise nearly one-third of all detected trafficking victims. Out of every three child victims, two are girls. In Africa and the Middle East, children comprise a majority of the detected victims; In Europe and Central Asia, however, children are vastly outnumbered by adults.

Every year, hundreds of thousands of women and children—primarily from Southeast Asia and Eastern Europe—are lured by the promise of good jobs and then end up forced into brothels or as circuit travelers in labor camps. Most go to wealthy industrialized countries. Japan now has more than 10,000 commercial sex establishments with 150,000 to 200,000 foreign girls trafficked into the country each year. India has experienced a large influx of foreign sex workers who are believed to be the source of the HIV epidemic that is sweeping the country. Traffickers import up to 50,000 women and children every year into the United States despite legal prohibitions (in addition to prostitution, some are brought in to work in sweatshops).

Global trafficking gangs use force, fraud, or coercion to exploit a person for profit. Victims are subjected to labor and/or sexual exploitation. Gangs prey on the weak, targeting vulnerable men, women, and children. They use creative and ruthless ploys designed to trick, coerce, and win the confidence of potential victims. Very often, these ruses involve promises of a better life through employment, educational opportunities, or marriage.

(Continued)

Trafficking for labor exploitation—the form of trafficking claiming the greatest number of victims—includes traditional slavery, forced labor, and holding people in bondage until they can pay off debts. Trafficking for sexual exploitation may include involvement in prostitution or pornographic films. The use of force or coercion can be direct and violent or psychological. Women may be kidnapped, beaten, raped, and led to believe they can never return home. If they still won't cooperate, their families and friends may be threatened or attacked.

Trafficking gangs are located in Latin America, Asia, and Eastern European nations such as Bulgaria and Russia. The UN report found that sex traffickers are often women, many of whom began as sex workers themselves. They are encouraged by their recruiter/trafficker to return home and recruit other women, often under the scrutiny of people working for the trafficker to make sure they don't try to escape.

Because it is a global enterprise, there is a great deal of cooperation in trafficking, so that in Eastern Europe, a single gang may include Russians, Moldavians, Egyptians, and Syrians. Cooperation allows sex slaves to be trafficked not only to neighboring countries but all around the globe. The UN found that victims from East Asia were detected in more than 20 countries in regions throughout the world, including Europe, the Americas, the Middle East, Central Asia, and Africa.

Combating Trafficking

The United States has made stopping the trafficking of women a top priority. More than 15 years ago, the "Memorandum on Steps to Combat Violence Against Women and the Trafficking of Women and Girls" was issued, directing the secretary of state, the attorney general, and the president's Interagency Council on Women to expand their work against violence against women to include work against the trafficking of women. Since then, a variety of government agencies have worked together to develop trainings to provide federal, state, and local law enforcement with the tools and strategies they need to identify human trafficking victims and prosecute offenders. Agencies that are cooperating include the Federal Law Enforcement Training Center,

US Immigration and Customs Enforcement (ICE), FBI, the Human Trafficking Prosecution Unit of the US Department of Justice, and the Department of Labor. There are now multi-agency specialized task forces called Anti-Trafficking Coordination Teams that focus primarily on the eradication of human trafficking gangs. The United States is not alone in its efforts. In the former Soviet Union, prevention education projects are aimed at potential victims of trafficking, and nongovernmental organizations have established hotlines for victims or women seeking information about the risks of accepting job offers abroad.

Despite increased awareness of the problem and increased efforts by law enforcement agencies, there are still very few convictions for trafficking in persons. About 40 percent of all affected countries report having 10 or more yearly convictions, and 15 percent report having no convictions at all. Fewer countries are reporting increases in the numbers of convictions, which remain very low. This may reflect the difficulties of the criminal justice systems to appropriately respond to trafficking in persons.

CRITICAL THINKING

1. If put in charge, what would you do to slow or end the international sex trade? Before you answer, remember the saying that prostitution is the oldest profession, which implies that curbing it may prove quite difficult.

2. Should men who hire prostitutes who are obviously involved in the sex trade against their will be punished more severely to deter them from getting involved in the exploitation of these vulnerable young women? Or is it unfair to expect someone to know the reasons their sex partner was involved in prostitution?

Sources: United Nations Office on Drugs and Crime, "Global Reports on Trafficking in Persons, 2014," http://www.unodc.org/documents/data-and-analysis/glotip/GLOTIP_2014_full_report.pdf (accessed March 2015); Federal Law Enforcement Training Center, "Combating Human Trafficking: A Look at the Federal Law Enforcement Training Center's Efforts," http://www.dhs.gov/blog/2013/01/25/combating-human-trafficking (accessed June, 2015); Mark Lusk and Faith Lucas, "The Challenge of Human Trafficking and Contemporary Slavery," *Journal of Comparative Social Welfare* 25 (2009): 49–57.

WEB APP 14.3 US Immigration and Customs Enforcement is the principal investigative arm of the US Department of Homeland Security (DHS) and the second largest investigative agency in the federal government, with more than 20,000 employees in offices in all 50 states and 47 foreign countries. To read about some or their antitransnational gang initiatives, go to **http://www.ice.gov/community-shield/**.

Transnational Crime Groups

Transnational crime networks may locate themselves in nations whose governments are too weak to present effective opposition. If they believe that the government may be interfering with their illegal activities that bring them immense profits, such as drug trafficking, they will carry out a terror campaign, killing police officials and using bribery, violence, or terror to achieve their goals. The political turmoil of the twenty-first century coupled with advances in telecommunications and computer technology have had the unintended effect of providing avenues for the rapid expansion of transnational organized crime activities.[73]

ASIAN GANGS Asian groups are involved in a number of global criminal conspiracies ranging from extortion and smuggling to arms dealing and human trafficking.[74] Among the best-known groups are the following:

- *Yakuza.* A Japanese criminal group often involved in multinational criminal activities, including human trafficking, gambling, prostitution, and undermining licit businesses.

- *Fuk Ching*. A Chinese organized criminal group in the United States involved in smuggling, street violence, and human trafficking.
- *Triads*. Underground criminal societies based in Hong Kong that control secret markets and bus routes and are often involved in money laundering and drug trafficking.
- *Heijin*. Taiwanese gangsters who are often executives in large corporations. They are often involved in white-collar crimes, such as illegal stock trading and bribery, and they sometimes run for public office.
- *Jao Pho*. Organized crime group in Thailand involved in illegal political and business activity.
- *Red Wa*. Gangsters from Thailand involved in manufacturing and trafficking methamphetamine.

There are several recent trends among Asian criminal enterprises:

- Criminal groups are now cooperating across ethnic and racial lines.
- Some gangs and criminal enterprises have begun to structure their groups in a hierarchical fashion to be more competitive.
- The criminal activities gangs engage in have become globalized.
- More of these criminal enterprises are engaging in white-collar crimes and are co-mingling their illegal activities with legitimate business ventures.

Asian criminal enterprises have been identified in more than 50 metropolitan areas in the United States, including Boston, Chicago, Honolulu, Las Vegas, Los Angeles, New Orleans, New York, Newark, Philadelphia, Portland, San Francisco, Seattle, and Washington, DC.

AFRICAN GANGS Nigerian criminal enterprises are the most significant of these groups and operate in more than 80 other countries.[75] Highly aggressive, they primarily engage in drug trafficking and financial frauds. Nigerian gangs deliver heroin from Southeast and Southwest Asian into Europe and the United States and cocaine from South America into Europe and South Africa. Large populations of ethnic Nigerians in India, Pakistan, and Thailand have given these enterprises direct access to 90 percent of the world's heroin production. The associated money laundering has helped establish Nigerian criminal enterprises on every populated continent of the world.

RUSSIAN TRANSNATIONAL CRIME GROUPS Since the collapse of the Soviet Union in 1991, criminal organizations in Russia and other former Soviet republics such as the Ukraine have engaged in a variety of crimes: drugs and arms trafficking, stolen automobiles, trafficking in women and children, and money laundering.[76] No area of the world seems immune to this menace, especially not the United States. America is the land of opportunity for unloading criminal goods and laundering dirty money.

Russian criminals make extensive use of the state governmental apparatus to protect and promote their criminal activities. For example, most businesses in Russia—legal, quasi-legal, and illegal—must operate with the protection of a *krysha* (roof). The protection is often provided by police or security officials employed outside their "official" capacities for this purpose. In other cases, officials are "silent partners" in criminal enterprises that they, in turn, protect. The criminalization of the privatization process has resulted in the massive use of state funds for criminal gain. Valuable properties are purchased through insider deals for much less than their true value and then resold for lucrative profits. Criminals have been able to directly influence the state's domestic and foreign policy to promote the interests of organized crime either by attaining public office themselves or by buying public officials.

In the United States, Russian criminal groups are extensively engaged in a broad array of frauds and scams, including health-care fraud, insurance scams, stock frauds, antiquities swindles, forgery, and fuel tax evasion schemes.[77] Russians are believed to be the main purveyors of credit card fraud in the United States. Legitimate businesses, such as the movie business and textile industry, have become targets of criminals from the former Soviet Union, and they are often used for money laundering and extortion.

MEXICAN DRUG CARTELS Mexican drug cartels have become large-scale suppliers of narcotics, marijuana, and methamphetamines In addition, an estimated 90 percent of cocaine entering the United States transits Mexico. Mexican drug gangs routinely use violence, and fighting for control of the border regions has affected US citizens: more than 60 Americans have been kidnapped, and Mexican drug cartel members have threatened to kill US journalists covering drug violence in the border region. And, as a result of their immense profits, Mexican cartels are the leading wholesale launderers of drug money from the United States.[78]

Of the numerous drug cartels operating in Mexico, the main ones are Gulf, Tijuana, Sinaloa, Juárez, Millennium, Oaxaca, and Colima. Some are dominant in local regions, while the major gangs—Gulf, Sinaloa, and Juárez—are present throughout all of Mexico. In recent years, new cartels have formed, and others have become allies in a constantly shifting landscape of drug activity. For example, the Tijuana cartel formed an alliance with the Gulf cartel, and several cartels (Sinaloa, Juárez, and Valencia) have also formed an alliance known as "the Federation."

LO8 List some of the most important transnational crime groups

Controlling Transnational Crime

Efforts to combat transnational organized crime are typically in the hands of federal agencies. One approach is to form international working groups to collect intelligence, share information, and plot unified strategies among member nations. The FBI belongs to several international working groups aimed at combating transnational gangs in various parts of the world. For example, to combat the influence and reach of Eurasian organized crime, the FBI is involved in the following groups and activities:

- *Eurasian Organized Crime Working Group.* Established in 1994, it meets to discuss and jointly address the transnational aspects of Eurasian organized crime that impact member countries and the international community in general. The member countries are Canada, Great Britain, Germany, France, Italy, Japan, the United States, and Russia.
- *Central European Working Group.* This group is part of a project that brings together the FBI and Central European law enforcement agencies to discuss cooperative investigative matters covering the broad spectrum of Eurasian organized crime. A principal concern is the growing presence of Russian and other Eurasian organized criminals in Central Europe and the United States. The initiative works on practical interaction between the participating agencies to establish lines of communication and working relationships, to develop strategies and tactics to address transnational organized crime matters impacting the region, and to identify potential common targets.
- *Southeast European Cooperative Initiative.* This is an international organization intended to coordinate police and customs regional actions for preventing and combating transborder crime. It is headquartered in Bucharest, Romania, and has 12 fully participating member countries. The United States has been one of 14 countries with observer status since 1998. The initiative's center serves as a clearinghouse for information and intelligence sharing, allowing the quick exchange of information in a professional and trustworthy environment. The initiative also supports specialized task forces for countering serious transborder crime such as the trafficking of people, drugs, and cars; smuggling; financial crimes; and terrorism.

ORGANIZED CRIME LAWS Congress has passed a number of laws that have made it easier for agencies to bring transnational gangs to justice. One of the first measures aimed directly at organized crime was the Interstate and Foreign Travel or Transportation in Aid of Racketeering Enterprises Act (Travel Act).[79] The Travel Act prohibits travel in interstate commerce or use of interstate facilities with the intent to promote, manage, establish, carry on, or facilitate an unlawful activity; it also prohibits the actual or attempted engagement in these activities. In 1970, Congress passed the Organized Crime Control Act. Title IX of the act, probably its most effective measure, is the **Racketeer Influenced and Corrupt Organization Act (RICO)**.[80] RICO did not create new categories of crimes but rather new categories of offenses in racketeering activity, which it defined as involvement in two or more acts prohibited by 24 existing federal and 8 state statutes. The offenses listed in RICO include state-defined crimes, such as murder, kidnapping, gambling, arson, robbery, bribery, extortion, and narcotic violations; and federally defined crimes, such as bribery, counterfeiting, transmission of gambling information, prostitution, and mail fraud. RICO is designed to limit patterns of organized criminal activity by prohibiting involvement in acts intended to do the following:

- Derive income from racketeering or the unlawful collection of debts and use or investment of such income.
- Acquire through racketeering an interest in or control over any enterprise engaged in interstate or foreign commerce.
- Conduct business through a pattern of racketeering.
- Conspire to use racketeering as a means of making income, collecting loans, or conducting business.

An individual convicted under RICO is subject to 20 years in prison and a $25,000 fine. Additionally, the accused must forfeit to the US government any interest in a business in violation of RICO. These penalties are much more potent than simple conviction and imprisonment.[81]

Why Is It So Difficult to Eradicate Global Crime?

While international cooperation is now common, and law enforcement agencies are willing to work together to fight transnational gangs, these criminal organizations are extremely hard to eradicate. The gangs are ready to use violence and are well equipped to carry out threats. Take for example the so-called war on drugs. One reason it has proven so difficult for law enforcement to combat the drug cartels is that they can use their firepower to intimidate police, judges, and potential witnesses. The shifting alliances and changes of location can confound law enforcement efforts. For example, the Zetas gang,

Racketeer Influenced and Corrupt Organization Act (RICO) Federal legislation that enables prosecutors to bring additional criminal or civil charges against people engaged in two or more acts prohibited by 24 existing federal and 8 state laws. RICO features monetary penalties that allow the government to confiscate all profits derived from criminal activities. Originally intended to be used against organized criminals, RICO has also been used against white-collar criminals.

LO9 Explain the methods law enforcement is now using to thwart transnational criminal syndicates

It is difficult to control the international drug trade since enemy states prevent U.S. law enforcement agents from entry. Here Afghan poppy farmers prepare the soil for their poppy seeds in the fields of Cham Kalai, a village located in Afghanistan's eastern Nangarhar province, a Taliban stronghold. Poppy cultivation in Nangarhar province has skyrocketed and profits have been used to fund terrorist activities.

AP Images/Anja Niedringhaus

whose core members are former members of the Mexican military's elite Special Air Mobile Force Group (*Grupo Aeromovil de Fuerzas Especiales,* GAFES) are able to carry out complex operations using their military training and sophisticated weaponry.[82] The Zetas, who began as enforcers for the Gulf cartel, are now their rivals. From their base in Nuevo Laredo, their sphere of influence extends across Mexico and deep into Central America, trafficking in arms, kidnapping, and competing for control of trafficking routes along the eastern half of the US–Mexican border. And when they feel threatened, they are quite willing to fight the law. It is estimated that more than 70,000 people have been killed by the drug gangs since 2006.[83]

Adding to control problems is the fact that the drug trade is an important source of foreign revenue, and destroying the drug trade undermines the economies of third-world nations. Even if the government of one nation was willing to cooperate in vigorous drug suppression efforts, suppliers in other nations, eager to cash in on the sellers' market, would be encouraged to turn more acreage over to coca or poppy production. Today, almost every Caribbean country is involved with narcotrafficking; illicit drug shipments in the region are worth more money than the top five legitimate exports combined. Drug gangs are able to corrupt the political structure and destabilize countries. Drug addiction and violent crime are now common in Jamaica, Puerto Rico, and even small islands such as St. Kitts. The corruption of the police and other security forces has reached a crisis point, where an officer can earn the equivalent of half a year's salary by simply looking the other way on a drug deal.[84] There are also indications that the drug syndicates may be planting a higher yield variety of coca and improving refining techniques to replace crops lost to government crackdowns.

The United States has little influence in some key drug-producing areas such as Helmon Province in Afghanistan—an area still controlled by the Taliban—and in rebel-held areas of Myanmar (formerly Burma).[85] War and terrorism also may make gang control strategies problematic. After the United States toppled Afghanistan's Taliban government, the remnants began to grow and sell poppy to support their insurgency; Afghanistan now supplies a significant percentage of the world's opium.[86] And while the Colombian guerillas may not be interested in joining or colluding with crime cartels, they finance their war against the government by aiding drug traffickers and "taxing" crops and sales.[87] Considering these problems, it is not surprising that transnational gangs continue to flourish.

ETHICAL Challenge

Would the torture of a suspected terrorist determined to destroy the government and harm innocent civilians ever be ethical? Although most people loathe the thought of torturing anyone, some experts argue that torture can sometimes be justified in what they call the ticking bomb scenario. Suppose the government found out that a captured terrorist knew the whereabouts of a dangerous explosive device that was set to go off and kill thousands of innocent people. Under these circumstances, would it be ethical to waterboard or otherwise torture this single suspect if it would save the population of a city? Before you answer, consider the fact that opponents of torture believe that even imminent danger does not justify state violence. There is a danger that torture would then become calculated and premeditated; torturers would have to be trained and be in place, ready to take action. We couldn't be running around looking for torturers with a bomb set to go off, could we? Because torturers would be part of the government bureaucracy, there is no way to ensure that they would use their skills only in certain morally justifiable cases. What happens if a superior officer tells them to torture someone, but they believe the order is unjustified? Should they follow orders, or risk a court-martial for being disobedient?

Ethical Challenge: Write an essay that presents an ethical argument for both sides of this issue: Is it ethical not to use torture in order to save thousands of lives? Is it ethical to use torture on someone who is only a suspect and not yet convicted in a court of law?

SUMMARY

LO1 *List the various forms of terrorism and their goals* There are a number of different forms of terrorism. Revolutionary terrorists use violence to frighten those in power and their supporters to replace the existing government with a regime that holds acceptable political or religious views. Political terrorists attack people or groups who oppose the terrorists' political ideology or whom the terrorists define as "outsiders" who must be destroyed. Nationalist terrorists promote the interests of a minority ethnic or religious group who believes it has been persecuted under majority rule and wants to carve out its own independent homeland. Retributive terrorists use violence as a method of influence, persuasion, or intimidation to get people to accept their social, religious, or political views. State-sponsored terrorists are part of a repressive government regime that forces its citizens into obedience, oppresses minorities, and stifles political dissent.

LO2 *Demonstrate how the USA Patriot Act is designed to combat terrorists* The USA Patriot Act helps control terrorist activity by granting or expanding four traditional tools of surveillance—wiretaps, search warrants, pen/trap orders (installing devices that record phone calls), and subpoenas. It gives the FBI greater power to check and monitor phone, Internet, and computer records. The act also enables the government to monitor more closely those people suspected of "harboring" and giving "material support" to terrorists and conducting surveillance of "lone wolves"—individuals suspected of terrorist-related activities not linked to terrorist groups.

LO3 *Evaluate the various forms of green crime* Green crimes involve the environment and include such activities as illegal fishing, pollution, dumping, forestry, and the like. In some instances, environmental criminals conduct activities overseas to avoid legal controls and enforcement.

LO4 *Comprehend the meaning of the term "cyber crime"* Cyber crime typically involves the theft and/or destruction of information, resources, or funds via computers, computer networks, and the Internet. Cyber theft is the use of computer networks for criminal profits. Illegal copyright infringement, identity theft, and Internet securities fraud are examples of cyber theft. Cyber vandalism, or technological destruction, involves malicious attacks aimed at disrupting, defacing, and destroying technology. Cyber war consists of politically motivated attacks designed to compromise the electronic infrastructure of the enemy and to disrupt its economy.

LO5 *Classify the methods now being used to thwart cyber criminals* Numerous organizations have been set up to provide training and support for law enforcement agents. In addition, new federal and state laws have been enacted to help discourage particular types of high-tech crimes. In the future, technological prowess may make it possible to identify cyber criminals and bring them to justice before they can carry out their attacks.

LO6 *Explain the influence of globalization on crime* Globalization has shifted the focus of crime from a local to a world perspective. With money and power to spare, criminal enterprise groups can recruit new members, bribe government officials, and even fund private armies.

LO7 *Interpret the concept of transnational crime* Transnational organized crime involves ongoing international criminal enterprise groups whose purpose is personal economic gain through illegitimate means. Transnational gangs are involved in money laundering; human smuggling; cyber crime; and trafficking of humans, drugs, weapons, body parts, or nuclear material. There is also a troubling overseas trade in prostitution. Transnational gangs export women from third-world nations for the purposes of prostitution. Some may be kidnapped or forced into prostitution against their will through violence and threats.

LO8 *List some of the most important transnational crime groups* Eastern gangs trace their origin to countries spanning the Baltics, the Balkans, Central/Eastern Europe, Russia, the Caucasus, and Central Asia. Russian organized crime is active in Europe, Africa, Asia, and North and South America. Asian gangs include the Yakuza Japanese criminal group, often involved in multinational criminal activities such as human trafficking, gambling, prostitution, and undermining licit businesses. Chinese groups are also involved in human trafficking—bringing large numbers of Chinese migrants to North America and essentially enslaving them for profit. A number of powerful Mexican drug cartels now dominate the cross-border drug trade into the United States.

LO9 *Explain the methods law enforcement is now using to thwart transnational criminal syndicates* Efforts to combat transnational organized crime are typically in the hands of federal agencies. One approach is for them to form international working groups to collect intelligence, share information, and plot unified strategies among member nations. US law enforcement agencies have cooperated in cross-border operations to eradicate gang activity.

KEY TERMS

REVIEW QUESTIONS

1. Should the US government use drones to spy on suspected terrorists on American soil?

2. Would you allow federal agents to use intense interrogation techniques such as waterboarding to pry information from terror suspects?

3. Should people who illegally download movies or music be prosecuted for theft?

4. How can Internet pornography be controlled considering that a great deal of adult content is available on foreign websites?

5. Considering the threat of transnational drug trafficking, should drugs be legalized and controlled by the government?

6. Should the Internet be more closely monitored and controlled to prevent the threat of cyber war?

7. Is there any point to placing economic sanctions on billion-dollar corporations? Should corporate executives be put in prison? Put another way, what is the purpose of incarcerating someone like 72-year-old Bernard Madoff? Is he really a threat to society?

GLOSSARY

A

actus reus An illegal act. The *actus reus* can be an affirmative act, such as taking money or shooting someone, or a failure to act, such as failing to take proper precautions while driving a car.

adjudication The determination of guilt or innocence; a judgment concerning criminal charges. The majority of offenders charged plead guilty; of the remainder, some cases are adjudicated by a judge and a jury, some are adjudicated by a judge without a jury, and others are dismissed.

adversarial procedure The process of publicly pitting the prosecution and the defense against one another in pursuit of the truth.

aggravated assault An unlawful attack by one person upon another, accompanied by the use of a weapon, for the purpose of inflicting severe or aggravated bodily injury.

antisocial (sociopathic, psychopathic) personality Individuals who are always in trouble and do not learn from either experience or punishment. They are loners who engage in frequent callous and hedonistic behaviors, are emotionally immature, and lack responsibility, judgment, and empathy.

appeal A request for an appellate court to examine a lower court's decision to determine whether proper procedures were followed.

appellate court A court that reconsiders a case that has already been tried to determine whether the measures used complied with accepted rules of criminal procedure and were in accordance with constitutional doctrines.

arson Any willful or malicious burning or attempting to burn, with or without intent to defraud, a dwelling house, public building, motor vehicle or aircraft, or personal property of another.

assigned counsel A lawyer appointed by the court to represent a defendant in a criminal case because the person is too poor to hire counsel.

B

bail The monetary amount for or condition of pretrial release, normally set by a judge at the initial appearance. The purpose of bail is to ensure the return of the accused at subsequent proceedings.

Bail Reform Act of 1984 Federal legislation that provides for both greater emphasis on release on recognizance for nondangerous offenders and preventive detention for those who present a menace to the community.

bench trial The trial of a criminal matter by a judge only. The accused waives any constitutional right to trial by jury.

Bill of Rights The first 10 amendments to the US Constitution that spell out specific freedoms granted to citizens and limit the power of the Federal government to conduct criminal prosecutions.

biosocial theory Human behavior is a function of the interaction of biochemical, neurological, and genetic factors with environmental stimuli.

bipolar disorder A psychological condition marked by mood swings between periods of wild elation and deep depression.

blameworthy Culpable or guilty of participating in a particular criminal offense.

blue curtain The secretive, insulated police culture that isolates officers from the rest of society.

boot camp A short-term militaristic correctional facility in which inmates undergo intensive physical conditioning and discipline.

broken windows hypothesis The view that deteriorated communities serve as a magnet for criminals and attract criminal activity.

broken windows model A term used to describe the role of the police as maintainers of community order and safety.

brutalization effect An outcome of capital punishment that enhances, rather than deters, the level of violence in society. The death penalty reinforces the view that violence is an appropriate response to provocation.

Bureau of Alcohol, Tobacco, Firearms, and Explosives (ATF) Federal agency with jurisdiction over the illegal sale, importation, and criminal misuse of firearms and explosives and the distribution of untaxed liquor and cigarettes.

burglary The unlawful entry of a structure to commit a felony or a theft.

C

challenge for cause A request that a prospective juror be removed because he or she is biased or has prior knowledge about a case, or for other reasons that demonstrate the individual's inability to render a fair and impartial judgment in a particular case.

child savers Late nineteenth-century reformers in America who developed programs for troubled youths and influenced legislation creating the juvenile justice system.

Children's Aid Society A child-saving organization begun by Charles Loring Brace; it took children from the streets in large cities and placed them with farm families on the prairie.

chivalry hypothesis The view that the low rates of female crime and delinquency are a reflection of the leniency with which police and judges treat female offenders.

chronic offender A delinquent offender who is arrested five or more times before he or she is 18 and who stands a good chance of becoming an adult criminal; these offenders are responsible for more than half of all serious crimes.

civil law All law that is not criminal, including the law of torts (personal wrongs) and contract, property, maritime, and commercial law.

cognitive behavioral therapy (CBT) A treatment approach that focuses on patterns of thinking and beliefs to help people become conscious of their own thoughts and behaviors so they can make positive changes.

commitment Decision of judge ordering an adjudicated and sentenced juvenile offender to be placed in a correctional facility.

common law Early English law, developed by judges, that incorporated Anglo-Saxon tribal custom, feudal rules and practices, and the everyday rules of behavior of local villages. Common law became the standardized law of the land in England and eventually formed the basis of criminal law in the United States.

community-oriented policing (COP) Programs and strategies designed to bring police and the public closer together and create a more cooperative working environment between them.

community service restitution An alternative sanction that requires an offender to work in the community at such tasks as cleaning public parks or working with disabled children in lieu of an incarceration sentence.

CompStat A program originated by the New York City police that used carefully collected and analyzed crime data to shape policy and evaluate police effectiveness.

compulsory process Compelling the production of witnesses via a subpoena.

concurrent sentences Prison sentences for two or more criminal acts served simultaneously and run together.

conduct disorder (CD) A pattern of repetitive behavior in which the rights of others or social norms are violated.

conflict view of crime The law is controlled by the rich and powerful who shape its content to ensure their continued economic domination of society. The criminal justice system is an instrument of social and economic repression.

confrontation clause A part of the Sixth Amendment that establishes the right of a criminal defendant to see and cross-examine all the witnesses against him or her.

congregate system Prison system first used in New York that allowed inmates to engage in group activities such as work, meals, and recreation.

consecutive sentences Prison sentences for two or more criminal acts, served one after the other.

consensus view of crime The majority of citizens in a society share common ideals and work toward a common good. Crimes are acts that are outlawed because they conflict with the rules of the majority and are harmful to society.

constable In medieval England, an appointed official who administered and supervised the legal affairs of a small community.

contract system The practice of correctional officials selling the labor of inmates to private businesses.

contract system (attorney) Providing counsel to indigent offenders by having attorneys under contract to the county handle all (or some) such cases.

convict-lease system The practice of leasing inmates to a business for a fixed annual fee.

corporate enterprise crime Conspiracies that involve bending the rules of legitimate business and commerce to make illegal profits in the marketplace. Enterprise crimes involve the violation of law in the course of an otherwise legitimate occupation.

corruption Exercising legitimate discretion for improper reasons or using illegal means to achieve approved goals.

court of last resort A court that handles the final appeal on a matter. The US Supreme Court is the official court of last resort for criminal matters.

courtroom work group The phrase used to indicate that all parties in the adversary process work together cooperatively to settle cases with the least amount of effort and conflict.

courts of general jurisdiction State or federal courts that have jurisdiction over felony offenses and more serious civil cases (i.e., cases involving more than a dollar amount set by the legislature).

crime A violation of societal rules of behavior as interpreted and expressed by a criminal legal code created by people holding social and political power. Individuals who violate these rules are subject to sanctions by state authority, social stigma, and loss of status.

crime control perspective A model of criminal justice that emphasizes the control of dangerous offenders and the protection of society. Its advocates call for harsh punishments as a deterrent to crime and support availability of the death penalty.

criminal justice process The decision-making points, from the initial investigation or arrest by police to the eventual release of the offender and his or her reentry into society; the various sequential criminal justice stages through which the offender passes.

criminal justice system The law enforcement, court, and correctional agencies that work together to effect the apprehension, prosecution, and control of criminal offenders. They are charged with maintaining order, enforcing the law, identifying transgressors, bringing the guilty to justice, and treating criminal behavior.

criminal procedure The rules and laws that define the operation of criminal proceedings. Procedural law describes the methods that must be followed in obtaining warrants, investigating offenses, effecting lawful arrests, conducting trials, introducing evidence, sentencing convicted offenders, and reviewing cases by appellate courts.

cross-examination The process in which the defense and the prosecution interrogate witnesses for the other side during a trial.

cruel and unusual punishment Physical punishment or punishment that is far in excess of that given to people under similar circumstances and is therefore banned by the Eighth Amendment. The death penalty has so far not been considered cruel and unusual if it is administered in a fair and nondiscriminatory fashion.

cultural transmission The passing of cultural values from one generation to the next.

culture of poverty The crushing lifestyle of slum areas produces a culture of poverty, passed from one generation to the next, marked by apathy, cynicism, feelings of helplessness, and mistrust of social institutions, such as schools, government agencies, and the police.

cumulative disadvantage The tendency of prior social problems to produce future ones that accumulate and undermine success.

Customs and Border Protection (CBP) Federal agency responsible for the control and protection of America's borders and ports of entry. Its first priority is keeping terrorists and their weapons out of the United States.

cyber crime Any criminal activity that employs the Internet or other computer-based systems for illegal gain.

cyber stalking Using the Internet, e-mail, or other electronic communications devices to stalk or harass another person.

cyber theft The use of computer networks for criminal profits. Illegal copyright infringement, identity theft, and Internet securities fraud are examples of cyber theft.

cyber vandalism Malicious attacks aimed at disrupting, defacing, and destroying technology.

cyber war Politically motivated attacks designed to compromise the electronic infrastructure of the enemy and to disrupt its economy.

cynicism The belief that most people's actions are motivated solely by personal needs and selfishness.

D

day fees A program requiring probationers to pay some of the costs of their treatment.

day fine A fine geared to the average daily income of the convicted offender in an effort to bring equity to the sentencing process.

day reporting center (DRC) A nonresidential community-based treatment program.

deadly force Force that is likely to cause death or bodily harm.

decriminalization Reducing the penalty for a criminal act but not actually legalizing it.

deinstitutionalization The policy of removing as many offenders as possible from secure confinement and treating them in the community.

deliberation Planning a criminal act after careful thought, rather than carrying it out on impulse.

demeanor The way in which a person outwardly manifests his or her personality.

denial-of-service attack Extorting money from an Internet service user by threatening to prevent the user having access to the service.

Department of Homeland Security (DHS) Federal agency responsible for preventing terrorist attacks within the United States, reducing America's vulnerability to terrorism, and minimizing the damage and assisting in recovery from attacks that do occur.

deposit bail The monetary amount set by a judge at a hearing as a condition of pretrial release; the percentage of the total bond required to be paid by the defendant.

detention The temporary care of a child alleged to be a delinquent or status offender who requires secure custody, pending court disposition.

determinate sentence A fixed term of incarceration, such as three years' imprisonment. Many people consider determinate sentences too restrictive for rehabilitative purposes; the advantage is that offenders know how much time they have to serve—that is, when they will be released.

deterrent effect Stopping or reducing crime by convincing would-be criminals that they stand a significant risk of being apprehended and punished for their crimes.

developmental theory Social interactions that are developed over the life course shape behavior. Some interactions, such as involvement with deviant peers, encourage law violations whereas others, such as marriage and military service may help people desist from crime.

direct examination The questioning of one's own (prosecution or defense) witness during a trial.

directed patrol A patrol strategy that involves concentrating police resources in areas where certain crimes are a significant problem.

directed verdict The right of a judge to direct a jury to acquit a defendant because the state has not proved the elements of the crime or otherwise has not established guilt according to law.

discretion The use of personal decision making and choice in carrying out operations in the criminal justice system. For example, police discretion can involve deciding whether to make an arrest; prosecutorial discretion can involve deciding whether to accept a plea bargain.

disposition For juvenile offenders, the equivalent of sentencing for adult offenders. The theory is that disposition is more rehabilitative than retributive. Possible dispositions include dismissing the case, releasing the youth to the custody of his or her parents, placing the offender on probation, or sending him or her to a state correctional institution.

diversion A noncriminal alternative to trial, usually featuring counseling, job training, and educational opportunities.

DNA profiling The identification of criminal suspects by matching DNA samples taken from their person with specimens found at the crime scene.

double marginality The social burden African American police officers carry by virtue of being both minority group members and law enforcement officers.

Drug Enforcement Administration (DEA) The federal agency that enforces federal drug control laws.

due process perspective Due process provides the basic rights of a defendant in criminal proceedings and the requirements for a fair trial.

E

electronic monitoring (EM) Requiring convicted offenders to wear a monitoring device as part of their community sentence. Typically part of a house arrest order, this enables the probation department to ensure that offenders are complying with court-ordered limitations on their freedom.

emotional intelligence The capability of monitoring one's own feelings and actions in order to guide action.

entrapment A criminal defense that maintains the police originated the criminal idea or initiated the criminal action.

equal justice perspective The view that all people should be treated equally before the law. Equality may best be achieved through individual discretion in the justice process.

equity The action or practice of awarding each person what is due him or her; sanctions based on equity seek to compensate individual victims and society in general for their losses due to crime.

e-tailing fraud Using the Internet to illegally buy or sell merchandise.

ex post facto **laws** Acts that retroactively change the legal status of actions that were committed before the enactment of a law and/or change the consequences once it was enacted.

exclusionary rule Evidence seized in violation of the Fourth Amendment cannot be used in a court of law.

F

Federal Bureau of Investigation (FBI) The arm of the US Justice Department that investigates violations of federal law, seeks to protect America from terrorist attacks, gathers crime statistics, runs a comprehensive crime laboratory, and helps train local law enforcement officers.

felony A more serious offense that carries a penalty of incarceration in a state prison, usually for one year or more. Persons convicted of felony offenses lose such rights as the right to vote, hold elective office, or maintain certain licenses.

fine A money payment levied on offenders to compensate society for their misdeeds.

first-degree murder Killing a person after premeditation and deliberation.

foot patrol Police patrols that take officers out of cars and put them on a walking beat to strengthen ties with the community.

forcible rape Under common law, the carnal knowledge of a female forcibly and against her will. Many states have made rape a gender-neutral crime. The FBI has created a new definition of rape for its UCR program: "The penetration, no matter how slight, of the vagina or anus with any body part or object, or oral penetration by a sex organ of another person, without the consent of the victim."

forensic science The use of scientific techniques to investigate questions of interest to the justice system and to solve crimes.

forfeiture The seizure of personal property by the state as a civil or criminal penalty.

furlough A correctional policy that allows inmates to leave the institution for vocational or educational training, for employment, or to maintain family ties.

fusion center A mechanism to exchange information and intelligence, maximize resources, streamline operations, and improve the ability to fight crime and terrorism by analyzing data from a variety of sources.

G

general deterrence The theory that crime rates are influenced and controlled by the threat of criminal punishment. If people fear being apprehended and punished, they will not risk breaking the law.

Gideon v. Wainwright The 1963 US Supreme Court case that granted counsel to indigent defendants in felony prosecutions.

globalization The process of creating a global economy through transnational markets and political and legal systems.

good faith exception The principle that evidence may be used in a criminal trial, even though the search warrant used to obtain it is technically faulty, if the police acted in good faith and to the best of their ability when they sought to obtain it from a judge.

grand jury A type of jury responsible for investigating alleged crimes, examining evidence, and issuing indictments.

grass eaters A term for police officers who accept payoffs when everyday duties place them in a position to "look the other way."

green crime Criminal activity that involves violation of rules and laws designed to protect the environment, including illegal dumping, polluting, fishing, logging, and so on.

H

halfway house A community-based correctional facility that houses inmates before their outright release so they can become gradually acclimated to conventional society.

hands-off doctrine The legal practice of allowing prison administrators a free hand to run the institution, even if correctional practices violate inmates' constitutional rights; ended with the onset of the prisoners' rights movement in the 1960s.

hearsay evidence Testimony that is not firsthand but, rather, relates information told by a second party.

hot spots of crime Places from which a significant portion of all police calls originate. These hot spots include taverns and housing projects.

house arrest A form of intermediate sanction that requires the convicted offender to spend a designated amount of time per week in his or her own home—such as from 5 P.M. Friday until 8 A.M. Monday.

hue and cry In medieval England, a call for assistance. The policy of self-help that prevailed in villages demanded that everyone respond if a citizen raised a hue and cry to get their aid.

hulks Abandoned ships anchored in harbors and used in eighteenth-century England to house prisoners.

hundred In medieval England, a group of 100 families responsible for maintaining order and trying minor offenses.

I

identity theft Using the Internet to steal someone's identity and/or impersonate the victim to conduct illicit transactions, such as committing fraud using the victim's name and identity.

incapacitation The policy of keeping dangerous criminals in confinement to eliminate the risk of their repeating their offense in society.

indeterminate sentence A term of incarceration with a stated minimum and maximum length, such as a sentence to prison for a period of 3 to 10 years. The prisoner would be eligible for parole after the minimum sentence has been served. Based on the belief that sentences should fit the criminal, indeterminate sentences allow individualized sentences and provide for sentencing flexibility. Judges can set a high minimum to override the purpose of the indeterminate sentence.

indictment The action by a grand jury when it finds that probable cause exists for prosecution of an accused suspect.

information Charging document filed by the prosecution that forms the basis of the preliminary hearing.

initial appearance A juvenile's first appearance before the juvenile court judge, in which the charges are reviewed and an effort is made to settle the case without a trial. If the child does not have legal counsel, an attorney is appointed.

inmate social code An unwritten code of behavior, passed from older inmates to younger ones, that serves as a guideline to appropriate inmate behavior within the correctional institution.

inmate subculture The loosely defined culture that pervades prisons and has its own norms, rules, and language.

in-presence requirement With a few exceptions, in order to make an arrest in a misdemeanor, a police officer must have witnessed the crime personally.

insanity A legal defense that maintains a defendant was incapable of forming criminal intent because he or she suffers from a defect of reason or mental illness.

intake The process in which a probation officer settles cases at the initial appearance before the onset of formal criminal proceedings; also, the process in which a juvenile referral is received and a decision is made to file a petition in the juvenile court, release the juvenile, or refer the juvenile elsewhere.

intelligence-led policing (ILP) The collection and analysis of information to generate an "intelligence end product" designed to inform police decision making at both the tactical and the strategic level.

intensive probation supervision (IPS) A type of intermediate sanction involving small probation caseloads and strict monitoring on a daily or weekly basis.

interactionist view of crime Criminal law reflects the values of people who use their social and political power to shape the legal system.

intermediate sanctions Punishments that fall between probation and prison ("probation plus"). Community-based sanctions, including house arrest and intensive supervision, serve as alternatives to incarceration.

internal affairs The branch of the police department that investigates charges of corruption or misconduct on the part of police officers.

J

jail A place to detain people awaiting trial, to serve as a lockup for drunks and disorderly individuals, and to confine convicted misdemeanants serving sentences of less than one year.

jailhouse lawyer An inmate trained in law or otherwise educated who helps other inmates prepare legal briefs and appeals.

judicial reprieve The common-law practice that allowed judges to suspend punishment so that convicted offenders could seek a pardon, gather new evidence, or demonstrate that they had reformed their behavior.

jury nullification A defense tactic that consists of suggesting that the jury acquit a defendant, despite evidence that he actually violated the law, by maintaining that the law was unjust or not applicable to the case.

jury trial The process of deciding a case by a group of persons selected and sworn in to serve as jurors at a criminal trial, often as a 6- or 12-person jury.

just desert The philosophy of justice asserting that those who violate the rights of others deserve to be punished. The severity of punishment should be commensurate with the seriousness of the crime.

justice of the peace Established in 1326 England, the office was created to help the shire reeve in controlling the county; it later took on judicial functions.

juvenile court A court that has original jurisdiction over persons defined by statute as juveniles and alleged to be delinquents or status offenders.

juvenile delinquency Participation in illegal behavior by a minor who falls under a statutory age limit.

K

Knapp Commission A public body that led an investigation into police corruption in New York and uncovered a widespread network of payoffs and bribes.

L

landmark decision A decision handed down by the US Supreme Court that becomes the law of the land and serves as a precedent for resolving similar legal issues.

larceny The unlawful taking, carrying, leading, or riding away of property from the possession or constructive possession of another.

latent trait A hidden trait that guides human behavior.

Law Enforcement Assistance Administration (LEAA) Funded by the federal government's Safe Streets Act, this agency provided technical assistance and hundreds of millions of dollars in aid to local and state justice agencies between 1969 and 1982.

legalization The removal of all criminal penalties from a previously outlawed act.

less-lethal weapons Weapons designed to disable or immobilize rather than kill criminal suspects.

lex talionis Latin for "law as retaliation." From Hammurabi's ancient legal code, the belief that the purpose of the law is to provide retaliation for an offended party and that the punishment should fit the crime.

life course theory Theory that focuses on changes in criminality over the life course brought about by shifts in experience and life events.

M

make-believe family In female institutions, the substitute family group—including faux father, mother, and siblings—created by some inmates.

mala in se Refers to acts that society considers inherently evil, such as murder and rape, and that violate the basic principles of Judeo-Christian morality.

mala prohibitum Crimes created by legislative bodies that reflect prevailing moral beliefs and practices.

mandatory sentence A statutory requirement that a certain penalty shall be set and carried out in all cases upon conviction for a specified offense or series of offenses.

Manhattan Bail Project The innovative experiment in bail reform that introduced and successfully tested the concept of release on recognizance.

maximum-security prison A correctional institution that houses dangerous felons and maintains strict security measures, high walls, and limited contact with the outside world.

meat eaters A term for police officers who actively solicit bribes and vigorously engage in corrupt practices.

medical model A correctional philosophy grounded on the belief that inmates are sick people who need treatment rather than punishment in order to help them reform.

medium-security prison A less secure institution that houses nonviolent offenders and provides more opportunities for contact with the outside world.

mens rea Guilty mind. The mental element of a crime or the intent to commit a criminal act.

minimum-security prison The least secure institution, which houses white-collar and nonviolent offenders, maintains few security measures, and has liberal furlough and visitation policies.

Miranda warning The requirement that police officers inform suspects subjected to custodial interrogation that they have a constitutional right to remain silent, that their statements can later be used against them in court, that they can have an attorney present to help them, and that the state will pay for an attorney if they cannot afford to hire one.

misdemeanor A minor crime usually punished by less than one year's imprisonment in a local institution, such as a county jail.

Missouri Plan A method of picking judges through nonpartisan elections as a way to ensure that judges adhere to high standards of judicial performance.

monetary restitution A sanction requiring that convicted offenders compensate crime victims by reimbursing them for out-of-pocket losses caused by the crime. Losses can include property damage, lost wages, and medical costs.

moral entrepreneurs People who wage moral crusades to control criminal law so that it reflects their own personal values.

motivational interviewing A technique that increases the probationers' awareness of their potential problems by asking them to visualize a better future and learn strategies to reach their goals.

motor vehicle theft The theft of a motor vehicle.

murder and nonnegligent manslaughter The willful (nonnegligent) killing of one human being by another.

N

National Crime Victimization Survey (NCVS) The ongoing victimization study conducted jointly by the Justice Department and the US Census Bureau that surveys victims about their experiences with law violation.

National Criminal Intelligence Sharing Plan (NCISP) A formal intelligence-sharing initiative that identifies the security and intelligence sharing needs recognized in the wake of the 9/11 terrorist attacks.

National Incident-Based Reporting System (NIBRS) Program that requires local police agencies to provide a brief account of each incident and arrest within 22 crime patterns, including incident, victim, and offender information.

neighborhood-oriented policing (NOP) Community-oriented policing efforts aimed at individual neighborhoods.

no bill The action by a grand jury when it votes not to indict an accused suspect.

nolle prosequi The term used when a prosecutor decides to drop a case after a complaint has been formally made. Reasons for a *nolle prosequi* include evidence insufficiency, reluctance of witnesses to testify, police error, and office policy.

nondeadly force Force that is unlikely to cause death or significant bodily harm.

nonintervention perspective A view of criminal justice that emphasizes the least intrusive treatment possible. Among its central policies are decarceration, diversion, and decriminalization. In other words, less is better.

O

obitiatry Helping people take their own lives.

official crime statistics Compiled by the FBI in its Uniform Crime Reports, these are a tally of serious crimes reported to police agencies each year.

order maintenance (peacekeeping) The order-maintenance aspect of the police role involves peacekeeping, maintaining order and authority without the need for formal arrest, "handling the situation," and keeping things under control by using threats, persuasion, and understanding.

P

parens patriae Latin term meaning "father of his country." According to this legal philosophy, the government is the guardian of everyone who has a disability, especially children, and has a legal duty to act in their best interests until they reach the age of majority.

parole The early release of a prisoner from imprisonment, subject to conditions set by a parole board.

Parole board A panel of people who decide whether an offender should be released

from prison on **parole** after serving the minimum portion of their sentence ordered by the sentencing judge.

Part I crimes The eight crimes for which, because of their seriousness and frequency, the FBI reports their incidence in its annual Uniform Crime Reports. The Part I crimes are murder, rape, assault, robbery, burglary, arson, larceny, and motor vehicle theft.

Part II crimes All other crimes except the eight Part I crimes. The FBI records all arrests made for Part II crimes, including race, gender, and age information.

penal harm A philosophy based on the belief that harsh treatment while serving a correctional sentence will convince offenders that crime does not pay, thereby lowering the chances of recidivism.

penitentiary A state or federal correctional institution for the incarceration of felony offenders for terms of one year or more.

penitentiary house Term used for early prisons, so named because inmates were supposed to have penitence for their sins.

Pennsylvania system The correctional model used in Pennsylvania that isolated inmates from one another to prevent them from planning escapes, to make them easy to manage, and to give them time to experience penitence.

peremptory challenge The dismissal of a potential juror by either the prosecution or the defense for unexplained, discretionary reasons.

phishing Also known as carding and spoofing, phishing consists of illegally acquiring personal information, such as bank passwords and credit card numbers, by masquerading as a trustworthy person or business in what appears to be an official electronic communication, such as an e-mail or an instant message. The term *phishing* comes from the lures used to "fish" for financial information and passwords.

plea bargaining Nonjudicial settlement of a case in which the defendant exchanges a guilty plea for some consideration, such as a reduced sentence.

police brutality Usually involves such actions as the use of abusive language, the unnecessary use of force or coercion, threats, prodding with nightsticks, stopping and searching people to harass them, and so on.

police chief The top administrator of the police department, who sets policy and has general control over departmental practices. The chief is typically a political rather than a civil service appointee and serves at the pleasure of the mayor.

Ponzi scheme An investment fraud that involves the payment of purported

returns to existing investors from funds contributed by new investors.

poor laws Seventeenth-century laws in England that bound out vagrants and abandoned children as indentured servants to masters.

preliminary hearing A hearing that occurs in lieu of a grand jury hearing, when the prosecutor charges via information. Three issues are decided: whether a crime was committed, whether the court has jurisdiction over the case, and whether there is sufficient probable cause to believe the defendant committed the alleged crime.

premeditation Considering the criminal act beforehand, which suggests that it was motivated by more than a simple desire to engage in an act of violence.

preponderance of the evidence The level of proof in civil cases; more than half the evidence supports the allegations of one side.

presentence investigation An investigation performed by a probation officer attached to a trial court after the conviction of a defendant.

presentment The report of a grand jury investigation, which usually includes a recommendation of indictment.

pretrial detention Holding an offender in secure confinement before trial.

pretrial diversion A program that provides nonpunitive, community-based alternatives to more intrusive forms of punishment such as jail or prison.

pretrial procedures Critical pretrial processes and decisions, including bail, arraignment, and plea negotiation.

preventive detention The practice of holding dangerous suspects before trial without bail.

prison A state or federal correctional institution for incarceration of felony offenders for terms of one year or more.

prisonization Assimilation into the separate culture in the prison that has its own set of rewards and behaviors, as well as its own norms, rules, and language. The traditional prison culture is now being replaced by a violent gang culture.

proactive policing A police department policy that emphasizes stopping crimes before they occur, rather than reacting to crimes that have already occurred.

probable cause The evidentiary criterion necessary to sustain an arrest or the issuance of an arrest or search warrant; less than absolute certainty or "beyond a reasonable doubt," but greater than mere suspicion or "hunch."

probable cause hearing Term used in some jurisdictions for a preliminary hearing to show cause to bring a case to trial.

probation A sentence entailing the conditional release of a convicted offender into the community under the supervision of the court (in the person of a probation officer), subject to certain conditions for a specified time.

probation rules Conditions or restrictions mandated by the court that must be obeyed by a probationer.

problem-oriented policing (POP) A style of police operations that stresses proactive problem solving, rather than reactive crime fighting.

proof beyond a reasonable doubt The standard of proof needed to convict in a criminal case. The evidence offered in court does not have to amount to absolute certainty, but it should leave no reasonable doubt that the defendant committed the alleged crime.

propensity theory The view that a stable unchanging feature, characteristic, property, or condition, such as defective intelligence or impulsive personality, makes some people crime prone.

pro se "For oneself"; presenting one's own defense in a criminal trial; self-representation.

prosecutor Representative of the state (executive branch) in criminal proceedings; advocate for the state's case—the charge—in the adversary trial. Examples include the attorney general of the United States, US attorneys, the attorneys general of the states, district attorneys, and police prosecutors. The prosecutor participates in investigations both before and after arrest, prepares legal documents, participates in obtaining arrest or search warrants, and decides whether to charge a suspect and, if so, with which offense. The prosecutor argues the state's case at trial, advises the police, participates in plea negotiations, and makes sentencing recommendations.

psychodynamic view Criminals are driven by unconscious thought patterns, developed in early childhood, that control behaviors over the life course.

public defender An attorney usually employed (at no cost to the accused) by the government to represent poor persons accused of a crime.

public law The branch of law that deals with the state or government and its relationships with individuals or other governments.

R

racial profiling The practice of police targeting minority groups because of a belief that they are more likely to be engaged in criminal activity.

racial threat hypothesis The view that the percentage of minorities in the population shapes the level of police activity.

Racketeer Influenced and Corrupt Organization Act (RICO) Federal legislation that enables prosecutors to bring additional criminal or civil charges against people engaged in two or more acts prohibited by 24 existing federal and 8 state laws. RICO features monetary penalties that allow the government to confiscate all profits derived from criminal activities. Originally intended to be used against organized criminals, RICO has also been used against white-collar criminals.

rational choice theory People will engage in delinquent and criminal behavior after weighing the consequences and benefits of their actions. Delinquent behavior is a rational choice made by a motivated offender who perceives the chances of gain as outweighing any perceived punishment or loss.

recognizance The medieval practice of allowing convicted offenders to go unpunished if they agreed to refrain from any further criminal behavior.

rehabilitation The strategy of applying proper treatment so an offender will present no further threat to society.

rehabilitation perspective The view that the primary purpose of criminal justice is helping to care for people who cannot manage themselves. Crime is an expression of frustration and anger created by social inequality and can be controlled by giving people the means to improve their lifestyle through conventional endeavors.

relative deprivation The view that extreme social and economic differences among people living in the same community exacerbate criminal activity.

release on recognizance (ROR) A nonmonetary condition for the pretrial release of an accused individual; an alternative to monetary bail that is granted after the court determines that the accused has ties in the community, has no prior record of default, and is likely to appear at subsequent proceedings.

residential community corrections (RCC) A nonsecure facility, located in the community, that houses probationers who need a more secure environment. Typically, residents are free during the day to go to work, school, or treatment, and they return in the evening for counseling sessions and meals.

restitution A condition of probation in which the offender repays society or the victim of crime for the trouble and expense the offender caused.

restorative justice perspective A view of criminal justice that advocates peaceful solutions and mediation rather than coercive punishments.

revocation An administrative act performed by a parole authority that removes a person from parole, or a judicial order by a court removing a person from parole or probation, in response to a violation on the part of the parolee or probationer.

risk classification Classifying probationers so that they may receive an appropriate level of treatment and control.

robbery The taking or attempting to take anything of value from the care, custody, or control of a person or persons by force or threat of force or violence and/or by putting the victim in fear.

S

search warrant An order issued by a judge, directing officers to conduct a search of specified premises for specified objects or persons and bring them before the court.

second-degree murder A person's wanton disregard for the victim's life and his or her desire to inflict serious bodily harm on the victim, which results in the victim's death.

Secret Service Federal agency responsible for executive protection and for investigation of counterfeiting and various forms of financial fraud.

self-defense A legal defense in which defendants claim that their behavior was legally justified by the necessity to protect their own life and property, or that of another victim, from potential harm.

self-report survey A research approach that requires subjects to reveal their own participation in delinquent or criminal acts.

sentencing circle A type of sentencing in which victims, family members, community members, and the offender participate in an effort to devise fair and reasonable sanctions that are ultimately aimed at reintegrating the offender into the community.

sentencing guidelines A set of standards that define parameters for trial judges to follow in their sentencing decisions.

sheriff The chief law enforcement officer in a county.

shire reeve In medieval England, the senior law enforcement figure in a county; the forerunner of today's sheriff.

shock probation A sentence in which offenders serve a short prison term before they begin probation to impress them with the pains of imprisonment.

Sixth Amendment The US constitutional amendment containing various criminal trial rights, such as the right to public trial, the right to trial by jury, and the right to confrontation of witnesses.

social bonds The ties people have to family, peers, social institutions, and significant others.

social conflict theory Human behavior is shaped by interpersonal conflict, and those who maintain social power use it to further their own interests.

social control The control of an individual's behavior by social and institutional forces in society.

social learning theory Behavior patterns are modeled and learned in interactions with others.

social process theory An individual's behavior is shaped by interactions with key social institutions—family, school, peer group, and the like.

social structure theory A person's position in the social structure controls his or her behavior. Those in the lowest socioeconomic tier are more likely to succumb to crime-promoting elements in their environment, whereas those in the highest tier enjoy social and economic advantages that insulate them from crime-producing forces.

specific deterrence A crime control policy suggesting that punishment should be severe enough to convince convicted offenders never to repeat their criminal activity.

split sentence A practice that requires convicted criminals to spend a portion of their sentence behind bars and the remainder in the community.

stalking The willful, malicious, and repeated following and harassing of another person.

stare decisis Latin for "to stand by decided cases." The legal principle by which the decision or holding in an earlier case becomes the standard by which subsequent similar cases are judged.

state courts of limited jurisdiction Courts that have jurisdiction over misdemeanors and conduct preliminary investigations of felony charges.

state (organized) crime Criminal acts committed by state officials within the context of their jobs as government representatives.

status offender A juvenile who engages in behavior legally forbidden to minors, such as running away, truancy, or incorrigibility.

stigmatize To characterize or brand someone as disgraceful in order to make them feel shameful and ruin their reputation.

sting operation An undercover police operation in which police pose as criminals to trap law violators.

stop and frisk The situation when police officers who are suspicious of an individual run their hands lightly over the suspect's outer garments to determine whether the person is carrying a concealed weapon. Also called a patdown or threshold inquiry, a stop and frisk is intended to stop short of any activity that could be considered a violation of Fourth Amendment rights.

strict liability crime Illegal act whose elements do not contain the need for intent, or *mens rea*; usually, an act that endangers the public welfare, such as illegal dumping of toxic wastes.

subculture A substratum of society that maintains a unique set of values and beliefs.

substantive criminal law A body of specific rules that declare what conduct is criminal and that prescribe the punishment to be imposed for such conduct.

substantive rights A number of civil rights that the courts, through a slow process of legal review, have established for inmates, including the rights to receive mail and medical benefits and to practice their religion.

suicide by cop A form of suicide in which a person acts in an aggressive manner with police officers in order to induce them to shoot to kill.

super-maximum-security prison The newest form of a maximum-security prison that uses high-level security measures to incapacitate the nation's most dangerous criminals. Most inmates are in lockdown 23 hours a day.

sureties During the Middle Ages, people responsible for the behavior of an offender released before trial.

suspended sentence A prison term that is delayed while the defendant undergoes a period of community treatment. If the treatment is successful, the prison sentence is terminated.

T

terrorism Politically motivated violence designed to intimidate governmental or civilian opponents to attain political or social objectives.

therapeutic communities Institutions that rely on positive peer pressure within a highly structured social environment to create positive inmate change.

time-in-rank system For police officers to advance in rank, they must spend an appropriate amount of time, usually years, in the preceding rank; for example, to become a captain, an officer must first spend time as a lieutenant.

tithing In medieval England, a group of 10 families who collectively dealt with minor disturbances and breaches of the peace.

tort A personal injury or wrong for which an action for damages may be brought.

total institution A regimented, dehumanizing institution such as a prison, in which inmates are kept in social isolation, cut off from the world at large.

trajectory theory The view that there are multiple independent paths to a criminal career and different types and classes of offenders.

transfer hearing The hearing in which a decision is made to waive a juvenile to the criminal court. Waiver decisions are based on such criteria as the child's age, her or his prior offense history, and the nature of the offense.

transnational organized crime Global criminal conspiracies designed to obtain power and influence or monetary gains that cross nation states and legal jurisdictions.

treatment The rehabilitative method used to effect a change of behavior in the juvenile offender, in the form of therapy, or educational or vocational programs.

true bill of indictment A written statement charging a defendant with the commission of a crime, drawn up by a prosecuting attorney and considered by a grand jury. If the grand jury finds sufficient evidence to support the indictment, it will issue a true bill of indictment.

U

Uniform Crime Reports (UCR) The FBI's yearly publication of where, when, and how much serious crime occurred in the prior year.

US magistrate judge A federal trial judge who is appointed by a district court judge and who presides over various civil cases with the consent of the parties and over certain misdemeanor cases.

US Marshals Service Federal agency whose jurisdiction includes protecting federal officials, transporting criminal defendants, and tracking down fugitives.

USA Patriot Act (USAPA) A law designed to grant new powers to domestic law enforcement and international intelligence agencies in an effort to fight terrorism.

V

venire The group called for jury duty from which jury panels are selected.

vice squad Police officers assigned to enforce morality-based laws, such as those on prostitution, gambling, and pornography.

victim impact statement A postconviction statement by the victim of crime that may be used to guide sentencing decisions.

vigilantes Groups of citizens who tracked down wanted criminals in the Old West.

voir dire The process in which a potential jury panel is questioned by the prosecution and the defense to select jurors who are unbiased and objective.

W

waiver (juvenile) A practice in which the juvenile court waives its jurisdiction over a juvenile and transfers the case to adult criminal court for trial. In some states, a waiver hearing is held to determine jurisdiction, whereas in others, juveniles may be automatically waived if they are accused of committing a serious crime such as murder.

Walnut Street Jail An eighteenth-century institution that housed convicted criminals in Philadelphia.

warez Copyrighted software illegally downloaded and sold by organized groups without license to do so.

watch system During the Middle Ages in England, men were organized in church parishes to guard at night against disturbances and breaches of the peace under the direction of the local constable.

widening the net of justice The view that programs designed to divert offenders from the justice system actually enmesh them further in the process by substituting more intrusive treatment programs for less intrusive punishment-oriented outcomes.

work release A prison treatment program that allows inmates to be released during the day to work in the community and then return to prison at night.

writ of certiorari An order of a superior court requesting that the record of an inferior court (or administrative body) be brought forward for review or inspection.

writ of *habeas corpus* A judicial order requesting that a person who detains another person produce the body of the prisoner and give reasons for his or her capture and detention. *Habeas corpus* is a legal device used to request that a judicial body review the reasons for a person's confinement and the conditions of confinement. *Habeas corpus* is known as "the great writ."

Z

zero tolerance The practice of seizing all instrumentalities of a crime, including homes, boats, and cars. It is an extreme example of the law of forfeiture.

50. David A. Ward, Mark C. Stafford, and Louis N. Gray, "Rational Choice, Deterrence, and Theoretical Integration," *Journal of Applied Social Psychology* 36 (2006): 571–585.

51. Melissa Thompson and Christopher Uggen, "Dealers, Thieves, and the Common Determinants of Drug and Nondrug Illegal Earnings," *Criminology* 59 (2012): 1057–1087; Christopher Uggen and Melissa Thompson, "The Socioeconomic Determinants of Ill-Gotten Gains: Within-Person Changes in Drug Use and Illegal Earnings," *American Journal of Sociology* 109 (2003):146–185.

52. Brandon C. Welsh and David P. Farrington, *Making Public Places Safer: Surveillance and Crime Prevention* (New York: Oxford University Press, 2008).

53. Stephanie Carmichael and Alex Piquero, "Deterrence and Arrest Ratios," *International Journal of Offender Therapy and Comparative Criminology* 50 (2006): 71–87.

54. James A. Densley, "It's Gang Life, But Not as We Know It: The Evolution of Gang Business," *Crime and Delinquency,* first published online April 4, 2012.

55. Ross Matsueda, Derek Kreager, and David Huizinga, "Deterring Delinquents: A Rational Choice Model of Theft and Violence," *American Sociological Review* 71 (2006): 95–122.

56. Alicia Sitren and Brandon Applegate, "Testing the Deterrent Effects of Personal and Vicarious Experience with Punishment and Punishment Avoidance," *Deviant Behavior* 28 (2007): 29–55.

57. Andrew Klein and Terri Tobin, "A Longitudinal Study of Arrested Batterers, 1995–2005: Career Criminals," *Violence Against Women* 14 (2008): 136–157.

58. Rudy Haapanen, Lee Britton, and Tim Croisdale, "Persistent Criminality and Career Length," *Crime and Delinquency* 53 (2007): 133–155.

59. Daniel Nagin and Greg Pogarsky, "Integrating Celerity, Impulsivity, and Extralegal Sanction Threats into a Model of General Deterrence: Theory and Evidence," *Criminology* 39 (2001): 865–892.

60. Cheryl L. Maxson, Kristy N. Matsuda, and Karen Hennigan, "Deterrability Among Gang and Nongang Juvenile Offenders: Are Gang Members More (or Less) Deterrable Than Other Juvenile Offenders?" *Crime and Delinquency* 57 (2011): 516–543.

61. Anthony Braga, Andrew Papachristos, and David Hureau, "The Effects of Hot Spots Policing on Crime: An Updated Systematic Review and Meta-Analysis" *Justice Quarterly* 31 (2014): 633–664.

62. Richard Timothy Coupe and Laurence Blake, "The Effects of Patrol Workloads and Response Strength on Arrests at Burglary Emergencies," *Journal of Criminal Justice* 33 (2005): 239–255.

63. Steven Durlauf and Daniel Nagin, "Imprisonment and Crime: Can Both Be Reduced?" *Criminology and Public Policy* 10 (2011): 13–54.

64. Robert Bursik, Harold Grasmick, and Mitchell Chamlin, "The Effect of Longitudinal Arrest Patterns on the Development of Robbery Trends at the Neighborhood Level," *Criminology* 28 (1990): 431–450; Theodore Chiricos and Gordon Waldo, "Punishment and Crime: An Examination of Some Empirical Evidence," *Social Problems* 18 (1970): 200–217.

65. John Paul Wright and Francis T. Cullen, "The Future of Biosocial Criminology: Beyond Scholars' Professional Ideology," *Journal of Contemporary Criminal Justice* 28 (2012): 237–253.

66. Todd A. Jusko, Charles R. Henderson Jr., Bruce P. Lanphear, Deborah A. Cory-Slechta, Patrick J. Parsons, and Richard L. Canfield, "Blood Lead Concentrations < 10 µg/dL and Child Intelligence at 6 Years of Age," *Environmental Health Perspectives* 116 (2008): 243–248; Joel Nigg, G. Mark Knottnerus, Michelle Martel, Molly Nikolas, Kevin Cavanagh, Wilfried Karmaus, and Marsha D. Rappley, "Low Blood Lead Levels Associated with Clinically Diagnosed Attention-Deficit/Hyperactivity Disorder and Mediated by Weak Cognitive Control," *Biological Psychiatry* 63 (2008): 325–331.

67. Lauren Wakschlag, Kate Pickett, Kristen Kasza, and Rolf Loeber, "Is Prenatal Smoking Associated with a Developmental Pattern of Conduct Problems in Young Boys?" *Journal of the American Academy of Child and Adolescent Psychiatry* 45 (2006): 461–467; "Diet and the Unborn Child: The Omega Point," *The Economist,* January 19, 2006.

68. Rick Nevin, "Understanding International Crime Trends: The Legacy of Preschool Lead Exposure," *Environmental Research* 104 (2007): 315–336.

69. David C. Bellinger, "Lead," *Pediatrics* 113 (2004): 1016–1022.

70. Centers for Disease Control and Prevention, "What Do Parents Need to Know to Protect Their Children?" http://www.cdc.gov/nceh/lead/ACCLPP/blood_lead_levels.htm (accessed April 2014).

71. Kevin Beaver, John Paul Wright, and Matthew Delisi, "Self-Control as an Executive Function: Reformulating Gottfredson and Hirschi's Parental Socialization Thesis," *Criminal Justice and Behavior* 34 (2007): 1345–1361.

72. Alice Jones, Kristin Laurens, Catherine Herba, Gareth Barker, and Essi Viding, "Amygdala Hypoactivity to Fearful Faces in Boys with Conduct Problems and Callous-Unemotional Traits," *American Journal of Psychiatry* 166 (2009): 95–102.

73. Thomas Crowley, Manish S. Dalwani, Susan K. Mikulich-Gilbertson, Yiping P. Du, Carl W. Lejuez, Kristen M. Raymond, and Marie T. Banich, "Risky Decisions and Their Consequences: Neural Processing by Boys with Antisocial Substance Disorder," *PLoS One* 5 (2010), published online, http://www.ncbi.nlm.nih.gov/pmc/articles/PMC2943904/ (accessed February 2013).

74. Thomas Brown, *Attention Deficit Disorder: The Unfocused Mind in Children and Adults* (New Haven, CT: Yale University Press, 2005).

75. Leonore Simon, "Does Criminal Offender Treatment Work?" *Applied and Preventive Psychology* (Summer, 1998); Stephen Faraone, Joseph Biederman, Belinda Krifcher Lehman, Thomas Spencer, Dennis Norman, Larry J. Seidman, Ilana Kraus, James Perrin, Wei J. Chen, and Ming T. Tsuang, "Intellectual Performance and School Failure in Children with Attention Deficit Hyperactivity Disorder and in Their Siblings," *Journal of Abnormal Psychology* 102 (1993): 616–623.

76. Anita Thapar, Kate Langley, Tom Fowler, Frances Rice, Darko Turic, Naureen Whittinger, John Aggleton, Marianne Van den Bree, Michael Owen, and Michael O'Donovan, "Catechol O-methyltransferase Gene Variant and Birth Weight Predict Early-Onset Antisocial Behavior in Children with Attention-Deficit/Hyperactivity Disorder," *Archives*

of *General Psychiatry* 62 (2005): 1275–1278.

77. Ronald L. Simons, Man Kit Lei, Eric A. Stewart, Steven R. H. Beach, Gene H. Brody, Robert A. Philibert, and Frederick X. Gibbons, "Social Adversity, Genetic Variation, Street Code, and Aggression: A Genetically Informed Model of Violent Behavior," *Youth Violence and Juvenile Justice* 10 (2012): 3–24; Kevin Beaver, John Paul Wright, and Matt DeLisi, "Delinquent Peer Group Formation: Evidence of a Gene X Environment Correlation," *Journal of Genetic Psychology* 169 (2008): 227–244.

78. Kevin Beaver, Chris Gibson, Michael Turner, Matt DeLisi, Michael Vaughn, and Ashleigh Holand, "Stability of Delinquent Peer Associations: A Biosocial Test of Warr's Sticky-Friends Hypothesis," *Crime and Delinquency* 57 (2011): 907–927.

79. Kevin M. Beaver, "The Effects of Genetics, the Environment, and Low Self-Control on Perceived Maternal and Paternal Socialization: Results from a Longitudinal Sample of Twins," *Journal of Quantitative Criminology* 27 (2011): 85–105.

80. Callie Burt and Ronald Simons, "Pulling Back the Curtain on Heritability Studies: Biosocial Criminology in the Postgenomic Era," *Criminology* 52 (2014): 223–262.

81. J. C. Barnes, John Paul Wright, Brian B. Boutwell, Joseph A. Schwartz, Eric J. Connolly, Joseph l. Nedelec, and Kevin M. Beaver, "Demonstrating the Validity of Twin Research in Criminology," *Criminology* 52 (2014): 588–626.

82. August Aichorn, *Wayward Youth* (New York: Viking Press, 1965).

83. Paige Crosby Ouimette, "Psychopathology and Sexual Aggression in Nonincarcerated Men," *Violence and Victimization* 12 (1997): 389–397.

84. Robert Krueger, Avshalom Caspi, Phil Silva, and Rob McGee, "Personality Traits Are Differentially Linked to Mental Disorders: A Multitrait-Multidiagnosis Study of an Adolescent Birth Cohort," *Journal of Abnormal Psychology* 105 (1996): 299–312.

85. Seymour Halleck, *Psychiatry and the Dilemmas of Crime* (Berkeley: University of California Press, 1971).

86. David Eitle and R. Jay Turner, "Exposure to Community Violence and Young Adult Crime: The Effects of Witnessing Violence, Traumatic Victimization, and Other Stressful Life Events," *Journal of Research in Crime and Delinquency* 39 (2002): 214–238. See also Albert Bandura, *Aggression: A Social Learning Analysis* (Englewood Cliffs, NJ: Prentice Hall, 1973); Albert Bandura, *Social Learning Theory* (Englewood Cliffs, NJ: Prentice Hall, 1977).

87. Ingrid Môller, Barbara Krahé, Robert Busching, Christina Krause, and Christina, "Efficacy of an Intervention to Reduce the Use of Media Violence and Aggression: An Experimental Evaluation with Adolescents in Germany," *Journal of Youth and Adolescence* 41 (2012): 105–120.

88. Christopher Ferguson and John Kilburn, "The Public Health Risks of Media Violence: A Meta-Analytic Review," *Journal of Pediatrics* 154 (2009): 759–763.

89. Elizabeth Cauffman, Laurence Steinberg, and Alex Piquero, "Psychological, Neuropsychological, and Physiological Correlates of Serious Antisocial Behavior in Adolescence: The Role of Self-Control," *Criminology* 43 (2005): 133–176.

90. Shadd Maruna, "Desistance from Crime and Explanatory Style: A New Direction in the Psychology of Reform," *Journal of Contemporary Criminal Justice* 20 (2004): 184–200.

91. Donald Lynam and Joshua Miller, "Personality Pathways to Impulsive Behavior and Their Relations to Deviance: Results from Three Samples," *Journal of Quantitative Criminology* 20 (2004): 319–341.

92. Tony Ward and Claire Stewart, "The Relationship between Human Needs and Criminogenic Needs," *Psychology, Crime and Law* 9 (2003): 219–225.

93. David Lykken, "Psychopathy, Sociopathy, and Crime," *Society* 34 (1996): 30–38.

94. Gisli Gudjonsson, Emil Einarsson, Ólafur Örn Bragason, and Jon Fridrik Sigurdsson, "Personality Predictors of Self-Reported Offending in Icelandic Students," *Psychology, Crime and Law* 12 (2006) 383–393.

95. Rolf Holmqvist, "Psychopathy and Affect Consciousness in Young Criminal Offenders," *Journal of Interpersonal Violence* 23 (2008): 209–224.

96. Lykken, "Psychopathy, Sociopathy, and Crime."

97. US Census Bureau, "Poverty," http://www.census.gov/hhes/www/poverty/data/threshld/ (accessed February 2014).

98. Sara Thompson and Rosemary Gartner, "The Spatial Distribution and Social Context of Homicide in Toronto's Neighborhoods," *Journal of Research in Crime and Delinquency* 51 (2014): 88–118.

99. Lincoln Quillian and Devah Pager, "Black Neighbors, Higher Crime? The Role of Racial Stereotypes in Evaluations of Neighborhood Crime," *American Journal of Sociology* 107 (2001): 717–769.

100. Oscar Lewis, "The Culture of Poverty," *Scientific American* 215 (1966): 19–25.

101. William Julius Wilson, *The Truly Disadvantaged* (Chicago: University of Chicago Press, 1987).

102. Xu Yili, Mora Fiedler, and Karl Flaming, "Discovering the Impact of Community Policing: The Broken Windows Thesis, Collective Efficacy, and Citizens' Judgment," *Journal of Research in Crime and Delinquency* 42 (2005): 147–186.

103. Kelly Socia and Janet Stamatel, "Neighborhood Characteristics and the Social Control of Registered Sex Offenders," *Crime and Delinquency* 58 (2012): 565–587.

104. Jonathan Crane, "The Epidemic Theory of Ghettos and Neighborhood Effects on Dropping Out and Teenage Childbearing," *American Journal of Sociology* 96 (1991): 1226–1259; see also Rodrick Wallace, "Expanding Coupled Shock Fronts of Urban Decay and Criminal Behavior: How U.S. Cities Are Becoming 'Hollowed Out,'" *Journal of Quantitative Criminology* 7 (1991): 333–355.

105. Barbara Warner, "The Role of Attenuated Culture in Social Disorganization Theory," *Criminology* 41 (2003): 73–97.

106. April Zeoli, Jesenia Pizarro, Sue Grady, and Christopher Melde, "Homicide as Infectious Disease: Using Public Health Methods to Investigate the Diffusion of Homicide," *Justice Quarterly* 31 (2014): 609–632; Jeffrey Fagan and Garth Davies, "The Natural History of Neighborhood Violence," *Journal of Contemporary Criminal Justice* 20 (2004): 127–147.

107. C. L. Storr, C. Y. Chen, and J. C. Anthony, "'Unequal Opportunity': Neighbourhood Disadvantage and the Chance to Buy Illegal Drugs," *Journal of Epidemiology and Community Health* 58 (2004): 231–238.

108. David Pyrooz, "Structural Covariates of Gang Homicide in Large U.S. Cities,"

Journal of Research in Crime and Delinquency, first published online August 17, 2011.

109. Steven Messner and Richard Rosenfeld, *Crime and the American Dream* (Belmont, CA: Wadsworth, 1994), p. 11.

110. David C. Pyrooz, Gary Sweeten, and Alex R. Piquero, "Continuity and Change in Gang Membership and Gang Embeddedness," *Journal of Research in Crime and Delinquency*, published online February 7, 2012.

111. Rebekah Levine Coley, Jodi Eileen Morris, and Daphne Hernandez, "Out-of-School Care and Problem Behavior Trajectories among Low-Income Adolescents: Individual, Family, and Neighborhood Characteristics as Added Risks," *Child Development* 75 (2004): 948–965.

112. Stacy De Coster, Karen Heimer, and Stacy Wittrock, "Neighborhood Disadvantage, Social Capital, Street Context, and Youth Violence," *Sociological Quarterly* (2006): 723–753.

113. Lisa Mufti, "Advancing Institutional Anomie Theory," *International Journal of Offender Therapy and Comparative Criminology* 50 (2006): 630–653.

114. Ibid.

115. Callie H. Burt and Carter Rees, "Behavioral Heterogeneity in Adolescent Friendship Networks," *Justice Quarterly*, first published online January 3, 2014.

116. Travis Hirschi, *Causes of Delinquency* (Berkeley: University of California Press, 1969).

117. Howard Becker, *Outsiders: Studies in the Sociology of Deviance* (New York: Macmillan, 1963), p. 9.

118. John Braithwaite, "Retributivism, Punishment, and Privilege," in *Punishment and Privilege*, ed. W. Byron Groves and Graeme Newman (Albany, NY: Harrow & Heston, 1986), pp. 55–66.

119. Michael Hallett, "Reentry to What? Theorizing Prisoner Reentry in the Jobless Future," *Critical Criminology* 20 (2012): 213–228.

120. Scott A. Bonn, *Mass Deception: Moral Panic and the U.S. War on Iraq* (New Brunswick, NJ: Rutgers University Press, 2010).

121. Marvin Krohn, Alan Lizotte, and Cynthia Perez, "The Interrelationship between Substance Use and Precocious Transitions to Adult Sexuality," *Journal of Health and Social Behavior* 38 (1997): 88.

122. Peggy Giordano, Stephen Cernkovich, and Jennifer Rudolph, "Gender, Crime, and Desistance: Toward a Theory of Cognitive Transformation?" *American Journal of Sociology* 107 (2002): 990–1064.

123. John Hagan and Holly Foster, "S/He's a Rebel: Toward a Sequential Stress Theory of Criminality and Gendered Pathways to Disadvantage in Emerging Adulthood," *Social Forces* 82 (2003): 53–86.

124. Patrick Lussier, David Farrington, and Terrie Moffitt, "Is the Antisocial Child Father of the Abusive Man? A 40-Year Prospective Longitudinal Study on the Development Antecedents of Intimate Partner Violence," *Criminology* 47 (2009): 741–780.

125. Gerald Patterson, Barbara DeBaryshe, and Elizabeth Ramsey, "A Developmental Perspective on Antisocial Behavior," *American Psychologist* 44 (1989): 329–335.

126. Robert Sampson and John Laub, "Crime and Deviance in the Life Course," *American Review of Sociology* 18 (1992): 63–84.

127. David Farrington, Darrick Jolliffe, Rolf Loeber, Magda Stouthamer-Loeber, and Larry Kalb, "The Concentration of Offenders in Families, and Family Criminality in the Prediction of Boys' Criminality," *Journal of Adolescence* 24 (2001): 579–596.

128. Alex R. Piquero and He Len Chung, "On the Relationships Between Gender, Early Onset, and the Seriousness of Offending," *Journal of Delinquent Justice* 29(2001): 189–206.

129. Mary Campa, Catherine Bradshaw, John Eckenrode, and David Zielinski, "Patterns of Problem Behavior in Relation to Thriving and Precocious Behavior in Late Adolescence," *Journal of Youth and Adolescence* 37 (2008): 627–640.

130. Kristin Carbone-Lopez and Jody Miller, "Precocious Role Entry as a Mediating Factor in Women's Methamphetamine Use: Implications for Life-Course and Pathways Research," *Criminology* 50 (2012): 187–220.

131. Lara DePadilla, Molly Perkins, Kirk Elifson, and Claire Sterk, "Adult Criminal Involvement: A Cross-Sectional Inquiry into Correlates and Mechanisms over the Life Course," *Criminal Justice Review* 37 (2012): 110–126.

132. Shawn Bushway, Marvin Krohn, Alan Lizotte, Matthew Phillips, and Nicole Schmidt, "Are Risky Youth Less Protectable as They Age? The Dynamics of Protection during Adolescence and Young Adulthood," *Justice Quarterly* 30 (2013): 84–116.

133. Alex Piquero, David Farrington, Jonathan Shepherd, and Katherine Auty, "Offending and Early Death in the Cambridge Study in Delinquent Development," *Justice Quarterly* 31 (2014): 445–472.

134. Alex Piquero, "Taking Stock of Developmental Trajectories of Criminal Activity over the Life Course," in *The Long View of Crime: A Synthesis of Longitudinal Research*, ed. Akiva Liberman (New York: Springer, 2008), pp. 23–78.

Chapter 3, Criminal Law: Substance and Procedure

1. WCVB.com, "Aaron Hernandez Indicted in Death of Semi-Pro Football Player Odin Lloyd Found Dead in June Near Former Pats' Player's Home," August 22, 2013, http://www.wcvb.com/news/local/boston-south/aaron-hernandez-indicted-in-death-of-semipro-football-player/21576582#ixzz30IpflEVf (accessed May 2015); Rick Hall, Susan Candiotti, and Catherine E. Shoichet, "Former New England Patriot Hernandez Charged with Murder," *CNN Justice* (June 27, 2013); Sasha Goldstein, "Aaron Hernandez Beats Down Fellow Inmate at Bristol County Jail: Report," February 25, 2014, http://www.nydailynews.com/news/crime/aaron-hernandez-beats-fellow-inmate-bristol-county-jail-report-article-1.1701678 (accessed May 2015),; Halimy Assafa and Chris Boyette, "Aaron Hernandez Sued by Families of 2012 Fatal Shooting Victims," *CNN US*, February 27, 2014.

2. Goldstein, "Aaron Hernandez Beats Down Fellow Inmate at Bristol County Jail: Report.".

3. Code of Hammurabi, available online at http://avalon.law.yale.edu/ancient/hamframe.asp (accessed February 2013).

4. See John Weaver, *Warren—The Man, the Court, the Era* (Boston: Little, Brown, 1967); see also "We the People," *Time*, July 6, 1987, p. 6.

5. *Kansas v. Hendricks*, 117 S.Ct. 2072 (1997); *Chicago v. Morales*, 119 S.Ct. 246 (1999).

6. *City of Chicago v. Morales et al.*, 527 US 41 (1999).

7. Daniel Suleiman, "The Capital Punishment Exception: A Case for

Constitutionalizing the Substantive Criminal Law," *Columbia Law Review* 104 (2004): 426–458.

8. *Calder v. Bull,* 3 US 386 (1798).

9. See, for example, *General Laws of Massachusetts, Part II: Real and Personal Property and Domestic Relations. Title III. Domestic Relations,* Section 209 (June 30, 2002).

10. Sheldon Krantz, *Law of Corrections and Prisoners' Rights, Cases and Materials,* 3rd ed. (St. Paul, MN: West, 1986), p. 702; Barbara Knight and Stephen Early Jr., *Prisoners' Rights in America* (Chicago: Nelson-Hall, 1986), ch. 1; see also Fred Cohen, "The Law of Prisoners' Rights—An Overview," *Criminal Law Bulletin* 24 (188): 321–349.

11. See *United States v. Balint,* 258 US 250, 42 S.Ct. 301, 66 L.Ed. 604 (1922); see also *Morissette v. United States,* 342 US 246, 72 S.Ct. 240, 96 L.Ed. 288 (1952).

12. *Regina v. Dudley and Stephens,* 14 Q.B.D. 273 (1884).

13. For a history and analysis of these types of defenses, see Eugene Milhizer, "Justification and Excuse: What They Were, What They Are, and What They Ought to Be," *St. John's Law Review* 78 (2004): 725–895.

14. William Blackstone, *Commentaries on the Law of England,* vol. 1, ed. Thomas Cooley (Chicago: Callaghan, 1899), pp. 4, 26. Blackstone was an English barrister who lectured on the English common law at Oxford University in 1753.

15. Henry Fradella, *From Insanity to Diminished Capacity: Mental Illness and Criminal Defenses of Excuse in Contemporary American Law* (Bethesda, MD: Academic Press, 2007).

16. Samuel M. Davis, *Rights of Juveniles: The Juvenile Justice System* (New York: Boardman, 1974; updated 1993), ch. 2; Larry Siegel and Joseph Senna, *Juvenile Delinquency: Theory, Practice, and Law* (St. Paul, MN: West, 1996).

17. "Criminal Law—Mutual Combat Mitigation—Appellate Court of Illinois Holds that Disproportionate Reaction to Provocation Negates Mutual Combat Mitigation—*People v. Thompson,* 821 N.E. 2d 664 (Ii. App. Ct. 2004)," *Harvard Law Review* 118 (2005): 2437–2444.

18. Florida Statutes, Home Protection; Use of Deadly Force; Presumption of Fear of Death or Great Bodily Harm, http://www.leg.state.fl.us/statutes (accessed February 2013).

19. Patrik Jonsson, "Is Self-Defense Law Vigilante Justice? Some Say Proposed Laws Can Help Deter Gun Violence. Others Worry about Deadly Confrontations," *Christian Science Monitor,* February 24, 2006.

20. 356 US 369, 78 S.Ct. 819, 2 L.Ed.2d 848 (1958); see also *Jacobson v. United States,* 503 US 540, 112 S.Ct. 1535, 118 L.Ed.2d 174 (1992).

21. Federal Criminal Code, Chapter 63—Mail Fraud and Other Fraud Offenses, Title 18, part 1, chapter 4, § 1028, http://www.law.cornell.edu/uscode/18/1028.html (accessed February 2013).

22. The CAN-SPAM Act of 2003 (15 USC. 7701, et seq., Public Law No. 108–187, was S.877), https://www.law.cornell.edu/wex/inbox/can-spam_act_core_requirements (accessed February 2015).

23. Matthew R. Lyon, "No Means No?: Withdrawal of Consent During Intercourse and the Continuing Evolution of the Definition of Rape," *Journal of Criminal Law and Criminology* 95 (2004): 277–314.

24. *Lawrence et al. v. Texas,* No. 02-102, June 26, 2003.

25. Marvin Zalman, John Strate, Denis Hunter, and James Sellars, "Michigan Assisted Suicide Three Ring Circus: The Intersection of Law and Politics," *Ohio Northern Law Review* 23 (1997): 230–276.

26. 1992 P.A. 270 as amended by 1993 P.A.3, M.C. L. ss. 752.1021 to 752.1027.

27. Michigan Code of Criminal Procedure, *Assisting a Suicide,* Section 750.329a.

28. National Institute of Justice, *Project to Develop a Model Anti-Stalking Statute* (Washington, DC: National Institute of Justice, 1994).

29. National Conference of State Legislators, Identity Theft Statutes, August 31, 2010, http://www.ncsl.org/issues-research/banking/identity-theft-state-statutes.aspx (accessed February 2013).

30. Environmental Protection Agency, Criminal Enforcement Division, http://www.epa.gov/compliance/criminal/ (accessed February 2013).

31. Drug Policy Alliance Network, "Medical Marijuana," http://www.drugpolicy.org/medical-marijuana (accessed February 2013).

32. State of New Jersey 213th Legislature, Senate Bill 119, http://medicalmarijuana.procon.org/sourcefiles/NJS119.pdf (accessed February 2013).

33. *Gonzales v. Raich,* 545 US 1 (2005).

34. 384 US 436, 86 S.Ct. 1602, 16 L.Ed.2d 694 (1966).

35. Daniel Suleiman, "The Capital Punishment Exception: A Case for Constitutionalizing the Substantive Criminal Law," *Columbia Law Review* 104 (2004): 426–458.

36. *Baze and Bowling v. Rees,* 553 US 35 (2008).

37. See "Essay," *Time,* February 26, 1973, p. 95; also, for a tribute to the Bill of Rights and due process, see James MacGregor Burns and Stewart Burns, *The Pursuit of Rights in America* (New York: Knopf, 1991).

38. *Griswold v. Connecticut,* 381 US 479 (1965).

39. 342 US 165, 72 S.Ct. 205, 95 L.Ed. 183 (1952).

40. *Herring vs. US,* 555, US 135, 1 (2009).

Chapter 4, Police in Society: History and Organization

1. Jeri Clausing, "Albuquerque Shooting Recordings to Be Given to FBI," *Associated Press,* March 28, 2014, http://news.yahoo.com/albuquerque-shooting-recordings-given-fbi-174702288.html (accessed April 3, 2014); see also Patrik Jonsson, "Feds Probe Albuquerque Camper Shooting as Police Rethink Use of Force," *Christian Science Monitor,* March 29, 2014, http://www.csmonitor.com/USA/Justice/2014/0329/Feds-probe-Albuquerque-camper-shooting-as-police-rethink-use-of-force-video (accessed April 3, 2014).

2. Larry Celona, Shawn Cohen, Jaime Schram, Amber Jamieson, and Laura Italiano, "Gunman Executes 2 NYPD Cops in Garner 'Revenge,'" *New York Post,* December 20, 2014, http://nypost.com/2014/12/20/2-nypd-cops-shot-execution-style-in-brooklyn/ (accessed January 28, 2015).

3. Federal Bureau of Investigation, "Law Enforcement Officers Killed and Assaulted, 2013," http://www.fbi.gov/about-us/cjis/ucr/leoka/2013 (accessed January 28, 2015).

4. This section relies heavily on such sources as Malcolm Sparrow, Mark Moore, and David Kennedy, *Beyond 911: A New Era for Policing* (New York: Basic Books, 1990); Daniel Devlin, *Police Procedure, Administration,*

and Organization (London: Butterworth, 1966); Robert Fogelson, *Big City Police* (Cambridge, MA: Harvard University Press, 1977); Roger Lane, *Policing the City, Boston 1822–1885* (Cambridge, MA: Harvard University Press, 1967); J. J. Tobias, *Crime and Industrial Society in the Nineteenth Century* (New York: Schocken Books, 1967); Samuel Walker, *A Critical History of Police Reform: The Emergence of Professionalism* (Lexington, MA: Lexington Books, 1977); Samuel Walker, *Popular Justice* (New York: Oxford University Press, 1980); John McMullan, "The New Improved Monied Police: Reform Crime Control and Commodification of Policing in London," *British Journal of Criminology* 36 (1996): 85–108.

5. Devlin, *Police Procedure, Administration, and Organization.*

6. McMullan, "The New Improved Monied Police," p. 92.

7. Phillip Reichel, "Southern Slave Patrols as a Transitional Type," *American Journal of Police* 7 (1988): 51–78.

8. Walker, *Popular Justice*, 61.

9. Christopher Thale, "Assigned to Patrol: Neighborhoods, Police, and Changing Deployment Practices in New York City Before 1930," *Journal of Social History* 37 (2004): 1037–1064.

10. Walker, *Popular Justice*, 8.

11. Dennis Rousey, "Cops and Guns: Police Use of Deadly Force in Nineteenth-Century New Orleans," *American Journal of Legal History* 28 (1984): 41–66.

12. Law Enforcement Assistance Administration, *Two Hundred Years of American Criminal Justice* (Washington, DC: Government Printing Office, 1976).

13. National Commission on Law Observance and Enforcement, *Report on the Police* (Washington, DC: Government Printing Office, 1931), pp. 5–7.

14. Pamela Irving Jackson, *Minority Group Threat, Crime, and Policing* (New York: Praeger, 1989).

15. James Q. Wilson and George Kelling, "Broken Windows," *Atlantic Monthly* 249 (1982): 29–38.

16. Frank Tippett, "It Looks Just Like a War Zone," *Time*, May 27, 1985, pp. 16–22; "San Francisco, New York Police Troubled by Series of Scandals," *Criminal Justice Newsletter* 16 (1985): 2–4; Karen Polk, "New York Police: Caught in the Middle and Losing Faith," *Boston Globe*, December 28, 1988, p. 3.

17. Staff of the *Los Angeles Times*, *Understanding the Riots: Los Angeles Before and After the Rodney King Case* (Los Angeles: *Los Angeles Times*, 1992).

18. David H. Bayley, "Policing in America," *Society* 36 (December 1998).

19. Ronald Burns, Keith Whitworth, and Carol Thompson, "Assessing Law Enforcement Preparedness to Address Internet Fraud," *Journal of Criminal Justice* 32 (2004): 477–493.

20. Brian A. Reaves, *Census of State and Local Law Enforcement Agencies, 2008* (Washington, DC: Bureau of Justice Statistics, 2011).

21. Bruce Smith, *Police Systems in the United States* (New York: Harper & Row, 1960).

22. Brian J. Reaves, *Census of State and Local Law Enforcement Agencies, 2008* (Washington, DC: Bureau of Justice Statistics, 2011).

23. *Texas Homeland Security Strategic Plan, 2010–2015,* http://governor.state.tx.us/files/homeland/HmLndSecurity_StratPlan2015.pdf (accessed March 2015).

24. Reaves, *Census of State and Local Law Enforcement Agencies, 2008.*

25. Harris County Homeland Security and Emergency Management, http://www.hcoem.org (accessed March 2015).

26. Montgomery County, Maryland, Office of Emergency Management and Homeland Security, http://www.montgomerycountymd.gov/oemhs/ (accessed March 2015).

27. Reaves, *Census of State and Local Law Enforcement Agencies, 2008.*

28. See, for example, Robert Keppel and Joseph Weis, *Improving the Investigation of Violent Crime: The Homicide Investigation and Tracking System* (Washington, DC: National Institute of Justice, 1993).

29. For an overview of the department's many counterterrorism initiatives, see http://www.nyc.gov/html/nypd/html/administration/counterterrorism_units.shtml (accessed March 2015).

30. NYPD SHIELD, http://www.nypdshield.org/public/ (accessed March 2015).

31. Elizabeth E. Joh, "The Paradox of Private Policing," *Journal of Criminal Law and Criminology* 95 (2004): 49–131.

32. David A. Sklansky, "The Private Police," *UCLA Law Review* 46 (1999): 1165–1287.

33. Elizabeth E. Joh, "Conceptualizing the Private Police," *Utah Law Review* (2005): 573–617, at 588–593.

34. Ibid., 588.

35. Clifford Shearing and Philip Stenning, "Say 'Cheese'?: The Disney Order That Is Not So Mickey Mouse," in *Private Policing* (Thousand Oaks, CA: Sage, 1987).

36. Andrea Elliott, "In Stores, Private Handcuffs for Sticky Fingers," *New York Times*, June 17, 2003, A1.

37. Sklansky, "The Private Police," p. 1168.

38. *Griffin v. Maryland*, 378 US 130 (1964).

39. See, for example, *Williams v. United States*, 341 US 97 (1951).

40. See, for example, *Wade v. Byles*, 83 F.3d 902 (7th Cir. 1996); *Gallagher v. "Neil Young Freedom Concert,"* 49 F.3d 1442 (10th Cir. 1995); *United States v. Francoeur*, 547 F.2d 891 (5th Cir. 1977); *People v. Taylor*, 271 Cal. Rptr. 785 (Ct. App. 1990); *United States v. Lima*, 424 A.2d 113 (DC 1980) (en banc); *People v. Toliver*, 377 N.E.2d 207 (Ill. App. Ct. 1978); *People v. Holloway*, 267 N.W.2d 454 (Mich. Ct. App. 1978); *State v. Buswell*, 460 N.W.2d 614 (Minn. 1990).

41. See, for example, *United States v. Antonelli*, 434 F.2d 335 (2d Cir. 1970); *City of Grand Rapids v. Impens*, 327 N.W.2d 278 (Mich. 1982).

42. See, for example, *United States v. Cruz*, 783 F.2d 1470, 1473 (9th Cir. 1986); *State v. Garcia*, 528 So. 2d 76 (Fla. Dist. Ct. App. 1988); *Perez v. State*, 517 So. 2d 106 (Fla. Dist. Ct. App. 1987); *People v. Gorski*, 494 N.E.2d 246 (Ill. App. Ct. 1986); *State v. Farmer*, 510 P.2d 180 (Kan. 1973); *Commonwealth v. Lindenmuth*, 554 A.2d 62 (Pa. Super. Ct. 1989).

43. Joh, "The Paradox of Private Policing," p. 64.

44. Larry Coutorie, "The Future of High-Technology Crime: A Parallel Delphi Study," *Journal of Criminal Justice* 23 (1995): 13–27.

45. This section is based on Derek Paulsen, "To Map or Not to Map: Assessing the Impact of Crime Maps on Police Officer Perceptions of Crime," *International Journal of Police Science and Management* 6 (2004): 234–246; William W. Bratton and Peter Knobler, *Turnaround: How America's Top Cop Reversed the Crime Epidemic* (New York: Random House, 1998), p. 289; Jeremy Travis, "Computerized Crime Mapping," *NIJ News* (National Institute of Justice), January 1999.

46. "Spotlight on Computer Imaging," *Police Chief* 66 (1999): 6–8.

47. See, generally, Ryan McDonald, "Juries and Crime Labs: Correcting the Weak Links in the DNA Chain," *American Journal of Law and Medicine*

24 (1998): 345–363; "DNA Profiling Advancement," *FBI Law Enforcement Bulletin* 67 (1998): 24.

48. Shumuriel Ratliff, "Hartselle Police Use Social Networking to Catch Crooks," http://www.waff.com/story /17316642/hartselle-police-use-social -networking-to-crack-down-on -crooks (accessed March 2015).

49. See http://www.facebook.com/note .php?note_id=10150225332920329 (accessed March 2015).

Chapter 5, The Police: Role and Function

1. Christopher Mathias, "Commissioner William Bratton Confirms NYPD Slowdown," *Huffington Post*, January 9, 2015, http://www.huffingtonpost .com/2015/01/09/nypd-slowdown _n_6446392.html (accessed February 3, 2015).

2. Ibid.

3. Ibid.

4. J. David Goodman, "New York Crime Keeps Falling, Mayor de Blasio Says; Cites Years of 'Momentum,'" *New York Times*, December 2, 2014, http://www .nytimes.com/2014/12/03/nyregion /violent-crime-in-new-york-has -dropped-to-historic-low-mayor -de-blasio-says.html?_r=0 (accessed February 3, 2015).

5. James Willis, Stephen Mastrofski, and David Weisburd, "Making Sense of COMPSTAT: A Theory- Based Analysis of Organizational Change in Three Police Departments," *Law and Society Review* 41 (2007): 147–188.

6. Matthew Durose and Patrick Langan, *Contacts Between Police and the Public, Findings from the 2005 National Survey* (Washington, DC: Bureau of Justice Statistics, 2007).

7. Brian A. Reaves and Pheny Smith, *Law Enforcement Management and Administrative Statistics, 1993: Data for Individual State and Local Agencies with 100 or More Officers* (Washington, DC: Bureau of Justice Statistics, 1995).

8. American Bar Association, *Standards Relating to Urban Police Function* (New York: Institute of Judicial Administration, 1974), standard 2.2.

9. Albert J. Reiss, *The Police and the Public* (New Haven, CT: Yale University Press, 1971), p. 19.

10. James Q. Wilson, *Varieties of Police Behavior: The Management of Law and Order in Eight Communities* (Cambridge, MA: Harvard University Press, 1968).

11. James Q. Wilson and Barbara Boland, "The Effect of Police on Crime," *Law and Society Review* 12 (1978): 367–384.

12. Robert Sampson, "Deterrent Effects of the Police on Crime: A Replication and Theoretical Extension," *Law and Society Review* 22 (1988): 163–191.

13. Richard Timothy Coupe and Laurence Blake, "The Effects of Patrol Workloads and Response Strength on Arrests at Burglary Emergencies," *Journal of Criminal Justice* 33 (2005): 239–255.

14. Lawrence Sherman, James Shaw, and Dennis Rogan, *The Kansas City Gun Experiment* (Washington, DC: National Institute of Justice, 1994).

15. For a thorough review of this issue, see Andrew Karmen, *Why Is New York City's Murder Rate Dropping So Sharply?* (New York: John Jay College, 1996).

16. Robert Davis, Pedro Mateu-Gelabert, and Joel Miller, "Can Effective Policing Also Be Respectful? Two Examples in the South Bronx," *Police Quarterly* 8 (2005): 229–247.

17. Mitchell Chamlin, "Crime and Arrests: An Autoregressive Integrated Moving Average (ARIMA) Approach," *Journal of Quantitative Criminology* 4 (1988) 247–255.

18. Stewart D'Alessio and Lisa Stolzenberg, "Crime, Arrests, and Pretrial Jail Incarceration: An Examination of the Deterrence Thesis," *Criminology* 36 (1998): 735–761.

19. Perry Shapiro and Harold Votey, "Deterrence and Subjective Probabilities of Arrest: Modeling Individual Decisions to Drink and Drive in Sweden," *Law and Society Review* 18 (1984): 111–149.

20. William Spelman and Dale K. William, *Calling the Police: A Replication of the Citizen Reporting Component of the Kansas City Response Time Analysis* (Washington, DC: Police Foundation, 1976).

21. Abdullah Cihan, Yan Zhang, and Larry Hoover, "Police Response Time to In-Progress Burglary," *Police Quarterly* 15 (2012): 308–327.

22. George Kelling and James Q. Wilson, "Broken Windows: The Police and Neighborhood Safety," *Atlantic Monthly* 249 (1982): 29–38.

23. Catherine Coles and George Kelling, *Fixing Broken Windows: Restoring Order and Reducing Crime in Our Communities* (New York: Free Press, 1998).

24. Anthony A. Braga and Brenda J. Bond, "Policing Crime and Disorder Hot Spots: A Randomized Controlled Trial," *Criminology* 46 (2008): 577–606.

25. Vincent Henry, *The Compstat Paradigm: Management Accountability in Policing, Business and the Public Sector* (New York: Looseleaf Law Publications, 2002).

26. For a view of the modern detective, see William Sanders, *Detective Work: A Study of Criminal Investigations* (New York: Free Press, 1977).

27. Mark Pogrebin and Eric Poole, "Vice Isn't Nice: A Look at the Effects of Working Undercover," *Journal of Criminal Justice* 21 (1993): 385–396; Gary Marx, *Undercover: Police Surveillance in America* (Berkeley: University of California Press, 1988).

28. Martin Innes, *Investigating Murder: Detective Work and the Police Response to Criminal Homicide* (Clarendon Studies in Criminology) (London: Oxford University Press, 2003).

29. John B. Edwards, "Homicide Investigative Strategies," *FBI Law Enforcement Bulletin* 74 (2005): 11–21.

30. Robert Langworthy, "Do Stings Control Crime? An Evaluation of a Police Fencing Operation," *Justice Quarterly* 6 (1989): 27–45.

31. Mary Dodge, Donna Starr-Gimeno, and Thomas Williams, "Puttin' on the Sting: Women Police Officers' Perspectives on Reverse Prostitution Assignment," *International Journal of Police Science and Management* 7 (2005): 71–85.

32. Peter Greenwood and Joan Petersilia, *Summary and Policy Implications,* vol. 1, *The Criminal Investigation Process* (Santa Monica, CA: Rand, 1975).

33. Mark Willman and John Snortum, "Detective Work: The Criminal Investigation Process in a Medium-Size Police Department," *Criminal Justice Review* 9 (1984): 33–39.

34. Janice Puckett and Richard Lundman, "Factors Affecting Homicide Clearances: Multivariate Analysis of a More Complete Conceptual Framework," *Journal of Research in Crime and Delinquency* 40 (2003): 171–194.

35. Police Executive Research Forum, *Calling the Police: Citizen Reporting of Serious Crime* (Washington, DC: Police Executive Research Forum, 1981).

36. John Eck, *Solving Crimes: The Investigation of Burglary and Robbery* (Washington, DC: Police Executive Research Forum, 1984).

37. A. Fischer, "CopLink Nabs Criminals Faster," *Arizona Daily Star,* January 7, 2001; A. Robbins, *PC Magazine* 22 (2003); M. Sink, "An Electronic Cop that Plays Hunches," *New York Times,* November 2, 2002.

38. Paul Johnson and Robin Williams, "Internationalizing New Technologies of Crime Control: Forensic DNA Databasing and Datasharing in the European Union," *Policing and Society* 17 (2007): 103–118.

39. For a general review, see Robert Trojanowicz and Bonnie Bucqueroux, *Community Policing: A Contemporary Perspective* (Cincinnati: Anderson, 1990).

40. Police Foundation, *The Newark Foot Patrol Experiment* (Washington, DC: Police Foundation, 1981).

41. John Worrall and Jihong Zhao. "The Role of the COPS Office in Community Policing," *Policing: An International Journal of Police Strategies and Management* 26 (2003), 64–87.

42. Jihong Zhao, Nicholas Lovrich, and Quint Thurman, "The Status of Community Policing in American Cities," *Policing* 22 (1999): 74–92.

43. Albert Cardarelli, Jack McDevitt, and Katrina Baum, "The Rhetoric and Reality of Community Policing in Small and Medium-Sized Cities and Towns," *Policing* 21 (1998): 397–415.

44. Brian Renauer, "Reducing Fear of Crime," *Police Quarterly* 10 (2007): 41–62.

45. Susan Sadd and Randolph Grinc, *Implementation Challenges in Community Policing* (Washington, DC: National Institute of Justice, 1996).

46. Donald Green, Dara Strolovitch, and Janelle Wong, "Defended Neighborhoods: Integration and Racially Motivated Crime," *American Journal of Sociology* 104 (1998): 372–403.

47. Robin Shepard Engel, *How Police Supervisory Styles Influence Patrol Officer Behavior* (Washington, DC: National Institute of Justice, 2003).

48. Amy Halsted, Max Bromley, and John Cochran, "The Effects of Work Orientations on Job Satisfaction among Sheriffs' Deputies Practicing Community-Oriented Policing," *Policing: An International Journal of Police Strategies and Management* 23 (2000): 82–104.

49. Venessa Garcia, "Constructing the 'Other' within Police Culture: An Analysis of a Deviant Unit within the Police Organization," *Police Practice and Research* 6 (2005): 65–80.

50. Kevin Ford, Daniel Weissbein, and Kevin Plamondon, "Distinguishing Organizational from Strategy Commitment: Linking Officers' Commitment to Community Policing to Job Behaviors and Satisfaction," *Justice Quarterly* 20 (2003): 159–186.

51. Michael Palmiotto, Michael Birzer, and N. Prabha Unnithan, "Training in Community Policing: A Suggested Curriculum," *Policing: An International Journal of Police Strategies and Management* 23 (2000): 8–21.

52. Lisa Riechers and Roy Roberg, "Community Policing: A Critical Review of Underlying Assumptions," *Journal of Police Science and Administration* 17 (1990): 112–113.

53. Yili Xu, Mora Fiedler, and Karl Flaming, "Discovering the Impact of Community Policing: The Broken Windows Thesis, Collective Efficacy, and Citizens' Judgment," *Journal of Research in Crime and Delinquency* 42 (2005): 147–186.

54. Ling Ren, Liqun Cao, Nicholas Lovrich, and Michael Gaffney, "Linking Confidence in the Police with the Performance of the Police: Community Policing Can Make a Difference," *Journal of Criminal Justice* 33 (2005): 55–66.

55. Jihong Zhao, Ni He, and Nicholas Lovrich, "Value Change among Police Officers at a Time of Organizational Reform: A Follow-Up Study of Rokeach Values," *Policing* 22 (1999): 152–170.

56. Herman Goldstein, "Improving Policing: A Problem-Oriented Approach," *Crime and Delinquency* 25 (1979): 236–258.

57. Jerome Skolnick and David Bayley, *Community Policing: Issues and Practices Around the World* (Washington, DC: National Institute of Justice, 1988), p. 12.

58. Lawrence Sherman, Patrick Gartin, and Michael Buerger, "Hot Spots of Predatory Crime: Routine Activities and the Criminology of Place," *Criminology* 27 (1989): 27–55.

59. Ibid., 45.

60. See, for example, Anthony Braga and David Weisburd, "The Effects of Focused Deterrence Strategies on Crime: A Systematic Review and Meta-Analysis of the Empirical Evidence," *Journal of Research in Crime and Delinquency* 49 (2012): 323–358.

61. Sherry Plaster Carter, Stanley Carter, and Andrew Dannenberg, "Zoning Out Crime and Improving Community Health in Sarasota, Florida: 'Crime Prevention through Environmental Design,'" *American Journal of Public Health* 93 (2003): 1442–1445.

62. Anthony Braga, David Kennedy, Elin Waring, and Anne Morrison Piehl, "Problem-Oriented Policing, Deterrence, and Youth Violence: An Evaluation of Boston's Operation Ceasefire," *Journal of Research in Crime and Delinquency* 38 (2001): 195–225; see also *Program Profile: Operation Ceasefire,* http://www.crimesolutions.gov/ProgramDetails.aspx?ID=207 (accessed February 2015); Braga and Weisburd, "The Effects of Focused Deterrence Strategies on Crime: A Systematic Review and Meta-Analysis of the Empirical Evidence."

63. Bureau of Justice Assistance, *Problem-Oriented Drug Enforcement: A Community-Based Approach for Effective Policing* (Washington, DC: National Institute of Justice, 1993).

64. Ibid., pp. 64–65.

65. David L. Carter and Jeremy G. Carter, "Intelligence-Led Policing: Conceptual and Functional Considerations for Public Police," *Criminal Justice Policy Review* 20 (2009): 310–325.

66. Global Intelligence Working Group, *National Criminal Intelligence Sharing Plan* (Washington, DC: Office of Justice Programs, 2003), p. 6.

67. Jerry Ratcliffe, *Intelligence-Led Policing* (New York: Willan, 2008).

68. Carter and Carter, p. 310.

69. Ibid., p. 312.

70. Ratcliffe, *Intelligence-Led Policing.*

71. Marilyn B. Peterson, "Toward a Model for Intelligence-Led Policing in the United States," in *Turnkey Intelligence: Unlocking Your Agency's Intelligence Capability* (Lawrenceville, NJ: International Association of Law Enforcement Intelligence Analysts, Law Enforcement Intelligence Unit, and National White Collar Crime Center, 2002), p. 5.

72. *National Criminal Intelligence Sharing Plan,* https://it.ojp.gov/documents/ncisp/ (accessed February 2015).

73. Fusion Center Guidelines: Developing and Sharing Information and Intelligence in a New Era, http://www.it.ojp.gov/documents/fusion_center_guidelines.pdf (accessed February 2015).

74. Charles R. Swanson, Leonard Territo, and Robert W. Taylor, *Police Administration: Structures, Processes, and Behavior,* 7th ed. (Upper Saddle River, NJ: Prentice Hall, 2008), pp. 77–78.

75. William Doerner and Terry Nowell, "The Reliability of the Behavioral-Personnel Assessment Device (BPAD) in Selecting Police Recruits," *Policing* 22 (1999): 343–352.

76. See, for example, Richard Larson, *Urban Police Patrol Analysis* (Cambridge, MA: MIT Press, 1972).

77. Brian A. Reaves, *Local Police Departments, 2007* (Washington, DC: Bureau of Justice Statistics, 2010).

78. Philip Ash, Karen Slora, and Cynthia Britton, "Police Agency Officer Selection Practices," *Journal of Police Science and Administration* 17 (1990): 258–269.

79. Dennis Rosenbaum, Robert Flewelling, Susan Bailey, Chris Ringwalt, and Deanna Wilkinson, "Cops in the Classroom: A Longitudinal Evaluation of Drug Abuse Resistance Education (DARE)," *Journal of Research in Crime and Delinquency* 31 (1994): 3–31.

Chapter 6, Issues in Policing: Professional, Social, and Legal

1. "Timeline: Eric Garner Death," http://www.nbcnewyork.com/news /local/Timeline-Eric-Garner -Chokehold-Death-Arrest-NYPD- Grand-Jury-No-Indictment-284657081. html (accessed February 2015).

2. Joseph Goldstein and Marc Santora, "Staten Island Man Died from Chokehold during Arrest, Autopsy Finds," *New York Times*, August 1, 2014, http://www.nytimes.com/2014 /08/02/nyregion/staten-island-man -died-from-officers-chokehold -autopsy-finds.html?_r=0 (accessed February 2015).

3. Jihong Zhao and Nicholas Lovrich, "Determinants of Minority Employment in American Municipal Police Agencies: The Representation of African American Officers," *Journal of Criminal Justice* 26 (1998): 267–278.

4. Brian A. Reaves, *Local Police Departments, 2007* (Washington, DC: Bureau of Justice Statistics, 2010).

5. T. David Murphy and John Worrall, "Residency Requirements and Public Perceptions of the Police in Large Municipalities," *Policing* 22 (1999): 327–342.

6. Jack Kuykendall and David Burns, "The African American Police Officer: An Historical Perspective," *Journal of Contemporary Criminal Justice* 1 (1980): 4–13.

7. Ibid.

8. Nicholas Alex, *Black in Blue: A Study of the Negro Policeman* (New York: Appleton-Century-Crofts, 1969).

9. Nicholas Alex, *New York Cops Talk Back* (New York: Wiley, 1976).

10. David Eitle, Lisa Stolzenberg, and Stewart J. D'Alessio, "Police Organizational Factors, the Racial Composition of the Police, and the Probability of Arrest," *Justice Quarterly* 22 (2005): 30–57.

11. Stephen Leinen, *African American Police, White Society* (New York: New York University Press, 1984).

12. Ni He, Jihong Zhao, and Ling Ren, "Do Race and Gender Matter in Police Stress? A Preliminary Assessment of the Interactive Effects," *Journal of Criminal Justice* 33 (2005): 535–547.

13. Joseph L. Gustafson, "Tokenism in Policing: An Empirical Test of Kanter's Hypothesis," *Journal of Criminal Justice* 36 (2008): 1–10.

14. For a review of the history of women in policing, see Dorothy Moses Schulz, "From Policewoman to Police Officer: An Unfinished Revolution," *Police Studies* 16 (1993): 90–99; Cathryn House, "The Changing Role of Women in Law Enforcement," *Police Chief* 60 (1993): 139–144.

15. Susan Martin, "Female Officers on the Move? A Status Report on Women in Policing," in *Critical Issues in Policing*, ed. Roger Dunham and Geoffery Alpert (Grove Park, IL: Waveland Press, 1988), pp. 312–331.

16. *LeBoeuf v. Ramsey*, 503 F.Supp. 747 (D. Mass 1980).

17. Michael Birzer and Delores Craig, "Gender Differences in Police Physical Ability Test Performance," *American Journal of Police* 15 (1996): 93–106.

18. Reaves, *Local Police Departments, 2007*.

19. Jill Harrison, "Women in Law Enforcement: Subverting Sexual Harassment with Social Bonds," *Women and Criminal Justice* 22 (2012): 226–238; James Daum and Cindy Johns, "Police Work from a Woman's Perspective," *Police Chief* 61 (1994): 46–49.

20. Mary Brown, "The Plight of Female Police: A Survey of NW Patrolmen," *Police Chief* 61 (1994): 50–53.

21. Matthew Hickman, Alex Piquero, and Jack Greene, "Discretion and Gender Disproportionality in Police Disciplinary Systems," *Policing: An International Journal of Police Strategies and Management* 23 (2000): 105–116.

22. Robin Haarr and Merry Morash, "Gender, Race, and Strategies of Coping with Occupational Stress in Policing," *Justice Quarterly* 16 (1999): 303–336.

23. Ibid.

24. Eric Poole and Mark Pogrebin, "Factors Affecting the Decision to Remain in Policing: A Study of Women Officers," *Journal of Police Science and Administration* 16 (1988): 49–55.

25. See, for example, Gary Cordner and AnnMarie Cordner, "Stuck on a Plateau? Obstacles to Recruitment, Selection, and Retention of Women Police," *Police Quarterly* 14 (2011): 207–226.

26. Reaves, *Local Police Departments, 2007*.

27. Bruce Berg, "Who Should Teach Police? A Typology and Assessment of Police Academy Instructors," *American Journal of Police* 9 (1990): 79–100.

28. David Carter and Allen Sapp, *The State of Police Education: Critical Findings* (Washington, DC: Police Executive Research Forum, 1988), p. 6.

29. John Krimmel, "The Performance of College-Educated Police: A Study of Self-Rated Police Performance Measures," *American Journal of Police* 15 (1996): 85–95.

30. See, for example, Richard Harris, *The Police Academy: An Inside View* (New York: Wiley, 1973); John Van Maanen, "Observations on the Making of a Policeman," in *Order Under Law*, ed. R. Culbertson and M. Tezak (Prospect Heights, IL: Waveland Press, 1981), pp. 111–126; Jonathan Rubenstein, *City Police* (New York: Ballantine Books, 1973); John Broderick, *Police in a Time of Change* (Morristown, NJ: General Learning Press, 1977).

31. Gary R. Rothwell, "Whistle-Blowing and the Code of Silence in Police Agencies: Policy and Structural Predictors," *Crime and Delinquency* 53 (2007): 605–632; Louise Westmarland, "Police Ethics and Integrity: Breaking the Blue Code of Silence," *Policing and Society* 15 (2005): 145–165.

32. Malcolm Sparrow, Mark Moore, and David Kennedy, *Beyond 911: A New Era for Policing* (New York: Basic Books, 1992), p. 51.

33. M. Steven Meagher and Nancy Yentes, "Choosing a Career in Policing: A Comparison of Male and Female

Perceptions," *Journal of Police Science and Administration* 16 (1986): 320–327.

34. Venessa Garcia, "Constructing the 'Other' within Police Culture: An Analysis of a Deviant Unit within the Police Organization," *Police Practice and Research* 6 (2005): 65–80.

35. Michael K. Brown, *Working the Street* (New York: Russell Sage, 1981), p. 82.

36. Stan Shernock, "An Empirical Examination of the Relationship between Police Solidarity and Community Orientation," *Journal of Police Science and Administration* 18 (1988): 182–198.

37. John Crank, *Understanding Police Culture*, 2nd ed. (Cincinnati: Anderson, 2003).

38. Eugene Paoline, "Taking Stock: Toward a Richer Understanding of Police Culture," *Journal of Criminal Justice* 31 (2003): 199–214.

39. Crank, *Understanding Police Culture*, pp. 359–363.

40. Egon Bittner, *The Functions of Police in Modern Society* (Cambridge, MA: Oelgeschlager, Gunn & Hain, 1980), p. 63.

41. Richard Lundman, *Police and Policing* (New York: Holt, Rinehart & Winston, 1980); see also Jerome Skolnick, *Justice without Trial* (New York: Wiley, 1966).

42. Robert Regoli, Robert Culbertson, John Crank, and James Powell, "Career Stage and Cynicism among Police Chiefs," *Justice Quarterly* 7 (1990): 592–614.

43. William Westly, *Violence and the Police: A Sociological Study of Law, Custom, and Morality* (Cambridge, MA: MIT Press, 1970).

44. Skolnick, *Justice without Trial*, pp. 42–68.

45. Milton Rokeach, Martin Miller, and John Snyder, "The Value Gap between Police and Policed," *Journal of Social Issues* 27 (1971): 155–171.

46. Wallace Graves, "Police Cynicism: Causes and Cures," *FBI Law Enforcement Bulletin* 65 (1996): 16–21.

47. Larry Tifft, "The 'Cop Personality' Reconsidered," *Journal of Police Science and Administration* 2 (1974): 268; David Bayley and Harold Mendelsohn, *Minorities and the Police* (New York: Free Press, 1969); Robert Balch, "The Police Personality: Fact or Fiction?" *Journal of Criminal Law, Criminology, and Police Science* 63 (1972): 117.

48. Lowell Storms, Nolan Penn, and James Tenzell, "Policemen's Perception of Real and Ideal Policemen," *Journal of Police Science and Administration* 17 (1990): 40–43.

49. Skolnick, *Justice without Trial*.

50. Carroll Seron, Joseph Pereira, and Jean Kovath, "Judging Police Misconduct: 'Street-Level' versus Professional Policing," *Law and Society Review* 38 (2004): 665–710.

51. Peter Salovey and John D. Mayer, "Emotional Intelligence," *Imagination, Cognition, and Personality* 9 (1990): 185–211.

52. Michael E. Burnette, *Emotional Intelligence and the Police* (Germany: VDM Verlag, 2008).

53. Ivan Y. Sun, Brian K. Payne, and Yuning Wu, "The Impact of Situational Factors, Officer Characteristics, and Neighborhood Context on Police Behavior: A Multilevel Analysis," *Journal of Criminal Justice* 36 (2008): 22–32.

54. Kenneth Litwin, "A Multilevel Multivariate Analysis of Factors Affecting Homicide Clearances," *Journal of Research in Crime and Delinquency* 41 (2004): 327–351.

55. Robert Kane, "Patterns of Arrest in Domestic Violence Encounters: Identifying a Police Decision-Making Model," *Journal of Criminal Justice* 27 (1999): 65–79.

56. Gregory Howard Williams, *The Law and Politics of Police Discretion* (Westport, CT: Greenwood Press, 1984).

57. Dana Jones and Joanne Belknap, "Police Responses to Battering in a Progressive Pro-Arrest Jurisdiction," *Justice Quarterly* 16 (1999): 249–273.

58. Allison Chappell, John Macdonald, and Patrick Manz, "The Organizational Determinants of Police Arrest Decisions," *Crime and Delinquency* 52 (2006): 287–306.

59. Westly, *Violence and the Police.*

60. Peter Liu and Thomas Cook, "Speeding Violation Dispositions in Relation to Police Officers' Perception of the Offenders," *Policing and Society* (March 15, 2005): 83–88.

61. Joseph Schafer and Stephen Mastrofski, "Police Leniency in Traffic Enforcement Encounters: Exploratory Findings from Observations and Interviews," *Journal of Criminal Justice* 33 (2005): 225–238; Richard Lundman, "Demeanor or Crime? The Midwest City Police-Citizen Encounters Study," *Criminology* 32 (1994): 631–653; Nathan Goldman, *The Differential Selection of Juvenile Offenders for Court Appearance* (New York: National Council on Crime and Delinquency, 1963).

62. David Klinger, "Bringing Crime Back In: Toward a Better Understanding of Police Arrest Decisions," *Journal of Research in Crime and Delinquency* 33 (1996): 333–336; "More on Demeanor and Arrest in Dade County," *Criminology* 34 (1996): 61–79; "Demeanor or Crime? Why 'Hostile' Citizens Are More Likely to Be Arrested," *Criminology* 32 (1994): 475–493.

63. Ambrose Leung, Frances Woolley, Richard Tremblay, and Frank Vitaro, "Who Gets Caught? Statistical Discrimination in Law Enforcement," *Journal of Socio-Economics* 34 (2005): 289–309.

64. Jennifer Schwartz and Bryan D. Rookey, "The Narrowing Gender Gap in Arrests: Assessing Competing Explanations Using Self-Report, Traffic Fatality, and Official Data on Drunk Driving, 1980–2004," *Criminology* 46 (2008): 637–671.

65. R. Steven Daniels, Lorin Baumhover, William Formby, and Carolyn Clark-Daniels, "Police Discretion and Elder Mistreatment: A Nested Model of Observation, Reporting, and Satisfaction," *Journal of Criminal Justice* 27 (1999): 209–225.

66. For a review, see Frank Schmalleger and John L. Worrall, *Policing Today* (Upper Saddle River, NJ: Pearson, 2010), p. 319.

67. Brian Withrow, "Race-Based Policing: A Descriptive Analysis of the Wichita Stop Study," *Police Practice and Research* 5 (2004): 223–240; Brian Withrow, "A Comparative Analysis of Commonly Used Benchmarks in Racial Profiling: A Research Note," *Justice Research and Policy* 6 (2004): 71–92; Amy Farrell, Jack McDevitt, Lisa Bailey, Carsten Andresen, and Erica Pierce, "Massachusetts Racial and Gender Profiling Final Report" (Boston: Northeastern University, 2004), http://iris.lib.neu.edu/cgi /viewcontent.cgi?article=1001&context =race_justice_pubs (accessed February 2015); Richard Lundman, "Driver Race, Ethnicity, and Gender and Citizen Reports of Vehicle Searches by Police and Vehicle Search Hits," *Journal of Criminal Law and Criminology* 94 (2004): 309–350; Michael Smith and Geoffrey Alpert, "Explaining Police Bias: A Theory of Social Conditioning and Illusory Correlation," *Criminal Justice and Behavior* 34 (2007): 1262–1283; *Interim Report of the State Police*

Review Team Regarding Allegations of Racial Profiling (Trenton, NJ: Office of the Attorney General, 1999).

68. David Eitle, Lisa Stolzenberg, and Stewart J. D'Alessio, "Police Organizational Factors, the Racial Composition of the Police, and the Probability of Arrest," *Justice Quarterly* 22 (2005): 30–57; Matt DeLisi and Robert Regoli, "Race, Conventional Crime, and Criminal Justice: The Declining Importance of Skin Color," *Journal of Criminal Justice* 27 (1999): 549–557; Jon Gould and Stephen Mastrofski, "Suspect Searches: Assessing Police Behavior Under the US Constitution," *Criminology and Public Policy* 3 (2004): 315–362; Joseph Schafer, David Carter, and Andra Katz-Bannister, "Studying Traffic Stop Encounters," *Journal of Criminal Justice* 32 (2004): 159–170; James Lange, Mark Johnson, and Robert Voas, "Testing the Racial Profiling Hypothesis for Seemingly Disparate Traffic Stops on the New Jersey Turnpike," *Justice Quarterly* 22 (2005): 193-223; Geoffrey P. Alpert, Roger G. Dunham, and Michael R. Smith, "Investigating Racial Profiling by the Miami-Dade Police Department: A Multimethod Approach," *Criminology and Public Policy* 6 (2007): 25–56.

69. Mathias Risse and Richard Zeckhauser, "Racial Profiling," *Philosophy and Public Affairs* 32 (2004): 131–170.

70. Karen Kruger and Nicholas Valltos, "Dealing with Domestic Violence in Law Enforcement Relationships," *FBI Law Enforcement Bulletin* 71 (2002): 1–7.

71. Lumb and Breazeale, "Police Officer Attitudes and Community Policing Implementation."

72. Donald Yates and Vijayan Pillai, "Frustration and Strain among Fort Worth Police Officers," *Sociology and Social Research: An International Journal* 76 (1992): 145–149.

73. For an impressive review, see Richard Farmer, "Clinical and Managerial Implications of Stress Research on the Police," *Journal of Police Science and Administration* 17 (1990): 205–217.

74. Lawrence Travis III and Craig Winston, "Dissension in the Ranks: Officer Resistance to Community Policing and Support for the Organization," *Journal of Crime and Justice* 21 (1998): 139–155.

75. Francis Cullen, Terrence Lemming, Bruce Link, and John Wozniak, "The Impact of Social Supports on Police Stress," *Criminology* 23 (1985): 503–522.

76. Merry Morash, Robin Haarr, and Dae-Hoon Kwak, "Multilevel Influences on Police Stress," *Journal of Contemporary Criminal Justice* 22 (2006): 26–43.

77. Farmer, "Clinical and Managerial Implications"; Nancy Norvell, Dale Belles, and Holly Hills, "Perceived Stress Levels and Physical Symptoms in Supervisory Law Enforcement Personnel," *Journal of Police Science and Administration* 16 (1988): 75–79.

78. Donald Yates and Vijayan Pillai, "Attitudes toward Community Policing: A Causal Analysis," *Social Science Journal* 33 (1996): 193–209.

79. Harvey McMurray, "Attitudes of Assaulted Police Officers and Their Policy Implications," *Journal of Police Science and Administration* 17 (1990): 44–48.

80. Lawrence Blum, *Force under Pressure: How Cops Live and Why They Die* (New York: Lantern Books, 2000).

81. Rose Lee Josephson and Martin Reiser, "Officer Suicide in the Los Angeles Police Department: A Twelve-Year Follow-Up," *Journal of Police Science and Administration* 17 (1990): 227–230.

82. Yates and Pillai, "Attitudes toward Community Policing," pp. 205–206.

83. Ibid.

84. Rosanna Church and Naomi Robertson, "How State Police Agencies Are Addressing the Issue of Wellness," *Policing* 22 (1999): 304–312.

85. Farmer, "Clinical and Managerial Implications," p. 215.

86. Peter Hart, Alexander Wearing, and Bruce Headey, "Assessing Police Work Experiences: Development of the Police Daily Hassles and Uplifts Scales," *Journal of Criminal Justice* 21 (1993): 553–573.

87. Scott R. Senjo and Karla Dhungana, "A Field Data Examination of Policy Constructs Related to Fatigue Conditions in Law Enforcement Personnel," *Police Quarterly* 12 (2009): 123–136.

88. Bryan Vila and Dennis J. Kenney, "Tired Cops: The Prevalence and Potential Consequences of Police Fatigue," *NIJ Journal* 248 (2002): 16–21.

89. Luenda E. Charles, Cecil M. Burchfiel, Desta Fekedulegn, Bryan Vila, Tara A. Hartley, James Slaven, Anna Mnatsakanova, and John M. Violanti, "Shift Work and Sleep: The Buffalo Police Health Study," *Policing* 30 (2007): 215–227.

90. Sean Griffin and Thomas Bernard, "Angry Aggression among Police Officers," *Police Quarterly* 6 (2003): 3–21.

91. Kim Michelle Lersch and Tom Mieczkowski, "Who Are the Problem-Prone Officers? An Analysis of Citizen Complaints," *American Journal of Police* 15 (1996): 23–42.

92. Samuel Walker, Geoffrey P. Alpert, and Dennis J. Kenney, *Early Warning Systems: Responding to the Problem Police Officer, Research in Brief* (Washington, DC: National Institute of Justice, 2001).

93. Michael D. White, "Controlling Police Decisions to Use Deadly Force: Reexamining the Importance of Administrative Policy," *Crime and Delinquency* 47 (2001): 131.

94. Steve Rothlein, *Conducting Integrity Tests on Law Enforcement Officers* (Indianapolis: Legal and Liability Risk Management Institute, 2010), http://www.patc.com/weeklyarticles/print/le_integrity_tests.pdf (accessed March 2015).

95. Samuel Walker, *Popular Justice*, 2nd ed. (New York: Oxford University Press, 1997), pp. 48–64.

96. Herman Goldstein, *Police Corruption* (Washington, DC: Police Foundation, 1975), p. 3.

97. Lawrence Sherman, *Scandal and Reform: Controlling Police Corruption* (Berkeley: University of California Press, 1978), p. 194.

98. Barbara Gelb, *Tarnished Brass: The Decade after Serpico* (New York: Putnam, 1983); Candace McCoy, "Lawsuits against Police: What Impact Do They Have?" *Criminal Law Bulletin* 20 (1984): 49–56.

99. Samuel Walker, *Police Accountability: The Role of Citizen Oversight* (Belmont, CA: Wadsworth, 2001); Liqun Cao and Bu Huang, "Determinants of Citizen Complaints against Police Abuse of Power," *Journal of Criminal Justice* 28 (2000): 203–213; Peter Finn, "Getting Along with Citizen Oversight," *FBI Law Enforcement Bulletin* 69 (2000): 22–27.

100. Christine Eith and Matthew J. Durose, *Contacts between the Police and the Public, 2008* (Washington, DC: Bureau of Justice Statistics, 2011).

101. Ibid.

102. Lawrence Sherman and Robert Langworthy, "Measuring Homicide

by Police Officers," *Journal of Criminal Law and Criminology* 4 (1979): 546–560.

103. Ibid.

104. Federal Bureau of Investigation, *Crime in the United States,* "Expanded Homicide Data," http://www.fbi .gov/about-us/cjis/ucr/crime-in -the-u.s/2013/crime-in-the-US-2013 /offenses-known-to-law-enforcement /expanded-homicide/expanded _homicide_data_table_14_justifiable _homicide_by_weapon_law_ enforcement_2009-2013.xls (accessed February 2015).

105. Richard Parent and Simon Verdun-Jones, "Victim-Precipitated Homicide: Police Use of Deadly Force in British Columbia," *Policing* 21 (1998): 432–449.

106. Anthony J. Pinizzotto, Edward F. Davis, and Charles E. Miller III, "Suicide by Cop: Defining a Devastating Dilemma," *FBI Law Enforcement Bulletin* 74(2005):8–20.

107. *Tennessee v. Garner,* 471 US 1 (1985).

108. Frank Zarb, "Police Liability for Creating the Need to Use Deadly Force in Self-Defense," *Michigan Law Review* 86 (1988): 1982–2009.

109. Brian A. Lawton, "Levels of Nonlethal Force: An Examination of Individual, Situational, and Contextual Factors," *Journal of Research in Crime and Delinquency* 44 (2007): 163–184.

110. Matthew J. Hickman, Alex R. Piquero, and Joel H. Garner, "Toward a National Estimate of Police Use of Nonlethal Force," *Criminology and Public Policy* 7 (2008): 563–604.

111. *Graham v. Connor,* 490 US 386 (1989).

112. Warren Cohen, "When Lethal Force Won't Do," *US News and World Report* 122 (June 23, 1997): 12.

113. Richard Lumb and Paul Friday, "Impact of Pepper Spray Availability on Police Officer Use-of-Force Decisions," *Policing* 20 (1997): 136–149.

114. Tom McEwen, "Policies on Less-than-Lethal Force in Law Enforcement Agencies," *Policing* 20 (1997): 39–60.

115. *Miranda v. Arizona,* 384 US 436 (1966).

116. *Colorado v. Connelly,* 479 US 157 (1986).

117. Marvin Zalman and Brad W. Smith, "Attitudes of Police Executives toward *Miranda* and Interrogation Policies," *Journal of Criminal Law and Criminology* 97 (2007): 873–942; Victoria Time and Brian Payne, "Police Chiefs' Perceptions about *Miranda*: An Analysis of Survey Data," *Journal of Criminal Justice* 30 (2002): 77–86.

118. Ronald Allen, "*Miranda*'s Hollow Core," *Northwestern University Law Review* 100 (2006): 71–85.

119. G. Daniel Lassiter, Jennifer Ratcliff, Lezlee Ware, and Clinton Irvin, "Videotaped Confessions: Panacea or Pandora's Box?" *Law and Policy* 28 (2006): 192–210.

120. *Fare v. Michael C.,* 439 US 1310 (1978).

121. *New York v. Quarles,* 467 US 649 (1984).

122. *Oregon v. Elstad,* 470 US 298 (1985).

123. *Colorado v. Connelly,* 479 US 157 (1986).

124. *Moran v. Burbine,* 475 US 412 (1986).

125. *Colorado v. Spring,* 479 US 564 (1987).

126. *Minnick v. Mississippi,* 498 US 146 (1990).

127. *Arizona v. Fulminante,* 499 US 279 (1991).

128. *Davis v. United States,* 512 US 452 (1994).

129. *Chavez v. Martinez,* 538 US 760 (2003).

130. *United States v. Patane,* 542 US 630 (2004).

131. *Missouri v. Seibert,* 542 US 600 (2004).

132. *Maryland v. Shatzer,* 559 US 98 (2010).

133. *Florida v. Powell,* 559 US ___ (2010).

134. *Berghuis v. Thompkins,* 560 US 370 (2010).

135. *J.D.B. v. North Carolina,* 564 US ___ (2011).

136. *Howes v. Fields,* 565 US ___ (2012).

137. *Chimel v. California,* 395 US 752 (1969).

138. *Riley v. California,* 573 US 2__ (2014).

139. *Terry v. Ohio,* 392 US 1 (1968).

140. *Illinois v. Wardlow,* 528 US 119 (2000).

141. Carroll v. United States, 267 US 132 (1925).

142. *United States v. Ross,* 456 US 798 (1982).

143. Drivers, *Pennsylvania v. Mimms,* 434 US 106 (1977); passengers, *Maryland v. Wilson,* 117 US 882 (1997) and *Arizona v. Johnson,* 555 US 323 (2009).

144. Mark Hansen, "Rousting Miss Daisy?" *American Bar Association Journal* 83 (1997): 22; *Knowles v. Iowa,* 525 US 113 (1998); *Wyoming v. Houghton,* 526 US 295 (1999).

145. *Arizona v. Gant,* 556 US 332 (2009); see also *Davis v. United States,* 564 US ___ (2011).

146. *Bumper v. North Carolina,* 391 US 543 (1960).

147. *Ohio v. Robinette,* 519 US 33 (1996).

148. Limitations on the plain-view doctrine have been defined in *Arizona v. Hicks,* 480 US 321 (1987); the recording of serial numbers from stereo components in a suspect's apartment could not be justified as being in plain view.

149. *Warden v. Hayden,* 387 US 294 (1967); *Minnesota v. Olson,* 495 US 91 (1990); *Breithaupt v. Abram,* 352 US 432 (1957).

150. *Kentucky v. King,* 563 US ___(2011).

151. *Plumhoff v. Rickard,* 572 US 2__ (2014).

152. *Weeks v. United States,* 232 US 383 (1914).

153. *Mapp v. Ohio,* 367 US 643 (1961).

154. William Greenhalgh, *The Fourth Amendment Handbook: A Chronological Survey of Supreme Court Decisions* (Chicago: American Bar Association Section on Criminal Justice, 1995).

155. *United States v. Leon,* 468 US 897 (1984).

Chapter 7, Courts, Prosecution, and The Defense

1. ABC News, "Florida Lawyer Fired for Posting Client's Leopard-Print Underwear," http://abcnews.go.com/ blogs/headlines/2012/09/florida -lawyer-fired-for-posting-clients -leopard-print-underwear/ (accessed March 2013).

2. Ibid.

3. Henry Gass, "An 'All-Star Team' to Defend Accused Boston Bomber Tsarnaev," *Christian Science Monitor,* January 2, 2015, http://www .csmonitor.com/USA/Justice/2015 /0102/An-all-star-team-to-defend -accused-Boston-bomber-Tsarnaev (accessed February 2015).

4. Ibid.

5. Zeninjor Enwemeka, "Who's Who in the Dzhokhar Tsarnaev Trial," http:// www.wbur.org/2015/01/05/dzhokhar -tsarnaev-bombing-trial-bios (accessed February 2015).

6. Sean Rosenmerkel and Donald Farole, Jr., *Felony Sentences in State Courts, 2006—Statistical Tables* (Washington, DC: Bureau of Justice Statistics, 2009), Table 4.4.

7. Greg Berman and John Feinblatt, *Problem-Solving Courts: A Brief Primer* (New York: Center for Court Innovation, 2001).

8. Ibid.

9. R. LaFountain, R. Schauffler, S. Strickland, and K. Holt, *Examining the Work of State Courts: An Analysis of 2010 State Court Caseloads* (National Center for State Courts, 2012).

10. US Constitution, Art. 3, Secs. 1 and 2.

11. David Klein and Robert Hume, "Fear of Reversal as an Explanation of Lower Court Compliance," *Law and Society Review* 37 (2003): 579–607.

12. See, for example, http://www.judicialselection.com (accessed February 2015).

13. Sari Escovitz with Fred Kurland and Nan Gold, *Judicial Selection and Tenure* (Chicago: American Judicature Society, 1974), pp. 3–16.

14. Judith McFarlane, Ann Malecha, Julia Gist, Kathy Watson, Elizabeth Batten, Iva Hall, and Sheila Smith, "Protection Orders and Intimate Partner Violence: An 18-Month Study of 150 Black, Hispanic, and White Women," *American Journal of Public Health* 94 (2004): 613–618.

15. Steven W. Perry and Duren Banks, *Prosecutors in State Courts, 2007* (Washington, DC: Bureau of Justice Statistics, 2011).

16. Ibid.

17. Jessie Larson, "Unequal Justice: The Supreme Court's Failure to Curtail Selective Prosecution for the Death Penalty," *Journal of Criminal Law and Criminology* 93 (2003): 1009–1031.

18. Kenneth C. Davis, *Discretionary Justice* (Baton Rouge: Louisiana State University Press, 1969), p. 180; see also James B. Stewart, *The Prosecutor* (New York: Simon & Schuster, 1987).

19. Barbara Boland, *The Prosecution of Felony Arrests* (Washington, DC: Government Printing Office, 1983).

20. Jeffrey Spears and Cassia Spohn, "The Effect of Evidence Factors and Victim Characteristics on Prosecutors' Charging Decisions in Sexual Assault Cases," *Justice Quarterly* 14 (1997): 501–524.

21. Ibid.

22. Myrna Dawson and Ronit Dinovitzer, "Victim Cooperation and the Prosecution of Domestic Violence in a Specialized Court," *Justice Quarterly* 18 (2001): 593–622.

23. Rodney Kingsworth, John Lopez, Jennifer Wentworth, and Debra Cummings, "Adult Sexual Assault: The Role of Racial/Ethnic Composition in Prosecution and Sentence," *Journal of Criminal Justice* 26 (1998): 359–372.

24. Michael Edmund O'Neill, "Understanding Federal Prosecutorial Declinations: An Empirical Analysis of Predictive Factors," *American Criminal Law Review* 41 (2004): 1439–1533.

25. Shaila Dewan, "Prosecutors Say Cuts Force Plea Bargains," *New York Times*, March 10, 2003, p. B3.

26. Charles D. Breitel, "Controls in Criminal Law Enforcement," *University of Chicago Law Review* 27 (1960): 427.

27. Cassia Spohn, Dawn Beichner, and Erika Davis-Frenzel, "Prosecutorial Justifications for Sexual Assault Case Rejection: Guarding the 'Gateway to Justice,'" *Social Problems* 48 (2001): 206–235.

28. "Prosecutor Conduct," editorial, *USA Today*, April 1, 1999, p. 14A.

29. *North Carolina v. Pearce*, 395 US 711 (1969).

30. *Blackledge v. Perry*, 417 US 21 (1974).

31. *Bordenkircher v. Hayes*, 434 US 357 (1978).

32. *Gideon v. Wainwright*, 372 US 335 (1963).

33. *Argersinger v. Hamlin*, 407 US 25 (1972).

34. *Douglas v. California*, 372 US 353 (1963).

35. *In re Gault*, 387 US 1 (1967).

36. *Coleman v. Alabama*, 399 US 1 (1970).

37. *Argersinger v. Hamlin*, 407 US 25 (1972).

38. *Morrissey v. Brewer*, 408 US 471 (1972).

39. *Gagnon v. Scarpelli*, 411 US 778 (1973).

40. *Ross v. Moffitt*, 417 US 600 (1974).

41. *Scott v. Illinois*, 440 US 367 (1979).

42. *Morris v. Slappy*, 461 US 1 (1983).

43. *Wheat v. United States*, 486 US 153 (1988).

44. *United States v. Monsanto*, 491 US 600 (1989).

45. *United States v. Gonzalez-Lopez*, 548 US 140 (2006).

46. *Rothgery v. Gillespie County*, 554 US 191 (2008).

47. Carol J. DeFrances, *State-Funded Indigent Defense Services, 1999* (Washington, DC: Bureau of Justice Statistics, 2001).

48. Data compiled by the Bureau of Justice Statistics, http://bjs.gov (accessed February 2015); see also Arye Rattner, Hagit Turjeman, and Gideon Fishman, "Public versus Private Defense: Can Money Buy Justice?" *Journal of Criminal Justice* 36 (2008): 43–49.

49. *Strickland v. Washington*, 466 US 668 (1984).

50. *Florida v. Nixon*, 543 US 175 (2004).

51. The following sections are based on Ron Bowmaster and John Cariotto, "Information Sharing in Nebraska," National Center for State Courts, 2003, http://ncsc.contentdm.oclc.org/cdm/ref/collection/tech/id/553 (accessed March 2013); Fredric I. Lederer, "The Road to the Virtual Courtroom? Consideration of Today's—and Tomorrow's—High-Technology Courtrooms," *South Carolina Law Review* 50 (1999): 799; "Criminal Court Records Go Online," *The Quill* 90 (2002): 39; Donald C. Dilworth, "New Court Technology Will Affect How Attorneys Present Trials," *Trial* 33 (1997): 100–114.

Chapter 8, Pretrial and Trial Procedures

1. Seattle Police Department, http://spdblotter.seattle.gov/2012/12/05/officers-shall-not-take-any-enforcement-action-other-than-to-issue-a-verbal-warning-for-a-violation-of-i-502 (accessed February 2015).

2. Terrence Petty, Associated Press, "Washington Could Become Pot Source for Neighbors," December 8, 2012, http://bigstory.ap.org/article/washington-could-become-pot-source-neighbors (accessed February 2015).

3. Associate Press, "2 States Challenge Colorado Marijuana Legalization," December 18, 2014, http://townhall.com/news/politics-elections/2014/12/18/2-states-challenge-colorado-marijuana-legalization-n1933837 (accessed February 2015).

4. *Stack v. Boyle*, 342 US 1 (1951).

5. Data in this section come from Thomas Cohen and Tracey Kyckelhahn, *Felony Defendants in Large Urban Counties, 2006* (Washington, DC: Bureau of Justice Statistics, 2010).

6. Traci Schlesinger, "Racial and Ethnic Disparity in Pretrial Criminal Processing," *Justice Quarterly* 22 (2005): 170–192.

7. Bob Burton, Director of Training and Surety Corporation Liaison, National Institute of Bail Enforcement, personal contact, September 17, 2004.

8. Cohen and Kyckelhahn, Felony Defendants in Large Urban Counties.

9. Vera Institute of Justice, *1961–1971: Programs in Criminal Justice* (New York: Vera Institute of Justice, 1972).

10. Public Law No. 89-465, 18 USC., sec. 3146 (1966).

11. 18 USC., sec. 3142 (1984).

12. See, generally, Fred Cohen, "The New Federal Crime Control Act," *Criminal Law Bulletin* 21 (1985): 330–337.

13. This section leans on John Clark and D. Alan Henry, *Pretrial Services Programming at the Start of the 21st Century: A Survey of Pretrial Services Programs* (Washington, DC: Bureau of Justice Assistance, 2003).

14. Ric Simmons, "Reexamining the Grand Jury: Is There Room for Democracy in the Criminal Justice System?" *Boston University Law Review* 82 (2002): 1–76.

15. John Gibeaut, "Indictment of a System," *ABA Journal* 87 (2001): 34.

16. Kirke D. Weaver, "A Change of Heart or a Change of Law? Withdrawing a Guilty Plea Under Federal Rule of Criminal Procedure 32(e)," *Journal of Criminal Law and Criminology* 92 (2001): 273–306.

17. Anne Piehl and Shawn Bushway, "Measuring and Explaining Charge Bargaining," *Journal of Quantitative Criminology* 23 (2007): 105–125.

18. George Fisher, "Plea Bargaining's Triumph," *Yale Law Journal* 109 (2000): 857–1058.

19. Fred Zacharis, "Justice in Plea Bargaining," *William and Mary Law Review* 39 (1998): 1121–1189.

20. Nathaniel J. Pallone, "Without Plea-Bargaining, Megan Kanka Would Be Alive Today," *Criminology and Public Policy* 3 (2003): 83–96.

21. William Stuntz, "Plea Bargaining and Criminal Law's Disappearing Shadow," *Harvard Law Review* 117 (2004): 2548–2569.

22. Mike McConville, "Plea Bargaining: Ethics and Politics," *Journal of Law and Society* 25 (1998): 526–555.

23. *Hill v. Lockhart,* 474 US 52 (1985).

24. *Boykin v. Alabama,* 395 US 238 (1969); *Brady v. United States,* 397 US 742 (1970).

25. Santobello v. New York, 404 US 257 (1971).

26. Ricketts v. Adamson, 483 US 1 (1987).

27. Bordenkircher v. Hayes, 434 US 357 (1978).

28. North Carolina v. Alford, 400 US 25 (1970).

29. United States v. Mezzanatto, 513 US 196 (1995).

30. Jeremy Ball, "Is It a Prosecutor's World? Determinants of Court Bargaining Decisions," *Journal of Contemporary Criminal Justice* 22 (2006): 241–260.

31. Deirdre M. Bowen, "Calling Your Bluff: How Prosecutors and Defense Attorneys Adapt to Plea Bargaining Strategies to Increase Formalization," *Justice Quarterly* 26 (2009): 2–29.

32. Stephen P. Lagoy, Joseph J. Senna, and Larry J. Siegel, "An Empirical Study on Information Usage for Prosecutorial Decision Making in Plea Negotiations," *American Criminal Law Review* 13 (1976): 435–471.

33. Keith Bystrom, "Communicating Plea Offers to the Client," in *Ethical Problems Facing the Criminal Defense Lawyer,* ed. Rodney Uphoff (Chicago: American Bar Association Section on Criminal Justice, 1995), p. 84.

34. American Bar Association, *Standards Relating to Pleas of Guilty,* standard 3.3; National Advisory Commission on Criminal Justice Standards and Goals, Task Force Report on Courts (Washington, DC: Government Printing Office, 1973), p. 42.

35. American Bar Association, *Standards Relating to Pleas of Guilty,* p. 73; see also Alan Alschuler, "The Trial Judge's Role in Plea Bargaining," *Columbia Law Review* 76 (1976): 1059.

36. Barbara Boland and Brian Forst, *The Prevalence of Guilty Pleas* (Washington, DC: Bureau of Justice Statistics, 1984), p. 3; see also Gary Hengstler, "The Troubled Justice System," *American Bar Association Journal* 80 (1994): 44.

37. National Institute of Law Enforcement and Criminal Justice, *Plea Bargaining in the United States,* p. 37–40.

38. For a discussion of this issue, see Michael Tonry, "Plea Bargaining Bans and Rules," in *Sentencing Reform Impacts* (Washington, DC: Government Printing Office, 1987).

39. Franklyn Dunford, D. Wayne Osgood, and Hart Weichselbaum, *National Evaluation of Diversion Programs* (Washington, DC: Government Printing Office, 1982).

40. Sharla Rausch and Charles Logan, "Diversion from Juvenile Court: Panacea or Pandora's Box?" in *Evaluating Juvenile Justice,* ed. James Kleugel (Beverly Hills, CA: Sage, 1983), pp. 19–30.

41. John Hepburn, "Recidivism Among Drug Offenders Following Exposure to Treatment," *Criminal Justice Policy Review* 16 (2005): 237–259.

42. *Tumey v. Ohio,* 273 US 510 (1927), at 523.

43. See, for example, Minn. R. Crim. P. 26.03, subd. 13(4).

44. *Riggins v. Nevada,* 504 US 127 (1992).

45. *Diaz v. United States,* 223 US 442 (1912); *Taylor v. Illinois,* 484 US 400 (1988).

46. *Illinois v. Allen,* 397 US 337 (1970).

47. *Maryland v. Craig,* 497 US 836 (1990).

48. *Washington v. Texas,* 388 US 14 (1967).

49. *Baldwin v. New York,* 399 US 66 (1970).

50. *Scott v. Illinois,* 440 US 367 (1979).

51. *Shelton v. Alabama,* 122 US 1764 (2002).

52. Faretta v. California, 422 US 806 (1975).

53. See American Bar Association, *Standards Relating to Speedy Trial* (Chicago: ABA, 1995).

54. Klopfer v. North Carolina, 386 US 213 (1967).

55. *Wilson v. Layne,* 526 US 603 (1999).

56. See *Brinegar v. United States,* 338 US 160 (1949); *In re Winship,* 397 US 358, 90 (1970).

57. *Brinegar v. United States,* 338 US 160 (1949), at 174.

58. See In re Winship, at 397.

59. Ibid., at 371, 90 S. Ct. at 1076.

60. Brian Kalt, "The Exclusion of Felons from Jury Service," *American University Law Review* 53 (2003): 65–189.

61. George Hayden, Joseph Senna, and Larry Siegel, "Prosecutorial Discretion in Peremptory Challenges: An Empirical Investigation of Information Use in the Massachusetts Jury Selection Process," *New England Law Review* 13 (1978): 768.

62. *Batson v. Kentucky,* 476 US 79 (1986); see also Alan Alschuler and Randall Kennedy, "Equal Justice—Would Color-Conscious Jury Selection Help?" *American Bar Association Journal* 81 (1995): 36–37.

63. John Schwartz, "As Jurors Turn to Web, Mistrials Are Popping Up," *New York Times,* March 17, 2009, http://www.nytimes.com/2009/03/18/us/18juries.html (accessed February 2015).

64. Arie Rubenstein, "Verdicts of Conscience: Nullification and the Modern Jury Trial," *Columbia Law Review* 106 (2006): 959–993.

65. Hilary Hanson, "Doug Darrell Acquitted of Marijuana Charges Through Jury Nullification in New Hampshire," *Huffington Post,* September 17, 2012, http://www.huffingtonpost.com/2012/09/17/doug-darrell-marijuana-jury-nullification_n_1890824.html (accessed February 2015).

66. David Pepper, "Nullifying History: Modern-Day Misuse of the Right to Decide the Law," *Case Western Reserve Law Review* 50 (2000): 599–643.

67. Chapman v. California, 386 US 18 (1967).

68. Douglas v. California, 372 US 353 (1963).

Chapter 9, Punishment and Sentencing

1. Bill Chappell and Steve Mullis, "Mistrial on Murder Charge in Florida Gas Station Shooting," http://www.npr.org/blogs /thetwo-way/2014/02/14/277033024 /mistrial-on-murder-charge-in -florida-gas-station-shooting (accessed February 2015).

2. Eyder Peralta, "Michael Dunn Found Guilty in Florida 'Loud Music' Shooting," http://www.npr.org/blogs /thetwo-way/2014/10/01/353058675 /michael-dunn-found-guilty-in -florida-loud-music-shooting (accessed February 2015).

3. Scott Neuman, "Florida 'Loud Music' Shooter Michael Dunn Gets Life in Prison," http://www.npr.org/blogs /thetwo-way/2014/10/17/356960741 /fla-loud-music-shooter-michael -dunn-gets-life (accessed February 2015).

4. Among the most helpful sources for this section were Benedict Alper, *Prisons Inside-Out* (Cambridge, MA: Ballinger, 1974); Gustave de Beaumont and Alexis de Tocqueville, *On the Penitentiary System in the United States and Its Applications in France* (Carbondale: Southern Illinois University Press, 1964); Orlando Lewis, *The Development of American Prisons and Prison Customs, 1776–1845* (Montclair, NJ: Patterson-Smith, 1967); Leonard Orland, ed., *Justice, Punishment, and Treatment* (New York: Free Press, 1973); J. Goebel, *Felony and Misdemeanor* (Philadelphia: University of Pennsylvania Press, 1976); Georg Rusche and Otto Kircheimer, *Punishment and Social Structure* (New York: Russell & Russell, 1939); Samuel Walker, *Popular Justice* (New York: Oxford University Press, 1980); Graeme R. Newman, *The Punishment Response* (Piscataway, NJ: Transaction Publishers, 2008); David Rothman, *Conscience and Convenience* (Boston: Little, Brown, 1980); George Ives, *A History of Penal Methods* (Montclair, NJ: Patterson-Smith, 1970); Robert Hughes, *The Fatal Shore* (New York: Knopf, 1986); Leon Radzinowicz, *A History of English Criminal Law*, vol. 1 (London: Stevens, 1943), p. 5.

5. *Crime and Punishment in America, 1999*, Report 229 (Washington, DC: National Center for Policy Analysis, 1999).

6. Sean Rosenmerkel, Matthew Durose, and Patrick Langan, *Felony Sentences in State Courts, 2006* (Washington, DC: Bureau of Justice Statistics, 2009), p. 6.

7. Patrick Langan and David Levin, *Recidivism of Prisoners Released in 1994* (Washington, DC: Bureau of Justice Statistics, 2002).

8. Faith Lutze, "The Influence of Shock Incarceration Program on Inmate Adjustment and Attitudinal Change," *Journal of Criminal Justice* 29 (2001): 255–266.

9. E. Ann Carson and William J. Sabol, *Prisoners in 2011* (Washington, DC: Bureau of Justice Statistics, 2012).

10. Tomislav Kovandzic and Lynne Vieraitis, "The Effect of County-Level Prison Population Growth on Crime Rates," *Criminology and Public Policy* 5 (2006): 213–244.

11. Raymond Liedka, Anne Morrison Piehl, and Bert Useem, "The Crime-Control Effect of Incarceration: Does Scale Matter?" *Criminology and Public Policy* 5 (2006): 245–276.

12. Ibid.

13. Charles Logan, *Criminal Justice Performance Measures for Prisons* (Washington, DC: Bureau of Justice Statistics, 1993), p. 3.

14. Alexis Durham, "The Justice Model in Historical Context: Early Law, the Emergence of Science, and the Rise of Incarceration," *Journal of Criminal Justice* 16 (1988): 331–346.

15. Andrew von Hirsh, *Doing Justice: The Choice of Punishments* (New York: Hill and Wang, 1976).

16. Shawn Bushway, "The Impact of an Arrest on the Job Stability of Young White American Men," *Journal of Research in Crime and Delinquency* 35 (1998): 454–479.

17. Lawrence W. Sherman, David P. Farrington, Doris Layton MacKenzie, Brandon Walsh, Denise Gottfredson, John Eck, Shawn Bushway, and Peter Reuter, *Evidence-Based Crime Prevention* (London: Routledge and Kegan Paul, 2002); see also Arnulf Kolstad, "Imprisonment as Rehabilitation: Offenders' Assessment of Why It Does Not Work," *Journal of Criminal Justice* 24 (1996): 323–335.

18. Francis Cullen, John Paul Wright, Shayna Brown, Melissa Moon, and Brandon Applegate, "Public Support for Early Intervention Programs: Implications for a Progressive Policy Agenda," *Crime and Delinquency* 44 (1998): 187204; Richard McCorkle, "Research Note: Punish and Rehabilitate? Public Attitudes toward Six Common Crimes," *Crime and Delinquency* 39 (1993): 240–252; D. A. Andrews, Ivan Zinger, Robert Hoge, James Bonta, Paul Gendreau, and Francis Cullen, "Does Correctional Treatment Work? A Clinically Relevant and Psychologically Informed Meta-Analysis," *Criminology* 28 (1990): 369–404.

19. Paula Ditton and Doris James Wilson, *Truth in Sentencing in State Prisons* (Washington, DC: Bureau of Justice Statistics, 1999).

20. Jo Dixon, "The Organizational Context of Criminal Sentencing," *American Journal of Sociology* 100 (1995): 1157–1198.

21. Michael Tonry, *Reconsidering Indeterminate and Structured Sentencing Series: Sentencing and Corrections: Issues for the 21st Century* (Washington, DC: National Institute of Justice, 1999).

22. *Blakely v. Washington*, 542 US 296 (2004).

23. *United States v. Booker*, 543 US 220 (2005).

24. Michael Tonry, "The Failure of the US Sentencing Commission's Guidelines," *Crime and Delinquency* 39 (1993): 131–149.

25. Sean Nicholson-Crotty, "The Impact of Sentencing Guidelines on State-Level Sanctions: An Analysis over Time," *Crime and Delinquency* 50 (2004): 395–410.

26. United States Sentencing Commission, "Final Report on the Impact of *United States v. Booker* on Federal Sentencing," March 2006, http://www.ussc.gov/sites /default/files/pdf/news/congressional -testimony-and-reports/submissions /200603-booker/Booker_Report.pdf (accessed February 2015).

27. Jeffrey T. Ulmer, Megan C. Kurlychek, and John H. Kramer, "Prosecutorial Discretion and the Imposition of Mandatory Minimum Sentences,"

Journal of Research in Crime and Delinquency 44 (2007): 427–458.

28. See, for example, John L. Worrall, *Crime Control in America: What Works?* (Boston: Allyn & Bacon, 2008), pp. 193–199.

29. Marc Mauer, *Americans Behind Bars: The International Use of Incarceration, 1992–93: Part II* (Washington, DC: The Sentencing Project, 1994).

30. For a review of the literature, see John L. Worrall, *Crime Control in America: What Works?* 2nd ed. (Boston: Allyn & Bacon, 2008), pp. 198–199.

31. Thomas B. Marvell and Carlisle E. Moody, "The Lethal Effects of Three-Strikes Laws," *Journal of Legal Studies* 30 (2001): 89–106; Thomas Kovandzic, John J. Sloan, III, and Lynne M. Vieraitis, "Unintended Consequences of Politically Popular Sentencing Policy: The Homicide-Promoting Effects of 'Three Strikes' in US Cities (1980–1999)," *Criminology and Public Policy* 1 (2002): 159–201.

32. *Lockyer v. Andrade*, 538 US 63 (2003).

33. *Ewing v. California*, 538 US 11 (2003).

34. Ditton and Wilson, *Truth in Sentencing in State Prisons.*

35. The most recent data as of this writing are found in Matthew Durose and Patrick Langan, *Felony Sentences in State Courts, 2006* (Washington, DC: Bureau of Justice Statistics, 2009), http://bjs.ojp.usdoj.gov/content/pub/pdf/fssc06st.pdf (accessed February 2015).

36. Ibid.

37. Brent Smith and Kelly Damphouse, "Terrorism, Politics, and Punishment: A Test of Structural-Contextual Theory and the Liberation Hypothesis," *Criminology* 36 (1998): 67–92.

38. Stewart D'Alessio and Lisa Stolzenberg, "Socioeconomic Status and the Sentencing of the Traditional Offender," *Journal of Criminal Justice* 21 (1993): 61–77.

39. Cecilia Saulters-Tubbs, "Prosecutorial and Judicial Treatment of Female Offenders," *Federal Probation* 57 (1993): 37–41.

40. See, for example, Janet Johnston, Thomas Kennedy, and I. Gayle Shuman, "Gender Differences in the Sentencing of Felony Offenders," *Federal Probation* 87 (1987): 49–56; Cassia Spohn and Susan Welch, "The Effect of Prior Record in Sentencing Research: An Examination of the Assumption that Any Measure Is Adequate," *Justice Quarterly* 4 (1987): 286–302; David Willison, "The

Effects of Counsel on the Severity of Criminal Sentences: A Statistical Assessment," *Justice System Journal* 9 (1984): 87–101.

41. Cassia Spohn, Miriam DeLone, and Jeffrey Spears, "Race/Ethnicity, Gender, and Sentence Severity in Dade County, Florida: An Examination of the Decision to Withhold Adjudication," *Journal of Crime and Justice* 21 (1998): 111–132.

42. Ellen Hochstedler Steury and Nancy Frank, "Gender Bias and Pretrial Release: More Pieces of the Puzzle," *Journal of Criminal Justice* 18 (1990): 417–432.

43. Shimica Gaskins, "Women of Circumstance—The Effects of Mandatory Minimum Sentencing on Women Minimally Involved in Drug Crimes," *American Criminal Law Review* 41 (2004): 1533–1563.

44. Shawn Bushway and Anne Morrison Piehl, "The Inextricable Link between Age and Criminal History in Sentencing," *Crime and Delinquency* 53 (2007): 156–183.

45. Dean Champion, "Elderly Felons and Sentencing Severity: Interregional Variations in Leniency and Sentencing Trends," *Criminal Justice Review* 12 (1987): 7–15.

46. Darrell Steffensmeier, John Kramer, and Jeffery Ulmer, "Age Differences in Sentencing," *Justice Quarterly* 12 (1995): 583–601.

47. Darrell Steffensmeier, Jeffery Ulmer, and John Kramer, "The Interaction of Race, Gender, and Age in Criminal Sentencing: The Punishment Cost of Being Young, Black, and Male," *Criminology* 36 (1998): 763–798.

48. Tracy Nobiling, Cassia Spohn, and Miriam DeLone, "A Tale of Two Counties: Unemployment and Sentence Severity," *Justice Quarterly* 15 (1998): 459–486.

49. Shawn Bushway and Anne Morrison Piehl, "Judging Judicial Discretion: Legal Factors and Racial Discrimination in Sentencing," *Law and Society Review* 35 (2001): 733–765.

50. Michael Tonry, *Malign Neglect: Race, Crime, and Punishment in America* (New York: Oxford University Press, 1995), pp. 105–109.

51. John Wooldredge, "Neighborhood Effects on Felony Sentencing," *Journal of Research in Crime and Delinquency* 44 (2007): 238–263.

52. Cassia Spohn, "Thirty Years of Sentencing Reform: A Quest for a

Racially Neutral Sentencing Process, in *Policies, Processes, and Decisions of the Criminal Justice System,* vol. 3, *Criminal Justice 2000* (Washington, DC: US Department of Justice, 2000), pp. 455–456.

53. Ibid.

54. Bruce Western, *Punishment and Inequality in America* (New York: Russell Sage Foundation, 2006).

55. *Payne v. Tennessee,* 501 US 808 (1991).

56. Robert Davis and Barbara Smith, "The Effects of Victim Impact Statements on Sentencing Decisions: A Test in an Urban Setting," *Justice Quarterly* 11 (1994): 453–469; Edna Erez and Pamela Tontodonato, "The Effect of Victim Participation in Sentencing on Sentence Outcome," *Criminology* 28 (1990): 451–474.

57. Rodney Kingsworth, Randall MacIntosh, and Jennifer Wentworth, "Sexual Assault: The Role of Prior Relationship and Victim Characteristics in Case Processing," *Justice Quarterly* 16 (1999): 276–302.

58. *Coker v. Georgia*, 433 US 584 (1977); see also *Lockett v. Ohio*, 438 US 586 (1978).

59. For more on this issue, read Hugo Adam and Paul Cassell, *Debating the Death Penalty: Should America Have Capital Punishment? The Experts on Both Sides Make Their Best Case* (London: Oxford University Press, 2003).

60. Stephen Layson, "United States Time-Series Homicide Regressions with Adaptive Expectations," *Bulletin of the New York Academy of Medicine* 62 (1986): 589–619.

61. James Galliher and John Galliher, "A 'Commonsense' Theory of Deterrence and the 'Ideology' of Science: The New York State Death Penalty Debate," *Journal of Criminal Law and Criminology* 92 (2002): 307.

62. Steven Stack, "The Effect of Well-Publicized Executions on Homicide in California," *Journal of Crime and Justice* 21 (1998): 1–12.

63. David Friedrichs, "Comment—Humanism and the Death Penalty: An Alternative Perspective," *Justice Quarterly* 6 (1989): 197–209.

64. *Sourcebook of Criminal Justice Statistics,* http://www.albany.edu/sourcebook/pdf/t2512013.pdf (accessed February 2015).

65. Alexis Durham, H. Preston Elrod, and Patrick Kinkade, "Public Support to the Death Penalty: Beyond Gallup," *Justice Quarterly* 13 (1996): 705–736.

66. Marvin Zalman, "Qualitatively Estimating the Incidence of Wrongful Convictions," *Criminal Law Bulletin* 48 (2012): 221–279.

67. The Innocence Project, http://www.innocenceproject.org (accessed February 2015).

68. Samuel R. Gross, Barbara O'Brien, and Edward H. Kennedy, "Rate of False Conviction of Criminal Defendants who are Sentenced to Death," *Proceedings of the National Academy of Sciences*, http://www.pnas.org/content/111/20/7230.full (accessed February 2015).

69. Julian Roberts, "Capital Punishment, Innocence, and Public Opinion," *Criminology and Public Policy* 4 (2005): 1–3.

70. *Sourcebook of Criminal Justice Statistics*, "Attitudes toward the Better Penalty for Murder," http://www.albany.edu/sourcebook/pdf/t2492010.pdf (accessed February 2015).

71. James Unnever and Francis Cullen, "Executing the Innocent and Support for Capital Punishment: Implications for Public Policy," *Criminology and Public Policy* 4 (2005): 3–37.

72. Scott Vollum, Dennis Longmire, and Jacqueline Buffington-Vollum, "Confidence in the Death Penalty and Support for Its Use: Exploring the Value-Expressive Dimension of Death Penalty Attitudes," *Justice Quarterly* 21 (2004): 521–546.

73. Gennaro Vito and Thomas Keil, "Elements of Support for Capital Punishment: An Examination of Changing Attitudes," *Journal of Crime and Justice* 21 (1998): 17–25.

74. Denise Paquette Boots, Kathleen Heide, and John Cochran, "Death Penalty Support for Special Offender Populations of Legally Convicted Murderers: Juveniles, the Mentally Retarded, and the Mentally Incompetent," *Behavioral Sciences and the Law* 22 (2004): 223–238.

75. James Unnever and Francis Cullen, "The Racial Divide in Support for the Death Penalty: Does White Racism Matter?" *Social Forces* 85 (2007): 1281–1301.

76. D. Nagin and J. Petter, *Deterrence and the Death Penalty*, Committee on Law and Justice at the National Research Council, April 2012, http://www.nap.edu/catalog/13363/deterrence-and-the-death-penalty (accessed February 2015).

77. Isaac Ehrlich, "The Deterrent Effect of Capital Punishment: A Question of Life or Death," *American Economic Review* 65 (1975): 397.

78. For a review, see William Bailey, "The General Prevention Effect of Capital Punishment for Noncapital Felonies," in *The Death Penalty in America: Current Research*, ed. Robert Bohm (Cincinnati: Anderson, 1991), pp. 21–38.

79. Bijou Yang and David Lester, "The Deterrent Effect of Executions: A Meta-Analysis of Thirty Years after Ehrlich," *Journal of Criminal Justice* 36 (2008): 453–460.

80. Rick Ruddell and Martin Urbina, "Minority Threat and Punishment: A Cross-National Analysis," *Justice Quarterly* 21 (2004): 903–931.

81. Marian Williams and Jefferson Holcomb, "Racial Disparity and Death Sentences in Ohio," *Journal of Criminal Justice* 29 (2001): 207–218.

82. Jon Sorenson and Donald Wallace, "Prosecutorial Discretion in Seeking Death: An Analysis of Racial Disparity in the Pretrial Stages of Case Processing in a Midwestern County," *Justice Quarterly* 16 (1999): 559–578.

83. Marian R. Williams, "Understanding the Influence of Victim Gender in Death Penalty Cases: The Importance of Victim Race, Sex-Related Victimization, and Jury Decision Making," *Criminology* 45 (2007): 865–891; Catherine Lee, "Hispanics and the Death Penalty: Discriminatory Charging Practices in San Joaquin County, California," *Journal of Criminal Justice* 35 (2007): 17–27.

84. Jefferson Holcomb, Marian Williams, and Stephen Demuth, "White Female Victims and Death Penalty Disparity Research," *Justice Quarterly* 21 (2004): 877–902.

85. Lawrence Greenfield and David Hinners, *Capital Punishment, 1984* (Washington, DC: Bureau of Justice Statistics, 1985).

86. Gennaro Vito and Thomas Keil, "Capital Sentencing in Kentucky: An Analysis of the Factors Influencing Decision Making in the Post-*Gregg* Period," *Journal of Criminal Law and Criminology* 79 (1988): 483–508.

87. Geoffrey Rapp, "The Economics of Shootouts: Does the Passage of Capital Punishment Laws Protect or Endanger Police Officers?" *Albany Law Review* 65 (2002): 1051–1084.

88. William Bailey, "Disaggregation in Deterrence and Death Penalty Research: The Case of Murder in Chicago," *Journal of Criminal Law and Criminology* 74 (1986): 827–859.

89. Gennaro Vito, Pat Koester, and Deborah Wilson, "Return of the Dead: An Update on the Status of Furman-Commuted Death Row Inmates," in *The Death Penalty in America*, ed. Bohm, (Cincinnati: Anderson, 1991) pp. 89–100; Gennaro Vito, Deborah Wilson, and Edward Latessa, "Comparison of the Dead: Attributes and Outcomes of Furman-Commuted Death Row Inmates in Kentucky and Ohio," in *The Death Penalty in America*, ed. Bohm, (Cincinnati: Anderson, 1991) pp. 101–112.

90. John Cochran, Mitchell Chamlin, and Mark Seth, "Deterrence or Brutalization? An Impact Assessment of Oklahoma's Return to Capital Punishment," *Criminology* 32 (1994): 107–134.

91. William Bailey, "Deterrence, Brutalization, and the Death Penalty: Another Examination of Oklahoma's Return to Capital Punishment," *Justice Quarterly* 36 (1998): 711–734.

92. *Hill v. McDonough*, 547 US 573 (2006).

93. Robert Johnson, *Death Work: A Study of the Modern Execution Process* (Pacific Grove, CA: Brooks/Cole, 1990).

94. LiYing Li, "The Tainted Milk Scandal: Punishing Economic Criminals in China," unpublished paper (Denver: Metropolitan College of Denver, 2011).

95. Tracy L. Snell, *Capital Punishment, 2011* (Washington, DC: Bureau of Justice Statistics, 2011), p. 12.

96. See, for example, Ernest Van Den Haag, *Punishing Criminals: Concerning a Very Old and Painful Question* (New York: Basic Books, 1975), pp. 209–211; Walter Berns, "Defending the Death Penalty," *Crime and Delinquency* 26 (1980): 503–511.

97. Thoroddur Bjarnason and Michael Welch, "Father Knows Best: Parishes, Priests, and American Catholic Parishioners' Attitudes toward Capital Punishment," *Journal for the Scientific Study of Religion* 43 (2004): 103–118.

98. Franklin Zimring, *The Contradictions of American Capital Punishment* (London: Oxford University Press, 2003).

99. Vance McLaughlin and Paul Blackman, "Mass Legal Executions in Georgia," *Georgia Historical Quarterly* 88 (2004): 66–84.

100. Austin Sarat, "Innocence, Error, and the 'New Abolitionism': A Commentary," *Criminology and Public Policy* 4 (2005): 45–53.

101. *Furman v. Georgia*, 408 US 238 (1972).

102. *Gregg v. Georgia*, 428 US 153 (1976).

103. Ibid., at pp. 205–207.
104. *Ring v. Arizona*, 536 US 584 (2002).
105. *Furman v. Georgia*, 408 US 238 (1972).
106. *Gregg v. Georgia*, 428 US 153 (1976).
107. *Woodson v. North Carolina*, 428 US 280 (1976).
108. *Coker v. Georgia*, 430 US 349 (1977).
109. *Lockett v. Ohio*, 438 US 586 (1978).
110. *Enmund v. Florida*, 458 US 782 (1982).
111. *Glass v. Louisiana*, 471 US 1080 (1985).
112. *Cabana v. Bullock*, 474 US 376 (1986).
113. *Ford v. Wainwright*, 477 US 399 (1986).
114. *Atkins v. Virginia*, 536 US 304 (2002).
115. *Ring v. Arizona*, 536 US 584 (2002).
116. *Roper v. Simmons*, 543 US 551 (2005).
117. *Deck v. Missouri*, 544 US 622 (2005).
118. *Oregon v. Guzek*, 546 US 517 (2006).
119. *Baze v. Rees*, 553 US 35 (2008).
120. *Kennedy v. Louisiana*, 554 U.S. 407 (2008).

Chapter 10, Community Sentences: Probation, Intermediate Sanctions, and Restorative Justice

1. Emily Strohm and Janine Rayford Rubenstein, "Teresa Giudice Sentenced to 15 Months in Prison on Fraud Charges," *People* (October 2, 2014) http://www.people.com/article/teresa-joe-giudice-sentenced-fraud (accessed January 2015).
2. Katherine Clarke, "Teresa Giudice, Joe Giudice Slash $500K Off Price of Palatial New Jersey Home in Run Up to Jail," *New York Daily News* (November 13, 2014) http://www.nydailynews.com/life-style/real-estate/teresa-giudice-slashes-500k-price-palatial-home-article-1.2010106 (January 2015).
3. Brandon Applegate, Hayden Smith, Alicia Sitren, and Nicolette Fariello Springer, "From the Inside: The Meaning of Probation to Probationers," *Criminal Justice Review* 34 (2009): 80–95.
4. For a history of probation, see Edward Sieh, "From Augustus to the Progressives: A Study of Probation's Formative Years," *Federal Probation* 57 (1993): 67–72.
5. Ibid.
6. David Rothman, *Conscience and Convenience* (Boston: Little, Brown, 1980), pp. 82–117.
7. Data in this section are from Erinn Herberman, and Thomas P. Bonczar, *Probation and Parole in the United States, 2013* (Washington, DC: Bureau of Justice Statistics, 2014), http://www.bjs.gov/content/pub/pdf/ppus13.pdf (accessed March 2015).
8. *Gall v. United States*, 552 US 38 (2007).
9. Sean Rosenmerkel, Matthew Durose, and Donald Farole, Jr., *Felony Sentences in State Courts, 2006* (Washington, DC: Bureau of Justice Statistics, 2009), http://bjs.ojp.usdoj.gov/content/pub/ascii/fssc06st.txt (accessed March 2015).
10. Ibid.
11. Heather Barklage, Dane Miller, and Gene Bonham, Jr., "Probation Conditions vs. Probation Officer Directives," *Federal Probation* 70 (2006), http://www.uscourts.gov/statistics-reports/publications/federal-probation-journal (accessed April 2015).
12. Karl Hanson and Suzanne Wallace-Carpretta, "Predictors of Criminal Recidivism among Male Batterers," *Psychology, Crime and Law* 10 (2004): 413–427.
13. *Higdon v. United States*, 627 F.2d 893 (9th Cir., 1980).
14. *United States v. Lee*, No. 01-4485 01/07/03, *United States v. Lee*, PICS N. 03-0023.
15. *United States v. Gallo*, 20 F.3d 7 (1st Cir., 1994).
16. Todd Clear and Edward Latessa, "Probation Officers' Roles in Intensive Supervision: Surveillance versus Treatment," *Justice Quarterly* 10 (1993): 441–462.
17. Jay Whetzel, Mario Paparozzi, Melissa Alexander, and Christopher Lowenkamp, "Goodbye to a Worn-Out Dichotomy: Law Enforcement, Social Work, and a Balanced Approach," *Federal Probation* 75 (2011): 7–12.
18. Joel Miller, "Contemporary Modes of Probation Officer Supervision: The Triumph of the 'Synthetic' Officer?" *Justice Quarterly.* 32 (2015): 314–336.
19. Jeffrey Lin, Joel Miller, and Mayumi Fukushima, "Juvenile Probation Officers' Dispositional Recommendations: Predictive Factors and Their Alignment with Predictors of Recidivism," *Journal of Crime and Justice* 31 (2008): 1–34.
20. Jill Viglione, Danielle Rudes, and Faye Taxman, "Misalignment in Supervision: Implementing Risk/Needs Assessment Instruments in Probation," *Criminal Justice & Behavior* 42 (2015): 263–285.
21. Lawrence Sherman, "Use Probation to Prevent Murder," *Criminology and Public Policy* 6 (2007): 843–849.
22. Melinda Schlager, "Validity of the Level of Service Inventory-Revised (LSI-R) among African American and Hispanic Male Offenders," *Criminal Justice and Behavior* 34 (2007): 545–554; Carolin Kroner, Cornelis Stadtland, Matthias Eidt, and Norbert Nedopil, "The Validity of the Violence Risk Appraisal Guide (VRAG) in Predicting Criminal Recidivism," *Criminal Behaviour and Mental Health* 17 (2007): 89–100.
23. Melissa Alexander, Bradley Whitley, and Christopher Bersch, "Driving Evidence-Based Supervision to the Next Level: Utilizing PCRA, 'Drivers,' and Effective Supervision Techniques," *Federal Probation* 78 (2014), http://www.uscourts.gov/statistics-reports/publications/federal-probation-journal (accessed May 2015).
24. Diana Wendy Fitzgibbon, "Deconstructing Probation: Risk and Developments in Practice," *Journal of Social Work Practice* 22 (2008): 85–101.
25. Nancy Ritter, "Predicting Recidivism Risk: New Tool in Philadelphia Shows Great Promise," *NIJ Journal* 271 (2013): 4–10, http://www.nij.gov/journals/271/Pages/predicting-recidivism.aspx (accessed April 2015).
26. "Rape Victim's Mom Sues Attacker and Probation Chief," Fox News Chicago (January 26, 2011), http://www.myfoxchicago.com/story/17807356/rape-victims-mom-sues-attacker-and-probation-chief (accessed March 2013).
27. National Law Enforcement Corrections Technology Center, "Community Corrections Directions," *Tech Beat* (Spring 2007), https://www.justnet.org/pdf/CommunityCorrections.pdf (accessed April 2015).
28. Mary McMurran, "Motivational Interviewing with Offenders: A Systematic Review," *Legal and Criminological Psychology* 14 (2009): 83–100; Scott Walters, Amanda Vader, Norma Nguyen, Robert Harris, and Jennifer Eells, "Motivational Interviewing as a Supervision Strategy in Probation: A Randomized Effectiveness Trial," *Journal of Offender Rehabilitation* 49 (2010): 309–323.
29. *Minnesota v. Murphy*, 465 US 420, 104 S.Ct. 1136, 79 L.Ed.2d 409 (1984).
30. *Griffin v. Wisconsin*, 483 US 868, 107 S.Ct. 3164, 97 L.Ed.2d 709 (1987).
31. *United States v. Knights*, 122 S.Ct. 587 (2001).
32. *Mempa v. Rhay*, 389 US 128, 88 S.Ct. 254, 19 L.Ed.2d 336 (1967).

33. *Morrissey v. Brewer*, 408 US 471, 92 S.Ct. 2593, 33 L.Ed.2d 484 (1972).

34. *Gagnon v. Scarpelli*, 411 US 778, 93 S.Ct. 1756, 36 L.Ed.2d 656 (1973).

35. *Beardon v. Georgia*, 33 CrL 3101 (1983).

36. *United States v. Granderson*, 114 Ct. 1259, 127 L.Ed.2d 611 (1994).

37. M. Kevin Gray, Monique Fields, and Sheila Royo Maxwell, "Examining Probation Violations: Who, What, and When," *Crime and Delinquency* 47 (2001): 537–557.

38. Kelli Stevens-Martin, Olusegun Oyewole, and Cynthia Hipolito, "Technical Revocations of Probation in One Jurisdiction: Uncovering the Hidden Realities" *Federal Probation* 78 (2014), http://www.uscourts.gov /statistics-reports/publications /federal-probation-journal (accessed May 2015); Nancy Rodriguez and Vincent Webb, "Probation Violations, Revocations, and Imprisonment: The Decisions of Probation Officers, Prosecutors, and Judges Pre- and Post-Mandatory Drug Treatment," *Criminal Justice Policy Review* 18 (2007): 3–30.

39. Christopher Krebs, Kevin Strom, Willem Koetse, and Pamela Lattimore, "The Impact of Residential and Nonresidential Drug Treatment on Recidivism among Drug-Involved Probationers: A Survival Analysis," *Crime and Delinquency* 55 (2009): 442–471.

40. Eladio Castillo and Leanne Alarid Fiftal, "Factors Associated with Recidivism among Offenders with Mental Illness," *International Journal of Offender Therapy and Comparative Criminology* 55 (2011): 98–117.

41. Joan Petersilia, Susan Turner, James Kahan, and Joyce Peterson, *Granting Felons Probation: Public Risks and Alternatives* (Santa Monica, CA: Rand, 1985).

42. Cassia Spohn and David Holleran, "The Effect of Imprisonment on Recidivism Rates of Felony Offenders: A Focus on Drug Offenders," *Criminology* 40 (2002): 329–359.

43. Daniel Mears, Joshua Cochran, and William Bales, "Gender Differences in the Effects of Prison on Recidivism," *Journal of Criminal Justice* 50 (2012): 370–378.

44. Paula M. Ditton, *Mental Health and Treatment of Inmates and Probationers* (Washington, DC: Bureau of Justice Statistics, 1999).

45. Kathryn Morgan, "Factors Associated with Probation Outcome," *Journal of Criminal Justice* 22 (1994): 341–353.

46. Naomi Freeman, "Predictors of Rearrest for Rapists and Child Molesters on Probation," *Criminal Justice and Behavior* 34 (2007): 752–768.

47. Kathryn Morgan, "Factors Influencing Probation Outcome: A Review of the Literature," *Federal Probation* 57 (1993): 23–29.

48. Fitzgibbon, "Deconstructing Probation."

49. Joan Petersilia, "Probation in the United States," in *Crime and Justice: A Review of Research* 21 (Chicago: University of Chicago Press, 1997), p. 185.

50. "Law in Massachusetts Requires Probationers to Pay 'Day Fees,'" *Criminal Justice Newsletter*, September 15, 1988, p. 1.

51. Peter Finn and Dale Parent, *Making the Offender Foot the Bill: A Texas Program* (Washington, DC: National Institute of Justice, 1992).

52. State of Arizona, Senate Bill 1476 (2008), http://www.azleg.gov/legtext /48leg/2r/bills/sb1476p.pdf (accessed March 2013).

53. Nicole Leeper Piquero, "A Recidivism Analysis of Maryland's Community Probation Program," *Journal of Criminal Justice* 31 (2003): 295–308.

54. Todd R. Clear, "Places Not Cases: Rethinking the Probation Focus," *Howard Journal of Criminal Justice* 44 (2005): 172–184.

55. Andrew Klein and Ann Crowe, "Findings from an Outcome Examination of Rhode Island's Specialized Domestic Violence Probation Supervision Program," *Violence Against Women* 14 (2008): 226–246.

56. Roberto Hugh Potter and Timothy Akers, "Improving the Health of Minority Communities through Probation-Public Health Collaborations: An Application of the Epidemiological Criminology Framework," *Journal of Offender Rehabilitation* 49 (2010): 595–609.

57. Private Probation Services, http:// www.privateprobationservices.com (accessed March 2013).

58. Christine Schloss and Leanne Alarid, "Standards in the Privatization of Probation Services: A Statutory Analysis," *Criminal Justice Review* 32 (2007): 233–245.

59. "HOPE in Hawaii: Swift and Sure Changes in Probation," National Institute of Justice, 2008, http://www.ncjrs .gov/pdffiles1/nij/222758.pdf (accessed March 2013).

60. "Evaluating Delaware's Decide Your Time Program for Drug-Using Offenders Under Community Supervision," National Institute of Justice, 2011, http:// www.nij.gov/nij/topics/corrections /community/drug-offenders/decide -your-time.htm (accessed March 2013).

61. Todd Clear and Patricia Hardyman, "The New Intensive Supervision Movement," *Crime and Delinquency* 36 (1990): 42–60.

62. Norval Morris and Michael Tonry, *Between Prison and Probation: Intermediate Punishments in a Rational Sentencing System* (New York: Oxford University Press, 1990).

63. Ibid., p. 8.

64. For a thorough review of these programs, see James Byrne, Arthur Lurigio, and Joan Petersilia, eds., *Smart Sentencing: The Emergence of Intermediate Sanctions* (Newbury Park, CA: Sage, 1993). Hereinafter cited as *Smart Sentencing*.

65. Michael Tonry and Richard Will, *Intermediate Sanctions* (Washington, DC: National Institute of Justice, 1990).

66. Sally Hillsman and Judith Greene, "Tailoring Fines to the Financial Means of Offenders," *Judicature* 72 (1988): 38–45.

67. George Cole, "Monetary Sanctions: The Problem of Compliance," in *Smart Sentencing*, pp. 51–64.

68. *Tate v. Short*, 401 US 395, 91 S.Ct. 668, 28 L.Ed.2d 130 (1971).

69. Doris Layton MacKenzie, "Evidence-Based Corrections: Identifying What Works," *Crime and Delinquency* 46 (2000): 457–472.

70. John L. Worrall, "Addicted to the Drug War: The Role of Civil Asset Forfeiture as a Budgetary Necessity in Contemporary Law Enforcement," *Journal of Criminal Justice* 29 (2001): 171–187.

71. C. Yorke, *Some Consideration on the Law of Forfeiture for High Treason*, 2d ed. (1746), pp. 26, cited in David Fried, "Rationalizing Criminal Forfeiture," *Journal of Criminal Law and Criminology* 79 (1988): 328–436.

72. Fried, "Rationalizing Criminal Forfeiture," p. 436.

73. James B. Jacobs, Coleen Friel, and Edward O'Callaghan, "Pension Forfeiture: A Problematic Sanction for Public Corruption," *American Criminal Law Review* 35 (1997): 57–92.

74. Worrall, "Addicted to the Drug War."
75. For a general review, see Burt Galaway and Joe Hudson, *Criminal Justice, Restitution, and Reconciliation* (New York: Criminal Justice Press, 1990); Robert Carter, Jay Cocks, and Daniel Glazer, "Community Service: A Review of the Basic Issues," *Federal Probation* 51 (1987): 4–11.
76. Frederick Allen and Harvey Treger, "Community Service Orders in Federal Probation: Perceptions of Probationers and Host Agencies," *Federal Probation* 54 (1990): 8–14.
77. Gail Caputo, "Community Service in Texas: Results of a Probation Survey," *Corrections Compendium* 30 (2005): 8–12.
78. Sudipto Roy, "Two Types of Juvenile Restitution Programs in Two Midwestern Counties: A Comparative Study," *Federal Probation* 57 (1993): 48–53.
79. Ibid.
80. Jodi Lane, Susan Turner, Terry Fain, and Amber Sehgal, "Evaluating an Experimental Intensive Juvenile Probation Program: Supervision and Official Outcomes," *Crime and Delinquency* 51 (2005): 26–52.
81. Sarah Kuck Jalbert, William Rhodes, Michael Kane, Elyse Clawson, Bradford Bogue, Chris Flygare, Ryan Kling, and Meaghan Guevara, "A Multi-Site Evaluation of Reduced Probation Caseload Size in an Evidence-Based Practice Setting," National Institute of Justice, Office of Justice Programs, 2010, https://www.ncjrs.gov/pdffiles1/nij/grants/234596.pdf (accessed March 2013).
82. Greg Warchol, "Intensive Supervision Probation: An Impact Evaluation," *Justice Professional* 13 (2000): 219–232.
83. James Byrne and Linda Kelly, "Restructuring Probation as an Intermediate Sanction: An Evaluation of the Massachusetts Intensive Probation Supervision Program," final report to the National Institute of Justice, Research Program on the Punishment and Control of Offenders, Washington, DC, 1989.
84. James Ryan, "Who Gets Revoked? A Comparison of Intensive Supervision Successes and Failures in Vermont," *Crime and Delinquency* 43 (1997): 104–118.
85. Angela Robertson, Paul Grimes, and Kevin Rogers, "A Short-Run Cost-Benefit Analysis of Community-Based Interventions for Juvenile Offenders," *Crime and Delinquency* 47 (2001): 265–284.
86. Linda Smith and Ronald Akers, "A Comparison of Recidivism of Florida's Community Control and Prison: A Five-Year Survival Analysis," *Journal of Research in Crime and Delinquency* 30 (1993): 267–292.
87. Robert N. Altman, Robert E. Murray, and Evey B. Wooten, "Home Confinement: A 90s Approach to Community Supervision," *Federal Probation* 61 (1997): 30–32.
88. Matthew DeMichele, Brian Payne, and Deeanna Button, "Electronic Monitoring of Sex Offenders: Identifying Unanticipated Consequences and Implications," *Journal of Offender Rehabilitation* 46 (2008): 119–135.
89. William Burrell and Robert Gable, "From B. F. Skinner to Spiderman to Martha Stewart: The Past, Present and Future of Electronic Monitoring of Offenders," *Journal of Offender Rehabilitation* 46 (2008): 101–118; Hugh Downing, "Emergence of Global Positioning Satellite (GPS) Systems in Correctional Applications," *Corrections Today* 68 (2006): 42–45.
90. Edna Erez and Peter Ibarra, "Making Your Home a Shelter: Electronic Monitoring and Victim Re-Entry in Domestic Violence Cases," *British Journal of Criminology* 47 (2007): 100–120.
91. Stephen Gies, Randy Gainey, Marcia Cohen, Eoin Healy, Martha Yeide, Alan Bekelman, et al., *Monitoring High-Risk Gang Offenders with GPS Technology: An Evaluation of the California Supervision Program Final Report* (Washington, DC: Office of Justice Programs, US Department of Justice, National Institute of Justice, 2013).
92. Kathy Padgett, William Bales, and Thomas Blomberg, "Under Surveillance: An Empirical Test of the Effectiveness and Consequences of Electronic Monitoring," *Criminology and Public Policy* 5 (2006): 61–91.
93. William Bales, Karen Mann, Thomas Blomberg, Gerry Gaes, Kelle Barrick, Karla Dhungana, and Brian McManus, *A Quantitative and Qualitative Assessment of Electronic Monitoring* (Tallahassee: Florida State University, College of Criminology and Criminal Justice, Center for Criminology and Public Policy Research, January 2010), http://www.ncjrs.gov/pdffiles1/nij/grants/230530.pdf (accessed March 2013).
94. Avdi Avdija and JiHee Lee, "Does Electronic Monitoring Home Detention Program Work? Evaluating Program Suitability Based on Offenders' Post-Program Recidivism Status," *Justice Policy Journal* 11 (2014): 1–15.
95. Omnilink Systems, http://www.omnilink.com (accessed March 2013).
96. "Evaluating a Location-Based Offender Monitoring System," National Institute of Justice (2015) http://www.nij.gov/topics/corrections/community/monitoring-technologies/Pages/location-based-monitoring.aspx (accessed February 2015).
97. See, generally, Edward Latessa and Lawrence Travis III, "Residential Community Correctional Programs," in *Smart Sentencing*, pp. 65–79.
98. Dale Parent, *Day Reporting Centers for Criminal Offenders: A Descriptive Analysis of Existing Programs* (Washington, DC: National Institute of Justice, 1990); Jack McDevitt and Robyn Miliano, "Day Reporting Centers: An Innovative Concept in Intermediate Sanctions," in *Smart Sentencing*, pp. 80–105.
99. David Diggs and Stephen Pieper, "Using Day Reporting Centers as an Alternative to Jail," *Federal Probation* 58 (1994): 9–12.
100. Michael Ostermann, "An Analysis of New Jersey's Day Reporting Center and Halfway Back Programs: Embracing the Rehabilitative Ideal through Evidence Based Practices," *Journal of Offender Rehabilitation* 48 (2009): 139–153.
101. Dae-Young Kim, Hee-Jong Joo, and William McCarty, "Risk Assessment and Classification of Day Reporting Center Clients: An Actuarial Approach," *Criminal Justice and Behavior* 35 (2008): 792–812.
102. Amy Craddock, "Day Reporting Center Completion: Comparison of Individual and Multilevel Models," *Crime and Delinquency* 55 (2009): 105–133; Sudipto Roy and Shannon Barton, "Convicted Drunk Drivers in Electronic Monitoring Home Detention and Day Reporting Centers," *Federal Probation* 70 (2006), http://www.uscourts.gov/statistics-reports/publications/federal-probation-journal (accessed March 2015).
103. Kathleen Daly and Russ Immarigeon, "The Past, Present, and Future of Restorative Justice: Some Critical Reflections," *Contemporary Justice Review* 1 (1998): 21–45.

104. John Braithwaite, *Crime, Shame, and Reintegration* (Melbourne, Australia: Cambridge University Press, 1989).

105. Gene Stephens, "The Future of Policing: From a War Model to a Peace Model," in *The Past, Present and Future of American Criminal Justice,* eds. Brendan Maguire and Polly Radosh (Dix Hills, NY: General Hall, 1996), pp. 77–93.

106. Kay Pranis, "Peacemaking Circles: Restorative Justice in Practice Allows Victims and Offenders to Begin Repairing the Harm," *Corrections Today* 59 (1997): 74.

107. Carol LaPrairie, "The 'New' Justice: Some Implications for Aboriginal Communities," *Canadian Journal of Criminology* 40 (1998): 61–79.

108. David R. Karp and Beau Breslin, "Restorative Justice in School Communities," *Youth and Society* 33 (2001): 249–272.

109. Paul Jesilow and Deborah Parsons, "Community Policing as Peacemaking," *Policing and Society* 10 (2000): 163–183.

110. Restorative Justice Online, Restorative Cautioning/Diversion by Police (2013), http://www.restorativejustice .org/police/1restorative-cautioning -police-diversion (accessed March 2013); Aidan Wilcox, Richard Young, and Carolyn Hoyle, "Two-Year Re-sanctioning Study: A Comparison of Restorative and Traditional Cautions," *British Home Office,* 2004, http:// webarchive.nationalarchives.gov .uk/20110220105210/rds.homeoffice .gov.uk/rds/pdfs04/rdsolr5704.pdf (accessed March 2013); Aidan Wilcox and Richard Young, "How Green Was Thames Valley? Policing the Image of Restorative Justice Cautions," *Policing and Society* 17 (2007): 141–163.

111. Natalie Kroovand Hipple, Jeff Gruenewald, and Edmund F. McGarrell, "Restorativeness, Procedural Justice, and Defiance as Predictors of Re-offending of Participants in Family Group Conferences," *Crime and Delinquency* 60 (December 2014): 1131–1157 (first published December 7, 2011).

112. Gordon Bazemore and Curt Taylor Griffiths, "Conferences, Circles, Boards, and Mediations: The 'New Wave' of Community Justice Decision Making," *Federal Probation* 61 (1997): 25–37.

113. Mark Umbreit and Rina Ritter, "Arab Offenders Meet Jewish Victim: Restorative Family Dialogue in Israel," *Conflict Resolution Quarterly* 24 (2006): 99–109.

114. John Braithwaite, "Setting Standards for Restorative Justice," *British Journal of Criminology* 42 (2002): 563–577.

115. Nancy Rodriguez, "Restorative Justice, Communities, and Delinquency: Whom Do We Reintegrate?" *Criminology and Public Policy* 4 (2005): 103–130.

116. John Braithwaite, "Setting Standards for Restorative Justice."

117. David Altschuler, "Community Justice Initiatives: Issues and Challenges in the US Context," *Federal Probation* 65 (2001): 28–33.

118. Lois Presser and Patricia Van Voorhis, "Values and Evaluation: Assessing Processes and Outcomes of Restorative Justice Programs," *Crime and Delinquency* 48 (2002): 162–189.

119. Sharon Levrant, Francis Cullen, Betsy Fulton, and John Wozniak, "Reconsidering Restorative Justice: The Corruption of Benevolence Revisited?" *Crime and Delinquency* 45 (1999): 3–28.

120. Dean Gromet and John Darley, "Restoration and Retribution: How Including Retributive Components Affects the Acceptability of Restorative Justice Procedures," *Social Justice Research* 19 (2006): 395–432.

121. Michael E. Smith, *What Future for "Public Safety" and "Restorative Justice" in Community Corrections?* (Washington, DC: National Institute of Justice, 2001).

Chapter 11, Corrections: History, Institutions, and Populations

1. The Associated Press, "Attica Corrections Officers Plead Guilty to 2011 Inmate Beating Just as Trial Begins" (March 2, 2015), http://www .nydailynews.com/news/crime /attica-corrections-officers-plead -guilty-inmate-beating-article -1.2134374 (accessed April 2015); Tom Robbins, "A Brutal Beating Wakes Attica's Ghosts: A Prison, Infamous for Bloodshed, Faces a Reckoning as Guards Go on Trial," *New York Times* (February 28, 2015), http://www.nytimes.com/2015/03/01 /nyregion/attica-prison-infamous-for -bloodshed-faces-a-reckoning-as-guards -go-on-trial.html (accessed May 2015).

2. E. Ann Carson, *Prisoners in 2013,* Bureau of Justice Statistics, 2014, http://www.bjs.gov/content/pub/pdf /p13.pdf (accessed March 2015).

3. See David Fogel, *We Are the Living Proof,* 2nd ed. (Cincinnati: Anderson, 1978); Andrew von Hirsch, *Doing Justice: The Choice of Punishments* (New York: Hill and Wang, 1976).

4. Francis Cullen, "The Twelve People Who Saved Rehabilitation: How the Science of Criminology Made a Difference," *Criminology* 43 (2005): 1–42.

5. Malcolm Feeley and Jonathan Simon, "The New Penology: Notes on the Emerging Strategy of Corrections and Its Implications," *Criminology* 30 (2006): 449–474.

6. E. Ann Carson, *Prisoners,* 2013; Roy Walmsley, *World Population List,* 10th ed. (Essex, England: International Centre for Prison Studies, 2013), http://www.prisonstudies.org/sites /prisonstudies.org/files/resources /downloads/wppl_10.pdf (accessed March 2015).

7. Paul Schupp and Craig Rivera, "Identifying Imprisonment Patterns and Their Relation to Crime Among New York Counties 1990–2000," *Criminal Justice Policy Review* 21 (2010): 50–75.

8. Ernest Drucker, A Plague of Prisons: The Epidemiology of Mass Incarceration in America, reprint ed. (New York: New Press, 2013).

9. Michelle Alexander, *The New Jim Crow: Mass Incarceration in the Age of Color Blindness* (New York: New Press, 2012).

10. Among the most helpful sources in developing this section were Mark Colvin, *Penitentiaries, Reformatories, and Chain Gangs* (New York: St. Martin's Press, 1997); Benedict Alper, *Prisons Inside-Out* (Cambridge, MA: Ballinger, 1974); Harry Elmer Barnes, *The Story of Punishment,* 2nd ed. (Montclair, NJ: Patterson-Smith, 1972); Gustave de Beaumont and Alexis de Tocqueville, *On the Penitentiary System in the United States and Its Applications in France* (Carbondale: Southern Illinois University Press, 1964); Orlando Lewis, *The Development of American Prisons and Prison Customs, 1776– 1845* (Montclair, NJ: Patterson-Smith, 1967); Georg Rusche and Otto Kircheimer, *Punishment and Social Structure* (New York: Russell and Russell, 1939); Samuel Walker, *Popular Justice* (New York: Oxford University Press, 1980); Graeme Newman, *The*

Punishment Response (Philadelphia: J. B. Lippincott, 1978); David Rothman, *Conscience and Convenience* (Boston: Little, Brown, 1980).

11. Frederick Pollock and Frederick Maitland, *History of English Law* (London: Cambridge University Press, 1952).

12. Marvin Wolfgang, "Crime and Punishment in Renaissance Florence," *Journal of Criminal Law and Criminology* 81 (1990): 567–584.

13. John Howard, *The State of Prisons,* 4th ed. (1972; reprint, Montclair, NJ: Patterson-Smith, 1973).

14. Alexis Durham III, "Newgate of Connecticut: Origins and Early Days of an Early American Prison," *Justice Quarterly* 6 (1989): 89–116.

15. Dario Melossi and Massimo Pavarini, *The Prison and the Factory: Origins of the Penitentiary System* (Totowa, NJ: Barnes and Noble, 1981).

16. Lewis, *Development of American Prisons and Prison Customs,* p. 17.

17. See, generally, David Rothman, *The Discovery of the Asylum* (Boston: Little, Brown, 1970).

18. Ibid., p. 144.

19. Walker, *Popular Justice,* p. 70.

20. Ibid., p. 71.

21. Beverly Smith, "Military Training at New York's Elmira Reformatory, 1880–1920," *Federal Probation* 52 (1988): 33–41.

22. William Parker, *Parole: Origins, Development, Current Practices, and Statutes* (College Park, MD: American Correctional Association, 1972); Samuel Walker, *Popular Justice.*

23. This section leans heavily on David Rothman, *Conscience and Convenience.*

24. Ibid., p. 23.

25. Ibid., p. 133.

26. 18 USC. 1761.

27. Barbara Auerbach, George Sexton, Franlin Farrow, and Robert Lawson, *Work in American Prisons: The Private Sector Gets Involved* (Washington, DC: National Institute of Justice, 1988), p. 72.

28. See, generally, Jameson Doig, *Criminal Corrections: Ideals and Realities* (Lexington, MA: Lexington Books, 1983).

29. Data in this section comes from Lauren Glaze and Danielle Kaeble, *Correctional Populations in the United States, 2013,* Bureau of Justice Statistics, 2014, http://www.bjs.gov /content/pub/pdf/cpus13.pdf (accessed March 2015); Todd Minton and Danielle Golinelli, *Jail Inmates at Midyear 2013: Statistical Tables,* Bureau of Justice Statistics, 2014, http://www.bjs.gov/content/pub/pdf /jim13st.pdf (accessed March 2015).

30. Tina Freiburger and Carly Hilinski, "An Examination of the Interactions of Race and Gender on Sentencing Decisions Using a Trichotomous Dependent Variable," *Crime and Delinquency* 59 (2013): 59–86.

31. National Institute of Corrections and the National Center on Institutions and Alternatives (NCIA), *National Study of Jail Suicide: 20 Years Later* (2010), http://nicic.gov/library/024308 (accessed March 2013).

32. Brandon Applegate, Ray Surette, and Bernard McCarthy, "Detention and Desistance from Crime: Evaluating the Influence of a New Generation of Jail on Recidivism," *Journal of Criminal Justice* 27 (1999): 539–548.

33. Federal Bureau of Prisons, Budget Summary 2012, http://www.justice .gov/jmd/2012summary/pdf /fy12-bop-bud-summary.pdf (accessed March 2013).

34. Human Rights Watch, *Prison Conditions in the United States,* http:// www.hrw.org/wr2k2/prisons.html (accessed March 2013).

35. "Suit Alleges Violations in California's 'super-Max' Prison," *Criminal Justice Newsletter,* September 1, 1993, p. 2.

36. Jeffrey Ian Ross (ed.), *The Globalization of Supermax Prisons* (New Brunswick, NJ: Rutgers University Press, 2013).

37. Jody Sundt, Thomas Castellano, and Chad Briggs, "The Sociopolitical Context of Prison Violence and Its Control: A Case Study of Supermax and Its Effect in Illinois," *Prison Journal* 88 (2008): 94–122.

38. Keramet Reiter, "Parole, Snitch, or Die: California's Supermax Prisons and Prisoners, 1997–2007," *Punishment & Society* 14 (2012): 530–563.

39. Keramet Reiter, "The Supermax Prison: A Blunt Means of Control, or a Subtle Form of Violence?" *Radical Philosophy Review,* first published online, September 20, 2014, http:// www.pdcnet.org/pdc/bvdb.nsf /purchase?openform&fp=radphilrev &id=radphilrev_2014_0999_9_16_23 (accessed April 2015).

40. Daniel Mears and William Bales, "Supermax Incarceration and Recidivism," *Criminology* 47 (2009): 801–836.

41. Daniel Mears, "An Assessment of Supermax Prisons Using an Evaluation Research Framework," *Prison Journal* 88 (2008): 43–68; Daniel Mears and Jennifer Castro, "Wardens' Views on the Wisdom of Supermax Prisons," *Crime and Delinquency* 52 (2006): 398–431; Daniel Mears and Jamie Watson, "Towards a Fair and Balanced Assessment of Supermax Prisons," *Justice Quarterly* 23 (2006): 232–270; Mears and Bales, "Supermax Incarceration and Recidivism."

42. James Anderson, Laronistine Dyson, and Jerald Burns, *Boot Camps: An Intermediate Sanction* (Lanham, MD: University Press of America, 1999), pp. 1–17.

43. Ibid., 328–329.

44. Doris Layton Mackenzie and James Shaw, "The Impact of Shock Incarceration on Technical Violations and New Criminal Activities," *Justice Quarterly* 10 (1993): 463–487.

45. Vanessa St. Gerard, "Federal Prisons to Eliminate Boot Camps," *Corrections Today* 67 (2005): 13–16.

46. Correctional Research Associates, *Treating Youthful Offenders in the Community: An Evaluation Conducted by A. J. Reiss* (Washington, DC: Correctional Research Associates, 1966).

47. Corrections Corporation of America, http://www.cca.com (accessed March 2015).

48. GEO Corporation, http://www .geogroup.com/facts (accessed March 2015).

49. Richard Harding, "Private Prisons," in *Crime and Justice: An Annual Edition,* ed. Michael Tonry (Chicago: University of Chicago Press, 2001), pp. 265–347.

50. E. Ann Carson, *Prisoners in 2013* (Washington, DC: Bureau of Justice Statistics 2014), http://www.bjs.gov /content/pub/pdf/p13.pdf (accessed March 2015)

51. William Bales, Laura Bedard, Susan Quinn, David Ensley, and Glen Holley, "Recidivism of Public and Private State Prison Inmates in Florida," *Criminology and Public Policy* 4 (2005): 57–82; Lonn Lanza-Kaduce, Karen Parker, and Charles Thomas, "A Comparative Recidivism Analysis of Releases from Private and Public Prisons," *Crime and Delinquency* 45 (1999): 28–47.

52. Charles Thomas, "Recidivism of Public and Private State Prison Inmates in Florida: Issues and

Unanswered Questions," *Criminology and Public Policy* 4 (2005): 89–99;

53. *Minneci et al. v. Pollard et al. 565 US ___ (2012)*, http://www.supremecourt.gov/opinions/11pdf/10-1104.pdf (accessed April 2015).

54. E. Ann Carson, *Prisoners* in 2013 (Washington, DC: Bureau of Justice Statistics, 2014), http://www.bjs.gov/content/pub/pdf/p13.pdf (accessed March 2015).

55. Ibid.

56. Sean Nicholson-Crotty, "The Impact of Sentencing Guidelines on State-Level Sanctions: An Analysis over Time," *Crime and Delinquency* 50 (2004): 395–411.

57. Pew Foundation Report, "Max Out, The Rise in Prison Inmates Released without Supervision," June 2014, http://www.pewtrusts.org/en/research-and-analysis/reports/2014/06/04/max-out (accessed April 2015).

58. Benjamin Steiner and John Wooldredge, "Comparing State-versus Facility-Level Effects on Crowding in US Correctional Facilities," *Crime and Delinquency* 54 (2008): 259–290.

59. Greg Greenberg and Robert Rosenheck, "Homelessness in the State and Federal Prison Population," *Criminal Behaviour and Mental Health* 18 (2008): 88–103.

60. Seena Fazel and John Danesh, "Serious Mental Disorder in 23,000 Prisoners: A Systematic Review of Sixty-Two Surveys," *Lancet* 359 (2002): 545–561.

Chapter 12, Prison Life: Living in and Leaving Prison

1. Stephanie Chen, "'Terrible Tommy' Spends 27 Years in Solitary Confinement," CNN, http://www.cnn.com/2010/CRIME/02/25/colorado.supermax.silverstein.solitary/ (accessed March 2015).

2. Taken from his website, https://thomassilverstein.wordpress.com/ (accessed April 2015).

3. Peter Wagner and Leah Sakala, "Mass Incarceration: The Whole Pie–A Prison Policy Initiative briefing," March 12, 2014, http://www.prisonpolicy.org/reports/pie.html (accessed March 2015); Sarah Lawrence and Jeremy Travis, *The New Landscape of Imprisonment: Mapping America's Prison Expansion* (Washington, DC: Urban Institute, 2004), http://www.urban.org/UploadedPDF/410994_mapping_prisons.pdf (accessed March 2015).

4. James Stephan and Jennifer Karberg, *Census of State and Federal Correctional Facilities, 2000* (Washington, DC: Bureau of Justice Statistics, 2003, updated 2008).

5. Timothy Hughes and Doris James Wilson, "Reentry Trends in the United States: Inmates Returning to the Community after Serving Time in Prison," Bureau of Justice Statistics, http://bjs.gov/content/pub/pdf/reentry.pdf (accessed March 2015).

6. Ros Burnett and Shadd Maruna, "So 'Prison Works,' Does It? The Criminal Careers of 130 Men Released from Prison Under Home Secretary Michael Howard," *Howard Journal of Criminal Justice* 43 (2004): 390–404.

7. Richard Berk, Heather Ladd, Heidi Graziano, and Jong-Ho Baek, "A Randomized Experiment Testing Inmate Classification Systems," *Criminology and Public Policy* 2 (2003): 215–242.

8. James A. Paluch, Jr., *A Life for a Life: Life Imprisonment (America's Other Death Penalty)* (Los Angeles: Roxbury Press, 2004), p. 4.

9. Margaret Leigey, "For the Longest Time: The Adjustment of Inmates to a Sentence of Life without Parole," *Prison Journal* 90 (2010): 247–268.

10. Manop Kanato, "Drug Use and Health among Prison Inmates," *Current Opinion in Psychiatry* 21 (2008): 252–254.

11. Gresham Sykes, *The Society of Captives* (Princeton, NJ: Princeton University Press, 1958).

12. Karen Lahm, "Inmate-on-Inmate Assault: A Multilevel Examination of Prison Violence," *Criminal Justice and Behavior* 35 (2008): 120–137.

13. Robert Johnson, *Hard Time: Understanding and Reforming the Prison* (Monterey, CA: Brooks/Cole, 1987), p. 115.

14. John D. Wooldredge, "Inmate Lifestyles and Opportunities for Victimization," *Journal of Research in Crime and Delinquency* 35 (1998): 480–502.

15. Attapol Kuanliang, Jon Sorensen, and Mark Cunningham, "Juvenile Inmates in an Adult Prison System: Rates of Disciplinary Misconduct and Violence," *Criminal Justice and Behavior* 35 (2008): 1186–1201.

16. Mark Kellar and Hsiao-Ming Wang, "Inmate Assaults in Texas County Jails," *Prison Journal* 85 (2005): 515–534.

17. Benjamin Steiner and John Wooldredge, "Inmate versus Environmental Effects on Prison Rule Violations," *Criminal Justice and Behavior* 35 (2008): 438–456.

18. Alan Prendergast, "Raped and Extorted by a Prison Gang, Scott Howard Was Called a 'Drama Queen' by Corrections Officials," *Denver Westword News* (February 2, 2011), http://www.westword.com/2011-02-03/news/211-crew-rapes-extorts-scott-howard-colorado-prison/ (accessed March 2013).

19. T. J. Parsell, *Fish: A Memoir of a Boy in a Man's Prison* (Cambridge, MA: Da Capo Press, 2007).

20. Christopher Hensley, Mary Koscheski, and Richard Tewksbury, "Examining the Characteristics of Male Sexual Assault Targets in a Southern Maximum-Security Prison," *Journal of Interpersonal Violence* 20 (2005): 667–679.

21. Wilbert Rideau and Ron Wikberg, *Life Sentences: Rage and Survival Behind Bars* (New York: Times Books, 1992), pp. 78–80.

22. Hensley, Koscheski, and Tewksbury, "Examining the Characteristics of Male Sexual Assault Targets in a Southern Maximum-Security Prison."

23. Mark Fleisher and Jessie Krienert, *The Myth of Prison Rape: Sexual Culture in American Prisons* (Lanham, MD: Rowman & Littlefield, 2009).

24. Allen Beck, Marcus Berzofsky, Rachel Caspar, Christopher Krebs, *Sexual Victimization in Prisons and Jails Reported by Inmates, 2011–12 Update* (Washington, DC: Bureau of Justice Statistics, 2014), http://www.bjs.gov/content/pub/pdf/svpjri1112.pdf (accessed April 2015).

25. Kristine Levan Miller, "The Darkest Figure of Crime: Perceptions of Reasons for Male Inmates to Not Report Sexual Assault," *Justice Quarterly* 27 (2010): 692–712.

26. Tonisha Jones and Travis Pratt, "The Prevalence of Sexual Violence in Prison," *International Journal of Offender Therapy and Comparative Criminology* 52 (2008): 280–295.

27. Allen Beck and Candace Johnson, *Sexual Victimization Reported by Former State Prisoners, 2008,* Bureau of Justice Statistics, 2012, http://www.bjs.gov/content/pub/ascii/svrfsp08.txt (accessed March 2013).

28. Nancy Wolff and Jing Shi, "Patterns of Victimization and Feelings of Safety

Inside Prison: The Experience of Male and Female Inmates," *Crime and Delinquency* 57 (2011): 29–55.

29. Mark Fleisher and Jessie Krienert, *The Culture of Prison Sexual Violence* (Washington, DC: US Department of Justice, National Institute of Justice, 2006).

30. S. 1435[108]: Prison Rape Elimination Act of 2003; Public Law No: 108–79.

31. John Irwin, "Adaptation to Being Corrected: Corrections from the Convict's Perspective," in *Handbook of Criminology*, ed. Daniel Glazer (Chicago: Rand McNally, 1974), pp. 971–993.

32. Donald Clemmer, *The Prison Community* (New York: Holt, Rinehart & Winston, 1958).

33. Gresham Sykes and Sheldon Messinger, "The Inmate Social Code," in *The Sociology of Punishment and Corrections*, ed. Norman Johnston, Leonard Savitz, and Marvin Wolfgang (New York: Wiley, 1970), pp. 401–408.

34. Ibid., p. 439.

35. James B. Jacobs, ed., *New Perspectives on Prisons and Imprisonment* (Ithaca, NY: Cornell University Press, 1983); James B. Jacobs, "Street Gangs Behind Bars," *Social Problems* 21 (1974): 395–409; James B. Jacobs, "Race Relations and the Prison Subculture," in *Crime and Justice*, vol. 1, ed. Norval Morris and Michael Tonry (Chicago: University of Chicago Press, 1979), pp. 1–28.

36. Matt DeLisi, Chad Trulson, James Marquart, Alan Drury, and Anna Kosloski, "Inside the Prison Black Box: Toward a Life Course Importation Model of Inmate Behavior," *International Journal of Offender Therapy and Comparative Criminology* 55 (2011): 1186–1207.

37. Nicole Hahn Rafter, *Partial Justice* (New Brunswick, NJ: Transaction Books, 1990), pp. 181–182.

38. Kathryn Watterson and Meda Chesney-Lind, *Women in Prison: Inside the Concrete Womb* (Boston: Northeastern University Press, 1996).

39. Merry Morash, Robin Harr, and Lila Rucker, "A Comparison of Programming for Women and Men in US Prisons in the 1980s," *Crime and Delinquency* 40 (1994): 197–221.

40. Pamela Schram, "Stereotypes about Vocational Programming for Female Inmates," *Prison Journal* 78 (1998): 244–271.

41. Morash, Harr, and Rucker, "A Comparison of Programming for Women and Men in US Prisons in the 1980s."

42. Vernetta Young and Rebecca Reviere, *Women Behind Bars: Gender and Race in US Prisons* (Boulder, CO: Lynne Rienner Publishers, 2006).

43. Margaret Leigey and Katie Reed, "A Woman's Life before Serving Life: Examining the Negative Preincarceration Life Events of Female Life-Sentenced Inmates," *Women and Criminal Justice* 20 (2010): 302–322.

44. Lauren Sharkey, "Does Overcrowding in Prisons Exacerbate the Risk of Suicide among Women Prisoners?" *Howard Journal of Criminal Justice* 49 (2010): 111–124.

45. Amanda Noblet, "Women in Prison: A Review of the Current Female Prison System: Future Directions and Alternatives," *Internet Journal of Criminology 2008,* http://www.internetjournalofcriminology.com (accessed March 2013).

46. Seena Fazel and John Danesh, "Serious Mental Disorder in 23,000 Prisoners: A Systematic Review of 62 Surveys," *Lancet* 359 (2002): 545–561.

47. Gary Michael McClelland, Linda Teplin, Karen Abram, and Naomi Jacobs, "HIV and AIDS Risk Behaviors among Female Jail Detainees: Implications for Public Health Policy," *American Journal of Public Health* 92 (2002): 818–826.

48. Breea Willingham, "Black Women's Prison Narratives and the Intersection of Race, Gender, and Sexuality in US Prisons," *Critical Survey* 23 (2011): 55–66.

49. Paula C. Johnson, *Inner Lives: Voices of African American Women in Prison* (New York: New York University Press, 2003), p. 203.

50. Christine Grella and Lisa Greenwell, "Correlates of Parental Status and Attitudes Toward Parenting among Substance-Abusing Women Offenders," *Prison Journal* 86 (2006): 89–113.

51. Lee Ann Slocum, Sally Simpson, and Douglas Smith, "Strained Lives and Crime: Examining Intra-Individual Variation in Strain and Offending in a Sample of Incarcerated Women," *Criminology* 43 (2005): 1067–1110.

52. Allen Beck, Marcus Berzofsky, Rachel Caspar, and Christopher Krebs, *Sexual Victimization in Prisons and Jails Reported by Inmates, 2011–12 Update* (Washington, DC: Bureau of Justice Statistics, 2014), http://www.bjs.gov/content/pub/pdf/svpjri1112.pdf (accessed April 2015).

53. Meda Chesney-Lind, "Vengeful Equity: Sentencing Women to Prison," in *The Female Offender: Girls, Women, and Crime,* ed. Meda Chesney-Lind and Lisa J. Pasko (Thousand Oaks, CA: Sage, 1997).

54. Rebecca Trammell, "Relational Violence in Women's Prison: How Women Describe Interpersonal Violence and Gender," *Women and Criminal Justice* 19 (2009): 267–285.

55. Candace Kruttschnitt and Sharon Krmpotich, "Aggressive Behavior among Female Inmates: An Exploratory Study," *Justice Quarterly* 7 (1990): 370–389.

56. Candace Kruttschnitt, Rosemary Gartner, and Amy Miller, "Doing Her Own Time? Women's Responses to Prison in the Context of the Old and New Penology," *Criminology* 38 (2000): 681–718.

57. Mark Pogrebin and Mary Dodge, "Women's Accounts of Their Prison Experiences: A Retrospective View of Their Subjective Realities," *Journal of Criminal Justice* 29 (2001): 531–541.

58. Shanhe Jiang and L. Thomas Winfree, Jr., "Social Support, Gender, and Inmate Adjustment to Prison Life," *Prison Journal* 86 (2006): 32–55.

59. Edna Erez, "The Myth of the New Female Offender: Some Evidence from Attitudes toward Law and Justice," *Journal of Criminal Justice* 16 (1988): 499–509.

60. Robert Ross and Hugh McKay, *Self-Mutilation* (Lexington, MA: Lexington Books, 1979).

61. Alyssa Whitby Chamberlain, "Offender Rehabilitation: Examining Changes in Inmate Treatment Characteristics, Program Participation, and Institutional Behavior," *Justice Quarterly* 29 (2012): 183–228.

62. Dianna Newbern, Donald Dansereau, and Urvashi Pitre, "Positive Effects on Life Skills Motivation and Self-Efficacy: Node-Link Maps in a Modified Therapeutic Community," *American Journal of Drug and Alcohol Abuse* 25 (1999): 407–410.

63. Rose Parkes and Charlotte Bilby, "The Courage to Create: The Role of Artistic and Spiritual Activities in Prisons," *Howard Journal of Criminal Justice* 49 (2010): 97–110.

64. Steven D. Vannoy and William T. Hoyt, "Evaluation of an Anger Therapy Intervention for Incarcerated Adult Males," *Journal of Offender Rehabilitation* 39 (2004): 40.

65. Retrieved from University of South Australia, School of Psychology, Social Work and Social Policy, http://www.unisa.edu.au (accessed March 2013).

66. Sesha Kethineni and Jeremy Braithwaite, "The Effects of a Cognitive-Behavioral Program for At-Risk Youth: Changes in Attitudes, Social Skills, Family, and Community and Peer Relationships," *Victims and Offenders* 6 (2011): 93–116; Patrick Clark, "Preventing Future Crime with Cognitive Behavioral Therapy," *National Institute of Justice Journal* 265 (2010), http://www.ojp.usdoj.gov/nij/journals/265/therapy.htm (accessed March 2013).

67. Mark Lipsey, Nana Landenberger, and Sandra Wilson, "Effects of Cognitive-Behavioral Programs for Criminal Offenders," *Campbell Systematic Reviews* (2007): 6, http://www.campbellcollaboration.org/lib/download/143/ (accessed March 2013).

68. Byron R. Johnson, "Religious Programming, Institutional Adjustment and Recidivism among Former Inmates in Prison Fellowship Programs," *Justice Quarterly* 21 (2004): 329–354.

69. Charles McDaniel, Derek Davis, and Sabrina Neff, "Charitable Choice and Prison Ministries: Constitutional and Institutional Challenges to Rehabilitating the American Penal System," *Criminal Justice Policy Review* 16 (2005): 164–189.

70. Lawrence T. Jablecki, "A Critique of Faith-Based Prison Programs," *The Humanist* 65 (2005): 11–16.

71. Ibid.

72. Corrections Corporation of America, "Inmate Programming with Corrections Corporation of America," http://cca.com/Media/Default/documents/CCA-Resource-Center/Inmate_Program_Overview.pdf (accessed July 2014).

73. Janeen Buck Willison, Diana Brazzell, and KiDeuk Kim, *Faith-Based Corrections and Reentry Programs: Advancing a Conceptual Framework for Research and Evaluation* (Washington, DC: Urban Institute, 2010), http://www.ncjrs.gov/pdffiles1/nij/grants/234058.pdf (accessed March 2013).

74. Dawn Daggett, Scott Camp, and Okyun Kwon, "Faith-Based Correctional Programming in Federal Prisons: Factors Affecting Program Completion," *Criminal Justice and Behavior* 35 (2008): 848–862.

75. Philip Magaletta, Pamela Diamond, Beth Weinman, Ashley Burnell, and Carl Leukefeld, "Preentry Substance Abuse Services: The Heterogeneity of Offender Experiences," *Crime and Delinquency,* 60 (2014): 193-215; *CASAColumbia,* "New CASA* Report Finds: 65% of All US Inmates Meet Medical Criteria for Substance Abuse Addiction, Only 11% Receive Any Treatment," February 26, 2010, http://www.casacolumbia.org/newsroom/press-releases/2010-behind-bars-II (accessed June 2015).

76. Federal Bureau of Prisons, *Substance Abuse Treatment*, http://www.bop.gov/inmates/custody_and_care/substance_abuse_treatment.jsp (accessed March 2015).

77. Kate Dolan, James Shearer, Bethany White, Zhou Jialun, John Kaldor, and Alex Wodak, "Four-Year Follow-up of Imprisoned Male Heroin Users and Methadone Treatment: Mortality, Re-Incarceration and Hepatitis C Infection," *Addiction* 100 (2005): 820–828.

78. Clayton Mosher and Dretha Phillips, "The Dynamics of a Prison-Based Therapeutic Community for Women Offenders: Retention, Completion, and Outcomes," *Prison Journal* 86 (2006): 6–31.

79. Sheldon X. Zhang, Robert E. L. Roberts, and Kathryn E. McCollister, "Therapeutic Community in a California Prison: Treatment Outcomes after 5 Years," *Crime and Delinquency* 57 (2011): 82–101; J. Mitchell Miller and Holly Ventura Miller, "Considering the Effectiveness of Drug Treatment Behind Bars: Findings from the South Carolina RSAT Evaluation," *Justice Quarterly* 28 (2011): 70–86.

80. Wayne Welsh, "A Multisite Evaluation of Prison-Based Therapeutic Community Drug Treatment," *Criminal Justice and Behavior* 34 (2007): 1481–1498.

81. Daniel Werb, Thomas Kerr, Will Small, Kathy Li, Julio Montaner, and Evan Wood, "HIV Risks Associated with Incarceration among Injection Drug Users: Implications for Prison-Based Public Health Strategies," *Journal of Public Health* 30 (2008): 126–132.

82. Karen Lahm, "Educational Participation and Inmate Misconduct," *Journal of Offender Rehabilitation* 48 (2009): 37–52.

83. Rosa Minhyo Cho and John H. Tyler, "Does Prison-Based Adult Basic Education Improve Postrelease Outcomes for Male Prisoners in Florida?" *Crime and Delinquency,* first published online November 30, 2010.

84. Bill Conlon, Scott Harris, Jeffrey Nagel, Mike Hillman, and Rick Hanson, "Education: Don't Leave Prison without It," *Corrections Today* 70 (2008): 48–52; David Wilson, Catherine Gallagher, and Doris MacKensie, "A Meta-Analysis of Corrections-Based Education, Vocation, and Work Programs for Adult Offenders," *Journal of Research in Crime and Delinquency* 37 (2000): 347–368.

85. Howard Skolnik and John Slansky, "A First Step in Helping Inmates Get Good Jobs after Release," *Corrections Today* 53 (1991): 92.

86. Federal Bureau of Prisons web page concerning UNICOR Federal Prison Industries, http://www.UNICOR.gov/Contracting.aspx (accessed May 2015).

87. Courtesy of the Prison Industry Authority, 560 East Natoma St., Folsom, CA, 95630–2200.

88. Douglas Lipton, Robert Martinson, and Judith Wilks, *The Effectiveness of Correctional Treatment: A Survey of Treatment Evaluation Studies* (New York: Praeger, 1975).

89. James Wilson and Robert Davis, "Good Intentions Meet Hard Realities: An Evaluation of the Project Greenlight Reentry Program," *Criminology and Public Policy* 5 (2006): 303–338.

90. Paula Smith, Paul Gendreau, and Kristin Swartz, "Validating the Principles of Effective Intervention: A Systematic Review of the Contributions of Meta-Analysis in the Field of Corrections," *Victims and Offenders* 4 (2009): 148–169.

91. Paul Gendreau and Robert Ross, "Effective Correctional Treatment: Bibliotherapy for Cynics," *Crime and Delinquency* 27 (1979): 463–489.

92. Mark W. Lipsey and Francis T. Cullen, "The Effectiveness of Correctional Rehabilitation: A Review of Systematic Reviews," *Annual Review of Law and Social Science* 3 (2007): 297–320.

93. Lucien X. Lombardo, *Guards Imprisoned* (New York: Elsevier, 1981); James Jacobs and Norma Crotty, "The Guard's World," in *New Perspectives on Prisons and Imprisonment,* ed. James Jacobs (Ithaca, NY: Cornell University Press, 1983), pp. 133–141.

94. Richard Tewksbury and Elizabeth Mustaine, "Correctional Orientations

95. Brie Williams, Marc Stern, Jeff Mellow, Meredith Safer, and Robert Greifinger, "Aging in Correctional Custody: Setting a Policy Agenda for Older Prisoner Health Care," *American Journal of Public Health* 102 (2012): 1475–1481.

96. Joseph Martin, Bronwen Lichtenstein, Robert Jenkot, and David Forde, "They Can Take Us Over Any Time They Want: Correctional Officers' Responses to Prison Crowding," *Prison Journal* 92 (2012): 88–105.

97. Eric Lambert, Nancy Hogan, Kelly Cheeseman Dial, Irshad Altheimer, and Shannon Barton-Bellessa, "Examining the Effects of Stressors on Organizational Citizenship Behaviors among Private Correctional Staff: A Preliminary Study," *Security Journal* 25 (2012): 152–172.

98. Eric Lambert, Nancy Hogan, and Irshad Altheimer, "An Exploratory Examination of the Consequences of Burnout in Terms of Life Satisfaction, Turnover Intent, and Absenteeism among Private Correctional Staff," *Prison Journal* 90 (2010): 94–114.

99. Stephen Owen, "Occupational Stress among Correctional Supervisors," *Prison Journal* 86 (2006): 164–181; Eugene Paoline, Eric Lambert, and Nancy Hogan, "A Calm and Happy Keeper of the Keys: The Impact of ACA Views, Relations with Coworkers, and Policy Views on the Job Stress and Job Satisfaction of Jail Staff," *Prison Journal* 86 (2006): 182–205.

100. Mike Vuolo and Candace Kruttschnitt, "Prisoners' Adjustment, Correctional Officers, and Context: The Foreground and Background of Punishment in Late Modernity," *Law and Society Review* 42 (2008): 307–335.

101. Dana Britton, *At Work in the Iron Cage: The Prison as Gendered Organization* (New York: New York University Press, 2003), ch. 6.

102. Associated Press, "One Dead, at Least 8 Injured during Prison Riot in Mississippi" May 20, 2012, http://www.foxnews.com/us/2012/05/20/one-dead-at-least-5-injured-during-prison-riot-in-mississippi/ (accessed March 2013).

103. David Duffee, *Corrections, Practice and Policy* (New York: Random House, 1989), p. 305.

104. Randy Martin and Sherwood Zimmerman, "A Typology of the Causes of Prison Riots and an Analytical Extension to the 1986 West Virginia Riot," *Justice Quarterly* 7 (1990): 711–737.

105. Benjamin Steiner, "Assessing Static and Dynamic Influences on Inmate Violence Levels," *Crime and Delinquency* 55 (2009): 134–161.

106. David Allender and Frank Marcell, "Career Criminals, Security Threat Groups, and Prison Gangs," *FBI Law Enforcement Bulletin* 72 (2003): 8–12.

107. Terri Compton and Mike Meacham, "Prison Gangs: Descriptions and Selected Intervention," *Forensic Examiner* 14 (2005): 26–31.

108. Jon Sorensen and Mark Cunningham, "Conviction Offense and Prison Violence: A Comparative Study of Murderers and Other Offenders," *Crime and Delinquency* 56 (2010): 103–125.

109. Steiner and Wooldredge, "Inmate versus Environmental Effects on Prison Rule Violations."

110. Kuanliang, Sorensen, and Cunningham, "Juvenile Inmates in an Adult Prison System: Rates of Disciplinary Misconduct and Violence."

111. Sorensen and Cunningham, "Conviction Offense and Prison Violence."

112. Grant Harris, Tracey Skilling, and Marnie Rice, "The Construct of Psychopathy," in *Crime and Justice: An Annual Edition,* ed. Michael Tonry (Chicago: University of Chicago Press, 2001), pp. 197–265.

113. For a series of papers on the position, see A. Cohen, G. Cole, and R. Baily, eds. *Prison Violence* (Lexington, MA: Lexington Books, 1976).

114. Lahm, "Inmate-on-Inmate Assault."

115. David M. Bierie, "Is Tougher Better? The Impact of Physical Prison Conditions on Inmate Violence," *International Journal of Offender Therapy and Comparative Criminology* 56 (2012): 338–355.

116. Scott Camp and Gerald Gaes, "Criminogenic Effects of the Prison Environment on Inmate Behavior: Some Experimental Evidence," *Crime and Delinquency* 51 (2005): 425–442.

117. Hans Toch, "Cumulative Default: The Cost of Disruptive Prison Careers," *Criminal Justice and Behavior* 35 (2008): 943–955.

118. Bert Useem and Michael Resig, "Collective Action in Prisons: Protests, Disturbances, and Riots," *Criminology* 37 (1999): 735–760.

119. Prison Litigation Reform Act P.L. 104-134, 110 Stat. 1321 (2006); 42 U.S.C. § 1997e (1994 ed. and Supp. II).

120. *Booth v. Churner,* US 731 (2001); *Porter v. Nussle,* 534 US 516 (2002).

121. ACLU, "Know Your Rights: The Prison Litigation Reform Act (PLRA)," http://www.aclu.org/images/asset_upload_file79_25805.pdf (accessed March 2013).

122. *Shaw v. Murphy* (99-1613), 2001.

123. *Cutter v. Wilkinson,* 544 US 709 (2005).

124. *Newman v. Alabama,* 92 S.Ct. 1079, 405 US 319 (1972).

125. *Estelle v. Gamble,* 429 US 97 (1976).

126. Ibid.

127. Lester Wright, "Health Care in Prison Thirty Years after *Estelle v. Gamble,*" *Journal of Correctional Health Care* 14 (2008): 31–35.

128. *Trop v. Dulles,* 356 US 86, 78 S.Ct. 590 (1958); see also *Furman v. Georgia,* 408 US 238, 92 S.Ct. 2726, 33 L.Ed.2d 346 (1972).

129. *Weems v. United States,* 217 US 349, 30 S.Ct. 544, 54 L.Ed. 793 (1910).

130. *Lee v. Tahash,* 352 F.2d 970 (8th Cir., 1965).

131. *Estelle v. Gamble,* 429 US 97 (1976).

132. *Robinson v. California,* 370 US 660 (1962).

133. *Gregg v. Georgia,* 428 US 153 (1976).

134. *Jackson v. Bishop,* 404 F.2d 571 (8th Cir. 1968).

135. *Johnson v. California,* 543 US 499 (2005).

136. *Bell v. Wolfish,* 99 S.Ct. 1873–1974 (1979); see "*Bell v. Wolfish:* The Rights of Pretrial Detainees," *New England Journal of Prison Law* 6 (1979): 134.

137. *Farmer v. Brennan,* 144 S.Ct. 1970 (1994).

138. *Rhodes v. Chapman,* 452 US 337 (1981); for further analysis of *Rhodes,* see Randall Pooler, "Prison Overcrowding and the Eighth Amendment: The Rhodes Not Taken," *New England Journal on Criminal and Civil Confinement* 8 (1983): 1–28.

139. Kristin Preston, "Right Place, Right Time: GPS Monitoring in Pinellas County," *Geography and Public Safety* 2 (2009): 3–5, http://nij.gov/topics/technology/maps/Documents/gps-bulletin-v2i1.pdf (accessed May 2015).

140. Joel Caplan and Susan Kinnevy, "National Surveys of State Paroling Authorities: Models of Service," *Federal Probation* 74 (2010): 34–42.

141. Thomas Bonczar and Erinn Herberman, *Probation and Parole in the United States, 2013,* Bureau of Justice

Statistics, 2014, http://www.bjs.gov /content/pub/ascii/ppus13.txt (accessed June 2015).

142. *Swarthout v. Cooke* and *Cate v. Clay* 562 US_(2011).

143. Alexia, Cooper, Matthew Durose, and Howard Snyder, *Recidivism of Prisoners Released in 30 States in 2005: Patterns from 2005 to 2010* (Washington, DC: Bureau of Justice Statistics, 2014), http://www.bjs.gov /index.cfm?ty=pbdetail&iid=4986 (accessed April 2015).

144. Pew Center on the States, *State of Recidivism: The Revolving Door of America's Prisons* (Washington, DC: Pew Charitable Trusts, April 2011), http://www.pewtrusts.org/en /research-and-analysis/reports /2011/04/12/state-of-recidivism -the-revolving-door-of-americas -prisons (accessed May 2015).

145. Benjamin Steiner, Lawrence Travis, Matthew Makarios, and Taylor Brickley, "The Influence of Parole Officers' Attitudes on Supervision Practices," *Justice Quarterly* 28 (2011): 903–927.

146. Jospeter Mbuba, "Lethal Rejection: Recounting Offenders' Experience in Prison and Societal Reaction Post Release," *Prison Journal* 92 (2012): 231–252.

147. Stephen Duguid, *Can Prisons Work? The Prisoner as Object and Subject in Modern Corrections* (Toronto: University of Toronto Press, 2000).

148. 148 Joan Petersilia, *When Prisoners Come Home: Parole and Prisoner Reentry* (New York: Oxford University Press, 2003); Joan Petersilia, "Hard Time Ex-Offenders Returning Home after Prison," *Corrections Today* 67 (2005): 66–72; Joan Petersilia, "When Prisoners Return to Communities: Political, Economic, and Social Consequences," *Federal Probation* 65 (2001): 3–9.

149. Michael Ostermann, "How Do Former Inmates Perform in the Community? A Survival Analysis of Rearrests, Reconvictions, and Technical Parole Violations," *Crime and Delinquency* 61 (2015): 163–187.

150. Michael Ostermann, "Parole? Nope, Not for Me: Voluntarily Maxing Out of Prison," *Crime & Delinquency* 57 (2011): 686–708.

151. Megan Kurlychek, Andrew Wheeler, Leigh Tinik, and Cynthia Kempinen, "How Long After? A Natural Experiment Assessing the Length of Aftercare Service Delivery on Recidivism," *Crime and Delinquency* 57 (2011): *778–800.*

152. Metraux and Culhane, "Recent Incarceration History among a Sheltered Homeless Population."

153. Beth Huebner and Mark Berg, "Examining the Sources of Variation in Risk for Recidivism," *Justice Quarterly* 28 (2011): 146–173; Beth Huebner, Christina DeJong, and Jennifer Cobbina, "Women Coming Home: Long-Term Patterns of Recidivism," *Justice Quarterly* 27 (2010): 225–254.

154. Catherine Hamilton, Louise Falshaw, and Kevin D. Browne, "The Link between Recurrent Maltreatment and Offending Behavior," *International Journal of Offender Therapy and Comparative Criminology* 46 (2002): 75–95.

155. Brent Benda, "Gender Differences in Life-Course Theory of Recidivism: A Survival Analysis," *International Journal of Offender Therapy and Comparative Criminology* 49 (2005): 325–342.

156. Mbuba, "Lethal Rejection: Recounting Offenders' Experience in Prison and Societal Reaction Post Release."

157. Petersilia, "Hard Time Ex-Offenders Returning Home after Prison."

158. Paul Hirschfield and Alex Piquero, "Normalization and Legitimation: Modeling Stigmatizing Attitudes toward Ex-Offenders," *Criminology* 48 (2010): 27–55.

159. Mark Berg and Beth Huebner, "Reentry and the Ties that Bind: An Examination of Social Ties, Employment, and Recidivism," *Justice Quarterly* 28 (2011): 382–410; Andy Hochstetler, Matt DeLisi, and Travis C. Pratt, "Social Support and Feelings of Hostility among Released Inmates," *Crime and Delinquency* 56 (2010): 588–607.

160. National Drug Strategy Network, "HUD Announces 'One Strike' Rules for Public Housing Tenants," May 1996, http://www.ndsn.org/may96 /onestrik.html (accessed March 2013).

161. Pew Charitable Trusts, *Collateral Costs: Incarceration's Effect on Economic Mobility* (Washington, DC: Pew Charitable Trusts, 2010), http:// www.pewtrusts.org/~/media/legacy /uploadedfiles/pcs_assets/2010 /CollateralCosts1pdf.pdf (accessed May 2015).

162. Richard Seiter, "Prisoner Reentry and the Role of Parole Officers," *Federal Probation* 66 (2002): 50–54.

163. Charis Kubrin and Eric Stewart, "Predicting Who Reoffends: The Neglected Role of Neighborhood Context in Recidivism Studies," *Criminology* 44 (2006): 165–197.

164. Ryken Grattet, Joan Petersilia, and Jeffery Lin, *Parole Violations and Revocations in California* (Washington, DC: National Institute of Justice, 2008).

165. John Hipp, Joan Petersilia, and Susan Turner, "Parolee Recidivism in California: The Effect of Neighborhood Context and Social Service Agency Characteristics," *Criminology* 48 (2010): 947–979.

166. Jeremy Travis, Anna Crayton, and Debbie Mukamal, "A New Era in Inmate Reentry," *Corrections Today* 71 (2009): 38–41.

167. Thomas Hanlon, David Nurco, Richard Bateman, and Kevin O'Grady, "The Response of Drug Abuser Parolees to a Combination of Treatment and Intensive Supervision," *Prison Journal,* 78 (1998): 31–44.

168. Kathleen Olivares, Velmer Burton, and Francis Cullen, "The Collateral Consequences of a Felony Conviction: A National Study of State Legal Codes Ten Years Later," *Federal Probation* 60 (1996): 10–17.

169. Dora Schriro, "Getting Ready: How Arizona Has Created a 'Parallel Universe' for Inmates," *NIJ Journal* 263 (2009), http://www.nij.gov/nij /journals/263/getting-ready.htm (accessed March 2013).

170. Stacy Adams, "Richmond Program Helps Former Female Inmates," *Crisis* 113 (2006): 8.

171. Anthony Braga, Anne Piehl, and David Hureau, "Controlling Violent Offenders Released to the Community: An Evaluation of the Boston Reentry Initiative," *Journal of Research in Crime and Delinquency* 46 (2009): 411–436.

172. Caitlin Taylor, "Tolerance of Minor Setbacks in a Challenging Reentry Experience: An Evaluation of a Federal Reentry Court," *Criminal Justice Policy Review* 24 (2013): 49–70.

Chapter 13, Juvenile Justice in the Twenty-First Century

1. Ed Lavandera, "What Was Motive to Kill the 'American Sniper'?", *Cnn.com*, http://www.cnn.com/2015/02/23/us

/eddie-ray-routh-american-sniper-motive/ (accessed February 2015).

2. Ibid.

3. Ibid.

4. Tasha Tsiaperas, "Defense Rests in Capital Murder Trial of Man Accused of Killing Navy SEAL Chris Kyle," *Dallas Morning News* (February 19, 2015), http://crimeblog.dallasnews.com/2015/02/defense-expected-to-call-mental-health-experts-today-as-american-sniper-murder-trial-continues.html/ (accessed February 2015).

5. BBC News, "Steven Miles Jailed for Murder of Girlfriend Elizabeth Thomas" (October 2, 2014), http://www.bbc.com/news/uk-england-29459516 (accessed February 2015).

6. Andy Campbell, "Teen Obsessed with 'Dexter' Given Life Sentence after Dismembering Girlfriend," *Huffington Post* (October 4, 2014), http://www.huffingtonpost.com/2014/10/04/steven-miles-elizabeth-thomas-dexter_n_5931474.html (accessed February 2015).

7. James Maynard, "'Dexter'-Obsessed Teen Stabs and Dismembers Girlfriend: 'Ed Made Me Do Something Bad'," *Tech Times* (October 5, 2014), http://www.techtimes.com/articles/17213/20141005/dexter-teen-stabs-dismembers-girlfriend-ed-made-something-bad.htm (accessed February 2015).

8. David S. Tanenhaus, *Juvenile Justice in the Making* (New York: Oxford University Press, 2004); Lawrence Stone, *The Family, Sex, and Marriage in England: 1500–1800* (New York: Harper & Row, 1977); Philippe Aries, *Century of Childhood: A Social History of Family Life* (New York: Vintage Press, 1962); Douglas R. Rendleman, "*Parens Patriae:* From Chancery to the Juvenile Court," *South Carolina Law Review* 23 (1971): 205–229; Anthony M. Platt, "The Rise of the Child-Saving Movement: A Study in Social Policy and Correctional Reform," *Annals of the American Academy of Political and Social Science* 381 (1979): 21–38; Robert S. Pickett, *House of Refuge: Origins of Juvenile Reform in New York State, 1815–1857* (Syracuse, NY: Syracuse University Press, 1969).

9. Anthony Platt, *The Child Savers: The Invention of Delinquency* (Chicago: University of Chicago Press, 1969), pp. 11–38.

10. See, generally, Anne Meis Knupfer, *Reform and Resistance: Gender, Delinquency, and America's First Juvenile Court* (London: Routledge, 2001).

11. This section is based on material from the New York State Archives, *The Greatest Reform School in the World: A Guide to the Records of the New York House of Refuge: A Brief History 1824–1857* (Albany: New York State Archives, 2001); Sanford J. Fox, "Juvenile Justice Reform: A Historical Perspective," *Stanford Law Review* 22 (1970): 1187.

12. Pickett, *House of Refuge.*

13. LaMar T. Empey, *American Delinquency: Its Meaning and Construction* (Homewood, IL: Dorsey Press, 1978), p. 515.

14. *Kent. v. United States,* 383 US 541 (1966).

15. *In re Gault,* 387 US 1 (1967).

16. *In re Winship,* 397 US 358 (1970).

17. *McKeiver v. Pennsylvania,* 403 US 528 (1971).

18. *Breed v. Jones,* 421 US 519 (1975).

19. *Fare v. Michael C.,* 442 US 707 (1979).

20. *Schall v. Martin,* 467 US 253 (1984).

21. *New Jersey v. T.L.O.,* 469 US 325 (1985).

22. *Vernonia School District v. Acton,* 515 US 646 (1995).

23. *Roper v. Simmons,* 543 US 551 (2005).

24. *Graham v. Florida,* 560 US ___ (2010).

25. *Miller v. Alabama,* 567 US ___ (2012).

26. Public Law 93-415 (1974).

27. For a comprehensive view of juvenile law, see, generally, Joseph J. Senna and Larry J. Siegel, *Juvenile Law: Cases and Comments,* 2nd ed. (St. Paul, MN: West, 1992).

28. Erika Gebo, "Do Family Courts Administer Individualized Justice in Delinquency Cases?" *Criminal Justice Policy Review* 16 (2005): 190–210.

29. Federal Bureau of Investigation, *Crime in the United States, 2013,* http://www.fbi.gov/about-us/cjis/ucr/crime-in-the-u.s/2013/crime-in-the-u.s.-2013/tables/table-32/table_32_ten_year_arrest_trends_totals_2013.xls (accessed February 2015).

30. Richard J. Lundman, "Routine Police Arrest Practices," *Social Problems* 22 (1974): 127–141; Robert E. Worden and Stephanie M. Myers, *Police Encounters with Juvenile Suspects* (Albany: Handling Criminal Justice Research Center and School of Criminal Justice, State University of New York, 2001).

31. *Fare v. Michael C.,* 442 US 707 (1979).

32. Ana Abates, Norman Hoffmann, and Ronald Anton, "Prevalence of Co-Occurring Disorders among Juveniles Committed to Detention Centers," *International Journal of Offender Therapy and Comparative Criminology* 49 (2005): 179–194.

33. Nancy Rodriquez, "Juvenile Court Context and Detention Decisions: Reconsidering the Role of Race, Ethnicity, and Community Characteristics in Juvenile Court Processes," *Justice Quarterly* 24 (2007): 629–656.

34. Barry Holman and Jason Seidenberg, *The Dangers of Detention: the Impact of Incarcerating Youth in Detention and Other Secure Facilities* (Washington, DC: Justice Policy Institute, 2006), http://www.justicepolicy.org/images/upload/06-11_rep_dangersofdetention_jj.pdf (accessed February 2015).

35. *Schell v. Martin,* 467 US 253 (1984).

36. See Juvenile Justice and Delinquency Prevention Act of 1974, 42 U.S.C., sec. 5633.

37. Catherine Van Dijk, An Nuytiens, and Christian Eliaerts, "The Referral of Juvenile Offenders to the Adult Court in Belgium: Theory and Practice," *Howard Journal of Criminal Justice* 44 (2005): 151–166.

38. *Kent v. United States,* 383 US 541 (1966).

39. *Breed v. Jones,* 421 US 519 (1975).

40. John Burrow, "Reverse Waiver and the Effects of Legal, Statutory, and Secondary Legal Factors on Sentencing Outcomes for Juvenile Offenders," *Crime and Delinquency* 54 (2008): 34–64.

41. Alan Karpelowitz, *State Legislative Priorities—1995* (Denver, CO: National Conference of State Legislatures, 1995), p. 10.

42. Sarah Hockenberry and Charles Puzzanchera, *Delinquency Cases in Juvenile Court, 2011* (Washington, DC: Office of Juvenile Justice and Delinquency Prevention, 2014), http://www.ojjdp.gov/pubs/248409.pdf (accessed February 2015).

43. Howard N. Snyder, Melissa Sickmund, and Eileen Poe-Yamagata, *Juvenile Transfers to Criminal Court in the 1990s: Lessons Learned from Four Studies* (Washington, DC: Office of Juvenile Justice and Delinquency Prevention, 2000).

44. James Austin, Kelly Dedel Johnson, and Maria Gregoriou, *Juveniles in Adult Prisons and Jails* (Washington, DC: Bureau of Justice Assistance, 2000).

45. Aaron Kupchik, "The Correctional Experiences of Youth in Adult and

Juvenile Prisons," *Justice Quarterly* 24 (2007): 247–270.

46. Benjamin Steiner and Emily Wright, "Assessing the Relative Effects of State Direct File Waiver Laws on Violent Juvenile Crime: Deterrence or Irrelevance?" *Journal of Criminal Law and Criminology* 96 (2006): 1451–1477.

47. Benjamin Steiner, "The Effects of Juvenile Transfer to Criminal Court on Incarceration Decisions," *Justice Quarterly* 26 (2009): 77–106; Megan Kurlychek and Brian Johnson, "The Juvenile Penalty: A Comparison of Juvenile and Young Adult Sentencing Outcomes in Criminal Court," *Criminology* 42 (2004): 485–517.

48. Barry Feld, "The Juvenile Court Meets the Principle of the Offense: Legislative Changes in Juvenile Waiver Statutes," *Journal of Criminal Law and Criminology* 78 (1987): 471–533. See also John Kramer, Henry Sontheimer, and John Lemmon, "Pennsylvania Waiver to Adult Court," paper presented at the annual meeting of the American Society of Criminology, San Francisco, November 1991; authors confirm that juveniles tried in adult courts are generally male, age 17 or older, and disproportionately minorities.

49. Jeffrey Fagan, Martin Forst, and T. Scott Vivona, "Racial Determinants of the Judicial Transfer Decision: Prosecuting Violent Youth in Criminal Court," *Crime and Delinquency* 33 (1987): 359–386; J. Fagan, E. Slaughter, and E. Hartstone, "Blind Justice: The Impact of Race on the Juvenile Justice Process," *Crime and Delinquency* 53 (1987): 224–258; J. Fagan and E. P. Deschenes, "Determinants of Judicial Waiver Decisions for Violent Juvenile Offenders," *Journal of Criminal Law and Criminology* 81 (1990): 314–347; see also James Howell, "Juvenile Transfers to Criminal Court," *Juvenile and Family Justice Journal* 6 (1997): 12–14.

50. Charles Puzzanchera and Sean Addit, *Delinquency Cases Waived to Criminal Court, 2010* (Washington, DC: Office of Juvenile Justice and Delinquency Prevention, 2014), http://www.ojjdp.gov/pubs/243042.pdf (accessed February 2015).

51. *In re Gault*, 387 US 1 (1967).

52. Melissa Sickmund and Charles Puzzanchera, *Juvenile Offenders and Victims: 2014 National Report* (Washington, DC: National Center for Juvenile Justice, 2014), p. 96.

53. Ibid.

54. See Joseph Goldstein, Anna Freud, and Albert Solnit, *Beyond the Best Interest of the Child* (New York: Free Press, 1973).

55. See Michael Serrill, "Police Write a New Law on Juvenile Crime," *Police Magazine* (September 1979): 47; see also A. Schneider and D. Schram, *Assessment of Juvenile Justice Reform in Washington State*, vols. 1–4 (Washington, DC: Department of Justice, Institute of Policy Analysis, 1983); T. Castellano, "Justice Model in the Juvenile Justice System—Washington State's Experience," *Law and Policy* 8 (1986): 479.

56. Emily Gaarder, Nancy Rodriguez, and Marjorie Zatz, "Criers, Liars, and Manipulators: Probation Officers' Views of Girls," *Justice Quarterly* 21 (2004): 547–578.

57. Office of Juvenile Justice and Delinquency Prevention, *Juveniles in Corrections*, http://www.ojjdp.gov/ojstatbb/corrections/qa08201.asp?qa-Date=2003 (accessed February 2015).

58. David Smith, "The Effectiveness of the Juvenile Justice System," *Criminal Justice: International Journal of Policy and Practice* 5 (2005): 181–195.

59. Barry C. Feld, *Bad Kids: Race and the Transformation of the Juvenile Court* (New York: Oxford University Press, 1999).

60. Alexes Harris, "Diverting and Abdicating Judicial Discretion: Cultural, Political, and Procedural Dynamics in California Juvenile Justice," *Law and Society Review* 41 (2007): 387–428.

61. John Johnson Kerbs, "(Un)equal Justice: Juvenile Court Abolition and African Americans," *Annals, AAPSS*, 564 (1999): 109–125.

62. Howard N. Snyder and Melissa Sickmund, *Juvenile Offenders and Victims: 2006 National Report* (Washington, DC: Office of Juvenile Justice and Delinquency Prevention, 2006), http://www.ojjdp.gov/ojstatbb/nr2006/downloads/NR2006.pdf (accessed February 2015).

63. Ibid.

64. National Council on Crime and Delinquency, *And Justice for Some: Differential Treatment of Minority Youth in the Justice System,* January 2007, http://www.nccdglobal.org/sites/default/files/publication_pdf/justice-for-some.pdf (accessed February 2015).

65. J. David Hawkins, Richard F. Catalano, and Associates, *Communities That Care: Action for Drug Abuse Prevention* (San Francisco: Jossey-Bass, 1992).

66. Richard F. Catalano, Michael W. Arthur, J. David Hawkins, Lisa Berglund, and Jeffrey J. Olson, "Comprehensive Community-and School-Based Interventions to Prevent Antisocial Behavior," in *Serious and Violent Juvenile Offenders: Risk Factors and Successful Interventions,* eds. Rolf Loeber and David P. Farrington (Thousand Oaks, CA: Sage, 1998).

Chapter 14, Crime and Justice in the New Millennium

1. FBI, "A Ponzi Scheme Collapses Financial Crime Ring Uncovered, Criminals Brought to Justice" (February 23, 2015), http://www.fbi.gov/news/stories/2015/february/a-ponzi-scheme-collapses/a-ponzi-scheme-collapses (accessed April 2015).

2. Nikos Passas and David Nelken, "The Thin Line between Legitimate and Criminal Enterprises: Subsidy Frauds in the European Community," *Crime, Law, and Social Change* 19 (1993): 223–243.

3. For a thorough review, see David Friedrichs, *Trusted Criminals* (Belmont, CA: Wadsworth, 1996).

4. Institute for Economics and Peace (IEP) Global Terrorism Index, 2014, http://www.visionofhumanity.org/sites/default/files/Global%20Terrorism%20Index%20Report%202014_0.pdf (accessed April 2015).

5. Title 22 of the U.S. Code section 2656f (d) (1999).

6. Paul Wilkinson, *Terrorism and the Liberal State* (New York: Wiley, 1977), p. 49.

7. Jack Gibbs, "Conceptualization of Terrorism," *American Sociological Review* 54 (1989): 329–340, at 330.

8. CNN, "Wisconsin Sikh Temple Shooting," http://www.cnn.com/specials/us/sikh-temple-shooting/index.html (accessed May 2015).

9. Clark McCauley and Sophia Moskalenko, "Two Possible Profiles of Lone-Actor Terrorists," National Consortium for the Study of Terrorism and Responses to Terrorism (START), 2013, http://www.start.umd.edu/publication/two-possible-profiles-lone-actor-terrorists (accessed May, 2015) .

10. Lawrence Miller, "The Terrorist Mind: A Psychological and Political Analysis, Part I," *International Journal of Offender Therapy and Comparative Criminology* 50 (2006): 121–138.

11. Gabriela Fried, "Piecing Memories Together after State Terror and Policies of Oblivion in Uruguay: The Female Political Prisoner's Testimonial Project (1997–2004)," *Social Identities* 12 (2006): 543–562.

12. Martin Miller, "Ordinary Terrorism in Historical Perspective," *Journal for the Study of Radicalism* 2 (2008): 125–154.

13. Stevan Weine, Chloe Polutnik, and Ahmed Younis, "The Role of Community Policing in Countering Violent Extremism," National Consortium for the Study of Terrorism and Responses to Terrorism (START) (February 2015), http://www.start.umd.edu /pubs/STARTResearchBrief _CommunityPolicing_Feb2015.pdf (accessed April 2015).

14. Jeremy Diamond, "NSA Surveillance Bill Passes after Weeks-Long Showdown," CNN (June 2, 2015), http:// www.cnn.com/2015/06/02/politics /senate-usa-freedom-act-vote-patriot -act-nsa/ (aaccessed June 2015).

15. H.R. 3361 – USA FREEDOM Act, 113th Congress (2013–2014), https:// www.congress.gov/bill/113th-congress /house-bill/3361 (accessed June 2015).

16. *Boumediene v. Bush,* 553 US 723 (2008).

17. FBI, "Ponzi Scheme Indictments: Five Charged in $7 Billion Ploy" (June 19, 2009), http://www.fbi.gov/news /stories/2009/june/stanford_061909 (accessed May 2015).

18. FBI, "2009 Financial Crimes Report," http://www.fbi.gov/stats-services /publications/financial-crimes-report -2009 (accessed March 2013).

19. Ibid.

20. Securities and Exchange Commission, "SEC Charges Bernard L. Madoff for Multi-Billion Dollar Ponzi Scheme" (December 11, 2008), http://www.sec .gov/news/press/2008/2008-293.htm (accessed March 2013); Joe Lauria, "Life Inside the Weird World of Bernard Madoff," *The Times* (March 22, 2009), http://www.thesundaytimes .co.uk/sto/business/article157099.ece (accessed May 2015).

21. Securities and Exchange Commission, "SEC Charges Bernard L. Madoff for Multi-Billion Dollar Ponzi Scheme"; Report of Investigation, US Securities and Exchange Commission Office of Inspector General, Case No. OIG-509, *Investigation of Failure of the SEC to Uncover Bernard Madoff's Ponzi Scheme,* https://www.sec.gov/news/studies/2009 /oig-509.pdf (accessed May 2015).

22. Sean Rosenmerkel, "Wrongfulness and Harmfulness as Components of Seriousness of White-Collar Offenses," *Journal of Contemporary Criminal Justice* 17 (2001): 308–328.

23. Jonathan Lechter, Daniel Posner, and George Morris, "Antitrust Violations," *American Criminal Law Review* 39 (2002): 225–273.

24. Mark Cohen, "Environmental Crime and Punishment: Legal/ Economic Theory and Empirical Evidence on Enforcement of Federal Environmental Statutes," *Journal of Criminal Law and Criminology* 82 (1992): 1054–1109.

25. Miami-Dade Mortgage Fraud Task Force, http://www.nij.gov/topics /crime/foreclosure-crime-meeting /documents/miami-dade-task-force .pdf (accessed March 2015).

26. Thomas Catan and Guy Chazan, "Spill Draws Criminal Probe," *Wall Street Journal* (June 2, 2010), http://www .wsj.com/articles/SB100014240527 48704875604575280983140254458 (accessed May 2015); Environmental Protection Agency press release, "Exxon to Pay Record One Billion Dollars in Criminal Fines and Civil Damages in Connection with Alaskan Oil Spill" (March 13, 1991), http://www2.epa .gov/aboutepa/exxon-pay-record-one -billion-dollars-criminal-fines-and -civil-damages-connection-alaskan (accessed May 2015); Tyson Slocum, "BP: The Worst Safety and Environmental Record of All Oil Companies Operating in the United States," *Monthly Review* (June 5, 2010), http:// mrzine.monthlyreview.org/2010 /slocum060510.html (accessed March 2013).

27. Helene Cooper and Peter Baker, "US Opens Criminal Inquiry into Oil Spill," *New York Times* (June 1, 2010), http:// www.nytimes.com/2010/06/02/us /02spill.html (accessed March 2013).

28. Department of Justice, "Transocean Agrees to Plead Guilty to Environmental Crime and Enter Civil Settlement to Resolve US Clean Water Act Penalty Claims from Deepwater Horizon Incident, Transocean to Pay Record $1 Billion in Civil Penalties and $400 Million in Criminal Fines" (January 3, 2012), http://www.fbi.gov /neworleans/press-releases/2013 /transocean-agrees-to-plead-guilty -to-environmental-crime-and-enter -civil-settlement-to-resolve-u.s. -clean-water-act-penalty-claims

-from-deepwater-horizon-incident (accessed March 2013).

29. Michael J. Lynch and Paul Stretesky, "Green Criminology in the United States," in *Issues in Green Criminology,* eds. Piers Beirne and Nigel South (Portland, OR: Willan, 2008), pp. 248–269, at 249.

30. Michael O'Hear, "Sentencing the Green-Collar Offender: Punishment, Culpability, and Environmental Crime," *Journal of Criminal Law and Criminology* 95 (2004): 133–276.

31. This section relies on Duncan Brack, *Illegal Logging* (London: Chatham House, 2007), http://www.illegal-logging .info/uploads/1_Illegal_logging_bp _07_01.pdf (accessed March 2013).

32. Ibid.

33. World Wide Fund for Nature, "Fishing Problems: Pirate Fishing," http:// wwf.panda.org/about_our_earth /blue_planet/problems/problems _fishing/fisheries_management /illegal_fishing/ (accessed March 2013).

34. Andrew Oliveira, Christopher Schenck, Christopher Cole, and Nicole Janes, "Environmental Crimes (Annual Survey of White-Collar Crime)," *American Criminal Law Review* 42 (2005): 347–380.

35. Environmental Protection Agency, Criminal Enforcement Division, http://www2.epa.gov/enforcement /criminal-enforcement (accessed May 2015).

36. Statement of Michael A. Vatis, director, National Infrastructure Protection Center, Federal Bureau of Investigation, on cyber crime before the Senate Judiciary Committee, Criminal Justice Oversight Subcommittee, and House Judiciary Committee, Crime Subcommittee, February 29, 2000.

37. Data provided from Vogon International, March 2013, http://www .vogon-investigation.com (accessed April 2013).

38. Michael Arrington, "Internet Porn Stats," Techcrunch, http://www .techcrunch.com/2007/05/12/internet -pornography-stats/ (accessed March 2013).

39. Ben Fritz, "Tough Times in the Porn Industry," *Los Angeles Times* (August 10, 2009), http://www.latimes .com/news/local/la-fi-ct-porn10 -2009aug10,0,3356050.story (accessed March 2013).

40. This section relies heavily on CERT® Coordination Center Denial of Service Attacks, http://www.cert.org

/tech_tips/denial_of_service.html (accessed March 2013).

41. These sections rely on "Phishing Activity Trends Report 2nd Quarter, 2014," Anti-Phishing Working Group, http://docs.apwg.org/reports/apwg _trends_report_q2_2014.pdf (accessed May 2015).

42. Identity Theft Resource Center (ITRC), "Scams and Consumer Alerts," http://www.idtheftcenter.org (accessed March 2015).

43. National Center on Addiction and Substance Abuse at Columbia University, "'You've Got Drugs!' V: Prescription Drug Pushers on the Internet" (May 2008), http://www.casacolumbia.org /addiction-research/reports/youve -got-drugs-perscription-drug-pushers -internet-2008 (accessed May 2015).

44. Anne Branscomb, "Rogue Computer Programs and Computer Rogues: Tailoring Punishment to Fit the Crime," *Rutgers Computer and Technology Law Journal* 16 (1990): 24–26.

45. Heather Jacobson and Rebecca Green, "Computer Crimes," *American Criminal Law Review* 39 (2002): 272–326.

46. National Conference of State Legislatures, "State Cyberstalking and Cyberharassment Laws" (January 2013), http://www.ncsl.org/issues -research/telecom/cyberstalking-and -cyberharassment-laws.aspx (accessed March 2013).

47. Janis Wolak, David Finkelhor, Kimberly Mitchell, and Michele Ybarra, "Online 'Predators' and Their Victims: Myths, Realities, and Implications for Prevention and Treatment," *American Psychologist* 63 (2008): 111–128.

48. This section leans heavily on Justin Patchin and Sameer Hinduja, "Bullies Move beyond the Schoolyard: A Preliminary Look at Cyberbullying," *Youth Violence and Juvenile Justice* 4 (2006): 148–169.

49. Ibid.

50. Mark Pollitt, "Cyberterrorism—Fact or Fancy?" FBI Laboratory, http:// www.sciencedirect.com/science /article/pii/S1361372300870098 (accessed March 2015).

51. Barry C. Collin, "The Future of CyberTerrorism: Where the Physical and Virtual Worlds Converge," http:// www.crime-research.org/library /Cyberter.htm (accessed May 2015).

52. James Lewis, "Assessing the Risks of Cyberterrorism, Cyber War, and Other Cyber Threats," report submitted to the Center for Strategic and International Studies (CSIS), Washington, DC, 2002, p. 1.

53. William J. Broad, John Markoff, and David E. Sanger, "Israeli Test on Worm Called Crucial in Iran Nuclear Delay," *New York Times* (January 15, 2011), http://www.nytimes.com/2011/01/16 / world/middleeast/16stuxnet.html (accessed March 2013).

54. Heather Jacobson and Rebecca Green, "Computer Crime," *American Criminal Law Review* 39 (2002): 273–326; Identity Theft and Assumption Act of 1998 (18 U.S.C. S 1028(a)(7)); Bruce Swartz, Deputy Assistant General, Criminal Division, "Justice Department Internet Fraud Testimony Before the House Energy and Commerce Committee, May 23, 2001"; Comprehensive Crime Control Act of 1984, PL 98-473, 2101-03, 98 Stat. 1837, 2190 (1984), adding 18 U.S.C. 1030 (1984); Counterfeit Active Device and Computer Fraud and Abuse Act Amended by PL 99-474, 100 Stat. 1213 (1986) codified at 18 U.S.C. 1030 (Supp. V 1987); Computer Abuse Amendments Act 18 U.S.C. section 1030 (1994); Copyright Infringement Act 17 U.S.C. section 506(a) 1994; Electronic Communications Privacy Act of 1986, 18 U.S.C. 2510-2520 (1988 and Supp. II 1990).

55. Computer Fraud and Abuse Act (CFAA), 18 U.S.C. section 1030 (1998).

56. Digital Millennium Copyright Act, Public Law 105-304 (1998).

57. Title 18, U.S.C., section 2319.

58. Title 17, U.S.C., section 506.

59. Identity Theft and Assumption Deterrence Act, as amended by Public Law 105-318, 112 Stat. 3007 (October 30, 1998).

60. *Ashcroft v. Free Speech Coalition,* 535 US 234 (2002).

61. The Prosecutorial Remedies and Other Tools to End the Exploitation of Children, 18 U.S.C. 1466A (2003).

62. *United States v. Williams,* 553 US 285 (2008).

63. PL 98-473, Title H, Chapter XXI, [sections] 2102(a), 98 Stat. 1837, 2190 (1984).

64. Statement of Mr. Bob Weaver, Deputy Special Agent in Charge, New York Field Office, United States Secret Service, Before the House Financial Services Committee, the Subcommittee on Financial Institutions and Consumer Credit, and the Subcommittee on Oversight and Investigations, US House of Representatives, April 3, 2003.

65. Andrew Nikiforuk, *Pandemonium: How Globalization and Trade Are Putting the World at Risk* (Queensland, NZ: University of Queensland Press, 2007).

66. David Friedrichs and Jessica Friedrichs, "The World Bank and Crimes of Globalization: A Case Study," *Social Justice* 29 (2002): 13–36.

67. Louise Shelley, "The Globalization of Crime and Terrorism," State Department's Bureau of International Information Programs (IIP), 2006, http://iipdigital.usembassy.gov/st/ english/publication/2008/06 /20080608103639xjyrrep4.218692e-02 .html#axzz3bxC0ACt9 (accessed May 2015).

68. Public Law No. 95-213, 101-104, 91 Stat. 1494.

69. Thompson Reuters News and Insight, "Pfizer Settles Foreign Bribery Case with US Government," August 7, 2012, http://www.reuters.com/article /2012/08/07/us-pfizer-settlement -idUSBRE8760WM20120807 (accessed May 2015).

70. United Nations, "The Globalization of Crime," 2010, http://www.unodc .org/unodc/en/data-and-analysis /tocta-2010.html (accessed March 2013).

71. Ibid.

72. US Department of State, "Trafficking in Persons Report 2010," http://www .state.gov/g/tip/rls/tiprpt/2010/ (accessed March 2013).

73. Louise Shelley, "The Globalization of Crime and Terrorism."

74. FBI, Asian Criminal Enterprises, 2015, http://www.fbi.gov/about-us /investigate/organizedcrime/asian (accessed March 2015).

75. FBI, African Criminal Enterprises, 2015, http://www.fbi.gov/about-us /investigate/organizedcrime/african (accessed March 2015).

76. Louise I. Shelley, "Crime and Corruption: Enduring Problems of Post-Soviet Development," *Demokratizatsiya* 11 (2003): 110–114; James O. Finckenauer and Yuri A. Voronin, *The Threat of Russian Organized Crime* (Washington, DC: National Institute of Justice, 2001).

77. Omar Bartos, "Growth of Russian Organized Crime Poses Serious Threat," *CJ International* 11 (1995): 8–9.

78. Colleen Cook, "Mexico's Drug Cartels, Congressional Research Service,

2007," http://ftp.fas.org/sgp/crs/row/RL34215.pdf (accessed March 2013).

79. 18 U.S.C. 1952 (1976).

80. Public Law 91-452, Title IX, 84 Stat. 922 (1970) (codified at 18 U.S.C. 1961-68, 1976).

81. Ibid.

82. William Booth, "Mexican Azteca Gang Leader Arrested in Killings of 3 Tied to US," *Washington Post* (March 30, 2010), http://www.washingtonpost.com/wp-dyn/content/article/2010/03/29/ AR2010032903373.html (accessed March 2013).

83. Ryan Villarreal, "Alms for the Dead: Mexico Sets Up Fund for Victims of Drug War," *International Business Times* (January 10, 2013), http://www.ibtimes.com/alms-dead-mexico-sets-fund-victims-drug-war-1007258# (accessed March 2013).

84. Orlando Patterson, "The Other Losing War," *New York Times,* January 13, 2007.

85. Declan Walsh, "Afghan Province to Provide One-Third of World's Heroin," *The Guardian* (June 14, 2006), http://www.guardian.co.uk/world/2006/jun/14/afghanistan.drugstrade (accessed March 2013).

86. Office of National Drug Control Policy, https://www.whitehouse.gov/ondcp/ (accessed March 2013).

87. Francisco Gutierrez, "Institutionalizing Global Wars: State Transformations in Colombia, 1978-2002: Colombian Policy Directed at Its Wars, Paradoxically, Narrows the Government's Margin of Maneuver Even as It Tries to Expand It," *Journal of International Affairs* 57 (2003): 135–152.

CASE INDEX

NAME INDEX

A

Alex, Nicholas, 133
Alexander, Michelle, 266
Allard, Robert, 336
Allen, Bryant, 93
Almodovar, Andrew, 258
Alonzo, Cristina, 53
Andrade, Leandro, 218
Ardalan, Aman, 164
Arias, Jodi, 202
Atkinson, Peter, 39
Atta, Mohammed, 68
Augustus, John, 238–239

B

Bales, William, 255, 278–279
Banasco, Raul, 276
Barajas, Johnny, 159
Barzee, Wanda, 15
Baxter, Jerry, 173, 196
Beall, Jim, 336
Becker, Gary, 56
Becker, Howard, 54
Beidler, John X., 90
Belton, David, 219
Bessey, Paul C., 152
Bin Laden, Osama, 346
Black, Daniel, 253
Blackstone, William, 69
Bobbitt, John, 71
Bobbitt, Lorena, 71
Bogenberger, David, 251
Boland, Barbara, 170
Bosworth, Anthony, 31
Boyd, James, 85
Brace, Charles Loring, 325
Brady, George, 159
Braithwaite, John, 257
Bratton, William, 86, 106, 113–114
Breitel, Charles, 171
Breivik, Anders Behring, 347
Breyer, Stephen G., 317
Brinsley, Ismaaiyl, 86, 141
Brockway, Zebulon, 215, 271, 272
Brown, Michael, 4, 6, 86
Brown, Nicole, 62
Browne, Avery, 21
Bruning, John, 180
Bush, George W., 298
Bush, Jeb, 298
Bushway, Shawn, 222
Butler, Sara, 111

C

Caine, Rebecca, 39
Calderon, Emilio, 65
Carr, Benjamin, 18
Carter, David, 123
Castro, Jennifer, 279
Cates, Kimberly, 168
Chapman, Piper, 297
Charles I of England, 210
Christie, Chris, 191
Clark, Patrick, 245
Clarke, Judy, 156
Clements, Tom, 235
Clutts, Merle, 288
Cole, Evelyn, 280
Colquitt, Joseph, 191
Conrad, Miriam, 156
Coolidge, Calvin, 91
Cooper, Bradley, 321
Cooper, Mike, 111
Correia de Abreu, Daniel Jorge, 60
Cosby, William, 203
Cullen, Francis, 302
Cunningham, Mark, 305

D

Dart, Tom, 102
Davis, Jordan, 208, 214, 215, 220
de Blasio, Bill, 106
Dorety, Jennifer, 152
Dorn, Richard, 50
Drucker, Ernest, 266
Dunn, Michael, 208, 214, 215, 220
Durham, Alexis, 226
Duriez, Stephanie, 250
Dwight, Theodore, 271

E

Earp, Wyatt, 7
Ebel, Evan, 235
Elliott, Jim, 185
Ewing, Gary, 218

F

Feld, Barry, 340
Ferdaus, Rezwan, 156
Fielding, Henry, 89
Fielding, John, 89

Figlio, Robert, 43
Florence, Albert, 317
Furtado, Safiro Teixeira, 60

G

Gacy, John Wayne, 102
Garcia-Jauregui, Jose Angel, 334
Garner, Eric, 18, 86, 106, 130, 138, 145, 146
Garrett, Pat, 7
Gendreau, Paul, 302
Giffords, Gabrielle, 15, 156
Ginsburg, Ruth Bader, 317
Giudice, Giuseppe "Joe," 96
Giudice, Joe, 236
Giudice, Teresa, 236
Goldman, Ron, 62
Goodell, Roger, 46
Goodson, Caesar R., Jr., 188
Graham, Hannah, 28, 56
Gray, Freddie, 188
Greaves, Theresa Rose, 118
Grunwald, Meagan, 334
Guzman, Joaquin "El Chapo," 362

H

Hall, Milton, 113
Harrington, Morgan, 28
Hayes-Tavares, Shawnna, 196
Healey, Russell, 208
Henry II, King, 64, 268
Hernandez, Aaron, 15, 60, 62, 94
Hirschfield, Paul, 314
Hirschi, Travis, 54
Hodge, Darryl, 15
Holmes, James, 15, 70
Holt, Gregory, 308
Hoover, Herbert, 7
Howard, John, 212, 267
Howard, Scott, 291–292

I

Innes, Martin, 116

J

Jackall, Robert, 116
Jackson, Frank, 133

SUBJECT INDEX

green crime, 346, 352–355
Gross, Samuel, 226
ground-penetrating radar (GPR), 277
Guantánamo Bay camp, 350
guardians, 272
guilty plea, 189–190
Gulf cartel, 366
Gulf oil spill, 75, 352–353
gun control, 76–77
gun courts, 160
guns. *See* Firearms

H

habeas corpus, 203, 204, 350
halfway houses, 280–281
Halliburton, 352–353
Hamas, 348
hands-off doctrine, 273, 307
Harris County, Texas, 97
hearsay evidence, 196
heartbeat monitoring, 277
Heijin, 365
"Hierarchy Rule," 33
high-risk sex offenders, and GPS technology, 312
HIV/AIDS treatment, 300
Homeland Security agencies, 94–95
homicide rate, trends in, 36
homosexuality, 292–293
Hong Kong, 365
HOPE program, 249–250
Horton, Willie, 273
HotSpot probation, 248
hot spots of crime, 112, 122
house arrest, 254–255, 257
House of Reformation, 325
hue and cry, 88
hulks, 268
human trafficking, 363–364
Human Trafficking Prosecution Unit, 364
hundred, 88
hung jury, 203
Hyundai Heavy Industries, 352

L

IACP (International Association of Chiefs of Police), 91
ICE (U.S. Immigration and Customs Enforcement), 364
identity theft, 74, 358, 360
Identity Theft and Assumption Deterrence Act of 1998, 360
Identity Theft Penalty Enhancement Act, 360
ignorance, as a criminal defense, 69
illegal touting, 358
Illinois Juvenile Court Act, 326, 328
ILP (intelligence-led policing), 123–125, 124t
immigration, effect of on crime trends, 37
impartial judge, right to, 195
impartial jury, right to, 196–197
imposition by statute, 67
inadequacy of counsel, 176
incapacitation, 213–214
incarceration, long-term effects of, 38
income, and victim patterns, 45
indenture, 324, 325
indeterminate sentences, 215
India, 363
indictment, 187
indictment process and grand jury, 187
indirect-supervision jails, 275–276
individual violence, 305–306
informal justice, 10, 16
informal justice system, 190

informal process, 14–16, 192–193
information, 11
information process and preliminary hearing, 187–188
information sharing, 178
information technology (IT), 117–118, 277
information theft, 357
infractions, 66
initial appearance, 336
initial contact, 10
Initiative 502, 180
inmate-balance theory, 306
inmate populations, 282–283
inmate social code, 293–294
inmate subculture, 293
Innocence Inquiry Commission, 227
Innocence Project, 226
in-presence requirement, 10
insanity, as a criminal defense, 69, 70
Insanity Defense Reform Act, 71
insanity defense standards, 71
Institute for Social Research (ISR), 37
institutionalization, 339
institutional racism, 41, 133
instructions to the jury, 202
intake process, 243, 332
intelligence-led policing (ILP), 123–125, 124t
Intelligence Working Group, 124
intensive probation supervision (IPS), 254, 257
interactionist view of crime, 30–31
Interagency Council on Women, 364
Interagency Telemarketing and Internet Fraud Working Group, 361
intermediate sanctions
    definition of, 249
    electronic monitoring, 235, 255, 257
    fines, 251–252, 257
    forfeiture, 252, 257
    global positioning system, 23, 255–256, 312
    house arrest, 254–255, 257
    intensive probation supervision, 254, 257
    overview of, 257
    residential community corrections, 256–257
    restitution, 214–215, 253, 257
    shock probation, 253, 257
    split sentencing, 240, 253, 257
internal affairs, 126
internal corruption, 143
International Association of Chiefs of Police (IACP), 91
Internet, 39–40, 178. *See also* cyber crime
Internet pornography, 357, 360–361
Internet securities fraud, 357–358
Internet spam, 73
interrogations and searches, 147–151
Interstate and Foreign Travel or Transportation in Aid of Racketeering Enterprises Act (Travel Act), 366–367
intoxication, as a criminal defense, 70
investigation, 10
investigation function, 115–119
investigations
    evaluation of, 116–117
    forensic science, 118–119
    technology, 117–118
Investment Advisers Act of 1940, 351
involuntary intoxication, 70
IPS (intensive probation supervision), 254, 257
Iran, 359
irresistible impulse test, 71
Islamic State of Iraq and the Levant (ISIL), 346, 348
ISR (Institute for Social Research), 37
Israel, 348
IT (information technology), 117–118, 277

J

jailhouse lawyers, 308
jails
    conditions in, 275
    definition of, 266
    gender trends in, 274, 274t
    juveniles in, 334, 336
    new-generation jails, 275–276
    populations and trends, 274–275
    suicide, 275
Jao Pho, 365
Japan, 363
JJDP Act (Juvenile Justice and Delinquency Prevention Act of 1974), 327, 328, 333
J-Net, 178
job stress, 140–141
Johnson & Johnson, 362
Joint Terrorist Task Force, 98
judges. *See also* judiciary
    and the justice system, 166
    role of in plea bargaining, 193
    selection methods, 167f
Judicial Act of 1789, 162
judicial reprieve, 238
judicial support staff, 165
judicial waiver, 335
judiciary, 164–167
jurisdiction, waiver of, in juvenile court, 334–336
jury, instructions to, 202
jury array, 199
jury nullification, 203
jury selection, 199–200
jury staff, 165
jury trial, 164, 199f
just desert, 214, 266
Justice Department, 364
justice of the peace, 88, 161f
justice policy, effect of on crime trends, 38–39
Justice Policy Institute, 333
justification defenses, 69, 71–73
juvenile correctional process
    aftercare, 340
    deinstitutionalization, 339
    institutionalization, 339
    probation, 338–339
juvenile court
    bail, 334
    detention process, 329, 332–334
    establishment of, 326–328
    intake process, 332
    plea bargaining, 329, 334
    waiver of jurisdiction, 334–336
juvenile delinquency, 328
juvenile gangs, 331
juvenile justice
    adjudication, 336–338
    vs. adult justice system, 329–330
    case flow through, 330f
    contemporary state of, 328–330
    development of, 326–327
    disposition and treatment, 337–338
    history of, 324–326
    important decisions, 327
    introduction to, 322, 324
    juvenile correctional process, 338–340
    juvenile court, establishment of, 326–328
    juvenile court process, 332–336
    police processing of juvenile offenders, 331–332
    problems of, 340–342
    sentencing reform, 338
    shifting philosophies of, 328

Juvenile Justice and Delinquency Prevention Act
   of 1974 (JJDP Act), 327, 328, 333
juvenile offenders
      discretion, 329, 331–332
      parole, 340
      police processing of, 331–332
      race/ethnicity, 341
      Uniform Crime Reports on, 331

K

Kansas City Gun Experiment, 112
Kit Carson Correctional Center, 309
Knapp Commission, 143
krysha, 365

L

labor exploitation, 364
labor unions, 91
landmark decision, 163
larceny, in Uniform Crime Reports, 32
latent trait, 56
Latinos/Hispanics
      crime and victimization trends, 41
      in jail populations, 275
      juvenile offenders, 341
      new inmate culture, 294
      prison inmate, profile of, 284
law enforcement. *See also* police and policing
      as component of criminal justice system, 8, 9f
      corporate crime, 352
      ethics and, 22
Law Enforcement Assistance Administration
      (LEAA), 8, 92
Law Enforcement Education Program, 92
law enforcer style of policing, 137
LEAA (Law Enforcement Assistance
      Administration), 8, 92
lead exposure, 48
lease system, 272
legalization, 19, 75
legal services for the indigent, 174, 175
legal staff, 165
less-lethal weapons, 146–147
less than probable cause, 198
lex talionis, 63–64
liberty, vs. security, 23
license plate recognition (LPR), 101–102
life course theory, 56
lifestyle crimes, 112
logging, illegal, 353
London Metropolitan Police, 7, 123
loss prevention, 99
loss prevention specialists, 100
lower courts, 161f
"low-visibility decision making," 138
LPR (license plate recognition), 101–102

M

Magna Carta, 187
magnetic resonance imaging (MRI), 277
mail fraud, 73
make-believe family, 297
mala in se, 64
mala prohibitum, 64
malware, 359
management styles, 120
mandatory-minimum sentencing laws, 283
mandatory parole release approach, 310
mandatory sentence, 216–218
Manhattan Bail Project, 185

marijuana, legalization of, 75, 180
marital status, and victim patterns, 45
market manipulation, 357
Massachusetts, 238–239
Massachusetts State Constables, 95
mass incarceration, 266
mass shootings, 38
maximum-security prisons, 276, 278
meat eaters, 143
media
      effect of on crime trends, 38
      influence on violence, 51
      and public trials, 197
medical marijuana, 75
medical model, 273
medical rights, 308
medical technology, effect of on crime trends, 38
medium-security prisons, 279
Megan's Law, 74
"Memorandum on Steps to Combat Violence
      Against Women and the Trafficking of
      Women and Girls," 364
men and prison life, 290–294
mens rea, 67, 68, 70
mental health courts, 158, 159
mental illness. *See also* insanity, as a criminal
      defense; psychological theory
      and criminal behavior, 50
      pretrial programs, 186
      treatment availability and crime trends, 38
metropolitan law enforcement agencies, 97–98
metropolitan police, core functions of, 97
Metropolitan Police Act, 89
Mexican drug cartels, 362, 366, 367–368
military courts, 162f
minimum-security prisons, 279
minorities. *See* race/ethnicity
Miranda rule, 101, 148
Miranda warning, 148, 329, 332
misdemeanor arrests, 10
misdemeanors, 66–67, 189f, 196–197, 240
Missouri Plan, 167
mistake, as a criminal defense, 69
mistral sprays, 277
M'Naghten rule, 71
Mollen Commission, 144
monetary restitution, 253
Monitoring the Future (MTF) study, 37
Montana Vigilantes, 90
Montgomery County, Maryland, 97
moral correctness, and capital punishment, 225
moral entrepreneurs, 30
Mortgage Fraud Task Force, 352
Mosaic Code of the Israelites, 63
motivational interviewing, 244
motor vehicle theft, in Uniform Crime Reports, 32
MRI (magnetic resonance imaging), 277
MTF (Monitoring the Future) study, 37
municipal court, 161f
murder and nonnegligent manslaughter, in
      Uniform Crime Reports, 32
Mutual Welfare League, 272

N

NAACP Legal Defense Fund, 307
National Center on Institutions and Alternatives
      (NCIA), 275
National Commission on Law Observance and
      Enforcement, 7
National Congress of Penitentiary and
      Reformatory Discipline, 271
National Council on Crime and Delinquency, 341
National Crime Victimization Survey (NCVS),
      33–34, 36–37, 44–47

National Criminal Intelligence Service (NCIS), 123
National Criminal Intelligence Sharing Plan
      (NCISP), 124
National DNA Database of England & Wales, 118
National Drugs Intelligence Unit, 123
National Employment Law Project, 316
National Incident-Based Reporting System
      (NIBRS), 33
National Information Infrastructure Protection
      Act (NIIPA), 361
National Institute of Bail Enforcement, 184
National Institute of Justice (NIJ), 8, 112
National Institute of Law Enforcement and
      Criminal Justice (NILECJ), 8
nationalist terrorism, 348
National Prison Project, 307
National Research Council, 227
National Security Agency (NSA), 349–350
National Youth Gang Center (NYGS), 38, 331
Native Americans, 258–259, 341
NCIA (National Center on Institutions and
      Alternatives), 275
NCIS (National Criminal Intelligence Service), 123
NCISP (National Criminal Intelligence Sharing
      Plan), 124
NCVS (National Crime Victimization Survey),
      33–34, 36–37, 44–47
Nebraska, 180
necessity, as a criminal defense, 73
neighborhood-oriented policing (NOP), 120
neurological factors in biosocial theory, 48–49
new crimes, creation of, 74–75
Newgate Prison, 268
new-generation jails, 275–276
new inmate culture, 294
The New Jim Crow (Alexander), 266
New Mexico State Penitentiary, 273, 305
new penology, 266
Newtown massacre, 38
New York City Police Department, 97
      controlling deadly force, 145
      Force-Related Integrity Testing, 142
      investigations, 115
      and terrorism, 98
      terrorism, 349
      work slowdown, 106, 120
New York Electronic Crimes Task Force
      (NYECTF), 361
New York House of Refuge, 324–325
New York system, 269–270
New Zealand, 211
NIBRS (National Incident-Based Reporting
      System), 33
Nigeria, 348, 365
NIIPA (National Information Infrastructure
      Protection Act), 361
NIJ (National Institute of Justice), 8, 112
NILECJ (National Institute of Law Enforcement
      and Criminal Justice), 8
Nixle, 104
no bill, 187
nolle prosequi, 11, 12, 170
nolo contendere, 189, 190
nondeadly force, 145–146
nonenforcement, 143
noninterventional perspective, 18–19
NOP (neighborhood-oriented policing), 120
Norway, 347
not guilty plea, 190
NSA (National Security Agency), 349–350
NYC Justice Corps, 315
NYECTF (New York Electronic Crimes Task
      Force), 361
NYGS (National Youth Gang Center), 38, 331
NYPD SHIELD, 98

O

obitiatry, 74
"objective reasonableness" standard, 145, 146
Office of Community Oriented Policing Services (COPS) program, 120
Office of Homeland Security and Emergency Management (OHSEM - Harris County, Texas), 97
Office of Juvenile Justice and Delinquency Prevention (OJJDP), 327, 334
official crime statistics, 31–33
Oil Pollution Act, 355
OJJDP (Office of Juvenile Justice and Delinquency Prevention), 327, 334
Oklahoma, 180
Old Bailey Court, 211
opening statements, 200
Operation Ceasefire, 122
Orange County (Florida) Youthful Offenders Program, 333
Orange Is the New Black, 297
"ordeal," 63
Order in Council of 1617, 211
order maintenance, 110
Organized Crime Control Act, 94, 367
outlaws, 6–7

P

Palm Beach Regional Fusion Center (PBRFC), 125
paper and pencil interviewing (PAPI), 34
paralegals, 169
parens patriae philosophy, 322, 328
parole
    definition of, 310
    development of, 271–272
    effectiveness, 311
    introduction to, 310
    juvenile offenders, 340
    legal right to, 311
    reasons for failure, 313–315
    and recidivism, 311–312, 311f
    reentry, 312–317
    supervision, 311–312
parole board, 310
Part I crimes, 32
Part II crimes, 32
Patriot Act, 349–350
patrol
    as a crime deterrent, 111
    directed patrol, 110–112
    improvement of, 110–114
    using technology, 113–114
patrol activities, 110
patrol function, 110–114
Patrolmen's Benevolent Association, 106
PBRFC (Palm Beach Regional Fusion Center), 125
PCR (police–community relations), 93, 119
PCRA (Post-Conviction Risk Assessment) scale, 243
peacekeeping, 110
penal harm, 274
penitentiaries, 212
Penitentiary Act, 267
penitentiary house, 269
Pennsylvania, 268–270
Pennsylvania system, 269–270
pepper spray, 146
peremptory challenges, 200
personal alarm location system, 277
personality theory, 51–52
persons in need of supervision (PINS), 328
Pew Foundation, 314

Pfizer, 362
Philadelphia Society for Alleviating the Miseries of Public Prisons, 269
phishing, 358
physician-assisted suicide, 74
PINS (persons in need of supervision), 328
plain-view search, 151
plea, 189–190
plea bargaining
    decision making, 192–193
    in juvenile court, 329, 334
    legal issues in, 192
    as part of criminal justice process, 11
plea bargaining reform, 193–194
plea negotiation, 190–192. *See also* plea bargaining
police and policing
    in the 20th century, 91–93
    African Americans police officers, 132–133
    as a career, 134
    changing role and community-oriented policing, 120–121
    community-oriented policing, 119–122, 123
    composition of, 132–135
    corruption, 142–144
    county law enforcement agencies, 96–97
    current state of, 93–101
    discretion, 137–140
    federal law enforcement agencies, 93–95
    history of, 88–90
    intelligence-led policing, 123–125, 124t
    introduction to, 86, 88
    investigation function, 115–119
    issues in, 130, 132
    metropolitan law enforcement agencies, 97–98
    organization, 108–109, 108f
    patrol function, 110–114
    private policing, 88–89, 98–101
    problems of, 140–144
    processing of juvenile offenders, 331–332
    profession, 135–137
    role and function, 106, 108
    roles of, 109–110
    searches and interrogations, 147–151
    state law enforcement agencies, 95–96
    styles of, 137
    support functions, 125–127
    technology and law enforcement, 101–103
    treatment of African Americans, 42
    use of force, 144–146
police brutality, 142
police chief, 108
police–community relations (PCR), 93, 119
police/court bail schedule, 183
police culture, 135–136
police discretion, 137–140
police field citation release, 183
police magistrate, 161f
police personality, 136–137
police/pretrial jail citation release, 183
police programs, and restorative justice, 259
police shootings, 4, 6, 85, 102
police station house citation release, 183
police unions, 92, 106
police values, 121
political terrorism, 347
polluting, illegal, 354
Ponzi, Charles, 346
Ponzi scheme, 344, 346, 351
poor laws, 211, 324
POP (problem-oriented policing), 122, 123
poppy cultivation, 367
pornography, 357, 360–361
POs (probation officers), 241, 242

postconviction remedies, 12
Post-Conviction Risk Assessment (PCRA) scale, 243
postrelease, 12
postrelease programs, 302
poverty
    crime and victimization trends, 42–43
    culture of, 52
    social structure theory, 52–53
preliminary hearing, 11, 187–188, 189f
premeditation, 60
preponderance of the evidence, 198, 327
prescriptive guidelines, 216
presentence investigation, 241–242
presentment, 187
President's Commission on Law Enforcement and Administration of Justice, 7–8
press, freedom of, 308
pretrial and trial procedures
    bail, 182–187
    charging the defendant, 187–194
    introduction to, 180, 182
    pretrial diversion, 194–204
pretrial detention, 182, 185, 329
pretrial diversion, 19
    introduction to, 194
    legal rights during trial, 195–198
    and restorative justice, 259–260
    trial, 195
    trial process, 198–204
pretrial publicity, 197
pretrial services, 186–187
prevention, 99
preventive detention, 186
prison brutality, 270
The Prison Community (Clemmer), 293
prison conditions, 305–306, 310
prisoner-made goods, 272
prisoners' rights, 307–310
prisoners' rights movement, 273
prison farms and camps, 279
prison industry, 270–271, 272
prison inmate, profile of, 284
prisonization, 293–294
prison life
    coping, 291
    correctional officers, 303–305
    correctional treatment, 297–302
    female inmates, 295–296
    female institutions, 295, 297
    inmate social code, 293–294
    introduction to, 288, 290
    men imprisoned, 290–294
    new inmate culture, 294
    parole, 310–317
    prisoners' rights, 307–310
    prison violence, 305–306
    sexual coercion, 291–293, 296
    women imprisoned, 294–297
Prison Litigation Reform Act, 307
prison population, 266, 283f
prison rape, 291–293, 296
Prison Rape Reduction Act of 2003, 293
prison riots, 273, 305
prisons
    in the 20th century, 272
    contemporary correctional institutions, 273–274
    definition of, 266
    development of, 268–269
    juveniles in, 336
    private prisons, 281–282
    rise of, 211–212
    state and federal populations, 283f
    type of, 276, 278–279

treatment
    in juvenile court, 337–338
    and probation, 244, 245–246
"Treatment of Youth of Color in the Justice
    System," 341
treatment orientation, 244
trends
    in crime, 35–39
    crime and victimization, 41–42, 45
    factors that influence, 37–39
    future, 39–40
Triads, 365
trial procedures. *See* pretrial and trial procedures
trial process
    appeals, 12, 203–204
    closing arguments, 202
    criminal defense, 69–73, 201–202
    deliberation and verdict, 202–203
    instructions to the jury, 202
    introduction to, 198–199
    jury selection, 199–200
    legal rights during, 195–198
    opening statements, 200
    overview of, 195
    as part of criminal justice process, 11
    prosecution's case, 200–201
    sentence, 203
Trojan horses, 359
true bill of indictment, 11
truth-in-sentencing laws, 218, 283
tunnel vision, 227
Twitter, 104
211 Crew, 291–292

U

Ukraine, 347
Unborn Victims of Violence Act of 2004, 64–65
unemployment, effect of on crime trends, 37–38
UNICOR, 301
Uniform Crime Reports (UCR), 109
    accuracy of, 32–33
    compilation of, 32
    crime trends in, 36
    introduction to, 31–32
    on juvenile offenders, 331
    National Incident-Based Reporting System
        (NIBRS), 33
unions, 91, 92
United Nations, 363–364
University of Virginia, 3
unsecured bond, 184
USA Freedom Act, 350
"us against the world" mentality, 136
USA Patriot Act (USAPA), 349–350
US Census Bureau, 33
U.S. courts of appeals, 162f, 163

U.S. district courts, 162–163, 162f
use of force, 144t
U.S. Immigration and Customs Enforcement
    (ICE), 364
U.S. Justice Department agencies, 94
U.S. magistrate judge, 166
U.S. Marshals Service, 94
U.S. Tax Court, 162f

V

vandalism, in Uniform Crime Reports, 32
venire, 199
Vera Institute of Justice, 185
verdict, 202–203
Vestal, New York, Police Department, 108f
vice squads, 116
victim characteristics
    and police discretion, 139–140
    and sentencing, 223
victim impact statement, 223
victimization, causes of
    biosocial theory, 48–49
    developmental theory, 55–56
    psychological theory, 49–52
    rational choice theory, 47–48
    social conflict theory, 54–55
    social process theory, 54
    social structure theory, 52–53
victim-offender relationships, 46
victim patterns of crime
    age, 44–45
    ecological factors, 45
    gender, 44
    income, 45
    marital status, 45
    race, 45
    repeat victimization, 46–47
    victim-offender relationships, 46
victims, role of in plea bargaining, 193
videoconferencing, 178
Vietnam War, 92
vigilantes, 89–90
violations, 66
violence
    within the correctional system, 273,
        305–306
    individual, 305–306
    and policing, 142
    prison conditions, 305–306
violent crimes, trends in, 36–37, 36f
Violent Offender Incarceration and Truth-in-
    Sentencing Incentive Grants Program,
    218
viruses, 359
vishing, 73, 74
Vivitrol, 245

vocational programs in prison, 301–302
voir dire, 199
voluntary and deliberate, 67

W

waiver, 335
waiver of jurisdiction, 334–336
Wall Street fraud, 350–351
Walnut Street Jail, 269, 300
warez, 357
war on terror, 95–96, 98. *See also* terrorism
warrantless searches, 150–151
Washington, 180
Washington Corrections Center For Women,
    273
watchman style of policing, 137
watch system, 88
water pollution, 354
weapons, 146–147. *See also* firearms
web defacement, 359
"wedding cake" model of justice, 14–16, 15f
Western Penitentiary, 270
white-collar crimes, 62
Wickersham Commission, 7
widening the net of justice, 19
WIT (Women Inspired to Transform), 317
witnesses, right to confront, 195–196
women. *See also* gender
    correctional officers, 304–305
    inmates, 295–296
    police officers, 133–135
    prison life, 294–297
    programs for reentry, 317
Women Inspired to Transform (WIT), 317
workhouses, 268
work release, 273, 301–302
work slowdown, 106, 120
worms, 359
writ of certiorari, 163
writ of *habeas corpus*, 203, 204, 350
wrongful convictions, 227

Y

Yakuza, 364
YMCA and YWCA, 341
Youthful Offenders Program, 333
youth gangs, 331
youth in adult courts, 335

Z

ZaZZZ vending machine, 75
zero tolerance, 252
Zetas gang, 367–368